Inдia

Discovery
CHANNEL

APA PUBLICATIONS L
Part of the Langenscheidt Publishing Group

ABOUT THIS BOOK

INSIGHT GUIDE

India

Editorial
Managing Editor
Maria Lord
Editorial Director
Brian Bell

Distribution

UK & Ireland
GeoCenter International Ltd
Meridian House, Churchill Way West
Basingstoke, Hampshire RG21 6YR
Fax: (44) 1256 817988

United States
Langenscheidt Publishers, Inc.
36–36 33rd Street 4th Floor
Long Island City, NY 11106
Fax: (1) 718 784 0640

Australia
Universal Publishers
1 Waterloo Road
Macquarie Park, NSW 2113
Fax: (61) 2 9888 9074

New Zealand
Hema Maps New Zealand Ltd (HNZ)
Unit D, 24 Ra ORA Drive
East Tamaki, Auckland
Fax: (64) 9 273 6479

Worldwide
**Apa Publications GmbH & Co.
Verlag KG (Singapore branch)**
38 Joo Koon Road, Singapore 628990
Tel: (65) 6865 1600. Fax: (65) 6861 6438

Printing

Insight Print Services (Pte) Ltd
38 Joo Koon Road, Singapore 628990
Tel: (65) 6865 1600. Fax: (65) 6861 6438

©2007 Apa Publications GmbH & Co.
Verlag KG (Singapore branch)
All Rights Reserved
First Edition 1985
Seventh Edition (Updated) 2007

The first Insight Guide pioneered the use of creative full-colour photography in travel guides in 1970. Since that time, we have expanded our range to cater for our readers' need not only for reliable information about their chosen destination but also for a real understanding of the culture and workings of that destination. Now, when the internet can supply inexhaustible (but not always reliable) facts, our books marry text and pictures to provide those much more elusive qualities: knowledge and discernment. To achieve this, they rely heavily on the authority and experience of locally based writers and photographers.

This fully updated edition of *Insight: India* is carefully structured to convey an understanding of the country and its culture, and to guide the reader through its many sights and activities:

◆ The **Features** section, indicated by a yellow bar at the top of each page, covers history and culture in a series of informative essays.

◆ The main **Places** section, indicated by a blue bar, is a complete guide to India's sights. Places of special interest are coordinated by number with the maps.

◆ The **Travel Tips** listings section, with an orange bar, provides information on travel, hotels, shops, restaurants and more.

The Contributors

This new edition was edited and updated by **Maria Lord**, an Insight Guides editor and writer. She wrote the panels on Adivasis and the political phenomona of Saffronisation and the chapters on Contemporary India and Dance and Music. She also added the new chapters on the states and regions of Ladakh, the Lakshadweep Islands, Uttaranchal,

The Taj Mahal from the Yamuna River

Jharkhand and Chattisgarh. In addition she thoroughly overhauled the Travel Tips as well as updating and expanding the History, Features and Places sections.

This seventh edition builds on the previous version produced by managing editor **Jane Hutchings**, a UK-based journalist with wide Insight Guides experience, and **Jan McGirk**, who also contributed the chapters on politics and wildlife, environment, temple architecture.

They were helped by **Farah Singha**, an energetic researcher, translator, producer and resident of Delhi, who wrote the Delhi and Andhra Pradesh chapters and worked on many other sections.

Savitri Choudhury, a correspondent for the Australian Broadcasting Corporation, previously revised the chapter on her native Assam. Broadcaster **Lea Terhune**, a long-time Delhi resident, wrote on Jammu and Kashmir.

Art critic and lecturer **Juliet Reynolds**, who has lived all her adult life in India, wrote the chapter on Indian art. **Gillian Wright**, who wrote the Uttar Pradesh section, is a translator and documentary film producer who knows all the byways between Delhi and Lucknow.

Other writers include the geographer **Dr Kamala Seshan**, who wrote about the land and climate. India's history was covered by **Professor Harbans Mukhia** and analysts **Prem Shankar Jha** and **Ajay Singh**.

The People chapter was written by **Radhika Chopra** with Jan McGirk, and the Religion chapter by **Professor V.S. Naravané**. **Royina Grewal** covered festivals and food. The movie industry was covered by **Anil Dharker** and Jan McGirk. Dharker also wrote about Maharashtra. **Laila Tyabji** detailed India's handicrafts. **Bill Aitken** covered train travel.

In the Places section, **Samuel Israel**, doyen of India's book-publishing editors, and **Bikram Grewal**, managing director of Dass Media, wrote about Mumbai; Grewal also wrote on Chennai. **Meenakshi Ganguly**, a *Time* reporter, returned to her home town to check the chapters on Kolkata and West Bengal. **Sardar Khushwant Singh**, a widely syndicated political commentator, wrote about Punjab and Haryana. **Aman Nath** and **Francis Wacziarg** covered Rajasthan.

A French writer, **Michel Vatin**, covered the Eastern and Northeastern states and wrote about tea. Madhya Pradesh was covered by conservationist **M.M. Buch**.

Usha Albuquerque wrote about Goa. **Jaya Jaitly** covered Gujarat, and **Pepita Noble** documented Kerala. **Vikram Sundarji**, a Tamilian Brahmin, wrote on Tamil Nadu.

Map Legend

— ·· —	International Boundary
— — — —	State Boundary
— • — —	National Park/Reserve
✈ ✈	Airport: International/Regional
Ⓜ	Metro
🚐	Bus Station
🅿	Parking
ⓘ	Tourist Information
✉	Post Office
∎ † ⸸	Church / Ruins
†	Monastery
☾	Mosque
✡	Synagogue
🏰	Castle / Ruins
∴	Archaeological Site
∩	Cave
⚊	Statue/Monument
★	Place of Interest

The main places of interest in the Places section are coordinated by number with a full-colour map (e.g. ❶), and a symbol at the top of every right-hand page tells you where to find the map.

Insight Guide INDIA

CONTENTS

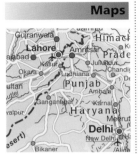

CONTENTS ◆ 5

The Asiatic
Society
Library,
Mumbai

Travel Tips

Getting Acquainted **346**

Planning the Trip **349**

Practical Info **352**

Getting Around **357**

Where to Stay **361**

Where to Eat **398**

Shopping **410**

Wildlife **413**

Language **415**

Further Reading **417**

◆ **Full Travel Tips index
is on page 345**

Information panels

The Environment **73**

The Adivasis **83**

Temple Architecture **92**

Saffronisation **101**

The Festival Year **109**

Tea **249**

Places

Introduction **159**

The North **163**

Delhi **167**

Uttar Pradesh **174**

Uttaranchal **182**

Punjab and Haryana **184**

Himachal Pradesh **190**

Jammu and Kashmir **196**

Ladakh **198**

Rajasthan **203**

The East **219**

Kolkata **221**

West Bengal **230**

Sikkim **238**

Northeastern States **241**

Bihar **250**

Jharkhand **254**

Orissa **257**

Andaman and
 Nicobar Islands **262**

The West **267**

Mumbai (Bombay)............... **269**

Maharashtra **276**

Gujarat **282**

Madhya Pradesh................. **289**

Chattisgarh **294**

Goa **297**

The South **307**

Chennai **309**

Tamil Nadu........................ **314**

Kerala **322**

Lakshadweep **328**

Karnataka **331**

Andhra Pradesh **339**

THE ALLURE OF INDIA

Travellers have been captivated since early times by India's awesome diversity of peoples, cultures and landscapes

India has a long history of welcoming new peoples, accommodating and absorbing them into its existing structures, which in time adapt and change to express the ideas and practices of the new arrivals. The contemporary visitor will encounter the same open-minded and welcoming attitude, and a fascinating complex of cultures and beliefs. Home to Hindus, Muslims, Christians, Sikhs, Jains, Buddhists and Jews, to political ideologies from peasant liberation-supporting communists to Hindu nationalists, and landscapes that range from the world's highest mountain ranges to tropical coasts, India has an almost endless variety of peoples and places to explore.

There is evidence, from the earliest times, of great movements of peoples across South Asia, sometimes replacing existing populations, sometimes integrating with them. Peoples from West and Central Asia came in massive sweeps through the lofty passes in the northwest, bringing with them the rudiments of the Hindu faith, later to be developed on Indian soil into a philosophically subtle and highly complex religion.

While it is only in recent years that Hinduism is again having a major influence outside the Indian subcontinent, Buddhism, which grew out of Hinduism, is a major world religion. But India has also absorbed Islam, Christianity, Zoroastrianism, and, on a very small scale but very significantly, Judaism. India has been the proverbial sponge, and not only in matters religious.

With various peoples and religions came a variety of ethnicities, their art, architecture, culture, languages, customs, literature, styles of music and dance, administrative structures, systems of thought, science, technology and medicine. Few of these have entirely lost their identity, all have had their influence, and many have found a permanent place in India's intricate mosaic.

While it is India's variety and complexity that give the country its identity, and make it attractive to the traveller, negotiating this heterogeneity can at times be a difficult task, both for the visitor and India's politicians. But despite the problems that can arise, India retains its allure for visitors eager to spend time in understanding what confronts them rather than judging it on first acquaintance. Everyone's perception is different. The English journalist James Cameron, one of India's greatest advocates, summed up its appeal when he wrote: "I like the evening in India, the one magic moment when the sun balances on the rim of the world, and the hush descends, and 10,000 civil servants drift homeward on a river of bicycles, brooding on the Lord Krishna and the cost of living." ❑

PRECEDING PAGES: the camel fair at Pushkar, Rajasthan; the bathing ghats in Varanasi; Dilwara Temple, Mount Abu; rules in a Mumbai restaurant.
LEFT: a welcoming Rajasthani.

INDIA'S TOP 10 SIGHTS

Huge and exceptionally diverse, India is impossible to cover in a single trip. Below are 10 suggested itineraries, going from north to south, each of which takes you round some of the country's most spectacular and fascinating locations.

The Far North: into the high Himalayas starting at Manali, and crossing over some of the highest passes in the world, amid breathtaking scenery, to the stark mountains and monasteries of Ladakh.

The Golden Triangle: starting at the capital of India, Delhi, this is a classic trip via Agra and the Taj Mahal, to the Rajasthani planned city of Jaipur, and the immense fort of Amber.

The Ganga Plain: from Delhi the floodplain of the Ganga stretches all the way to Kolkata. En route it passes the fascinating cities of Lucknow and Varanasi, and the Buddhist sites of Bihar.

The East: from the lively cultural city of Kolkata, either go south to the fabulous temple towns of Orissa, or north to the hill station of Darjeeling and on into the little-explored northeast.

Rajasthan: one of India's greatest destinations, full of palaces, forts and temples. Of the many places to explore, some of the finest are Udaipur, Mount Abu, Jodhpur and Jaisalmer.

Central India: on from the temples at Khajuraho to some of India's finest wildlife reserves at Kanha, Bandhavgarh and Indravati.

The West: the great city of Mumbai, India's brash cinematic and commercial heart, has in its hinterland the fabulous rock-cut temples at Ajanta and Ellora.

The Deccan: the Deccan Plateau dominates peninsular India; on it are the ruins at Hampi, and the contrasting cities of Bangalore and Mysore.

Tamil Temples: from Chennai, a bastion of Tamil culture, south to the stunning temples of Mamallapuram, Thanjavur and Madurai.

The Malabar Coast: a trip through beautiful Kerala, taking in Thiruvananthapuram and its nearby beaches, via the Backwaters, to the port of Kochi.

△ **JAISALMER (page 215)**
This desert citadel with its golden sandstone fort and wonderful *havelis* is the oldest Rajput capital. It also has some beautiful and ornate Jain temples.

△ **THE TAJ (page 175)**
India's most recognisable sight, this truly stunning monument in white marble is seductive in its perfect proportions and fine details.

◁ **MADURAI (page 318)**
The Minakshi temple is one of Tamil Nadu's most holy sites, with brightly painted and towering *gopurams*.

◁ **VARANASI (page 180)**
The most sacred place on India's most sacred river, the bathing ghats and *galis* (alleyways) of Varanasi present a spectacle that covers the panoply of human existence. One of the world's oldest cities, in its streets you will encounter births, marriages, intense displays of religious devotion and death.

◁ **DARJEELING (page 234)**
A summertime retreat for the British Raj, this hill station, surrounded by neat tea plantations, has extraordinary views over the eastern Himalayas. It is reached by a "Toy Train", itself a World Heritage Site.

◁ **KERALA BACKWATERS (page 326)** The intense greens and blues of these inland waterways, overhung by innumerable coconut palms, encapsulate tropical India like nowhere else.

▷ **HAMPI (page 337)**
The deserted Vijayanagar capital at Hampi is perhaps India's most evocative ruin. A World Heritage Site, the Vittala Temple has a wealth of sculptural detail.

△ **KHAJURAHO (page 290)**
The life-affirming and minutely carved temples at Khajuraho in Madhya Pradesh date back to the 10th century. They are the product of an immense outpouring of creativity, devotion and sensuality.

◁ **AJANTA (page 279)**
Dating back to the 2nd century BC, the carved rock temples of Ajanta lie in a beautiful, forested valley. The stunning frescoes are some of the greatest works of Buddhist art.

▷ **LADAKH (page 198)**
A Himalayan Buddhist kingdom, high up on the Tibetan Plateau, and surrounded by stark, bare peaks. Ladakh's impressive *gompas* (monasteries) contain numerous art treasures.

LAND AND CLIMATE

Few countries encompass as richly varied a landscape as India's,
watered by the monsoon and burnished by the sun

Beneath its distinctive bulge, India narrows like an elephant's trunk to drink from the Indian Ocean, the Bay of Bengal and the Arabian Sea. Such thirst is understandable. Three of the world's greatest deserts – the Mexican, the Sahara and the Arabian – lie at the same latitude. But India extends far beyond its Thar desert, and extra altitude allows for rainforests, alpine meadows and glaciers.

Weather patterns

The southwest monsoon dominates most of the country from late June to the end of September, bringing high humidity and heavy rain. As these winds retreat in October, the land dries out and humidity levels fall. The southeastern coasts, however, have rain and cyclonic squalls until January.

In November, with the strength of the sun diminishing, the winter season starts in the northern plain. Until February the weather remains cold (below 5°C/41°F) in the Himalaya and its foothills (where skiing is possible), pleasant in the plains (between 15°C/59°F and 20°C/68°F), and warm (above 20°C/68°F) in South India, except in the cooler uplands.

India's summer, which runs from March to May, is hot and dry, with flurries of wind raising a dusty curtain over the northern plain and maximum daytime temperatures averaging 40°C (104°F). South India is sultry and hot but temperatures are usually bearable, between 27°C (80°F) and 29°C (84°F).

Tracking the monsoon

Come June, the intense heat of the northern plain causes the upper air currents to move north of the Himalaya and draw the monsoon across the entire country. Starting from the southwestern coast, it branches eastward and northward, and on reaching the Ganga delta follows the wide river valleys bounded by the Himalaya with its heavily forested foothills.

LEFT: harvest landscape, Uttar Pradesh.
RIGHT: Kerala backwater in southwest India.

Luxuriant rainforests blanket the hills along the southwest coast, in Kerala, where the lowland lagoons are canopied by coconut trees. The coast stretches north to the estuarine plains of Goa where wide sunny beaches are lapped by the gentle waves of the Arabian Sea. The rest of the coast is mostly rocky, rising to the low

red lateritic plateaus and then more steeply to the black, forest-covered slopes of the Western Ghats. Further north, in Kathiawar, the coast becomes salt-encrusted with marshy lowlands rich with flamingo.

Inland, open country covered with cotton and sunflower fields merges into rocky desert. From the Rann (saline marshlands) of Kutch in the west to the Luni River is the Great Desert, and further north between Jaisalmer and Jodhpur is the Little Desert. Here is open scrub country with rocky hills often capped by the forts of the Rajput kings. Wandering herds of sheep and goats, and camels carrying cotton and marble, are seen in this area.

Separating the desert from the Gangetic plain and the Deccan lava tableland are the rugged plateaus of Malwa, Bundelkhand and Rewa. Stony, harsh and covered with only a thin layer of soil, the plateau is drained by the Chambal, Ken and Betva rivers. Badlands are formed by the ravines made by the rivers, and fields of mustard and wheat form a patchwork of green and gold.

On the west, steeply rising from the plain to the lava plateau, is the Vindhya range of hills. The Narmada river, flowing through a narrow gorge, and the river Tapi, through a broad valley, are separated by the Satpura range. South of the Tapi are the hills housing the carved and

The steel city of Jamshedpur and the coal and iron-ore mines contribute to India's increasing pollution and deforestation. The plateau is flanked in the east by the Rajmahal Hills, which descend steeply to the Ganga plain where the river takes a sharp bend to the sea.

Deccan peninsula

It was on the "table-tops" of the steep-sided hills of the black lava-covered Deccan that the Marathas built a series of impregnable fortresses. Cut across by the Krishna, Godavari and Kaveri rivers flowing east, the wet Karnataka plateau has dense sandal, teak and sissu forests,

painted caves at Ajanta and Ellora. At the mouth of the Tapi is the ancient port city of Surat, famous for its gold and silver brocade (*zari*). It was here, in 1608, that the British East India Company set up its first "factory", as its trading centres were called.

By 15 June, the eastward-moving monsoon winds reach the Chota Nagpur plateau in Jharkhand, which is drained by the Damodar. It is a wide plateau with conical and dome-shaped hills that look like gigantic bubbles.

During the three long monsoon months the brown forests of sal, bamboo and teak turn green and Adivasi peoples collect lac (the secretion of a forest insect) and mahua flowers.

where elephants roam wild. The Telengana plateau to the east has only a thin cover of red lateritic soils with rocky humps between. Thorny scrub and wild Indian date palms grow on this soil. Tanks are built in the dried river channels to hold water when the rivers are briefly in flood. Here is the former princely state of Hyderabad, the pearl city, surrounded by vineyards.

Southwest of the plateau, separated from Kerala by the blue Nilgiris, with coffee and tea plantations, and the cloud-covered Palani Hills in the rain shadow, is the Coimbatore plateau, which extends east to the coast near Chennai. The Kaveri, which rises here, flows east into the Tamil Nadu plains. The fertile Kaveri delta is the rice bowl of Tamil Nadu, its prosperity expressed in the exuberant temple architecture of towns such as Thanjavur.

Looking east

India's stony east coast, with vast exposed spaces scattered with aloes and palm trees and swampy alluvial shores, merges northwards into the fertile deltaic lowlands of the Krishna, Godavari and Mahanadi rivers. Wooded forests replace fields of sugar cane and tobacco in places reached by the summer monsoon.

Replenishing itself in its passage over the Bay of Bengal, the southwest monsoon continues westwards along the wide Ganga plain and eastward along the Brahmaputra gorge.

Eastwards, the Brahmaputra Valley cuts across the Shillong plateau, by the Garo, Khasi and Jaintia hills, through the Assam-Burma range. The Brahmaputra swings across its wide valley in an immense rocky corridor. Tiny hamlets are surrounded by rice fields and tea plantations. On the slopes tussar silkworms are bred on mulberry trees, and pineapple plantations are prolific.

Mangrove delta

The Brahmaputra reaches the wet Ganga delta dominated by the port of Kolkata. Criss-crossed by the distributaries of an ever-growing delta, the mangrove forests offer cover for the endangered Bengal tiger. Inland, jungle has been cleared to cultivate barley and pulses.

Following the monsoon winds westwards comes the Middle Ganga plain where the annual rainfall decreases from 140 cm (55 inches) to 80 cm (31 inches) near Delhi. North of this plain are the foothills of the Himalaya across which the tributaries of the Ganga flow through steep reed-filled courses in sal forests. Here, as in the Dooars of Bengal, the Terai has jungles of sisoo and tamarisk that afford excellent hideouts for tigers.

When the now comparatively dry monsoon winds reach the upper course of the Ganga, the fields are ready for sowing. The canal-irrigated wheat plains of Punjab merge into the dry land of Haryana to the southwest. Delhi, the gateway to the Ganga plain, is located here. Northward, the foothill ridges of the Shivaliks and the gravel vales rise through ridges and valleys to the snow-capped peaks of the Himalaya. The ascent is from around 300–600 metres (980–1,960 ft) above the plain to 4,800 metres (15,750 ft) in the middle Himalaya where the peaks of Nanda Devi rise up to 7,000 metres (22,970 ft).

The Teesta Valley in the Eastern Himalaya lies opposite the Ganga delta at the head of which is Sikkim. Orchids and rhododendrons grow wild here and the musk deer and rhinoceros are found in these dense forests. The valleys are a patchwork of paddy fields, and on the terraced slopes are yellow maize and millet fields. ❏

LEFT: gathering in the harvest near Tiruchirappalli in Tamil Nadu.
RIGHT: the lush Nilgiri Hills, western Tamil Nadu.

NOMADIC ROUTES

The Central Himalaya, in Himachal Pradesh, is a favourite for trekking and fishing. Here the golden snowcapped Dholadhar ranges separate the River Beas from the Ravi. At the head of the Beas are apple orchards and the Kullu Valley. Chir and deodar jungles enclose the sloping river terraces of the Sutlej, covered with potato and rice fields. From Kullu the traditional routes of the Bhutia shepherds enter the upland pastures of Ladakh. The lowest valleys of the Himalayan foothills, the Terai, are hot and sultry in summer and have heavy rainfall in July. Here the nomadic ways of the Bhutias are replaced by a settled pastoral economy on the forest edge, and farming in the valleys.

Decisive Dates

EARLY HISTORY

c. 2500–1600 BC: Urban settlements of Harappa and Mohenjodaro established in the Indus Valley.
c. 1500 BC: Peoples from Central Asia invade northern India. Sacred texts of the *Vedas* are written.
521–486 BC: The Persian king, Darius, occupies Punjab and Sind. Buddhism and Jainism develop.
321–184 BC: Northern India is ruled by the Mauryan emperors; the most notable is Ashoka (269–232 BC).
AD 319–606: Gupta Empire is established in the north. Science, literature and arts flourish.

550–1190: The Chalukya and Rashtraka dynasties rule central India from Karnataka. The Pallava and Chola dynasties rule the South and establish trading links with Indonesia.

THE RAJPUT PERIOD: 900–1200

c. 850: Anangpal builds Lal Kot, Delhi's first city.
1000–1300: Hoysala Empire rules the South.
1192: Muhammed of Ghor invades the north and makes Qutb-ud-Din Aibak Delhi's first ruler.

THE DELHI SULTANATE

1206: Qutb-ud-Din becomes sultan of Delhi. His dynasty is overthrown in 1296 by Feroz Shah, a Turk, who builds Delhi's second city east of Lal Kot.

1321: Ghias-ud-Din Tughlaq is proclaimed sultan. He starts building Tughlaqabad, the third city of Delhi.
1325: Muhammad-bin Tughlaq becomes sultan and builds Jahanpanah, the fourth city. In 1351 Feroz Shah Tughlaq builds Ferozabad, the fifth city.
1414: Power passes to the Sayyids.
1451: Buhlbal Lodi, an Afghan noble, captures the throne and founds the Lodhi dynasty.
14th–16th century: Islam is established throughout the north. The South remains independent under the Hindu Vijayanagar dynasty.
1498: Vasco da Gama establishes Portuguese trading posts, followed by the Dutch, French and English.

THE MUGHAL DYNASTY: 1526–1857

1526: Babur, from Samarkand, defeats the Sultan of Delhi at the Battle of Panipat, and proclaims himself the first Mughal emperor.
1540: Humayan succeeds his father, Babur, and starts to build Purana Qila, Delhi's sixth city.
1556: Akbar is enthroned, aged 13. He pushes the borders of the Mughal empire three-quarters of the way across South Asia.
1565: Akbar starts to build the Red Fort in his capital city, Agra. Meanwhile, Muslim forces bring down the Vijayanagar dynasty in the South, which in turn are conquered by the Mughals.
1569–74: Akbar moves his capital to Fatehpur Sikri, near Agra, but the court returns to Agra ten years later. Akbar then starts to build his tomb at Sikandra.
1600: Queen Elizabeth I grants a trading charter to the British East India Company, and in 1608 English merchants set up a trading base at Surat in Gujarat.
1605: Akbar is succeeded by his son, Jahangir.
1627: Shah Jahan, Akbar's grandson, becomes emperor. In 1632 he starts to build the Taj Mahal in memory of his wife. In 1638 he moves the capital from Agra to Delhi and lays the foundations for Shahjahanabad, the seventh city. He begins work on Lal Qila (the Red Fort) in 1639.
1659–1707: Aurangzeb becomes emperor by imprisoning his father, Shah Jahan, in the Red Fort, Agra, and killing his brothers. Following his death the Mughal empire declines. Calcutta begins to expand as a trading post of the East India Company.
1739: Persian king Nadir Shah invades Delhi and slaughters 30,000 residents of Shahjahanabad before returning to Persia with the Peacock Throne and the Koh-i-noor Diamond.
1756–63: In the Seven Years' War the British East India Company ousts the French from Bengal.
1857: Uprising against British rule breaks out in Meerut. The campaign spreads across India, causing much

bloodshed. The British defeat the insurgents. Bahaudur Shah, last of the Mughal emperors, is exiled to Burma. The reign of the East India Company comes to an end.

THE BRITISH RAJ: 1858–1947
1858: The British Crown imposes direct rule and appoints a viceroy as the sovereign's representative.
1877: Queen Victoria is proclaimed Empress of India.
1885: The first political party, the Indian National Congress, is founded.
1911: George V, King and Emperor, announces that the capital will be transferred from Calcutta to Delhi.
1908: The Muslim League is set up.
1915: Mohandas Gandhi, dubbed "Mahatma" (great soul) by Rabindranath Tagore, returns from South Africa and starts to campaign against British rule.
1919: General Dyer orders his Gurkha troops to open fire on a peaceful anti-British protest meeting in Amritsar, killing at least 379 and wounding 1,200.
1930: Gandhi's non-cooperation movement gains momentum with his Dandi Salt March from Ahmadabad to protest against taxes on Indian-produced salt.
1931: New Delhi inaugurated as the capital of India.
1935: Mohammed Ali Jinnah, head of the Muslim League, calls for a new Muslim nation of Pakistan.

INDEPENDENCE (1947–PRESENT)
1947: India gains independence at midnight on 15 August. Jawaharlal Nehru becomes first prime minister. India is divided in two: the mainly Hindu nation of India and the Muslim nation of Pakistan. During Partition more than 10 million migrate in each direction across the divided Punjab. Communal violence between Hindus, Sikhs and Muslims claims between 200,000 and 1 million lives.
1948: Mahatma Gandhi is assassinated on 30 January by a Hindu nationalist.
1950: The constitution of India comes into force.
1964: Nehru dies. In 1965 his successor, Lal Bahadur Shastri, defeats Pakistan in a war over Kashmir.
1966: Indira Gandhi, Nehru's daughter (no relation to Mahatma Gandhi) becomes prime minister.
1971: War with East Pakistan leads to the creation of the new independent nation of Bangladesh.
1975–77: Indira Gandhi imposes a State of Emergency, suspends civil liberties and imprisons her political opponents. She is defeated in the 1977 elections.
1977–79: Janata Party in power under Morarji Desai.
1980: Indira Gandhi returns as prime minister.

PRECEDING PAGES: mural of a royal hunt, Jodhpur.
LEFT: the son of the Nawab of Banda *circa* 1844.
RIGHT: Mahatma Gandhi (1869–1948).

1984: Sikhs demand independence for Punjab; 1,000 people die when the army storms the Golden Temple in Amritsar. Indira Gandhi is assassinated on 31 October. Her son, Rajiv Gandhi, becomes prime minister.
1990: Communal and civil disturbances in Jammu and Kashmir and Assam. Religious violence in Punjab.
1991: Rajiv Gandhi is assassinated. Congress forms a minority government led by Narasimha Rao.
1992–93: Destruction of Babri mosque in Ayodhya by Hindu militants provokes riots nationwide.
1996: A leftist coalition under Deve Gowda, later succeeded by I.K. Gujral, takes office.
1998: BJP-led coalition; Atal Bihari Vajpayee becomes prime minister. Nuclear tests in the Thar Desert.

God is Truth
MKGandhi

1999: A BJP-led coalition (the NDA) under Atal Bihari Vajpayee wins a general election. Fighting breaks out in the Kargil Valley between India and Pakistan.
2000: India's population passes 1 billion.
2001: Huge earthquake hits western Gujarat.
2002: Communal violence kills many in Gujarat.
2004: India and Pakistan begin talks to resolve "all outstanding issues". Congress-led coalition wins general election, Manmohan Singh is prime minister. A tsunami devastates the Andaman and Nicobar Islands and parts of the Tamil coast.
2005: The first bus service starts between Indian-Administered- and Pakistan-Occupied-Kashmir.
2006: More than 100 people die from bombs placed in Mumbai's transport network. ❑

BEGINNINGS

Evidence points to a number of complex urban settlements

existing in India as early as 2500 BC

The strikingly complex mix of societies that comprises India, Pakistan and Bangladesh was until 1947 a single political entity: India. The history of the region can be traced back several millennia and many facets of human existence have contributed to the changes it has undergone: ecology, craft skills and labour, social divisions and the ensuing frictions, and not least culture and religion.

A cardinal feature of the Indian ecology, which exercised a considerable influence on the historical development of South Asia, was the very high fertility of its land. The topsoil in the river basins was renewed annually by the summer monsoons, which deposited enormous quantities of fertile silt from the mountains. The Indus and Ganga alone are estimated to bring down a million tons of suspended matter daily. Cultivation came to be densely concentrated in the valleys of these great rivers, and most Indian soils yielded an average of two crops a year.

The contrast between the high agricultural yield and the low level of consumption by the population made large surpluses available to maintain a substantial number of towns at an impressive level of material comfort.

Harappa culture

The earliest known urban settlements in India, the starting point of Indian history, were already thriving by around 2500 BC. Discovered in the 1920s, they were initially thought to have been confined to the valley of the Indus, hence their early identification as the Indus Valley Civilisation. Of the towns, two earned great renown: Mohenjodaro and Harappa, both in Pakistan.

Later archaeological excavations established the spread of these peoples across an area in northwestern and western India, far beyond the valley of the Indus; hence "Harappan culture" is the more recent label put on these discoveries.

LEFT: the lion capital of an Ashokan pillar, the emblem of the Indian government.
RIGHT: a dancing figure from Mohenjodaro.

Among the Indian sites are the ones at Ropar in Punjab, and Lothal and Kalibangan in Gujarat and Rajasthan.

The towns at Mohenjodaro and Harappa were well planned, with streets criss-crossing one another at right angles, a system of sewage and a fairly clear division of localities and types of

houses earmarked for the upper and the lower strata of society. There were also public buildings, the most famous being the Great Bath at Mohenjodaro, and the granaries.

Production of metals such as copper, bronze, lead and tin was undertaken as some remnants of furnaces have survived to bear evidence. There were two kilns to make the burnt bricks, used extensively in domestic as well as public buildings. The Harappan culture had developed its own pictographic script; unfortunately, the script still hasn't been definitively deciphered.

Among the discoveries at Harappan sites are a couple of thousand seals in quadrangular shapes and sizes, each with a human or an animal figure carved on it. It is likely that these seals served as the trademarks of merchants, for the Harappan culture had extensive trade relations with neighbouring regions and distant lands in the Persian Gulf and Sumer in Iraq.

Evidence shows that Harappan society was divided between rich and poor, traders, artisans and peasants. It can be safely assumed that they had an organised government even if we know little about its form or actual working. We know, however, that the Harappans worshipped gods and goddesses represented in male and female forms. But we know little else for certain about their religious life.

were a pastoral people who gradually familiarised themselves with agriculture. Cattle-breeding and settled agriculture came to complement each other. However, the notion of individual landholdings was slow to grow; in early Vedic literature, cattle and enslaved women are the only movable forms of property mentioned.

The local inhabitants whom the Central Asian peoples had displaced and enslaved might have been employed in the fields. The plough drawn by oxen was the primary agricultural implement; the Indian brahmin bull had mercifully been provided with a hump by nature, making the yoking of the plough so

By about 1700 BC the Harappan culture was starting to disappear, partly due to repeated flooding of towns located on river banks and partly because of ecological changes that forced agriculture to yield to the spreading desert. When the initial migrations into India of people probably from northeastern Iran and the region around the Caspian Sea began around 1500 BC, the Harappan culture had already practically disappeared.

The Vedic Age

Deriving its name from the four *Vedas*, the earliest Hindu scriptures, the Vedic Age was spread over several centuries. The new immigrants

much easier. The crops cultivated were barley, sesamum, cucumber, bittergourd and sugar cane. The Harappa culture, too, had used the plough and was known to have grown rice, wheat and cotton besides sesamum and peas, but early Vedic literature makes no reference to the first three of these crops. Cattle were highly valued, and beef-eating was reserved for very honoured guests.

The new invaders were initially organised into tribes. Tribal chiefship gradually became hereditary, though the chief operated with advice from either a committee or the entire tribe and, in time, the giving or taking of advice was institutionalised.

With work specialisation, the internal division of society developed along caste lines. The early division was between the fairer-skinned newcomers and the darker-skinned indigenous populations; hence, perhaps, caste was known as the *varna* (colour). The rulers came to be grouped into the Brahmana (priests), Kshatriya (warriors), Vaishya (merchants/traders) and Sudra (agriculturalists). It was, at first, a division of occupations, which was open and flexible. Later, caste-status and occupation came to

The relationship of one's life with the universe was a subject of speculation, and the notion of a cycle of lives in various forms through which the soul had to pass was hinted at, if not yet fully articulated. This was later to grow into the doctrine of *Karma* (one's deeds), according to which one's next status in, or even form of, life depended on one's deeds in the present life. This doctrine served as a major deterrent to protest against oppression, for a person's current misery would be easily attributed to his or

depend on birth, and any change from one caste to another became more difficult.

The prosperity generated by agriculture and cattle breeding and the employment of enslaved labour provided adequate leisure time in which to meditate and seek answers to fundamental questions about the origin of the universe. Their language, Sanskrit, was Indo-European and for a considerable period remained without a script. Imparting of knowledge was done orally and through repetitive memorising (the oral scriptures were written down as the *Vedas*).

LEFT: depiction of a prehistoric hunt from Central India.
ABOVE: the rock-cut Kailasa temple, Ellora.

her past misdeeds, for which the person must undergo appropriate punishment in order to ensure a better life next time.

Discovery of iron

Around 1000 BC iron was discovered in India, which was to lead to several changes in society. Since iron axes made clearing of forests easier, a considerable amount of forest land gave way to the plough; agricultural expansion was also facilitated by an iron ploughshare, sickle and hoe.

One could perhaps assume that extension of the cultivated area led to a growth of population, a greater degree of specialisation of functions and more trade. It certainly led to a second urbanisation. With land gaining prominence as a form of individual property and with demand for it growing faster than could be met through forest clearing, society came to be divided even further between the rich and the poor.

Popular teachings

In the 6th century BC this stark contrast between miserable poverty and luxury led two men, Mahavira and Buddha, both of them Kshatriyas, to seek answers to the question of why people suffer. In the end both Mahavira and Buddha came upon the same ideas as answers: a moderate, balanced life based on non-violence,

EMPEROR ASHOKA

Emperor Ashoka, the 3rd-century BC Mauryan ruler, inherited an empire that covered most of northern India, with the exception of Kalinga, modern-day Orissa. This Ashoka conquered, but the sight of the battlefield littered with dead bodies so shocked the emperor that he asked himself, what was the result of worldly ambition? The answer that satisfied him was the one that the Buddha had given. Ashoka became a convert to Buddhism. He is renowned for the edicts he had carved on pillars throughout his empire calling for wise government and a moral lifestyle in accordance with the Buddha's teachings. Many of these can still be seen today.

abstinence, truthfulness and meditation would free one of greed and therefore of suffering. These teachings won popular acceptance owing to their immediacy and practicality; the sermons of both were preached in commonly spoken languages. Both movements, Jainism and Buddhism, were, at least initially, essentially atheistic and therefore a challenge to Brahmanical orthodoxy.

With land becoming property and society being divided, conflicts and disorders were bound to arise. Organised power to resolve those conflicts emerged, giving rise to fully fledged state systems, including vast empires. The best known of these was the Magadha Empire, with its capital near modern-day Patna in Bihar, ruled by the Maurya dynasty. The Emperor Ashoka was its most famous figure. He ruled from 269 BC to 232 BC.

Mauryan India

The Mauryan economy was largely agrarian. Huge state-owned and private farms were cultivated by various forms of labour. While the state mobilised slaves, labourers and prisoners to work its lands, private fields were tilled by bonded or wage labourers and perhaps sharecroppers. The mighty Mauryan state also had among its sources of income gambling houses and brothels; but the chief source was taxes collected on land, trade and the manufacture of handicrafts.

The Greeks came in contact with India in the 6th and 5th centuries BC, through their conflict with the Persian Empire, which bordered northwestern India. In 327 BC Alexander of Macedon crossed into northwest India. When his armies seemed to have lost heart on the banks of the fifth river of Punjab and forced their chief to turn homewards, Alexander left behind governors to rule over the conquered territories. Over time, these territories lost out to Indian states.

But there was another sphere where contact between the two cultures left a far more lasting impact: art. Sculpture, especially of this region, bears a marked Hellenic influence.

The Mauryan empire did not long survive Ashoka. Its disintegration was an open invitation to invaders, mainly from Central Asia, to seek their fortunes in India. Among them were the Bactrian Greeks, survivors of Alexander's men who had settled in Iran and Afghanistan, the Parthians, the Shakas and the Kushanas.

They established kingdoms in the northwestern and northern regions that lasted for varying lengths of time. Over the decades they were submerged in the mainstream of Indian life, just as it happened with several earlier and later groups of invaders.

Literary heritage

South India at this time was divided into several states. They gave birth to a durable aspect of South Indian society which was then evolving: its culture, particularly a collective literature. This was emerging in the form of poems composed, so legend has it, during assemblies of

well as Java, Sumatra and Bali. The Romans imported spices, textiles, precious stones and birds from India and paid for them in gold. It was in Malabar, in present-day Kerala, that India first came into contact with Christianity and, later, Islam.

The Gupta Age

The second huge empire in Indian history emerged in the 4th century AD. It, too, covered a large part of South Asia, though not as large as the Mauryan Empire, and its administration was not as highly centralised. This was the Gupta Empire, which lasted more than two cen-

wandering poets and bards. Three such assemblies are said to have been held at Madurai, then capital of Tamil Nadu. At the third assembly more than 2,000 poems were collectively composed: these are known as the Sangam literature, an invaluable source of information about early Tamil society, culture and policy.

Control over the eastern and western coasts of South Asia also facilitated the establishment of trade relations between the Chola kingdom of Tamil Nadu and the distant Roman empire as

LEFT: one of the highly ornate gateways at the Buddhist stupa at Sanchi.
ABOVE: Jain sculptures at Gwalior Fort.

turies, its borders fluctuating with each successive ruler.

In the Gupta Age, orthodox Hinduism reasserted itself against the heretical sects that had sprung up. This was facilitated by the patronage the rulers extended to the Hindu religious tradition. However, there is little evidence of the use of violence to re-establish Hindu supremacy; indeed, we have the evidence of the Chinese traveller, Fa Hsien, who came to India in the beginning of the 5th century, that Buddhists and Brahmans lived in peaceful co-existence. The Buddhist monastery at Ajanta, cut into the hills and decorated with breathtaking murals, was a creation of this period. The caste system became far more rigid, however, and those below the lowest caste came to be treated at subhuman levels; even the sight of them was sufficient to pollute the upper castes.

Yet this age registered considerable achievements in literature and science, particularly in the areas of astronomy and mathematics. The most outstanding literary figure of the Gupta period was the writer Kalidasa whose choice of words and imagery brought Sanskrit drama to new heights. Aryabhatta, the astronomer, had argued that it was

> **SCIENTIFIC HEIGHTS**
>
> The Iron Pillar, erected in Delhi in the 4th century, still stands today, upright and without trace of rust, evidence of the Gupta's considerable knowledge of metallurgy.

the earth that moved round the sun, but he was completely ignored, though not persecuted.

It was also during the Gupta period that Hinduism broke with strict Vedic practices and turned towards devotional religion – posited on a personal relationship with the divine – *bhakti*.

Post-Gupta India witnessed many significant changes. The Indian economy had always been agrarian, though supplemented by trade and handicraft production. But with the end of the Gupta Age, trade declined dramatically and this led to a greater ruralisation of the economy. The amount of money in circulation also contracted. Land became the primary source of state as well as private income.

The centuries following the breakdown of the Gupta Empire witnessed a great deal of economic innovation, especially in agricultural production. From the 8th to the 12th centuries there were impressive works of irrigation. In northwestern and northern India various kinds of wheels were used to draw water from ponds or wells. These were initially manually operated; later on, from about the 13th century, a geared wheel was drawn by a pair of oxen – this was the Persian wheel, which can still be seen in use today.

In South India, water tanks provided the chief source of irrigation. Small tanks were constructed by the individual farmer, bigger ones by the village, or by the state. Canals and water channels also marked the rural landscape. In this way, new lands were brought under cultivation and new crops experimented with.

A new society

This economic expansion was creating greater social and economic disparities. While the Persian wheel could ensure water supply, its installation was a costly affair. Only the upper stratum of peasants could make the investment and reap the benefit.

The operation of caste laws excluded some of the lower castes from holding land of their own; it was their labour that came to be used by the entire community of cultivators, irrespective of its own stratification. This also introduced a paradox; a class of landless agricultural labourers was created in the context of an abundance of land. This was a peculiarly Indian solution to the problem of labour scarcity; medieval Europe had solved the same problem through the system of serfdom.

Greater agricultural production also meant greater resources for the rulers, who began to appropriate a large part of the produce in the form of land revenue. This in turn necessitated a greater centralised control over the system of revenue collection. On a small scale, such developments had already taken place in the regional kingdoms of the 11th and 12th centuries all over South Asia. ❑

LEFT: 4th-century Iron Pillar at Qutb Minar, Delhi.
RIGHT: sculpture of Yakshi, the tree spirit, from Barhut, Madhya Pradesh, 2nd century BC.

THE SULTANATES AND AFTER

Under the sultans and emperors of the 13th–18th centuries
India grew prosperous, and culture and science flourished

At the outset of the 13th century, a new wave of invaders from Central Asia made its way to North India. This time they had come to stay. They professed a different religion, Islam. A new state was established in 1206, which came to be known as the Delhi Sultanate. By the first quarter of the 13th

century it had brought under its direct or indirect control the greater part of North India. During the course of the 320 years of its existence, the throne of the Delhi Sultanate changed hands among six dynasties.

The process of centralisation of administrative control over revenue collection reached its climax under the sultans of Delhi.

Land revenue was legally fixed at half the produce; soldiers and officers were assigned territories to collect revenue that equalled their annual salary. Other high officials were given charge of large territories from which they were to collect the revenue, maintain an army and, of course, themselves, and look after law and

order. About 6 percent of the state revenue was given away in charity to religious institutions and pious individuals.

While this picture suggests a considerable resemblance to feudal Europe, there were some crucial differences. The assignees had no right over the land, which belonged to the peasants; they had the right merely to collect the revenue due to the state. Secondly, the officials (or assignees) were actually transferred from one territory to another every three or four years. This was to pre-empt corruption and their sinking of local roots and gaining personal control over the administrative apparatus.

This is how the growth of a permanent landed aristocracy, with power based on control over land, was cleverly prevented until the 19th century. It was only under the aegis of colonial rule that such a class took root in India.

The revenue system

Although a large majority of the administrative officials of the Sultanate were Muslims, the bulk of the revenue collection machinery was still run by Hindus. Often the tensions generated by conflicts of interests between the two sections were portrayed as being religious in nature. Inevitably, the establishment of the new state created manifold tensions, at times interregional, religious, and sectarian.

The increased produce from the land was beginning to find its way into an expanding network of markets. This process was accelerated when the Sultanate began to show its preference for the collection of revenue in cash rather than grain. This gave a spurt to the growth of urban centres, as well as to markets.

The Sultanate also introduced several new crafts and promoted or changed old ones. The spinning wheel, though of uncertain origin, is first encountered in India in the 14th century; its productivity compared to that of the distaff was five to six times higher. This led to a greater production of coarse cotton textiles, worn by the poor. Paper also came to India at this time, as did gunpowder, both perhaps from China.

The break-up of the Delhi Sultanate began in the second quarter of the 14th century, during the reign of the controversial ruler, Muhammad bin Tughlaq. Tughlaq was an intellectual *par excellence*, enamoured of the force of reason, possessing a powerful imagination, impatient with those who failed to keep pace with his ideas, but who achieved little. His reign of 26 years was marked by 15 rebellions of his nobles. Among the parts of the Sultanate that broke away were two southern regions, each harbouring an independent dynasty, one Hindu, the other Muslim. Both these, the Vijayanagar Empire and the Bahmani Kingdom, have left behind some of the most magnificent architectural monuments, though they now lie in ruins.

> ## SULTAN ARCHITECTURE
> The Sultanates introduced new styles of architecture: minarets, as at Qutb Minar; the perfect round dome on a square or rectangular base; and the true arch.

The much-contracted empire of the Sultans of Delhi lingered on as several of its regions established independent kingdoms. The remainder of the "empire", much weakened, provided an irresistible temptation to any Central Asian adventurer with a strong army to reach out here for plunder. The most devastating of these plundering raids was led by Timur in 1398; among the prized loot that he carried home were numerous Indian artisans.

The Mughal Empire

An Uzbek prince, who had failed to protect his kingdom against his cousins' intrigues and battles, was to follow the old invaders' route of northwestern mountain passes into India in 1526. This was Zahiruddin Muhammad Babur, a descendant of Timur as well as Chingiz Khan, founder of the Mughal Empire in India. It was during the reign of his grandson Akbar, who ruled over North India and parts of the South from 1556 to 1605, that the basic institutions and policies of the empire were framed.

Ascending the throne at the age of 13, Akbar began to take interest in the affairs of state only after spending another four years in adolescent playfulness. However, at the age of 17 he took full charge of the situation and never looked back. Akbar realised that if the empire was to attain stability, it must grow local roots and

seek support from the local ruling groups. He thus began altering the predominantly alien character of the nobility by recruiting groups of indigenous rulers from various regions.

The most powerful among these were the Rajputs of Rajasthan. He took the daughters of several Rajput houses as his wives, respected their customs, bestowed upon them some of the highest imperial offices, but dealt ruthlessly with those who refused to surrender. Gradually, he reduced every group in the higher nobility to

a minority, including his Mughal brethren. The result was that each group had to tolerate and co-operate with the others.

The administrative institutions of the Delhi Sultanate were modified and a new bureaucratic framework was evolved. Under this, every official, from the lowest to the highest, was recruited and paid by the imperial department of the army. This greatly tightened central control. The system of transfer of officials was rigorously implemented. Payment of salaries was first made in cash; gradually, however, the old system of revenue assignment came back into vogue. But then a person might be posted in Gujarat and yet his revenue assignment might

LEFT: Mughal Emperor Jahangir at Fatehpur Sikri, the town built near Agra by his father, Akbar.
RIGHT: Sher Singh, a Sikh chieftain.

be located in Bengal. This necessitated revenue collection in cash.

Land was classified into four categories according to productivity, and a graduated land tax was imposed on peasants, going by the period for which their land had remained fallow. The ideal was, of course, two regular crops each year from every field. Peasants were given documents stating their liabilities.

Himself illiterate, Akbar took great interest in intellectual discussions on matters of religion and metaphysics; he called assemblies of theologians professing various religions, including Christians, and engaged in an exchange

A keen interest in cultural pursuits was characteristic of the Mughal Empire. Both its founder and his last descendant were eminent poets; several of the emperors and princes were deeply concerned with problems of metaphysics, some were writers of superb memoirs. Jahangir, besides leaving behind one such book, was a connoisseur and patron of the art of painting; Shah Jahan's fame rests on the creation of the Taj Mahal in memory of his queen who had died giving birth to his 14th child.

Aurangzeb, the third of Shah Jahan's four surviving sons, has been much maligned by generations of historians. His rise to power was

AKBAR

The greatest Mughal is said to be Akbar, who in 1556 inherited the throne when barely in his teens and went on to rule for 49 years and build an empire that lasted two centuries more. He was politically astute and a hyperactive military genius. It took him just nine days to march 1,000 km (621 miles) from Fatehpur Sikri to Ahmadabad in Gujarat, where his swift mounted warriors defeated enemy troops after just two days' rest. He controlled virtually all of North and Central India and most of Afghanistan. Akbar became a patron of literature and the arts although he was illiterate. A part-time mystic given to collecting emeralds, he had 300 wives and 5,000 concubines; he allowed his Hindu wives to practise their rites within the Red Fort. Rajputs were permitted to keep their kingdoms and pride, and happily supplied soldiers to this Mughal overlord who curtailed excessive taxation. Akbar received ambassadors from Elizabethan England and Jesuit priests from Portugal, and synthesised a new religion with himself as God King. He delighted in hunting cheetahs into old age.

of ideas with them, refusing to accept the absolute primacy of Islam. He also patronised the writing of history and a monumental historical work was compiled during his reign: the *Akbar Nama* (the "Book of Akbar").

In his numerous and massive buildings at Fatehpur Sikri and Agra, where he had established his capital, there is an exquisite assimilation of Islamic and Hindu architectural styles.

Akbar's son and grandson, Jahangir and Shah Jahan, continued to expand and strengthen the empire, and are notable for their extensive patronage of the arts and architecture. Monuments left by Shah Jahan include the Taj Mahal, and the Red Fort and Jama Masjid in Delhi.

no more ruthless than that of his father, and his reputation for religious intolerance is undeserved. He came to the throne after imprisoning his father (Shah Jahan is said to have spent his last years gazing at the Taj Mahal from the battlements of Agra fort) and killing his brothers.

His 48-year reign was marked by a firm administrative hand and by attempts to put down the Marathas led by Shivaji and to expand the empire into southern India. Towards the end of his life he became a religious ascetic, spending his time in prayer and copying out the Qur'an. The eventual break-up of the empire owed more to internal problems of administration than to any misrule.

Europe comes to India

During the 17th century, India had also been host to a very large number of West European travellers; among them were Italians, English, French and Dutch. Some had come to India for reasons of commerce, others in pursuit of knowledge, and others bitten by the travel bug. Some, like the French doctor François Bernier, rose high in the confidence of princes; others went around on their own, noting down impressions to be published later.

Beside individual travellers, organised European intervention in India's commerce took place during the 17th century when England, France, the Netherlands and Denmark floated East India Companies. Chartered as trading companies by their respective governments, they sought chiefly Indian textiles, both silk and cotton, indigo and, at times, other items. The spices of Malabar (Kerala) had attracted the Portuguese in the 15th century when, in 1498, Vasco da Gama had landed at Calicut, sailing via the Cape of Good Hope. Early in the 16th century, the Portuguese had already established their colony in Goa; but their territorial

LEFT: Akbar, 16th-century Mughal emperor.
ABOVE: Shah Jahan's 17th-century Mughal masterpiece, the Taj Mahal, was a tribute to his empress.

and commercial hold in India remained rather limited. During the late 16th and the 17th century they remained unrivalled as pirates on the high seas; but inland the other European companies were making their presence felt, though entirely in commercial terms.

The companies were trading in a sellers' market, competing with one another to purchase finished Indian goods. They had brought with them woollen cloths and garments, but these commanded a rather limited market, given India's tropical climate. At any rate, woollens were produced in India, too. They also brought knives and clocks, but knives could hardly be transported and sold on a scale to balance the purchase of textiles and indigo, and clocks were not a great success because the measurement of time was done altogether differently. They therefore had to make their purchases by paying mostly in gold and silver.

Valuable as the European trade was, it formed a very small fraction of commercial activity, and had no effect on agriculture. Trade carried on by Indian merchants was far higher in value. One great Indian merchant of the 17th century in Surat, Abdul Ghaffoor, had greater assets at his disposal than the Indian assets of all the East India Companies together. There were many other merchants scattered in Surat and elsewhere in the country, not as rich as Abdul Ghaffoor, but nonetheless important. Indeed, the companies had often to depend upon individual merchants for loans to pay for their transactions.

For the ruling class, India in the 17th century presented a picture of agreeable prosperity and dynamism. The immensely fertile lands of the river valleys had not been fully brought under cultivation. The economy was essentially agrarian, yet trade and money had penetrated to almost every village. Monetary

transactions had given rise to a highly skilled, and locally powerful, professional class of moneychangers and moneylenders. Insurance and bills of exchange had also reached a high degree of complexity.

If the Indian economy was predominantly agrarian, there was a strong urban streak in it. One writer at the end of the 16th century enumerated 3,200 cities and towns across the Mughal Empire.

The degree of centralisation of control over the administration of the vast empire was unparalleled in the contemporary world; this was combined with a high degree of centralised control over the empire's resources. It has been

> **CASH RICH**
>
> Indian currency in the 17th century was struck in gold, silver and bronze. Anyone who had these metals could walk into a mint and have them coined.

estimated that only 73 individuals (0.9 percent of the nobles) had under their command 37.6 percent of the revenues of the empire in the mid-17th century and they did not include the emperor himself. The concentration of such economic wealth and control can explain the grandeur that has almost become synonymous with the word "Mughal".

But then the collapse of such authority usually occurs with comparable enormity; as it certainly did in this case.

Religion and literature

If impressive progress in the sphere of music, painting and, above all, architecture occurred under the emperor, literature developed outside the imperial precincts. Sanskrit and Tamil were "classical" languages with highly complex poetry predating the empires by several centuries; but many regional languages, such as Hindi, Urdu, Gujarati, Marathi and Bengali, had begun to take shape from around the 15th century (earlier in the south with Kannada, Telugu and Malayalam). By the 17th century, each had acquired a distinct identity with its own literature.

By the 17th century India had also learnt to live with a number of religious communities. Hindus still constituted the preponderant part of the population. Among Muslims, the Sunnis predominated, though the Shias too had pockets of large population. In Kerala, Indian Christians were a familiar sight. Among the older religions, the Jains continued to dominate trade in western India. Buddhism had ceased to exist in any significant magnitude.

The medieval period, especially from the late 15th to the 17th century, also witnessed the evolution of a new group in Punjab: the Sikhs. This sect, commanding the support of hardy peasants, cultivating the most fertile of Indian plains, denounced the caste system and emphasised social equality and devotion to God and the word of their Guru (teacher). Founded by a gentle and compassionate Guru, Nanak, the sect came into violent conflict with the Mughals who executed two of its 10 Gurus. In self-defence, it transformed itself into a truly militant religion. Hospitable and generous to a fault, the Sikhs have adhered to a tradition of militancy whenever their religious institutions have been tampered with.

Even as clashes occurred between the Mughal state and various groups that were to form regional kingdoms in the 17th and 18th centuries – and these groups comprised Hindus in Maharashtra, Sikhs in Punjab and Muslims in several other regions – medieval Indian society was almost completely devoid of communal religious tensions.

RELIGIOUS TOLERANCE

Travellers in India in the 17th century noted how the various religious groups lived in harmony compared to the hostilities between Christians in Europe.

An empire crumbles

The 18th century was to witness a sea change in the overall scene in India. After 1707, the

rein to officials to fleece the peasants; the peasants in turn resisted this by taking up arms. The regional states that inherited the Mughal Empire were not of uniform character. Some of them had been established by eminent Mughal nobles who had broken away from the empire: among these were Bengal, Avadh and the newly founded state of Hyderabad; others had come into existence following popular rebellions against the imperial authority – these included the Maratha kingdom in Maharashtra and the

mighty Mughal Empire began to crumble and give way to smaller regional kingdoms. Such of the empire as survived was riven with friction and intrigue. The ever-expanding class of officials was beginning to find the resources at its disposal utterly unequal to the demand; this led to intense struggles among officials at every level to grab whatever they could and strive to hold on to whatever others were seeking to wrest from them. The consequent loss of control over the administrative setup gave free

LEFT: 18th-century depiction of the monsoon.
ABOVE: an Indian artist's impression of local government at the beginning of British rule.

state of an Afghan people called Rohillas who had settled in Uttar Pradesh. Inevitably, the Mughal model continued to exercise overwhelming influence on the evolution of regional policies in these states.

The Maratha Empire

The power that came closest to imperial pretensions was that of the Marathas. Starting from scratch, the non-Brahman castes in the Maharashtra region had been organised into a fighting force by their legendary leader, Shivaji. He led an extraordinary life, still remembered in song and legend, in which he was always one step ahead of his adversaries; he even went to the

Mughal court in Delhi to negotiate a truce, which broke down due to mistrust on both sides. In one notable episode, Shivaji killed the Bijapur representative Afzal Khan by embracing the general with iron claws attached to his fingers. During their heyday in the 18th century, the Marathas moved like lightning and suddenly appeared in areas where least expected. They always went home with their hands full of plunder. States began to pay them vast amounts in "protection money", insurance against their plundering raids.

COLONIAL ECONOMICS

It was the Dutch success in taking what is now Indonesia that drove the British to concentrate their efforts on India in an attempt to acquire profitable Asian territories.

By the third quarter of the 18th century, the Marathas had under their direct administration enough Indian territory to justify the use of the term "the Maratha Empire", though it never came near the dimensions of the Mughal Empire. The Marathas also never sought to formally substitute themselves for the Mughals; they often kept the emperor under their thumb but still paid him formal obeisance. Their ruthlessness in the wake of their battles against Aurangzeb's armies, especially towards Muslim populations, meant they were not trusted to the same degree as the Mughal administration had been, a further factor in their inability to form an extensive empire.

The disintegration of the Mughal Empire was also an invitation to foreign invasions – a scenario common in Indian history. Nadir Shah, an Iranian ruler leading an attack in 1739, killed about 30,000 troops and civilians and plundered the capital, carrying off the famous Peacock Throne that had stood in the Red Fort, and the 105-carat Koh-i-noor diamond, the largest in the world. The second invasion in the 18th century, under the command of the ruler of Afghanistan, led to more permanent consequences. In 1761 the Afghan armies met the Marathas in battle near Delhi. The decisive defeat of the Marathas put an end to their imperial ambitions. The road was now wide open for the British to move in and colonise India.

The European companies had organised their trade around the "factories" (their overseas agents were called factors) they had established in several towns; these factories were in reality mere warehouses for the commodities they had purchased. As the power of the Mughal Empire to protect them declined, they began to fend for themselves, recruiting their own miniature armies and using European weapons that were often superior to the Indian ones. This provided an irresistible temptation to the groups engaged in ousting each other from positions of power in the states. The Europeans, too, were eager to sell their services to the highest bidder. Bit by bit they acquired a foothold in the political and administrative setup in several of these states. Inevitably, different European groups often stood in opposite Indian camps; their own rivalries, operating through their Indian patrons, contributed greatly to the prevailing friction.

Of the European East India Companies that had come to trade in India, the Dutch had shifted their focus to Indonesia; the Portuguese held on to Goa, but were no contenders for imperial status; the Danes were never a significant factor. The real contest was between the English and the French. The English ultimately outwitted the French to become rulers of India for nearly two centuries. ❑

LEFT: Maharaja Pratap Singh of Alwar, Rajasthan.
RIGHT: Jantar Mantar, the observatory at Jaipur, built with precision by Maharaja Jai Singh II in 1716.

THE YEARS OF THE RAJ

India was described as the "brightest jewel in the British Crown", but for the people of India Independence was the prime objective

It was in Bengal that the English made the first successful bid for rule in India. In 1757 and again in 1765 they defeated the Bengal ruler and, during the intervening years, engaged in the most unscrupulous intrigues at his court. The battle of 1765 was followed by an atrocious division of authority: while the local ruler was responsible for the administration, the British took charge of the revenues. The chaos that resulted led, in the words of a Bengali poet, to "a night of eternal gloom for India".

The English East India Company continued its commercial activities, of course, but it no longer needed to import gold and silver into Bengal to purchase textiles for export to Britain and thence to Europe; it could make the purchases with the fabulous Bengal revenues. There was, besides, private trade carried on by private British citizens as well as the Company's servants. Nor was there any lack of financial corruption on the part of British officials, including governors.

A new aristocracy

Towards the end of the 18th century, the East India Company started planning for a long stay. For this purpose it required local support. This was obtained by creating a class of landed aristocracy akin to the feudal aristocracy of Europe.

In Mughal India, while officials were entitled to a part or all of the revenue due to the state, the land belonged to the peasants. The British devised "Permanent Settlement", which altered this situation and created a class that held its vast lands permanently, so long as it paid revenues to the state. The peasants were at the mercy of this class. Grateful that they had been granted unfettered rights, this aristocracy was to remain loyal to the British cause up until Independence. The demand for revenue by the British was passed on to those least able to pay – the peasants.

In the early 19th century the British extended their hold. A large part of South Asia was brought under direct administration; some local rulers were retained as subsidiaries of the Company. By 1857 "the British empire in India had become the British empire of India". Although the activities of the Company were regularly

and closely supervised by the British Parliament, there was little possibility of placing any real restraints on the Company's functioning, for the revenues drained from India in money and in trade brought prosperity on a large enough scale in Britain to create a vested interest in the colonisation of India.

This interest was apart from the personal benefit that many Members of Parliament derived from involvement in the Company's enterprises; not infrequently the Company or its retired employees invested money to purchase seats in the House of Commons for its agents. Among its patrons the Company could count even the sovereign.

LEFT: Bahadur Shah Zafar, the last Mughal emperor, who was exiled to Burma by the British in 1857.
RIGHT: Independence celebrations, Kolkata, 1947.

The British hold over the Indian economy and society, too, underwent a substantial change in the first half of the 19th century. If the peasant was carrying the ever-rising burden of supporting the government and the indigenous landed aristocracy, the artisan could still sell his goods to the Company, for which the demand had not contracted. This was particularly true of silk and cotton textiles, though the market for indigo was shrinking, for a better-quality indigo was being manufactured in the West Indies. The superior

TAXING TEXTILES

The threat to the British textile industry from quality Indian goods was such that in 1760 an English woman was fined £200 for using an Indian-made handkerchief.

quality of Indian textiles, however, posed a threat to the English textile industry throughout the 18th century and heavy duties and fines were imposed.

Yet the demand for textiles did not decline. The decisive shift came with the industrialisation of cloth manufacture in Britain. The very scale of its production and low price began to drive out the handloom-manufactured textiles.

In 1794 the value of British cotton manufactures sold in India amounted to £156; in 1813 it had risen to £110,000. Under pressure of the manufacturers, Parliament in 1833 abolished the Company's monopoly over the Indian trade and opened the floodgates to British goods, the custom duties for which were fixed at nominal levels. By 1856 British imports into India were valued at £6.3 million. Inevitably, the Indian textile industry was ruined. Instead, Indian raw cotton was exported to Britain to be turned into finished goods and then sent back to the Indian market.

For capturing the vast Indian market, it was necessary to develop the country's transport and communications. Steamships started navigating the network of Indian rivers; roads were repaired and improved; and in 1853 railways arrived. In the same year the telegraph was also introduced.

Along with these modern means of transport and communications came certain modern concepts of social organisation. A separation of civil administrative functions from those of the army and the police, and the notion of the rule of law and equality before the law were all major departures from the then existing forms of social functioning. So also was the attempt at rooting out some of the social customs such as a widow burning herself at the funeral pyre of her husband (*sati*), or the infanticide of female children. Western sciences and philosophy taught through the medium of English were also first experimented with in 1835, in Bengal.

There was considerable support for these measures among many Indian intellectuals and social reformers who had had the opportunity to compare traditional Indian with modern European educational and social systems. Clearly these changes were only the first step towards a transformation of Indian society; the overwhelming part of it still remained steeped in tradition, not all of which was admirable.

The progress of British rule in India had understandably generated various kinds of resentment in different locales. The princely houses that had been deprived of their territories and power could hardly relish the goings-on; the Company's high civil and military officials seldom adhered to their own declared principles, for it was after all not easy to sacrifice the prospect of territorial expansion for the sake of any scruples. Impoverishment of ruling houses brought in its wake misery for vast numbers of those directly or indirectly dependent on court patronage for their livelihood – courtiers, soldiers, servants, merchants, artists.

Artisans, especially textile weavers, suffered directly when the Company sought to depress the wages of labour and prices of goods, and later flooded Indian markets with British goods. Several towns, centres of textile production, were ruined. In the countryside, the peasants were being subjected to an ever-rising demand for revenue.

The Uprising of 1857

The British hold on India and the unfolding of its political and economic policies were marked by

SATI BAN

The British ban on a widow's self-immolation at her husband's funeral pyre was seen by some Indians as an unwelcome interference with an age-old custom.

in Delhi, which housed his palace, and whose "revenue" was a pension settled on him by the Company. Yet this old man was to become the centre and the symbol of the massive rebellion.

The immediate cause of the rebellion was an order issued by the Company's army commanders to the Indian sepoys to bite the cartridges before putting them into their rifles. A rumour spread that the cartridges were greased with the fat of cows and pigs. Since cows were held sacred by the Hindus and there were few sins

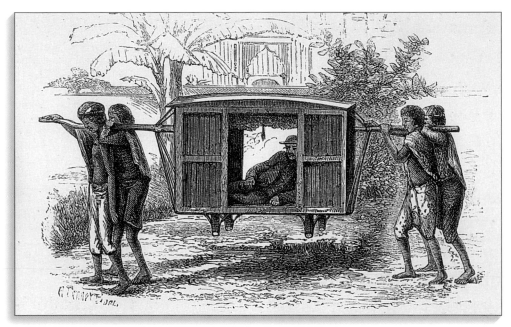

sporadic and local uprisings in several regions. What happened in 1857, however, was a concerted effort on a grand scale in large parts of India to be rid of alien rule. This was an endeavour in which the Mughal emperor, a number of princely states in the regions, artisans and peasants and Indian sepoys of the Company's army joined hands against the common enemy.

"Mughal" was a hallowed name, although the emperor was an aged man, whose "empire" did not extend beyond the walls of the Red Fort

LEFT: some rajas became British vassals and saw their states survive intact until after Independence.
ABOVE: an early 18th-century sahib in a palanquin.

greater than eating beef, this order was greatly upsetting. The Muslims were also hurt by the utter indifference to their religious sentiment, which forbade them even to touch pork, held unclean by them. Thus, irrespective of the truth of the rumour, both Hindu and Muslim sepoys were alienated at one go. The fact that the rumour was easily believed pointed to the general level of alienation of the government from the people, and it served as a spark to set the forest of discontent on fire.

On 10 May 1857, sepoys stationed at Meerut, near Delhi, mutinied. This was the beginning of the rebellion. From Meerut the sepoys marched to Delhi where they were joined by the local infantry who killed their British officers and carried off the "emperor" to "lead" them. From Delhi, the revolt spread to northern and central India, and into the ranks of townsmen and peasants. However, the landed aristocracy that the British had created through the Permanent Settlement stood by its master. It was a fight to the end on both sides with bloodshed, violence and hatred fully unleashed. But the outcome did not favour India. While vast numbers of Indians rose in revolt, many groups and regions

JOB VACANCIES

No Indian was allowed to rise to an officer's position in the army until after 1910. Indians could compete for high Civil Service jobs, but few were successful.

stood by silently and there were others who joined hands with the British. The latter were also better armed and had more efficient means of communication, including the railways and telegraph. The "emperor" did not possess the capacity of leadership in a situation in which leadership was of critical importance.

The uprising lasted a year and a half; by the end of 1859 the "emperor" had been deported to Burma where he died a lonely death, bringing to a formal end the grand era of Mughal rule in India.

Even in its failure, the Mutiny produced a sense of unity between the Hindus and the Muslims. This was one of the chief lessons the

government was to draw from 1857; that such unity must be pre-empted through "divide and rule" policies. Immediately after the Mutiny, Muslims were discriminated against by the government: they were denied employment opportunities in the government and barred from the modern education to ensure they remained at a disadvantage to Hindus, which meant that they would forever be in contention with them.

The uprising saw the end of the Company's rule in India. Power was transferred to the British Crown in 1858 by an Act of British Parliament. The Crown's viceroy in India was to be the chief executive. The army was reorganised with a far greater number of British officers than had been the case hitherto. The highest posts in most administrative departments were reserved for the British subjects of the Crown.

The new government sought to accommodate some of the princely states that had stood by the British in 1857; they were to be the bulwark of Britain's Indian Empire. But, of course, this accommodation was to be allowed within the framework of complete subordination to imperial authority.

Gone, too, was the zeal for social reform; the government began carefully to refrain from interfering with any of the social customs of Indians. Enthusiasm for imparting a Western education to wider Indian society also began to wane, and university education remained confined for a long time to the three cities – Kolkata, Mumbai and Chennai – where universities had been established in 1857.

Onset of industrialisation

The Indian contact with Britain's growing industrialisation had initially undermined the market for the products of India's artisans. Gradually, however, this contact also brought modern industry to India. The first textile mill began operating in Mumbai in 1853 and the first jute mill in Bengal two years later. By 1905, more than 200 cotton textile mills and 36 jute mills were functioning. A large iron and steel plant was established in Jharkhand, which continues to operate today. Some of these mills and factories were established by Indians, but most were under the control of British capital, which saw enormous profits in the cheap raw materials and labour and a vast market in India and abroad. The introduction of modern industry brought with it incipient conflict between British and Indian entrepreneurs. The government extended all patronage to British-owned industries, and plantations such as tea, indigo and coffee, and discriminated against Indian capital.

Political activity

There was a remarkable degree of social awakening in the second half of the 19th century;

USE OF FORCE

The army was used to suppress protest against British rule and in campaigns against Burma and Afghanistan. In 1904 it used up 52 percent of India's revenue.

were to be effective. The crucial new method was to be based on organised strength, challenging the government on its own ground, within the framework of British laws and policies. This clearly required a class of highly educated Indians, especially lawyers. British-trained Indian lawyers were indeed to play a crucial role in Indian National Movement, the political vehicle for India's liberation In 1885, a national-level organisation was formed that was to play a decisive role in the country's subsequent

apparent were the growth of modern ideas and realisation of the need for removing social evils. At times it took on a religious mantle so that religious movements were often covers for protests against such evils as child mariages, or the stigma on widows remarrying.

Above all, there was a growing political consciousness that encompassed all other spheres of activity. The violent uprising of 1857 had ended in failure; new methods of protest against alien rule had to be adopted if protest

history: this was the Indian National Congress. The initial thrust for its creation came from a retired English civil servant, Allan Octavian Hume, who recruited eminent educated Indians in Mumbai and held the organisation's first session. He had seen it as a "safety valve" against the spread of popular discontent. In his own words, "A safety valve for the escape of great and growing forces generated by our own action was urgently needed."

To begin with, Congress sought to air reservations against the government's laws and political and administrative measures. Gradually, various strands began to appear within the organisation. The "moderate" and the "extremist"

LEFT: Queen Victoria, Empress of India, from a painting at Fort St George Museum, Chennai.
ABOVE: Western India Turf Club, Pune, *circa* 1900.

wings began to make their appearance by the beginning of the 20th century. While the "moderates" sought gradual reform within the structure of law and government and expressed their aspirations through speeches and petitions, the "extremists" were hostile to the notion of an alien government and were prepared to use violence to achieve their objective.

The perils of partition

A major departure in the growth of Indian nationalism occurred in 1905. In that year an order was issued for the partition of Bengal into two units. The public justification for this order

was that this would make the two provinces administratively more viable; privately, officials at various levels admitted that the objective was to stem the tide of nationalism then on the rise among Bengalis, by separating East and West Bengal and isolating them from the people of other linguistic regions (Assam, Bihar, Jharkhand and Orissa), which together constituted a single province. Leaders of the National Movement understood the purpose of this move and prepared to oppose it tooth and nail.

If nothing else mobilised the masses of Indian people into opposition of the government, the proposed partition of Bengal did. There were hunger strikes, general strikes, marches, demonstrations and public meetings, in all of which large numbers of people participated. Above all, a new weapon, likely to touch the British where it hurt most, was adopted: the boycott of British goods and use instead of Indian-made commodities. This gave an enormous spurt to Indian industry in various sectors. The movement, with its nerve centre in Kolkata, began to spread throughout the country in diverse forms, from peaceful strikes and protest marches to acts of terrorism.

The government countered with unprecedented repression, of which imprisonment was the mildest form. A political manoeuvre on the government's part was to have a more lasting impact on India's future: calculated steps were taken to create dissensions between the predominantly Muslim East Bengal (now Bangladesh) and Hindu West Bengal, which proved easy to provoke. This was to become a central issue in the National Movement and lead to serious consequences. Several vain attempts were made to find a solution to this problem.

The British policy of weakening the National Movement by creating dissensions within it bore its first fruit in 1906 when the All India Muslim League was founded. It stood up in support of the partition of Bengal and demanded special concessions from the government for the Muslims, such as proportionate reservation of government jobs for them. However, the League's claim to be the representative of all the Muslims of India was challenged by a large number of Muslim leaders who had pledged their support to the Congress. Even so, two political entities, one representing the Muslims exclusively, the other the Hindus predominantly, began to operate. At times they entered into agreements with one another, at others they adopted mutually antagonistic postures. In either case their separate identities persisted.

While the government responded to the growing Movement by resorting to repression and division, it also sought to appease public opinion by amending its legal structure. It began to introduce legislatures with elected as well as nominated members and with some control over a few of the departments of administration. Voting rights were, however, severely restricted. Such measures fell short of the goals that the National Movement had set for itself.

Most of the leaders of the Movement were lawyers who had had their legal training in

England and had familiarised themselves with the working of the parliamentary system there. These leaders, while participating in these legislatures, were dissatisfied with the severe limitations that were placed on them. But they were frequently willing to resign collectively, an act that would paralyse the entire functioning of the legislatures.

The Gandhi era

In 1917 a new phase began in the developing struggle for India's freedom. In 1915, Mohandas Karamchand Gandhi had returned to India from South Africa where he had experimented

the moral protest latent among the victims, so unleashing the energy and power of the multitudes without incurring any expense on arms.

The story of Gandhi's experiments had reached India, his homeland. When he returned in 1915 he was already a well-known figure. Before launching himself into the struggle, Gandhi sought to familiarise himself with conditions in India. He undertook extensive tours of various regions of the country and saw for himself the immense poverty and degradation suffered by the masses at the hands of both their Indian and foreign masters. The misery of the lower castes, perpetrated by the upper castes,

M.K. GANDHI

Mohandas Karamchand Gandhi (1869–1948) was a British-trained lawyer and a radical proponent of non-violence. He left Mumbai in 1893 for South Africa to work as a lawyer, where he become involved in the struggle for workers' rights. In 1915 he returned to his homeland and became involved in the movement for Indian self-rule. Gandhi revived the hunger strike as a potent political protest and his passive resistance tactics inspired freedom movements worldwide. His followers called him "Mahatma" (Great Soul), though many preferred "Bapu" (Little Father). An ascetic, he preferred village to urban life and adopted the villagers' dress of *dhoti* and shawl. Gandhi led a Salt March in 1930 in defiance of British tax demands. In 1947 he negotiated an end to 190 years of British colonial rule. The following year he was assassinated at the age of 78 by a Hindu nationalist who objected to his continued religious tolerance, following the savage communal violence that accompanied Partition.

with new forms of resistance to the racism he had found there. He had gone to South Africa to practise as a lawyer after his training as barrister-at-law in England. In South Africa he witnessed and experienced humiliation because of the colour of his skin. In protest he began to organise the Indian victims of segregation to wage a completely non-violent protest. The victims were to violate the unjust law publicly and take the punishment willingly. The strategy was to appeal to the conscience of the oppressors, and arouse

LEFT: Bhagat Singh, leading member of a 1930s revolutionary group, who was hanged by the British.
RIGHT: Mahatma Gandhi called for Independence.

the inhuman treatment of bonded farm labourers, the deprivation from which Indian women suffered everywhere – all these facets of inhumanity came clear to him as he travelled in crowded trains, bullock-carts and on foot.

Gandhi also realised that most of India still lived in villages, and that it was in those villages that India's real strength lay. This resource could be tapped only if relief was brought to Indian peasants from exploitation both at the hands of Indian landlords and the British government and planters.

Gandhi reached a similar conclusion about the industrial workers. He strongly believed that their living conditions must improve and

Indian mill owners must sacrifice a part of their profit for this purpose. From the beginning, Gandhi waged a moral protest against oppression by defying unjust laws and willingly taking punishment. He would often undertake fasts lasting several weeks until his demands had been conceded.

Defying laws frequently led him into prison. Following him, other leaders went to jail for the same offence; then masses of people, moved by his inspiring leadership, followed suit. Gandhi, however, always imposed one inviolable condition: defiance of law, or "civil disobedience" as it came to be called, must

NON-COOPERATION

In 1920 a "Non-Cooperation Movement" was launched jointly by Congress and Muslims to protest against unwarranted killings in Punjab, and against the British government going back on its promise to Muslim Turkey during World War I that Turkey would not be deprived of "the rich and renowned lands of Asia Minor and Thrace which are predominantly Turkish in race" once the war was over; yet Thrace was detached from Turkey just as war ended. The British treatment of the Turkish Caliph hurt Muslims in India who treated him as the head of their world. Congress hoped the movement would win over Muslims for joint struggles against the British.

always be completely peaceful. The government had been familiar with the passing of resolutions at annual Congress sessions; it was familiar, too, with demonstrations, public meetings and terrorist activity; but this was altogether a new form of protest, which it did not know how to handle. Consequently, it reacted clumsily. If it imprisoned the leaders, as it often did, multitudes of Indians would line up to fill the jails; they had to be released because prisons could no longer hold them. If it opened fire on unarmed and peaceful protestors, as it did in 1919 in Punjab, its own pretensions to civilised behaviour would be exposed and its legitimacy questioned. It was willing to give some concessions, but these fell short of the demand.

In 1921 and 1922 unprecedented scenes of mass participation in the newly formed Non-Cooperation Movement were witnessed throughout India. People of all communities, regions and ages responded to the call by giving up their studies, jobs, everything. Women joined the movement in massive numbers. Boycott of European cloth became a public cry and bonfires of imported cloth were made. Hindus and Muslims forgot all about their differences.

The government reacted as usual with imprisonment and gunfire, which only helped to bring even more people into the movement. But the government was saved by Gandhi himself at a time when the movement was attaining ever higher peaks: he suddenly withdrew from the struggle because in a village in eastern Uttar Pradesh some policemen had fired upon a procession of 3,000 peasants and the peasants had, in a moment of rage, burnt down the police station and caused the death of 22 policemen. Gandhi's condition of non-violence had been violated; he would have nothing to do with any protest that carried even a suggestion of violence. He called off non-cooperation and the rebellion ended.

This was an anticlimax that was not appreciated by most of the leaders of the National Movement, both old and young. Among the latter was Jawaharlal Nehru. The Movement began to drift without much force and without a clear aim. But this mood was not to last long. Late in the 1920s a new strand of leadership was beginning to emerge, both within the Congress and outside. This strand comprised a younger group of men and women inspired by the socialist ideas of Marx and Lenin.

In 1925 the Communist Party of India had been formed; its membership remained rather small, but its influence, particularly among workers, peasants and the intelligentsia, was disproportionate to its numerical strength.

Within the Congress, leadership was beginning to pass into the hands of younger men, who also carried distinctly socialist sympathies, men such as Subhash Chandra Bose and Jawaharlal Nehru. There were, besides, young men and women who constituted a stream of revolutionary terrorists. They were moved by a commitment to the vision of remoulding Indian society as much as by anti-imperialist sentiment.

expression in their writings and speeches. This concern, in turn, brought even larger numbers of India's poor masses into the struggle.

The demand for Independence

It was this mood that was reflected in the resolution of the Congress passed in 1929: the resolution demanded complete Independence for India. Jawaharlal Nehru presided over the session. The day the resolution was adopted, 26 January 1930, was later known as Republic Day, the anniversary of which was to be observed by Indians by unfurling a new tricoloured flag and taking the Independence pledge, which

The most famous of these revolutionaries was Bhagat Singh, who was put to death for throwing a bomb into the central legislative assembly hall during a session. He was 23 and still studying the writings of socialist thinkers when he was sent to the gallows.

The influence of socialist ideas brought the concern with economic issues to the centre of the Movement's thinking. The shape of things after British rule was terminated began to emerge in the minds of leaders; it also found

declared that it was "a crime against man and God" to submit to British rule.

A second movement of civil disobedience was launched early in 1930; this was to defy laws that were considered unjust. Gandhi chose to dramatise this defiance by taking up an item that touched the poorest of households. The government had a monopoly on the manufacture of salt from which it derived a large revenue. Gandhi decided symbolically to "manufacture" salt on the Gujarat coast without paying any tax. After declaring his intention, he set out on foot to march to the coast about 250 km (150 miles) away, accompanied by a few supporters. He was 60 years old. As he walked

LEFT: *Illustrated London News* report, 1946.
ABOVE: Mahatma Gandhi (centre) and Jawaharlal Nehru (left) in discussion at a Congress meeting.

people joined him in their thousands, a substantial number of them women. Once again, mass participation in this movement eliminated differences of community, region, language and gender.

The government's response was predictable: imprisonment and firing on unarmed people. It also called a Round Table Conference in London where representatives of various groups would confer on the future of India. The Congress demanded preparatory steps towards complete Independence, but that was unthinkable for the British. Negotiations broke down; the Civil Disobedience Movement was resumed, but it had to give way in the face of the terror and repression unleashed by the government.

GLOBAL SUPPORT

The new superpowers to emerge following World War II, the USA and USSR, were both in favour of seeing India a free nation, an important boost to Independence.

greater, though not full, control over the administrative departments. The Congress opposed the Act, but nonetheless decided to contest elections and form governments. Except in Bengal and the Punjab, Congress swept the polls.

War clouds gather

Between 1935 when the Act was implemented and World War II, the world was in ferment. The growth of Nazism in Germany and Fascism in Italy and Japan contrasted with colonial people's determined struggles for liberation. Sympathy

In 1935 the Government of India Act was passed by the British Parliament. This proposed a bicameral legislature at the centre, to which the princes would nominate their representatives and about 14 percent of the people of India, who had been given the right to vote, would elect the others.

Even with this balance between people's representatives and the government's allies, the legislature had limited powers. In the provinces, however, the elected assemblies had much

in India clearly lay with these struggles all over the world, even as it was willing to side with its own imperialist master and its allies in the fight against Nazism.

India's support of Britain in the war was not unconditional. If India were to help Britain retain its freedom against possible enslavement by Hitler, surely this could not be done by India itself remaining enslaved. A free India would be able to render much more effective assistance in resisting the Nazi onslaught than an India in bondage. The government would not even consider such a proposition. Events came to a head in 1942. The Congress gave a call to Indians to ensure that the British "Quit India";

Indians were called upon to "do or die" in this endeavour. Once again, a massive movement was underway to achieve freedom; once again it was matched by massive repression.

Subhash Chandra Bose, who had quit the Congress earlier, organised Indians in Southeast Asia into a powerful armed force called the Indian National Army. He sought Japanese help to lead this army into India and free it from British control. The defeat of Japan in the war put an end to this dream.

The Allies had won the war but Britain was no longer a great power. There was growing support for India's demand for independence

government was spreading and the government could no longer depend on this spirit keeping within the bounds of non-violence. Also, the government's grip over the mainstay of its authority, the army and the bureaucracy, was beginning to loosen.

Sympathy for Bose's Indian National Army was often visible in the ranks of the Indian armed forces. In 1946 the ratings of the Indian Navy mutinied in Mumbai and waged a pitched battle with British forces There were widespread strikes in the Indian Air Force, the Signals Corps and the police. All this was in tandem with widespread strikes by workers everywhere.

in Britain. If Winston Churchill's Conservative government had been adamant in retaining India – which had once been described as "the brightest jewel in the British Crown" – and if the prime minister had declared that he had not been elected to that office "to preside over the liquidation of the empire", the new Labour government of 1945, headed by Clement Attlee, was less moved by considerations of past imperial glory than by the visible writing on the wall. The spirit of rebellion against the alien

LEFT: Mountbatten (centre), with Nehru to his right and Jinnah to his left, in Independence negotiations.
ABOVE: the Mountbattens bid farewell to India.

Attlee's government was sensitive to these developments and also to the weakness of Britain's position and, for the first time, Independence for India became negotiable.

The Muslim League

There was, however, one major development that was to embitter the taste of Independence for millions of Indians. The Muslim League, which always enjoyed the government's patronage, sought guarantees from the government as well as the Congress that the rights of the Muslim minority (about 10 percent of the population) would be safeguarded. The Congress was willing to give them oral assurances, but it was argued that the fact that the Congress itself had a strong wing of leaders who were Hindu communalists justified a degree of scepticism.

Since the Congress commanded the support of the majority community, the Hindus, it could always camouflage its own communalism under the slogan of nationalism as well as democracy, it was said. No one doubted the personal integrity of leaders like Gandhi and Nehru when they spoke of Muslims as their brothers: but much more was at stake than the promise of honest

> **A LOST DREAM**
>
> On the eve of Independence Gandhi wept over the loss of all that was closest to his heart: non-violence, humanity and compassion irrespective of colour, religion or creed.

had been Muslims, and not all Muslims sympathised with the League, anyway. Yet the Congress contested elections on the basis of separate electorates while never giving up its reservations concerning them.

Separate electorates could only have reinforced the communal division. The paths of the Congress and the League began to diverge more sharply than ever. In 1940 the League raised the demand for a separate independent state for the Muslims and frequently reiterated it. The state was to be called Pakistan.

The new state of Pakistan

The tension that this demand created led to widespread communal rioting as the prospect of independence began to take shape. Hindus and Muslims participated in mass butchery in 1946, each blaming the other for the first killing. There were, too, heroic people on both sides who laid down their lives in defence of brethren of the other community; but in a situation of such large-scale turbulence their effort was too feeble to bridge the gap that had opened between the communities. The British Government decided to move quickly.

By early 1947 the decision to grant freedom to India had been taken; but this freedom would be accompanied by the partition of the country to create the new state of Pakistan. Not all the effort on the part of leaders of the Congress and the Muslim League could resolve the communal problem. Pakistan was to comprise two regions, one in the west and the other, separated by nearly 2,000 km (1,300 miles) of Indian territory, in East Bengal, now Bangladesh. Large numbers of Hindus from the regions that were to constitute Pakistan, and Muslims from India, began to emigrate. Millions moved in opposite directions, and many of the Sikhs – whose homeland of Punjab had been cut in two – moved into India. Many of the migrants were murdered by religious extremists as they crossed the borders, and freedom finally came to India at midnight on 15 August 1947 in the midst of human tragedy. ❑

persons. How could the Muslims be certain that the future, too, would produce leaders of the same calibre and integrity?

A solution that the British government had worked out was to establish separate electorates for the Hindus and the Muslims, each community electing its representatives. This was tantamount to validating the theory that the League had begun to propound, namely that the Hindus and the Muslims were two separate nations, thus equating religion with nation. The Congress had never accepted this theory, for it implied that the Congress could not enrol Muslims as members, nor represent them. Some of the most illustrious presidents of the Congress

LEFT: freedom comes to India – Nehru addresses the crowds at Delhi's Red Fort on 15 August 1947.
RIGHT: palace guards in the princely state of Mysore.

INDEPENDENT INDIA

India's democracy is a triumph in a land of multitudinous ethnic,
religious and secessionist interests

Although India is often praised as the world's largest democracy, most of its institutions are in need of reform. The British-based judicial system, for instance, is gridlocked but often seems to be the only institution able to put any restraints on the wilder excesses of politicians. The country has, however, managed to sustain a working electoral system since 1947, with only a 19-month gap in the mid-1970s when Prime Minister Indira Gandhi declared emergency rule. This achievement is considerable and some analysts believe elections have helped to keep the poor, heterogeneous country together since achieving Independence from Britain in 1947.

The new republic

Jawaharlal Nehru, India's first prime minister, believed that economic power should rest with the state. He gave India a planned economy, in which the government owned basic industries, such as steel and power generation, and had control over what the private sector produced. Manufacturers were licensed to produce goods in certain quantities, at certain prices, and were issued with raw materials. This, in conjunction with the "India First" policy of self-sufficiency, made considerable headway in improving the economic condition of the country. The Green Revolution also contributed to turning India from a net importer of food to a major exporter.

Pessimists warned it was premature to give the vote to the illiterate masses in 1947 and unwise to adopt Britain's political system, designed for such different circumstances. Nehru, however, was vindicated in arguing that it was precisely what India needed. It would, he thought, keep under control the cultural, ethnic and religious differences that might otherwise tear the country apart. To achieve unity, more than 500 Indian princes had to give up their titles. This tricky diplomatic task was accomplished in

LEFT: Jawaharlal Nehru, India's first prime minister, unfurls the new national flag.
RIGHT: Indira Gandhi, an authoritarian prime minister.

1950 by Nehru's deputy, Sardar Vallabhai Patel, a communal right-winger trusted by those who lived off inherited wealth.

The decision to base the new state boundaries on regional languages led to problems. Inevitably a multitude of dialects had to be ignored. The ethnic and language divisions of

the states were never satisfactorily settled and violent disputes still occasionally flare.

Initially, the communal violence of Partition (the separation of the country into a predominantly Muslim Pakistan and a predominantly Hindu India) was traumatic. Hindus and Muslims clashed bitterly, slaughtering thousands and forcing countless others to flee their homes. Although Nehru tried to separate political and public life, confining religion to the private sphere, the distinction was never fully accepted by large parts of the population, who regarded their spiritual and secular lives as indivisible.

Nehru aimed to transform a feudal society into one of equal opportunity. He placed his faith in Democratic Socialism, a middle way between a capitalistic welfare state and a Soviet-styled centrally controlled economy. Encouraging self-reliance would, he hoped, stimulate free enterprise, but avoid polarising wealth. Imports were restricted, business excesses were checked by state institutions and key industries were kept under state control.

On the foreign front, India helped to establish the Non-Aligned Movement and advocated in the 1950s that China be given international status. But Nehru's admiration of China blinded him to its territorial ambitions, which led to war in 1962 over claims on the remote Aksai Chin

landowners, guaranteeing her an agrarian power base well into the 1980s.

It was a turbulent time. When, in June 1975, the Allahabad High Court found Gandhi guilty of corrupt political practices, she reacted by imposing a State of Emergency that was to last two years. The press was censored, 100,000 political opponents and activists were imprisoned, slums were cleared and enforced sterilisations were carried out. Inevitably, there was a backlash. Her Congress (Indira) party decisively lost the 1977 election, which brought to power the Janata Dal party, led by the octogenarian Morarji Desai. In a political drama

area. India suffered a disastrous defeat. Nehru determined to build up India's arms capability, but was opposed by the United States and Great Britain. He turned instead to the Soviet Union.

Nehru dynasty

Jawaharlal Nehru died in 1964, but a dynasty had been born. Two years later his daughter, Indira Gandhi, took over the reins of power and championed Democratic Socialism.

Her authoritarian manner helped to establish her as the undisputed leader of a divided Congress party, as did India's 1971 victory over East Pakistan (now Bangladesh). Her Green Revolution turned tenant farmers into

unusual even by Indian standards, Gandhi was put briefly behind bars. Against all odds, however, she was back in office in 1980.

Her joy was short-lived, for later that year her son, Sanjay, died in an air crash. Although his ruthlessness had won him scant popularity, Sanjay was being groomed by Gandhi as her heir apparent. On his death she persuaded her second son, Rajiv, a pilot with Indian Airlines, to make his first appearance on the political stage.

Problems in Punjab

Also making headlines in 1980 was Sant Jarnail Singh Bhindranwale, a charismatic, turbaned militant leader based in the Golden Temple in

Amritsar, the holiest of Sikh shrines. Surrounded by a group of young, educated and fanatical Sikhs, he demanded greater rights for the Sikh community and separation of the state of Punjab from the rest of India. Indira Gandhi's tactic of pitting Sikh groups against each other only aggravated the crisis and the Sant's followers were able to terrorise, rob and murder Hindus unhindered.

By 1984 the threat had reached the capital, and Gandhi sent the army into the Golden Temple, large parts of which were destroyed. Much blood was shed and the Sant was killed. Revenge was not long in coming: on 31 October, Indira Gandhi was assassinated by her Sikh bodyguards.

A shocked Congress party elected Rajiv Gandhi prime minister. It seemed to some a rash decision, given his inexperience, but the electorate overwhelmingly endorsed Congress's decision by sweeping Rajiv to power in the subsequent elections. His manifesto was ambitious, promising to revive industry with new technology and management techniques. It was an appealing mix in a year that had seen a shattering accident at Bhopal in Madhya Pradesh, when gas leaked from a pesticide plant owned by the US multinational Union Carbide, killing 2,000 local residents and affecting hundreds of thousands of people.

Five years later, amid allegations of political corruption, Congress (I) was defeated catastrophically in the polls. A key issue was the Bofors scandal, in which suspect commissions had been paid by a Swedish arms manufacturer in order to supply guns to the Indian army. Rajiv's defence minister, V.P. Singh, resigned in 1987 alleging Congress corruption in the affair and formed a new party, the National Front. In the 1989 election he won enough votes to form a minority government, which was toppled in 1990 over caste and religious issues.

Rajiv, believing that he had lost the 1989 election by being too aloof, plunged into a populist campaign, driving in an open Jeep through milling crowds. In Tamil Nadu a woman approached him with a sandalwood garland and detonated the bomb on her belt. Gandhi and 20 others were killed in the blast. Such had been

the grip of the Nehru succession over the Congress (I) party that no obvious successor existed. Desperate attempts were made to draft Rajiv's Italian-born widow, Sonia, as his successor, but she resisted until 1998, when she campaigned to salvage the reputation of the dynastic party and then was chosen to head it.

Demise of Congress

In the meantime, power devolved to P.V. Narasimha Rao, a Congress party stalwart from South India. It was a classic compromise, but Rao's staying power was underestimated. Rao made the rupee convertible and allowed foreig-

LEFT: graffiti depicting the assassination of Indira Gandhi by her Sikh bodyguards in 1984.
RIGHT: Narasimha Rao, prime minister, early 1990s.

STATE OF THE PARTIES

The political kaleidoscope of India is forever changing, creating unlikely patterns and alliances. Parties with a wide constituency include the Congress (Indira), which still plays on the Nehru legacy; the Bharatiya Janata Party (BJP), Hindu nationalists; the Left Front, a coalition of parties, including the Communist Party of India and the Communist Party of India (Marxist); and the Samajwadi Party, representing the low-castes and Muslims. Regional parties include the Sikh activists, Akali Dal; two Dravidian parties in Tamil Nadu, the AIADMK and their rivals, DMK; the Telugu Desam Party from Andhra Pradesh; and the Hindu and Maratha extremist Shiv Sena based in Mumbai.

ners to control 51 percent of their joint ventures. Import tariffs were cut and foreigners were allowed to buy and sell shares on India's 20 stock exchanges. But the old demons would not easily disappear. The fight for independence in Kashmir rumbled on, with stories of appalling atrocities. In 1992 tens of thousands of Hindu zealots used their bare hands to tear down a mosque in Ayodhya *(see page 101).*

Mumbai was rocked by a dozen bombs in a single day in March 1993. Terrified Muslims fled the city and gangsters appropriated valuable downtown land. The BJP (Bharatiya Janata Party) triumphed in the next state elections. Bal

Thackeray, sinister leader of the Hindu chauvinist Shiv Sena (Shiva's army), called for state borders to be closed to all non-residents.

Under Rao, Congress lost considerable support. Reports of a cash-crammed suitcase left as a blatant bribe, and profiteering from import scams, surfaced in the newspapers. Economic liberalisation measures were criticised for lining the pockets of the rich while doing little to help the poor.

The rise of the Sangh Parivar

The demise in support for Congress gave the BJP its chance to bid for power. Formed in 1980 out of the Jana Sangh Party, part of the Janata

Party coalition that had ousted Indira after the Emergency, the BJP is the political wing of the Sangh Parivar, a collection of right wing Hindu organisations that includes the RSS, the VHP (Vishva Hindu Parishad) and the youth wings of the Bajrang Dal and Durga Vahini *(see page 101).* In elections in 1989 it was part of a short-lived coalition government that was replaced by left-leaning coalitions under prime ministers Deve Gowda and I.K. Gujral. However, the momentum gained through the 1992 destruction of the Babri Masjid continued to grow, and in 1998 the BJP found itself at the head of a coalition government.

As well as persuing a virulently neo-liberal economic agenda (after ditching its pre-election claim to promote *swadeshi*, Indian-made goods) the BJP oversaw a communalisation of education and encouraged intolerance towards minority communities.

India, once hailed for its doctrine of non-violence, continued to flex its muscles in the region. As well as maintaining the largest standing army in the world, Prime Minister Atal Bihari Vajpayee in 1998 authorised five surprise nuclear underground tests at Pokhran in the Rajasthan desert, 24 years after Indira Gandhi first pushed the button. In 1999 he formed a more durable coalition government called the National Democratic Alliance (NDA) with the support of regional parties including the TDP (Telugu Desam Party) and Akali Dal.

An election upset

That same year India and Pakistan engaged in a 50-day war in the Kargil Valley in Kashmir that threatened to escalate into a much broader conflict. Pakistani infiltrators were eventually pushed back, though not before more than 1,000 soldiers had been killed. Patriotic fervour, whipped up by politicians, created an ugly mood in the country. Tensions continued to increase between the neighbouring countries, reaching their height in 2002 when the two nuclear powers teetered on the brink of all-out war.

However, geopolitics held little interest for the great mass of Indians who still lacked electricity and had to make do with poor sanitation and filthy water. When they were given a chance to make their voices heard in the general election of 2004, the judgment of the 380 million people who voted came as a complete shock to the political class. They decisively rejected the BJP-led alliance in favour of a Congress-led alliance.

The shock was compounded by the fact that the Congress party's leader was Sonia Gandhi. The thought of having a 59-year-old Italian-born woman as prime minster was anathema to many, and the stock market, fearing that the new government might be less business-friendly, took a tumble. Sonia Gandhi, having listened to her "inner voice", declined the premiership and appointed instead Manmohan Singh, previously a Congress finance minister, who thus became India's first Sikh prime min-ister Palaniappan Chidambaram, have maintained the neo-liberal economics of their predecessors while, admittedly, putting money into social relief programmes.

However, there have been some important changes: school books are being re-examined and re-written to remove any communal bias; a Common Minimum Programme was agreed with the Left Front – comprising the Communist Party of India (Marxist), the Communist Party of India, the Forward Bloc and the Revolutionary Socialist Party – who continue to support the government from the outside; and, perhaps most importantly, India's relations

ister. Perhaps, some mused, Sonia Gandhi was consoled by the hope that the family succession might eventually pass to her son Rahul, who in the same election won a seat in his father's old constituency of Amethi in Uttar Pradesh by more than 100,000 votes.

After the event

As it turned out, the stock market need not have been jittery about the new government. The new prime minister, along with the new finance min-

LEFT: an election poll worker updates the results.
ABOVE: the new prime minister, Manmohan Singh, confers with Sonia Gandhi in 2004.

with Pakistan are the best they have been for many years.

Ongoing peace talks started between Pakistan's General Pervez Musharraf and Prime Minister Vajpayee in 2003. Since the accession of Congress and its allies to power these have continued apace and a great deal of progress has been made over the divisive, and central, issue of Kashmir. In early 2005 this received a boost with the adoption of "confidence building measures", including the opening of a bus route between Srinagar and Muzaffarabad in Pakistan-Occupied-Kashmir. With both countries describing the peace process as "irreversible" there is hope that a final settlement might at last be in sight. ❏

CONTEMPORARY INDIA

Indian society is being challenged by a new economic orthodoxy,
rising religious intolerance and desperate levels of poverty

An observation often made of India is that it is "timeless" or "unchanging"; this, of course, is sheer drivel. No society or culture is unchanging, and India is no exception. Equally, a mistake is made by commentators who have become excited about the rise of the "new Indian middle class", assuming this appetite for change and development is a recent phenomenon manifested in India's embrace of neo-liberalism (confusing an economic doctrine with modernity). In reality, as ever, the situation is more complex.

Economic acceleration

At a governmental level, India has become a paragon of economic virtue as it adopts Western orthodoxy. A huge programme of "disinvestment" (privatisation) has been put in place and inward investment has greatly increased; largely to the benefit of the much-lauded Indian middle class. At the same time, attitudes to social welfare have hardened among policy makers, with large tax breaks given to the well-off, while the nation's poor become increasingly marginalised in both the political and economic debate.

Much effort has been spent since the 1990s undoing the structures put in place by post-Independence Congress governments. These championed state ownership, industrialisation and an "India first" policy — indigenous production and consumption coupled with protectionist import policies. Alongside these were promulgated the belief in secularisation and, to borrow a government slogan of the time, "unity through diversity". The irony is that these nation-building ideas were radical solutions to the economic difficulties and fragmented nature of India's post-colonial society. The British left India in a woeful state, in terms of both economic and human development. There was

hardly any indigenous industry and literacy rates were exceptionally low. Recent economic commentators have tended to denigrate the legacy of Nehru (it was largely he who pushed through the post-Independence industrial policies), without acknowledging that the industrial base that they are so keen to see privatised,

and the literate workforce that they foresee taking over call centre jobs from the West, are the products of precisely these earlier policies.

Religion and identity

The political discourse around the millennium was dominated by reactionary, right-wing Hinduism as espoused by the BJP, and economic liberalisation. Although at first these seem strange bedfellows, given the disruption neo-liberal policies cause to people's lives, religion and an aggressive promotion of the national myth are useful tools in keeping the populace onside while state and national governments push through unpopular measures.

PRECEDING PAGES: bullock carts; travelling to school by rickshaw, Tamil Nadu.
LEFT: women at the Pongol festival, Tiruvanathapuram.
RIGHT: monitoring components, Bangalore.

In an Indian context this saw an individualisation of Hindu identity, while at the same time there was an attempt to homogenise a highly disparate and eclectic group of beliefs and practices. Modern Hinduism, at least as promoted by the Sangh Parivar, is increasingly coming to resemble evangelical Christianity. An individual's relationship with a deity and personal observance of ritual, rather than action for the social good, are seen as the key to salvation. Thus, limiting consumption and displays of wealth in the face of deprivation is of less spiritual importance than, say, taking part in the building of a new temple to Ram at Ayodhya.

This move away from Gandhian ideals has been accompanied by a more canonical approach to the religious text. Writings such as the *Vedas*, *Bhagavad Gita* and *Ramayana* have acquired the status of historical document rather than spiritual tract; they are statements of absolute fact, rather than guides towards universal truths that are open to interpretation. Modern right-wing Hinduism is far more interested in having a rigid rule book of rights and wrongs, than in the traditional subtleties of religious debate, which in the past made the Hindu world relatively inclusive and tolerant.

As with any hegemonic insistence on the

THE INDIAN POVERTY LINE

Most international organisations such as UNICEF and the World Bank have a working poverty line for developing nations, such as India and China, as US$1 or below per day ($365 per year). By contrast, the Indian Government defines poverty as earning less than Rps10 per day (around US$75 per year) which would barely keep you alive. The Indian figures give a population of around 300 million people living below the poverty line (coincidentally around the same number as estimates for the total middle class). If the international figure is taken then some 70 percent of all Indians (some 790 million people) live below the poverty line, a sobering thought.

observance of a series of rules, minority viewpoints suffered. In India this had the greatest effect on the country's 100 million-plus Muslims. The national myth promoted by the BJP was fiercely anti-Islamic. For all the recent talks between the two countries, the external bogeyman has been largely identified as Pakistan, while Muslim Indian nationals were portrayed as an Islamic fifth column. The most distressing and vicious manifestation of this occurred in Gujarat in 2002, where at least 1,000 Muslims were killed in communal rioting. The BJP Chief Minister, Narendra Modi, was heavily implicated in the carnage but continues to enjoy the party's protection.

The rich and poor

The BJP-led National Democratic Alliance (NDA) was trounced in the 2004 general election, as the majority of people could see no truth in its "India Shining" slogan; giving some hope for a change in direction from the new Congress-led, and Left Front-supported, United Progressive Alliance. "India Shining", however, was firmly aimed at India's middle and upper classes, for whom a huge increase in consumer debt has fuelled an equally large orgy of spending, on anything from mobile phones to the latest foreign car.

However, such riches, apparent on any trip to one of the large "metros" (Delhi, Mumbai,

was supposed to bring much-needed jobs to India but unemployment has risen, from 9.2 percent in 2000 to 10.1 percent in 2004. The loss of jobs has also affected the non-agricultural sector, which includes the area celebrated by many as India's saviour: the IT and service industries. The service industry accounts for around 51 percent of jobs, much of it extremely badly paid. The country has attracted much business process outsourcing (BPO) by Western companies, which has benefitted the middle class, though the work itself is not highly skilled, and most of its operators are vastly overqualified. India exports $25 billion a year

of these services, though there have already been reports of companies relocating from India to places such as Ghana where the workforce is even cheaper. In any case, it has been argued that such work merely diverts the best-educated workers into servicing US and European bank and utility accounts rather than into more productive employment – in essence, an internal brain drain.

At the same time, the employment figures mask the true scale of the problem. Only 61 percent of the adult population (between 15 and 65 years old) are seeking employment, and of those who do actually find work, most will be underemployed. Just to satisfy the middle class alone

Kolkata and Chennai), are available to only the 10 percent of the population that comprises the Indian urban middle class. What, then, about the other 90 percent? Life for them, it seems, might not be so rosy. Since 1991, the country has undergone huge economic change, and the adoption of neo-liberal policies, and while this has given a huge boost to the 300 million who count themselves as the Indian middle class, conditions for the vast majority have not improved, and in many cases have become much worse.

Economic reform got off to a shaky start. It

LEFT: Bandra basti, and, **ABOVE:** very expensive real estate, Mumbai.

it is estimated that at least 10 million well paid jobs a year need to be created.

Health and education

Meanwhile failures (some created by the misinformed planting of genetically modified crops) and hardship in agricultural regions, which still support around 72 percent of the population whilst accounting for only 21 percent of GDP, have led to an unprecedented number of suicides by farmers. On other indicators of public well-being, India is also faring badly. Public spending is declining, particularly on health, as tax cuts are given to the better off. According to the UN,

less than 50 percent of the population have access to essential drugs and there is a chronic shortage of health facilities (in rural India there are only 44 hospital beds per 100,000 people; in the UK there are around 470).

The list of statistics goes on to point out that in a country with one of the lowest levels of health spending as a percentage of GDP, only 30 percent of people have access to adequate sanitation and some 66 percent of children under the age of three suffer from malnutrition. It is not only on health that India faces difficulties; education also has a lot of catching up to do. One in three of the world's illiterate people lives

THE MIDDLE CLASS

The exact figure for the percentage of the population that comprises the middle class is hard to come by, though most observers put it at around 300 million. It is this part of society that has been so prominent in the media and has become the darling of foreign leaders who see, in their apparent inexorable rise, economic opportunities.

In terms of lifestyle the middle class, and particularly its younger members, are easy to spot on the streets of Delhi or Mumbai. They are the ones with one of India's 19 million mobile phones glued to their ears, or those getting out of their newly acquired foreign cars, or perhaps, if they are on the way up, dismounting from the "two wheeler"

(scooter) which they hope to upgrade someday soon. At home they have televisions, fridges and perhaps a washing machine, cook on gas and live in concrete houses.

These are the people that multinational companies have in their sights – it is a huge market for their consumer goods. Mall heavens have gone up in places such as Gurgaon, a satellite city of New Delhi, to sell all the global brands. Annually burning £10 billion of cash, young adults are an easy catch for the retailers. And their spending is going up around 12 percent every year, outpacing the country's economy, much of it financed by a huge rise in credit and by "selling off the family silver".

in India. This is a staggering number and a trend that looks set to continue. Only around 50 percent of girls are enrolled in primary education, and for this there is a 10 percent drop-out rate.

Child labour also continues. Based on government figures (which nearly all NGOs and independent commentators consider to be wildly overoptimistic) UNICEF has reported that at least 35 million children (14 percent of those of school age) work as, overwhelmingly rural, labourers (some breaking stones in quarries to provide for

> ## LITERACY
>
> India has 61 percent adult literacy. Kerala has the highest rate at 90 percent, Bihar the lowest at 47 percent. 54 percent of women are literate (20 percent in Rajasthan).

projects of around US$36.5 billion by 2010.

Evidence for the great divide between haves and have-nots can be seen all over the country. In Gurgaon, middle-class enclave extraordinaire, house prices start at Rps10 billion, about 270 times the average annual income. Close by in Delhi, 32 percent of the population live in *jhuggis* (slums), although the city has a Bentley showroom. Meanwhile, poverty-stricken survivors of the 2004 tsunami in Tamil Nadu have resorted to selling their kidneys in order to survive.

LEFT: glaring inequalities on a Delhi street.
ABOVE: the young middle class of Bangalore.

European patios). A huge amount of these are "bonded", effectively a form of slavery.

In a further blow to the poor, the government has embarked on creating a series of "special economic zones" (SEZs), effectively tax havens for rich multinational companies as an incentive for their inward investment. This has entailed a huge land grab, with millions being displaced with little or no compensation. The promise is that these SEZs will bring employment and prosperity. However, the Indian Ministry of Finance has said that there would be a net loss on these

Electoral fightback

In the past India has shown a great capacity for reinvention. The 2004 election showed that politics are alive and kicking, particularly at a grass roots level. Believing their own propaganda, the NDA aimed their campaign squarely at the middle class, imagining that the dreams of the affluent minority would prove sufficiently alluring to the poor majority to carry the election. This was not to be the case. The BJP saw its vote plummet, losing 44 seats, while Congress (the largest party) went up from 114 to 145. Perhaps even more telling were the gains for the left-wing, with the two communist parties (CPI and CPI(M)) winning in 53 seats (up from 37 in 1999), and the overwhelming defeat of the arch-liberaliser Chandrababu Naidu's TDP (Telugu Desam Party) in Andhra Pradesh, which went down from 29 to five seats.

Social attitudes

As with so much else in contemporary India, people's attitudes towards everything from religion, to clothes, to sex are multifarious and complex. To take one example, it is generally true that the position of women in society has improved over the past 50 years. After all, India had a female prime minister years before the UK, and it is not uncommon to see women in

have seen their prospects and freedoms open up, while their poorer sisters concern themselves with the struggle for survival.

In moving away from traditional roles and becoming a target in the marketplace, women find themselves facing new challenges. Body image has become a major concern. Women are now bombarded with advertisements for creams, shampoos and beauty treatments, promoted by sylph-like creatures with fair skins. "Fair and Lovely", a skin-lightening cream, is the best-selling beauty product in the country, highlighting the implicit racism in the widely promoted ideal image. Anorexia, unheard of in India a few

the workplace. On the streets of central New Delhi you can now see young women wearing miniskirts, unthinkable 10 years ago; though it is true that this is still an exception, the norm being either jeans and a T-shirt or *salwar kamiz*.

However, these advances are not universal. In many areas women are still restricted to the domestic sphere or, if they are poor, undertake gruelling physical work for little reward. Female infanticide (now gone illicitly hi-tech through foetal screening) is still a huge problem, and astonishing levels of rape and abuse are under-reported.

As with many things, middle-class women, with their access to education and health care,

years ago (going without food was not fashionable in a country where so many people are malnourished), has now reared its ugly head as movie stars and models parade their skinny bodies across the television and cinema screens.

Indians are caught between competing discourses: liberalisation or the Nehru-Gandhi legacy; frugality and saving or consumption and spending; religious orthodoxy or newly acquired social freedoms. In the past they have proved themselves humane and inventive, giving us hope for the future. ❑

ABOVE: religious traditions and multinational companies; India in the 21st century?

The Environment

According to a report by the TERI organisation for the Indian Ministry of Environment and Forests, the country "holds the dubious honour of suffering from poverty-induced environmental degradation at the same time as pollution from affluence and a rapidly growing industrial sector".

New Delhi has more than 4 million vehicles, with 200,000 added each year. The air had become so thick with flying ash and particulate pollutants that the city's administration forced all public transport (including autos) to convert to CNG (compressed natural gas), as well as building a new metro system.

Steady population growth puts pressure on resources, and Indians cope with polluted air and an alarmingly diminishing water table. The sacred rivers teem with bacteria. Development schemes and environmental control measures are often at odds, and legislation is difficult to enforce.

Timber, paper and mining industries have depleted the forest cover. The Chipko activists, tree-hugging Adivasi women who put themselves in the way of saws and axes to stop the loss of their forests in the Garwal Himalayas in 1973, inspired green protests across the planet. The forest protection measures that followed may now be bearing fruit. Between 1999 and 2006 forest cover grew from 19.39 to 20.64 percent of the country.

The damming of rivers and flooding of valleys continues to be a focus for eco-activists, who oppose the dam projects on the Narmada river, the dam at Tehri in Uttaranchal, a region prone to earthquakes, as well as the Sardar Sarovar project in Maharashtra. Tourism has also taken its toll. Many trekking routes in the Himalayas are vertical rubbish heaps, particularly from plastic bottles used for water. In Ladakh local projects have been set up to provide clean, boiled water to visitors. Ancient marble monuments such as the Taj Mahal show erosion due to chemical emissions.

Unenforced regulations in industry and official and management callousness have led to environmental disasters. In 1984 more than 3,500 people were killed in their sleep when toxic methyl ico-cynate leaked from the Union Carbide factory in Bhopal, Madhya Pradesh. The first fire in the Jharia coalfields in Bihar started in 1916 and there are currently around 70 still burning, causing asthma, chronic bronchitis and skin and lung diseases. Mer-

RIGHT: deforestation is a major problem.

cury poisoning is becoming a huge problem. Dumping of the highly toxic chemical by multinational companies such as Unilever (which makes thermometers for the US market in Kodaikanal, Kerala) causes birth defects, tumours and damage to the central nervous system, lungs and kidneys. The North Koel river in Bihar has up to 700 times above the permissible level of mercury.

Soft drinks multinationals are also culpable. The Coca-Cola plant at Plachimada, Kerala, was using up to 1.5 million litres of ground water daily until it was banned from doing so by the State Government. It has also been dumping toxic waste, high in heavy metals, on farmland. In 2003, both Coca-

Cola and Pepsi Cola were found to have "shocking" levels of pesticides in their bottled drinks.

Fightback is occurring: the Narmada Bachao Andolan are particularly active as is the more radical Mumbai Resistance. And when the French aircraft carrier Clemenceau, riddled with asbestos and due to be broken up in Alang's shipyard in 2006, was recalled to France in a wave of protests worldwide, many saw this as an opportunity for India to improve conditions for its shipyard workers.

On a more practical level, India practises recycling on many levels – ragpickers sort rubbish so efficiently that plastic bags, paper and wire are sold off by weight – providing social institutions from which sustainable systems can develop. ❑

PEOPLE

India's greatest resource is the number and variety of its people,
but the social order is complicated by ancestry and caste

It would be almost impossible to pick out a single person as a typical Indian. The diversity among more than 1 billion citizens is mind-boggling: from the Adivasi societies of the Northeast to the Tamil-speakers of the South, this incredible array of humanity spices up the spectacle of crowd-watching. Any description of this huge variety of societies and cultures must, of necessity, be highly simplified, and for each assertion made there are bound to be many examples that contradict it.

India's melting pot

At least six different sets of peoples converge in present-day India, after millennia of traders, conquerors, colonisers, mercenaries and missionaries that swept through South Asia from outside.

The first settlers are thought to be the forebears of the present-day Adivasis. These peoples still dwell in mountainous or jungle zones in a belt that stretches from Arunachal Pradesh's high forests to India's southern tip at Kanniyakumari *(see page 83)*.

The Dravidian-speaking peoples, who drove the Adivasis into the margins, away from plains lush with sugar cane and rice, now live mainly in the south Deccan. Apparently related to the pre-Hellenic Aegeans and Cretans, they brought the Harappan culture to its zenith at the cities of Harappa and Mohenjadaro. (The most impressive archaeological ruins are sited in what is now Pakistan.) The Dravidians were in turn pushed back by peoples who galloped into India from Central Asia and dominated the Indo-Gangetic plain from around 1,500 BC.

These new peoples were warriors and herdsmen who found the urban settlements of the Indus Valley peoples alien to their traditional way of life as nomadic herders. However, as they spread out across the plains of North

India they began to settle in agricultural village communities. The language of their earliest writings (hymns of the Rig Veda, *circa* 1000 BC), Sanskrit, and Latin share many root words and a basic grammar pattern, pointing to a common ancestry with peoples in southern Europe. From the Bharatas, a domi-

nant Indo-European speaking people, comes Bharat, the official name for India – the "B" in BJP, the Bharatiya Janata Party, which won political power in the late 1990s.

This wave of invaders was followed by Arab Semites from the area now comprising Afghanistan, Iran and Central Asia. They settled in large numbers. Jews escaping from Nebuchadnezzar arrived around 600 BC at the Malabar coast and became spice traders. Refugee Zoroastrians fled from Persia in the 10th century, and ended up in Mumbai. Persecuted Baha'is from modern Iran arrived more recently. In the Himalayas and on the northeastern frontier with Burma (Myanmar), most

---

PRECEDING PAGES: dressed in their finest *salwar kamiz* for a wedding in Himachal Pradesh.
LEFT: portrait of a Rajasthani.
RIGHT: bejewelled Adivasi woman from the Northeast.

peoples have more in common, in terms of both culture and history, with neighbouring societies to the north and east than with people of the Hindi-speaking belt of the central plains. Added to these are several million Tibetans in exile, who have taken sanctuary in India since 1959 and cluster in mostly mountain communities, although there are some monasteries as far south as Karnataka.

Early European court visitors and explorers included Portuguese, Danes, British and French, and long-term settlers soon followed. Eurasians, as the offspring of many mixed marriages were called during the British Raj

(often now known as Anglo-Indians), are acutely aware of the slightest skin tone variance even today. Bleaching away a suntan with harsh chemicals is a standard practice in beauty parlours. There are few coy euphemisms about racial distinctions in polite society because they are one obvious key to prestige. Yet ancestry is only one component of India's complex social hierarchy.

Caste

India's caste system is based on the twin concepts of *dharma* and *karma*, the duties one must fulfil in this life and the effects one's actions will have on any future lives. These, coupled with the principle of hereditary occupation and strong concepts of pollution, produced a highly stratified society which, due to its flexibility, was one that could absorb new peoples with little trouble.

The Laws of Manu (*circa* AD 150) spell out codes for life in a multiracial society. Each individual is born into a particular *jati* or caste that predetermines both profession and status, regardless of the wealth of the parents. These castes are said to fall into four basic divisions, or *varna*. The Brahmans are intellectuals and priests – the link between mortals and millions of Hindu deities. Kshatriyas are rulers and warriors, in charge of justice and administration. Both Brahmans and Kshatriyas are considered "twice-born" and display their status with a sacred thread worn over the shoulder. Below them are the Vaishyas, merchants or traders, and the Shudras, agriculturalists. However, the most menial tasks were reserved for the outcastes, in practice the peoples conquered by higher castes and considered unworthy to be part of the system. These jobs include cleaning latrines, sweeping the streets, scavenging, burning corpses and gathering dead animals (which extends to working with leather, making shoes and playing drums at funerals or weddings).

A wedding, the ultimate family occasion, will bring out latent caste differences even in liberal-thinking modern professionals who have earned degrees for jobs forbidden them by birth. Every Sunday, classified advertisements in Indian newspapers list brides and grooms available for arranged marriages under specific headings of caste. Only occasionally – if the bride is over 30 years old, for example, or the groom is HIV-positive – will these "wanted" advertisements

RELIGIOUS MARKS AND BINDIS

Vivid multi-striped foreheads in earth tones of white, yellow, or saffron are not decoration, but a marking that denotes affiliation to a particular deity or a sign of religious devotion. They range from a simple *tilak*, a divine mark smeared with a vermilion-dipped thumb, to elaborate patterns daubed across the forehead. Don't confuse these marks with the *bindi (bhindhya, kum-kum, tikka)*, worn by women over their "third eye". The round red forehead dot traditionally signifies that a woman is married. But the glittery stick-on *bindis* sold in the bazaar are decorative and just for fun. Grandmothers, teenagers, movie stars, and even babies wear *bindis*.

say "Caste no bar". Otherwise, the demands are blatantly racist, often requiring a "fair complexion", "sharp features", or a minimum height ("must be over 135 cm"). Income and astrological signs are usually specified, too.

There are thousands of sub-divisions possible within the four major caste divisions, and these *jati* really matter. They determine the degree of superiority within society's pyramid. Caste is not something that can be easily lied about. It may be encoded in a surname – one reason why tra-

ON-LINE MATCHMAKING

The Internet has become a useful tool in widening the search for a suitable marriage partner, and is used both in India and by NRIS looking for a South Asian spouse.

ment has forced many Hindus to desert the old village ways in order to eke out a living in contemporary India. Originally, the needy could approach sympathetic members of their own *jati*, who would provide a meal, a job or shelter. The traditional division of labour is breaking down, albeit slowly. K.R. Narayanan was born a Dalit *(see overleaf)* and had to fight convention for an education. Following years as a high-profile lawyer and diplomat, he was President of the Republic between 1997 and 2002.

ditional families still insist on an arranged marriage. A child will inherit the caste of the father, so inter-caste marriages are tolerated by the bride's relatives if it is the groom who marries down. For consenting to such a match, a bigger dowry is demanded by the groom's family.

Hindu scriptures predict a time of chaos and deprivation when the Code of Manu will be forgotten, and the caste structure will come crashing down. Some claim these bad times, called *kaliyuga*, are here already. Unemploy-

LEFT: a Brahman wearing the religious mark of a devotee of Visnu.
ABOVE: young girl at a wedding in Mumbai.

In India's big cities, people from different castes often end up as neighbours and can't help rubbing shoulders on the bus or in cinema halls. Unlike in the villages, where caste groups tend to live in segregated areas and traditionally only eat with their own caste members, there is some leeway for intermingling in the cities. Living in such close proximity occasionally sparks confrontation between different caste groups, especially those jockeying for position. Attempts to prove status are as crucial for career advancement as for family alliances. Opportunities, whether through quotas or connections, hinge on an Indian's caste and community.

Although banned by the Indian constitution for 50 years, atrocities against the lowest castes occur daily. In the early 20th century Mahatma Gandhi insisted that everyone must take turns cleaning the toilet, and renamed outcastes (then known as "Untouchables") the Harijans ("Children of God"). But many now prefer the less patronising term Dalit (literally "the oppressed"), which is more forthright than the bureaucratic acronym SC & ST (Scheduled Castes and Scheduled Tribes). This terminology comes from the Indian constitution, written by B.K. Ambedkar, an early Dalit campaigner and brilliant lawyer, who converted to Buddhism in protest at what he saw as the divisive Hindu veneration of caste.

When New Delhi tried to implement an affirmative action plan to set aside half of all federal jobs for the officially underprivileged – which make up 85 percent of India's population – dozens of middle-class students burnt themselves alive to protest at their loss of opportunities. These so-called "caste martyrs" contributed to the overthrow of Prime Minister V.P. Singh, and reservation continues to be a controversial issue in many areas of the country.

In parts of rural India, particularly in Bihar, private armies enforce the status quo for feudal

A THIRD GENDER?

In India there are an estimated 750,000 transgendered people, known as Hijras, who live together in small groups under the leadership and protection of a *guru*. Out of these, about 2 percent are considered to be hermaphrodites, with sex organs that are ambiguously male or female; many of the others are castrated males. While they traditionally have the right to take hermaphroditic babies, there are numerous tales of forcible abduction and castration.

Hijras tend to live in cities and earn money as performers. Rural fairs and auspicious openings always attract a band of Hijras to work the superstitious crowd. All Hijras are considered to possess powers to bestow fertility or to cast misfortune. While traditionally they survive through singing and dancing at weddings, many are prostitutes. Others band together and work as roving beggars, commonly seen on trains, lewdly demanding payment for a blessing or else threatening to linger.

There is a long tradition of eunuchs in India, pre-dating the Mughal *zenanas* (harems), with their burly castrated guards. The Hindu epic Mahabharata includes a eunuch, and the *Kamasutra* mentions special positions suitable only for Hijra. Today, even in the modern cities, few people dare to annoy them if confronted; a curse from a Hijra is considered particularly potent.

landlords who still keep low-caste bonded fieldworkers in appalling conditions. Oppression is also meted out on women with, at its most extreme, the smothering of newborn girls and "dowry-deaths", the burning of young brides unable to pay illegal dowry demands.

This discrimination is being challenged in many ways. Peasants' rights activists oppose the brutalities of landlords, even to the extent of taking up arms as the "Naxalites" of Bihar and Andhra Pradesh (named after the village of Naxabari in West Bengal where the insurrection started). Urban women's rights activists gather support in tenements and suburbs, among housewives and bank-tellers, washerwomen and weavers, organising co-operatives (most famously SEWA, the Self-Employed Women's Association, in Gujarat) and lobbying politicians.

Placing the stranger

It is difficult for any newcomer to be accepted until the locals can slot the person into a category. The inevitable grilling, "What is your native place?" is not just some tiresome gambit to keep a conversation from flagging. The responses are of intense interest, for the name of someone's village, town or locality reveals a great deal to the knowledgeable.

Being able to pigeonhole a newcomer in the social hierarchy eases tensions between strangers. Indians are open and noticeably unneurotic because they are confident that their social responses are completely correct. If a guest is not shown proper respect, it is taken as a deliberate insult towards his or her group, and the onus is upon the insulted to figure out why. Such caste concerns meant that the adoption of orphans with unknown origins was quite rare until the late 1990s. Now, more couples dare to adopt an abandoned child, usually a girl.

Converts to different religions, particularly Christianity and Buddhism, often maintain their caste links and sometimes never entirely relinquish their Hindu beliefs. Modern-day Mazbhis of Punjab, adherents of the Sikh faith, recognise the primacy of their caste origin (sweeper) in intermarriages with sweepers who converted to Christianity. Though the bride wears white,

a vermilion spot on her forehead symbolises her married status in a traditionally Hindu way.

Religious order

Schisms and sects combined with caste to complicate India's religious order, even across religions that claim to have transcended caste, such as Islam.

Buddhism and Jainism were early religious and social movements that revolted against a strict caste structure and against the Brahmanical rigidities of Vedic ritual sacrifice. Buddhism was perceived as an assertion of Kshatriya power against Brahman supremacy.

FAR LEFT: a Kumaon woman, Uttaranchal.
LEFT: a Gharwali.
RIGHT: a Gypsy from western India.

UNTOUCHABILITY

A verse in the *Upanishads* (*circa* 700 BC onwards) vividly emphasises the religious discrimination that Dalits faced. Only through a life of rigorous virtue could they expect to improve their lot in their next life. In no way, however, could they aspire to boosting their current status in this world through self-improvement:

"Those whose conduct on earth has given pleasure can hope to enter a pleasant womb, that is the womb of a Brahman, or a woman of the princely class.

"But those whose conduct on earth has been foul can expect to enter a foul and stinking womb, that is, the womb of a bitch, or a pig, or an outcaste".

Pali, the language of early Buddhist texts, became a vehicle of protest against elitist Brahmanical Sanskrit. Jainism found support among the trading caste. Neither movement completely severed its links with Hinduism and in turn lost much support with the rise of *bhakti*, devotional Hinduism.

Modern movements, the rationalist philosophy of the Brahmo Samaj and the evangelical fervour of the Arya Samaj's *shuddi* conversions, may be seen as Western and Christian in inspiration. However, explanation was also sought from within Hindu philosophy – a characteristic accommodation of new ideas and influences.

Even today, language represents power and access to knowledge. Riots erupt if regional languages are seen to be snubbed by the English- and Hindi-speaking élite. When television newscasts were broadcast only in Hindi, Tamil Nadu erupted in violence. This was a grassroots refusal to accept the tongue of the conqueror, and some South Indian politicians are actively lobbying for Tamil to be ranked alongside Hindi and English as an official language for government documents.

Proselytising religions, particularly Islam and Christianity, encountered resistance at first, but both could offer concepts of immediate salvation to the dispossessed and, more crucially, both were associated with ruling powers of long tenure. Caste Hindus sometimes resent any favouritism shown to these groups by government authorities.

A mingling of cultures

In Punjab, the entrance hall of so many invasions, the impact of Islam was strong and deep. Here, Hindu dress disappeared. The sari was dropped in favour of the Islamic *salwar kamiz*, the modest tunic worn over drawstring pants. The rivalry between the stitched clothing of the Muslim and the unstitched draped garments of the Hindu was an expression in daily life of competing notions of civilised propriety. With so much interaction, the two religions – one with a god of a thousand names and another with 330 million deities – mingled. A new Indian identity evolved. It is epitomised in the linguistic amalgam of Hindi and Urdu, which is spoken across much of North India.

Muslims are outnumbered, almost 10 to one, yet India ranks as one of the largest Islamic populations on earth, with 110 million people. Consequently, Indian airports are overcrowded during Haj (February–March), the time of pilgrimage to Makkah.

Family terms

Extended family life in a densely populated country can be fraught with problems of privacy. Most societies in India are patriarchal and a daughter must leave her parents to set up a household with the groom's family.

There are a bewildering number of terms for family relationships. It can sometimes seem that everyone in a room is distantly related in some fashion. "*Bahu*", the daughter-in-law, and "*Sas*", the mother-in-law, are important adversaries in the Indian family and a focus for conflicts about duty, obedience and respect.

Brother, "*Bhai*", and older sister, "*Didi*", are affectionate and respectful terms of address, even for people outside the nuclear family. It is even more common to call a visitor "Aunty" or "Uncle", and older people may call you son, "*Beta*", or daughter, "*Beti*". "*Mata*" and "*Pita*" are terms for mother and father (often with the respectful tag, *ji*, added), and there are many other names for relatives that show the birth order and branch of the family. ❑

LEFT: a venerable Muslim, Old Delhi.

The Adivasis

Also known as "tribals", the Adivasi (indigenous/aboriginal) peoples of India are found from the Nilgiris to the Himalaya, and from Rajasthan to Arunachal Pradesh. This blanket term refers to a hugely diverse selection of societies and cultures, and is used as a catch-all for peoples who are not easily categorised in terms of India's dominant groups or ideologies.

Many Adivasi peoples, particularly those living in a forest belt that stretches across Central India, from Orissa and Bihar, to Madhya Pradesh, may be the descendants of the first inhabitants of South Asia. Linguistically and culturally distinct from the peoples that make up the majority of India's population, it is thought their presence in South Asia predates the two waves of immigration from the north and west that brought the now-dominant groups of the North and South.

As these new peoples moved in through the passes of the northwest they displaced the existing inhabitants, forcing them into the hills and forests where there was less pressure for land. Over time there was interaction between these different groups, but due to their relative isolation in sparsely populated regions many Adivasi peoples have retained highly individual identities.

The northeastern states have, after Madhya Pradesh, Chattisgarh and Orissa, the highest concentration of Adivasis. The groups who live here have more in common culturally and linguistically with peoples living in Burma (Myanmar) to the east, than they do with, say, the Todas or Kotas of Kerala and Tamil Nadu. Even within the state of Arunachal Pradesh, one of the very few areas of India where Adivasis have any control over their affairs, there are over 60 distinct groups.

What does unite many of these peoples, however, is the degree of discrimination they have suffered and continue to face. Where Adivasis have had close contacts with the dominant Hindu population their place within the caste system has been considered extremely low, working as agricultural labourers or undertaking menial tasks (often those believed to be "polluting" by high-caste Hindus).

Traditionally, land-ownership patterns among Adivasi groups tend to be collective and not governed by individual ownership laws, making it easy for unscrupulous politicians and landowners

RIGHT: a Maria Gond from Madhya Pradesh.

to appropriate Adivasi lands. This process of appropriation accelerates as the general pressure for land increases, and those areas where the Adivasis are relatively protected from exploitation become fewer and fewer.

Some of the worst offences of this kind have been committed by the state. Many large dams, such as the controversial Narmada projects, have flooded areas populated by Adivasis, and provide power and drinking water to urban areas while handing out pitiful, or no, compensation to the people they displace. Land reform programmes in states such as Kerala, while laudable in many respects, redistributed land that had traditionally

supported Adivasi groups practising low-level rotational agriculture and hunter-gathering. Logging has decimated many of the forests previously inhabited by Adivasi groups, and areas such as Jharkhand, which are rich in mineral wealth, have seen the displacement of many people, as well as widespread pollution of their lands.

Southern Bihar is now the new state of Jharkhand, and eastern Madhya Pradesh is now the state of Chattisgarh. Both have large Adivasi populations and, in theory, the Adivasis themselves should be able to lobby the state governments more efficiently than before. How far these new states will go towards protecting the interests of the Adivasis, however, remains to be seen. ❑

RELIGIONS OF INDIA

A multitude of faiths exist side by side in India, shaping the country's heritage, its life, culture, traditions and mythology

Four of the world's major faiths meet on Indian soil: Hinduism, Buddhism, Islam and Christianity. The first two were born in India, while the latter arrived through conquest, trade and missionary activity. Of those religions largely restricted to India itself, the two most significant are Jainism and Sikhism, in addition to which there are countless minor cults and regional sects. India has also given refuge to Jews and Zoroastrians fleeing persecution elsewhere.

Prehistoric times

There was a time when historians looked on the peoples who came to India in the second millennium BC as the founders of the Indian cultural tradition. But recent archaeological studies have changed the picture. It is now realised that existing elements played an important part in shaping religious practices. These were the indigenous inhabitants of India, the Dravidians, and the people of the Harappan Culture, to whom the Dravidians were probably related and who worshipped a Mother Goddess, and several animal deities.

Many features of later Hinduism were anticipated by the Harappans. A statuette from this period shows a man meditating in a yogic posture. Figures of ascetics, standing rigidly, point to a world-negating attitude. The worship of images seems to have been popular. One of the images, which appears on clay seals, is that of a god carrying a three-pronged weapon, surrounded by an elephant, a tiger and other animals. This figure has been described as proto-Shiva because it anticipates many features of Pashupati (Lord of the Beasts), a form of Shiva still worshipped several centuries later in many Hindu temples.

The arrival of Indo-European speaking peoples, probably from southern Russia, marks the beginning of the religious tradition known historically as Hinduism.

LEFT: Rath (Chariot) Festival at Puri in Orissa.
RIGHT: praying at the Jama Masjid, Old Delhi.

Hinduism

A "museum of religions" – that would seem to be the only way to describe Hinduism. No other religious tradition is so eclectic. It is the only global religion that has not been traced to a specific founder, and, unlike Islam or Christianity, does not have a holy book as the one and only

scriptural authority. One may regard the *Rig Veda* as one's personal holy text, or one may turn to the *Upanishads*, or the *Bhagavad Gita*; or one may dispense with all sacred texts and still claim to be a good Hindu. One may worship Vishnu or Shiva or some other gods or goddesses; or one may not worship any specific deity and meditate on the Supreme Spirit dwelling within one's own heart. Some Hindus visit temples for prayer, worship or devotional music; others prefer sacrificial ritual, or to bathe in holy rivers, or to go on pilgrimages; others regard all rituals as redundant. The same flexibility can be seen in Hindu theories of creation or the nature of God.

Hinduism thrives on contrasts. At one end is the most abstruse metaphysical speculation about Ultimate Reality; at the other there are popular practices based on the propitiation of tree-spirits and animal deities. Absolute monism goes hand in hand with extreme pluralism. On the one hand, Hinduism accepts the validity of many paths leading to the same goal, and is willing to recognise the divinity of the prophets of other religions. But along with this tolerance one sees rigid adherence to caste distinctions and custom-ridden practices. Defying attempts to codify it, this heterogeneity is perhaps Hinduism's most defining characteristic.

The Vedic Age

The Harappan cities were supplanted by a new wave of peoples. They brought with them a new language, Sanskrit, and their own concepts of the cosmos. Their reverence for the Divine was recorded in beautiful hymns and prayers, which have been collected in the four *Vedas* (from the Sanskrit root *vid*, to know). The most important is the *Rig Veda*. The hymns were transmitted orally for centuries and were not written down until the beginning of the first millennium AD.

The Vedic hymns, composed between 1600 and 1000 BC, were addressed to gods and goddesses who were regarded as personifications of the powers of nature: Indra, god of rain and thunder; Prajapati, lord of the creatures; Agni, god of the sacred fire; the Maruts, gods of winds and storms; Savitr, the sun god; Ushas, goddess of dawn; and Varuna, god of the sea and upholder of the moral law. The hymns are believed to have been composed by *rishis* (sages) who were divinely inspired.

The *Vedas* are regarded as the fountainhead of Hinduism. They contain ideas and suggestions that have shaped the entire Hindu tradition and show a tendency to move from pluralism to monism. Although different gods were, and continue to be, worshipped, they were increasingly seen as manifestations of a single Divine Principle. The Vedic concept of *rita* (cosmic law) points to a single rhythmic force animating the entire universe.

Also, by combining religion with philosophy and poetry, the *Vedas* initiated a typical Hindu concept of perfection, the concept that the man of wisdom must combine the intellectual clarity of the philosopher with the faith of the sage and the aestheticism of the artist.

Vedic religion consisted mainly of sacrificial ritual. The sacred flame was kindled in the centre of a raised platform. The sacrificer offered oblations to the flame while the priest chanted hymns and invocations. In the centuries that followed, the mystical and symbolic meaning of the *yajna* (sacrifice) receded into the background. The ritual became all-important. Every detail had to be meticulously followed: the kindling of the fuel, the shape of the vessel containing the holy water, the intonation of the words. The Brahmans, who performed this ritual, became the dominant class of society.

The *Upanishads* (800–400 BC) represent a reaction against this decline in values. They are dialogues between teachers and disciples and are regarded as a continuation of the *Vedas*.

The most popular text in the Vedic tradition is the *Bhagavad Gita* (Song of God). Although it is a part of the Mahabharata, an epic poem that belongs to a later period, the *Bhagavad Gita* is strongly influenced by the *Upanishads*. The *Upanishads* are the cows, says a Sanskrit couplet, and the *Gita* is the sweet, nourishing milk that the cows yield. M.K. Gandhi once described the *Gita* as his spiritual dictionary.

LEFT: Lord Hanuman, the monkey god.
RIGHT: Radha and Krishna.

The Mahabharata

The Mahabharata revolves around the conflict between the five Pandava brothers, their joint wife Draupadi, and the Pandavas' cousins, the Kauravas, who had wrongly usurped the kingdom. Krishna, an incarnation of the God Vishnu, became the charioteer of Arjuna, the commander of the Pandava army. On the eve of battle Arjuna was beset with doubt and refused to fight against his kith and kin. In this dramatic setting, Krishna gave him a discourse on the immortality of the soul and his obligation to fulfil his *dharma* (sacred duty).

Krishna's discourse, with occasional questions from Arjuna, covers almost every aspect of human life. The *Gita's* tremendous appeal derives from its earnestness, optimism and tolerance. As with many popular religious texts, there is something in it for everyone. The *Gita* accepts the validity of three different paths leading to the common goal of self-realisation: the path of *Jnana* (Knowledge), the path of *Bhakti*

> ### KRISHNA'S WORDS
>
> "Whichever path you tread, you can reach me. Offer me but a flower, a fruit … or a little water. I will accept it if you come to me with a pure and loving heart."

WHO'S WHO IN THE HINDU PANTHEON

Vishnu (Narayana) is the highest of the gods. When he is asleep, the universe is in a state of dissolution. When he wakes up, the universe evolves. Periodically, Vishnu descends to earth to protect truth and virtue and to destroy evil. His earlier *avataras* (incarnations) were in animal forms. In his seventh, eighth and ninth incarnations, Vishnu appeared as Rama, Krishna and the Buddha respectively. Vishnu's wife is **Lakshmi**, the Goddess of Prosperity.

Shiva has many roles. He is the Great Yogi meditating on Mount Kailash. He is Nataraja (Lord of Dance), creating and destroying. In another aspect he is the seed of life and his phallic symbol is worshipped in many temples.

Shiva's spouse is **Shakti** (female power). In her beneficent form she is Parvati, while in her terrifying form she appears as Kali.

Of all the Hindu gods, **Krishna** is the most human. We see him as a child, stealing butter and being punished by his mother. Then we see him as a handsome youth. All the *gopis* (female cowherds) are in love with him. Among them, Radha is his favourite. The romantic love of Radha and Krishna is interpreted symbolically as the relationship of the human soul with the Divine Spirit. In his mature years, Krishna appears as the wise philosopher whose teaching is embodied in the *Bhagavad Gita*.

(Devotion and Love), and the path of *Karma* (Work). These are said to equate with the intellectual, the emotional and the practical sides of human nature. In addition, the special path, the path of *Yoga*, is also recognised. The central message of the *Gita* is sometimes said to be: work without attachment, dedicating the fruit of your work to the Divine.

The Ramayana

The *Ramayana*, whose author, Valmiki, is a legendary figure, has exerted a deep influence on the religious and cultural life of India. Rama, eldest son of King Dasharatha of Ayodhya, was

Mythology and local deities

In India, mythology has always been very close to the actual life of the people. There are hundreds of myths about gods, goddesses, heroes, sages, demons, and natural phenomena like the sun and the moon, lakes, rivers, mountains, trees, flowers and animals. They are kept alive through fairs and festivals, in traditional songs, dramas and dances, and provide the main motifs in court and stage performances.

As the Vedic deities (such as Brahma and Surya) lost some of their importance, other gods, particularly Rama and Krishna, probably local hero-gods that were absorbed into Hindu

banished for 14 years through the machinations of his stepmother. He went into the forest, accompanied by his wife, Sita, and younger brother, Lakshmana. Sita was kidnapped and taken to Sri Lanka on the orders of the demon-king, Ravana. Rama, supported by an army of monkeys led by Hanuman, defeated Ravana and rescued his wife. Rama, an incarnation of Vishnu, emerges from the narrative as *Purushottama* (Perfect Man). He is the ideal king, the ideal brother, the ideal son. Stories of Rama's devotion to his parents and teachers, his courage and compassion, have been woven into the poem. There are vivid descriptions of the regions through which he passed.

mythology, became popular. Vishnu and Shiva, who were minor deities in the *Vedas*, became predominant in the later Hindu pantheon.

The two great epic poems are a treasure house of mythology. Stories from these epics, and other myths derived from various sources, were later elaborated in a literature known as the *Puranas*. Of these, the *Siva Purana*, the *Visnu Purana* and the *Bhagavata* are especially important since they contain myths of Shiva, Vishnu and Krishna respectively.

However, it is not necessarily these canonical deities that are closest to the lives of many, particularly rural, Indians. It is their complex of local village gods and, more often, goddesses that claim the greatest attention. These local deities perform vital functions in delineating and protecting the village. Goddesses, in particular, are associated with disease – most commonly smallpox, as with the powerful South Indian goddess Yellama – and their propitiation is an essential yearly ritual.

The shrines of the more powerful, and hence most dangerous, deities are often to be found outside the village boundaries, where they are not only at a safe distance, but form a protective ring around the dwellings, warding off disaster such as famine or disease. The *pujaris*, or priests, of these local deities are generally not

Canonical Hinduism

The Hindu epics were probably composed in the 1st century AD, and the later *Puranas* were completed by 500 AD. The basic principles of Hinduism received fresh support from the *Vedanta* philosophy. Based on the *Upanishads*, *Vedanta* was brilliantly systematised by Shankaracharya in the 8th century. This Sanskritised orthodoxy has attained the status of what might be described as a "Hindu canon".

In the *Vedanta* it was asserted that, from the transcendental viewpoint, Brahman is the sole Reality and everything else is a mere appearance. But from the empirical viewpoint, the

the Brahmans of the village temple, but are drawn from the lower castes.

Not only does this caste division emphasise the divergence of the Sanskritised pan-Indian Hindu tradition from local religion, but also points up differences in ritual. The local goddesses often demand blood sacrifices, of a buffalo, goat or chicken, thought of as "polluting" by the higher castes, and the rituals are often accompanied by drumming, an activity also associated with the lower castes as animal skins also carry the stigma of "pollution".

LEFT: *terukuttu* performers from Tamil Nadu.
ABOVE: a sacred tree near Kollam, Kerala.

reality of the world and the values and distinctions of human life must be accepted. The fundamentals of canonical Hinduism might be summarised as:

Goal and Paths. The ultimate goal is *moksa*, liberation from the cycle of existence.

Karma and Rebirth. Until *moksa* is attained, all human beings are subject to rebirth. The conditions of life in each birth are determined by the cumulative results of the *karma* (deeds) that were performed in previous lifetimes.

Four Objectives. In addition to *moksa*, three proximate ends are recognised as legitimate: *kama* (pleasure, including sex), *artha* (prosperity, fame) and *dharma* (truth, righteousness).

Four Stages in Life. These are: the stage of the learner, demanding self-control and abstinence; the stage of the householder, when *kama* and *artha* are valid ends; the stage of detachment; and the stage of renunciation, when one leads a wholly spiritual life, preparing for *moksa*.

Four Castes. Differences in aptitudes and temperaments are reflected in society's division into four castes: *Brahmans* (priests, teachers); *Kshatriyas* (warriors, rulers); *Vaisyas* (traders, merchants); and *Sudras* (agriculturalists).

Yoga. Through *yoga* (inner integration) one can proceed from physical to mental control, to the recognition of one's own reality as Pure Spirit.

Historical developments

The coming of Islam to India in the 12th century was a turning point in the evolution of Hinduism. The Sikh religion, founded by Guru Nanak in the 15th century, played an important part in bringing the two faiths (Islam and Hinduism) together. In the 16th century, Catholic missionaries came to India and Hinduism began to feel the impact of Christianity. However, Hinduism remained the dominant religion.

In the Middle Ages, poetry, rather than philosophy, was the chief medium of religious expression. This was the age of the great poet-saints whose songs are still performed.

SADHUS

A feature of Indian religious life is the presence of numbers of *sadhus* (wandering hermits). They can be seen in cities and villages, in forests, on the banks of rivers and, of course, in the Himalaya. Usually dressed in saffron or ochre robes, their bodies smeared with ash and foreheads anointed with sandal-paste, the *sadhus* carry all their possessions with them: a bowl, a staff, a blanket. Some move alone, others in small groups. Some have taken vows of silence, others preach or chant hymns, sometimes bursting into songs of religious ecstasy. One is not supposed to ask questions about their homes or destinations. They are simply spiritual wanderers.

The consolidation of British rule in India at the end of the 18th century exposed India to new influences from the West: Western liberalism and humanism, scientific thought and technology. Hinduism once again showed its diversity and power to assimilate elements from other traditions while retaining its own basic identity.

Hinduism reacted to the West in two divergent ways. There was a strong movement for reform, led by Raja Ram Mohan Roy, with a positive approach to Western culture. There was also a revivalist trend represented by Dayanand Sarasvati, founder of the Arya Samaj, and others who felt that the West had little to offer. They pressed for a Vedic revival.

In the 20th century, two Hindus, M.K. Gandhi and the poet Rabindranath Tagore, emphasised Hinduism's tolerance and creativity. Gandhi described himself as orthodox, but believed firmly that the essential message of all religions was the same. His ancestors were Jains and some of his closest friends were Muslims. In interpreting Hinduism he gave primacy to Truth and Non-violence. While Gandhi represented a moral force in 20th-century Hinduism, Tagore focused on its creative and aesthetic achievements.

> ### FOUR NOBLE TRUTHS
>
> Suffering is universal; suffering is caused and sustained by craving; suffering *can* be prevented and overcome; there is a *way* leading to the removal of suffering.

centuries before it became a pan-Asian one.

Siddhartha, who was later known as the Buddha, the Enlightened One, was the son of King Shuddhodana of Kapila-vastu and his queen, Maya. He was born at Lumbini in the Himalayan foothills. His family name was Gautama and he belonged to the Shakya clan. Hence he is sometimes called Shakyamuni (Shakya Sage) or Shakyasimha (Shakya Lion). Among his other epithets are Amitabha (Infinite Light) and Tathagata (He Who Has Arrived At Perfection).

Buddhism

The personality and teachings of the Buddha have illuminated the lives and thoughts of millions in Asia. It was in India that the light was first kindled. The Buddha was born in India, and he lived and died there. His teachings were imparted in the context of his Indian heritage. A thousand years after his death, he was accepted as an incarnation of Vishnu, one of the three highest gods in the Hindu pantheon. Buddhism remained an Indian religion for many

LEFT: Brahmans distributing offerings at the Kapalesvara temple, Chennai.
ABOVE: keeping watch over a funeral pyre.

Queen Maya died a week after delivering the prince. At Siddhartha's birth, the royal astrologer prophesied that he would one day become disillusioned with worldly pleasures and become a mendicant in search of the wisdom to overcome suffering. Siddhartha grew up into a handsome youth, gentle and compassionate, skilled in all the arts. The king, remembering the astrologer's prophecy, tried to save his son from unpleasant sights. He was surrounded by luxury. The king found for him a lovely wife, Yashodhara, princess of a neighbouring kingdom. Yashodhara bore him a son. But the seeds of disenchantment had already sprouted in Siddhartha's heart. He named his son Rahula (Impediment).

Symbolic Design

Religious buildings in India come in all shapes and sizes and their architecture varies from region to region. Hindu temples *(mandir)* are built with beams, and feature low ceilings, narrow doorways, and hundreds of pillars, unlike the Indian mosques *(masjid)*, which have spacious interiors reflecting the introduction of the true arch in Muslim architecture.

Hindu temple architecture is highly symbolic – a cosmology in miniature planned to entice a particular deity back to visit a place (there are said to be 300

million different gods). Complex astrological and numerological calculations come into play. Temple blueprints follow *vastu-shastras*, sacred principles similar to the Feng Shui of the Far East, which can correct any on-site imperfections.

Most temples started out as a simple shelter over a sacred spot beneath a tree or beside a river. Many have become awesome stone monuments as worshippers have built elaborate extensions. Water, which represents the place where spirits may cross over to the far shore of wisdom *(tirth)*, is integral to the temple's layout. Ritual cleansing takes place here.

The sacred sanctum, where an idol of the presiding deity resides in a darkened chamber, is almost always square-shaped and must be orientated towards one of the cardinal points. East is most auspicious because it represents the constancy of sunrise.

Depending on the time of year, the temple was constructed and to which deity it is devoted, this womb chamber *(garbha griha)* may face elsewhere. West denotes Varun, ever-changing domain of the ocean god; north, towards the navigators' North Star, represents permanence; south, the domain of Yama, the Lord of Death, denotes decay or destruction. Regardless of the direction, the inner sanctum must be enclosed on three sides.

The main entrance is flanked by sculpted river goddesses, and niches on the outer walls depict various manifestations of the god within, whose face will be carved in the middle of the main lintel. Protective mythological guardians deter evil. The *vahana*, or the animal vehicle of a god, is placed directly in front of the shrine, near a lamp that symbolically eliminates ignorance.

A towering roof structure soars above the inner sanctum to make the holy place visible from a distance. Called *shikharas*, these sloping towers vary in shape according to region. An elaborate cluster of multiple carved layers represents the Himalayan mountains, where Hindu gods dwell. Always balanced on top is a *kalash*, an emblem for a pot of ambrosia, which symbolises the ultimate end of prayer – freedom from the cycles of rebirth.

Smaller shrines for related deities are often added to a temple complex. Ancient Hindu temples in the South and Orissa include additional pavilions for dance and food distribution.

There are no set rules for designing Sikh temples *(gurdwara)*. The Golden Temple, Amritsar, for instance, is a mixture of Muslim and Hindu styles.

Early Buddhist temples centre on *stupa*, which contain relics of the Buddha or sages, and worshippers circumambulate clockwise to show respect. The image of the Buddha and an interior place for worship were late developments, and normally placed at the end of a hallway or quadrangle. The earliest examples of temples were cut from rocks, but were sculpted to resemble timber constructions. Later, freestanding temples were built using bricks.

Devout Jains specialise in high-density temple construction. Shatrunjaya, in Gujarat, numbers more than 900 temples on a single hill. ❑

LEFT: the ornate 10th-century Muktesvar Temple, Bhubaneshwar, an example of Orissan architecture.

As prophesied, Siddhartha saw the three signs of suffering: sickness, old age and death. On the night of the full moon in the month of *Vaisakha*, corresponding with April-May in the Western calendar, Siddhartha prepared for the Great Renunciation. He stood at the door of his bedchamber, looked at his sleeping wife and son for a few moments, and then left the palace.

Siddhartha sat at the feet of famous masters, but none of them could explain to him the cause of sorrow. For a while he joined a group of ascetics and performed severe physical austerities. He became extremely weak in body and mind, and realised that wisdom could not be attained through self-mortification. At last, meditating under a tree near Gaya, he attained Bodhi (Illumination). Prince Siddhartha had become the Buddha, the Fully Awakened One. And the tree that had sheltered him came to be known as the Bodhi Tree.

After becoming enlightened, Gautama the Buddha could have immediately released himself from the cycle of rebirths and attained Nirvana, supreme liberation. But the compassionate side of his nature prevented him from tasting the fruit of liberation so long as a single living creature was in pain. His first sermon was preached in the Deer Park at Sarnath, near the ancient holy city of Varanasi. The ascetics from whom he had parted company a few months earlier became his first audience. According to legend, deer from the forest listened enraptured to the Buddha, sensing that his message was for all living beings. It contained the Four Noble Truths, which form the basis of Buddhist thought.

As the number of his followers increased, the *Bhikshusangha* (Order of Monks) was formed. At first, only men were admitted. But later, urged by his foster mother Gotami, the Buddha admitted women and an Order of Nuns was formed.

After a few months the Buddha visited Kapilavastu and met his father, wife and son. He had left as a prince: he returned as a mendicant. He was hailed as a hero, a conqueror in the spiritual realm.

RIGHT: following in the Buddha's footsteps – a priest at Mahabodhi Temple in Bodhgaya, Bihar.

WHAT IS NIRVANA?

Asked what Nirvana was like, the Buddha merely smiled and when pressed for an answer, he said, "*Shantam Nirvanam*: Nirvana is peace, silence."

During the remaining 40 years of his life the Buddha travelled from village to village, except during the rainy season when travel would be impossible, preaching the message of love, compassion, tolerance and self-restraint. He led a humble life, and he died in 483 BC, in his 80th year, at Kusinara, not far from the place of his birth. His last words were to his favourite disciple, Ananda: "A Buddha can only point the way. Become a lamp unto yourself. Work out your own salvation diligently."

Buddha's teachings

While Hindu thought was preoccupied with the essential nature of Absolute Reality, the Buddha avoided metaphysical controversies. "The arising of sorrow, the termination of sorrow, that is all I teach," he once said. Two philosophical principles are implicit in the Buddha's teaching. First, there is the Law of Impermanence. Everything in the phenomenal world is subject to change. The second assumption is the Law of Causation. Nothing happens by chance. Apart from natural causes, we are subject to the operation of our *karma*. It follows that the popular notion of a soul that somehow survives the body is illusory. The Buddha urges us to discard this illusion. He did not, however, reject the Universal Spirit of Self *(Atman)* of the *Upanishads*.

The Buddha's first sermon is called the Sermon of the Middle Way and steers between two sets of extremes: on the ethical plane, the extremes of self-indulgence and asceticism; on the philosophical plane, the extremes of naive acceptance of everything as real and the total rejection of everything as unreal. The Middle Way now becomes the Eightfold Path of the good life,

> ### WAVING THE FLAG
>
> The colours of the Indian flag have religious significance: saffron represents Hinduism, green is the colour of Islam, and white represents all the other faiths.

of war, became a Buddhist. Ashoka's conversion marked the beginning of a period of Buddhist expansion. Ashoka set up inscriptions throughout South Asia exhorting his subjects to follow the Buddha's message of compassion and tolerance.

In modern India, there has been a revival of interest in Buddhism, particularly among Dalits following Dr Ambedkar's public conversion. Yet Buddhists constitute a very small proportion of the Indian population. This has led some people to assert

consisting of right conduct, right motive, right resolve, right speech, right livelihood, right attention, right effort and right meditation.

By following this path of restraint and self-perfection, one can conquer craving. Then one is within sight of Nirvana, the transcendental state of complete emancipation.

Shortly after the Buddha's death, his oldest disciple, Kashyapa, convened a Council at Rajagriha. The master's teachings were classified into three sections, known as *Tripitaka* (Three Baskets). These, along with later commentaries, became the scriptures of Buddhism.

In the 3rd century BC the great Mauryan emperor, Ashoka, saddened by the bloodshed

that India banished Buddhism. But something that has been assimilated until it flows through the very bloodstream of Indian culture cannot be said to have been rejected simply because we cannot see it on the surface. Even when there was an ideological conflict between Hinduism and Buddhism, the Buddha's personality and character attracted the admiration of Hindus and Buddhists alike.

The Buddha's emphasis on compassion, love and non-violence has become a permanent part of India's spiritual heritage. Buddhism has inspired some of the finest architecture, sculpture and painting. The stupas of Sanchi and Amaravati, the frescoes of Ajanta, the remains of the university of Nalanda, the monasteries of Bodhgaya and Rajagriha and, above all, the Buddha images of the Mathura and Sarnath schools – all these bear witness to the fact that the influence of Buddhism has endured. Refugee communities of Tibetan Buddhists and Dalit converts have significantly boosted the numbers of Indian Buddhists since the 1960s.

Jainism

About the same time as the Buddha was preaching his *dharma*, and in the same region, another religious tradition was being established. Vardhamana, better known by his title Mahavira (Great Hero), was an elder contemporary of the Buddha. The two teachers had much in common: both were *Kshatriyas* of royal descent but renounced the worldly life; both rejected caste barriers and questioned the sacredness of the *Vedas*. Globally Mahavira's fame has been eclipsed by the Buddha's; Jainism, the religion preached by Mahavira, counts more than 3 million adherents in India today, whereas the Buddha's faith has almost twice as many, with many more outside the country.

The theme of self-conquest, common to many religions, is supremely important to the Jains. The very word Jain is derived from *jina* (conqueror). Carrying the idea of self-conquest to its extreme, Jainism has become the world's most rigorously ascetic faith. God has little or no place in this system. The popular gods of Hinduism are accepted, but they are placed lower than the *jinas*, who are regarded as the true focus of devotion.

Mahavira, though usually accepted as the founder of the faith in the context of history, is said to be the last of a line of 24 *jinas*. All of them are said to have attained perfect wisdom *(Kaivalya)* through different penances, to vanquish desire and break their bonds with the material world. The *jinas* are also known as *Tirthankaras* (crossing-makers). The crossing refers to the passage from the material to the spiritual realm, from bondage to freedom.

Jainism not only rejects the notion of a Personal God, but also the idea of a single impersonal Absolute Reality. It regards each living being as an independent *jiva* (soul). In its mundane condition, the soul is permeated by material particles through the working of *karma*. To attain liberation, a double process is necessary: the incursion of new *karma*-particles must be stopped; and those that have already tainted the soul must be expelled. This is possible only through right faith, right knowledge and right conduct: the *tri-ratna* (three jewels) of Jainism.

Right conduct is seen as the rejection of falsehood, theft, lust, greed and violence. Of these five sins violence is the most heinous. The highest virtue is the total abjuration of any thought or action that can hurt a living being.

Ahimsa paramo dharma (non-violence is the supreme religion): this Jain motto was adopted by Mahatma Gandhi. Sometimes the Jains carry their non-violence, like their asceticism, to extreme limits. For instance, Jain monks are often seen with their nose and mouth covered by a fine cloth mask to ensure that they do not involuntarily kill insects while breathing, and use a whisk to sweep their path clear.

Jains have made valuable contributions in many areas of Indian culture: philosophy, literature, painting, sculpture and architecture. The greatest glory of Jain religious art lies in temple architecture, particularly at Girnar, Palitana and Mount Abu.

LEFT: sleepy Buddhist monks.
RIGHT: Jain nuns wear a cloth over their face to ensure they do not kill insects while breathing.

Opposites together

In orthodox terms, no two religions in the world appear on the surface to be as dissimilar as Hinduism and Islam. Islam was founded by a historical person and has a specific scripture, the *Qur'an*; Hinduism's origins lie in a speculative distant past. Hinduism is eclectic and pluralistic; Islam is homogeneous and has a definite concept of God. The Hindu temple is enclosed on three sides, and there is mystery in the dark inner sanctum; the Muslim mosque is open on all sides, exposed to light and air. Hindus worship sculptured images of deities; to the Muslim, idol worship is a most grievous sin.

Hinduism tends to shun proselytisation; Islam welcomes converts.

Yet these two faiths met in India, influenced each other and, after initial conflict, enriched each other. Within a few decades of their arrival in India, Muslims began to consider India as their home. Between the 13th and the 18th centuries, northern India witnessed a synthesis of Hindu and Islamic elements in almost every sphere of life. This unique syncretic Indo-Islamic culture gave rise to a huge flowering of cultural endeavour, in poetry, painting, architecture and music. Indeed, India is unimaginable without Islam, its influence is everywhere, from food to music to architecture.

The origins of Islam

Islam is a religion derived from the revelations of the prophet Muhammad. These are claimed to have been passed down to him by the Archangel Gabriel and they now form the text of the Muslim holy book, the *Qur'an*, which builds on the texts of the Jews and Christians. It is upon this text that Muslims base their lives.

Muhammad was born at Makkah (Mecca) in AD 570, a fatherless child. His mother died when he was four. Muhammad's childhood was not a happy one. As a boy, he earned a paltry living doing odd jobs for traders in caravans. He was 25 when he married Khadijah, a wealthy widow who had employed him. Arabia was at that time a battleground for warring tribes. Religion was pantheistic and centred around the worship of stone images of deities. Muhammad, introspective and sensitive by nature, felt opposed to this and often sought solitude in the desert. He had his first mystical experience at the age of 40. The archangel Gabriel appeared before him in a vision, hailed him as the *Rasul* (Messenger) of God and called upon him to proclaim the glory of Allah, "the one true God". Gabriel again appeared and showed Muhammad a written text which later became a part of the *Qur'an*.

As the number of his followers increased, Muhammad became bolder in his denunciation of idolatry. The tribesmen harassed and threatened him. In AD 622 Muhammad left Makkah and went to Medina, a town 200 miles to the north, at the invitation of some merchants. The Islamic calendar is dated from this migration *(hijrah)*. In Medina, he consolidated his new religion, Islam (Submission to God). His followers, the Muslims ("Those Who Have Submitted"), now numbered thousands.

Eight years later he returned to Makkah and defeated his opponents in battle. He died in 632. Within two decades, the Muslims had conquered Iraq, Syria, Egypt and eastern Turkey. By AD 670 the Arabs were masters of Iran and the whole of northern Africa. Their success was the result of their faith in the Prophet and the holy book, their strong sense of brotherhood and equality of all Muslims, and the precision and simplicity of their creed. Its success cannot be attributed to force alone. Muhammad himself was a man of deep generosity and wisdom. The God of Islam is compassionate and merciful *(Rahman* and *Rahim)*.

Islam in India

Arab traders came to India as early as the 7th century and the first Muslim – Arab – invaders came as far as Daibul, close to present-day Karachi, and Multan, both now in Pakistan, in 712. Islam gradually spread north through missionary activity, and in 977 Mahmud of Ghazni, a Turkish ruler from Central Asia, invaded India as far as the Ganga. His descendants consolidated their hold over the Punjab and, when the Ghaznivad dynasty was replaced by Muhammad Ghauri at the end of the 12th century, Islamic influence reached Delhi and Ajmer. By the beginning of the 13th century the Delhi Sultanate

In its first phase, Islamic rule in India was aggressive, but it was not through the temporal power of the Islamic armies that the vast majority of converts were made; the mystics of Islam, known as Sufis, played an important part in spreading the message of universal love. The Sufi saints, or *pirs*, taught their disciples through *zikr*, or the repetition of religious formulas. The message of Islamic mysticism was also conveyed effectively by the classical Persian poets, particularly by Rumi, who expressed the spirit of Sufism through beautiful symbols and images. Persian, not Arabic, was the court language during Muslim rule.

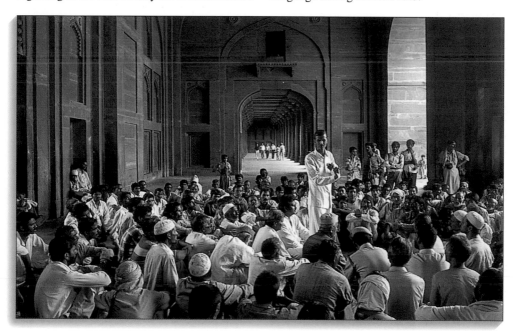

was established and Muslim rule gradually extended eastwards and southwards.

When the sultanate's power declined, the Mughal Empire, founded by Babur in 1506, replaced it as the ruler of North India. One of the greatest Mughal emperors was Akbar (1556–1605), whose policy of religious tolerance brought Hindus and Muslims together. The later emperor Aurangzeb (1658–1707), however, gained notoriety for destroying many temples and thereby alienating many Hindus.

LEFT: a Hindu *sanyasi* in the Asiatic Society library in Mumbai.
ABOVE: a meeting at the Jama Masjid, Fatehpur-Sikri.

THE FIVE PILLARS OF ISLAM

In order to be a good Muslim one must follow five basic precepts and practices:
• to assert that "There is no God but Allah, and Muhammad is his Prophet",
• to pray, preferably five times a day,
• to perform acts of charity,
• to observe a fast from dawn to dusk throughout the month of Ramadan (this is a holy month for Muslims because the Prophet received his divine revelation in this month),
• to go on a pilgrimage to Makkah (Mecca) at least once during one's lifetime.

Renowned *pirs* settled in India. Among these, Mu'inuddin Chishti of Ajmer and Nizamuddin Aulia of Delhi were the most influential. Annual festivals in their honour are celebrated. Amir Khusrau, poet, musician and historian, was a disciple of Nizamuddin. Khusrau was famous as a poet in the classical Persian tradition, but he also wrote religious poetry in Urdu. The prevalent spirit of Hindu-Muslim integration was reflected admirably in Khusrau's work. The tombs of these poet-saints are still places of worship and pilgrimage for both Muslims and Hindus, particularly at the time of the saint's *urs* (the anniversary of the saint's death).

THE SIKH IDENTITY

The Sikh community forms around 2 percent of India's population. Since its founding by Guru Nanak in the 15th century, it has evolved its own unmistakeable identity. It is opposed to the caste system, and all Sikh men carry the last name Singh (lion). Idol worship is rejected as in Islam, but the ideas of *karma* and rebirth are accepted. In their religious life and ritual, Sikhs are very close to Hindus. It is not uncommon for a Hindu to bring up one of his sons as a Sikh and there are frequent intermarriages. Sikh men grow beards and wear turbans over their uncut hair. Every Sikh considers it an obligation to wear a *kara* (steel bangle).

The Sikhs

This process of bringing Hinduism and Islam close to each other was continued by Kabir and Nanak. Born into a Brahman family, Kabir was brought up by Muslim foster parents. He was a disciple of Ramananda, a famous Hindu saint, but he was also deeply influenced by Sufism and used Sufi terminology in many of his poems. Inspired by Kabir, Guru Nanak (1469–1539) founded the Sikh religion with the avowed purpose of synthesising Hinduism and Islam. Islam's spirit of brotherhood helped in loosening the rigidity of the caste system.

Nanak came from the Punjab, a region where Hindus and Muslims had come in closer contact than in any other part of India. A Hindu by birth and training, Nanak was attracted from his childhood towards Hindu as well as Muslim saints and poets. He visited the sacred places of Hinduism and also made the pilgrimage to Makkah. He saw the essential teaching of both religions as being the same. Nanak began to preach his message of unity. He attracted many followers and soon came to be known as Guru Nanak. His disciples came together, and a new religious tradition was born. The term Sikh is derived from the Sanskrit *shishya* (disciple).

Angad succeeded Nanak as the Guru of the Sikhs, and started compiling Nanak's writings. He also used a script that was used by some Punjabis, called *Gurmukhi*, and it became the official script of the Sikhs. Guru Arjun, the fifth in succession, started building the temple at Amritsar, which later became the holiest Sikh shrine. Arjun also systematised the collection of sacred hymns and poems by Nanak, Kabir and other saints. This collection became the holy scripture of the Sikhs. It is known as *Adi Granth* (The First Book), or *Granth Sahib* (Book of the Lord).

The spread of the Sikh faith alarmed orthodox Muslims. The Sikhs were persecuted. Guru Arjun was put to death on a charge of sedition in 1606. Arjun's martyrdom convinced his successors that Sikhs must have military training to defend themselves. The 10th Guru, Govind Singh, transformed the pacifist Sikh sect into a martial community. He introduced rites of initiation into a well-organised Sikh army known as the *Khalsa*. Govind Singh also decided to terminate the succession of gurus. He asked his followers to look upon the *Granth Sahib* as the sole object of veneration. The Holy Book became the symbol of God.

Christianity

According to a strong tradition prevalent in the South, Christianity in India is as old as Saint Thomas, one of the apostles of Jesus Christ. The saint is said to have spent a few years near Chennai (Madras) and to have died there. Other legends describe Saint Bartholomew as the first Christian missionary in India. Latin historians in the Middle Ages made frequent references to Christian settlements in India.

Indian Christians, who number nearly 25 million, represent almost every denomination: Catholic, Methodist, Baptist, Presbyterian, Maronite, Seventh-Day Adventist and others.

structures and practices are very similar to those of Keralan high-caste Hindus; it is thought that they were originally converts from the Brahman Nambudiri caste.

Christian missionary activity from Western Europe began with the arrival of the Jesuit Saint Francis Xavier in 1542. His tomb in Goa, a stronghold of Catholicism in India, is still visited by thousands of Catholics every year. Saint Francis Xavier was succeeded by Portuguese missionaries. Some of them visited Akbar's court, and even entertained the hope of converting the emperor. Other Catholic countries soon began to send missionaries to India. In the

However, it is the Syrian Catholics who hold historical primacy. They trace their origins in South Asia back to Saint Thomas (who is thought to have travelled in South India between AD 52 and 72). Certainly they can date back their activities to the 6th century, when orthodox Syrian Christians embarked on missionary activity in South Asia.

Found in the southwestern state of Kerala, the Syrian Catholics follow the Syrian order of service and, until recently, the liturgy was in ancient Syriac. Although Christian, their social

LEFT: Sikh priest reads from the *Guru Granth Sahib*.
ABOVE: St Mary's church, Kerala, founded in 427.

18th century, Protestant missionaries, especially from Denmark, Holland and Germany, started their work in India.

The British conquest naturally gave the Anglican Church an advantage over others. William Carey and Alexander Duff played key roles in establishing Christianity. Carey founded the Seminary at Serampore. Alexander Duff came to India in 1830 and continued Carey's work. Throughout the 19th century, Catholic as well as Protestant missionaries, besides preaching Christian doctrines, made contributions to education and scholarship. Most Indian Protestants are now members of the Anglican Church of North or South India.

Jewish India

India has two ancient, but now greatly depleted, indigenous Jewish communities: the Malayalam-speaking Cochinis who are restricted to Kochi in Kerala; and the Marathi-speaking Bene Israel (children of Israel), concentrated in Mumbai, Kolkata, Old Delhi and Ahmadabad. Today, migration to Israel, England, the United States and Canada has reduced the Indian Jewish population to 5,000.

The Jews of Kochi claim their origins reach back to refugees who fled Palestine in AD 70 after the destruction of the Temple in Jerusalem. The Bene Israel claim to have been in India since the 2nd century BC; however, the earliest report of Indian Jews dates from a traveller's account of the early 11th century. The communities were well established and showed great similarities to neighbouring peoples, indicating a long period of settlement, possibly starting with trade along India's west coast.

Later Jewish immigrations, in the 17th and 18th centuries, came from present-day Iran and Central Asia. These settlers gave Mumbai India's largest Jewish community.

Religion in contemporary India

Religion still has a tremendous hold on contemporary India. Mahatma Gandhi, one of the leaders of the Indian Independence movement, was deeply religious, and some of the worst excesses of recent history can be ascribed to intolerance between religious communities *(see opposite)*. In the 20th century India captured the religious imagination of the West, as many religious leaders established spiritual centres that continue to attract thousands of people.

South Asia has been a meeting ground for all the major religions of the world. Even today, Muslim Sufi saints are venerated all over India. Meher Baba, the silent sage of Maharashtra, was a Parsi. Mother Teresa was given a state funeral following her death in Kolkata in 1997 and was considered an Indian treasure, even though she was a Roman Catholic.

India is a secular republic. The protection of religious minorities is recognised as one of the obligations of the state and the constitution of India guarantees the right of religious freedom to all citizens. While almost all political parties pay lip service to this ideal, recently the concept of secularisation has been at the centre of a political storm, with many claiming that the overtly Hindu BJP is trying to subvert this constitutional obligation.

In the beautiful national anthem, composed by Rabindranath Tagore, a tribute is paid to the different religions of India. Addressing the Divine Power as *Bharata-bhagya-vidhata* (the dispenser of India's destiny), the poet says: "Your call goes out to the Hindus, the Buddhists, the Sikhs, the Jains, the Parsis, the Muslims and the Christians. They all come, gather around your throne, and weave a garland of love for your worship." ❑

PARSIS

Parsis are the descendants of Persians, who emigrated to India in the 8th century. They brought with them the ancient Persian religion founded by Zoroaster in the 6th century BC, based on the worship of Ahura Mazda (Wise Lord) who is eternally in conflict with Ahriman, the Evil Force. Their scripture, the *Avesta*, includes the *gathas* (songs) composed by Zoroaster. In their *agiaries* (fire temples) the sacred flame is always kept burning. Although conservative in their religion, Parsis have identified with their fellow countrymen and have greatly contributed to the educational, scientific and industrial progress of India.

LEFT: stringing garlands for a temple, Mumbai.

Saffronisation

India's most disturbing political phenomenon in recent years has been the rise of the chauvinistic Hindu right, in a process dubbed "saffronisation" after the colour associated with high-caste Hinduism. This was most dramatically illustrated by the destruction of the Babri Masjid (mosque) in Ayodhya in 1992, seen by many as the defining moment in modern Indian politics. However, the roots of Hindu communalism run back to the Independence struggle, and can even be seen in the pre-Independence Congress party, perceived by many Muslims as Hindu-dominated from its very inception.

Anti-Muslim riots at Partition saw the prominent Congressmen Sardar Vallabhai Patel, India's first Home Minister, and Rajendra Prasad call for the withdrawal of protection for Muslim citizens and the sacking of Muslim civil servants. However, the cause of Hindu nationalism suffered a severe setback when Gandhi, who preached tolerance, was assassinated by Nathuram Ghose, a Marathi Brahman with links to the RSS (Rashtriya Swayamsevak Sangh, a hard-line Hindu nationalist organisation). This gave Nehru the chance to outlaw communalist organisations, thus burying the ambitions of the Hindu right for the next two decades.

Ironically, Nehru's daughter, Indira Gandhi, indulged in communal politics. Although she declared allegiance to the secular ideals of her father, she actively courted Hindu support by surrounding herself with Hindu holy men and being seen to participate in Hindu rituals, particularly after her defeat in 1977 by a coalition government, which included a fledgling BJP (Bharatiya Janata Party).

The flirtation of Congress with communal politics (not only Hindu but also, with more immediately disastrous consequences, Sikh separatism in the Punjab) broke the taboo that had existed since Gandhi's assassination, and the 1980s saw a steady rise in support for overtly communal parties, aided by disillusionment with the corruption-ridden Congress.

The main challenger was the BJP led by veteran politician L.K. Advani, formed out of the Janata Party of the late 1970s and with close links to the RSS and Sangh Parivar (a collection of right-wing Hindu groups). They campaigned on a high-caste, right-wing agenda, espousing the ideal of *Hindutva*, a Hindu homeland.

RIGHT: a *sadhu* in Madurai, Tamil Nadu, wearing the traditional saffron robes of a Hindu holy man.

The BJP got its first taste of power in 1989 as part of the coalition government of V.P. Singh. This did not last for long. Advani started to campaign for the destruction of the Babri Masjid, which Hindus were claiming was built on the site of the birthplace of Rama and of an earlier temple. He embarked on a country-wide *yatra* (pilgrimage) to raise support for the building of a new temple, culminating in a visit to the site at Ayodhya itself. Advani was arrested and the government fell. However, the campaign continued to gather support and in 1992 hundreds of *kar sevaks* (Hindu volunteers) tore down the mosque. This led to some of the worst communal rioting India has ever seen, in which many Muslims and Hindus

were killed, particularly in Mumbai. In 2002, Hindu extremist mobs in Gujarat killed and displaced thousands of Muslims, in what can only be described as ethnic cleansing. Numerous mosques and shrines have also been destroyed, allegedly with the connivance of the BJP-led state government.

The BJP-led national government had given saffronisation momentum. Religious minorities came under attack, and school books were even rewritten glorifying India's mythological "Aryan" past, describing *kar sevaks* as national heroes and vilifying Islamic contributions to society. Even after the fall of the BJP-led government, attacks against Muslims have continued, and Christians, too, have been set upon by Hindu militants. ❑

FESTIVALS

*On almost every day of the year there is a festival in some part of
India when colour and pageant merge with ritual and worship*

Festivals are part of everyday life in India – inevitable perhaps, given the thousands of deities, saints, prophets and gurus named by the six major religions who must be worshipped, propitiated and remembered.

A large number of these festivals stem from Hinduism. Myriad practices and an enormous body of legend and history bring an extensive range of significance and association to most major Hindu religious occasions.

Dussera commemorates both the victory of the warrior-goddess Durga (consort of Shiva) over the buffalo-demon Mahisasura, and that of Rama, a god king (an incarnation of Vishnu), over Ravana, the 10-headed king of Lanka, who had abducted Rama's wife, Sita. Worship of the goddess is significant as it represents the female deity's supremacy over the male gods who were unable to destroy the demon.

Navratri is a nine-day festival when the goddess is venerated as the supreme mother. Images installed in homes are worshipped every day and *kathas* (stories) are narrated. In Gujarat, the women dance the *garba* with swaying steps and rhythmic clapping around an earthen lamp.

In Bengal, the main festivals are Kali Puja and Durga Puja when rituals at the Mahakali Temple in Kolkata and other temples attract large crowds. In Durga Puja praises to Devi are sung and much cultural activity is initiated. On the tenth day, buffaloes representing Mahisasura are ritually slaughtered and offered to the goddess. Images of Durga are taken out in procession and immersed.

Durga worship also has social implications. As goddess of war, she is a particular favourite of the Kshatriyas, the warrior caste. After the sacrifice on the tenth day, it was customary to embark on the season's military campaigns. Today this is symbolically re-enacted in the magnificent Dussera processions of Mysore

and Jaipur. The erstwhile ruler, seated in state on an elephant, rides in glittering procession from the centre of the city to a point just outside its gate. Trumpets blare and war drums boom. Richly caparisoned elephants, soldiers in ceremonial uniforms and nobles in traditional attire are in attendance.

Meanwhile, preparations are being completed for the evening's spectacle commemorating Rama's victory and symbolising the triumph of good over evil in his 10-day battle against Ravana. Over nine evenings the epic story (the *Ramlila*) is narrated. On the tenth night colourful effigies of Ravana, his son and his brother, are burnt, setting off a fusillade of crackers – good is established for another year.

Continuing the story of Rama, Divali or Dipavali (literally, "a row of lights") is celebrated 20 days after Dussera. It commemorates the hero-king's return from voluntary exile undertaken to fulfil a father's rash vow. Twinkling oil lamps *(diyas)*, candles or even electric bulbs,

---

PRECEDING PAGES: Krishna plays Holi (*circa* 1780).
LEFT: dressed to play Rama during Dussera.
RIGHT: every town and village has its annual festivals.

light up every home, symbolising the lifting of spiritual darkness. Fireworks explode. Ritual devolves on the worship of Lakshmi (consort of Vishnu), goddess of wealth and prosperity, of whom Sita was an incarnation. The beginning of a new financial year, Divali is significant for traders and businessmen. Old books are closed, new accounts opened.

Lakshmi is a fastidious goddess. Houses are cleaned to ensure her favour, while in villages walls are plastered with insulating and antiseptic cowdung paste. Decorative designs are painted on floors and walls; families gather and sweets are distributed.

Vishnu is invoked in his human incarnations as Rama and Krishna on their birth anniversaries in the festivals of Ramanaumi and Janmastami respectively. Thousands of pilgrims converge on the temples of Ayodhya and Ramesvaram, which are closely connected with the events of the *Ramayana*, to participate in Ramanaumi festivities. Colourful processions carry images of Rama, Sita (the epitome of self-sacrificing Indian womanhood), Lakshmana and Hanuman, Rama's monkey general.

Janmastami is extravagantly recalled in the temples around Vrindavan, Uttar Pradesh. The *Rasalila* is performed to recreate incidents in

FESTIVAL OF HOLI

On the day after the full moon in early March, North India goes wild in a celebration of the springtime festival of Holi. People throng the streets, smearing each other with brightly hued powder *(gulal)* or squirting coloured water. Marijuana-based *bhang* or *thandai* adds to the relaxation of the usual social restraints of sexual propriety (this can be threatening, sometimes dangerous, for women, so be careful). Originally a fertility festival, later legends have ascribed varied origins to Holi. One speaks of a king so arrogant that he demanded that his people worship him. Only his young son, Praladh, dared refuse. Attempts to kill the prince failed. Finally his father's sister, Holika, said to be immune to burning, sat with

the boy in a huge fire. So potent was Praladh's devotion, that he emerged unscathed while Holika burnt to death. Huge bonfires are lit on the eve of Holi in commemoration, and the grain of the harvest is thrown into the flames. The playing of Holi is closely associated with the Radha-Krishna story. In Vraj, legendary homeland of the pastoral god, the festival is spread over 16 days. Apart from the usual fun with *gulal* and coloured water, there are processions with music, song and uninhibited dance, and boisterous scenes in and around temples. Kama, god of love, and his consort, Rati (passion), are also worshipped on Holi in commemoration of Kama's destruction and resurrection by Shiva.

Krishna's life. The image of the divine infant is bathed and placed in a silver cradle. Toys are offered and devotional songs sung.

Festival fairs

Secular asides to major festivals are the *melas* (fairs). One of the best-known fairs is held at Pushkar in Rajasthan on the eighth day after Divali. The fair has become the annual market for livestock. Bullock-cart and camel races add to the excitement. Similar fairs are held at other hallowed sites. At Sonepur in Bihar there's a brisk buying and selling of elephants.

The greatest and most important of Hindu fairs, the Kumbha Mela, is held every sixth and twelfth year at Prayag (Allahabad). The city's supreme sanctity as the confluence *(sangam)* of the Ganga, Yamuna and the mythical Sarasvati, is accentuated by the story behind the gathering. When the gods wrestled the jar *(kumbha)* of immortal nectar from the *asuras* (demons), four drops of the precious liquid fell to earth. Prayag was one of the places where a drop fell (the others are Haridwar, Ujjain and Nasik). The extensive river bed draws crowds unparalleled anywhere else in the world.

Temple festivals

Each Hindu temple has an annual festival in honour of the particular deity it enshrines. These festivals are important regional events.

The Floating Festival in Madurai, Tamil Nadu, commemorates the birth of Tirumala Nayak, a 17th-century king. Elaborately decked images are taken in procession to a tank and placed in a barge illuminated by thousands of lamps.

At Puri in Orissa, a major temple festival celebrates Lord Jagannath. Considered a living manifestation of Krishna, the unfinished image is invested with tremendous sanctity and attracts huge crowds. The high point is the drawing of the temple deities through the city to their country residence on giant chariots *(raths)*.

Onam, a Keralan festival, reveres the memory of the demon king, Mahabali, who was ousted from his kingdom by Vishnu. So attached was the king to his subjects, that he was allowed to return once a year. For his amusement, snake boats manned by 100 oarsmen, rowing to the

rhythm of cymbals and drums race at Aranmula, Champakulam and Kottayam. Some Hindu festivals are connected with the the seasons. Nationwide festivities mark the beginning of the northward journey of the sun. Pongal or Sankranti in the South marks the withdrawal of the southeast monsoon and the reaping of the harvest. During the Assamese Ranguli Bihu rituals are performed for the welfare of the herds and for a good harvest, and young men collect orchids for young women.

Adivasi festivals

Celebrating the sun god and local deities, most

Adivasi festivals retain much of their ancient traditions. The harvest, hunting expeditions, marriage and other social events are welcome opportunities for the expression of joy. Quantities of local brew are imbibed and feasting is followed by dancing. The focus in many festivals is on a shaman, who, possessed by the spirits of the dead, enthrals the people with pronouncements.

Non-Hindu festivals

Islamic festivals occurring throughout the year range from major events to localised *urs* held at the tombs of various Muslim saints. Visits to mosques, much feasting, visiting relatives, and

LEFT: bathing at the Kumbha Mela, Allahabad.
RIGHT: a Durga image immersion in Kolkata.

the donning of new clothes mark all Muslim festivals. But there is little to actually see except at Muharram, which is not a festival in the celebratory sense as it mourns the martyrdom at Karbala of Imam Hussain, grandson of the prophet. Despite their connotation of grief, the memorial processions are colourful and dramatic. Songs of praise and lamentation are accompanied by drums and oboes.

Buddha Jayanti, the birth anniversary of the Buddha, is widely celebrated. But this and other Buddhist festivals have less visual interest than the Lamaistic festivals of the Himalayan states. Celebrations commemorating the birth of Padmasambhava at the Hemis Gompa in Ladakh and in Towang in Arunachal Pradesh are particularly vital. Masks worn by the dancers symbolise the power and fearsome ability of the deities as well as the malignancy of the demons.

Jainism tends not to mark its festivals with any great public spectacle. Dip Divali, however, commemmorating its founder Mahavira's liberation from the cycle of life, is celebrated 10 days after Divali. Illuminations are said to be an endeavour to mitigate the darkness caused by the passing of the "light of the world" and are particularly splendid at Mount

THE GOD OF WISDOM

Ganesh, elephant-headed son of Parvati and leader of Shiva's attendants, is widely venerated as the vivacious and munificent god of wisdom. The festival in his honour reaches its peak in Mumbai. Areas vie with one another to produce the most impressive idols. Elaborate arrangements for lighting, decoration, devotional singing and cultural activity are organised for the two to 10 days during which Ganesh is fervently worshipped. On Ganesh Chaturthi thousands of processions converge on Chowpatti beach, bringing their images with them for immersion. Drums beat and devotees dance and sing, calling upon the god to return early next year.

Girnar near Junagadh. The festivals of the Parsis, too, are not demonstrative. Pateti, their New Year, and Jamshedji Navroz, two major festivals, occasion visits to the fire temple and prayer.

Christian festivals in India follow the same patterns as elsewhere. Catholic Goa comes to life with the carnival preceding the Lent period of penance. Similar to Mardi Gras, it is a boisterous event. A colourful carnival parade, presided over by Momo, king of the underworld, is accompanied by much drinking, song

ABOVE: the Republic Day parade, 26 January, New Delhi.

The Festival Year

Here is a selection of the annual highlights in India's festival calendar. In addition, every town, village and temple celebrates its own deities and auspicious occasions during the year.

Moveable
Id-ul-Fitur. All India. End of month-long Ramzan fast.
Muharram: Delhi, Hyderabad, Lucknow. Commemorates martyrdom of Muhammad's grandson.

January
New Year (1 January): Goa, Kerala, cities.
Pongal (Sankranti): Tamil Nadu, Karnataka, Andhra Pradesh. Four-day harvest festival.
Republic Day (26 January, public holiday): All India. Spectacular parade in New Delhi.
Basant Panchami: West Bengal, Madhya Pradesh. Hindu festival of learning; kite flying.

February
Desert Festival: Jaisalmer (Rajasthan). Camels.
Float Festival: Madurai. Colourful floats.

February/March
Shivaratri: All India. Celebrates Shiva's dance of creation and marriage to Parvati.
Holi: Northern India. Coloured powder and water are thrown in this boisterous spring celebration.

March/April
Gangaur. Rajasthan, Bengal and Orissa. Festival of Parvati. Women dress in a blaze of colour.
Carnival: Panaji (Goa). Mardi Gras.
Spring Festival: Kashmir. First almond blossoms.
Ugadi (New Year): Andhra, Karnataka, Tamil Nadu. Hindu solar New Year.

April/May
Baisakhi: North India, Amritsar. Foundation of Sikh brotherhood; New Year celebration in West Bengal.
Puram: Trichur. Elephant procession; fireworks.
Minakshi Kalyanam: Madurai. Procession of temple chariots celebrates the marriage of the goddess.
Buddha Purnima: Sarnath, Bodhgaya. Marks the birth, enlightenment and the death of the Buddha.

June/July
Rath Yatra: Puri. Honours Lord Jagannath. Parade of huge temple chariots.

July/August
Teej: Rajasthan. Women welcome the monsoon.
Amarnath Yatra: Amarnath. Pilgrimage to an icicle.
Nag Panchami: West India. Fair and festival honouring a cobra deity.

RIGHT: a deity dressed in all its finery and surrounded by fresh blooms for festival day.

August/September
Raksha Bandhan: Northern India. Brothers, sisters and platonic friends pledge kinship by the girls tying threads around the boys' wrists.
Independence Day (15 August, public holiday): All India. Commemorative parades.
Janmastami: All India. Birthday of Lord Krishna; dance dramas.
Ganesh Chaturthi: All India, particularly Maharashtra. Festival of Lord Ganesh; fairs, cultural events. Mumbai parades take the image of the god for immersion in the sea.
Onam: Kerala. Harvest festival; four days of feasting, dancing and snake-boat races.

September/October
Dussera: Delhi, Kullu, West Bengal, Uttar Pradesh, Mysore, South India. Dance dramas, exhibitions.
Gandhi Jayanti (2 October, public holiday): Raj Ghat in Delhi. Birthday of Mahatma Gandhi.

October/November
Divali (Dipavali): All India. Festival of lights; fireworks; considered New Year for many people.
Pushkar Fair. Pushkar. Spectacular crowds of pilgrims at the lake; camel fair.
Guru Purab: Amritsar, Punjab. The birthday of the founder of the Sikh religion, Guru Nanak.

December
Christmas Day (25 December): Goa, Kerala. Christians in these states celebrate this festival.   ❑

CINEMA

The prolific output from Indian film studios draws audiences in their millions with a penchant for melodramas and masala westerns

In most Indian cities, you can give directions to the rickshaw-wallah by naming the cinema hall nearest to your destination. Movies are big in India. More blockbusters are cranked out here than in Hollywood – upwards of 900 new films a year. Their incessant sound-track tunes are broadcast by loudspeakers on buses, in bazaars and at five-star discos.

Gaudy outsize posters advertise the latest releases, and avid film buffs buy tickets in 12,000 cinemas every day. Gossipy fan magazincs such as *Filmfare, Stardust* and *CineBlitz* scrutinise the love lives of the various heroes and villains and the latest vampish heroines.

Since 1897 films have grown to be the ideal mass entertainment in India, reaching out to a mostly illiterate audience. By bringing to different strands of society the same images, a powerful pop culture was created. After silent films became *passé* in the early 1930s, regional cinema began to flourish in India. Bombay Talkies pioneered sound in 1932 and musicals were born. Films today are lengthy two-hour-plus melodramas, masala westerns, or blatant rip-offs of foreign hits.

Analysing Indian cinema

Indian films arc largely unrealistic morality tales that uphold traditional virtues: the intrinsic goodness of the poor, the pre-eminence of familial loyalty, the importance of chastity and faith in God. These are values associated with the temple, church or mosque and close to the heart of an audience that is mostly religious, poor and not highly literate.

These virtues, however, are not what one might call the stuff of entertainment. Indian cinema solves this problem by concentrating on the antithesis of these values. Thus films will generally feature characters whose wealth is displayed with ostentatious garishness, who frequent cabaret shows of startling vulgarity and

LEFT: cinema hoardings, Chennai.
RIGHT: on set in "Bollywood" during the filming of *Lahoo ke do rang* ("Two Bloods Clash").

whose attempts at violating feminine purity are shown in graphic detail. These are the bad guys. They get their comeuppance at the hands of the good guys who overcome picturesque poverty with impossible standards of goodness.

There is, of course, catharsis involved in all this and that's why critics of Indian cinema

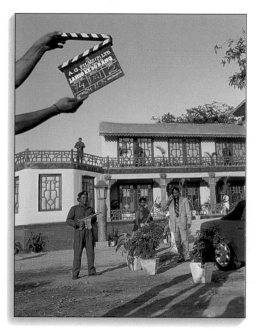

often accuse it of pandering to the establishment: the disadvantaged who make up the bulk of the audience get their wish fulfilment at the movies and accept the inequalities of real life with greater equanimity. Supporters of Indian cinema, on the other hand, see virtue in this: movies help to keep the lid closed tight and prevent a blow-up in Indian society.

The plot

The supporters of Indian film-making also say that almost all Indian movies drum home the message of religious harmony, of vital importance in India's frequently strife-torn multi-religious society. *Amar, Akbar, Anthony,* directed by the successful film-maker Manmohan Desai, is the story of three brothers, separated by accident in their childhood from their parents and each other. Each child drifts away to be adopted by a family belonging to one of India's three dominant religious groups, Hindu, Muslim and Christian (hence the title of the film). The long arm of coincidence, often stretched beyond yogic proportions by Indian scriptwriters, brings the three brothers together as adults. "We are like brothers," they proclaim in many songs, unaware how near the truth they are.

The end of the film sees them defeat the villains in a long-drawn-out fight that leaves

them wounded. Urgent blood transfusion is needed; their blood is of the same type (they are like *blood* brothers!); the type is rare. But a donor is found. It's an old lady, and as she lies in a hospital bed, connected by rubber tubes to the three men into whose veins her blood flows directly, we discover that she is, in fact, one of the lost parents. The film fades on that image of Mother India.

The biology may be weak, but the symbolism is strong and it pervades Indian cinema. Also coursing through its veins is an adherence to traditional theatrical forms which lay strong emphasis on the *nava rasa* (nine emotions), plots and subplots plus song and dance. The *nava rasa* theory means that a single film runs through the entire gamut of feelings, from farcical comedy to wrenching tragedy. The subplots make a film's seemingly excessive length (about 150 minutes) an absolute necessity: each film isn't dealing with one story, but three or even four.

Star attraction

Only 25 percent of films recover their investment, but it's the 5 percent that are big box-office successes – plus the glamorous image of the cinema – that act as siren songs. They are produced in many of India's languages and dialects, but mostly in Hindi (generally made in Mumbai), Telugu (Hyderabad), Tamil (Chennai) and Malayalam (Trivandrum). The largest of the South Indian industries is based in Hyderabad at the huge complexes of Ramanaidu Studios and Ramoji Film City. At times Telugu production has even beaten that of Bollywood (overall the South Indian film industry is larger than that of Hindi cinema).

Actors' fees not only use up 40 percent of a film's budget, but the excessive reliance by producers on a few bankable names means that a few stars are so much in demand that they work in a number of films simultaneously to a system of dates and shifts. "Dates" are the days of a month when the star will act in your film; "shift" indicates the hours in that day (a day consists of three shifts) in which he or she will be available to you. At the peak of his career Shashi Kapoor was signed on for 140 films at one time and good-humouredly called himself the "Taxi Star of India": you could take him anywhere as long as you paid the fare. No wonder films take such a long time to make. Two years is considered fast; four years is not uncommon.

The New Wave

It was not just disenchantment with this system gone haywire, but also with the industry's values and its essential vulgarity that led to the formation of a small breakaway group of film-makers, which critics often refer to as the New Wave. Unlike the French *Nouvelle Vague*, this was not a cohesive group united by a single ideology; the New Wave's members often did not speak the same language. The one language they did share was cinema and through it they were determined to

MOVIE BLUES

Video piracy and the spread of cable TV in the late 1980s threatened the film industry. It has adapted by cashing in on the burgeoning telefilm market.

opment Corporation), other directors began to emulate his example. Mrinal Sen, also from Ray's Kolkata, was notably successful, both critically and commercially, with *Bhuvan Shome,* financed by the FFC. This success was the spur the movement needed and soon outstanding movies were being made in regional languages. It was not only Bengali directors that made significant contributions; many excellent films were made in Kerala (by P.N. Menon), Karnataka (B.V. Karanth) and Assam (by Jahnu Barua).

portray the reality of India. Almost all of these film-makers also wanted to get away from the star system (although ironically, many New Wave actors and actresses have now become stars of the larger film industry themselves).

The initial inspiration came from the Bengali director Satyajit Ray, who brought India into the international film scene with *Pather Panchali* (*The Song of the Road,* 1955). Later, aided by the government-funded Film Finance Corporation (FFC, now the National Film Devel-

LEFT: final touches are made to the star's make-up during the filming of the TV series *Life of Shiva.*
ABOVE: Sri Devi and Sanjay Dutt.

New Wave directors shattered a well-nurtured myth of the Indian film industry: Hindi is the national language, crossing regional boundaries not only of language but culture. So, the myth held, to draw in disparate audiences, the Hindi film must appeal to the lowest common denominator. The statement is still occasionally heard, but it is now made with less conviction.

Initially, the focus of the New Wave was almost entirely on rural India, where 70 percent of India still lives and where development takes time to catch up, but the emphasis moved on to contemporary problems in the cities, areas spiritually and physically much closer to the film-makers themselves.

After a flowering of Hindi realist cinema during the 1980s (including such films as Satyajit Ray's *Shatranj Ke Khilari*; "The Chess Players"), by the 1990s the New Wave had lost its way, and much of its already small audience. Aside from one or two films by indigenous directors, the headlines have been grabbed by expatriate film-makers such as the controversial Deepa Mehta (for *Fire*, 1998) and the more popular Meera Nair (for *Monsoon Wedding*, 2001). The Indian box-office cinema and the New Wave live warily with each other, one envious of the other's popularity, the other resentful of the critical acclaim and prizes denied to it.

Box-office hits

The majority of viewers go to see films such as Ramesh Sippy's movie, *Sholay* (1975), which became one of the biggest box-office successes in Indian cinema history. A name was coined for the genre, the "Curry Western", a tribute to its inspiration, the Italian "Spaghetti Western", which was itself a derivative of the Hollywood Western.

Sholay invented a country of kind desperadoes fighting a gang of vicious bandits. Critics aimed their intellectual six-shooters at its appalling violence and its make-believe world, but even as they pulled the trigger they could not but admit that the film was entertaining. For an audience that wants to forget the tribulations and indignities of life in India, films like *Sholay* are the perfect answer.

Foreign competition

In cinema, as in television, competition has arrived from the West. For years Hollywood served as an inspiration for Indian directors (inspiration implying the plagiarisation of American technique, car chases and sometimes even entire plots). Yet Hollywood itself could make little headway in India, mainly due to the language barrier.

The dubbing of blockbusters into various Indian languages has vastly expanded the market. *Jurassic Park*, the first dubbed experiment, collected half a million dollars in a fortnight from Indian viewers compared to the US$160,000 earned by *Indecent Proposal* in English over a whole year. Many film industry hot shots are also moving into allied businesses of setting up studios and celebrity marketing.

THE TELEVISION REVOLUTION

For decades, until the early 1980s, television was controlled by government and concentrated on a heavy-handed mix of education and propaganda. It reached only 13 percent of the country. Then the focus shifted from social development to entertainment; the government liberalised the import of colour TVs and VCRs, and television proliferated, along with pirated videos. The launch of Star TV in 1991 brought an entertainment channel, Star Plus, Prime Sports, MTV and the BBC World Service to Indian screens. In 1992, a Hindi channel was added to Star. Zee, with its talk shows, games, sitcoms and soaps, turned out to be a huge hit with the young and burgeoning middle classes. Stung by this competition, Doordarshan, the Indian state-owned television network, launched an entertainment channel, Metro. Independent entrepreneurs also jumped into the fray by hiring transponders on various satellites and floating channels in Hindi and other Indian languages. A substantial segment of this new programming was film-based, but social issues were tackled; one channel even took to telecasting a late-night "adult" film on Saturdays. Now there are more than 350 channels across the country, and the four major cities have accesss to around 90 cable channels, more than half of which are free. This has made India the world's third-largest TV market; 119 million households are daily tuned in.

Top film stars like Amitabh Bachchan (who has reinvented himself as a kindly elder figure rather than the action hero of his younger days) and Sri Devi, and directors such as Subhash Ghai and Mukul Anand have tried launching public issues to raise funds for their new companies.

Film scores

Succour for the ailing film industry has also come from a new source, or rather the expanded potential of an old source: music. Music has always been an integral part of Indian cinema *(see page 121)*. In fact, the film song, performed by a variety of characters in myriad situations and locations, can be said to be the precursor of the contemporary music video. Despite their undeniable significance, songs were always considered appendages to the film. But by the late 1990s a spate of top-20-style television programmes based on film songs, combined with the proliferation of tape recorders and cheap audio cassettes, had created an enormous demand for film music.

Sales of popular scores run into millions. The busiest people in the film world today are the music directors (composers) and choreographers. According to the prominent weekly *India Today*, the amount spent on a single song in a film has increased tenfold in five years.

The surging attraction of film songs has also blurred age-old boundaries. One of the most sought-after musicians in "Bollywood" (the common term for Mumbai's Hindi film industry) is A.R. Rahman, who made his mark with South Indian films. Rahman's fame spread when his musical *Bollywood Dreams* was produced by Andrew Lloyd Webber in London's West End.

The strict division between film and non-film music is also fast disappearing. In the old days the only popular indigenous music was Hindi film music. The emergence of MTV Asia provided exposure to other, non-film musicians such as rock bands Indus Creed and Apache Indian, and rapper Baba Sehgal. Channel V, the music channel that apes MTV on the Star network, now devotes almost 50 percent of its time to both film and non-film Indian music.

BOX OFFICE BABYLON

Hindi dubbing of English films started with *King Kong* and returned with *Jurassic Park. Titanic*, with its overwrought tale, broke all records for dubbed films.

While films such as *Sholay* played on an appetite for violence, the 1990s also saw the rebirth of family drama. Films such as *Hum Aapke Hain Kaun, Raja Hindustani* and *Maine Pyar Kiya* managed the difficult task of promoting traditional family values while chaste but scantily-clad actresses (such as Aishwarya Rai, Karisma Kapoor and Preity Zinta) and muscle-bound heroes (current favourites include Salman, Shah Rukh and Amir Khan) flirt and revel in material excess. The link between these conflicting messages and the prevailing political climate is not hard to make *(see pages 67–72)*.

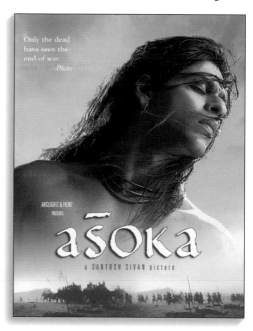

Crossovers

Bollywood is now trendy outside South Asia, due in part to bland, location-neutral films expressing middle-class concerns, and targetting lucrative NRI (non-resident-Indian) populations. Shilpa Shetty's headline-grabbing encounter with *Big Brother* in 2007 also spread the word abroad. The trade is not all one way; Amitabh Bachchan's kinder image is due to his appearance on *Kaun Banega Crorepati*, India's version of *Who Wants to be a Millionaire?*, subsequently hosted by heartthrob Shahrukh Khan. ❑

LEFT: a street scene in Goa is recreated for the shooting of a movie at the Film City studios, Chennai.
ABOVE: a poster for a recent blockbuster.

DANCE AND MUSIC

Dance and music traditions in India play important roles in society and act as expressions of Indian identity

South Asia's myriad performing arts traditions are as diverse as its peoples. They vary from the so-called "classical" styles of *bharata-natyam* and *kathak* dance, and Hindustani (North Indian) and Karnatak (South Indian) music, to rural local traditions associated with life-cycle and calendrical rituals, to

urban film and popular music styles. However, through this diversity runs the unifying influence of devotional religion. While there are many music and dance forms that directly form part of, or have their roots in, religious ritual, many more take their inspiration either through their texts, social function (for weddings, funerals, childbirth, and so on) or underlying theoretical ideology, from the powerful complex of religious belief and practice that runs through South Asian societies. Another important factor lies in the relatively distinct worlds of South Asian men and women, often thought of as the "public" and "private" respectively, that govern both the mode and space of performance.

Dance

As with music *(see page 118)*, Indian dance forms may be conveniently divided into those that are now concert forms (though their origins lie elsewhere) and those that continue to be performed as part of local or calendrical rituals and festivals. There are seven dances that have largely become concert forms, and are regarded as "classical" (partly through the project of nation-building): the temple/ritual dances *bharata-natyam*, *manipuri* and *odissi*, the dance dramas *kathakali* and *kucipudi*, the devotional *mohiniattam,* and the court dance *kathak*. These have a wide geographical spread, variety of origins and variation in musical accompaniment.

These South Asian dance styles share basic concepts of movement and expression. Dance is broadly divided into *nrtta* and *nrtya*. *Nrtta* refers to abstract movement to music, while *nrtya* is the use of movement and facial expression to convey emotion. Movement is also divided into two types, *anga*, the movement of the torso, head, arms and legs, and *upanga*, facial expression. The close relationship between dance and sculpture can be seen in the shared system of poses, based on *sutra* (the vertical and horizontal planes) and *bhanga* (the bending of the body).

Bharata-natyam

This is the most popular South Asian dance style, which, although originating in Tamil Nadu, is now taught and performed across India as well as overseas. Its origins lie in Tamil temple dance and it has been a concert form since the early 20th century.

The female hereditary temple dancers *(devadasis)* took part in rituals in praise of the temple deity and were considered "married" to the god. This made them auspicious women as they could never become widowed. They would also be the sexual partners of the temple priests and local king (sponsor of the temple). It was this aspect of their duties that outraged Victorian sensibilities and an "anti-nautch" (from the Sanskrit *naca*, "dance") was started –

largely by middle-class Indians who had taken on the social mores of the colonial power. This culminated in the 1947 Madras Devadasi (Prevention of Dedication) Act, which effectively banned temple dancing.

At the same time as the antinautch campaign sought to ban dance in the temples, growing Indian nationalism was seeking to legitimise claims for independence by presenting elements of South Asian culture as evidence of a strong national identity. Tamil temple dance was seized on as a

pellet bells *(ghungru)* around their ankles which add to the rhythmic texture of the music. A *bharata-natyam* performance ideally consists of seven pieces: the introductory *alarippu* which is a prayer to the presiding deity; a *jatisvaram*, a technical piece using *nrtta*; the *sabda*, which introduces *nrtya*; a complex dance known as *varnam*, that uses both *nrtya* and *nrtta*; a *padam*, a piece expressing love through *nrtya*; a technical and fast *tillana*; and a concluding *sloka* (rhythmic recitation of a religious verse).

perfect example and, led by the Brahman dancer and teacher Rukmini Devi, moves were made to establish a "pure" form of the dance on the stage – the result was present-day *bharata-natyam*.

It is a solo dance, still performed largely by women, with an accompaniment of Karnatak music played by an ensemble known as the *cinna melam* and led by the *nattuvanar*, who keeps time with a pair of cymbals and calls out the dance patterns, or *jati*. The dancers wear

LEFT: Kucipudi dancer, Andhra Pradesh.
ABOVE: Kathakali dancer from Kerala playing Hanuman, the monkey god.

Other dance styles

Odissi stems from the Orissan tradition of temple dance. The *devadasis* (known in Orissa as *maharis*) at the Jagannath temple in Puri were affected by the ban on temple dance and by the 1950s the dance style was in danger of dying out. Dance scholars from all over India gathered for a conference at which the style was reinvented as a concert form, drawing greatly on Orissan temple sculpture.

The ritual dance *manipuri* is the only "classical" dance from northeastern India, although the masked dance drama *chau* found in parts of West Bengal, Bihar and Orissa is sometimes considered "classical". *Manipuri* is performed by Vaishnava Hindus living in the Manipur valley. It includes solo, duet and group dances known as *rasalila*, in praise of Krishna and depicting his exploits with the *gopis* (female cowherds).

Kathakali and *kucipudi* are dance dramas from Kerala and Andhra Pradesh respectively. Both are performed only by male dancers, in contrast to *mohiniattam*, a Keralan devotional dance performed only by women. *Kathakali* is characterised by its dramatic make-up and costumes and is danced to poetic

> **NADA**
>
> Musical sound, *nada*, is considered in South Asia to be intrinsically auspicious, hence its widespread use in ritual and to accompany religious festivals.

texts taken from the Ramayana and Mahabharata. *Kucipudi* comes from the eponymous village in the Krishna-Godavari delta and is said to have been invented somewhere between 1350–1450 by Sidhyendra, a Telugu Brahman. It takes its themes from the *Parijatapaharana*, the story of Krishna and his consort Bhama, and the *Golla Kalapam*, a philosophical discussion between a milkmaid and a Brahman.

The origins of *kathak* are closely linked to the rise of Hindustani music at the North Indian courts, particularly *khayal*, *thumri* and *dadra*. Traditionally danced by courtesans, it is characterised by its fast pirouettes and rhythmic patterns created by pellet bells worn on the ankles.

Music

The musical traditions of South Asia differ between north and south, urban and rural environments, and men and women. The music most commonly associated with India in the West is that of the North Indian concert stage, whose genres have their roots in the Muslim and Rajput courts. South India has its own concert traditions, also in part stemming from the musics of the southern courts, but also owing a great deal to a strong tradition of devotional song.

The concert musics of South Asia use a basic collection of seven pitches *(svara)* within an octave – *sa, ri, ga, ma, pa, dha, ni, (sa)* – which roughly correspond to the Western doh, re, mi etc., and also have upper and lower ("sharp" and "flat") variants. However, they differ radically from Western pitches by not having a fixed value; for example, *sa* is fixed at a convenient level (higher or lower) for each individual musician, to suit an instrument, or his or her voice. Also essential to both Hindustani and Karnatak music are the twin concepts of *raga* and *tala*.

Raga (Sanskrit "colour") designates which pitches it is permissible to play during the performance of a piece, and also (as different *ragas* share the same collection of pitches) characteristic phrases, "ornamentations" as well as – although this is now less common – the time of day at which individual *ragas* should be played. This is particularly true of North India; in the South concepts of *raga* tend to rely much more on the classification of different collections of pitches. Often misrepresented as merely a "scale" or "mode", a *raga* is more than a lineally arranged group of pitches (although this is often the most convenient way of notating them), but also implies the approach the musician should take towards the *svara*.

Tala (Sanskrit "clapping") is the name for the repeating rhythmic cycles that underpin the metred sections of any Hindustani or Karnatak performance. Different *talas* consist of different numbers of beats *(matra)*, and the first beat of a cycle, known in the North as *sam*, provides a reference point, not only for the musicians, but also the audience. At a performance of Karnatak music it is common to see the audience collectively marking the cycle through claps and waves on strong and weak beats respectively.

The northern concert tradition

The *gharana* (literally "household", denoting male lineages of musical instruction, usually hereditary) of the court musicians generally traced their ancestry back to Tansen, a musician at the court of Akbar (1556–1605). He is said to have been one of the greatest performers of *dhrupad*, a vocal genre held by many musicians to be the "purest" form of *raga* music. Although initially very popular at the courts, during the time of Muhammad Shah (1719–48) *dhrupad* was supplanted by *khayal*. Muhammad Shah's court musician, Niyamat Khan, is usually credited with popularising the form.

unmetred section introducing the *raga* (mode or pitch collection), followed by the *ciz*, which is in *tala* (rhythmic cycle), the most common of which is the 16-beat *tintal*. It is accompanied by the *tabla* (paired kettledrums) and, traditionally, the bowed lute, *sarangi* (this is now usually replaced by the harmonium, a small hand-pumped organ introduced to South Asia by French missionaries). The drone-lute *tambura* provides a constant background, sometimes played by a supporting singer and usually tuned to *sa* and *pa* (roughly corresponding to the Western doh and soh). The compositions are explored in a series of elaborations and improvisations.

Khayal, which legend has it was invented by Sultan Husain Sharqi in the 15th century, is now the vocal genre most commonly heard in the concert hall. A *khayal* composition *(bandish* or *ciz)* comprises two short sections, known as *sthayi* and *antara*, which are in contrasting registers. Usually two compositions are presented, the first in a slow tempo, known as a "big" *(bara) khayal*, the second, a "small" *(chota) khayal* in a faster tempo, which speeds up towards the end of the performance. A *khayal* concert starts with a short

Instrumental music, particularly of the *sitar* and *sarod* (both plucked lutes), follows a slightly different pattern, and draws on both *khayal* and *dhrupad* traditions. Compositions are known as *gat* (analogous to those of *khayal*); they are preceded by a long *alap* section, an unmetred presentation of the *raga* introducing each note in turn, in a similar fashion to that of *dhrupad* singers. The soloist then uses a variety of improvisational techniques to explore the material presented in the *gat*, and will usually present two different compositions, the second of which is faster. Instrumentalists usually consider themselves part of the Seniya *gharana*, which is traced back to Tansen.

LEFT: *Bharata-natyam*, a dance from Tamil Nadu.
ABOVE: Ravi Shankar, one of India's leading sitar players.

The southern concert tradition

Although sharing similar basic concepts of *raga*, *tala* and *svara*, Karnatak music differs quite considerably from the concert musics of the North, perhaps most evidently in its performance of fully composed pieces, a lesser degree of improvisation and an important tradition of devotional song. Also, Karnatak music has tended to be a Brahmanical tradition, as opposed to that of either the Muslim or lower-caste musicians of the North.

The first Karnatak compositions are generally held to be those of the Tallapakam composers, Annamacharya, Peda Tirumalacharya and Chinnanna (father, son and grandson), of the 15th–16th century. They are remembered for their Telugu *kirtanas* (devotional songs), written in the tripartite form of *pallavi*, *anupallavi* and *caranam* (ABC) – the basic structure of much present-day Karnatak music. Although none of their actual melodies survive, many of their texts, which indicate the *raga* in which they are to be performed, have been preserved on copper-plate inscriptions.

At around the same time, Purandaradasa (1484–1564), known as the "father of Karnatak music", was writing his *kirtana*, following the old two-part form of *pallavi* and *caranam*.

LOCAL TRADITIONS

Local performance traditions in India are usually associated with life-cycle and calendrical rituals, and also village festivals, often for local deities. Births, deaths and weddings are all accompanied by music, particularly by women singing. Marriage processions are usually accompanied by bands, traditionally playing oboes and drums, but now more commonly by brass bands playing covers of film songs. Funerals have traditionally been accompanied by low-caste drummers. Music and dance also accompany festivals such as *Holi* and the yearly Ganapati *puja*. At other times people gather in temples to collectively sing *bhajan* (devotional songs).

Some of his melodies have survived and are still sung in concerts. However, he is chiefly famous for composing the basic exercises that all students of Karnatak music still learn.

These early composers were followed by the great "trinity" of Karnatak composers, Tyagaraja (1767–1847), Muttusvami Diksitar (1775–1835) and Syama Sastri (1762–1827), all of whom were born in the temple town of Tiruvarur in the Kaveri delta. Their compositions are generally thought by Karnatak musicians to be the finest in the repertory. They were primarily responsible for transforming the *kirtana* form into the *kriti* through the addition of composed variations known as *sangati*.

Karnatak music is overwhelmingly oriented towards vocal performance, especially with its emphasis on devotional texts. Other vocal forms often included in concerts include the *varnam* and *ragam-tanam-pallavi*. The latter form, in contrast to the devotional *kirtana* and *kriti*, stems from the musical traditions of the South Indian courts and is considered a great demonstration of technical skill. Comprising three sections, the *ragam* and *tanam* are close in style to the *alap* and *jor* of Hindustani music, the third section takes a short composition, the *pallavi*, through a demanding series of melodic and metrical variations, all improvised.

A Karnatak ensemble usually consists of a soloist, usually a singer but who may also be a *vina* (long-necked, plucked lute) player, accompanied by violin (introduced into Karnatak music in the 18th century by Muttusvami Diksitar's brother, Baluswami), *mrdangam* (double-headed barrel drum) and *tambura* (drone lute), now sometimes replaced by an electronic drone known as a *sruti*-box. The ensemble may be augmented by a *ghatam* (clay pot used as an idiophone) and *kanjira* (small framedrum).

Film and popular musics

The audiences for the concert musics of North and South India tend to be restricted to a small portion of the middle class. The Indian music with the largest audience is *filmi git* (film song). The first Indian "talkie", *Alam Ara*, was made in Mumbai in 1931. Following the conventions of traditional theatre the action was broken up by songs and dances that served to push the action forward and represented the passing of time. These early films gained great popularity, and, as a consequence, so did the songs.

The singers in the early films were the actors and actresses themselves, but when recording technology allowed the songs to be dubbed in the late 1930s, most songs became prerecorded and specialists, known as playback singers, took over. By this time film song had become phenomenally popular and playback singers became musical superstars.

LEFT: a *periya melam* ensemble, Kerala.
RIGHT: a young girl learning the *vina*, Thiruvananthapuram, Kerala.

TEMPLE MUSICIANS

In South Indian temples, processions of the deities are accompanied by the *periya melam* ensemble of *nagasvaram* (oboe) and *tavil* (barrel drum).

The most popular, and enduring, of all playback singers is Lata Mangeshkar. She, her sister Asha Bhosle and singers such as Geeta Dutt, perform in a high-pitched style, very different to the lower, richer voices of the singers of the 1930s, and this has now become the dominant female film music vocal style. Popular male singers include Mohammad Rafi and Mukesh.

The music itself was initially based on the sung poetic forms of *ghazal* and *thumri*, associated with the *tawa'if* or *kalavant* (courtesans).

However, the music directors (film song composers) soon began to draw on an eclectic range of sources, from traditional *bhajan* (devotional songs), to South American genres, to modern Western rock and pop.

Although for a long time film song dominated the Indian market for popular music, since the availability of cheap recording technology, regional popular musics have reached a much wider audience in the past couple of decades. In addition, the major cities now have thriving pop and rock scenes that draw on the popular musics of Europe and the US, which now have a wide audience through TV music channels such as MTV. ❑

ART

Indian art since the earliest cave paintings has been dominated by the gentle forms of animals and sensuous beings

The art traditions of India are among the oldest and richest in the world. They are also unique in that they reflect a continuity of ethos and aesthetic sensibility across many thousands of years, albeit with a remarkable ability to remake themselves by absorbing, retaining and shaping incoming styles, artists and ideas.

Early rock paintings

The first Indian art works were painted during the Palaeolithic era on the walls of shallow caves or rock shelters. The largest concentration of rock art sites belongs to the region of the Narmada river in Madhya Pradesh; the most extensive site is Bhimbetka in the same state. A distinct Indian character is discernible in the earliest paintings. The images are mainly of large animals, such as the bull or bison, and are similar to those created by European cave dwellers during the Upper Palaeolithic. In style they tend towards naturalism. Compared to the fearsome beasts of the French and Spanish caves, the Indian animals are gentle creatures with an almost anthropomorphic quality. Animals have since remained a dominant motif in Indian art – whether in a temple carving, a Mughal miniature, or the work of a modern master, they express an intimate and affectionate relationship with the natural world.

The largest number of rock paintings belong to the Mesolithic Age, when technological advances enchanced the efficiency of hunting and food-gathering, resulting in a population increase. Human stick figures appeared in abundance, engaged in activities ranging from fishing and dyke-building to dancing and ritual theatre. Among the most striking are dancing priests or shamans; in them we see harbingers of Shiva Nataraja, the Lord of Dance, sculpted many millennia later in the great temples of Ellora and Elephanta in Madhya

Pradesh, Aihole and Badami in Karnataka, and in South Indian bronzes.

Many of Bhimbetka's paintings also belong to the ages of the first cultivators and of the historic empires, up to Mughal times. Thus the site is a museum recording the history of the region's Adivasi people, but it is also a record of the

early flowering of artistic genius among the Indian people. Many images are visually magical. Executed with remarkable sleight of hand, they express a wide range of moods or feelings, including harmony, joy and humour. These are qualities to be encountered again and again in Indian art.

Sculptural figures

Another enduring quality of Indian art is a sublime sensuality, particularly in the female figure. In the bronze statuette of a dancing girl, representing South Asia's first urban settlements – the early cities of the Indus Valley – one meets the first example. Wearing only

LEFT: fresco detail from the Ajanta Caves, Maharashtra, dating from between 200 BC and AD 650.
RIGHT: hunting scene, part of court life in Udaipur.

chunky jewellery, this little figure is utterly absorbed in her rhythmic dance; in her elongated modelling and pose, she reminds us of the prehistoric images, but in expression and feeling she is close to the voluptuous celestial women and goddesses of the Buddhist shrines and Hindu temples created more than two millennia later.

In keeping with the unambitious character of the Harappan Culture cities, noted above all for their superb urban planning, their other surviving art works are also hand-held objects. These include a nude male torso, carved with a robust naturalism, and a group of exquisite seals bearing animals or motifs of religious import; there

paintings at times of festivity. That they are lost to us is due to their perishability.

India's first stone monuments belong to the 3rd century BC. To propagate his message of peaceful coexistence, Emperor Ashoka, a Buddhist convert, ordered the raising of pillars, inscribed with edicts, at public meeting places across his territories. The pillars were crowned with animal sculptures. The best known is the lion capital at Sarnath, Uttar Pradesh, now the emblem of the Indian Republic. Another group of monuments founded by Ashoka were *stupas* (tumuli), in which the relics of the Buddha or his followers were interred. Intended for

is also a large number of terracotta figurines and toys, most of them zoomorphic and, like the animals on the seals, delightfully realistic.

Monuments in stone

There are very few visual records of the era that followed the decline of the Harappan Culture (*circa* early 2nd millennium BC) – the era that witnessed the composition of the *Vedas*, the coming of the Iron Age, the growth of new cities and the life of Buddha. But it would be wrong to assume that artistic activities ceased. Later literary records attest to the contrary; Buddhist stories allude to the fabled "galleries" of kings and descriptions of cities adorned with

circumambulation by worshippers, they were originally surrounded by wooden railings, with *toranas* (gateways) at their cardinal points. Around the end of the 2nd century BC, these began to be replaced by stone replicas.

Attesting to this period of material transition are the remains of Barhut in Madhya Pradesh. The railing here was carved with Buddhist stories and parables, voluptuous demi-goddesses, donor couples, lush vegetation and other motifs. Although a little basic in execution, the work expresses a fervour and celebratory philosophy of life. Examples of Barhut art can be seen in the Indian Museum in Kolkata. The same qualities are evident in the gateways at

Sanchi, Madhya Pradesh, sculpted about a century later, but here they are achieved with greater delicacy. A masterpiece at Sanchi is the *yaksi* (maiden) of the eastern gateway, a rare surviving example of Indian sculpture in the round. Carved under a laden mango tree, a symbol of fertility, this dancer-like figure is at once provocative, dignified and graceful.

One of ancient India's most important art schools was situated at Mathura, Uttar Pradesh, a flourishing centre of commerce and pilgrimage that attracted the adherents of numerous sects, many unorthodox. The style that evolved here in the early centuries AD is superbly exemplified in several *yaksi* figures bearing symbols of earthly bounty and wearing the same mysterious half-smile as their sisters at Sanchi. In the figure of an adolescent sage, with aristocratic physique and clothing, we find another fine example. Represented in the moments following his surprise introduction to sexual pleasure, the sage is lost in wonder and is infused with a feeling of exquisite tenderness.

At other Buddhist monuments across the land, joyfully sensuous female and male figures reappear, often as loving couples *(mithuna)* in playful dalliance. Sites abundant in such figures were concentrated in the western and eastern extremes of the Deccan, in the excavated cave sanctuaries at Karle and Ajanta in Maharashtra, and in the remains of the great stupas from Amaravati and Nagarjunakonda in Andhra Pradesh. In frieze fragments from the latter, narrative panels are intercut by unabashedly amorous couples.

The Buddha's influence

The Buddha had ruled that only abstract motifs were suitable for the eyes of monks. In the centuries following his death this was largely adhered to. That it was broken so flagrantly had practical reasons: monasteries were generally established at existing cult spots and were close to trade routes. With the expansion of Buddhism's sphere of influence – economic as much as ideological – grew the need for

BUDDHIST IMAGERY

The depiction of the Buddha, the "Enlightened One", in painting or sculpture represented one of the highest aspirations of human art and human thought.

popular appeal. The Buddhist hierarchy realised that the means to attract and hold adherents of all classes and sects was a powerful figurative art rooted in popular tradition. The same need governed the appearance of Buddha images at Mathura and Gandhara (the northwestern seat of the Greco-Roman Buddhist school in the province that straddled what is now the frontier between Pakistan and Afghanistan) around the 1st century AD.

The earliest examples show evidence of experimentation, but both schools soon began

to refine the image. It was not until the 4th and 5th century (the Gupta Age) that the masters of Mathura came close to expressing the Buddhist ideal in stone. This goal was achieved in the late 5th century, as we see at Sarnath in the sublime sitting Buddha, a tensionless yogic figure composed in perfect geometric harmony, yet made real and human through its subtle corporality and sensitive details.

The ideal of the sage or deity whose calm cannot be shaken was hardly exclusive to Buddhist thought or art. If we compare, for example, three heads from Mathura – the Buddha, the Jina (founder of Jainism) and the great Hindu god, Vishnu – we can see the same qualities of

LEFT: erotic sculpture at Khajuraho, Madhya Pradesh.
RIGHT: Chola bronze showing Siva Nataraja performing a cosmic dance.

form and feeling. Later, we encounter images of majestic serenity such as the Bodhisattva of Compassion painted at Ajanta, the towering Trimurthi and androgynous Siva at Elephanta, or Vishnu asleep on the cosmic ocean at Mamallapuram (Tamil Nadu); even the mighty Shiva Nataraja at Ellora remains calm in his fiery cosmic dance, which was performed to maintain the harmony of the universe.

In fact, together with sensuousness, the most pervasive quality or mood of Indian classical art is a deep calm and equilibrium. These combine potently in the great female figures in the Ajanta murals, in the dancing and flying god-

BOOK ILLUSTRATION

In the Sultanate courts of the 13th–15th centuries book production was encouraged. The Mughals that followed were also a literary dynasty, with Babur, the 16th-century founder, having written his memoirs in the first guidebook to Hindustan, in which with the eye of a naturalist he described the different species of flora and fauna of Hind. His son, Humayan, brought over the great painters Mir Sayyid Ali and Abd us-Samad from Persia. Almost 100 years later his grandson, Jahangir, wrote his memoirs and in a move to outdo Babur he employed the master painter of animals, Mansur, to illustrate his descriptions of the natural world. The Emperor Akbar, who is reputed to have been illiterate, became a great patron of painting. Illustrated histories of the Mughals were commissioned as official chronicles – the *Babur Nama*, *Timur Nama* and *Akbar Nama* – and artists recruited from all over India. The style was bold and dynamic, fusing Islamic and Hindu elements. Mughal painting introduced a quality of portraiture still unsurpassed today.

desses at Aurangabad (Maharashtra), Badami (Kanataka) and Aihole, and in the goddess Ganga at Ellora who seems to have been modelled on an Adivasi queen. We find a further example at Mamallapuram where the goddess Durga battles the Buffalo Demon, a work of immense theatricality. These figures underline the intimate relationship between the visual arts, music, dance and drama.

Mamallapuram – southern glory

Like the earlier Buddhist site of Amaravati in Andhra Pradesh, Hindu Mamallapuram was one of the glories of South Indian art, distinguished by its elongated style of figuration. This shore site's rock-cut temples (7th century) are clear reminders of the Indian conceptual unity between sculpture and architecture.

The intimate structures, hewn from granite, are each a finely detailed sculpture. But the masterpiece here is a relief narrating the story of the descent of the Ganga from the long locks of Shiva in his Himalayan abode. Carved across two massive boulders, scores of figures – divine, human and animal – surge in graceful rhythm towards the central cleft that forms the river. Of special note are the gentle and often humorous animal figures.

Together with the Kailasa Temple at Ellora, the world's largest monolithic structure created a century later, Mamallapuram marks the twilight years of India's great monumental traditions. These would now be carried eastward to shape the art of Indonesia, ancient Cambodia and Vietnam (Kamboj and Annam).

Medieval manuscript painting

The medieval age in India was one of political confusion and social ferment. Temple art became remote from the life of the people, tending increasingly towards over-ornateness and mannerism. But exceptions are to be found at sites such as Khajuraho in Madhya Pradesh, famous for its carvings of couples in coitus *(maithuna)*, and at Bhubaneshwar and Konarak in Orissa. The Sun Temple at Konarak, Orissa, also famed for its erotic imagery, is a masterpiece of architectural design and sculptural imagination.

The next chapter of Indian art opens in the medieval period when the first manuscript paintings were commissioned by the Jains and Buddhists. This form later became popular in the Rajput courts, where passages from the great epics, the Mahabharata and Ramayana, and other sacred texts were colourfully illustrated in a style derived from folk traditions. The paintings were often based on, or related to, nature's seasons and moods, like the *ragas* of Hindustani music – in the *Ragamala* series the musician's moods are given visual form.

It was largely under Mughal patronage that manuscript painting became a fine art. Although illiterate, the Emperor Akbar had learned to paint; he was also a ruler with a sense of history and a keen interest in all religions. The result was the commissioning of the chronicles of the Mughal dynasty and the translation into Persian of the Hindu epics. The works illustrating the texts fuse Persian and Rajput elements, but they are more realistic and refined.

Mughal miniature painting reached its peak under Akbar's son, Jahangir, a patron so discerning that he could recognise the brushwork of each of the many masters attached to his court. In the documents of his reign, we see the full flowering of a secular art, most notably in portraiture; in many works the emperor is surrounded by numerous figures, finely detailed, each with individual features and demeanour.

PAPERLESS ART

Prior to the introduction of paper in the 14th century, writings and illustrations were inscribed on palm leaves or parchment and "bound" in wooden covers wrapped in cloth.

Rajasthan and the Himalayan foothills (the Pahari kingdoms).

Pahari miniatures often illustrated literary texts like those describing the amorous exploits of Lord Krishna. With such themes, great emphasis was placed on the female figure, ever delighting in her sensuality. But the high point of Pahari narrative painting is the landscape element; the forms and colours of nature are rendered with such intense delight that they almost become the *raison d'être* of the work.

ABOVE: painting during the Raj era, *The Hirkarah Camel*, by William Daniell, *circa* 1835.

Many also record the life of the ordinary people of the times, from wandering holy men, soldiers and musicians to artisans and villagers, all painted with the same loving care. Artistic contacts with Europe had made their mark. The modelling of figures to suggest roundness, lost since the Ajanta period, was reintroduced by the Mughal painters, and elements of perspective were used for the first time. When the Mughal Empire began to disintegrate in the late 17th century, patronage declined and many masters moved to the courts of the Deccan,

The colonial era

In the earlier phase of the colonial age, dominated by the East India Company, local artists were employed to document human activities and the natural wonders of India, as well as their patrons' way of life; they continued to work in the traditional opaque watercolour medium but often incorporated elements of British academic painting. Although the socio-historic value of these works is considerable, few match the Mughal or Pahari miniatures in skill, expressive content or feeling; the exceptions are mainly portraits and animal paintings.

In the imperial phase of colonial rule, Indian art was shaped by two contradictory forces. On the one hand, it was deemed primitive and decadent, and in order to train a native elite according to Victorian aesthetic standards, Western art schools were established in Kolkata, Mumbai and other metropolises. On the other hand, archaeologists were fast rediscovering India's grand past, leading to a reawakening among the educated elite and to the introduction of indigenous traditions into art school syllabuses.

This return to lost roots was further fuelled by the emergent nationalist movement; this promoted indigenous art as a symbol of national pride. From these contradictions emerged the foundations of modern Indian art.

At Shantiniketan, West Bengal, Rabindranath Tagore established his famous university; while the masters who taught here were encouraged to experiment with non-Indian forms and techniques, they put down firm roots in indigenous traditions. But their subjects were rooted in everyday life. The Bengal landscape, its cultivators and fishermen, as well as portraits of intimates, were rendered with new and freer expression by each generation of masters. The main names associated with the Bengal School are Abanindranath Tagore (nephew of the Nobel laureate Rabindranath), Nandalal Bose, Benode Behari Mukherjee and the sculptor-painter, Ram Kinkar.

In the meantime, Raja Ravi Varma, the artist-prince from Kerala, had popularised oil painting across the country through his portraits and mythological themes. A breakthrough in this medium was made by the half-Hungarian Amrita Sher-Gil, trained in Paris. Although she died young, she achieved a synthesis of European modern art and Indian classical forms. While her sources were the Ajanta murals and miniature paintings, her subjects were ordinary people and sights. Other important figures include M.F. Hussain who started off painting cinema hoardings in Mumbai, and Jamini Roy who drew on traditional rural forms. In sculpture, a breakthrough was later made by Dhanraj Bhagat, trained in Lahore. In their starkly simple elongated forms, his images of Shiva Nataraja are close to Brancusi. But they also return us full circle to the dancing shamans of the prehistoric era.   ❑

LEFT: *British Raj*, M.F. Husain (born 1915).
RIGHT: detail from *Tree of Life*, S.H. Raza (born 1922).

CONTEMPORARY INDIAN ART

In the years following Independence, Indian art was dominated by the Progressive Artists of Mumbai, including Ara, Souza, M.F. Husain, Raza, Ram Kumar and Kishen Khanna, most of whom are now at the top of the contemporary art ladder. Unlike the masters of the earlier Modern Movement, the Progressives styled their Indian themes in the modern European mould, and their followers have become increasingly influenced by the avant-garde movements of the West. This is one of the main reasons why so much contemporary work appears derivative. But it must be remembered that many artists are genuinely inspired by the modern urban environment with its Western influences.

It is also important to note, when touring the galleries (the National Gallery of Modern Art in Delhi is a good place to start getting a feel for different styles), that the hallmark of contemporary Indian art is diversity. Artists work in a wide range of media and styles and with an immense variety of themes and motifs. It is possible to see everything from installations to narrative paintings, from landscapes and portraits to abstracts and works with Adivasi and local motifs. Although quality also varies substantially, the discerning eye may pick out very accomplished and expressive works from the mediocre. Kolkata and Delhi are the best cities in which to find interesting art to buy.

CRAFTS AND TEXTILES

A feast of colours, textures and motifs awaits the traveller. Every village
has its skills, evidence of which can be traced back 5,000 years

Crafts in India can be divided into two streams: those created for personal use and adornment by people whose livelihood is agriculture or animal husbandry, which only incidentally find markets elsewhere; and those made by professional craftsmen on commission for a particular market or buyer.

Some states and regions predominate in one kind of craft and others in another. In the hill states and Gujarat, every village surface, utensil and garment is vibrantly alive with colour and ornamentation, while the equally skilled hands of Uttar Pradesh and Kashmir make almost entirely market-orientated shawls, silverware, carpets, ivories and brocades. Is it history, geography, economics or the weather that impels the directions creativity takes? If it is the dry, brown parched landscape of the Bani desert that causes the contrasting exuberance of Kutchi craft, and the green fertility of Kerala that evokes the austere simplicity of its architecture, bronze vessels and white cotton weaves, how does one explain the flowering lushness of Kashmiri craft motifs? Visitors can buy papier-mâché, crewel embroidery and carpets, all vibrant with the flowing imagery and colour of the foliage, flora and fauna of Kashmir's landscape.

Craftspeople traditionally have had the status of artists, tracing their descent from Visvakarma, "Lord of the Many Arts, Master of a Thousand Handicrafts, Carpenter to the Gods, Architect of Their Celestial Mansion, Designer of All Ornaments, the First of All Craftsmen".

Hammered in metal

Brass, copper, silver and gold – hammered, beaten or cast; engraved, enamelled or repoussé – have been used for centuries in shapes consecrated by tradition to temple ritual or court ceremonial, or simply to carry water. Each metal has its ascribed attribute: according to an

LEFT: hand-made string puppets, called *kathputli*, on display in Rajasthan.
RIGHT: potter at work in Gujarat .

ancient text, the *Kalika Purana*, gold "removes the excesses of the three humours and promotes strength of vision", silver is "favourable and inimicable to bile, but calculated to increase the secretion of wind and phlegm", bronze is "agreeable and intellectual", but brass is "wind-generating, irritating", and iron is "beneficial

in overcoming dropsy, jaundice and anaemia".

Techniques and traditional craft forms worth looking out for are the engraved and enamelled *minakari* brassware of Rajasthan and Uttar Pradesh, known as *siakalam* and *marori* work. The designs are chased on tinned brass, then filled in with black or coloured lacquer applied with a hot tool and finally polished. The coloured patterns, generally flowing arabesques of flowers and foliage, stand out on the glittering metal. In Jaipur and Udaipur you will also find exquisitely enamelled silver and gold ornaments and *objets d'art*, with precious stones embedded among the brilliant blues, greens and deep reds.

Stunning in black and white is *bidri*, the silver damascene or inlaid metal originating in old Hyderabad. Stylised motifs are engraved and set in silver leaf on boxes, bowls and vases made of an alloy of copper, zinc and lead treated with a solution of copper sulphate and saltpetre, which turns it jet black.

The more common form of damascene wirework – the base of brass or bronze, with gold and silver wire ornamentation – which travelled to India via Iran and Afghanistan from Damascus, was patronised by the Emperor Akbar. His warriors went to war with Koranic verses inscribed in golden *koftagiri* calligraphic arabesques

on their sword hilts. In Udaipur, Alwar and Jodhpur you can still see daggers and shields made by descendants of the royal armourers who now occasionally turn their hands to nutcrackers and betelnut cutters.

Intricate inlay

When two metals are used in conjunction, either by inlaying or embossing, or welding them together, the resulting contrast of colour and texture is known as *Ganga-Jamuna* (the confluence of India's two rivers). This is a favourite technique all over India, from the Thanjavur plates of the South, with mythological figures encrusted in high relief in white metal on copper, to the brass and copper utensils of the hill states in the northeast.

Cire perdue, the lost-wax technique of casting brass, bronze and bell metal objects, is also used all over India. Made in this way are the life-size bronzes of Hindu deities from Svamimalai in Tamil Nadu; the austerely elegant ritual vessels of Kerala; and the delightful *dhokra* toy animals of Madhya Pradesh and Bengal. The object is moulded in clay, coated with wax, and encased in more clay. The molten metal is poured in through a small hole in the outer layer, melting the wax which runs out, with the metal taking its place and hardening. The clay coating is then removed and the object polished, chased and finished on a lathe.

Carved in stone

An enduring image of India is the Taj. Its exquisite marble mosaics and inlays and delicate trellises are still reproduced in Agra. Boxes, table tops, plates and bowls are made from

A TREASURE CHEST OF WOOD

India was once called "the land that has no furniture", but wood was always extensively used, not only in architecture and sculpture but also for ceremonial carriages and palanquins, dowry chests, screens and myriad smaller articles. Sandalwood was the most auspicious, and finely carved statuettes, fans, frames and boxes are made of this delicate, aromatic wood. Walnut in Kashmir; black wood, mahogany, redwood and ebony in the south and east; teak everywhere, are carved in a variety of ways, though the ancient Shilpasastras sagely prohibited the use of wood from trees struck by lightning or disease; those in which birds had built nests; those growing near burial or crema-

tion grounds; or those trampled by elephants. The *sadeli* marquetry work of Surat in Gujarat; the *tarkasi* brass wire inlay of Rajasthan and Uttar Pradesh; ivory and mother-of-pearl inlay in the south; the brass sheet inlay *pattara* dowry chests and doors of Saurashtra; the *kamangiri* figurative painted woodwork of Jodhpur and Jaipur; the brilliantly-hued lacquer work of Sankheda, Nirmal and Sawantwadi; the lattice lace of *jali* screens from Saharanpur; the flowers and foliage carved into the satin finish of Kashmiri walnut; the gesso and goldleaf of Bikaner, are all worth looking for. Kondapalli in Andhra, Udaipur and Sankheda all make delightful, painted wooden toys.

translucent white marble or alabaster inlaid in Mughal flower designs with mother-of-pearl, lapiz and cornelian.

Other stoneware to look out for is the granite statuary of Mamallapuram (Mahabalipuram), which echoes the vibrant, powerful themes of South Indian temple art; the green serpentine or rust Gaya stone; rock crystal and alabaster boxes, bowls and animal figures of Jaipur, Varanasi and Bihar; the black chlorite utensils of Orissa; and the wonderful red and buff sandstone pillars, balconies and windows of domestic and temple architecture all over Rajasthan and Gujarat, whose stone lattice work is often described as "frozen lace".

Ceramic ware

Ceramics and terracotta are not the most durable of souvenirs for the tourist to take home but no visitor to India should miss the sight of the village potter turning his wheel with his big toe and producing, with a few flicks of his thumb, a shape identical to that which was thrown in Mohenjodaro 5,000 years ago.

The famous Blue Pottery of Jaipur is not turned on a wheel but moulded. Made of ground felspar mixed with gum rather than clay and painted a pure opaque white with turquoise and cobalt blue floral and figurative designs, it is reminiscent both of Persian tiles and Chinese porcelain and yet is richly, eclectically Indian in feel. Other lovely shapes and glazes are the blue and green cutwork pottery of Khurja, the black ware of Chinhat and Azamgarh in Uttar Pradesh, and the huge terracotta horses found outside village temples in Tamil Nadu and Bengal.

Woven fabrics

The richness of colour and motif in Indian textiles is overwhelming. The *Visnudharmottaram* speaks of five white tones – ivory, jasmine, the August moon, August clouds after rain, and mother-of-pearl.

The fine muslins used as shrouds for royal Egyptian mummies draped Mughal emperors

---

CLOTHED IN MUSLIN

Emperor Aurangzeb rebuked his daughter for appearing naked. She showed him that her muslin drapes were wound seven times round her body.

3,000 years later, and were given poetic names like "running water" *(abrawan)*, "evening dew" *(shabnam)*, and "woven air" *(bafthava)*, by court poets. Now many of them are commissioned by European fashion houses who recognise their superb quality. A *tanchoi* brocade from Varanasi will play on the contrast of one delicately differing shade against another in shadow and sun, while a south Indian temple sari might have a body of shocking pink and a border of parrot green with stylised elephants and peacocks.

Woven, waxed, embroidered, appliquéd, brocaded, block-printed, painted, tie-dyed, tinselled: whether cheap or expensive, there is something for every season and ceremony. Often seen abroad are block-printed cottons and Saurashtrian mirrorwork, Indian silks and brocades, Kashmiri carpets and shawls. The celebrated "ring-shawl" is made from the fleece the wild Himalayan ibex – now a protected species – sheds on rocks and bushes and is so fine that a metre-length passes through a man's signet ring. Textiles have been among India's major exports since the days of the Pharaohs.

Fascinating lesser-known techniques are the tie-dyed *bandhani* saris and scarves of

---

LEFT: *zari* (gold embroidery) decorates a cover for a palanquin at Jodhpur.
RIGHT: the traditional art of carving in soapstone.

Rajasthan and Gujarat, in which fine cotton or silk is knotted into minute patterns with waxed string and dyed in successive deepening shades of different colours. The knots are untied later to produce delicate spotted designs, each dot often no bigger than a matchhead, all over the body of the fabric. In *laheria bandhani* the cloth is tied to make fine diagonal stripes of contrasting colour. When the Prince Regent's passion for snuff in the late 18th century made snuff-taking a European fashion, and coloured handkerchiefs

bunch of steel wires attached to a wooden handle with which the melted beeswax is painted on to cloth before it is dyed, is another beautiful and subtle textile, similar in technique to Indonesian batik, but with very different colouring and designs. There are two main centres in coastal South India: Machlipatnam, specialising in the delicate, all-over floral trellis designs that were the origin of chintz *(chint)*; and Kalahasti for bold, black-outlined, heavily stylised mythological panels where calligraphy and pageantry,

to hide the ensuing stains became a painful necessity, it was the *bandhani* or *bandanna* spotted kerchief that came to the rescue.

Allied to the *bandhani* technique is *ikat*. In the case of the *patola, pochampalli, telia rumal* and *mashru* weaves of Gujarat, Andhra and Orissa, the warp and weft threads are separately tie-dyed before being woven into intricate, stylised designs of flowering shrubs, birds, elephants and fish set in geometric squares and stripes. Both *bandhani* and *patola* are associated with marriage, and no bride's trousseau is complete without one or the other.

Kalamkari, literally "the art of the pen", a wax-resist technique taking its name from the

goddesses and warriors riot together in baroque curlicues. Both styles use indigo and *myrobalam* vegetable dyes on handspun fabric with deep blue, ochre and dun as the predominant colours.

Two differing but equally exciting techniques are the *phulkari* (flower-craft) of Punjab and the *chikan* work of Uttar Pradesh. In its bold surface satin stitch in vivid satin floss oranges, pinks and flames, the *phulkari* reflects the vigour and vibrant energy of the Punjabi peasant; while the *chikan's* typical delicate white on white floral net and shadow work shows the subtlety and refinement of the Mughal court, where, legend has it, Nurjahan, Queen Consort to the Emperor Jahangir, devised the craft.

Delightful too are the *kantha* quilts of West Bengal. *Kantha* means rag, and the quilts are made with old saris laid one on top of the other and sewn with white asymmetrical circles and swirls. Coloured threads are then extracted from the borders of the saris and used to embroider folk motifs of animals, humans and trees all over the quilt, either in a spiral formation, starting with a central lotus, or in squared-off panels, each with a different design.

Patterns of embroidery

All over India, embroidery, unlike weaving, is a female occupation. Secluded by custom or religion from the public eye, women get together and sew either for money or their daughters' dowry chests. Designs and stitches are handed down from generation to generation, as are the wooden pattern blocks. In Kutch, villages less than a couple of kilometres apart will each have their own distinctive stitches, patterns and colours.

The exceptions in this female-dominated field are Uttar Pradesh and Kashmir, two states whose crafts have traditionally been practised by skilled professionals for patrons, originally the Imperial Court and local nobility, but which are now for exporters and the tourist trade. The gold and silver sequin and *zardozi* embroidery of Uttar Pradesh, and the *crewel*, *kani* and *kashida* of Kashmir, are all done by men. Making the various coiled and twisted gold and silver wires, spangles, sequins and braid is a craft in itself.

Centuries-old skills

Images of Indian crafts are inescapably accompanied by images of their makers. It may be an 80-year-old ivory carver in the shadow of the Jama Masjid, curved over an ivory that's already taken him seven years, calmly speculating whether he'll live the further two he'll need to finish it; a Rajasthani cobbler embroidering gold peacocks on shoes whose turned-up toes echo the ends of his moustache; or a papier-mâché painter chasing a squirrel for new hairs for his brush. However, so many of these images are now of old men and women whose descendants no longer carry on the tradition.

LEFT: *ikat* sari being woven, Andhra Pradesh – the warp and weft threads are tie-dyed before weaving.
RIGHT: detail showing appliqué work.

In stark contrast are the distressing images of children used as a cheap labour force, whether stitching footballs for Western sports companies, or working at Kashmiri carpet looms. Existing as virtual slaves, they are paid, if at all, barely subsistence wages, and work in cramped and dangerous conditions. There are many campaigners working against the exploitation of Indian workers, including children, and these now have numerous outlets for ethically sourced handicrafts. Organisations include SEWA (the Self-Employed Women's Association), a Gujarati group, and the Rajasthani-based shop, Anokhi. ❑

THE LANGUAGE OF COLOUR

The contemporary artist Kamladevi Chattopadhya says that every Indian colour has its tradition, emotional content and rich significance. "Red, the colour of marriage and love; orange, saffron, the colour of the ochre earth and the yogi who renounces that earth; yellow, the colour of spring, young mango blossoms, of swarms of bees, of southern winds and the passionate cry of mating birds. Blue, the colour of indigo, also the colour of Krishna, the cowherd child god... he that is of the colour that is in the newly-formed cloud, dormant with that darkness that is rain. Even the great gods had their colour – Brahma was red, Shiva was white and Vishnu was blue."

FOOD

The cuisines of India are as diverse as the country's culture, from the "tandoor"
of the Northwest Frontier to the chilli-hot curries of the south

Characteristic of the many and diverse styles of Indian cookery is the use of spices, used not only for flavour but also as appetite stimulators and digestives. Care is taken to ensure that the spices enhance rather than dominate the basic flavour. Traditionally, the ingredients in each meal were governed by the time of the year and classifications of heating or cooling foods, age, and even personality. Once there were also injunctions on the six *rasas* or flavours to be included in every meal: sweet, salty, bitter, astringent, sour and pungent. Each was believed to have its particular physical benefit and was prescribed in specific ratio to the others.

Essential ingredients

Other than spices, the important ingredients in Indian cuisine include milk and milk products, particularly *ghee* and *dahi* (curd). To the orthodox, a meal is "pure" only if cooked in *ghee*; an emphasis that derives not just from its distinctive fullness and unique flavour but from its acclaimed preservative qualities.

Dahi is part of almost any Indian menu. Served to mitigate the chilli "hotness" of some dishes, it is often mixed with vegetables or fruit and is lightly spiced to create the *raitas* of the North and the *pachadis* of the South. An important ingredient in several recipes, *dahi* is also churned and salted or sweetened to taste and served in summer as *lassi*, a cooling drink.

Dals (split lentils) are common to most parts of the country. Regional preferences and availability have resulted in a bewildering variety, from the thick tamarind-flavoured *sambars* of the South and the sweetish dals of Gujarat to the delicious *makhani dal* of North India.

Vegetarian variety

The style of vegetable cooking is determined by the cereal or main dish with which they are served. Deep-fried vegetable crisps are perfect accessories to the *sambhar* and rice of Tamil

LEFT: boiling milk for sweets, Agra, Uttar Pradesh.
RIGHT: selling bananas, Tiruchirapalli, Tamil Nadu.

Nadu. The thick *avial* stew of Kerala cooked in coconut oil, or the *kaottu* in a coconut and gram sauce, are perfect for rice-based meals. *Sarson ka sag*, mustard greens, eaten with *maki ki roti* (maize bread), is a particular favourite in the Punjab, while the delicately flavoured *chorchori* of Bengal complements Bengal's rice and fish.

India presents a vast range of vegetarian cooking. The roasted and steamed food of the south is lighter than northern cooking. Rice is the basis of every meal. It is served with *sambar*, *rasam* (a thin peppery soup), vegetables, both dry and in a sauce, and *pachadi*. Coconut is used in cooked foods as well as chutneys. Made of fermented rice and *dal* batter, the *dosa*, *vada* and *idli* are South Indian snacks popular all over the country.

The semolina-based *upma*, cooked with curry leaves and garnished with nuts and copra, is another favourite. Other in-between bites found everywhere are the *samosa*, a three-cornered deep-fried pastry parcel with potatoes, and *pakoras* or *bhajiyas* – vegetables coated in a gram batter and deep-fried. In Gujarat, another region famous for its vegetarian food, gram flour, a source of protein, is used in bread-making and as a component of various dishes.

Kadi, which is made from *dahi* and gram with spices, is popular. *Gur* or *jaggery* (unrefined sugar) adds a hint of sweetness to piquant sauces. *Am rasa*, the puréed pulp of mangoes eaten with *puris*, is a special treat on summer days.

Although Bengali food is never actually sweetened, it is customary to serve a sweet along with the other food as a foil to the hot chillies, or for a change in flavour. In keeping with religious mandates, Gujarati (especially

Meat and fish delicacies

Muslim influence is most evident in the cooking of meats. The major contribution was the *tandoor*, the conical earthen oven from which emerged a delectable array of *kababs* and *rotis*. This was the origin of the famous *tandoori* cooking, brought from the Northwest Frontier, but available all over the country – the *tandoori* chicken, *seekh*, *boti* and *barra kababs*, and *tandoori* fish. Among the *rotis* are the elongated *naan*, the *tandoori roti*, or its richer equivalent, the *tandoori paratha*. All are delicious breads.

The fastidious Mughals transformed local recipes, developing what has become known

Jain) and Bengali vegetarian food is often cooked without the garlic, ginger, onions, and the "heating" or stimulating spices.

Possibly the "purest" form of North Indian vegetarian food is the Banarsi. Lightly spiced, many specialities are based on *panir* (soft cheese). A good source of protein, it is cooked in innumerable ways, with spinach *(palak panir)*, in a gravy with peas *(matter panir)* or lotus seeds *(panir phulmakhana)*.

Then there are the deep-fried or stuffed breads, made of combinations of refined and wholemeal flour; the golden puffs called *puris*, the *parathas*, *baturas* and so on. Most widely eaten is the simple *chapatti*, baked on a griddle.

as Mughlai cuisine, with its luscious sauces of *dahi*, cream and crushed nuts. An amazing variety is on offer, including: the rich *kormas* and *nargisi koftas* (meatballs shaped around a hard-boiled egg) of Lucknow; the *pasandas* or mutton steaks cooked in an almond sauce; the *biriyani*, a layered rice and meat concoction famous in Hyderabad; and a variety of *kababs* that literally melt in the mouth.

Laden with nuts, dried fruits and saffron, Kashmiri Muslim food is a gourmet's joy and bears much in common with Persian food. *Haleem*, mutton pounded with wheat; *gaustaba*, incredibly light meatballs; and *rogan josh* are well-known Kashmiri specialities.

Although rice is not the staple cereal of the North, it is an important accessory to many meals. Indeed, a good *pilau* (rice cooked in stock, with meat, vegetable or nuts) is considered the supreme test of a good cook.

Vinegar lends a different taste to the meat dishes of Goa. The pork *sorpotel*, *vindaloo*, the Goan sausages and the chicken *shakuti* or *cafreal* are inimitable.

Fish, too, is prepared in many ways: the mustard-flavoured *macher jhol* and *malai* or cream prawns of Bengal, the chilli-hot curries of Andhra, the coconut and curry-leaf flavoured specialities of the south and the memorable fish and shellfish curries of Goa. *Hilsa*, a Bengali speciality, has spiky bones that support meltingly delicate flesh and requires careful chewing. Dried fish, misleadingly known as Bombay Duck, is cooked with vegetables or *dals* and adds interest to the simpler fare of Maharashtra.

The Parsis also contributed interesting dishes. *Dhansak*, meat cooked with five different *dals* and an unusual blend of spices, and *patrani machi*, lightly spiced fish steamed in banana leaves, are just two examples.

Chutneys and pickles, sweet, sour, hot, or all three, stimulate the appetite and add relish to a meal. Many ingredients can be used: mint, coriander, mango, ginger, lime and vegetables with extravagant spices or just salt.

Papads (or *papadams*), roasted or fried savoury crisps, add crunch. They are made from a previously prepared dough of *dal*, rice, or vegetable flour.

Sweets

Often too sweet for the non-Indian palate, the huge array of Indian confections and desserts is largely milk-based. Bengal is particularly well-known for its confections. These include the *rasagulla*, *sandesh*, *rasamalai* and the steaming hot *gulab-jamuns*. Typical of the north are the *barfis* (milk cakes), some of pure milk, others of coconut or various types of nuts. Crisp golden *jelabis*, dripping with syrup, made even in the tiniest bazaars all over the country, are breakfast and tea-time favourites.

Kheer, the Indian equivalent of rice pudding; *shahi tukra*, a variation on bread pudding; *phirni*, made of powdered rice and served in

earthenware bowls; and *kulfi*, a rich nutty ice cream, are common northern desserts. Sweets from the South include Mysore *pak* and the creamy *payasam*, while the Gujaratis are partial to *srikhand* made of drained, sweetened and spiced *dahi*. *Halvas* are created from ingredients as diverse as carrots, semolina, *dals*, eggs, or even wholemeal flour.

Finally, there is the satisfying ritual of the after-dinner *pan*, which is lauded for its digestive and medicinal, if addictive, properties. It is a fragrant combination of betel leaf, areca nut, catechu, cardamom, cloves and other fragrant ingredients. ❑

SOUTHERN MEALS

Meals in the South revolve around rice, eaten with *dal*-based soups, thin and spicy *rasams* and the thicker *sambars*, often flavoured with tamarind. To these are added "sambar powder", made up of spices such as coriander, *methi* (fenugreek) seeds, cumin and the pungent asafoetida. Often they are finished by "tempering", chillies and whole spices heated in oil until the important black mustard seeds "pop"; the whole lot is then poured on the top of the dish. Dry vegetable dishes (and in certain places, notably Andhra Pradesh and Kerala, spicy meat and fish preparations) are also served with the rice, to which is added copious quantities of curd (yoghurt) and fiery pickles.

LEFT: ingredients laid out on a banana leaf, Goa.
RIGHT: nuts and *dals* for sale.

FLORA AND FAUNA

Habitats are vanishing and poachers flout the laws, but the astonishing variety of animal, reptile, bird and plant life in India can still be glimpsed

Animals are never far away in India. Even common house pests could include such exotics as a red-rumped monkey or a mongoose, besides the geckoes flexing on the wall or a scorpion hiding inside a shoe. Mynah birds and an occasional cobra in the garden come as no surprise. Camels and elephants wander in the street traffic and humped cattle sometimes outnumber the vehicles on the road. Water buffalo loll beside the dhobi ghats, where laundry is done. Huge birds of prey – vultures or pariah kites – spiral overhead.

Lions, tigers and bears – savage and shy – inhabit South Asia from Himalayan cloud forests to desert scrub. Land-clearing has encroached on much of the former hunting grounds, and without the game reserves and sanctuaries many more might disappear. There's no chance of spotting a cheetah now; the last of these died in 1994. The government of India continues to permit the destruction of big cats which are proven man-eaters, and so-called "cattle lifters" are often gunned down for revenge as well. These can be leopards, panthers, or tigers, though snow leopards and the daintier clouded leopard are often spared.

Hundreds of stocky Asiatic lions prowl the Gir Forest Reserve in Gujarat, the only place in the world where they thrive. Unlike African lions, these cats don't have much mane, but carry most of their shaggy hair on the tip of their tails and elbows. In the 1990s some young males strayed outside the park and were neutered by rangers, who were anxious that local cattleherders shouldn't start shooting the lions if they dared put a paw outside their sanctuary. Striped hyenas feed on the lions' leftovers and there are more panthers visible in the Gir – pronounced "gear", not "Grrrr" – than at any other Indian park.

Bears are more aloof. Himalayan brown bears are heavy-set and larger than their black cousins, who live below the tree line on Himalayan slopes. Sloth bears, found over much of India, are mostly nocturnal. All three varieties can climb trees and swim if put to the test. The sloth bear grunts with pleasure or anger, and digs for termites and other grubs. It gobbles bees, but prefers honeycomb or sweet

fruits and berries. The bears are hunted for their gall bladders, sold for Chinese fertility medicine. Miserable sloth bears can be seen in cities, shuffling along in chains and a muzzle, and earning a few rupees for their captors. In the forests of the northeast red pandas, resembling slim, auburn raccoons, are found.

Big beasts

The one-horned Indian rhinoceros keeps mainly to the northeastern woods around Kaziranga in Assam, though a number have been reintroduced to Dudhwa park in Uttar Pradesh, nudging India's total of rhinos to around 1,700. They stand about 1.6 metres (5.5 ft) at the shoulder

---

PRECEDING PAGES: egrets in flight at Bharatpur.
LEFT: a slender loris from South India.
RIGHT: saltwater crocodile with its catch, Orissa.

and weigh around 1,820 kg (4,000 lbs). Adult males are larger than females, with horns that are usually thicker at the base and often broken or split at the tip (the horn of the female is usually slender and unbroken). Adult females may also be accompanied by calves.

Floodplain grassland interspersed with marsh, swamp and lake, and the adjoining riverine forest, are their favoured habitat. Rhinos prefer to feed on short grasses and seek shelter in thick stands of tall grass, sometimes 6–8 metres (20–25 ft) high.

Rhinos are usually viewed from elephant back. These mounts are domestic elephants.

ELEPHANTS

Elephants make large demands on their environment; an adult animal consumes something like 200 kg (450 lbs) of green fodder a day, probably wasting an equal amount in the process. The elephant has few natural enemies, calves are jealously guarded by their mothers and tigers seldom have the opportunity to take them. The elephant, therefore, is an apex species and an excellent indicator of the health of their habitat. A habitat that is good for the elephant is also good for its associate species, such as the sambar deer, spotted deer and barking deer, which in their turn — as prey species — support predators like the tiger or the leopard.

Wild tuskers found in the jungles are feared, with good reason. Some may roam close to villages, developing a taste for alcohol after drinking the contents of a still. Others stampede through villages, mowing down everything in their path – usually after being provoked by villagers defending their crops. Yet spying a herd of wild elephants tearing calmly through the shrubbery is a definite thrill. Such enormous beasts can move with surprising silence.

There are an estimated 9,000 wild elephants in India, with thousands more working at temples, logging camps, game parks, or hired out for weddings. Periyar, in Kerala, is the best place to view elephants in the wild. Parks in West Bengal and Assam are also good bets.

Game tourism

Indian game viewing began on a grand scale in the 1950s, and even today the arrangements sometimes resemble gentlemen's shooting parties of that era. Creature comforts are not ignored in the wild, and some tents are quite luxurious, though many forest houses are rustic, and safari suits are now worn mostly by chauffeurs for the middle class.

Wild animal-watching in India takes patience. Many of the most spectacular beasts hide in the shadows, lone predators waiting for their opportunity. Game reserves are not easily accessible (except for Ranthambore in Rajasthan, near a railway connection). A few parks require special permits in advance, usually for a minimum group of four. In the northeast, where shy pandas and macaques hide, militants and Adivasis often do, too. The government limits visits near strategic borders or guerrilla areas. It is always wise to check before setting out, since situations change without warning. At any sanctuary, dress in sensible camouflage and keep quiet; the creatures are easily frightened. Yet with almost 350 species of mammal, a couple of thousand types of bird, and at least 30,000 kinds of insect (more than you want to know personally), India provides an unmatched range that justifies several trips.

Tigers

Tiger sightings are very rare these days. The 2001–2 census by Project Tiger (http://project-tiger.nic.in) recorded only 3,642 tigers in India (over half of the world's total), slightly up on 1997. A typical day's kill on a hunt in the days of the British Raj would be close to 100. Now, dead tiger parts are sold clandestinely to Chinese pharmacists for use in what is, quite frankly, outright quackery. The poachers rarely use guns, especially since there is no longer a premium on intact pelts. Instead a carcass is wired to a few sticks of dynamite, and a curious tiger comes along and triggers an explosion. Often they simply poison the tiger's own kill, or lay snares. Poorly paid game wardens are no match for the organised poachers working in remote game parks.

AQUATIC TIGERS

Tigers are powerful swimmers and are found in the Sunderban tidal-swamp and mangroves, where they eat fish, sea turtles, water monitors, chital and wild pigs.

of its kill, a tiger may feed on it for four to five days. By the end, it will have eaten all the flesh, small bones, skin and hair.

The tiger's choice of quarry is not chosen by species. It is, rather, by size; the bigger the better. With very large prey, such as the gaur or the buffalo, a tiger will generally go for the sub-adults. When a tigress is training her cubs, many monkeys and langur are killed, regardless of size: this is the only form of communal hunting seen among tigers.

A formidable hunter, the tiger usually takes its quarry from behind, laying its chest on the back of the animal, grabbing the neck in its canines, sometimes bracing a forearm on the forelimb of the quarry and trying to pull it down by their combined weight. The tiger's sharp retractile claws also play a significant role in capturing and holding on to its quarry. A swipe of the forearm is sometimes used to stop a fleeing animal or to kill very small prey like monkey or peafowl. Depending on the size

LEFT: sambar hind, Bandhavgarh, Madhya Pradesh.
ABOVE: one of the 35 tigers under the auspices of Project Tiger at Ranthambore, Rajasthan.

Dominant males may occupy very extensive territories, as large as 50 to 100 sq km (20 to 40 sq miles). Up to three or even five females may occupy mutually exclusive sub-territories within a large male territory. The females in such an organisation are assured of food supply for themselves and their offspring and, in return, owe allegiance to the territorial male.

The best bet for glimpsing a tiger in the wild is to visit an Indian sanctuary before it is too late. At Kaziranga (Assam), Bandhavgarh or Kanha (Madhya Pradesh), Dudhwa or Corbett (Uttar Pradesh) or Bandipur (Karnataka) odds are more favourable than at parks where poachers penetrate. Even during the dry season, when thirsty animals slow down and are visible against the parched leaves, luck is still a key ingredient. Dusk or dawn is a likely hour. Jeeps, elephants, and even dugout canoes carry visitors deep into the bush, and few will be disappointed by the experience, even if they only see the pug marks of big predators.

Other creatures

Such expeditions readily produce other specimens. Look out for the pangolin, a scaly anteater that resembles an armadillo but lives high in the treetops. This nocturnal creature, found mainly in dense eastern rainforest, hisses and

rolls up into an armoured ball when agitated. The rare slow loris curls into a fuzzy ball by day, then moves hand over hand through the trees, hunting in slow motion.

Mugger crocodiles are extremely adaptable and live in any freshwater (sometimes even brackish water) habitats, from large reservoirs to small streams. During extreme dry months or drought they make deep tunnels or even trek miles overland throughout India but, again because of hunting pressure, are now confined to a few protected reservoirs and rivers. Narrow-nosed gharial live well on fish, growing up to 5 metres (16 ft) long in Indian rivers. In winter, they emerge to sun themselves and are more easily spotted. The huge saltwater crocodiles (the biggest in the world) are confined to the Andaman Islands, the Sunderbans in West Bengal, and Bhitar Kanika in Orissa.

Of the 238 snake species in India, the four most common poisonous snakes are the cobra, krait, Russell's viper and the saw-scaled viper. Together, they cause 10,000 snakebite deaths every year in India alone. There are several species of non-venomous "garden snakes" common throughout the region. The large rat snake is often mistaken for a cobra but has a more pointed head, large eyes and of course does not spread a hood. The biggest snake in India is the reticulated python which grows up to 10 metres (30 ft) in length.

Elsewhere on the plains, groups of black buck, recognisable by their elegant antlers, cluster together. Other antelopes, such as the large nilgai (or blue cow), prefer open forest. The widespread sambar deer can be found from the Himalayas to Kanniyakumari; and on the higher

FLORA

You will frequently spot huge versions of familiar houseplants growing wild in India. There are some 15,000 different species, including rare ladyslipper orchids, groves of precious sandalwood, or pines interwoven with scarlet rhododendrons. Tangled mangrove swamps compete with casuarina trees. Thickets of bamboo thrive in the northeastern states, where it is used for paper making, amongst other things. Delicate wildflowers carpet high Himalayan meadows in the summer and salt breezes toss the fronds of several types of palm. Although the mixed deciduous forests have been severely depleted, fire-resistant stands of sal trees or teak (which is also virtually termite-proof) are still found. Banyan trees with multiple trunks, sacred pipal figs and Ashoka trees with spear-shaped leaves remain quintessentially Indian. What often fascinate visitors are the flowering trees that shade city parks: jacarandas unfurl blooms like lavender-blue fans, while white magnolia flowers gleam against glossy leaves. Feathery gulmohar trees suddenly blaze bright crimson. Flame of the Forest's large orange flowers are used to make yellow dye, while the bark produces a blue stain. Blossoms of the frangipani (temple tree) can be cream, pink, or deep fuschia. Most fragrant of all are tamarind and jamun plum trees, the blossoms of which emit a scent to rival tuberose or jasmine.

slopes of the Himalayas ibex clamber freely. Brow-antlered deer, one of the country's rarest creatures, hide in the dense northeastern forests.

Himalayan flowers seem to hover above the meadows, until closer inspection reveals that they are in reality butterflies evaporating dew from their iridescent wings. Gazelles or wild boar, leatherback turtles or blind river dolphins (often spotted playing the Ganga), porcupines or flying squirrels – many species take sanctuary in game reserves around the country.

OLIVE RIDLEY TURTLES

One of the major nesting sites for these marine turtles is the Bhitkar Kanika Sanctuary in Orissa. More than 200,000 turtles come ashore over just three or four days.

Keoladeo Ghana sanctuary at Bharatpur, near Agra, is renowned for the number and spectacular variety of its visiting species. However, in most recent years the Siberian cranes that usually spend winter at the park have failed to show up. Scientists blame fighting in Afghanistan, which lies beneath their migratory flight path, for the disruption of their journey.

Another major problem is the near extinction of the once widespread vulture, whose numbers have declined by 98 percent in the

Bird life

Many rare birds stop over in India, joining the beauties that reside year round. Heavy-headed hornbills fly in pairs over northeastern and southern jungles. Apart from the ubiquitous crows and kites, raucous flocks of rose-ringed parakeets wheel over the trees in city parks, while in rural areas look out for the bright blue flash of the common kingfisher. Other waterbirds include herons, spoonbills, flamingoes, egrets, or teal ducks.

LEFT: poinsettias glow against a mountain backdrop near Darjeeling, West Bengal.
ABOVE: a fine specimen of gaur.

last 10 years or so. At first it was thought that an unknown virus was to blame, but researchers have now found a link between the drug diclofenac (widely used as a veterinary pain-killer in South Asia) and kidney failure in vultures. Vultures perform the vital function of scavenging rotting carcasses (from which they absorb the diclofenac). This helps prevent the spread of disease and keeps down the population of feral dogs. The Parsis of Mumbai are also facing problems because it is the vultures who dispose of corpses from their Towers of Silence.   ❑

● *For full coverage of the flora and fauna of South Asia, see* Insight Guide: Indian Wildlife.

INDIAN RAILWAYS

For a true taste of India, its people and landscape, nothing beats travelling by train on one of the most comprehensive networks in the world

Indian Railways is a huge state-run conglomerate, the world's largest employer. It moves 14 million passengers a day yet still remains remarkably efficient and uniquely poetic. There is no better way to get the pulse of South Asia than to view the changing scene from a carriage window. Incidentally, a window in the non-air-conditioned sleeper class comprises several layers to keep out the sun, dust and ticketless travellers.

British colonialists laid most of the 63,140 km (39,230 miles) of track, and left sturdy Victorian relics – clocks, scales and benches – on platforms across India. Things have moved on since then, however, and now the fast track inter-city services, known as *Rajdhani* and *Shatabdi*, run to various state capitals and major cities from Delhi and other centres. In the 1990s, the overnight switch of political power from North India to the constituencies of the South resulted in the conversion of metre gauge to broad gauge, a decision that had been considered unrealistic under North Indian prime ministers.

Yet in spite of political interference the working of the railways is impressive. Serving under the Rail Minister is the Railway Board, whose chairman is invariably a railway engineer. The system is divided into nine zones, which derive in part from the reach of the imperial private companies. For example, today's Central Railway has inherited the extent and style of the Great Indian Peninsular lines. Zonal profiles vary considerably, with the southern states profitably in command of their assets (borne out by the smart livery of both rolling stock and railwaymen), while those in the north and east wilt under the burden of saturation.

Reservations are now computerised at most stations of any size and special quotas are available for foreign tourists. Indrail Rover Tickets, bookable in India and abroad, can be very convenient for the frequent rail traveller.

LEFT: all clear down the line. Rail travel is the best way of soaking up the scenery.

RIGHT: railway art – a mural decorates a station.

Luxury service

Service on speciality trains such as the Palace on Wheels through Rajasthan is unrivalled, with two turbaned valets for each carriage. For the luxury of service, if not for speed and fittings, the first-class air-conditioned compartments of Indian Railways are as good as any in the world.

When you compare what the railways give you for about the comparable price of a plane ticket with all the delays and charmlessness of airports, then you travel more meaningfully by train. Following a relaxed journey, you arrive in the middle of town. Budget travellers can also go by second class in an air-conditioned or three-tier air-conditioned sleeper coach so that the heat and dust is filtered out.

On board, there are rules and there are rules. Officially, no drinking is allowed, but those most likely to benefit from abstention are the least troubled by warnings. Just as first-class passengers are generally free to indulge, so are they allowed to take their pets on board.

The age of steam

Steam locomotives are officially on the scrap-heap. (Rumour had it that the constant pilfering of coal was a major factor in the fate of steam.) Luckily, one famous route has been reprieved, that of the line to Udhagamandalam (Ooty) in the Nilgiris. The famous line up to Darjeeling in the Himalayas has recently been converted to diesel traction but still occasionally runs steam engines (this is now a World Heritage Site and there is a Darjeeling Himalayan Railway Society; www.dhrs.org). *Tweed* and *Mersey* (1873 vintage) unfortunately no longer get up steam each winter to cart sugar cane on the metre gauge

east of Gorakhpur in Uttar Pradesh. However, Tipong Colliery in Assam still runs two narrow-gauge steam locomotives, and the Riga sugar mill in Bihar sometimes uses a metre-gauge steam engine to haul sugar cane.

There seems to be a change of heart at the railway ministry as they realise the tourist potential of running steam services (particularly on the popular hill services). There are plans to resume steam traction on the Matheran railway near Mumbai, and as well as "specials" (information on these can be had from the Indian Steam Railway Society; www.indian steamrailway.org) there are the yearly steam-hauled Royal Orient and Fairy Queen luxury tourist trains.

Prime lines

Not all progress is forwards. Until 1994 the traveller could cover the entire subcontinent by one gauge, but since then the metric has been sacrificed to a broader option that does not (nor probably ever will) have such extensive coverage. However, the broad-gauge network stretches from Ledo in eastern Assam to Bhuj in western Gujarat, a journey of 3,776 km (2,346 miles); and from Kanniyakumari in the south to Jammu Tawi in the north, 3,581 km (2,225 miles). The journeys take you through some startling changes of scenery: from the lush rhino tracks of the Brahmaputra, through the rice paddies of West Bengal and the wheat fields of Uttar Pradesh, to the flat desert of the Rann of Kutch; or, from tropical Kerala, over the high Deccan Plateau, down to the Ganga Plain, and then up, through the foothills, to the edge of the Himalayas.

STATION ATTRACTIONS

Whiling away time on an Indian station waiting for a late-running connection need not be as tedious as you might imagine. As well as being dragged into conversation by curious fellow passengers, there are other amenities to help you pass the time.

Platform booksellers (Wheelers in the North and Higginbothams in the South) sell low-priced local editions of India's finest authors to read during the journey. They also sell timetables such as *Trains at a Glance* and the comprehensive *Indian Bradshaw*.

There will always be a magazine stall, either a small shop or a cart that is pushed alongside the trains as they come into the station. They stock a wide variety of reading matter, from the latest editions of the daily newspapers, to news magazines such as *Frontline* and *India Today*, to the women's magazine *Femina* and the Bollywood gossip publication *Cine-Blitz*.

Food from stalls on the platform can be surprisingly good – particularly in Kerala where tasty fish curry and rice comes wrapped in banana leaves. There will often be a stall cooking up fresh omelettes, and railway buffets can serve up good, and cheap, dishes such as *biryani* and "meals".

For a treat, try the Himachal Pradesh government apple juice stalls, found on stations all over the country.

The coasts on both sides of the subcontinent offer some fine scenery but the Coromandel leading to Chennai is more impressive. With the new length of Konkan Railway from Mumbai to Mangalore, a fabulous stretch of coastal scenery has opened up. Probably the most sensational coastal run of all is to Ramesvaram, on the isle of Pamban. Until a storm obliterated it in 1965, this line ran another 20 km (12 miles) along a narrow spit of sand to Danushkodi.

Inland, the hill railways of India are famous for their character and quaintness. Not far from Mumbai is the climb to Matheran by tiny narrow-gauge stock. Darjeeling's toy railway

The world's highest broad-gauge track is notable for the triple-headed trains that carry iron ore for export from Kirinul to the port of Visakhapatnam in Andhra Pradesh, a modern engineering triumph of Indian expertise. A daily mixed train from Vizag runs up this line and over the Eastern Ghats to the Adivasi capital of Bastar. Other impressive crossings, this time of the Western Ghats, are from Tenkasi to Quilon and the newer and more dramatic alignment from Mangalore to Hassan. Yet another memorable ghat line is over the Aravalli range from Jodhpur to Udaipur in Rajasthan, past craggy forests and the highest point on the Western Railway. ❏

is well known. Ooty's also is widely loved but, contrary to popular notions about its "rack" (which only runs as far as Coonoor), this is not a narrow-gauge railway but metric. Whereas the Darjeeling engines were Scottish, those that push up the Ooty train are Swiss, with an extra set of pistons to work the rack mechanism. While the hill line to Simla is famous for its 103 tunnels, a better view of the Himalayan peaks can be had from its sister narrow-gauge line that runs through the Kangra Valley.

LEFT: the Toy Train winds its way up through the spectacular Nilgiri Hills to the cool of Ooty.
ABOVE: bicycles on the rails.

ON TRACK

To photograph Indian Railways' property, permission must be obtained from HQ in New Delhi. Entry to the immaculate portals of Rail Bhavan will be an eye-opener to those who thought all Indian government offices were run-down and stained by betel-nut juice. Restrictions usually apply to prohibited areas and military installations. Make sure your permit states a time frame, or officials may argue that it is valid only on the day of issue.

Timetables: *Newman's Indian Bradshaw* is published monthly in Kolkata. Express trains are numbered according to a code that lists their point of origination; locos are classified according to gauge and duty.

PLACES

*A detailed guide to the entire country, with principal sites
clearly cross-referenced by number to the maps*

No one feels neutral about India. It slams you in the face with heat, spice and dirt, then seduces you with colour and sensual pleasure. Time distorts and assumes surreal yogic contortions: distances take longer to travel, minutes crawl during interminable waits, then vanish into a blur of hours, even days. The constant chaos can charm or repulse.

There are so many different facets of India: the 28 states and six Union Territories and the National Capital Territory of Delhi offer a bewildering number of travel options. Trekking to Adivasi villages in the Western Ghats is a physical challenge. Chugging across the Deccan Plateau in a three-tiered sleeper car while the other passengers snore is a mental one. The pride of an artisan working at a potter's wheel or loom is obvious; the appeal of rural villages trimmed with intricate murals is unforgettable.

Visit an old Portuguese fort or an ancient Jewish synagogue. Take refuge in a remote pleasure palace a full day's camel ride away from the rest of the world. Barter in a bazaar for old silver, new rugs, inlaid daggers, or go for the miniature paintings brushed with a squirrel's whisker, the antique opium boxes, or new jewellery made with crushed gemstones: it's all spread out before your eyes in a former caravanserai.

Other visitors come to India seeking something within themselves, some spiritual calm beyond the cacophony. Some enrol in meditation centres, others opt for social or environmental work, either can teach you something more about yourself.

India's travel experiences can be similarly uplifting, from boating down a river where elephants bathe, to the colour and spectacle of a religious festival. White-water rafting down the Ganga, practising yoga on a sunrise beach, tracking wildlife in game sanctuaries, climbing a Himalayan peak, sketching wildflowers in a hill station meadow, or examining erotic sculpture at Tantric temples: it would need immense stamina to undertake all the travel possibilities in India. The following pages will help readers to awaken their wanderlust and give a rounded view of the people and places that might otherwise be omitted from a journey because of shortage of time.

Some run away from India; others keep returning. ❑

PRECEDING PAGES: valley in Ladakh; Hampi, Karnataka; waiting for the morning bus outside CST station in Mumbai.
LEFT: the Durbar hall, Samode Palace, Rajasthan.

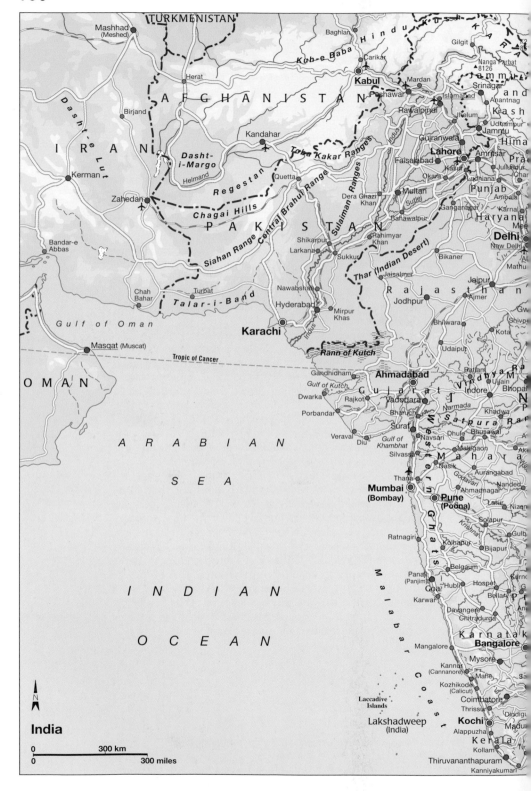

India

| 0 | 300 km |
| 0 | 300 miles |

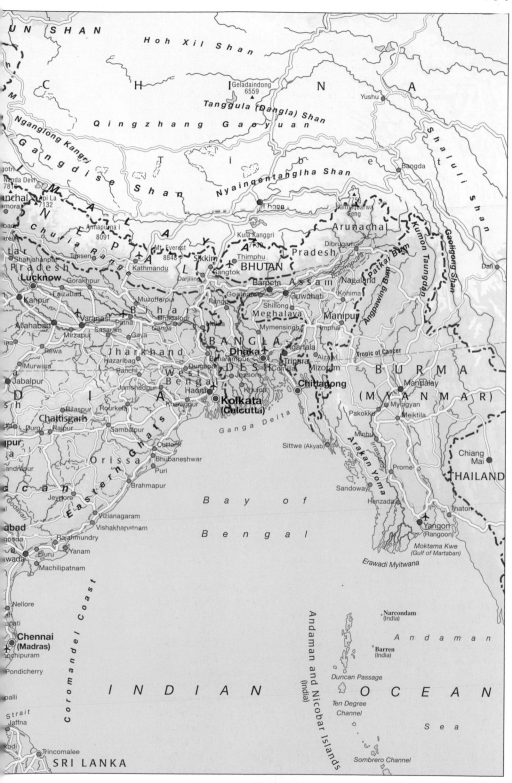

THE NORTH

*North India covers a great swathe of South Asia,
seducing travellers with its infinite contrasts*

In the cities of North India boisterous crowds jostle past and new-comers attract plenty of stares. Colours and voices are loud. So are the sound systems of the temples and the mosques. The place can be fascinating and infuriating in turn.

The landscape goes to extremes – sand dunes in the Thar desert compete with glaciers glittering on distant peaks. Craggy Himalayan provinces loom over the plains, and the roads are under constant repair from the onslaught of monsoon rains or searing temperatures. Colonial cities are still slightly haunted by memories of the Sepoy Uprising and the Nawabs. Gung-ho adventure tourists try to tame the rapids of snowmelt rivers while pilgrims seek the source of the Ganga. At Varanasi a multitude swirls away the ashes of its dead in the green waters where blind river dolphins swim like torpedoes.

There are people milling everywhere. Uttar Pradesh (UP), the most populous state, is right in the middle of what is known as the Cow Belt. This is not particularly a cattle-raising zone (though you may often see stolid black water buffalo lolling on the wayside). It is the heartland of the Holy Cow, the conservative Hindu stronghold, as well as being a bastion of Muslim culture.

Punjab, closer to Pakistan, is home to proud Sikhs and prosperous Jat farmers. Radiating around Ladakh and in high Himalayan valleys, refugee Tibetan communities maintain their rituals and traditional dress. India's elite enrols its children in up-country boarding schools, well away from the distractions of the city.

Despite satellite TV, North India resists an overwhelming same-ness. Delhi is grand with monuments and its buzz as the seat of gov-ernment, as well as its mosques or bazaars. Rajasthan provides a spectacle of camels, veiled women and enormous turbans. Polo is played on elephant-back while peacocks flutter the eyes in their tails.

Jammu and Kashmir's heartbreaking beauty is defined by lakes, orchards and snowy peaks, while Agra is home to the Taj Mahal, one of the world's great monuments to love.   ❏

LEFT: balancing jars of well water to be used for cleaning one of the many 15th-century Jain temples at Ranakpur, Rajasthan.

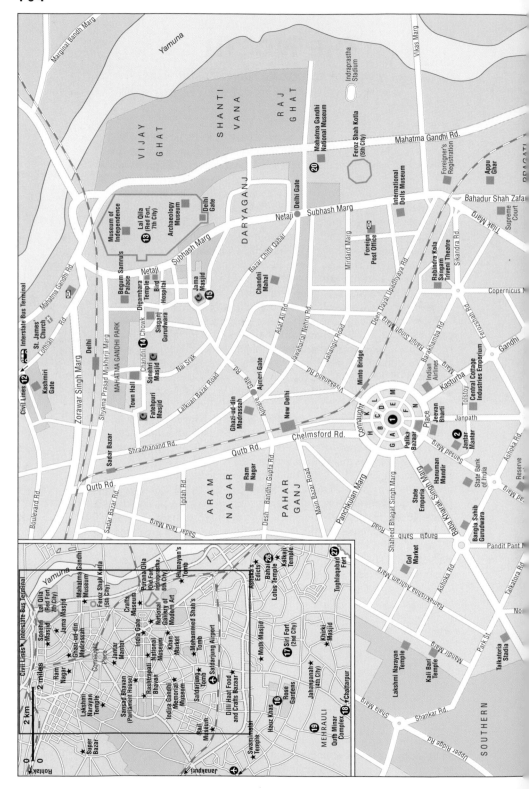

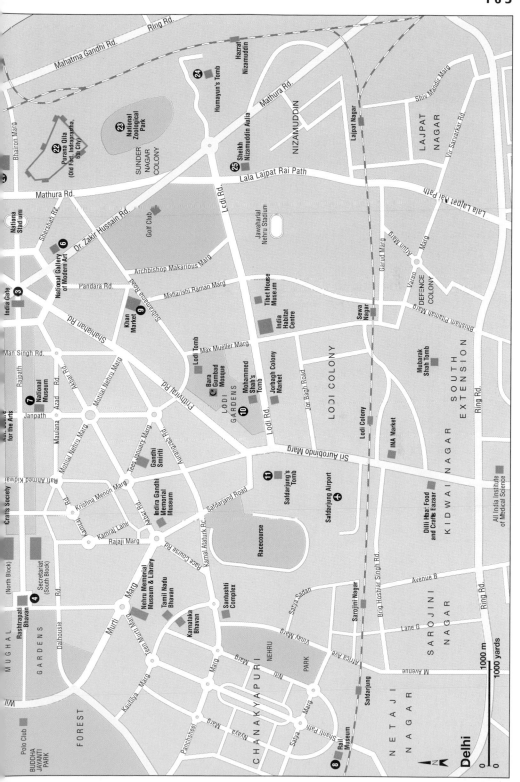

Delhi

DELHI

The capital of India presents a captivating combination of ancient and modern. As a major cultural centre, Delhi offers a glimpse of the diversity of the country's many states

Map on pages 164–5

Delhi is the political and administrative centre of the world's largest democracy. It has a population of more than 13.7 million and covers 1,500 sq km (579 sq miles). Presenting a curious mixture of old and new, this sprawling city has two main parts, Old Delhi (former Shahjahanabad) and New Delhi (the former British capital), consisting of ancient villages and sites that have been engulfed by newer residential areas (colonies). The city struggles to cope with the effects of expansion – pollution, traffic congestion, shortages of water and power, continual construction – and an extreme climate. Recent positive moves include the conversion of all public transport from diesel to compressed natural gas, and the opening of the first stages of a metro system. There are three lines, which are constantly expanding – visit www.delhimetrorail.com to check their progress. Line 1 runs from Shahdara across the Yamuna to Kashmiri Gate before heading north to Rithala. Line 2, of more use to visitors, runs from Vishwa Vidyalaya in the north, crossing line 1 at Kashmiri Gate, before running down to the Central Secretariat via Connaught Place. Line 3 runs from Barakhamba to Dwarka.

Ancient cities of Delhi

Strategically located between the Aravalli hills and the Yamuna river, Delhi has been the site of more than a dozen cities. It is named after an earlier settlement, "Dillika". The first of the cities was Indraprastha, legendary capital of the Pandavas, epic heroes of the *Mahabharata*. Recent excavations at Purana Qila (Old Fort) date the settlement to between the 1st century BC and the 4th century AD.

The next documented city was Lal Kot, founded in the 8th century AD by Tomara Rajputs. It was captured and renamed Qila Rai Pithora by the Chauhan Rajputs in the 12th century. Later it was occupied by the Slave King Qutb-ud-din, who founded the Delhi Sultanate and began construction of the Qutb Minar. The monuments and ruins from this era stand in and around the Qutb Minar complex in South Delhi. The ruins of Siri, a capital established by the Turkish Ala-ud-Din Khilji, can be seen around Hauz Khas colony. In 1320 Ghias-ud-Din Tughlaq moved to his fortress city of Tughlaqabad, east of Qutb Minar. His tomb, overrun by monkeys, stands across the road from the ruins.

Ferozabad, once the richest city in the world, was founded in 1351 by his successor, Feroz Shah Tughlaq, on the banks of the River Yamuna. The ruins of his palace and other monuments are situated in Feroz Shah Kotla, south of the memorials on the Ring Road.

They were followed by the Sayyids and the Lodis, whose tombs stand in Lodi Gardens, south of India Gate. Their defeat by the Central Asian invader Babur, in the 16th century, marked the end of the Delhi Sul-

LEFT: crowds on the streets of Old Delhi.
BELOW: at the mosque of the Qutb Minar.

tanate and the dawn of the Mughal Empire. Din-Panah fort (Purana Qila) was built above the Yamuna River by Babur's son, the studious Humayun, who was forced to flee by Sher Shah, an Afghan invader. Sher Shah began constructing his new capital of Shergarh, but Humayun won back Delhi in 1555 only to die a few months later when he fell down his library stairs. Akbar, Humayun's son, moved his capital to Agra. His grandson, Shah Jahan, builder of the Taj Mahal, returned to Delhi in 1638 to build the glorious Shahjahanabad. This walled capital, bound by 14 gates, included most of Old Delhi, Jama Masjid (Friday Mosque), the bazaars around Chandni Chowk and Lal Qila (Red Fort) from where he ruled his empire. Successive invasions from Persia reduced the power of the Mughals until the British took over Delhi in the 19th century.

In 1911, during the visit of King George V, Delhi was declared the capital of the British Empire in India. The present city of New Delhi, designed by Edwin Lutyens and Herbert Baker, was completed by 1931.

Lutyens' Delhi

The circular shopping arcade of **Connaught Place** ❶ (properly Rajiv Chowk) forms the heart of modern Delhi. The colonnaded corridors were built for the British to shop in style. Concentric roads create an inner, middle and outer circle lined with shops, restaurants, street stalls and cinemas. The underground **Palika Bazaar** on the Outer Circle has tiny shops overflowing with tourist tat and touts. The tourist theme continues to the north, with the backpackers' ghetto of **Paharganj Bazaar**, opposite New Delhi Railway Station, which offers cheap food and accommodation, and colourful shops: most of which is best avoided.

To the west, Baba Kharak Singh Marg has a row of State Government Emporia

New Delhi Station can be confusing at first; ignore all the touts trying to distract you and then, to avoid the queues for tickets, go in the main entrance and up the stairs on the right to the helpful Tourist Bureau.

BELOW: Rashtrapati Bhavan and North and South Blocks seen from Rajpath.

where regional handicrafts are sold at regulated prices. Also here is the popular Coffee Home cafe. Opposite is **Hanuman Mandir**, a temple dedicated to the monkey god Hanuman, much revered by wrestlers. At the end of this road, to the left, rises the golden dome of **Bangla Sahib Gurudwara**, the city's principle Sikh Temple. Going southwest along Sansad Marg (Parliament Street) is the red sandstone **Jantar Mantar ❷**, an open-air observatory built by Maharaja Jai Singh I of Jaipur (open sunrise to sunset), a focal point for political protests. To the south, **Janpath** is popular for its street stalls, Tibetan market, women from western India peddling embroidered fabrics and the huge **Central Cottage Industries Emporium** (CCIE), which offers a glimpse of the wide range of handicrafts available in India.

Kasturba Gandhi Marg leads southeast to India Gate past the cultural centres of the UK and the US, which have good libraries and reading rooms in addition to cultural programmes. To the southeast, Barakhamba (Twelve Pillar) Road leads to the cultural circle with **Rabindra Kala Sangam**, **Triveni Theatre** and cafe, and various auditoria hosting regular performances of dance, music and theatre.

The area around **India Gate ❸** formed the British administrative centre of Delhi with the local "Champs Elysées" of **Rajpath** surrounded by lawns and shady trees, water channels and fountains. India Gate, a 42-metre (138-ft) high archway, was built by Lutyens at the eastern end in 1931 to honour Indian soldiers who died during World War I and on the Northwest Frontier.

Rashtrapati Bhavan ❹, the presidential residence (former Viceregal Lodge), can be seen at the western end of Rajpath with the circular **Sansad Bhavan ❺** (Parliament House) nearby. Flanking the approach to Rashtrapati Bhavan are the North and South Block Secretariats, housing the Ministries of Finance and Home Affairs, and Ministries of Foreign Affairs respectively. At the eastern end of Rajpath (by India Gate) are two magnificent residences, **Hyderabad House** and **Baroda** House, built for the two most powerful rulers of the so-called princely states of British India. Beyond India Gate lies the National Stadium.

South of Rashtrapati Bhavan is Teen Murti Bhavan (open Tues–Sun 10am–3pm; free), which houses the **Jawarharlal Nehru Memorial Museum** in the prime minister's former residence. Nehru's study, sitting room and bedroom have been preserved and there is a very detailed exhibition of the history of the Independence struggle. The modesty of the interiors reflects well on one of India's greatest leaders.

The story of the Nehru/Gandhi dynasty is continued at the **Indira Gandhi Memorial Museum** (open Tues–Sun 9.30am–5pm; free) at 1 Safdarjang Road. This bungalow was her residence and the place where she was killed by her bodyguards. Blood stains are still visible at the spot in the gardens. Inside you can see her study and her wedding sari, woven by Nehru. Close by, on Tees January Marg, is the site of another political assassination, the **Gandhi Smriti** (open Tues–Sun 9am–5.30pm), museum and memorial, in the house of the industrialist G.D. Birla. In the garden, the place where Mahatma Gandhi was shot in 1948 is marked by a simple memorial.

Southeast of India Gate is the **National Gallery of Modern Art ❻** (open Tues–Sun 10am–5pm; free), in the former Delhi home of Jaipur's royal family. Its per-

Map on pages 164–5

The Rabindra Kala Sangam on Mandi House Chowk also contains the contemporary art gallery of the Lalit Kala Akademi and the Sangeet Natak Akademi museum of musical instruments.

BELOW: Jantar Mantar, the open-air observatory.

Avoid visiting Lal Qila on Sunday, if possible, when the Chandni Chowk bazaars are closed and the fort is very crowded.

manent collection includes 1930s paintings by Jamini Roy and Nandalal Bose and 18th-century Indian landscapes by Thomas and William Daniell. The ground floor is devoted to contemporary Indian artists. The **National Museum** ❼ (open Tues–Sun 10am–5pm; entrance fee; www.nationalmuseumindia.gov.in), south of Rajpath on Janpath, is noted for its Indian sculpture and jewellery collections, Chola bronzes and a Buddhist gallery, including a carved Buddhist gateway from Sanchi. Especially good, on the second floor, is the Verrier Elwin collection of Adivasi art, from northeastern, central and southern Indian states.

Southwest of Rajpath is **Chanakyapuri**, the diplomatic enclave where the majority of foreign missions and embassies are located. The **Rail Museum** ❽ (open Oct–Mar 9.30am–5pm, Apr–Sept 9.30am–7.30pm; entrance fee; www.rail-museum.org), just off Shanti Path, is worth a visit. There are some interesting period coaches and a large array of steam engines, including the huge Garratt, built in 1930 in Manchester; there is also an unusual working steam monorail. Nearby is the **Santushti Complex** (opposite the Ashoka Hotel), with shops of Indian designers and the pleasant Basil and Thyme restaurant.

Around Lodi Gardens

South of India Gate lie most of the sites of the former cities of Delhi and many good shopping areas, such as **Khan Market** ❾, which has good bookshops and up-market stores selling everything for the house, including fresh flowers.

A short walk southwest along Subramania Road brings you to the beautiful **Lodi Gardens** ❿ (open sunrise to sunset), with fascinating tombs set in well-maintained lawns lined with rows of flowerbeds, immense trees, a bridge and walkways. At the Lodi Road end is the octagonal tomb of the Sayyid ruler **Muhammad Shah** (1434–44), and by the lake near Subramania Road is another octagonal tomb, of Sikandar Lodi (1489–1517). In the centre of the gardens is the large Shish Gumbad, another tomb from the Lodi period.

Cross Lodi Road to **Jorbagh Colony Market** for the Steak House selling a variety of Indian-made natural cheeses (yak's milk, cheddar, mozzarella) and other foodstuffs. C. Lal & Sons sells handicrafts. East along Lodi Road is the **India Habitat Centre**, a cultural and conference centre with offices. Just along from the centre, in the Institutional Area, is the **Tibet House Museum** (open Mon–Fri, 9.30am–5.30pm; free), with some fine exhibits, including *thankas* and Tibetan musical instruments.

Safdarjung's Tomb ⓫ (open sunrise to sunset; entrance fee) and its adjoining rose garden are just across Aurobindo Marg. This huge monument, dating from 1753, is the last significant piece of Mughal architecture to be built in Delhi. Turning south past Safdarjung Airport brings you to the

LAL QILA, THE RED FORT

If there be paradise on the face of earth,
It is this! Oh it is this! Oh it is this!

This Persian couplet by the court poet Amir Khusrau is inscribed on the walls of the Diwan-e-Khas (private audience hall) in the magnificent **Lal Qila** (open Tues–Sun 7am–6.30pm; entrance fee), which once housed the legendary Peacock Throne and the Koh-i-noor diamond (later looted by Persian forces). Shah Jahan, the Mughal emperor, built the immense red sandstone fort with its palaces and halls in 1648. The entry point is Lahori Gate. Inside, passing through the Chatta Chowk covered market, one enters Shah Jahan's elaborate gardens. To the far right is Mumtaz Mahal's former harem and next to it the Rang Mahal (Palace of Colours, open 10am–5pm, closed Fri), and Khas Mahal, the emperor's private apartments. The octagonal tower was used for royal public appearances (including that of Britain's George V and Queen Mary during their visit to India in 1931). Other buildings include the Diwan-e-Am (public audience hall); the royal baths; and the tiny white marble Moti Masjid (Pearl Mosque). Now that the Yamuna has retreated, the fort, originally built on its banks, overlooks a large open ground, previously the site of Chor Bazaar (the thieves' market, now held near the Jama Masjid).

Map on pages 164–5

popular INA fruit and vegetable market consisting of warrens of covered shacks selling meat, fish, poultry and every imaginable household good. Across the road is the **Dilli Haat Food and Crafts Bazaar**, which provides a pavilion for regional craftspeople from all the Indian states and an opportunity to taste their varied cuisine (open 10.30am–10pm; entrance fee) from the very hygienic stalls.

Old Delhi

The peaceful 18th-century **Qudsia Gardens**, near the Inter-State Bus Terminal (ISBT) and Kashmiri Gate, mark the southern boundary of British Delhi (which was strung out to the east of the Northern Ridge) with its cantonment bungalows and administrative buildings of the **Civil Lines** ⑫ and the **University** campus. South of the gardens lies Mughal **Shahjahanabad**, Delhi's seventh city, with the spectacular **Lal Qila** ⑬ (Red Fort, *see box opposite*) facing Chandni Chowk (meaning moonlit or silver crossroads), once the central avenue of an ancient bazaar that is still an important commercial centre.

Each side street around **Chandni Chowk** ⑭ has its own speciality: silver and gold at Dariba Kalan, wedding paraphernalia and theatrical props at Kinari Bazaar, silk saris, copper and brassware and a fascinating wholesale spice market (with dry fruit and nuts from Kabul) at Naya Bazaar. On Main Street is **Digambara Temple**, the oldest Jain Temple in Delhi, and the **Bird Hospital**, where injured birds are nursed back to health.

The **Sisganj Gurudwara** (Sikh temple), **Sunehri Masjid** (Golden Mosque), and **Fatehpuri Masjid** (1650) are some of the sites crowded between stalls selling a jumble of wares, street photographers using ancient cameras, and hawkers and touts. The famous sweetmeat shop of **Ghantewala**, established

The temple of Sisganj Gurudwara in Old Delhi is dedicated to the guru Tegh Bahadur, who was killed by Aurangzeb in the 17th century for refusing to give up his faith.

BELOW: view of Old Delhi from Jama Masjid minaret.

Old Delhi's Jama Masjid throngs with people every Friday, the Muslim day of prayer.

BELOW: Purana Qila, Delhi's third city.

in 1790, is worth a visit. Specialities include *sohn halva* and *sohn papri* (caramelised sweets made with clarified butter). South of Central Road, follow Dariba Kalan to the massive red sandstone and white marble **Jama Masjid**  (Friday Mosque), the focal point for Delhi's Muslims. Commissioned by Shah Jahan in 1644, the mosque can hold 20,000 people in its huge courtyard, in the centre of which is a tank used for ritual ablutions. The mosque and fort, opposite each other, were integral to the complex plan of the walled city.

South Delhi

Hauz Khas Village ⑯, poised at the edge of a 14th-century water reservoir, and *madrasa* and tomb of Feroze Shah Tughlaq, is south along Aurobindo Marg from Lodi Gardens. Although the village has been transformed into an enclave of expensive boutiques, art galleries (particularly good is the Village Gallery which has a wide selection of modern and contemporary Indian art), and restaurants, it still retains much of its greenery and charm. Traditional dance performances are sometimes held here in the evenings.

Monuments dot the area: the ruins of **Siri Fort** ⑰, now very overgrown and difficult to see, stand near the Asian Games Village complex to the east (open only to members). Southwards on Aurobindo Marg, past the Outer Ring Road and Aurobindo Ashram, stands **Qutb Minar Complex** ⑱ (open sunrise to sunset; entrance fee). This remarkable 72-metre (278-ft) high tower, engraved with verses from the Koran, was built in the 13th century by Qutb-ud-Din-Aibak, the first Muslim sultan of Delhi, to celebrate his victory over the Hindu kings. In the grounds, Aibak's **Quwwat-ul-Islam Mosque** is believed to be the oldest in India, built using parts of demolished Hindu and Jain temples. In the mosque courtyard is a 4th-century iron pillar, remarkable for having never shown any sign of corrosion. The ruins of **Lal Kot**, Delhi's first city, are also in this area.

Other historic sites dot **Mehrauli Village** ⑲ to the west amid a labyrinth of old Indian bazaars. Further west on Gurgaon Road the tombs of **Jamali Kamali**, noted for their coloured ceilings, and a giant statue of Mahavira face each other. Turn south again to see the spectacular modern temples and ashram complexes of **Chattarpur**. These offer courses in yoga, naturotherapy, colour therapy, pyramid power and more traditional religious studies.

On the banks of the Yamuna

Eastward, behind the Red Fort, the Ring Road along the River Yamuna is connected by three bridges to the Trans-Yamuna residential areas. On the river bank from Red Fort south to ITO Bridge are the cremation grounds, now memorial parks dedicated to national leaders such as Nehru, Lal Bahadur Shastri, Indira and Rajiv Gandhi. The biggest complex here is **Rajghat** where Mahatma Gandhi was cremated, and there are two museums dedicated to him here. **Gandhi Darshan** (open Tues–Sun 10am–5pm; free; www.gandhismriti.nic.in) has a good collection of paintings and photos, and charts the history of the *Satyagraha* (non-violence) movement. Close by is **Gandhi Smarak Sangrahalaya** (open Fri–Wed 9.30am–

Map on pages 164–5

5.30pm; free; www.gandhismriti.nic.in), which houses a display of Gandhi's personal belongings and has a library of recordings of his speeches.

Further south is **Pragati Maidan** – a huge exhibition complex – site of the Appu Ghar entertainment park. The adjoining **Crafts Museum** ㉑ (open Tues–Sun 10am–5pm; entrance fee) has demonstrations by regional craftsmen, huts built in regional styles and a good crafts shop. The fascinating exhibition galleries have displays of Adivasi art, woodcarving and textiles. There are *bhuta* figures from Karnataka, brightly decorated Naga objects from the northeast and some wonderful bronzes from Orissa. The textile galleries are superb – the collections run to over 22,000 objects – as well as some astounding, especially the Kashmiri, examples of embroidery. There are also weaving demonstrations.

Facing its entrance stand the ramparts of the **Purana Qila** ㉒ (open sunrise to sunset; entrance fee; daily "Light and Sound Show"), with panoramic views of the city. The fort was built by Afghan ruler Sher Shah Suri (1540–45) and was taken over by Mughal Emperor Humayun when he regained the throne in 1555–56. Its Qila-e-Kunha-Masjid is the best preserved Lodi mosque in Delhi. The **Sher Mandal** pavilion, library and a lake (once part of the moat) surround the fort.

Delhi Zoo ㉓ is next door. Indian zoos are particularly depressing, resembling concentration and torture camps rather than, at best, places to breed endangered species (for further information visit www.petaindia.com, www.aapn.org and www.zoocheck.com). The zoo shares a border with the wealthy **Sunder Nagar colony**, with a market famous for antique/reproduction shops and sweet stalls.

Mathura Road leads to **Humayun's Tomb** ㉔ (open sunrise to sunset; entrance fee). Set in beautiful gardens, the red sandstone monument is the finest Mughal building in Delhi and the prototype for the Taj Mahal. It was commissioned by Humayun's senior widow, Bega Begum, and completed in 1565. Also in the grounds are the remains of the octagonal tomb of Isa Khan. To the north, easily visible from the gardens, is the modern Damdama Sahib Gurudwara.

Close by is the shrine, or *dargah*, of the Sufi saint of the Chisti order, **Sheikh Nizamuddin Aulia** ㉕ (1236–1325), after whom the surrounding colonies are named. The *dargah* is a haven of peace in this busy Muslim area; the tomb of the saint is in a pavilion with beautiful marble screens (note: women are not allowed in the tomb itself). Also buried here are the Mughal Emperor Muhammad Shah (1719–48) and the saint's disciple and poet Amir Khusrau.

South of Nizamuddin, the modern white marble, lotus-shaped **Baha'i Lotus Temple** ㉖ (open Apr–Sept Tues–Sun 9am–7pm, Oct–Mar Tues–Sun 9.30am– 5.30pm; free) stands on Kalkaji Hill. This was completed in 1986 as a pilgrimage site for the Baha'i sect. Visitors must walk barefoot. Nearby, the colony markets (M & N Block) of Greater Kailash offer good shopping and restaurants.

South, on the Mehrauli-Badarpur road, the 14th-century ruins of **Tughlaqabad Fort** (open sunrise to sunset) and **Adilabad** ㉗, Delhi's third city, dominate the landscape. Remains of ramparts, water-storage tanks and subterranean passages can be explored, but this area can be dangerous to visit alone. ❑

The reinstigated Delhi–Lahore bus service leaves twice a week (on Tuesdays and Fridays) from the Dr Ambedkar Bus Terminal at Delhi Gate, close to Rajghat.

BELOW: studying at Humayun's tomb.

Map on page 176

UTTAR PRADESH

Spread out across the plains of the Ganga, the great state of Uttar Pradesh contains some of the most sacred sites of Buddhist and Hindu culture

Uttar Pradesh, with 166 million inhabitants, would be the seventh most populous country in the world if it were independent. As it is, the state is the heartland of the world's largest democracy and politics here are lively. UP has a broad industrial base but is still predominantly agricultural, with wheat, maize, rice and sugar cane among the main crops. Uttar Pradesh means "northern state" and it is made up of two regions. The largest part of the state covers the rich, alluvial plain of the Ganga and its tributaries. To the south are the Vindhya hills and the plateau of peninsular India. Although UP is famous worldwide for the Taj Mahal at Agra, it attracts devout Hindus to the many pilgrimage places along the River Ganga, which flows through the holy cities of Allahabad and Varanasi. Buddhists are drawn to the deer park at Sarnath where the Buddha preached his first sermon. Fifteen percent of the population is Muslim and in addition to historic mosques and Sufi shrines, UP has some of the most prestigious Muslim theological colleges.

Agra: city of the emperors

The old part of **Agra ❶**, 204 km (127 miles) southeast of Delhi, is like a medieval city, with narrow lanes and colourful shops selling local handicrafts, especially gold and silver thread embroidery and imitation Mughal inlay on marble. Among its culinary specialities is *petha*, crystallised pumpkin. The city achieved greatness first under the Mughals, and particularly the emperors Akbar (1556–1605), Jahangir (1605–27) and Shah Jahan (1628–58).

Agra Fort (open 6am–6.30pm, entrance fee), on the banks of the River Yamuna, began to take shape from 1564. Akbar constructed the 2.4-km (1½-mile) surrounding walls of local sandstone. It was said of Agra Fort that "from top to bottom the fire-red stones, linked by iron rings, are joined so closely that even a hair cannot find a way into their joints". Of Akbar's "500 edifices of red stones in the fine styles of Bengal and Gujarat" only the Jahangiri Mahal still stands. This was the main part of the women's quarters, constructed in a local Indian style to suit the needs of the emperor's Hindu wives. Akbar's other buildings were demolished to make way for the imperial quarters of Shah Jahan, combining Hindu and Islamic styles of architecture. The Mussaman Burj (Octagonal Tower) is said to be the place where Shah Jahan lay on his deathbed gazing out at the Taj Mahal.

The tomb of **Itimad-ud-Daula** (open sunrise to sunset; entrance fee), across the river from the fort, is the most intimate of the three great monuments in Agra. Itimad-ud-Daula was father-in-law and *vazir* (principal minister) to Emperor Jahangir. Nur Jahan, Jahangir's queen, undertook the construction of her father's tomb (1622–28) using white marble inlaid with coloured

BELOW: a *jali* screen on the tomb of Salim Chisti.

stone. Also on the east side of the river, hidden behind the lovely nurseries along Aligarh Road, are the **Chini ka Rauza**, the tomb of Afzal Khan, a courtier to Jahangir and Shah Jahan, and, further on, the **Aram Bagh**, gardens believed to have been laid out by the Emperor Babur (both sites open sunrise–sunset).

Within sight of Agra Fort, the **Taj Mahal** (open Sat–Thur 6am–7.30pm; entrance fee) stands in a Mughal garden on a terrace beside a bend in the Yamuna. It is the tomb of Mumtaz Mahal, wife of Emperor Shah Jahan. She was married to him for 19 years, during which she accompanied him on his military campaigns and shared his confidence on all matters of state. She bore 13 children, seven of whom, including the next emperor, Aurangzeb, survived into adulthood. In 1631 she died in childbirth. Shah Jahan was desolate and built the Taj Mahal in her honour *(see box)*. He was later deposed by Aurangzeb and imprisoned in Agra Fort.

Fatehpur Sikri: Akbar's capital

Early morning is the best time to visit **Fatehpur Sikri ❷** (open sunrise to sunset; entrance fee), Akbar's imperial capital, 35 km (20 miles) southwest of Agra. The well-preserved remains include the palace and the royal Jama Masjid (mosque) where the Sufi saint Shaikh Salim Chisti is buried. Akbar is said to have visited the saint on this site when he was anxious for an heir. He was told that he would have three sons, and when his words came true Akbar chose Sikri for his capital.

Fatehpur, "town of victory", was built of sandstone quarried from the hill on which it stood. It was only occupied for 14 years before Akbar shifted his capital to Lahore. Everyone at Fatehpur Sikri will tell you that it was because the water ran out, but it may also have been for strategic reasons. The palace buildings draw on the style of local Indian architecture, with the craftsmen replicating wooden houses

The system of entrance fees in Agra is quite complicated. Levies are charged by the Agra Development Authority (ADA) and the Archaeological Survey of India (ASI). Presently there is a 500 rupee ADA ticket, valid for one day, that covers the Taj, Fort, Fatehpur Sikri, the Itimad-ud-Daula, Sikandra and Aram Bagh. The ASI charges a further fee of between 100 and 250 rupees for each site.

BELOW: entrance to the Taj Mahal, Agra.

TAJ MAHAL

In terms of design the Taj Mahal marks the summation of Mughal architecture. Its proportions are stunningly simple. Its height is equal to the width of the plinth on which it stands. The height of its facade is equal to the height of the bulbous double dome above it.

Built between 1631 and 1648 by Emperor Shah Jahan to house the tomb of his beloved wife Mumtaz Mahal, the plan owes much to Humayun's tomb in Delhi. It is believed to have been designed by Ustad Ahmad Lahori, a master architect. White marble, brought from Makrana 300 km (186 miles) away in Rajasthan, adds to its ethereal beauty. So do the floral decorations, bands of black marble Arabic caligraphy, and carved marble screens. The queen's tomb is complemented by the four minarets, which lean slightly outward so as not to fall on the main building in the event of an earthquake. To the west of the enclosure is a mosque, to the east its replica, known as the *javab* (reply). It cannot be used for prayer as its central arch does not face Mecca.

According to legend, Shah Jahan planned to build a similar tomb for himself out of black marble, but it remained a dream. He is buried in the Taj Mahal beside his wife. The colour of the white marble varies with the light and, if you have time, try and see it at different times of day.

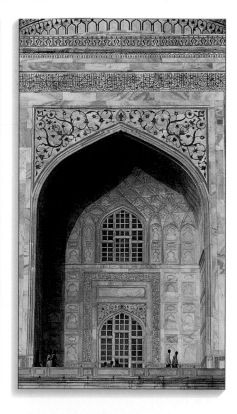

in stone. The finest monuments include Diwan-e-Khas where Akbar debated religious matters; the Turkish sultan's house with its minute carvings; Mariam's house with its wall paintings; and the Jama Masjid (free).

Akbar also designed his own resting place. The tomb, completed in 1613, is at **Sikandra** (open sunrise–sunset; entrance fee), 12 km (7 miles) northwest of Agra. The mausoleum is four storeys high; the first three are of red sandstone, the fourth of white marble containing the false tomb of the emperor. The real tomb, as in all such mausoleums, is in a crypt below. Blackbuck wander the gardens.

Braj

The area around **Mathura** ❸, on the banks of the River Yamuna, 30 km (19 miles) north of Agra on the Delhi road, is known as Braj and is popularly believed to have been the birthplace and home of Lord Krishna, who in one of the greatest Hindu texts, the *Bhagavad Gita*, explains the world and how best to live in it. According to legend, the young Krishna was brought up in a family of

On the High Gate of Fatehpur Sikri's mosque is a verse from the Koran: "Said Jesus, on whom be peace: The world is but a bridge; pass over it but build no houses on it."

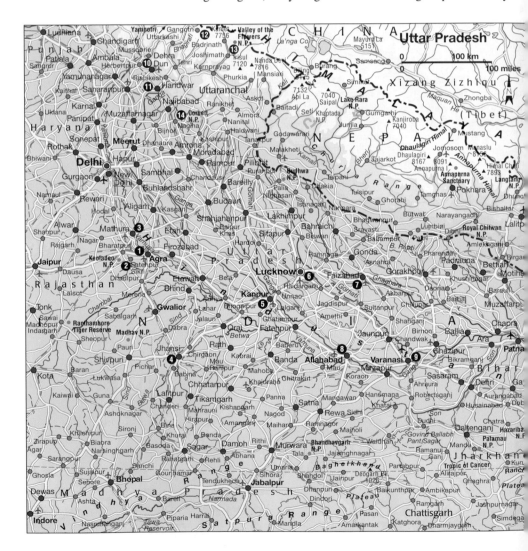

Map on page 176

cowherds, where he performed miracles for the good of the villagers, and played tricks on them, and where all the *gopis* (milkmaids) fell helplessly in love with him. He was, Hindus believe, an incarnation of the god Vishnu.

Mathura today is an industrial town notable for its oil refinery. Its highlights include the **Kesava Deo Mandir**, built on the spot where Krishna was born; the stepped tank where his clothes were washed, **Potara Kund**; and the numerous riverside ghats, of which **Vishram Ghat** is best known. Pilgrims gather to bathe at the ghats on the Yamuna and to visit temples such as the **Dvarkadhish shrine** in the crowded marketplace. Around the town are numerous sites associated with Vishnu. The most impressive is **Vrindavan**, 10 km (6 miles) north of Mathura, home to many Hindu widows who earn a tiny sum each day singing hymns to the Lord. Among the fine temples are those to **Govind-dev** (1590); **Jugal Kishor**, **Radha-Vallabh** and **Madan-Mohan** (17th century); **Ranganathji** and **Shahji** (19th century); the **Bankebehari shrine**; and the temple of **Pagal Baba**. Mathura was once a thriving centre of Buddhism and Jainism. Sculptures made by local artists between the 2nd century BC and the 6th century AD are on display at the museum (open Tues–Sun, July–Apr 10.30am–4.30pm; May–June 7.30am–12.30pm).

Every year in Mathura and Vrindavan scenes from the life of Lord Krisna are enacted. These are known as "Ras Lilas".

Southern Uttar Pradesh

The area bordering Madhya Pradesh can be explored from **Jhansi** ❹, 188 km (117 miles) south of Agra. Jhansi is dominated by its hill fort (open dawn to dusk), from where the Rani of Jhansi, one of the heroines of the popular uprising against the British in 1857, directed her operations. There is a museum here (open Tues–Sun, July–Mar 10.30am–4.30pm; Apr–June 7.30am–12.30pm).

From Jhansi it's a three-hour drive east to the village of **Khajuraho** (in Madhya Pradesh), renowned for its 1,000-year-old temples and erotic carvings *(see page 290)*. The pilgrimage centre of **Chitrakut**, 235 km (146 miles) east of Jhansi, looks like a mini-Varanasi, with ghats on the banks of the narrow Mandakani River.

Central and Eastern UP

The route from Delhi, 446 km (277 miles) east to the state capital of Lucknow, passes through Aligarh, site of the Aligarh Muslim University founded by Sir Syed Ahmad Khan in 1875 to provide the Muslim community of India with a modern, scientific education.

Kanpur ❺, on the Ganga 70 km (44 miles) southwest of Lucknow, is the state's leading industrial city. In the uprising of 1857 the British garrison at Kanpur was besieged by Indian forces, and in the face of starvation agreed to an offer of safe passage. As they crossed the river bank they were massacred. **All Souls' Memorial Church** (1875) contains the names of those who died.

Lucknow

Uttar Pradesh's state capital, **Lucknow** ❻, a two hour journey from Kanpur, stands on the Gomti river, a tributary of the Ganga. It was once a city of gardens but many have disappeared under the onslaught of offices, shopping centres and residential colonies.

If you enter the city via the airport at Amausi, you will pass **Dilkusha**, a former royal hunting lodge

BELOW: the Jama Masjid Fatehpur Sikri, Akbar's capital city.

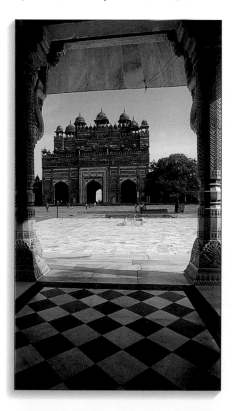

Jama Masjid,
Lucknow, built by
Mohammad Ali
Shah in the
mid-19th century.

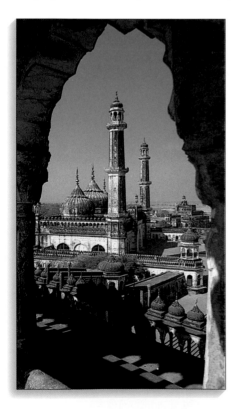

designed like a Ruritarian castle and a key site in the 1857 uprising. Several British officers died here, including General Havelock, who is buried in the **Alambagh**.

La Martinière College, one of the city's most extravagant estates, lies on its eastern outskirts. It was built as a home for the French businessman adventurer Claude Martin, who bequeathed his huge fortune to the running of educational institutions for Anglo-Indians. In front of Constantia, the college's main building, is the Lord Cornwallis, a canon cast by Claude Martin and used in the Battle of Seringapatam against Tipu Sultan. Major Hodson, who killed the sons of the last Mughal emperor Bahadur Shah in Delhi, is buried in the park, as is Martin's Indian wife Martin himself is buried in the basement of Constantia. Visitors are welcomed but permission must be granted by the Principal's office at the college's east end.

Heading west there is Claude Martin's former armoury, now the state governor's residence, and beyond it the Anglican Church, post office and state legislature, built in 1932 when the capital of Oudh was shifted from Allahabad to Lucknow. Nearby is Lucknow's main shopping area, **Hazratganj**, the Gentleman's Market. On Hazratganj itself is the **Imambara Sibtainabad**, built by the last nawab Wajid Ali Shah as a mausoleum for his father.

Heading north from Hazratganj on Shah Najaf Marg is the Shah Najaf Imambara and **Sikandarbargh**, a 24-hectare (60-acre) botanical garden named after the Nawab's wife. West, along Rana Pratap Marg, is **Kurshid Manzil**, shaped like a moated English castle, now the La Martinière Girls School. Adjoining it is the **Taron Wali Kothi**, the Nawab's observatory, now the State Bank of India.

Heading west towards the Residency, you pass Farhat Baksh, Claude Martin's principal residence, now the Central Drug Research Institute (no entry permitted). All of this area, as it leads to the Residency, was the scene of ferocious fighting during the Great Uprising.

The **Residency Compound** is a complex that housed about 3,000 mostly European residents prior to the Siege of Lucknow in 1857. After the five-month conflict only 1,000 of these inhabitants were still alive. The buildings are part of a **museum** marking this event (open 8am–5pm; entrance fee).

About a 2 km (1 mile) west is the **Bara Imambara** (open 8.30am–6pm, closed during Muharrum entrance fee). This architectural marvel contains an entertaining maze on the upper floor. Built in the time of famine in 1784 as a food-for-work programme without steel, cement or pillars, it nevertheless has a hall 50 metres (163 feet) long with acoustics so good you can hear a paper tear at the other end. Its maintenance is by the Hussainabad Trust and a single ticket allows you to visit this and the **Hussainabad Imambara** next to it, with its fabulous chandeliers and silver pulpit, the Picture Gallery housing portraits of the Nawabs, the Hussainabad Clock Tower and the Jama Masjid. Also in this area, south of Victoria Park, is the **Chowk**, or the street of the silversmiths, that now sells chikan goods and local handicrafts.

Travelling east

The Nawabs' influence is also apparent at **Faizabad** ❼, 150 km (93 miles) east of Lucknow, and for a while the capital of the province of Avadh. This busy town as fine monuments, including Bahu Begum's tomb and Gulab Bari, the mausoleum of one of the first rulers of Avadh, Shuja-ud-Daula.

Six kilometres (4 miles) further east is the temple town of **Ayodhya**, standing on the banks of the Ghaghara River. This is believed by Hindus to be the capital and birthplace of Lord Rama, another incarnation of Vishnu and hero of the *Ramayana* epic. Popular devotion to Rama increased in the 16th century after Tulsi Das wrote his great version of the *Ramayana* in Avadhi – the language of the people. The Nawabs of Avadh and their courtiers gave donations to various temples, and the oldest and most beautiful buildings of Ayodhya date from this period. One of the most notable is **Hanumangarhi**, the fort of Hanuman, the monkey god, greatest devotee of Rama, and Sita. Steep steps lead up to the main temple (open dawn to dusk) and monkeys are ready to snatch offerings from pilgrims' hands. It is run by an order of celibate ascetics, who have a militant history and are fond of wrestling. The peace of the town was broken in 1992 when Hindu extremists demolished a mosque that they believed stood on the birthplace of Rama, "Ram Janambhoomi".

Gorakhpur, 130 km (80 miles) east of Faizabad, is named after Guru Gorakhnath, a pre-medieval saint, whose temple and *matha* (monastery) stand here. During the Khichri Mela, which climaxes on 14 January each year, villagers offer rice and lentils, which are thrown onto a pile in front of an image of the saint.

Buddhist sites

Khushinagar, 53 km (33 miles) east of Gorakhpur, is identified as the spot where the Buddha left this world and attained *parinirvana* in the 5th or 6th century BC. Here the **Muktabandhana stupa** is said to have been built to preserve the relics of the Buddha by the Mallas who ruled at the time he died. A smaller shrine nearby

Map on page 176

Close to Kanpur, at Bhitargaon, is a brick temple from the 3rd–7th century AD, which is thought to be the oldest such example to survive in its original, though eroded, form.

BELOW: bathing at dawn on the auspicious day of 14 January at the 2001 Kumbh Mela.

Ornate gilded ceiling of Akbar's tomb at Sikandra. The emperor built many forts along the Ganga; remains of the largest can be seen at Allahabad.

BELOW: on the ghats at Varanasi during Holi.

contains a reclining statue of the Buddha. Other pilgrimage sites within reach of Gorakhpur are **Piprahva**, 90 km (56 miles) away, where the Buddha spent his early years, and **Lumbini**, 8 km (5 miles) across the border with Nepal, where he is believed to have been born. To the west, near the Nepal border, is **Sravasti** where the Buddha spent 25 rainy-season days. The founder of the Jain religion, Lord Mahavira, a contemporary of Buddha, was also a frequent visitor to Sravasti. Two Ashokan pillars stand at the gate of the **Jetavana**, the excavated ruins here.

Allahabad

One of the most sacred places of Hinduism is **Allahabad** ❽, 188 km (117 miles) southeast of Kanpur. Here the Yamuna flows into the Ganga. Hindus believe the invisible River Saraswati joins the Ganga at this point. Allahabad is known as "Tirth Raj", the king of pilgrimage places. At the sacred confluence a religious fair, the *Magh Mela*, is held each January and February, and once every 12 years the greatest religious festival of northern India, the *Mahakumbha Mela*, takes place. To bathe at the confluence at the most sacred times is said to wash away the sins of many births; in 2001 an estimated 66 million people bathed here. Rowing boats will take you to the spot where the milky waters of the Ganga meet the blue waters of the Yamuna. The city itself is crowded and somewhat dilapidated. **Anand Bhavan** (open Tues–Sun 9.30am–5pm; entrance fee) was the home of the Nehru family and a nerve centre of the independence movement. At **Kausambi**, 45 km (28 miles) away, are the ruins of one of the great metropolitan forts built during the first millennium BC. Courtyard houses were protected by massive walls of burnt brick. Kausambi was occupied from the 8th century BC to the 6th century AD. Its main Buddhist stupa measured 25 metres (80 ft) across.

Varanasi

The most sacred stretch of the Ganga is at **Varanasi** ❾ (Benares), one of the oldest living cities in the world. For more than 2,500 years it has attracted seekers and pilgrims. The heart of the city lies between the streams of the Varuna and the Assi which flow into the Ganga. Varuna and Assi together form the name Varanasi. But the city's other name, "Kashi", probably derives from the Sanskrit "to shine or look brilliant". That light is the god Shiva's, Varanasi is his home. Shiva literally means auspiciousness or happiness and, according to a local saying, every single pebble and stone in Kashi is Shiva. To his devotees, Shiva is the one great God. To die here in his city on the banks of the holy river is to achieve *moksha*, liberation from the cycle of life and death. Death is not hidden in India. It is part of life, and one reason why you find cremation grounds in the very centre of Varanasi.

Dawn on the Ganga is a fabulous sight. The river flows south to north, with the city on the west bank and fields and trees to the east. As the sun rises, the golden rays fall on the innumerable temples and 70 bathing ghats, on the priests under their tilted umbrellas, and devout Hindus taking a purifying dip. The one notable mosque on the skyline was built by the Mughal Emperor Aurangzeb. Rowing boats take visitors along the ghats from Assi in the north to Raj Ghat.

Map on page 176

Within the city, the **Vishvanath temple**, built in the late 18th century, is the main Shiva sanctuary. It is closed to non-Hindus, but visitors can climb surrounding buildings to see the gilded dome. If Siva is king of Varanasi, the goddess Annapurna is queen. Her temple is close to Vishvanath's. She is the perfect mother, a gentle goddess, who provides food *(anna)* and life. Another of the city's busiest temples is in the south and dedicated to Durga, one of its fierce goddess guardians. The temple is often called the **monkey temple** because of the hordes of red macaques which have made it their home.

Nearby is the most popular shrine to the monkey god Hanuman, the **Sankat Mochan**. One of Hanuman's main strengths is to turn away difficulties, and on Tuesdays and Saturdays devotees gather to ask for his help. The chief priest lives in a house overlooking the Ganga on Tulsi Ghat where Gosvami Tulsi Das is said to have written his Ramayana epic.

Across the river is **Ramnagar**, home of the Raja of Benares, whose fort houses a private museum (open summer 9am–noon, 2–5pm, winter 10am–1pm, 2–5pm; entrance fee). He is the patron of the Ramnagar Ram Lila, a traditional month-long enactment of the Ramayana, performed in October and November.

About 6 km (4 miles) to the north of Varanasi is **Sarnath**, the deer park where the Buddha preached his first sermon after attaining enlightenment, and returned to spend the rainy season several times during his life. It is one of the most important Buddhist pilgrimage sites. Most impressive of the ruins is the **Dhamekh Stupa**, which is said to mark the exact spot where the Buddha preached, and an Ashokan pillar (3rd century BC). The lion capital of the pillar, now the emblem of the Government of India, is one of several outstanding exhibits in the nearby museum (open Sat–Thur 10am–5pm; entrance fee). ❑

The narrow galis (alleyways) and busy bazaars of Varanasi are worth exploration. The city is famous for its sweets and richly brocaded silk.

BELOW: bathing ghats on the River Ganga, Varanasi.

Map
on page
176

UTTARAKHAND

This northern state consists of the Himalayas and their foothills,
the Shivaliks, the site of popular hill stations and the forests
of Corbett National Park

The mountain districts to the north of Uttar Pradesh form the region of Uttarakhand and also make up the new state of the same name (known formerly as Uttaranchal) which split off from Uttar Pradesh in 2001. Hinduism regards mountains as the dwelling places of gods, and these Himalayas are especially sacred as the source of the streams that join to form the Ganga and Yamuna rivers. Among the highest peaks is Nanda Devi rising 7,817 metres (25,646 ft) above the Nanda Devi National Park, which is a World Heritage Site owing to its exceptional natural beauty and populations of rare and threatened mammals.

Dehra Dun ⑩ at the foot of the hills is a fast-expanding town and capital of the new state is notable for its prestigious institutions, including the Wildlife Institute of India, the Forest Research Institute and the Indian Military Academy. On a ridge above Dehra Dun is the hill station of **Mussoorie**, home to the Lal Bahadur Shastri National Academy of Administration, which trains entrants to the elite Indian Administrative Service, successor to the British colonial Indian Civil Service.

At **Haridwar** ⑪, 50 km (30 miles) southeast of Dehra Dun, the Ganga flows out of the mountains into the plains, making it one of the seven most sacred cities of India. Like Allahabad, Haridwar hosts a Kumbha Mela religious festival, once every 12 years. The evening *arati* (worship) of the river Ganga is held every day

BELOW: sacred
rivers meet at
Deoprayag in the
Himalayan foothills.

at **Har-ki-Pauri**, the main ghat. **Rishikesh**, a town of temples and ashrams surrounded by forest, is 25 km (15 miles) upstream. The northern part of the town, **Muni-ki-Reti**, is very attractive, and the best views can be seen from either of the two footbridges suspended across the river, the Ram Jhula and the Laksman Jhula.

Sacred sites of the Himalayas

Haridwar, Rishikesh and Dehra Dun are the starting points for pilgrimages to the four most sacred places in the Himalayas: Yamunotri, source of the Yamuna; Gangotri, the source of the Ganga; and the temples of Kedarnath and Badrinath.

Yamunotri can be reached from Dehra Dun or Rishikesh. The road stops 13 km (8 miles) short of the temple at **Hanuman Chatti**. From here there is a trek along the riverbank. Pilgrims cook rice and potatoes in the water of a hot spring near the temple and offer it to the goddess Yamunotri.

The road to **Gangotri** ⑫ runs steeply from Rishikesh to Narendra Nagar, Tehri (where a controversial dam is being built), Uttarkashi, and to Ganga's shrine, Gangotri at 3,140 metres (10,300 ft). From here it's a day's trek to **Gaumukh** ("cow's mouth") where the Ganga springs from the base of a glacier.

The road to **Badrinath**, home of Lord Vishnu, rises slowly from the steep valley of Deoprayag to the old Garhwal capital of **Srinagar**. From here the route leads to **Joshimath**, seat of the great Hindu reformer and sage of the 8th century, Adi Shankaracharya. He is credited with establishing the temples at Badrinath and Kedarnath. The **Narsingh Bhagwan temple** here is the main centre of worship to Vishnu when his shrine at Badrinath is closed during winter. Beyond Joshimath, at Govindghat, is the starting point for treks to the **Valley of the Flowers National Park** ⑬ (best seen June–Aug), carpeted with flowers during the monsoon, and to the modern Sikh temple at **Hemkund**. The road continues up to Badrinath. The route for **Kedarnath** branches off before Badrinath. The shrine here is dedicated to Shiva and contains one of the 12 *Jyotirlingas*, or *lingas* of light. The temple stands at the head of the Mandakani River, in a stunning valley surrounded by snow-covered mountains.

In Kumaon to the east are the popular hill stations of Nainital, Ranikhet and Almora. **Nainital**, built around a lake surrounded by forested hills, was originally the summer capital of the government of United Provinces, as UP and Uttaranchal were known under the British. **Ranikhet**, home of the Kumaon Regiment, is one of the least spoilt of the hill stations. **Almora** is an ideal starting point for exploring the oak forests of **Binsar**, or for visiting the 150 magnificent temples at **Jagesvar**.

The best of the terai forests are in Nainital District in the **Corbett National Park** ⑭ (open mid-Nov–mid-June), 300 km (186 miles) north of Delhi. India's premier national park is populated by tigers (around 137), elephants and deer, and a variety of birds, including the maroon oriole, fairy bluebird, green magpie and red-breasted falconet. The Ramganga River provides a habitat for crocodiles and gharial, as well as the impressive mahseer. The park was named after the hunter-turned-conservationist Jim Corbett. His gung-ho adventures, *The Maneaters of Kumaon* and *The Maneating Leopard of Rudraprayag*, are perennial best-sellers. ❏

The Nehru Institute of Mountaineering in Uttarkashi (tel: 01374 222 123; www.nimindia.org) runs mountaineering courses and can give up-to-date advice on trekking and rafting in the region.

BELOW: pilgrims at the temple in Badrinath.

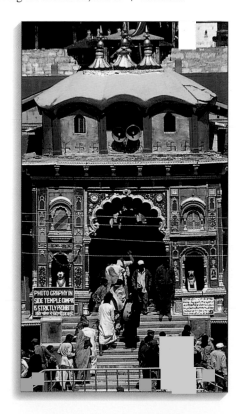

Map
on page
186

BELOW:
Sikh agricultural
labourers, Punjab.

PUNJAB AND HARYANA

The states of Punjab and Haryana form a flat, sunburnt agricultural landscape sloping gently from the Himalayan foothills to the deserts of Rajasthan and the central plains

The Punjab at one time extended northwestward to the River Indus and was known to the Greeks as Pentopotamia, because of the five rivers that ran through it. The Persians named it *Panj* (five) *ab* (waters) – a name which has stuck. In 1947 when India was partitioned, the larger part of Punjab went to Pakistan. Nevertheless, both Pakistan and India retained the name "Punjab" for their respective states since Punjabi is spoken on both sides of the border. In 1966, after Sikh agitation, the Indian, smaller, part was divided into three: Punjab, Haryana and Himachal Pradesh.

The people of the Punjab and Haryana have much in common. The farmers are largely Jatt (to rhyme with gut) or, in Haryana, Jat (to rhyme with part). Tall, brawny and rugged, they are renowned for their pugnacity and fierce attachment to the soil. Townsmen are equally go-ahead as entrepreneurs. While Pakistani Punjabis are Muslims, Indian Punjabis are Sikhs or Hindus. Haryana is predominantly Hindu and its language is a dialect of Hindi.

The climate ranges from bracing cold in winter to scorching heat in summer with winter and summer monsoons. Spring comes with Basant Panchmi, a festival in early February. The countryside becomes an ocean of mustard yellow broken by green squares of sugar cane. As the mustard is harvested, wheat and

barley take its place. The sounds of brown partridges calling to each other and the monotonous *kooh kooh* of flourmills pervade the countryside. Spring gives way to a long summer, with fresh foliage. Silk cotton, coral, flame of the forest and flamboyant trees are a scarlet red; laburnum which flowers in late May is like burnished gold. The partridges are silent; instead the screaming of koels in mango groves and the metallic call of barbets are heard. By the time the wheat is harvested the summer is full on. The blazing inferno lasts from April to the end of June. By mid-July, the monsoon comes and within a few days the heavy downpour turns the land into a swamp. Life begins anew.

By the time the monsoon is over, it is cool again. A new crop of rice, maize, millet and pulses is sown. Traditionally this is the time when farming communities dance *bhangra*, accompanied by the *dhol* (double-headed, cylindrical drum). Through October to the festival of lamps (Divali), usually in November, there is a succession of fairs and festivals. Then once more it is wintertime, when nights are cold, the days full of blue skies and bright sunshine.

"The sun scorches, the earth burns like an oven. Waters give up their vapours, yet it burns and scorches relentlessly." GURU NANAK, 1469–1539, FOUNDER OF SIKHISM

Historical sites

There are several Mughal monuments in Haryana, of which the most popular is **Pinjore Gardens** at the base of the Shivalik hills, 20 km (12 miles) north of Chandigarh on the road to Simla. Inside the Mughal battlements is a beautifully laid out garden with fountains and cascades.

Close to Delhi is **Suraj Kund**, an 8th-century Hindu sun temple, and beyond it the **Badkhal Lake** with a resthouse overlooking its stretch of water. The **Sultanpur Bird Sanctuary**, is 46 km (28 miles) southwest of Delhi *(see page 189)*, and beyond it the hot spring of **Sohna**.

BELOW:
Le Corbusier's
Chandigarh.

Punjab and Haryana contain some of the earliest evidence of Indian societies. Archaeologists have found implements made of quarzite fashioned over 300,000 years ago. Agricultural tools made of copper and bronze prove the existence of rural communities around the 25th century BC. Later excavations have unearthed whole cities built around that period.

Both Punjab and Haryana have more history than historical monuments, more facilities for tourists than places of tourist interest. It is through these two states that invaders from the northwest – Greeks, Turks, Mongols, Persians and Afghans – entered India, and where many battles were fought. Their sites are marked with commemorative stones and mausoleums of kings and commanders. The most famous of these are at **Panipat** (also site of the shrine of the Muslim saint Abu Ali Kalandar) and **Karnal** in Haryana. There are innumerable forts scattered all over the countryside, including those of **Bathinda**, **Faridkot** and **Anandpur Sahib** *(see page 189)*. Both states have developed wildlife sanctuaries along lakes, swamps and rivers, with attractive tourist bungalows.

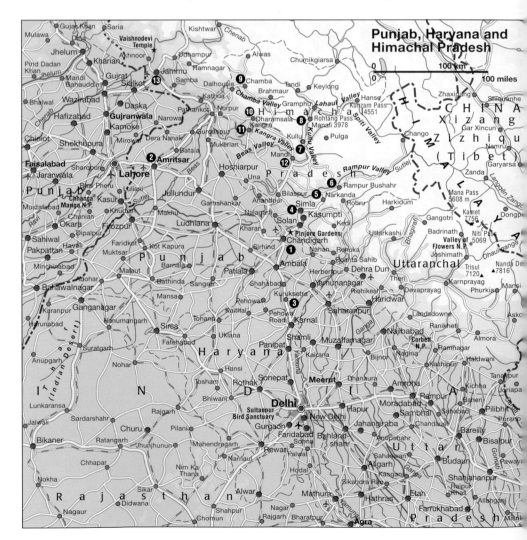

Le Corbusier's city

There are many things that Punjab and Haryana have in common; the most important of these is the common capital, **Chandigarh ❶**. Since both states have laid claims to the city, it is administered by the Central Government as a Union Territory until a final decision regarding its future is made. However, in the same city reside governors of the two states; in the same office buildings but on different floors are their separate secretariats and their respective High Courts. For the visitor, more interesting than the wrangle over its future is the city itself, which is beautifully located below the Shivalik range of hills.

Two hill torrents were tamed to form a large lake with a most attractive boulevard, along which the citizens take the morning and evening air and watch waterfowl which have made **Sukhna Lake** a halting place on their migrations from Central Asia to India and vice versa.

The layout of the city was designed in the mid-20th century by the Swiss-born architect Le Corbusier, assisted by his cousin, Jeanneret, and an English husband-and-wife team, Maxwell Fry and Jane Drew. Le Corbusier himself designed most of its important public buildings, including the **Secretariat**, the **Legislative Assembly** and the **High Court** (for those who are interested in the city's design there is a **City Museum** with displays of the original plans and models). Many of these buildings are on stilts, an architectural style copied by many private institutions and homes. Chandigarh is a very green city with a large variety of flowering trees. It has an extensive **Rose Garden** with more than 1,000 varieties. The **Government Museum and Art Gallery** (open 10am–4.30pm, closed Mon; entrance fee) was also designed by Le Corbusier. It has a good collection of Gandharan sculpture and miniature painting.

Map on page 186

The town of Kalka, just to the north of Chandigarh, is the starting point of the spectacular hill train ride up to Simla in Himachal Pradesh (see pages 151 and 191).

BELOW: Sikh resident of Punjab.

TURBANS

Sikhs wrap up their long hair in distinctive turbans. Typically, they use at least 4.5 metres (5 yards) of cloth, sometimes stitched into a double width. You will see all shapes, colours and sizes. Often the hair is first wrapped into a bun and placed into a hanky. (On casual occasions, the outer turban is left off.) Many Punjabi turbans are tidy, especially compared to the enormous desert turbans seen in Rajasthan up to 7 metres (8 yards) long. Fastidious city Sikhs use a dust cover, like a tea cozy, for two-wheeler rides around town (beard nets are also commonly seen). Motorcycle helmets will not accommodate a turban, so protective goggles are strapped on for safety.

It is considered a humiliating offence to knock someone's turban from his head. Be ready for a fight if you witness this. Abject apology is shown by removing one's own turban and placing it at another man's feet. In hot lands across the Muslim world, turbans protect men from the heat and blows to the head. Persian invaders brought a refined aesthetic to the Mughal courts, with turban gems and feather adornments to indicate status.

Today, Hindus, Muslims and Sikhs all wear varieties of this distinctive headgear. Turbans are macho: women usually drape a large scarf to keep cool.

Chandigarh's top attraction is the popular Rock Garden, a huge sculptural complex made out of recycled and found objects put together by Nek Chand, a local government inspector (open 9am–1pm, 3–7pm).

BELOW: the Golden Temple at Amritsar.

Temples of the Punjab

The Punjab's largest city is **Amritsar ❷** with its **Golden Temple**, the holiest of holy Sikh shrines, and, in the past, a flashpoint for religious and political conflict. The temple was stormed by government troops in 1984.

Amritsar was founded a little over 400 years ago by Guru Ram Das, the fourth of the 10 Sikh Gurus. His son and successor, the fifth guru, Arjun, raised a temple in the middle of a pool, sanctified its waters and installed the Sikhs' holy scripture, the *Granth Sahib*, in its inner sanctum. The city takes its name from the sacred pool – *amrit* (nectar) *sar* (pool). In 1803, the Sikh ruler Maharaja Ranjit Singh (1780–1839) rebuilt the temple in marble and gold. Ever since, it has been known as the Golden Temple. The Sikhs refer to it as the *Harimandir* (the temple of God) or *Darbar Sahib* (the court of the Lord).

It is worthwhile spending an hour or two in the temple complex (be sure to have your head covered and feet bare), listening to the hymn-singing and watching the thousands of pilgrims at worship. The complex has a number of shrines of historical importance, notably the **Akal Takht** (throne of the timeless God) facing the temple where arms of the warrior gurus, their dresses and emblems can be seen, and the eight-storeyed **Baba-Atal tower**.

Besides the Golden Temple, there is its Hindu counterpart, the 16th-century **Durgiana Temple**; and **Jallianwala Bagh** where, in one of the worst atrocities of British rule, on 13 April 1919, General Dyer fired on a peaceful, unarmed crowd and killed at least 300 people, shocking the nation. The garden has a monument commemorating the event. Amritsar is also an important industrial and commercial centre and, away from the peace of the Golden Temple complex, is an extremely busy and congested city.

There are many other Sikh temples in the Punjab. In the foothills of the Himalaya is **Anandpur** where, in 1699, the last of the Sikh gurus, Govind Singh, baptised the first five Sikhs into the militant fraternity he called the *Khalsa* ("the pure"). Here are several temples and a fortress, **Kesgarh**. A large complex of temples, palaces and forts is to be seen at **Sirhind** near Patiala.

The industrial city of **Ludhiana** is known as the "Manchester of India", but aside from being a good place to buy textiles there is little to see. **Patiala** was the capital of one of the richest "princely states" in British India, and the Shish Mahal palace of the ruling family is worth a visit.

Haryana

Haryana has very few famous sites of tourist interest, however, this state could rightly claim to be the birthplace of the most sacred religious scripture of Hinduism. At **Kuruksetra** ❸, 155 km (96 miles) north of Delhi, a legendary battle was fought between two sets of cousins, the Kuruvas and the Pandavas. On the eve of the battle, Sri Krishna, an incarnation of Vishnu, persuaded Arjuna, the reluctant commander of the Pandava army, to wage war on his relatives. This sermon known as the *Bhagavad Gita* discusses *dharma*, the moral principle of doing one's duty without consideration of reward, victory or defeat. Kurukshetra is full of temples and tanks where pilgrims come to bathe on auspicious days. Holy men arrive during eclipses.

Also in Haryana, in Gurgaon District close to Delhi, is the **Sultanpur Bird Sanctuary**. Set up in 1971, the sanctuary is based around a *jhil*, or seasonal lake. A large number of bird species can be seen here, including common hoopoe, white ibis and painted stork, as well as nilgai and blackbuck antelopes. ❑

At the festival of "hola mohalla" in Anandpur, Sikh Nihangs take part in mock combat displays on horseback.

BELOW: interior of the Golden Temple.

Map on page 186

HIMACHAL PRADESH

Nestling in the northwestern lap of the Himalayas, the high valleys and green slopes of Himachal Pradesh are much loved by walkers, climbers and those in search of tranquillity

Himachal Pradesh straddles the Himalaya from the foothills, over snowy peaks, to the valleys of Lahaul and Spiti. Its capital, Simla, had the distinction of serving as the summer capital of India in the days of the British viceroys, a refuge for the sahibs from the heat of the plains.

In summer, the fragrance of fresh flowers pervades these enchanting hills and the coolness of the melting snow tempers the heat. The monsoon brings a spectacle of lush greenery and cascading waterfalls. Autumn is marked by pleasant sunny days, clear views and gorgeous sunsets. Winter brings snow.

A large majority of Himachalis are Hindus, but Buddhism is also a major influence, particularly with the presence of the exiled Dalai Lama at Dharamsala and the large settlements of Tibetan refugees in the state. As many as 6,000 temples are spread all over the area of this comparatively small state. Each year sees a cycle of rituals and ceremonies. Local fairs and festivals are often associated with deities and traditional dances form part of the celebrations.

Himachal Pradesh is noted for its wide range of traditional songs and dances. *Nati* is the most widely performed dance, in which the masked dancers link hands and form a chain. In Kinnaur and Lahaul-Spiti, some dances depict the perpetual strife between gods and demons.

BELOW: a Himachal village.

The state is predominantly rural and its towns are small. The traditional village house is of special interest: the lowest storey is occupied by the household cattle; the middle provides space for storing grain and other things, but also for sleeping in winter; the top floor *(dafi)* provides living space.

Simla to Kinnaur

Simla ❹ (Shimla) lies on a ridge at a height of 2,100 metres (6,900 ft). It was previously the official summer location for the government of British India and much British influence survives in the upper town. The town is linked to the plains by the Kalka–Simla narrow-gauge railway, which opened to freight in 1891 and passengers in 1903. There are four departures a day in each direction and the train slowly winds its way up the picturesque mountainside in about six hours. The level ground of the ridge is a favourite evening rendezvous, particularly Scandal Point, and Simla's main street, the Mall (from which Indians were infamously banned), is the place for shopping. In spite of considerable growth since India became independent, Simla, perhaps more than any other spot in India, is reminiscent of an attempt to recreate England in India. Its colonial domestic architecture and Christchurch (the second church to be built in North India) give it the air of a neglected Edwardian town. It was the setting of many of Rudyard Kipling's stories in his book *Plain Tales from the Hills*, and the bazaar below the ridge was famously described in his novel *Kim*. Simla is a pleasant place to relax and around the town there are excellent walks through the woods. The green slopes are covered with fir, rhododendron, pine and Himalayan oak.

    Narkanda ❺, at a height of about 2,700 metres (8,850 ft), 64 km (40 miles) from Simla on the Hindustan–Tibet road, is famous for its apple orchards and scenery. It is one of the state's ski resorts and is a convenient starting point for visiting the heart of Himachal Pradesh. Travelling east from Narkanda along the valley of the River Sutlej brings you to the border region of **Kinnaur**.

    On the bank of the Sutlej, **Rampur ❻**, 140 km (90 miles) from Simla, is one of the biggest towns of Himachal Pradesh and is a good place to pick up a permit to visit Kinnaur. It is noted for its three-day market fair, *Lavi*, in November. While the days are spent in making bargains, the evenings are given over to song and dance.

    Kinnaur is one of the most unspoilt and least-visited regions of Himachal Pradesh. Its proximity to the Tibetan border makes it a restricted zone but permits are now easy to obtain. **Rekong Peo** is the main town, but a better place to head for is **Kalpa**, a little way along the main road, which has stunning views of the Kinner-Kailash mountains and a wider choice of accommodation. Buses run from Rekong Peo and Kalpa to **Sangla** in the beautiful valley of the Baspa river.

    There are some lovely treks in the region. The old Hindustan–Tibet road is recommended; starting in Sarahan, passing through Kalpa and continuing into Upper Kinnaur (for which an Inner Line permit is needed) and the Rupa Valley. Another spectacular trek is the pilgrims' circuit of the Kinner-Kailash range.

Visit the Kullu Valley in October when the Dussera festival is celebrated. Highlights include statues of the gods in festive palanquins and nightly dance competitions.

BELOW: Simla Bazaar.

Many of the peaks in Himachal Pradesh are still unscaled. However, some of the more accessible mountains provide a good training ground for climbers.

BELOW: woman dressed in regional costume.

The Valley of the Gods

The **Kullu Valley** ❼ on the River Beas, at an altitude of 1,200 metres (3,900 ft), is renowned for apple orchards, beautiful scenery, wooden temples and its music and dances. It offers scope for trekking, climbing, rafting and angling.

Kullu itself has fewer attractions to detain travellers than places further up the valley. However, there are two temples in the town that are worth seeing: the Raghunathji temple, the chief deity of the valley, and the cave-temple of Vaisno Devi. Kullu really comes to life during the *Dussera* festival, when tourists and locals flood into the town to see the spectacular celebrations. Accommodation should be booked well in advance.

The most remarkable temple of the valley is **Bijli Mahadeva**, 8 km (5 miles) southeast of Kullu town. It is built of large blocks of stone without the use of cement and its 20-metre (65-ft) high flagstaff is reputed to attract lightning which, according to local legend, is an expression of divine blessing. Every time the flagstaff is struck by lightning, the Shiva *lingam* (phallic symbol) inside the temple is shattered. It is put back together each time by the priest and stands until another flash repeats "the miracle".

Kullu's airport is at Bhutar, 10 km (6 miles) south of the town. This is also the turning-off point for the **Parvati Valley**, which runs to the northeast. Along the valley are the hot springs at **Manikaran**, a Sikh and Hindu pilgrimage spot. Although the valley is best explored on foot, several trekkers have recently been attacked or have disappeared in the area, so if you wish to trek along the valley, hire an experienced guide and travel in a group.

The road from Kullu to Manali runs along the rushing torrents of the Beas. It is flanked by lofty mountains and spreading forests. Near Katrain is the small town of **Naggar**, where the Castle Hotel is said to be haunted. The town has been made famous by the late Russian painter Nicholas Roerich, whose gallery can be seen here (open Tues–Sun 9am–1pm, 2–5pm, entrance fee).

Manali ❽ is circled by beautiful glades of deodars and flowering horse chestnuts. It is an ideal place for walks, climbs, treks and picnics. It was an important trading centre, and in recent years has become a popular resort for Indian honeymooners, as well as Western tourists. The town is split into two parts: the new town is where the bus-stand and most of the hotels are, while along The Mall (the main street) and over the Manalsu river is the more atmospheric old village, where it is possible to find accommodation in traditional houses. The Hindu **Dhungri Temple**, dedicated to the goddess Hadimba, is believed to be more than 1,000 years old, while Manali's large Tibetan population has built two new *gompas* (monasteries), both of which may be visited by tourists – remember always to walk around a Buddhist shrine clockwise.

Three kilometres (two miles) up the valley from Manali are the hot springs of **Vashisht**. The temple complex here has separate outdoor baths for men and women. The Kullu Valley ends as the road passes the ski resort of Solang and winds up through rocky ranges to the Rohtang Pass, gateway to the enchanting Lahaul and Spiti valleys.

Map on page 186

Lahaul and Spiti

In the northeast of Himachal Pradesh, across the 3,955-metre (13,050-ft) **Rohtang Pass**, lie the two valleys of **Lahaul** and **Spiti** at a height of 3,000–4,800 metres (9,800–15,700 ft). Both valleys are cut off from the rest of the world for much of the year. The Rohtang Pass is open only from May to October, and it is only during this period that one may cross the still higher **Kunzam Pass** at an altitude of 4,500 metres (14,800 ft) to enter the Spiti Valley. The people of these two valleys have distinct cultures: Lahaul is half-Buddhist, half-Hindu, while Spiti is almost entirely Buddhist.

The district capital of **Keylong** is a convenient place to stop between Manali and Leh and it has a number of *gompas* within easy reach. The major crops of Lahaul are potatoes and hops, which have made its agricultural communities relatively well off. Spiti has a much less hospitable landscape. The town of **Kaza** is the place to plan treks and get permits for Inner Line areas, and is a good base from which to visit the spectacular *gompa* at **Kyi** 12 km (7 miles) away. Some of the world's greatest examples of Buddhist painting and sculpture can be seen 46 km (28 miles) further up the valley in the *gompa* at **Tabo**.

It is said that the goddess Renuka was beheaded by her son on her husband's orders. As a reward, the son asked for his mother to return to life. An annual fair at Parshuram Tal (tank) near Renuka commemorates the event.

Milk and honey

The romantic valley of **Chamba**, a former princely state, has few rivals for scenic beauty. Its valleys, meadows, rivers, lakes, springs and streams have a unique charm. **Chamba town ❾** is situated on the right bank of the River Ravi at an altitude of 900 metres (2,950 ft). It is noted for its ancient Shiva and Vishnu temples, some of which date back to the 10th century. The **Bhuri Singh Museum** (open Tues–Sun 10am–5pm) in Chamba is a treasure house of exquisite paintings

BELOW: trekking and climbing country around Manali.

TREKKING ROUTES

There is no end to the trekking possibilities in Himachal Pradesh and the routes are generally far less crowded than in Nepal.

Manali–Chandratal 11 days: Chikka, 2,956 m (13 km); Chatru, 3,360 m (16 km); Chota Dara (16 km); Batal (16 km); Chandratal (18 km); Topko Yongma (11 km); Topko Gongma, 4,730 m (10 km); Baralacha 4870 m (10 km); Patseo 3,820 m (19 km); Jispa (14 km); Keylong, 3,340 m (21 km).

Manali–Deo–Tibba 7 days: Khanul, 2,020 m (10 km); Chikka (10 km); Seri (5 km); Chandratal, 4,570 m (10 km).

Manali–Solang Valley 7 days: Solang, 2,480 m (11 km); Dhundi; Beas Kund, 3,540 m and back (10 km); Dhundhi-Shigara Dugh (8 km); Marrhi, 3,380 m (10 km).

Dharamsala–Chamba via Lakagot and Bharmaur 8 days: Lakagot is at the foot of Indrahar Pass, 5,660 m. **Chamba District** Pangi Valley and the Manimahesh mountains are particularly attractive.

Shimla District Shimla to Kullu via Jalori Pass; Shimla to Mussoorie via Tuini; and Shimla to Churdhar via Fagu.

Manali–Chandrakhani–Malana 7 days: Ramsu, 2,060 m (24 km); Chandrakhani, 3,650 m (6 km); Malana (6 km); Kasol (8 km); Jari (14 km); Bhuntar, 1,900 m (11 km).

of the famous Kangra and Basohli schools and has a mass of epigraphical material relating to the history of the region.

Among the innumerable fairs and festivals celebrated in Himachal Pradesh, the most important is the *Minjar* Fair of Chamba, held around August to celebrate the coming of the rains and the flowering of maize. A procession of decorated horses and banners marks the beginning of the week-long fair.

Some 56 km (35 miles) from Chamba town is **Dalhousie**, a quiet hill station located on five hills, which offer pleasant walking. **Brahmaur**, the ancient capital of Chamba, is famous for the Pahari architecture of its ancient temples and its lovely location, and **Nurpur** is known for its textiles.

Cannabis is easily available in Himachal Pradesh, particularly in the Kullu Valley. Don't be tempted to buy any. Being caught in possession by the local police would be a very unpleasant experience.

The Kangra District

Kangra is one of the most beautiful valleys in the Himalaya. **Dharamsala** , the headquarters of the district at the foot of the Dhauladhar Range, consists of a lower and an upper town, its altitude varying from 1,000 to 2,000 metres (3,280 to 6,560 ft). Upper Dharamsala, better known as McLeodganj, is the home of His Holiness the Dalai Lama and the Tibetan Government in Exile. The large Tibetan population supports many organisations, including TIPA (Tibetan Institute of Performing Arts) who preserve and arrange performances of traditional Tibetan music and dance, particularly the drama, *lhamo*. In the lower town is the **Museum of Kangra Art** (open Tues–Sun 10am–1.30pm, 2–5pm), housing a collection miniature paintings and other local artefacts.

The ancient town of **Kangra** , 48 km (30 miles) away, is well known for its temples, whose riches were plundered by a number of invaders, the most popular being the one dedicated to the goddess Vajresvari. Also worth visiting is Kangra's fort, once the palace of the local Katoch kings, with an outstanding view over the valley below.

Lying 34 km (22 miles) southwest of Dharamsala are the 10th-century rock-cut temples of **Masrur**, similar in style to those at Ellora in Maharashtra, though not as well preserved.

BELOW: Buddhists at prayer in Dharamsala.

Fair town

Mandi , on the left bank of the River Beas at an altitude of 750 metres (2,460ft), is 165 km (102 miles) from Simla. The town has several stone temples with beautiful carvings. For the *Shivratri* Fair (February/March) devotees put the *rathas* (carriages) of their village family gods and goddesses on their shoulders and process to Mandi town. They present themselves at the **Raj Madhan Temple** and pay homage to Lord Shiva at **Bhutnath Temple**. On this day, a week-long fair of selling, music and dance begins.

Bilaspur is 90 km (56 miles) from Simla. Among the town's major attractions are **Vyas Gufa** (cave) and the **Lakshmi Narayan** and **Radheshyam temples**. The **Shri Naina Devi Temple**, which attracts thousands of pilgrims during its many fairs, is situated at the top of a triangular hillock just 57 km (35 miles) from Bilaspur. This sacred place provides an unparalleled view of the holy **Anandpur Sahib**, the birthplace of a Sikh guru, on one side, and Govind Sagar (named after the guru) on the other.

Poanta Sahib, 45 km (30 miles) from the small holiday resort of **Nahan**, is a pilgrimage centre for the Sikhs. Its impressive *gurdwara* (temple) on the bank of the River Yamuna is thronged by pilgrims during the Hola festival in March. **Renuka** is a picturesque lake town 45 km (30 miles) from Nahan.

Map
on page
186

Sports

Kufri, 16 km (10 miles) from Simla, is the centre for winter sports. The ice skating rink is the only one in this part of the world. The skiing season starts in the last week of December and lasts until the end of February, depending on the weather. Skiing opportunities are also available at **Narkanda**, 64 km (40 miles) from Simla, and **Solang**, 10 km (6 miles) from Manali. There is a sporadic heli-ski service from Manali

Himachal Pradesh is also a centre for adventure sports, including trekking, mountaineering and rafting. The trekking options are numerous *(see page 193)*; it is a good idea to check out the various options carefully, finding a route that suits your ability and time. The mountaineering institutes in Manali and Dharamsala are useful sources of advice on both trekking and climbing. Rafting and kayaking down the Beas river are now available in Manali (enquire at the Western Himalayan Institute of Mountaineering and Allied Sports).

Naldera, 23 km (14 miles) from Simla, has one of the oldest golf courses in the country. **Chail**, 63 km (39 miles) from Simla, was once the summer capital of the Maharaja of Patiala and is now a lovely tourist resort. Its cricket pitch is reputed to be the highest in the world and certainly one of the most scenic. The town and its environs provide excellent facilities for fishing, tennis, squash, bird and wildlife enthusiasts. ❑

The Indian Institute of Skiing and Mountaineering in New Delhi (Dept. of Tourism, C 1 Hutments, Dalhousie Road, tel: 011-2301 6179) can give advice on trekking and skiing in Himachal Pradesh.

BELOW: prayer flags flying over the Rohtang Pass.

Map
on page
197

Delhi

JAMMU AND KASHMIR

*Jammu stands sentinel on the plains guarding the route north to the
legendary beauties of Kashmir, sadly out of bounds to travellers,
while Ladakh nurtures the ancient culture of Tibet*

Although talks have restarted between the Indian and Pakistani governments which will eventually address the intractable problem of the partition of Kashmir, the state is still a highly dangerous place as militant and army activity continues (it was, after all, only a short while ago that the two countries were on the point of going to war over the disputed territory). It is not safe to travel here; foreign tourists have been kidnapped, even killed, and it is strongly advised that you do not visit any part of Kashmir. The brief description below is for information only. So far the northern region of Ladakh has largely escaped the troubles; although it is a sensitive border area *(see pages 198–201)*.

Geography

Jammu and Kashmir is divided into three regions. Jammu is on the plains, populated by Dogras and Punjabis, who are primarily Hindu and Sikh. Punjabi, Dogri, Kashmiri, Urdu and Hindi are all spoken here. Kashmir includes the Kashmir Valley and surrounding mountains that stretch from Banihal north into Pakistan. The third region, Ladakh, is dealt with in a separate chapter *(see pages 198–201)*. Much of northern Kashmir is controlled by Pakistan. The present border between the two countries (known as the Line of Control) is the ceasefire line from the 1948–49 war. At Independence it was still undecided which country Kashmir was to enter. The Hindu ruler took his majority Muslim population into the Indian Union in 1948, under circumstances that are still heavily disputed, particularly by Pakistan. The referendum on the issue of accession, promised by Nehru, has never been allowed to take place.

BELOW: Mughal
garden of Nisat,
Srinagar.

Jammu

Jammu Tawi ❶ is the only railhead in the state of Jammu and Kashmir. Situated amid the Shivalik hills, its low elevation (300 metres/984 ft) makes it hot and humid in summer. Traditionally it is a stopover on the way to the Kashmir Valley or for pilgrims visiting the Vaishnodevi cave temple.

Two temples of note in Jammu town are the **Ranbireshwar Temple**, dedicated to Shiva, and the **Raghunath Temple**, dedicated to Rama. Both temples were constructed in the 19th century under Dogra *rajas*. Dogra kings were patrons of the arts, and there is a collection of miniatures from the Basholi, Jammu and Kangra schools in the **Dogra Art Gallery**.

Out of the town centre is the **Bahu Fort**, perched on a hill across the Tawi River. Within is a temple dedicated to the goddess Kali. At the northern edge of town sits **Amar Mahal Palace**, now a museum with some fine Pahari miniatures, which has an excellent view of the surrounding countryside and city.

Kashmir

Spread out across the Kashmir Valley are fertile fields of rice bordered by poplar trees, and orchards of fruit for which Kashmir is famous. **Srinagar ②**, located on Dal Lake and ringed by high mountains, is the centre of activity in the valley. People still live on the houseboats on Dal Lake, also the location of a daily floating vegetable market and home to many varieties of birds. Sadly, the lakes of Srinagar are dying, polluted by the city's sewage. Several Mughal gardens are located on The Boulevard that skirts Dal Lake: **Chasma Shahi**, built by Shah Jahan; **Nishat** and **Shalimar**, both with fountains, marble terraces and latticed marble pavilions; and the smaller garden of **Harwan**. Near Harwan are the ruins of a Buddhist college. There are several important mosques and *dargahs* in Srinagar. The huge **Jama Masjid** dates from the late 17th century. The **Shah Hamadan Mosque** is famous for the papier-mâche work on its walls and ceiling, and for its construction without nails or screws. Across the river is the stone **Pather Masjid** (1623). In Nagin the modern, lakeside **Hazratbal shrine** is said to preserve a hair of the Prophet Muhammad.

Elsewhere in the valley, **Pahalgam** (east of Srinagar) is from where pilgrims – amid tight security – make a four-day trek to a Hindu shrine held sacred to the god Shiva, the **Amarnath Cave ③**. Off the road from Pahalgam to Anantnag to the south of Srinagar, at Mattan, are the ruins of the **Martand Temple** complex and a sacred spring. South of Anantnag are **Achabal**, site of elaborate Mughal gardens, and more gardens at **Verinag**, while towards Srinagar there are more temple ruins at **Avantipur**. Around Srinagar are the resort of **Gulmarg ④**, used as a backdrop for old Hindi films, and the alpine meadows at **Sonamarg ⑤**, once a popular stopping place for Ladakh-bound travellers. ❑

The road between Jammu and Srinagar is very scenic as it runs along the Chenab and Jhelum rivers. En route, you pass a large Mughal sarai at Akhnu and an important Hindu cave temple at Katra. The Jawahar Tunnel, more than 1.5 km (1 mile) long, marks the entry to Kashmir.

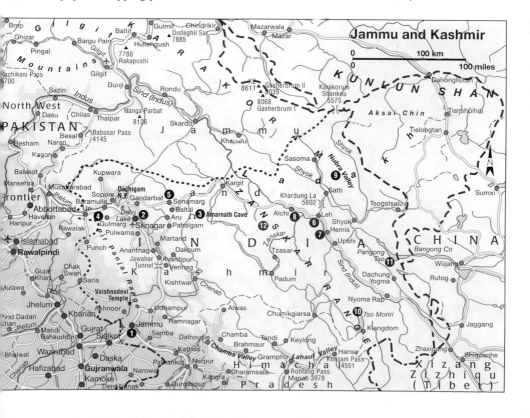

Jammu and Kashmir

Map on page 197

LADAKH

This former Buddhist kingdom, high up in the Himalayas, contains some of India's most impressive scenery as well as some wonderful monasteries

The far-northern region of Ladakh was formerly a kingdom of Western Tibet, but following invasions by the Dogras in the 19th century it was annexed by India. Geographically and culturally it has more in common with Tibet than with India and provides travellers with an insight into that fascinating region. Ladakhi is closely allied to Tibetan, and Buddhism is the predominant religion, although there are many Muslim Ladakhis. This identity, very different to the rest of the state, has lead to calls for either separate statehood or for separate administration from Delhi as a Union Territory; in part to disassociate Ladakh from the troubles elsewhere in Jammu and Kashmir.

The best time to visit is June to mid-September, when you can travel by road, and seasonal tourism is now an important part of the Ladakhi economy. Travellers either fly into Leh from Delhi, or cross the 5,328-metre (17,476-ft) Taglang Pass from Manali in Himachal Pradesh (the route via Srinagar and Kargil is not safe for visitors). The landscape changes from lush to stark as you emerge onto the Tibetan Plateau. Such mineral-streaked mountains against a brilliant blue sky can only be seen in the high Himalayas. It is 475 km (295 miles) from Manali to **Leh ❻**, the Ladakhi capital, a two-day journey. Flights to Delhi, Chandigarh and Srinagar operate all year at Leh. However, winter flights can be suspended for days on end without warning owing to bad weather conditions, and summer flights are often heavily overbooked. The view of the snowy Himalayas from the air is truly spectacular. If you plan to fly one-way into or out of Leh, it is best to fly in and take the bus out. The 5,328-metre (17,476 ft) Taglang Pass will be very uncomfortable if you are unacclimatised.

On arrival in Ladakh, it is essential that you allow yourself a day or two to acclimatise to the altitude by doing absolutely nothing. Drink plenty of water – 3 litres/6 pints a day is not excessive – and not only when you are acclimatising, since the dry air and altitude mean you still have to take in a lot of fluid. Ladakh is a very sensitive environment and bottled water should be avoided at all costs (India's "plastic bottle mountain" is huge and in any case bottled water in Ladakh is often beyond its sell-by date). Take your own water bottle and fill it for a nominal fee with pressure-boiled water from one of the eco-projects such as Dzomsa *(see opposite)*.

The traditional staples of the Ladakhi diet are *tsampa* (roasted barley flour), yoghurt, salt tea and butter. Tibetan dishes are widely available, particularly *momos* (dumplings) and *thukpa* (noodle soup). The most useful word of Ladakhi for travellers is "*Jullay!*", which can mean "hello", "goodbye", "please" or "thank you".

BELOW: woman from Ladakh.

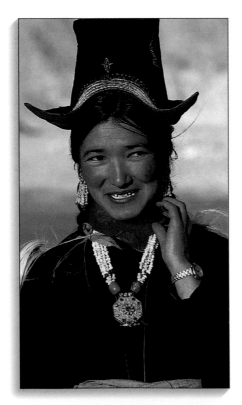

Leh

Leh's bazaar was once a trading post on the route between India, China and Central Asia. When the Chinese border closed in the 1950s its importance soon declined, but it is still a pleasant place to wander. The shopping, dominated by refugee Tibetans, is nothing great and most items are expensive; much better items and prices are available from Ladakhis. However, good Tibetan food is available in the restaurants. It is quite difficult to change or obtain money in Leh (and few places accept credit cards) so make sure you have plenty of cash.

The most ambitious walk in town is up to the imposing and partially ruined 16th-century **Leh Palace** (open 7–9.30am, entrance fee), home to the kings of Ladakh until the early 1940s when the royal family moved out to Stok. If you are fit and energetic, you can visit the **Tsemo Gompa** (Tibetan, "monastery"; open 7–9am, entrance fee), perched on Namgyal hill, above the palace. The narrow streets of **Old Leh** below the palace evoke the medieval town it once was; close by, on Main Street, is the new **Soma Gompa**. An interesting place to visit is the **Ecology Centre**, run by the Ladakh Ecological Development Group (LEDeG). The group aims to promote ecological awareness and sustainability through traditional methods. The centre has a library and craft shop. **Dzomsa**, at the end of Main Street, has an ecological laundry, recycling bins and pressure-boiled water, as well as local produce such as dried apricots and apples for sale.

The village of **Changspa** (a continuation of Leh to the west), with its small vegetable gardens and peaceful guesthouses, is a pleasant place for a stroll. At the end of Changspa Lane is the new **Shanti Stupa**. A steep line of steps leads up to this Japanese-built peace shrine, and the views from the top are wonderful; there is also a small cafe in which you can recover your breath.

Taxi and jeep hire in Ladakh is regulated by the Ladakhi Taxi Operator's Union who can be found on Fort Road in Leh (tel: 253 089). They operate to a fixed tariff, making getting around easy and ensuring you are not overcharged.

BELOW: Leh Palace.

Ladakh's *gompas*

Within a day's journey of Leh are some spectacular *gompas*. It is easy to arrange for a driver, and guide, from either a travel agency, or the Taxi Operator's Union. Prayer halls in monasteries are decorated with silk hangings in auspicious colours and sacred paintings, called *thankas*, and the walls are lined with stacks of Buddhist texts swathed in silk. Shrines dedicated to the Buddha and Bodhisattvas were traditionally lit with smoky, pungent butter lamps, now oil lamps, and are heaped with offerings of incense, water, tea, food or money. Most monasteries charge entrance fees towards their upkeep and are administered by the Archaeological Survey of India.

Ladakh is also known for its "oracles". According to Tibetan Buddhist belief, an oracle is a person who goes into a trance to heal people or animals, or predict the future. Oracles are possessed by benevolent spirits, serving as their channels, for the good of all beings. Several monasteries and villages have a resident oracle; Mulbekh, on the Srinagar–Leh road, has one, as does Stok, the royal residence near Leh.

There are two basic routes around the monasteries, one up, and one down, the Indus valley. The road leading south from Leh up the **Indus River** to Hemis Gompa passes a number of monasteries of importance, including the small but interesting **Sankar**

*The Ladakh Festival,
run by Jammu and
Kashmir Tourism,
is held during the
first two weeks in
September (a ruse
to extend the tourist
season). If possible,
try and coincide
your trip with the
festival in order to
see the exhibitions,
and dance and music
performances
(including the ritual
cham masked dance).*

BELOW: appearance
of the oracle at
Shey Gompa.

monastery on the way out of town. Along this road is **Shey**, the 17th-century summer palace of Ladakhi kings, which houses the largest Buddha in Ladakh. The 600-year-old **Shey Gompa** is here, too. Hundreds of *chortens* – whitewashed reliquaries – can be seen scattered around the barren plains. **Tikse** is a large hilltop monastery noted for its monumental statue of the Maitreya Buddha.

Hemis  (45 km/28 miles from Leh) lies across the Indus River at the end of a winding road. Founded in the 1630s, Hemis is the largest monastery in Ladakh, known for its religious festival in June which features a traditional dance-drama. The greatest treasure of the *gompa* is its enormous embroidered *thanka*, only shown every 12 years – the next display is in 2016.

The rough road back to Leh on the southern side of the Indus travels past **Stagna**, noted for its images of Bodhisattvas, and **Matho**. Just before the bridge that crosses the Indus is a turnoff to the 18th-century **Stok Palace** (open 7am–7pm, entrance fee), the more recent home of the kings of Ladakh and of the present Gyalmo. The palace houses a well-labelled display of some of the royal family's most precious ritual and ceremonial objects.

Heading west from Leh, down the Indus, brings you to one of the most beautiful monasteries at **Alchi** ❽ *(see box below)*. **Spitok** and **Phyang** monasteries lie along this route. Beyond Spituk, as the road emerges from a steep gorge, is the confluence of the Indus and Zanskar rivers. The view here is spectacular and the different colours of the two waters can be clearly seen. Beyond, up a newly paved road, is the monastery of **Likir**, a Gelugpa *gompa* with a small museum and beautiful prayer hall. A right turn after **Saspul**, noted for its apricots, and the bridge which takes you over the Indus and to Alchi, brings you via an impressive gorge to **Rezong** *gompa*, perched high up at the end of a valley.

ALCHI

Perhaps the most exquisite of Ladakh's monasteries is that at Alchi, some 60 km (40 miles) from Leh, west along the River Indus. Unique in being built on the flat valley floor, Alchi was established in the 11th century by the Tibetan Kal-dan Shes-rab. Much of the monastery, now no longer in use but maintained by the monks of nearby Likir, is made of locally grown willow. However, it seems to have been constructed by artisans from Kashmir; their work is seen in the intricate woodcarving and painted ceilings. The paintings are some of the oldest and most extensive surviving examples of Kashmiri Buddhist art.

The earliest temple is that of Du-Khang, with its ornately carved doorway and walls decorated with mandalas. The walls of the three-storeyed Sum-tsek temple are also covered with mandalas; the carving of the wooden structure is very fine. The square shrines of Lotsava Lha-Khang and Manjusri Lha-Khang are side by side; the walls of the latter are covered with representations of the 1000 Buddhas. The figures in the temples are of Bodhisatvas, including Avalokitesvara and Manjusri.

Alchi is currently being restored and there is a nominal entrance fee to help with its upkeep; if you are with a local guide they will help you gain access to the locked shrines.

Further afield

Many areas previously out of bounds to travellers have now opened up. Chief among these is the **Nubra Valley** ❾ which lies over the Khardung La (5,600m/18,370 ft), one of the highest motorable roads in the world. The valley itself is surprisingly green after the heights of the pass; the microclimate is warm enough to grow apricots, apples and walnuts. Panamik, at the far end of the valley, has hot springs, while the most important local *gompa* is at Deskit.

The lakes of **Tso Moriri** ❿ and **Pangong Tso** ⓫ lie to the southeast, each a three-day trip from Leh. Tso Moriri is an important nesting site for the barheaded goose and brahminy duck. Some 130 km (80 miles) long and wonderfully clear, Pangong Tso crosses over into Tibet proper. The small kingdom of **Zanskar** ⓬ lies to the southwest, over a fearsome range of peaks. This remote area is cut off by snow for seven months of the year and this limited access has helped preserve its stong Buddhist identity. The capital, **Padum**, lies over the Pensi La (4,400m/14,400 ft); the only other access is to walk in along the Zanskar River.

Trekking can be one of the most rewarding ways of exploring the region. Popular treks include the Markha Valley, which takes in the Nimaling plain and the 5,200-metre (17,056-ft) Kongmaru pass, and the trek from Lamayuru to Alchi or Chiling, which has some stunning views. One of the best, but more arduous, routes is over to the beautiful Zanskar valley. But short treks may also be taken to the monasteries near Leh, and along the Indus. It is strongly recommended that you hire an experienced guide and ponies, that you have the necessary permits and are well equipped and provisioned. Ladakh has a delicate ecosystem, with little rain, and here supplies are scarce. Take as much food, water and fuel as possible, and bring *all* rubbish back out with you. ❑

Map on page 197

Buddhist fresco at Tikse Gompa, Ladakh.

BELOW: hilltop monastery, Ladakh.

RAJASTHAN

A desert state this might be, but Rajasthan is bursting with colour and exuberance. Ornamental palaces, impregnable forts and painted towns all vie for attention

Map on page 204

Many people come to the desert state of Rajasthan in search of its past. Visitors can ride caparisoned elephants, stay in palace hotels and explore imposing forts. Both the Thar Desert and the Aravalli Ranges contribute to the landscape. The rugged skyline over dunes seems diametrically opposed to palaces, pavilions and peacocks, but both are typical.

The first dwellers

It is now thought that the ancient cities of the Indus Valley had their precursors in north Rajasthan. It seems that this area was inhabited by the Bhils and Minas who were dispersed when, around 1400 BC, horse-riding nomads from the north-west moved into Rajasthan. These new arrivals had come to stay, like the Afghans, Turks, Persians and Mughals who followed, first in war then in peace, giving the Rajputs a martial ancestry. From the reign of Harsha (7th century AD) to the time when the Delhi Sultanate was founded by the Muslims (1206 AD), Rajasthan fragmented into competing kingdoms. Powerful sons of rajas claimed genealogies linking them to the sun, the moon and the fire god. After the 14th century, prosperity declined. In the 16th century the Mughals made North India their home. Winning over Rajasthan was the achievement of Akbar who mixed military might with the soft touch of religious toler-ance. His trump card was matrimonial alliances with the Hindu Rajputs, which turned them from dangerous enemies into faithful allies.

Many princesses from Jaipur and Jodhpur married into the Mughal royal line, but when the Mughals weakened, the Rajputs were quick to reassert their sovereignty. In 1757, the British captured Bengal, but Rajasthan resisted. However, by the beginning of the 19th century, the maharajas had surrendered most of their powers to the British. Rajputana was Rajasthan's old name under the British, "land of the Rajputs". The Maharana of Mewar (Udaipur) was the acknowledged head of their 36 states. When India became indepen-dent, 23 princely states were consolidated to form the State of Rajasthan, "home of rajas".

The pink city

Jaipur ❶ (the city of *jai* or victory), the capital of Rajasthan, was not always pink. The original city was light grey, edged with white borders and motifs. In honour of the visit in 1883 of Prince Albert it was ordered to be painted the traditional colour of wel-come, which has been retained in the walled, old city.

The city was laid out in 1728 in a simple grid pat-tern by young Bengali, Vidyadhar Bhattacharya, architect to Maharaja Sawai Jai Singh II. This royal house had ruled from Amber, 11 km (7 miles) away,

LEFT: *haveli* rooftop, Jaisalmer.
BELOW: inside Amber Fort, near Jaipur.

since the early 10th century. Seven blocks of buildings are divided by wide tree-lined avenues; at the heart of the city is the palace *(see below)* which covers a further two blocks. These rectangular divisions represent the nine divisions of the universe. The whole is surrounded by a crenellated wall with seven imposing gates *(pols)*, still in use today. Each of the blocks houses *mohallas*, districts given over to the practice of various crafts or trades, from bangle-making to fabric dying, to *minakari* (enamel work), for which the city is famous.

The **City Palace** (palace and museum open 9.30am–4.30pm, entrance fee) remains the residence of Jaipur's royal family. Several gateways lead from the crowded streets into the palace, but the museum entrance is recommended through the courts of justice to the **Jantar Mantar** (open 9.30am–4.30pm entrance fee), the observatory of Maharaja Jai Singh. The construction and precision of the observatory were a unique achievement in 1716. Jai Singh's Delhi observatory had preceded this and three others followed: in Mathura, Ujjain and Varanasi, where the maharaja travelled as governor of Agra. The 16 instruments each have a specific role, tracing the movements of the stars and planets

Jaipur's Sawa Man Singh II Museum contains the two large silver urns used by Maharaja Madho Singh to carry a six-month supply of holy Ganga water with him to the coronation of King Edward VII in London in 1901.

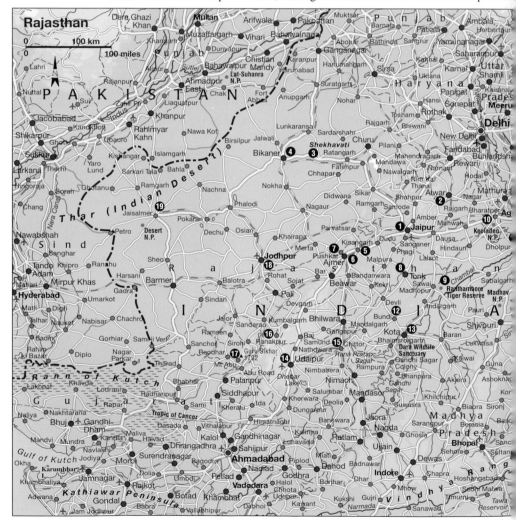

Map
on page
204

The **Sawa Man Singh II Museum** has extensive collections, with displays of textiles, arms, carpets, paintings and manuscripts. One of the most exquisite parts of the palace is the **Pritam Niwas Chowk**, or "Peacock Courtyard", named after the colours with which its doorways are decorated. Perhaps the best-known sight in Jaipur is the **Hawa Mahal** ("Palace of Winds"; open 10am–4.30pm Sat–Thur, entrance fee), built in 1799 and adjoining the outside palace wall. It is not, in fact, a palace, but an extraordinary facade of 953 airy niches and windows, used by the women of the palace, who were kept in *purdah* (secluded from the public), to watch the outside world of the streets below.

Outside of the city walls, in the centre of the Ram Niwas gardens, is the Albert Hall containing the **Central Museum** (open 10am–4.30pm Sat–Thur, entrance fee). The ornate Indo-Saracenic building houses a rather disorderly collection of costumes, ivory, brasswork and jewellery, as well as some unintentionally amusing models of Rajasthani festivals, occupations and trades.

Surrounding Jaipur stand impressive forts. **Nahargarh Fort** provides a marvellous view of Jaipur city and, en route, of the **Jal Mahal**, the lake palace of Jaipur. The cenotaphs of the Jaipur maharajas at Amber and Gaitor, as well as the *chatris* (memorials) of the maharanis, are well worth a visit.

Amber (open 9am–4.30pm, entrance fee), 11 km (7 miles) from Jaipur, was once the capital of the Minas – believed to be the original inhabitants of this area. Painted elephants take visitors up the hill to admire the massive gateways, pillared pavilions and palaces that recall the glory and wealth of Amber's association with the Mughals. Raja Man Singh was the commander-in-chief of Akbar's army and Mirza Raja Jai Singh was a powerful ally of Jahangir. Of special interest are the **Diwan i Am**, Jai Singh's audience hall, and the **Shish Mahal**, the palace of mirrors, where the walls are inlaid with exquisite mirrored motifs that dance to the flame of even a single candle.

Within walking distance is **Jaigarh Fort** (open 9am–4.30pm, entrance fee), opened to the public in the late 1990s after being sealed for seven years following a rumour that an enormous treasure in gold was buried in vaults under deep reservoirs. The vast purity of its austere spaces is admirable. The highlight of the fort, apart from its views back over Amber, is the Jaya Vana, the largest antique cannon in India.

About 10 km (6 miles) along the Jaipur–Agra road are the holy springs of **Galta**. Here the **Hanuman Temple** is particularly lively on Tuesdays.

Northeast to Alwar

Five major roads lead out of Jaipur. National Highway No. 8 leads north to Delhi. One can branch off right about 60 km (35 miles) from Jaipur, turning northeast to **Alwar ❷**, picturesque and dotted with historical sites. At **Bairath** or **Viratnagar** are ancient Buddhist rock edicts of Emperor Ashoka, a 3rd-century BC Buddhist *chaitya* (temple), and a painted garden pavilion, which was built around 1600 AD.

Founded in 1771, Alwar is one of the most recent of the princely states of Rajasthan. Beginning as distant cousins of Jaipur, they manoeuvred their way through the chaos of the 18th century, changing sides for quick gains, until the British finally acknowledged and

The Moti Dhungri on Jawaharlal Nehru Road is a bizarre fort shaped like a Scottish castle. One of its most famed inhabitants was Gayatri Devi, the third wife of Man Singh II. During a tax inspection in 1975 one room was found to contain over £2 million worth of gold.

BELOW: Hawa Mahal, Palace of the Winds, Jaipur.

Some of the forts, palaces and havelis of Shekhavati have been converted into hotels. Apart from Samode Palace, other notable buildings in which to stay include Castle Mandawa, Roop Niwas in Nawalgarh, and Dundlod Fort.

BELOW: brightly painted Shekhavati facade.

rewarded them for their help against the Marathas. But the affairs of Alwar remained troubled, with only a few scattered years of peace. Yet Alwar has some handsome palaces, built from half the state exchequer – a high proportion even by feudal standards. In Alwar's **museum** (open 10am–4.30pm, closed Fri), in the City Palace, is a fine collection of miniature paintings, manuscripts, arms and a solid-silver dining table. Outside is a reservoir with delicate temples, kiosks and symmetrical stairs considered masterpieces of Indo-Islamic architecture

The **Sariska Palace**, 37 km (23 miles) from Alwar, was once a hunting lodge and is now a hotel on the outskirts of a wildlife sanctuary.

Decorated towns

The second northern road (National Highway No. 11) leads to the painted towns of **Shekhavati ❸** *(see below)*, and on to Bikaner. Wealthy Marwari traders relocated to Shekhavati in order to service the Silk Route caravans that linked them to 19th-century Kolkata. Their tall houses were built to combat the heat and glare. Owners hired Rajput artists to enliven the great expanses of blank plaster with heroic or whimsical frescoes – all protected by jutting eaves. Traders vied to outdo their neighbours with garish colours or glimpses of sophisticated gadgetry. Havelis were embellished with blue-faced gods or pink-faced colonials on elephants. Erotic motifs were camouflaged in niches, such as those at Sara Haveli, Mandawa, near a steaming locomotive and a gramophone. Sarog Haveli, Fatehpur, shows a laden paddle steamer, while Sikar's clock tower and the vast Somani haveli nearby are eclectic marvels, and Ramgarh's Saturn temple is exquisitely painted. Nearly all Shekhavati's 30 principal towns lie in Jhunjhunu and Sikar districts, a morning's drive from Delhi, Jaipur or Bikaner

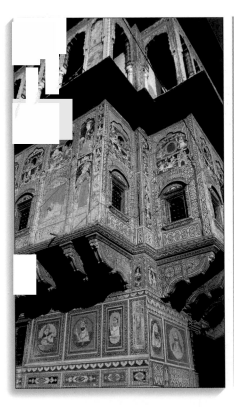

EXPLORING SHEKHAVATI

Shekhavati was once subordinate to Jaipur to its south, but in 1471 Rao Shekhav asserted his independence, giving Shekhavati his name. Located on the caravan route from the Gujarat ports and from Central India to Delhi, trade in opium, cotton and spices flourished. Merchants built palatial *havelis* (mansions), cenotaphs and reservoirs, temples and caravanserais. Most of these buildings are covered with frescoes painted between 1760 and 1920. The *havelis* were fortified houses that walled in the secluded life of the women who spent their days in the *zenana* (ladies' apartments) around an inner courtyard. The men conducted their business on the white cotton mattresses of their sitting rooms.

The streets of **Nawalgarh**, 120 km (75 miles) north of Jaipur, are lined with richly painted facades and the market bustles with activity. A garden palace on the outskirts provides a cool stopover. From Nawalgarh the road leads north to **Dundlod** and **Mandawa**. The rugged forts are now hotels with a medieval charm. **Fatehpur**, 20 km (12 miles) west of Mandawa, offers a wealth of painted *havelis*. A detour from the road to Bikaner leads to the fascinating towns of **Ramgarh** and **Churu**, where there is some of the best art and architecture of the region.

Map on page 204

Thirty-one km (20 miles) from Jaipur is **Samode**, a palace hotel set among steep hills. It doubled for Afghanistan in the shooting of *The Far Pavilions*. Its durbar hall is painted with frescoes, among the most delicate in Rajasthan.

Desert towns

Bikaner ❹ 190 km (118 miles) west of Fatehpur, was founded 29 years after Jodhpur, in 1488. A younger but more intelligent son of Jodphur's founder Rao Jodha, Rao Bika, was given an army and asked to seek his own fortune to avoid a war of succession. Thus Bikaner was founded in the heart of the wilderness called Jangaldesh. Perhaps the very bareness of the landscape spurred the human hand to create beauty. The royal family resides in the restrained **Lalgarh Palace**, parts of which function as a luxury hotel. Designed by Sir Swinton Jacob (architect of Jaipur's Albert Hall), it's less alluring than its predecessor, but harbours old photographs and royal memorabilia in the **Shri Sadul Museum** (Mon–Sat 10am–5pm, entrance fee), plus ancient Sanskrit and illuminated Persian manuscripts in the **Anup Sanskrit Library** (same hours; free).

The umconquered 15th century **Junagarh Fort** (open 10am–4pm, entrance fee) contains palaces and temples of great refinement. Bikaner's art of miniature painting is highly rated; the **Durbar Hall** has breathtaking frescoes, gilded stucco mouldings, floral patterns and delicate carpets. The Old Town has a number of lovely *havelis*, the finest along Rampuria Street and Purana Bazaar.

The Bikaner Camel Corps is still a showpiece of the Indian Army's display parade in Delhi on Republic Day. On the outskirts of Bikaner, the **camel farm** (open 3–5pm, Mon–Sat) makes an interesting visit, particularly at sunset when herds of camels return from the dunes.

The temple of Karni Mata at Deshnoke (28 km/17 miles) from Bikaner) is inhabited by rats, which are revered and roam free – a unique sight for those who don't feel too queasy.

BELOW: a camel cart in the dusty streets of Mandawa.

One of the many pilgrims who gather in Pushkar for the annual camel fair in November.

Outside Bikaner, the countryside is still rugged, dotted with intricately carved 16th-century Jain temples. **Devi Kund**, 8 km (5 miles) from Bikaner, is where the cenotaphs of the rulers of Bikaner were built, and **Gajner**, 31 km (20 miles) from Bikaner, has beautiful palaces set around a lake.

North of Bikaner, between Suratgarh and Anupgarh (both on the railway), is the Harappan site of **Kalibangan**, dating back to around 3,000 BC. The two largest sites, Mohenjodaro and Harappa, are now in Pakistan, but Kalibangan, a citadel on the banks of the Ghaggar River, is the third city. The excavation and finds show, as at all Harappan sites, a high degree of social organisation, with a well-designed sewage system and a uniform system of weights and measures.

Kisangarh ❺ is an interesting city of palaces and lakes, 100 km (60 miles) west of Jaipur towards Ajmer. The **City Palace**, the **Phul Mahal** and the **Kalyan Raiji Temple** are located beside a lake. From there one can walk the narrow streets of the walled city. The largest collection of paintings of the renowned Kisangarh School is at the **Majhela Palace** and can be viewed by prior appointment.

Kisangarh is a convenient starting point for visits to the marble cenotaph at **Karkeri**, the **Krishna Temple** of the Nimbarkachari sect at Salemabad, and the fort and palace of **Rupangarh**. A little further away, the salt lake of **Sambhar** is a unique sight along with the marble quarries at **Makrana**, source for the Taj Mahal. It continues to be exploited today. Nearby, **Kuchaman** has one of the most beautiful lived-in fortresses of Rajasthan.

Sacred sites

About 135 km (80 miles) southwest of Jaipur lies **Ajmer** ❻, the most sacred of all Sufi pilgrimage places in India. Its Muslim history began in 1193, when Prithviraj Chauhan lost Ajmer to Sultan Muhammad of Ghori. The Persian saint, Khwaja Mu'inuddin Chisti, who had come with Ghori, settled and preached here. The **Dargah Sharif**, where the saint is buried, lies at the foot of Taragarh Hill. When Akbar captured Ajmer in 1556 he made it his military headquarters and visited the tomb on foot to pray for a son. The request was granted and Ajmer's reputation soared. Large cauldrons *(deg)* were presented by Akbar to be filled with food for distribution among the pilgrims at the shrine; this continues today, but the original *deg* were replaced in the 19th century. Important monuments within the *dargah* include the delicate white marble mosque of Shah Jahan (*c.* 1650).

The **Arhai din ka Jhonpra** mosque is just west of the *dargah*. This Sanskrit college was converted to a mosque in 1210 by Qutb-ud-Din-Aibak. It is one of the finest monuments of medieval India, with beautiful decorations and ornate calligraphic inscriptions. Just off Station Road is Akbar's red-sandstone palace, the **Daulat Khana**. Above the town is the large **Taragarh Fort**, built in the 12th century by Ajaipal Chauhan.

Not far from here is the pleasant sight of **Ana Sagar**, a lake constructed in the early 12th century. There are cool marble pavilions built by Shah Jahan and a circuit house constructed by the British.

Pushkar ❼, 14 km (9 miles) from Ajmer, is considered high up in the hierarchy of Hindu places of pilgrimage. It has one of the few temples to Brahma, the Creator. Here every year, on the full moon of November, hundreds of thousands of pilgrims gather to bathe in the sacred lake. This is the occasion for one of the largest cattle and camel markets in Rajasthan, where the abundance of colour, jewellery, turbans and moustaches is unmatched.

Map on page 204

The road to Tonk

South of Jaipur, the airport road leads 12 km (7 miles) to **Sanganer**, a name synonymous with fine block-printing on fabric. It is said that the water of Sanganer makes the colours fast. Traditionally, only coarse cotton was printed for the ankle-length flared skirts of Rajasthani women. A 15th-century Jain temple and a Krishna temple are among spots worth visiting in Sanganer.

Continuing south, the road winds past **Chaksu**, where large numbers gather at the temple every year to pay reverence to Shitala Mata, the goddess of smallpox. Although this disease has now been eradicated from India, the goddess continues to have her following.

Some 80 km (50 miles) from Jaipur lies **Tonk ❽**, once ruled by Muslim Nawabs, descendants of Pathan tribesmen from Afghanistan, who had come to India in search of *Zan, Zar, Zamin* – women, gold and land – possibly in that order. Tonk has charming painted mosques and a host of colonial buildings. Of particular interest is the **Sunehri Kothi** or golden mansion. Its interior is studded like a jewel box. An inlay of coloured glass, mirrors, gilded stucco and trappings, painted and polished lime floors, and stained window panes, all add up to an extraordinary opulence.

From Tonk, the road continues south to Bundi and Kota. However, eastwards

The Padma *(lotus)* Purana *tells the story of Brahma killing a demon with a lotus. The petals fell at three spots where lakes appeared, the most important of which is at Pushkar. Bathing here is considered especially auspicious by devout Hindus.*

BELOW: women constructing a road in rural Rajasthan.

Ranthambore National Park in southeast Rajasthan is a Project Tiger reserve. The best time to visit is between October and April.

BELOW: City Palace and Lake Palace Hotel, Udaipur.

the road leads to **Sawai Madhopur** where the royal Jaipur household used to come for big hunts accompanied by their VIP guests. Overlooking the wildlife sanctuary of **Ranthambore ❾**, 13 km (8 miles) from the town, is the formidable fortress of Rao Hamir, which was conquered by Ala-ud-Din Khilji in the 14th century and then again by Akbar in 1569. Even though in ruins, its palaces, temples and cenotaphs are well worth a visit. It is possible to spend a night at the maharaja's former hunting lodge. Ranthambore itself is famous for its tigers though the population is in severe decline.

Jat states

The Jaipur–Agra road leads east to **Bharatpur ❿** and **Dholpur ⓫** – unusually both Jat states in the predominantly Rajput stronghold of Rajasthan.

The **Bharatpur Palace** houses a museum with exhibits of mixed antiquity, but what makes Bharatpur famous is its 29 sq-km (11 sq-mile) **Keoladeo Ghana Sanctuary** (open dawn–dusk, entrance fee), with the largest concentration and variety of birdlife in Asia. Prior to 1940, this was the favourite shooting ground of the British viceroys, with a record kill of 4,273 birds in a single day. Sunrise or sunset from October to February is the best time to see the birds. You may see one of the few Siberian crane that still make the long migration, although visits have been very rare in recent years; other species include Sarus cranes, the tiny Scops owl, egrets, spoonbills and kingfishers.

The wondrous palaces of **Deeg**, 30 km (18 miles) from Bharatpur, are set at the water's edge with cool channels, fountains and water alleys below, where iron balls were made to roll and rumble like monsoon thunder. The rooms have an exquisite beauty.

Southeast Rajasthan

Founded in 1342, the ancient kingdom of **Bundi** ⑫ (from *bando nal*, "narrow passage") in southeast Rajasthan lies well protected in the ranges of the rugged Aravalli Hills that drop into rocky ravines traversed by four narrow passes. The highlight of Bundi is its stunning palace-fort, the **Chattar Mahal** (open 8am–5pm, entrance fee), which reflects the changing colours of the greenish serpentine of its walls in the **Naval Sagar** lake. Incredible ramps and stairs zig zag between the ramparts as overhanging balconies frame perfect views.

Besides its architecture, the palace is famous for the **Chitra Shala** (open 7.30am–6pm, free), a gallery of refined frescoes painted in the 17th and 18th centuries, unmatched in their harmony of blues, greens and terracotta colours.

The Bundi territory was first claimed by Udaipur and later by Jaipur. Part of it was given in 1579 as patrimony for a favoured younger son. This tract, set in the open plains, grew to be **Kota** ⑬, larger than its parent state and bustling with the youth of a commercial city.

Bundi, in contrast to the rapidly industrialised Kota, has gracefully mellowed into old gold. Its secluded position saved it, so to speak, from the hybridisation of the 19th century, even though the British virtually controlled its affairs from 1818. "Bundi is deliciously behind the times," wrote the Maharaja of Baroda.

A rather curious feature of the main Bundi market street is the height at which the shops are built. The monsoon overflow from the town's reservoir, which is atop the hill in the **Taragarh Fort**, is emptied when the sluice gates open. Water gushes out like a cloudburst, flooding the streets. But everyone is forewarned and there has never been damage to life or property.

Kota had to be on constant alert because its strategic location on the plains along the Chambal River drew the envy of Udaipur, Jaipur, the Marathas and also the British – to whom it was the first to accede, due to the foresight of Zalim Singh, the Regent. Spasmodic spells of peace led to spurts of architecture and a melange of pillared halls, kiosks, commemorative gateways, carving and painting. Some of the finer frescoes and miniature paintings of India belong to the Bundi-Kota school. The **City Palace** (open 10am–4.30pm, Sat–Thur, entrance fee) at Kota abounds in ornamentation and a small museum shows treasures from the ruler's private collection. The most exquisite room is the hall hung with paintings from the Mughal to British periods.

Famous hunting paintings from Kota depict scenes from what is now the **Dara Wildlife Sanctuary**, where tiger, bear, wild boar and spotted deer roam – well worth visiting for lovers of wildlife.

Udaipur

The royal house of Mewar, now better known as **Udaipur** ⑭, has two reasons for pride. The first is that it can trace its recorded history back to Bapa Rawal (728 AD), whereas Jaipur and Jodhpur lag behind by 200 and 483 years respectively. The second pride in being Hindu and not losing honour to Muslim invaders. Mewar alone of all the Rajput states resisted such alliances – at least 50 years more than the others. This sense of history and pride persisted

Map on page 204

The small Jat state of Dholpur, 55 km (34 miles) south of Bharatpur, supplied the stone for the president's palace in New Delhi.

BELOW: mosaic at the City Palace, Udaipur.

Ancient carved plinths in the Thar Desert around Jaisalmer in western Rajasthan. Camel safaris across the dunes can be arranged in town.

BELOW: Jodhpur's splendid palace.

during the British period, earning them the highest gun salute in Rajasthan: 19 guns as against the 17 each of Jaipur, Jodhpur, Bundi, Bikaner, Kota and Karauli. Maharana Fateh Singh of Udaipur had the distinction of not attending the Delhi Durbar for King George V in 1911.

Udaipur has a profusion of palaces, lakes, temples and cenotaphs. The **City Palace**, now a museum (open 9.30am–4.30pm, entrance fee), is a labyrinth of courtyards richly decorated with inlaid mirror-work, galleries covered with frescoes, temples and kiosks from where one can see the **Pichola Lake** . An island on the lake houses the elegant **Jag Niwas**, built in 1746 as the rulers' summer residence, and now the **Lake Palace Hotel**. **Jag Mandir**, another island, is worth a visit at sunset. This is where Prince Khurram, who was later to become Emperor Shah Jahan, took refuge in 1624 and lived for a while. In the old town the **Jagdish Temple**, built in the mid-17th century, has a remarkable bronze statue of Garuda (a mythical bird) facing his revered Lord Vishnu. The shops and craftsmen's studios in the narrow streets of the bazaar justify endless walks.

The temple of Eklingji, the Saiva patron deity of the Udaipur royal house, is 24 km (15 miles) by road from Udaipur. On the way are the ruins of the ancient city of **Nagda**, where exquisitely carved temples, both Hindu (10th century) and Jain (15th century), are a treat for the eyes. **Eklingji Temple** is carved from marble and even today the Maharana of Udaipur, who is the *Divan* of the temple makes it a point to visit every Monday.

Also nearby is the famous, and rich, **Srinathni Temple** at Nathdwara (non-Hindus not admitted). It contains a black marble image of Krishna, brought from Mathura in the 17th century to protect it from the advance of Aurangzeb's army. Nathdwara is also famous for *pichwai* painting.

HERITAGE HOTELS

Thikaras, *havelis*, small palaces and forts are opening their doors to visitors. Some old feudal families are now playing host to guests for brief stays for a reasonable charge – usually less than 2,500 Rs a night, though some are considerably more expensive. You may get to see local traditional musicians, sleep in historic bedrooms and lounge around on the terrace. The decor is often spectacular with antique furniture and traditionally decorated walls. Food in the larger hotels usually takes the form of a buffet of seven or so different Rajasthani and North Indian dishes. Heritage Hotels started in Rajasthan, but the network is extending across India.

For the latest listings, contact the Indian Heritage Hotels, Mandawa Haveli, Sansar Chandra Road, Jaipur, tel: 014 237 1194 (www.indianheritagehotels.com).

There is also a Paying Guest Scheme that places guests with local families. It operates in Ajmer, Bikaner, Bundi, Jaipur, Jaisalmer, Jodhpur, Mt Abu, Pushkar and Udaipur. Rates vary depending on the quality of the accommodation. For details, contact your nearest Government of India Tourist Office, or the Department of Tourism, Paryatan Bhavan, M.I. Road, Jaipur, tel: 0141 511 0591 (www.rajasthantourism.gov.in).

The forts of Mewar

In the erstwhile princely state of Mewar there were three almost impregnable forts: **Chittor** (112 km/70 miles from Udaipur), **Kumbalgarh** (64 km/40 miles from Udaipur) and **Mandalgarh** (near Kota). Kumbalgarh is not easily accessible, but the adventurous will be well rewarded. This fort was built by Rana Kumbha in the 15th century. It is surrounded by 13 mountain peaks, which keep watch over distant horizons. Seven gateways lead up to the palaces.

In a shaded valley, 160 km (100 miles) northwest from Udaipur, lie the superb Jain temples of **Ranakpur**, which were built in the mid-15th century. The **Risabji Temple** has 1,444 columns, each different. The nearby **Sun Temple** is worth a visit, both for its carvings and its unusual plan.

Chittor became the first capital of Mewar in the early 13th century under the reign of Jaitra Singh (1213–53). The siege of Chittorgarh in 1303 by the Sultan of Delhi, Ala-ud-Din Khilji, is notorious. The sultan had heard of the beauty of Princess Padmini, wife of Maharana Rawal Ratan Singh, and determined to bring her back to his harem. Despite a courageous Rajput defence, the citadel was captured by the sultan's force. Rather than face dishonour, the women committed *johar*, mass suicide. Chanting verses from the Gita, they threw themselves on the funeral pyre. Chittor was later recaptured by the Rajputs. However, two centuries later, in 1535, Chittor was attacked by the Sultan of Gujarat, Bahadur Shah, and 13,000 Rajput women sacrificed themselves in the flames.

Abu, 100 km (62 miles) west of Udaipur, is one of the most sacred places of Jain pilgrimage. According to the Jain tradition, Mahavira, the last of the 24 *Tirthankara* (saints), spent a year there. **Mount Abu**, situated at an altitude of 1,220 metres (4,000 ft), is the only such hill resort in Rajasthan. Many princes

Near Jhalavar (87 km/54 miles south of Kota) is Jhalra Patan, "city of bells", and the ruins of the 10th century Surya Temple, one of the finest sun temples in India.

BELOW: the blue city of Jodhpur, seen from the fort.

built summer bungalows and small palaces around Nakki Lake, and visitors flock there during the summer months to take advantage of the cooler temperatures. The surrounding countryside is wooded and has many pleasant walks.

The main attractions, and one of the great sights of India, are the **Dilwara Jain temples** (open 12–6pm, free). Of the five main temples here, **Adinath** and **Neminath** display the finest carving in white marble. Adinath, the most celebrated, was built in 1031 and is dedicated to the first Tirthankar. The lotus ceiling in the main shrine is carved from a single block of marble. Neminath was erected in 1230 to celebrate the 22nd Tirthankar, and the **Hall of Donors** is particularly fine. Of the other three, the Chaumukha Temple is later and built of sandstone, the Risah Deo Temple is unfinished, while the Dagambar Temple is much less highly decorated. The 24 elite Chauhan clans of Rajasthan claim descent from the holy fire that springs from the peak of Mount Abu.

A pleasant stop on the road north from Udaipur to Kumbalgarh is the cool royal lake of Rajsamand at Kankoli. From the dam the view of the town is magnificent.

Jodhpur

The Rathors of Kanauj (in UP) moved in 1211 AD to Marusthal, the blazing desert land in the heart of Rajasthan. Their land came to be called Marwar. In 1459 Rao Jodha founded **Jodhpur** ⓲ after the old capital of Mandore had proved too vulnerable. Some five centuries later (1929–43), Maharaja Umaid Singh had completed for himself one of the largest private homes in the world (with 347 rooms), to create employment as a famine relief measure (now the sumptuous Umaid Bhawan Palace Hotel).

The hugely impressive **Meherangarh Fort** (open 9am–5pm, museum closed 1–2.30pm, entrance fee) sits on a mighty rock 120 metres (400 ft) high. A fairly steep climb leads up, winding through seven gateways. By the strongest of

BELOW: Jaisalmer Fort dominates the town below.

these, **Loha Pol**, or "Iron Gate", are a series of *sati* prints, the handprints of royal widows burnt on the maharajas' pyres. The palaces within are sculpted from a hard sandstone and were designed to catch the breeze to keep them cool. An extensive museum displays *howdahs*, paintings, thrones, banners, doors, weapons, and a spectacular 17th-century tent made for Shah Jahan. The city of Jodhpur and its bazaar, below the fort, is an intriguing place to explore, with its complex system of narrow streets.

The old capital of **Mandore**, 8 km (5 miles) north of Jodhpur, now has landscaped gardens surrounding temples and the *chatris* of the Marwar rulers. The **Hall of Heroes**, with larger-than-life figures painted in gaudy colours, and the temple of the black Bhairav and the white Bhairav (manifestations of Lord Shiva), where the idols are pasted over with layers of foil paper, are curious.

The **Osian temple** complex, 65 km (40 miles) north of Jodhpur, has 16 very fine Hindu and Jain temples, dating from the 8th–12th century. The first group, of 11, represents the earliest phase of temple building in Rajasthan. The largest, **Mahavira**, temple has a sanctum dating from 783–93. As well as rich decoration, the halls are open, with balustrades rather than walls, to provide more light. This group also contains one of the few temples to Surya (the sun god). The second group is later and contains the fine 12th-century **Sachiya Mata temple**.

Khimsar, located 90 km (55 miles) north of Jodhpur, features the 15th-century **Khimsar Fort** with its carved stone, which is now a charming hotel. Continuing northeast, **Nagaur** (135 km/84 miles from Jodhpur) celebrates the Ramdeoji Fair in February and the Tejaji Cattle Fair in August, named after local heroes and considered to be among the biggest livestock fairs in the world. Camel races are included among the activities, which attract thousands of people from outlying areas.

Jaisalmer

Jaisalmer ⑲, land of the Bhatti princes, born of the moon, is by far the oldest Rajput capital, dating from 1156 AD. The skyline holds kiosks with parapets, balconies and terraces. The beauty of the Jain temples (12th–15th century) leaves visitors breathless.

Jaisalmer's imposing fort, built in 1156, is like a city in itself with houses, shops and hotels. The maharaja's palace, the **Rajmahal**, has a number of interesting Hindu and Jain temples (open 9am–6pm, entrance fee). The Rani ka Mahal, the maharani's palace, has been restored by the organisation **JiJ** and now houses the **Jaisalmer Heritage Centre. Manik Chowk**, by the entrance to the palace, is where merchants from as far as North Africa gathered on their way across the Thar desert; the city's role as a trading post was the source of much of its wealth.

Down in the city are a number of beautiful *havelis*. The *silavats* (stone carvers) of Jaisalmer were famous and they reached the peak of their skill during the 18th and 19th centuries. The *havelis* of Salim Singh, Nathmalji and the Patwon are three of the finest, owing much of their character to the yellow-gold Jaisalmer sandstone. Also in the city is a group of 12th- to 15th-century Jain temples, including the **Risabdevji**, **Sambhavnath** and **Astapadi** *mandirs*. ❑

Map on page 204

Desert camel safaris are available from Jaisalmer. Sights they pass through include: the sand dunes at Sam (40 km/25 miles to the west); the remains of a petrified forest at Aakal (17 km/10 miles); and the ancient Bhatti capital of Lodurva (16 km/10 miles), passing by enormous sand dunes patterned by the wind.

BELOW: a young Rajput.

THE EAST

Largely unexplored by tourists, this region
offers a feast of scenic and spiritual splendours

East India is the least-visited region in the country, despite its beauty and natural bounty. The waters of the River Ganga and the great Brahmaputra provide a lifeline to civilisation when roads are washed away. Startlingly ornate temples attract throngs of worshippers in Orissa, especially the Konarak Sun Temple with its great carved chariot and annual dance festival. The original juggernauts (enormous wheeled vehicles that haul the gods through the streets) come from the main temple in Puri and continue to rumble through the city once a year. Adivasis in Orissa, though usually isolated from outsiders, add spice to weekly markets near the Adivasi crossroads of Koraput.

Devout Buddhists descend on Bihar to trace the Buddha's footsteps. Bodhgaya, where meditation under the holy Bodhi tree first took place, draws scholars from around the world and has in recent years metamorphosed into a sampler of international temple architecture. More rustic pleasures are on offer at the Sonepur fair, where working elephants are sold to the highest bidder.

The Sunderban swamps, bordering Bangladesh, attract adventurous wildlife lovers. Honey gatherers and fishermen wear masks on the back of their heads to fool predatory swimming tigers, who reputedly will only pounce on a prey's backside.

Kolkata (formerly Calcutta), despite its undeserved reputation for misery, has gracious mansions, a horse track and cricket pitches dating from the British Raj. Pavement hawkers, rickshaw pullers, and political activists help to give the city of Kali a chaotic frenzy. Conversations are easy to strike up with opinionated and widely read Bengalis. Throughout Bengal, women have a special status derived from the worship of powerful female goddesses, Kali and Durga. In the northeast, many matriarchal societies pass down property rights through the mother's side. Although the area is gradually opening up, separatist guerillas make some areas here out of bounds to travellers.

Darjeeling, the largest hill station in the east, is reached by an 88-km (55-mile) journey on a toy train that provides dramatic Himalayan views and steaming cups of home-grown tea. Sikkim adds orchids to this compelling list of attractions.

Across the deep channel towards Burma (Myanmar) are the scattered islands of Andaman and Nicobar, hit by the 2004 Indian Ocean tsunami. Remote islands are home to still uncontacted indigenous peoples, and the deep, tropical forest is full of exotic birds. ❑

PRECEDING PAGES: tea plantations stretch across the Himalayan foothills around Darjeeling in West Bengal.
LEFT: traditional transport on the Ganga Delta in West Bengal.

KOLKATA (CALCUTTA)

From its beginnings as a small east-coast trading settlement, Kolkata (formerly Calcutta) became a city of palaces in the heyday of the Raj. Today it is recognised as a vibrant cultural centre

Map on page 222

Until 1999 when it took on the local Benghali name of Kolkata, the capital of West Benghal was known to the world as Caluctta. Its history dates back to 1686, when Job Charnock, chief of the East India Company's factory in Hugli, looking for new factory sites, selected a group of three villages – Kalikata, Govindapur and Sutanuti – where Armenian and Portuguese traders had already settled. A factory was established in Kalikata on 24 August 1690, and Calcutta was born. A fort was built, named after King William I.

The community's lifestyle was distinctly marked by the profile of the European population, most of whom were young bachelors. Punch houses, brawls and duels were common. The young "writers", as Company employees were called, usually lived with local mistresses, their "sleeping dictionaries".

In 1773, Calcutta became the headquarters and potential capital of the British administration in India. By that time, the European population had swollen from a few hundred to 100,000 through the arrival of new writers, traders, soldiers and what the administration called "cargoes of females". The city was flourishing, a home away from England with an Esplanade and a Strand. Decline started when the capital of British India was moved to Delhi in 1911. Then, with the partition of South Asia when India became an independent country, and the flow of refugees across the newly created borders, the city had more people than it could house. Following the 1971 Bangladesh war, there was a further sudden increase. This brought services to the verge of collapse. However, two developments helped alleviate the transport situation: the metro, the first in India, opened in 1984, and a suspension bridge over the river at Hastings to relieve some of the pressure on the Haora Bridge.

Kolkata is the second-largest city in India, with a population of over 13.2 million. Descriptions of its misery, however, are exaggerated. It is a lively city with a strong tradition of left-wing politics and a long-standing Communist administration. There is always something happening, be it a religious celebration, concert, cricket match, theatre or movie festival, or political demonstration; and although decaying, the architectural heritage is still there.

Kolkata's reputation as a city of intellectuals and culture is unrivalled in South Asia. It was the home not only of India's first, and so far, only Nobel laureate for literature, Rabindranath Tagore in 1913, but also its first, and again only, Oscar winner, Satyajit Ray in 1991, "in recognition of his rare mastery of the art of motion pictures, and of his profound humanitarian outlook…". During the 20th century, the city also produced some of India's most important painters and sculptors, including Jamini Roy and Nandalal Bose.

LEFT: street scene, Kolkata.
BELOW: a statue of Curzon in front of the Victoria Memorial.

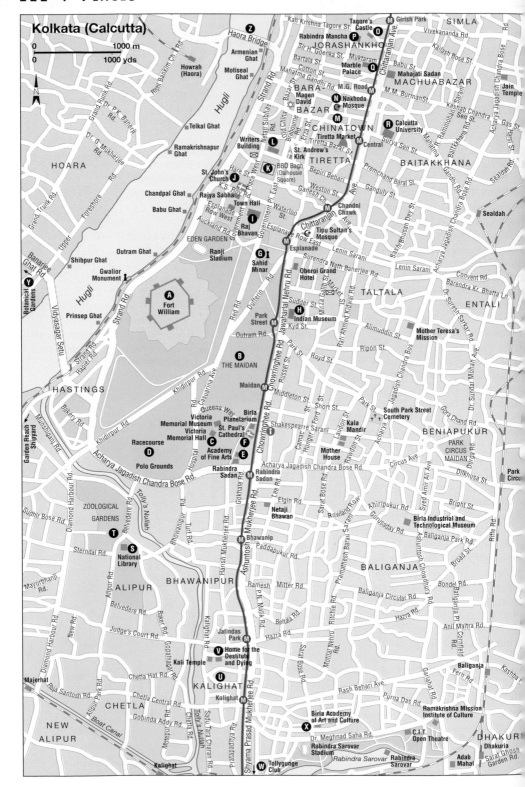

Kolkata (Calcutta)

0 ——————— 1000 m
0 ——————— 1000 yds

SIMLA

JORASHANKHO

MACHUABAZAR

BARA-BAZAR

CHINATOWN

BAITAKKHANA

TIRETTA

HOARA

HASTINGS

THE MAIDAN

TALTALA

ENTALI

BENIAPUKUR

PARK CIRCUS MAIDAN

BHAWANIPUR

ALIPUR

BALIGANJA

KALIGHAT

CHETLA

NEW ALIPUR

DHAKUR

Downtown

Kolkata was built around **Fort William** **Ⓐ**. On its western side is the **Strand** and the **Hugli River**, a branch of the Ganga; on the eastern side is the Maidan.

The **Maidan** **Ⓑ** is a huge open park surrounding Fort William. This was set up in 1758 by Clive who cleared tracts of forest around the new Fort William (now the eastern headquarters of the Indian army) to open up lines of fire for the guns. The main construction on the Maidan is the **Victoria Memorial** **Ⓒ** (open Tues–Sun 10am–5pm, entrance fee; www.victoriamemorial-cal.org), a massive domed building of white marble from Rajasthan. It was inaugurated in 1921 by the Prince of Wales. It houses an excellent collection of Victorian memorabilia as well as a huge number of items on Bengal, including paintings, miniatures and manuscripts. In the park in which the memorial stands are statues of Queen Victoria and Lord Curzon. Here people picnic, families meet for matchmaking, and pilgrims bring flowers to the statue of "Maharani Victoria".

Behind the memorial, on A.J.C. Bose Road, is the **Presidency General Hospital** where, in 1898, Sir Ronald Ross identified the carrier of malaria, the female anopheles mosquito. South of the Maidan is the **Racecourse** **Ⓓ**, opened in 1819, and in its central oval are the **Kolkata Polo Club** grounds where the game has been played since 1861.

To the southeast is Cathedral Road starting at **Rabindra Sadan**, a concert hall named after Rabindranath Tagore. The nearby **Academy of Fine Arts** **Ⓔ** (open Tues–Sun 3–6pm) has a collection of textiles, miniatures, Mughal swords, Tagore memorabilia and modern Bengali art. The adjacent **St Paul's Cathedral** **Ⓕ** was consecrated in 1847. It is a tall Gothic building with rows of fans hanging from a wooden ceiling, stalls and pews of heavy wood, and a stained-glass window by Edward Burne-Jones, *The Destruction of Sodom*. On the walls are commemorative slabs to the British killed during the 1857 uprising and those who lost their lives in various wars.

Near the cathedral are the **Birla Planetarium** (open Tues–Sun 12.30–6.30pm, entrance fee), one of the largest in the world, and the **Nehru Children's Museum** (open Tues–Sun noon–8pm, entrance fee). The latter displays a collection of toys and two dioramas of the Ramayana and Mahabharata shown in 61 scenes.

At the northern end of the Maidan, the 48-metre (158-ft) high **Saheed Minar** **Ⓖ** (Ochterlony Monument) was erected to celebrate Sir David Ochterlony's victories in the Nepal wars. In the 19th century the monument was used by Young Bengal nationalists to hoist the French flag as a sign of rebellion against the British Raj. The monument has been renamed Saheed Minar to honour martyred freedom fighters.

Nowadays the Maidan Mela is a 24-hour-a-day show. At sunrise joggers appear; the West Bengal Mounted Police hack their horses; army units do their morning drills; goats and sheep browse on the course of the **Calcutta Golf Club**. Later, trams start plying, bringing people to work. Football or cricket then takes over, and *sadhus* and bards gather audiences under trees near the **Gandhi Statue** and the **War Memorial**. At night, action concentrates around **Sri Aurobindo's Statue** opposite the Victoria Memorial.

Map on page 222

Many place names have changed in Kolkata: Harrison Road is now M.G. Road, Theatre Road is Shakespeare Sarani and Howrah is now spelt Haora.

BELOW: at the city's racecourse.

To find out what's on in this city renowned for its cultural life, pick up a copy of Kolkata this Fortnight, *available from tourist offices.*

BELOW: St Paul's Cathedral, Kolkata.

To the east of the Maidan, **Chowringhee** (now Jawaharlal Nehru Road), once a jungle path leading to the Kali Temple, and the **Esplanade** symbolise Kolkata's past grandeur with late 19th-century buildings such as the **Oberoi Grand** and the **Indian Museum** ⓗ *(see box on page 226).* Chowringhee's glory is no more: many of the facades are decaying and the old buildings are being displaced by modern high-rise developments. Hawkers, shoe-shine boys, beggars and touts now crowd the pavement.

Raj Bhavan ⓘ on East Esplanade was built in 1803 by Governor-General Wellesley, who believed that India should be governed "from a palace, not from a counting-house". Towards the river are the **Rajya Sabha** (Assembly House), the old **Town Hall** and the **High Court** built in 1872 on the model of the Gothic belfry of Ypres in Flanders. The Town Hall has been restored and now houses the **Kolkata Museum** (open Mon–Sat 10.30am–5.30pm, entrance fee) which outlines the history of the city through sound and light shows. **Eden Gardens**, north of the Maidan, is the famous site of test match cricket. The park was laid out on the site of Respondentia Walk, a fashionable promenade, and the pagoda here was brought to Kolkata from Prome in Burma by Lord Curzon.

To the north of Raj Bhavan is **St John's Church** ⓙ, built in 1784. Inside is a *Last Supper* by Zoffany. Job Charnock, the founder of the city, was buried in the cemetery here. In the garden stands the Halwell Monument to the victims of the "Black Hole", when 146 British prisoners were crammed into a small room after Fort William was stormed in 1756, and 113 suffocated and died. Beyond is **Dalhousie Square**, renamed **BBD Bagh** ⓚ in memory of three brothers, Binoy, Badal and Dinesh, who were hanged for having conspired to kill Lord Dalhousie, the Lieutenant-Governor of Bengal.

Facing the tank that once used to be Kolkata's only source of drinking water stands the **Writers Building ❶**, seat of the West Bengal Government. It was built in the late 19th century. The first Writers Buildings that stood here housed "writers" (clerks) of the East India Company. Opposite stands **St Andrew's Kirk**, opened in 1818 and built on the site of the old Court House. It is reputed to have the best organ in India. The offices of Kolkata's most prestigious companies – tall Victorian buildings, with art nouveau staircases, brass signs, marble floors and wood panelling – are on the old **Clive Row**, now **Netaji Subhas Road**. These streets are now choked with hawkers, cars and taxis. Even the **Stock Exchange** has spilled over onto the street opposite Jardine Henderson's. The Stock Exchange building on the corner of Lyon's Range, erected in 1917, houses a number of official bodies and associations. In India Exchange Lane, near the **Jute Balers Association**, speculators on the jute market operate from booths equipped with telephones projecting from the buildings along the street. Buyers shout their orders to sellers who stand in the street.

Diverse communities

Starting at the northeastern corner of the Maidan, in **Bentinck Street** there is a succession of Chinese shoemakers, Muslim tailors and sweet and tea shops. **Tiretta Market** nearby, named after its former owner, a friend of Casanova's who had to flee Venice, sells dry fish, vegetables and meat.

Chinatown ⓜ is in Tangra where the Chinese settled at the end of the 18th century. A whole area in Kolkata once was a Cantonese town, but since 1962, when Indian and Chinese troops clashed at the frontier, it has been greatly reduced. There are still some 5,000 Chinese citizens – the community has been greatly depleted by emigration – and most of the Chinese buildings have disappeared. Tangra still has a large number of Chinese restaurants and the **Sea Ip Temple** on Chatawala Gully is still going. The **Kuomintang Press**, on Metcalfe Street, publishes two daily papers in Chinese, the *Seong Pow* and the *Chinese Journal of India*.

In **Old China Bazaar**, west of Brabourne Road, Parsis have an *agiary* (fire temple), the Ismailis have a mosque, and the Gujarati Jains a temple, possibly one of the most charming in Kolkata. There are also two working synagogues, one of which, **Magen David**, was built in 1884. Kolkata's Jews came from Iraq in the 19th century and formed a prosperous community, but emigration to Israel, the US and the UK since the end of World War II has left less than 100 Jewish families in the city.

Off Old China Bazaar Lane stands the **Armenian Church of Our Lady of Nazareth**. It was built in 1724 and is said to have the oldest working clock in Kolkata. Coming as traders from Isfahan in the 17th century, the Armenians were already here and in Chinsura, upriver on the Hugli, when Job Charnock founded the city. A grave in the church cemetery is dated 1630. In and around Kolkata, the Armenians, of which there are now only a few hundred, have several churches, a school, a club and also one of India's best rugby teams.

Map on page 222

Kolkata's clean and efficient Metro system operates Mon–Sat 7am–9.15pm, Sun 3–9.15pm. Platform TVs show films while you wait. Avoid peak hours (see also http://business.vsnl.com/metrorly).

BELOW: Tagore's Castle, 1867.

A controversial figure to some, Mother Teresa (1910–97) spent her life among the destitute and dying of Kolkata.

BELOW: Belur Math, headquarters of the Ramakrishna Mission.

Along Chitpur Road, now Rabindra Sarani, stands the **Nakhoda Mosque** , built in red sandstone with four floors. The model was Akbar's tomb at Sikandra near Agra. It has room for a congregation of 10,000. The area around the mosque is full of Muslim shops and some good restaurants.

Stately homes

Jorashankho, with verandahed houses on Sir Hariram Goenka Street and mansions around Kali Krishna Nagore and Jadulal Mullick streets, has a character all its own. The most eccentric of the mansions is **Tagore's Castle** on Darpanarain Tagore Lane. It was built in 1867 and is reminiscent of the Bavarian castle of Neuschwanstein. Overbuilt structures have, unfortunately, altered its silhouette. At the end of Dwarkanath Tagore Lane is **Rabindra Mancha** (open Mon–Fri 10am–5pm, Sat 10am–1.30pm), an 18th-century house where the poet Rabindranath Tagore was born in 1861, and where he died in 1941. Adjoining the house is a library and **Rabindra Bharati University**, the Tagore Academy. The University's museum (www.rabindrabharatiuniversity.net) is devoted to the poet's life and to the Young Bengal Movement, as well as a collection of almost 2,000 of Tagore's paintings.

In **Kumartuli**, further north, lives a community of artisans making clay images of the goddesses Durga, Laksmi and Sarasvati for festivals. In **Rajabazar** on Badni Das Temple Road are four Jain temples of the Digamber sect, built at the end of the 19th century. Known collectively as the **Parasnath Mandir**, the best known is that dedicated to Sital Nath. Its architecture is a mixture of Mughal, Baroque, neoclassical and local styles, and its interior is decorated with mosaics, coloured glass, mirrors, coloured stones, crystal and marble.

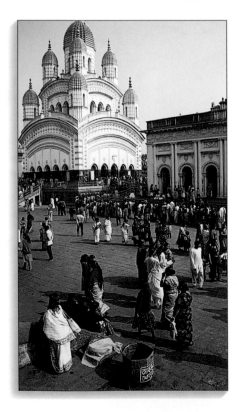

INDIAN MUSEUM

This huge museum, certainly the largest in the country, if not all of Asia, is opposite the Maidan on Jawaharlal Nehru Road. It was founded in 1814 but it was not opened to the public until 1878. Also known as the *jadu ghar*, "house of magic", it attracts a large number of visitors from the surrounding area as well as abroad.

The 36 galleries contain a large variety of exhibits and you will need to put aside a whole morning or afternoon to see the best of them. Prize archaeological exhibits include a 3rd-century BC Mauryan lion capital, excellent finds from Mohenjadaro and Harappa, and pieces from the 2nd-century BC stupa at Barhut in Madhya Pradesh. The museum also contains extensive geological and natural history galleries (although these are a legacy of rather unenlightened research methods). In addition there are collections of textiles, Kalighat paintings, miniatures and sculpture, including many Gandharan works and some excellent Pala bronzes. The new painting galleries are particularly good, with collections of Bengali art.

The museum publishes a useful guidebook to help you find your way around the vast collections (open Tues–Sun. Mar–Nov 10am–5pm, Dec–Feb 10am–4.30pm, entrance fee; www.indianmuseum-calcutta.org).

At Chorebagan ("the thieves' garden"), the **Marble Palace Q** (open Tues–Wed, Fri–Sun 10am–4pm) on Muktaram Babu Street was built in 1835 by Raja Mullick in Italian marble. The Raja's descendants still live here, but most of it can be visited. In dark halls are assembled paintings, clocks, statues, crystal and china. Among them there is said to be a Napoleon by Houdin, one Arnold, one Gainsborough, three Rubens and a statue by Michelangelo. In the yard is the family temple, and a collection of parrots, doves and mynahs.

Calcutta University R on College Square was founded in 1857 and moved to this location in 1873. It has, in the past, been the scene of many demonstrations and many of its walls are periodically covered with political grafitti. In the **University Senate** building is the **Ashutosh Museum**, presenting a collection of Pala sculptures, terracotta, bronzes, *thankas* (Buddhist religious paintings on cloth) and examples of Bengali traditional art (open Mon–Fri 10am–5.30pm; www.caluniv.ac.in). The **Coffee House**, on Bankim Chatterjee Street, is the traditional meeting place for the city's intellectual and student circles.

On R.N. Mukharji Road, to the west of BBD Bagh, is the **Old Mission**. This was built in 1770 by a Swedish missionary and is the oldest church in Kolkata. On Gurusady Road is the **Birla Industrial and Technological Museum** (open Tues–Sun 10am–5pm, entrance fee). As well as a number of models it features a life-size replica of part of a working coal mine.

Behind Chowringhee is where the Europeans used to live. It is an area of mansions slowly being replaced by modern buildings. **Park Street**, the main thoroughfare, was laid during the first quarter of the last century. The **Freemasons' Hall** on this street was built in the 19th century. It houses the Star of the East Lodge, the oldest outside Britain. The **Asiatic Society**, also at the beginning of

Map on page 222

BELOW: a clay image of the god Ganesh.

Map on page 222

The Kali Temple is said to stand on the spot where Sati's little toe landed after her dead body had been dismembered by Vishnu – to stop Shiva's destructive dance of mourning – and scattered across the earth.

BELOW: new bridge on the Hugli.

Park Street, was founded in 1784 by Sir William Jones. It houses a permanent exhibition of oriental manuscripts, prints and paintings that can be visited on request (open Mon–Fri 10am–8pm, Sat–Sun 10am–5pm; www.indev.nic.in/asiatic).

Another landmark is **La Martinière College** on Acharya Jagadish Chandra Bose Road, founded by a Frenchman, Claude Martin. A former bodyguard to the French Governor of Pondicherry, Martin later joined the service of the East India Company and ended his career as a Major General. He died in 1800, bequeathing his fortune to set up schools in Lyons, Kolkata and Lucknow, and donated a sum of Rs50,000 to the Church of the Sacred Heart in Chandernagore.

Park Street used to be called European Burial Road and once ended at the **South Park Street Cemetery**, the oldest extant in Kolkata. It was opened in 1767. Here are buried Major General Charles "Hindoo" Stuart, an Irishman who adopted the Hindu religion; Robert Kyd, founder of the Botanical Gardens; William Makepeace, Thackeray's father; Rose Aylmer, "who died of eating too many pineapples"; the poet Henry Derozio, founder of the Young Bengal Movement; and Sir William Jones, the father of the Asiatic Society.

Nearby, in Bhavanipur, is **Netaji Bhavan** on Elgin Road, the house from which Netaji Subhas Bose, the nationalist leader, escaped during World War II to establish the Indian National Army in Japanese-occupied Southeast Asia. It is now a museum (www.netaji.org).

South Kolkata

This is essentially residential, with upper-class alternating with middle-class neighbourhoods. Warren Hastings' first residence, at Alipore, now an institute of education, is said to be haunted by its former owner. The **National Library ⑤**, on Belvedere Road, was once the Winter Viceregal Lodge (open Mon–Fri 9am–8pm, Sat–Sun 9.30am–6pm; www.nlindia.org). The collections are extensive and are divided into sections corresponding to the major Indian languages.

The **Zoological Gardens ⑦**, close to the National Library, were established in 1876. Like all Indian zoos, a visit here can be a very depressing experience (for more information see www.petaindia.com, www.aapn.org and www.zoocheck.com).

Kalighat ⑪ is a middle-class neighbourhood on **Tolly's Nullah**. In 1775 Colonel Tolly drained the silted canal to bring Ganga water to the **Kali Temple**. The present *mandir* was built in 1809 by Sobarna Chowdhury on the site of a 16th-century, Kali temple, although some kind of temple has probably been here since early times. The temple is still owned by the founder's descendants, the *paladas*, who have a monopoly over rituals. Pilgrims make offerings to Kali (an *avatar* of Sati) of milk mixed with Ganga water and *bhang* (cannabis). Human sacrifices are known to have taken place, but today only goats are sacrificed. Kali's image, inside the central shrine, is made of black marble and the goddess is seen with four arms, garlanded with a chain of human heads, and with a hand, tongue and eyebrows made of gold; her eyes and tongue are painted blood-red. The temple is closed to non-Hindus.

Next door, the late Mother Teresa's **Home for the Destitute and Dying ⓥ**, or Nirmal Hriday, is the first of several missions run by her Sisters of Charity in the city *(see margin text)*. The nuns, in their white saris, can be seen all across town.

There are more temples further south on Alipore Chetla and Tollygunge roads. Nearby is the **Tollygunge Club ⓦ**. An indigo plantation was laid out here in 1781 by the Johnson family. Later the exiled family of Tipu Sultan lived in the Johnson mansion, which was subsequently converted into the club. It became the Tollygunge Club in 1895 and offers its facilities (golf, tennis and squash) to visitors on a daily basis. It is also possible to stay here (contact the club secretary in advance at: 120, Deshapran Sasmal Road, Kolkata 700 033; tel: (033) 2473 4539; www.thetollygungeclub.com).

Northeast of Tollygunge, around **Rabindra Sarovar lake**, are rowing clubs and the **Birla Academy of Art and Culture ⓧ** (open Tues–Sun 4–8pm) on Southern Avenue, a museum that is never crowded, with a whole floor of miniatures from all the major schools, a modern art gallery and old statues.

The **Ramakrishna Mission Institute of Culture** on Gol Park, near the lake, is a branch of the Ramakrishna Mission of Belur Math. It has a school of languages, a library, a museum of Indian art and a Universal Prayer Room.

Ghats on the Ganga

From the ghat near the Garden Reach shipyard, a ferry periodically crosses to the **Botanical Gardens ⓨ** (open sunrise to sunset). Set up in 1787, these once boasted the largest banyan tree in the world. The trunk was struck by lightning in 1919 and was subsequently removed. About 1,500 offshoots remain, forming a circle with a diameter of more than 10 metres (33 ft). It is also the location of the Central National Herbarium of India.

The **Metiaburuz Shiite Mosque**, where the last nawab, Wajid Ali Shah was exiled, on Garden Reach Road was built and lavishly decorated by the royal family of Avadh in the 19th century.

The riverside ghats off Strand Road, like any on the Ganga, are most active at dawn and sunset. During festivals thousands of devotees converge on **Babu**, **Outram** and **Princep Ghats** to immerse clay images of Durga, Kali, Laksmi or Sarasvati into the river. Other communities hold festivals too. On Chat, Biharis dip fruit in the river and Sindhis, on Chetti Chand, immerse statues of the god Jhulelal. On Strand Road, in January, a transit camp is arranged for the thousands of pilgrims on their way to the holy island of Sagardwip. Every morning the ghats swarm with people washing and praying.

On the riverfront promenade is the **Gwalior Monument**, called the "Pepper Pot" because of its shape, and erected to commemorate a British victory in the Maratha Wars. At Princep Ghat dinghies are available for hire on an hourly basis.

The 1941 **Haora Bridge ❷** over the Hugli has eight traffic lanes, which is not enough for the daily flow of trams, buses, trucks, rickshaws, pedestrians, buffaloes, sheep, goats, taxis and bullock-carts. On hot days its length can increase by one metre (3 ft). It has been supplemented by a new suspension bridge at Hastings. ❑

Map on page 222

Map on page 222

People interested in volunteering at the Nirmal Hriday should contact the Mother's House in advance, at: Missionaries of Charity, 54 A.J.C. Bose Road, Kolkata 700 017; tel: 033-2244 7115.

BELOW: an Ambassador taxi with St Andrew's in the background.

Map
on page
232

WEST BENGAL

*From the swamps of the Sunderbans to the peaks of the Himalayas,
this extraordinarily diverse state has attracted traders and
colonisers, poets and philosophers, all of whom have left their mark*

West Bengal stretches from the Himalayas to the Bay of Bengal. Early
mention of Bengal can be found in the Mahabharata and in Ptolemy's
geography. Bengal was then a seafaring nation, sending traders to Sri
Lanka, Sumatra and Java and being visited by Greeks, Chinese and Persians.

From the end of the 19th century onwards Bengal was one of the most
prosperous territories of the British Empire. Temples were built, and the Bengali language was enriched by poets and writers such as Bankim Chandra Chatterjee and Rabindranath Tagore, and major religious philosophers such as
Ramakrishna and Vivekananda emerged.

Early colonisers

On the right bank of the Hugli, just north of **Kolkata ❶**, along the Grand Trunk
Road, are sleepy little towns with palaces, old churches, riverfront promenades
and colonial houses and cemeteries – remains of the old Danish, Dutch and
French settlements. The Grand Trunk Road is reached by the Bally Bridge
crossing the Hugli at **Dakshinesvar** 20 km (12 miles) north of Kolkata, where,
on the left bank, stands the 9th-century **Kali Bhavatarini Temple** complex
containing a central temple to Kali, one to Radha-Krishna and 12 small temples

BELOW: a young boy
tends his grazing
cows, Vishnupur.

to Shiva. The philosopher Ramakrishna lived here and his room is now a museum. Downstream across the river is **Belur Math**, headquarters of the Ramakrishna Mission, founded by Ramakrishna's disciple Vivekananda. The main building, the **Sri Ramakrishna Temple**, 75 metres (246 ft) long and 35 metres (115 ft) high, reflects Ramakrishna's call for harmony between religions. The gate is Buddhist, the structure above the entrance South Indian, the windows and balconies Mughal and Rajput, and the floorplan is that of a Christian cross.

The first erstwhile foreign settlement north of Kolkata is **Serampore**, 25 km (15 miles) from Kolkata. The Danish East India Company carried on trade here from the late 17th century until 1845, when the Danes sold to Britain all their possessions in India. In 1799 William Carey, an Englishman, and two fellow Baptist missionaries established a press here and were pioneers of printing in several Asian languages. In 1819 Carey founded the **Serampore College**, incorporated in 1827 as a university by Danish Royal Charter. Still active, the college is now a Baptist theological institute. It stands on the banks of the Hooghly, among other 18th- and 19th-century mansions. Slightly inland is **Saint Olaf's Church**, built in 1747.

A gate bearing the motto of the French Republic, *Liberté, Egalité, Fraternité*, marks the entrance to **Chandernagore**, a French *Etablissement* almost continuously from 1673 to 1952. A French atmosphere still persists along the shaded Quai Dupleix, now Strand Road, with its public benches exactly like those in Parisian parks.

To the northwest, at **Palpara** and **Narvah**, are groups of Shiva temples. The most important of these is the 18th-century **Nandadulal Temple** at Lal Bagan, dedicated to Krishna, a good example of flat-roofed Bengali architecture.

The Dutch settled at **Chinsura**, 1 km (½ mile) south of Hooghly, in 1625 and ceded it to Britain in 1826 against Bencoolen in Sumatra. A Dutch barracks, church and cemetery still remain from that period. Chinsura's Armenian community built **St John's Church** in 1695 and, once a year, on Saint John's day, in January, the Armenians of Kolkata gather here to hold religious services. To the north, on the riverside, is the **Imambara**, a Shiite place of worship with a clock tower donated by Queen Victoria.

The Portuguese founded nearby Bandel de Ugolim, now **Hugli**, in 1580, and controlled most of the trade passing through Bengal, until the arrival of other European nations.

The **Church of Our Lady of Bandel** is all that remains of the Portuguese past. Consecrated in 1599, it was rebuilt after it was destroyed by Shah Jahan in 1632, but without the usual exuberance of Portuguese churches. It has remained a pilgrimage centre. Even today, each Christmas Eve, a Mass is celebrated.

Holy cities

There are two temples at **Bansberia ❷**, 6 km (4 miles) north of Hooghly. The small **Vasudeva Temple**, built in the 17th century, has sculptured terracotta tiles representing ships, Portuguese soldiers and scenes from

The annual Mahesh Yatra *(car festival) takes place at the Jagannpath Temple, Mahesh (3 km/2 miles from Serampore) in June/July. Images of the goas are placed on massive cars for a procession.*

BELOW: mangrove and palm-covered islands of the Sunderbans.

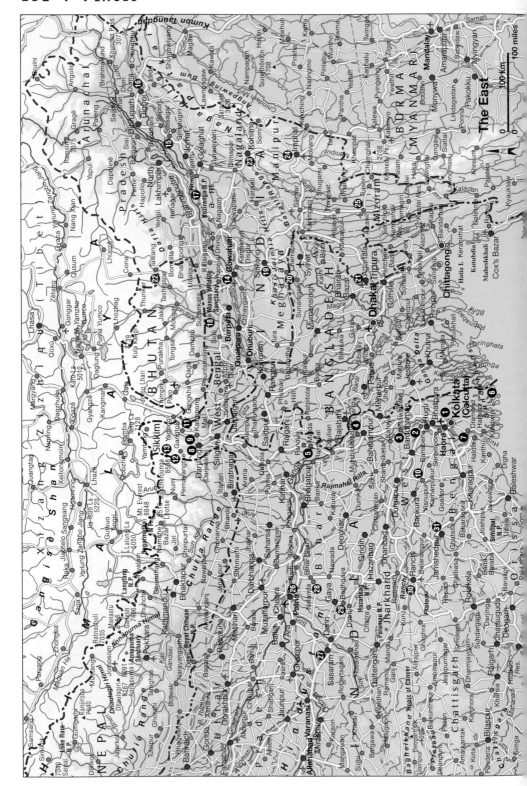

Map on page 232

the *Ramayana*. **Hangsesvari Temple**, with its 13 towers, was founded in the early 19th century. Rajah Deb started building it following a dream, but died before completion. His widow was about to commit *sati* (self-immolation) but was saved at the last moment by the religious reformer Ram Mohan Roy, founder of the Brahmo Samaj movement. She lived on and finished the temple.

Tribeni, 50 km (30 miles) north of Bansberia, is a holy place at the confluence of two rivers where twice a year, at Dussera and during the festival of Varuna, the god of water, pilgrims visit the little **Benimadhava Temple** complex and take a bath in the Ganga. On the southern side is the **Darya Zafar Khan**, Bengal's oldest Muslim building, erected in the 13th century using material from dismantled Buddhist and Hindu temples.

Nawadwip ❸, 125 km (78 miles) north of Kolkata, also known as **Nadia**, is built on nine formerly distinct islands on the Ganga, called Bhagirathi here. It was the capital of Bengal in the 11th and 12th centuries and is among the holiest of places in West Bengal. Chaitanya Mahaprabhu, said to be an incarnation of Vishnu, taught the Vaishnava philosophy here in the 16th century. Every year in March, over 500,000 pilgrims come to Nadia for the *padikrama*, a pilgrimage on foot, that takes them along a 50-km (30-mile) loop around places and temples associated with Chaitanya. Nearby is Sri Mayapur, the headquarters of the International Society for Krishna Consciousness (ISKON).

Murshidabad and Malda

Some 50 km (30 miles) north of the battlefield of Plassey, **Murshidabad ❹** was the capital of Bengal in 1705, when the diwan (Mughal viceroy) of Bengal, Bihar and Orissa, Murshid Kuli Khan, transferred his capital here from Dacca. Most of the monuments are ruined, but Siraj-ud-Daula's grave at Khusbagh (across the river), Murshid Kuli Khan's tomb inside the Katra Mosque and the Jafarganj cemetery can still be seen. There are also palaces like the Jafarganj Deorhi palace, where Siraj-ud-Daula was assassinated; and **Hazarduari**, the nawab's palace, built in 1837 in Gothic style, now a museum containing old arms, china and special plates called *ghauri* used by the nawab that, it was believed, would crack if the food were poisoned (open Sat–Thur 10am–4.30pm). Murshidabad is still well-known for its fine silk, and ivory carving.

Nearby, at **Baranagar**, are 18th-century terracotta temples. Further north, 340 km (210 miles) from Kolkata, is **Malda ❺**, formerly called English Bazaar, a foreign settlement dating from 1680, where the Dutch, the French, and then the East India Company carried on trade.

Gaur, nearby, was the capital of the Pala and Sen dynasties. The now deserted city was destroyed by the Afghan rulers of Bengal, and you can see the Barasona Baroduari Mosque completed in 1526; the Ferze Minar, a minaret built in 1486; the ruined Chika Mosque with Hindu idols on the doors and lintels; and the now dilapidated Lattan mosque. Portions of Hindu monuments from Malda were used to build the new capital of **Pandua** where the most important building is the Adina mosque.

Berhampore, 11 km (7 miles) from Murshidabad, is noted for its silk production. An interesting visit can be made to the Government Silk Research Centre here.

BELOW: Sunderbans family at home.

Sunderbans Wildlife Sanctuary is a Project Tiger centre, but visitors are more likely to see deer, monkeys and wild pigs than the elusive Bengal tigers.

BELOW: transport in the mountains near Darjeeling.

South to the Sunderbans

South of Kolkata start the **Sunderbans ❻**, "beautiful forest" in Bengali, formed by the Ganga-Brahmaputra delta, and extending across the northern shore of the Bay of Bengal. A World Heritage Site, two-thirds of which is in Bangladesh, this is an area of marshy mangrove jungle, the largest estuarine forest in the world. It is also the land of the Royal Bengal Tiger, which swims and has been known to attack fishermen.

There are few roads, and water transport is often the only way of communication. A permit is required to enter this area. Check with the West Bengal Tourist Promotion Board, particularly for the **Sudhanyakali** and **Sajankali** wildlife sanctuaries. The chances of seeing a tiger are slim, but there are estuarine crocodiles, the largest in the world, usually seen sleeping on mud flats along the river, as well as fishing cats, water monitors and turtles.

At **Bratacharingam**, 15 km (9 miles) south of Kolkata, on the road to Diamond Harbour, is **Gurusaday Museum** (open 10am–5pm), a collection of Bengali traditional art: terracotta temple plaques, clay figurines, wood sculptures, Kalighat paintings, scroll painting and *kanthas*, which are used cotton saris, stitched together and embroidered.

On the Hugli, at the end of Budge-Budge Road, branching off Diamond Harbour Road, is **Achipur**, named after Ah-Chi, the first Chinese to migrate to Bengal in modern times (end of the 18th century). His red-painted grave facing the river is probably the only Chinese tomb along the Ganga. There is also a Taoist temple with inscriptions dating back to the 18th century. On every Lunar New Year, the Chinese community of Kolkata comes here on pilgrimage, transforming this Bengali village into a Chinese community for one day.

Diamond Harbour ❼, 50 km (30 miles) down the Hugli from Kolkata, a natural harbour, is a former stronghold of the Portuguese pirates. Remains of their fort can still be seen along the riverfront.

The last island before the ocean is **Sagardwip** where the Ganga meets the sea. Every year, in mid-January, a religious festival, Gangasagar Mela, is celebrated here. Over half-a-million pilgrims take a holy dip and then converge at the **Kapil Muni Temple**. An independent trip to Sagardwip can be arranged with accommodation on board the boat.

On the west coast of the Bay of Bengal 240 km (150 miles) southeast of Kolkata, on the Orissa border is **Digha**, which has a good beach, and is very popular with Indian tourists.

North to the hill station

Every year, at the beginning of the monsoon, the viceroys of India, and after 1911 the lieutenant governors of Bengal, would move to **Darjeeling ❽** situated at an altitude of 2,134 metres (7,000 ft), facing the Himalaya. In the 1840s tea planting was introduced in the area. Darjeeling "orthodox" tea is now famous for its delicate flavour. Darjeeling is a three-hour drive up a winding road from Bagdogra airport near Siliguri. It can also be reached from New Jalpaiguri railway station by **Toy Train**. Completed in 1881, the line climbs 1,500 metres (5,000 ft) through

mountains and tea gardens. The steep ride takes seven hours – at one point the train goes so slowly that one can buy from hawkers alongside. During the monsoon the service may be disrupted.

Darjeeling is an abrupt change from the plains. The population is Nepali, Lepcha, Tibetan and Bhutia. At the town centre is the **Mall**, Darjeeling's commercial street, lined with souvenir shops. Photo stores sell prints of old black-and-white pictures from the early 1900s. The Mall leads to **Chaurastha**, a square with a bandstand, a bookshop with old books on India and Tibet, and antique shops. On **Observatory Hill** is perhaps the oldest built-up site in Darjeeling. A Nyingmapa Buddhist monastery, **Dorjeling**, "the place of the thunderbolt", once stood here but was destroyed by the Nepalis in the 19th century. A Shiva temple and an old-fashioned hotel now occupy the site.

On Birch Hill to the north stands the Shrubbery, the residence of the governor of West Bengal, and further down along Birch Hill Road is the **Himalayan Mountaineering Institute**, once headed by the late Tenzing Norgay, the Sherpa guide who conquered Everest with Sir Edmund Hillary on 29 May 1953. A museum displays the equipment used (open 9am–1pm, 2–4pm; entry through zoo). The **Zoological Park** specialises in high-altitude wildlife – yaks, Himalayan black bears, pandas, but it also has four Siberian tigers (open 10am–4pm; entrance fee). Dominating the Mall is the **Planters' Club**, which visitors can join and where they can stay on a daily basis. The **Lloyd Botanical Gardens** (open Mon–Sat 6am–5pm) were laid out in 1878 on land donated by the owners of Lloyd's Bank. They present a collection of Himalayan and Alpine flora. Nearby is the Tibetan Refugee Self-Help Centre with its temple, school, hospital, and a shop selling carpets, textiles and jewellery.

Map on page 232

The Himalayan Mountaineering Institute (Jawahar Parbat, Darjeeling, tel: 0354-225 4083) runs mountaineering courses and can advise on trekking and climbing in the region.

BELOW: Darjeeling, developed by the British as a resort.

Mount Kanchenjunga can be seen from Observatory Hill, but a much better view of the peak is that from **Tiger Hill**, 10 km (6 miles) south of Darjeeling. Taxis take visitors there to watch the sunrise. On most winter days the range can be clearly seen, with **Kanchenjunga** (8,598 metres/28,208 ft) in the middle, flanked by **Kabru** (7,338 metres/24,074 ft) and **Pandim** (6,691 metres/21,952 ft).

To the right are the Three Sisters, **Everest** (8,848 metres/29,028 ft), **Makalu** (8,482 metres/27,828 ft) and the **Lhotse** (8,500 metres/27,887 ft), and to the east, Tibetan peaks. On the way back the taxis stop at Ghum. The small Tibetan monastery by the roadside is often mistaken for the nearby **Yiga Cholang Gelugpa Buddhist Temple**, built in 1875 and hosting a 5-metre (16-ft) statue of Lord Buddha.

Along the top

With a plunging view of the plains, **Kurseong** (1,458 metres/4,783 ft), 35 km (22 miles) south of Darjeeling, marks the point where the Toy Train starts running parallel to the road. Branching off at Ghum, a road leads to **Mirik** 40 km (25 miles) southwest of Darjeeling set in attractive forests. It has an artificial lake in a small valley where boats can be hired.

A five-hour drive (57 km/35 miles to the west) from Darjeeling is the trekking centre **Sandakphu**, which is situated 130 km (80 miles) from Everest as the crow flies. As well as being the most convenient place from which to start a trek, Sandakphu deserves a visit by itself as it commands a particularly fine view of the main Himalayan range. **Phalut**, 22 km (14 miles) from Sandakphu, has spectacular views of Kanchendzonga.

Kalimpong ❾, east of Darjeeling, is reached after a two-hour journey. Driving among forests and tea gardens, the road crosses the one-lane bridge over the Teesta River, near its confluence with the Rangeet at Pashoke, finally reaching Kalimpong 51 km (32 miles) from Darjeeling. The Lepchas say the two rivers are lovers who fled the mountains to hide their love. One came down in a straight line, led by a partridge, the other zigzagged, led by a cobra, and they were united at Pashoke. Kalimpong was once the starting point for the land route to Tibet. Twice a week, on Wednesday and Saturday, a market, a *hat*, is still held here selling spices, fruit and traditional Tibetan medicines, textiles, wool and musk.

There are two Gelugpa Buddhist monasteries in Kalimpong. **Tharpa Choling** at Tirpai houses a library of Tibetan manuscripts and *thankas*. **Zangdog Palrifo Brang Monastery**, on Durpin Dara Hill, is smaller and of more recent construction.

East of Kalimpong, along the Bhutan border, are the **Dooars**, a tea garden and jungle area little known to tourists, which can be reached by rail from New Jalpaiguri and by plane via Cooch Behar or Bagdogra. At **Jaldapara** there is a Wildlife Sanctuary, with abundant wildlife including one-horned rhinos, elephants, deer, gaur and wild boar. The Tourist Lodge at nearby **Madarihat** is a villa on stilts built entirely in timber. Nearby is Phuntsholing, across the border in Bhutan.

The British brought tea to Darjeeling in the 1840s. Visit the Happy Valley Tea Estate from April to November to see tea picking and processing (open 8am–noon, 1–4.30pm, closed Mon, Sun pm).

BELOW: tea gardens cover the hills around Darjeeling.

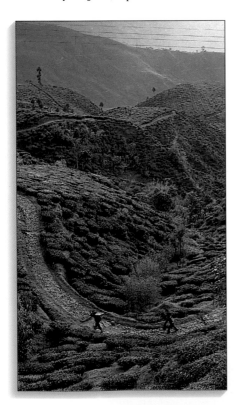

West of Kolkata

The **Tarakeshwar Temple**, built around a black stone *lingam* of Tarakesvar Babu, an *avatar* (incarnation) of Shiva, 57 km (35 miles) west of Kolkata, has little architectural interest but is one of West Bengal's most active pilgrimage centres. At Sivaratri in February and Kastamela in August, barefooted pilgrims carry Ganga water from Kolkata to the temple in earthen pots decorated with flowers and pour it over the *lingam*.

Kamarpukur, 60 km (37 miles) further west, a group of three hamlets surrounded by paddy fields, is religious philosopher Ramakrishna Paramhansdeb's birthplace. There is a temple with a marble statue of Ramakrishna.

Vishnupur , 200 km (125 miles) west of Kolkata, was the capital of the Malla kings. In the 17th and 18th centuries Vishnupur became an important cultural centre, developing its distinctive style of brick-built temple architecture, as well as being a centre for *dhrupad* singing.

Vishnupur's temple architecture is inspired by the curved roofs of Bengali village huts.

The most impressive building in Vishnupur is **Rashmancha**, a Vishnu shrine that takes the form of a flat pyramid-like structure resting on the arches of three circumambulatory galleries. Nearby, opposite the Tourist Lodge, is **Dalmadal**, a huge cannon, almost 4 metres (13 ft) long, whose boom saved the city from the Maratha armies in 1742. There are temples all over the city, most of them dedicated to Radha and Krishna. The most remarkable ones are: the **Kalachand Sri Mandir**; the **Shyam Rai Mandir**, perhaps the finest terracotta temple of Bengal, with scenes from the *Ramayana* and the *Mahabharata*; **Jor Bangla**, covered with tiles depicting naval battles and hunting scenes; the **Madan Mohan**, dating from 1694; and **Madan Gopal**, resembling a church more than a temple, with its five towers.

North of Vishnupur, 136 km (85 miles) from Kolkata, is **Shantiniketan**. In 1861 Rabindranath Tagore's father founded an ashram here. The poet spent most of his Nobel Prize money to make it an educational institution. Then, with the help of the Maharaja of Tripura, he upgraded it to the level of a university in 1921. Here the poet revived the traditional Indian way of teaching in the open air, under a tree, in close contact with nature. Shantiniketan soon became one of the hubs of intellectual life. One of the university's most famous alumni is the late Indira Gandhi.

An annual festival is celebrated near Shantiniketan, at **Kendubilwa**, the birthplace of Jaidev, another great Bengali poet and keen propagator of Vaishnava philosophy. In mid-January, Bengali bards, known as *bauls*, gather here and hold a four-day nonstop recital of the poet's work.

To the north of Shantiniketan are two pilgrimage centres. **Bakresvar**, 58 km (36 miles) towards the Bihar border, is a place of Kali worship, where the space between the goddess's eyebrows is said to have fallen when she was cut into 51 pieces. Bakresvar is famous as well for its hot sulphurous springs.

The other centre is **Tarapith**, 80 km (50 miles) from Shantiniketan, which is a small village dominated by a temple to Tara, an avatar of Kali, whose third eye is said to have landed here. ❑

BELOW: teaching in the open air at Shantiniketan.

Map on page 232

Delhi

About 660 species of orchids can be found in Sikkim. See them bloom from mid-April to early May.

BELOW: Gangtok, capital of Sikkim.

SIKKIM

High in the Himalayas, bordering Tibet, the former kingdom of Sikkim is a land of flowers, forests and holy splendours, still relatively untouched by commercialism

Sikkim is India's highest state, with peaks above 6,330 metres (21,000 ft). Kanchenjunga (8,598 metres/28,208 ft), the third highest summit in the world, is believed to be the abode of a god of the same name, a fiery character with a red face who wears a crown made of five skulls and rides a snow lion. Legend has it that, at the peak, this god buried five sacred treasures – salt, gems, sacred books, medicines and a suit of armour.

Until the 18th century, the inhabitants of Sikkim were mainly Lepchas, cultivators of Mongol origin who came from Tibet in the 8th century. The first kings of Sikkim were the Namgyals descended from the Minyaks of Tibet. Khye-Bumsa, a Namgyal prince, helped in the building of the Sa-Kya Monastery in Central Tibet in 1268. He befriended the Lepchas, and swore a blood brotherhood with their chief, Thekongtek. When Thekongtek died, the Lepchas turned for leadership to Guru Tashi, Khye-Bumsa's fourth son, who was consecrated king *(chogyal)* in 1642. In 1700 the Bhutanese invaded Sikkim and the young *chogyal*, Chador, was forced into exile. He built monasteries at Pemayangtse and Tashiding and invented the Lepcha alphabet. He was assassinated in 1717 on the orders of his pro-Bhutanese half-sister, Pei Womgmo.

In the early 19th century the East India Company entered the Himalayas with a view to opening up trade with Tibet. In 1814, in the Anglo-Nepal wars, Sikkim sided with the Company and received as a reward in 1816 parts of the Nepal Terai. As a friendly gesture, King Tsugphud Namgya gave the East India Company the hill of Darjeeling for development as a resort. Relations soured and, following a quarrel over the illegal collection of taxes by the British in Sikkim, the British annexed the Terai and established a protectorate over the kingdom. Since the 18th century Nepalis have flowed into Sikkim and they now constitute 75 percent of the population.

When British rule in India ended, the government of independent India entered into a similar arrangement with the *chogyal*. Sikkim was not wholly merged with the Indian Union. In 1975, however, the Sikkim Parliament voted for the incorporation of the kingdom into India. The monarchy was abolished and Sikkim became a state.

Gangtok

The capital, **Gangtok** ⓫, "the hill made flat", lies at an altitude of 1,640 metres (5,400 ft), facing Kanchenjunga. It is reached by road from Darjeeling, Bagdogra airport (110 km/70 miles), or New Siliguri railway station (125 km/77 miles). The most important building in the town is the **Chogyal's Palace**, usually closed to visitors except for the Tsuklakhang Royal Chapel, where ceremonies are held. The palace itself

opens once a year, during the last week of December, for the Pong Labsal festival during which lamas wearing masks perform a dance to Kanchenjunga around a banner-pole.

The **Research Institute of Tibetology**, built in 1958 by the last *chogyal* to preserve Tibetan culture, houses a library of more than 30,000 books on Buddhism, astrology, medicine and philosophy, as well as a collection of *thankas* (Tibetan religious paintings on cloth). The **Deer Park** was set up in homage to a Bodhisattva who was reincarnated as a musk deer. The **Orchid Sanctuary** is where 250 different types of orchids bloom. Nearby is a **Tibetan Refugee Craft Centre** and the well-known **Hotel Tashi Delek**.

Monastery treks

The **Rumtek Monastery**, 24 km (14 miles) west of Gangtok, belongs to the Karmapa school, a reformist branch of Tantric Buddhism, founded in the 15th century. The monastery, built in the 1960s, is a replica of one in Tibet destroyed at the time of the Chinese takeover.

About 100 km (62 miles) further west, **Pemayangtse** ⓬ has a **Red Hat Ningmapa Monastery**, built in 1705. Its walls and ceilings bear frescoes of gods and demons. A one-day trek north leads to **Tashiding Ningmapa Monastery**, dating from 1706. A longer trek can be organised from Pemayangtse. As the path approaches **Kanchenjunga** ⓭, the altitude rises to 4,270 metres (14,000 ft) and terraced rice paddies and barley fields give way to apple orchards, then fir trees and mountain lakes. **Yakshun**, reached after six hours, is a small town where the first *chogyal* was crowned in 1642. The next stages are **Bakkhin** (five hours) and **Dzongri** (six hours), with a close-up view of Kanchenjunga. ❑

Access to Sikkim requires an Inner Line Permit, obtainable from Indian foreign missions when applying for a visa. The 15-day permit is extendable in Gangtok. The eastern part of the state, the Nathu-la and Jelep-la passes leading to Tibet and the north, are closed to tourists.

BELOW: lamas at a Tibetan monastery in Sikkim.

NORTHEASTERN STATES

Map on page 232

Situated in a sensitive border region with limited road access, the northeast is India's predominant Adivasi region. As restrictions ease, visitors have a greater chance to explore this fascinating area

ike the topography, the people of the northeast, both culturally and historically, have more in common with their neighbours to the east and southeast than the rest of India. This is one of the least visited yet most fascinating areas of South Asia, and the Indian Government continues to ease travel restrictions to the northeastern states, opening up many new areas for exploration. Each of the seven states is described below; visitors should check with the Indian Government before travelling, to find out what the current entrance restrictions are.

Assam

Assam, meaning undulating, best describes this state of rolling plains dissected by the Brahmaputra and its many tributaries. One of the world's widest rivers, at places the Brahmaputra spills across several kilometres, making it impossible to see the opposite bank. The river often floods during the July monsoon, and in successive years recentlyAssam has experienced terrible deluges, due largely to excessive deforestation, in which more than a million people are displaced.

Early Assamese history

The name Assam is probably derived from the Ahoms – the dynasty that ruled Kamrupa, as Assam was known, from the 13th to the early 19th century. Legend has it that the first king of Assam was Narakasur, son of the Hindu god Vishnu and Dharitiri (Mother Earth). Narakasur was killed by Vishnu for his unreligious behaviour and was succeeded by his son Bhagadatta.

From the earliest times Assam has been a melting-pot of peoples. In 1228, the Ahoms, a Buddhist people from northern Thailand, raided Assam and defeated the ruler of Kamrupa. They established their own kingdom with their capital in Charideo (now Sibsagar). The Ahoms converted to Hinduism, but there are isolated villages in Upper Assam where Buddhist customs are still practised and the inhabitants speak Khan Thai. The Ahoms established a powerful kingdom that flourished along the south bank of the Brahmaputra. On several occasions the Mughals tried to subdue the "rats of Assam", but each time the Ahoms proved more than a match for the invaders.

British rule

The Ahom dynasty's grip on power started weakening from the 17th century. In 1792 Burma invaded Assam and the king, Gaurinath Singh, was forced to ask the East India Company for assistance. The Anglo-Burmese war of 1824–26 was followed by the Treaty of Yandaboo, whereby Burma ceded a large part of northeast India, including Assam, to the British. The

BELOW: chital, the swift-footed Indian spotted deer.
LEFT: one-horned Indian rhinoceros.

colonists gradually established their hold over the region and during World Wa
II Assam played a strategic role as an important supply route to both China an
Burma. A testament to Assam's British legacy is the region's 300 tea estates
Braving the inhospitable terrain and climate, the British, with the help o
labourers from central India, transformed large areas of malaria-infested trop
ical jungle into well-manicured carpets of tea for which the state is renowned

The site of Hajo's Hayagribha Maghadeva Mahadap temple, west of Guwahati, is believed by some to be the place where the Buddha attained nirvana.

Modern Assam

Since Independence in 1947 Assam has been fragmented into several smalle
states. Today it only occupies the plains of the Brahmaputra valley, south o
Arunachal Pradesh and the kingdom of Bhutan. The fragmentation has deepene
the crisis facing Assam. Its major problem is a growing imbalance betwee
ethnic Assamese and immigrants – Bengali Hindus displaced by Partition i
1947 and Muslim immigrants fleeing poverty in Bangladesh.

The fear of being swamped by outsiders triggered a popular student-led revol
in the 1980s, which snowballed into violent secessionist movements. The ULF.
and Bodo militants now have a powerful presence in the state and are wagin;
wars against Indian Army soldiers. As a result, Assam was shut to foreig
tourists until the 1990s. The state is now open, but visitors should keep an ey
on the political situation and take reasonable care when travelling around.

BELOW: an Adivasi fisherman in Kaziranga National Park.

Guwahati

Pragjyotishpur, the ancient capital of the Kamrup kings, is now **Guwahati** ⑭
a city with a population of around 600,000 people. Despite its dramatic locatio
on the south bank of the Brahmaputra, Guwahati is not a pretty city. There ar

spectacular views of the river from the hill 3 km (2
miles) southeast of the centre where **Raj Bhavan**, th
governor's residence, and **Belle Vue Hotel** are situ
ated, or take a boat cruise at sunset.

Close to the railway station, opposite the Dighal
Pukhuri tank, is the **State Museum** (open 10am–4pm
closed Sun, Mon and alternate Sats), housing rar
stone sculptures from the Kamrup period. Guwahat
features some unusual temples: on a small promontor
along the river is the 10th-century **Sukhlesva
Janardhan Temple**, which was rebuilt in the 17t
century. It has a statue of Lord Buddha in a rare coex
istence with Hindu deities. Nearby, in the middle o
the river on **Umananda** (Peacock Island), is a sma
Siva temple, which can be reached by boat from one o
the ghats along the bank. During the winter month
there's a daily sound and light show on Assamese his
tory on the adjoining island.

Navagraha Mandir, the Temple of Nine Planets, i
located on Chitrachala Hill. The temple was an astro
logical centre, hence the city's earlier name of Pragjy
otishpur, the "Eastern City of Astrology".

Guwahati's most important temple is **Kamakhy:
Mandir**, 10 km (6 miles) southwest of the city centr
along the banks of the Brahmaputra on Nilachal Hill
Legend goes that to stop Lord Shiva's fearful dance o
destruction, provoked by the sight of the dead body o
his consort, goddess Shakti, the lesser gods stealthil,

ismembered and scattered her body far and wide. Shakti's *yoni* (reproductive rgan) landed on Nilachal Hill. Kamakhya is one of India's main centres of the 'antric cult and human sacrifices were once common here.

Along Guwahati's boundary wall and water tank one can still see the ruins of 1e original temple destroyed in 1553 by Kalapahar, a powerful Brahman who onverted to Islam after being ostracised by his community for marrying a Mus- m princess. The present structure, with its high beehive spire and long turtle- ack hall, is typical of early Assamese religious architecture.

Map on page 204-5

around Assam

'ravelling east, about 372 km (230 miles) along the south bank of the Brahma- utra, is the old Ahom capital of **Charideo**, now called **Sibsagar** ⑮ Few mon ments have survived Assam's torrential monsoons and the tropical undergrowth 1at threatens to overrun every abandoned structure. Among those still standing re the water tank along with adjoining Devi, Shiva and Vishnu temples, an val-shaped pavilion from where the kings watched elephant fights and the *harideo* (necropolis) of the Ahom kings.

Surrounded by thick forests, 100 km (62 miles) northeast of Sibsagar, are 1e oil towns of **Duliajan** and **Digboi** ⑯. The British struck oil here in 1867 and uilt India's first refinery at Digboi.

Assam also has what may be the largest river island in the world, **Majuli** hough being subject to severe erosion and flooding it may not hold this place or long). The centre of Assamese Vaisnaivism, the island is dotted with *satras*, illage-like centres where Vishnu is worshipped through the performances of ance-dramas. The island is also a haven for many species of birds.

A pilgrimage to the hillside mosque of Pao Mekka, 25 km (15 miles) southwest of Guwahati, is said to be equivalent to one-fourth or "pao" of a Haj to Makkah.

BELOW: sunrise over the Brahmaputra river, Assam.

*A slow loris
from Manipur.*

National Parks

Kaziranga National Park , 23 km (145 miles) northeast of Guwahati, is th
main sanctuary for the Indian one-horned rhinoceros. Nearing extinction at th
turn of the 20th century, it's now being rehabilitated. Despite stringent protectiv
measures, a number are still poached every year and their horns are smuggled t
traditional medicine markets in East Asia.

To the northwest, 176 km (109 miles) from Guwahati, is the **Manas Wildlif
Sanctuary** ⓲, a thick tropical jungle set along the Bhutan border. The park is
sanctuary for several endangered species, including rhinos, tigers, pygmy hog an
golden langur. The river flowing through the park is an angler's paradise fo
mahaseer, a local variety of carp. Angling camps are also organised on the Ji
Bharali river in the **Nameri Sanctuary**, 200 km (124 miles) from Guwahati.

Meghalaya

Meghalaya, "the abode of clouds", south of Assam, was previously part o
Assam. It became a separate state of the Indian Union in 1972. It is a hill
region, and very foggy in winter, causing the traffic police to dress in fluorescen
clothing. It is inhabited by three Adivasi groups: the Garos in the west, the Kha
sis in the centre, and the Jaintias in the east. They originally constituted inde
pendent little township kingdoms, the Seiyams, which the British annexed on
by one to British India in the 19th century.

The Garos are Tibetan. They once practised human sacrifice as part of thei
local religion. In 1848, under a treaty with the British, they agreed to stop display
ing skulls in their houses. Archery stakes, a peculiar local form of gamblin
using arrows, is still a common amusement.

BELOW: the Great
Escarpment Cliffs,
Cherrapunji.

The Khasis are Mon-Khmers related to the Shans o
Burma. Their religion, Seng Khasi, holds that God i
everywhere and should not be represented or adore
in a specific form. There are no temples, just prayer
halls for specific celebrations. The Khasis adorn them
selves in jewellery made of gold and amber. T
commemorate their dead, they erect *mawbynnas*
monoliths arranged in groups of three or more tha
can be seen in most villages. The Pnars, generall
known as Jaintias, are closely related to the Khasis

The three peoples have matrilineal and matriloca
family systems. Missionaries in the 19th centur
converted most of them to Christianity but old tradi
tions persist, especially their dances. A major danc
festival, the *Shat Suk Myasiem*, the Festival of the Joy
ful Heart, is held in Shillong in April. In Novembe
the Garo 100-drum festival in Tura celebrates the en
of the harvesting season.

Shillong ⓳, the capital of Assam until 1972 an
of Meghalaya since then, lies 100 km (60 miles) sout
of Guwahati, a three-hour drive through hills covere
with pineapple and betel plantations, and pine forests
It passes along **Bara Pani** (Umian Lake).

Shillong has been called the "Scotland of the East
because of its climate and its location at an altitude o
1,500 metres (4,900 ft). Here the British and rich Ben
galis built cottages, a golf course and polo grounds.
is a small city with a market, **Bara Bazaar**, sellin

Nepali silver and Khasi gold jewellery, spices and textiles. Shillong spreads across hills covered with English-style country houses, the largest being **Raj Bhavan**, the summer residence of the governor of Assam and Meghalaya, and the **Pinewood Hotel**. Nearby are the **Ward Lake** and **Botanical Garden**. The highest point in the state is **Shillong Peak** (1,965 metres/6,440 ft), which offers a fine view of the neighbouring hills.

Cherrapunji ㉒, 56 km (35 miles) to the south, is said to be the world's wettest place, with 11,500 mm (450 in) of rain each year. The most interesting spot is **Mawphluang**, 24 km (15 miles) further south, a barren and windy plateau covered with monoliths. Beyond Mawphluang is **Mawsynram**, which has beaten Cherrapunji for the amount of annual rainfall. The road takes you along the side of a spectacular gorge. This whole region is riddled with caves, many with spectacular formations and river passages.

Access to **Garo hill country** from Shillong is difficult, via Guwahati and then southwest to **Tura**. The villages in this region have retained their traditional architecture and some traditional buildings like the bachelors' dormitory at Rongreng (Williamnagar). The highest point in the Garo Hills is Nokrek Peak (1,412 metres/4,630 ft); the rich flora in this area is now protected as part of a biosphere reserve. Also in the hill region is **Balpakram National Park** (167 km/ 103 miles from Tura), set around a huge gorge.

Tripura

Well-forested **Tripura** was the former princely state of Tipperah. The population, mostly of Tibeto-Burmese origin, took up Vaishnava Hinduism early, and was ruled by rajas until Indian independence. Other major groups in Tripura are the Kukis, related to the Shans of Burma, Chakmas, Moghs, Lusharis and Riangs. Tripura had been at war with her neighbours when the British, taking advantage of a feud between Maharajah Krishna Manikya and the Nawabs of Bengal, intervened and established a protectorate. Following independence, Tripura joined the Indian Union in 1949 and became a state in 1972.

Agartala ㉑, the capital, is a small town of 60,000 people, surrounded by hills on three sides. One of the main sights is the large **Ujjayanta Palace**, built 1899–1901 by Maharaja Radha Kishore Manikya. Much of the building is very fine and is set in pleasant Mughal-style gardens; it is now the home of the State Legislature. The **Pushbanta Palace** was erected in 1917 by Maharaja Birendra, a philanthropist who helped Rabindranath Tagore to finance the Shanniketan University in Bengal. The palace is now the residence of the Governor of Tripura. The **Tripura Government Museum** (open Mon–Sat 10am–1pm, 2–5pm, entrance fee) has an interesting array of archaeological finds and a good display of Tripura crafts.

In Udaipur (55 km/34 miles from Agartala), the ancient capital of Tripura, is the temple to **Tripura Sundari**. Said to be built on the spot where the right foot of Sati fell *(see page 228)*, it is also known as Kurma ("turtle") Pith as its shape resembles a turtle's back. By the temple is a pool containing enormous turtles which you can feed.

Map on page 232

At present foreign visitors do not need special permits to visit the states of Assam, Meghalaya and Tripura.

BELOW: monoliths erected by the Khasi, Meghalaya.

Arunachal Pradesh

North of Assam lies **Arunachal Pradesh**, kept isolated for years by its strategi location on the frontier between India and China. The area has 600,00 inhabitants divided into 82 different peoples, the largest groups being the Apata nis, Khamptis, Padmas and Miris. Most are Buddhists. **Itanagar**, the state cap ital, has a couple of interesting sights, including Itar Fort, a brick-built citade said to have been constructed by the Ahoms, and the Jawaharlal Nehru Museum which has good coverage of the state's customs and peoples.

At **Tawang 🏵**, over the Sela Pass (4,215 metres/13,820 ft), is India's larges Buddhist monastery. Founded in 1642, this Gelugpa *gompa* (monastery) is wher the 6th Dalai Lama was born. The monastery is very similar to those in Tibet, with colourfully painted windows and murals, and there is also a huge gilded statue o the Buddha. The monastery celebrates its major festival in December/January However, perhaps the main attraction is its spectacular location, at an altitude o 3,048 metres (10,000 ft); the views and surrounding scenery are breathtaking

To the east, near the border with China and Burma, the Brahmaputra forms lake, **Brahmakund**, before entering the plains of Assam. Bathing here i believed to wash away one's sins, and Hindus come by the thousands on Maka Sankranti day in mid-January. The old road to Mandalay begins at **Ledo**.

In the south of the state is the **Namdapha National Park** which has retaine much of its pristine state due to its very inaccessibility. It covers a wide variet of environments, ranging from around 200 metres (650 ft) to 4,500 metre (14,750 ft) above sea level. The remote sanctuary is home to the very rar Hoolock gibbon, and four cat species – tigers, leopards, clouded leopards an snow leopards – as well as the endangered red panda.

Foreign tourists intending to visit Arunachal Pradesh need a Restricted Area Permit. This is valid for 10 days and only for a group of four or more travellers. There is a charge of $50 per head and you must book through a locally approved tour operator. The local Indian high commission or embassy can supply more details.

BELOW:
Manipuri dancers.

Nagaland

Remote **Nagaland** is inhabited by a variety of Tibeto-Burmese peoples, speaking more than 20 different dialects, the largest groups being the Aos, Angamis and Konyaks. These Nagas were once headhunters, but the practice was abandoned two generations ago.

Cacharis, one of the Naga peoples, once established a Hindu kingdom at **Dimapur** from where they used to raid Assam and Burma. The Ahoms of Assam established their authority over the Cacharis at the end of the 17th century, but as soon as Burma invaded Assam in 1816, the Naga raids on the plains were resumed. In 1832, the British, while establishing a road link between Assam and Manipur, met the Nagas for the first time. For a few years they made attempts to control them, Naga raids being followed by punitive expeditions. In 1879 the British outpost at **Kohima** ㉓ came under Naga siege for a month. A state of permanent peace was finally reached in 1889.

During World War II the Japanese and the Indian National Army launched an attack on Kohima, taking half of the city in 1943. The objective was to reach Dimapur, a vital railhead for supplies to British Army units in forward areas. Kohima proved to be the furthest point west reached by the Japanese. The War Cemetery at Kohima contains Commonwealth graves, and a memorial with the inscription: "When you go home tell them of us and say, 'For your tomorrow we gave our today.'"

In the war against the Japanese, the Nagas were of great help to the allied forces, carrying supplies to the front, evacuating the wounded, and spying behind enemy lines. Following Indian independence, some Nagas grouped in a Naga National Council and demanded autonomy, but soon successionist elements were asking for independence. In November 1975, at Shillong, the Government of India and Naga leaders reached an agreement, whereby the Nagas accepted the Indian Constitution, but there are still occasional outbreaks of violence. Naga villages are usually perched on hills and are surrounded by a stone wall. One, **Barra Basti**, is a suburb of Kohima. To the east of Kohima, at the railhead of Dimapur, are the remains of the former capital of the Cachar Hills razed by the Ahoms in 1536.

Manipur

This is another former princely state on the Burmese border. Meitheis, a Tibeto-Burmese people related to the Shans, form 60 percent of the population. They live in the valleys and have developed *Jagoi*, a Manipuri dance style which is performed at festivals and is accompanied by the *pung* (a double-headed barrel drum). The 29 other peoples, most of them Tibeto-Burmese and now mostly Christian, form one-third of the population and live in the hills. The largest of these groups are the Lotha, the Konyak and the Nagas.

Manipuris are reputedly fierce fighters. They excel in martial arts, including: *thangta*, practised by both men and women, and accompanied by drumming; the spear dance *(takhousarol)*; the sword fight *(thangjicol)*; and wrestling *(mukna)*. The Manipuris have a history of conflict with their neighbours in Arakan and

Map
on page
232

Foreign visitors to Nagaland must acquire a Restricted Area Permit. They can visit the district headquarters and other specified places for 10 days, extendable if they are in a group of four or more, or are a married couple. Contact the Ministry of Home Affairs (Foreigners Division), see overleaf.

BELOW: an Adivasi dancer.

Map on page 232

Both Manipur and Mizoram require a Restricted Area Permit for foreign visitors. This can be obtained from: Ministry of Home Affairs (Foreigners Division), Lok Nayak Bhavan, Khan Market, New Delhi 110 003. Apply at least four weeks before your visit.

BELOW: Manipuri drum-maker.

other border regions of Burma, which they invaded in 1738. In 1819, the Raja o Manipur, who previously had paid tribute to the Burmese crown, did not attend the coronation of Burma's new King Bagyidaw. The Burmese sent out a punitive expedition. The Anglo-Burmese War was caused partly by this incursion.

Burma was defeated, and by the Treaty of Yandaboo, on 24 February 1826 recognised British sovereignty over Manipur. After years of relative peace a revolt took place in 1891 during which the British chief commissioner o Assam was killed. The rising was crushed and its leader, Tikenderjit Singh the maharaja's brother, hanged. There was trouble again in 1930, when a self styled prophet, Jadonang, announced the imminent departure of the British He was executed and the priestess of his cult, Rani Gaidiniliou, who was only 17, was sentenced to life imprisonment. She was released when India gained its independence. In 1944, the Indian National Army and the Japanese pu Imphal under siege from March to June. They were repulsed, and in March 1945, General Slim's 14th Army marched to Mandalay from the Manipur hills In 1949 Manipur became a Union Territory and a fully fledged state of the Indian Union in 1972.

Imphal , the capital, can be reached by road from Kohima after a 130-km (80-mile) drive along the famous road to Mandalay. The most impressive sigh is the huge Kwairamband Bazaar, a women's market selling food and crafts. The **Manipur State Museum** (open Tues–Sun 10am–4.30pm) has a good display o Adivasi artefacts. Also worth seeing are the two well-maintained war cemeter ies, the Raja's Palace and Royal Polo Grounds. Nearby, at **Langthabal**, is the Raja's Summer Palace. **Moirang**, 45 km (28 miles) from Imphal, has the **Thankgjing temple**, dedicated to a forest god, and is also known as the head quarters of the Indian National Army *(see page 53)*.

Mizoram

The former Lushai Hills District, **Mizoram** is bor dered by Bangladesh on one side and Burma on the other. The region has deep river gorges, the sides o which are densely forested with bamboo. Related to the Shan, Mizos are a group of peoples (Lushais Hmars, Pawis) that came relatively recently to India They started raiding tea plantations in 1871. The Brit ish retaliated and established control over the area in 1872, but could not establish peace until 1892. The British then introduced the Inner Line system. Only missionaries were allowed through. As a result, 9 percent of the population is Christian and literacy ha reached 86 percent in some areas. At Indian independ ence Mizoram became a Union Territory, and wa granted full statehood in 1987.

The capital, **Aizawl** , is built along a ridge. In tow is Bara Bazaar, the central shopping area where loca people in traditional costume sell their produce, includ ing river crabs in small wicker baskets. The small **Mizoram State Museum** (open Mon–Fri 9am–5pm Sat 9am–1pm) has an interesting collection of loca artefacts. Other places of interest include the **Dampha Wildlife Sanctuary** on the Bangladesh border, and the busy town of **Champhai**, from where you can visit the traditional Mizo village of **Ruantlang**.

Tea

Chinese tradition points to India as the original home of tea. A Brahman, Dharma, went as a missionary to China. He was so tired that he fell asleep on reaching his destination. When he awoke, he was so angry at his own weakness that he tore out his eyebrows. The hair took root and became tea plants. He ate the leaves and fell into meditation.

Tea had been identified in Assam by English travellers as early as in the last years of the 18th century. When the East Indian Company's monopoly of importing tea into Britain from China was abolished in 1823, the Honourable Company decided to look into the possibility of growing tea in India.

Expeditions were sent to Assam, and in 1826, following the Burmese wars, the Company's troops brought back a tea bush as evidence of the existence of tea in the area. On Christmas Eve 1844, the Governor General, Lord Bentinck, officially announced the discovery of tea in India and called for the development of the industry. Production started in Assam in 1836, in Bengal in 1839, and in the Nilgiris in the South in 1863. Plantations were introduced around Darjeeling in the early 1840s. The bushes were not indigenous; they had been smuggled out of China.

The first Indian teas were of low quality and Chinese experts were brought to Assam to supervise the processing of tea leaves. India became a major grower and, by 1900, was supplying Britain with 150 million pounds of tea against 15 million brought from China.

Today, India is the world's largest producer of the fragrant leaf, with an output of 635,000 tonnes (total world production, 2 million tonnes). India's area under tea (400,000 hectares/ 990,000 acres) is the largest in the world. More than half of Indian tea is grown in Assam, one quarter in West Bengal and one fifth in the southern Nilgiris.

There are two sorts of Indian tea. CTC tea, the most common, takes its name from the Cut-Twist-Curl process in which the leaf is broken. It gives a strong liquid of dark colour.

Most CTC production is for the home market. "Orthodox" teas have a lighter colour (they are said to be "bright") and yield a weaker liquid: one kilo makes 350 cups against 500 for CTC tea. Most of the Orthodox tea is exported, the best varieties being Darjeeling and Assam Golden Flower Orange Pekoe.

Some 60 percent of the Indian production is sold through auctions, including all export teas. There are auction centres at Guwahati, in Assam; Kochi, Coimbatore and Coonoor, in the South; and at Siliguri and Kolkata, in West Bengal. The Kolkata centre has two auction rooms (one for the home market, the other for exports), and the largest tea-tasting room in the world.

From having been consumed only by the hill peoples 150 years ago, tea has become the national drink of India. However, on average, each cup of tea consumed by an Indian is matched by approximately six consumed by an English person.

Tea gardens can be visited in Darjeeling and in the South, where the whole process of tea preparation can be observed. ❑

RIGHT: Darjeeling tea-pickers at work. India is the world's largest producer of tea.

Map on page 232

Delhi

BIHAR

Landlocked Bihar is one of the poorest states in India, but for travellers interested in Buddhism and Jainism it offers a wealth of historic sites

Bihar lies in the eastern Gangetic plain. It was the seat of several of the most famous ancient Indian dynasties and the cradle of Jainism and Buddhism. The name Bihar is itself derived from *vihara* (Buddhist monastery). Although the state is situated on the fertile alluvial soils of the floodplain of the Ganga, this is one of the very poorest parts of India. Bihar is notorious for its extreme divisions of caste, manifested in sporadic outbreaks of caste-based violence, adding to the state's lawless reputation. On one side are the brutal private armies of the landlords, and ranged against them, Naxalite communist insurgents with close links to Nepal's Maoist Nepal Communist Party. Travellers visiting Patna and the major Buddhist sites should face few problems, but visitors travelling off the beaten track should be alert to the possiblity of trouble.

Patna 26, the capital of Bihar, is a city of more than a million lying beside the Ganga. Under the name of Pataliputra it was the capital of the Magadha empire. Patna is divided in two by a large square known as the Maidan. To the west lies **Bankipur**, a cantonment and administrative area with colonial buildings, including **Raj Bhavan**, the governor's residence; the **Maharaja's Palace**, now the Bihar State Transport Corporation; **Patna Women's College**, an early 20th-century neo-Mughal complex; and 1920s bungalows for government officers.

The **Patna Museum** near the **High Court** houses a collection of Hindu and Buddhist stone statues, bronzes and terracotta sculptures, 18 of which were stolen in 2006, even though the police station is next door. Among the exhibits is a 15-metre (49-ft) long fossil tree said to be 2,000 million years old and the longest tree fossilised in the world (open Tues–Sun 10.30am–4.30pm). At the entrance of the hall, on the left, is the **Didarganji Yakshi**, a buff-coloured Mauryan sandstone statue of a woman, remarkable for her brilliant polish, her firm rounded breasts, her navel, and her aggressive belly and hips. It is considered to be one of the greatest examples of Indian art of all times. Between the Maidan and the Ganga stands the **Golghar**, a beehive-shaped structure, built in 1786 as a granary. It is 27 metres (88 ft) high and can hold 150,000 tonnes of wheat. Two stairways lead to the top, offering a fine view of Patna.

Old Patna lies to the east of the Maidan. In this district of bazaars, a few buildings stand out: the **Khuda Baksh Oriental Library**, which contains rare Islamic manuscripts, including some from the Moorish University of Córdoba in Spain; **Padri-ki-Haveli** (St Mary's Church), built in 1775; **Sher Shah Masjid** and **Patther-ki-Masjid**, mosques erected respectively around 1540 by Sher Shah, and in 1621 by Parvez Shah, son of Jahangir and Governor of India.

Haramandirji, a *gurdwara* in old Patna, is one of

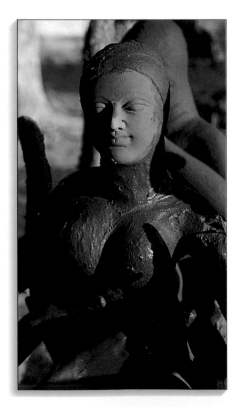

BELOW: a mud statue for a religious festival.

the holiest places for Sikhs. Guru Govind Singh, the 10th and last Sikh Guru, was born and died here. The *gurdwara*, built in the 19th century around the room where the Guru was born, is a white marble building housing a museum of the Sikh religion. On top is a terrace with marble kiosks from where one can watch the sun going down over the city while loudspeakers broadcast the recitation from the Holy Granth.

Near the *gurdwara*, and visited only by appointment with the owner, is **Qila House**, a private residence built on the ruins of Sher Shah's fortress, which houses a collection of jade, Chinese paintings, silver filigree work of the Mughal period, and a bed that once belonged to Napoleon.

At **Gulzaribagh**, further east near the Mahabir Ghat, is a former East India Company Factory, now a Government Printing Press. Visitors can see the opium godowns, the former ballroom and the hall where Shah Alam II was crowned Emperor of Delhi (under the protection and patronage of the East India Company) on 12 March 1761. In the same area, to the south at **Kumhrar**, a park has been created around the remains of **Pataliputra**. Here are the foundations of Emperor Ashoka's palace, wooden beams from structures in the former city, ramparts, and the pond where Ashoka is said to have thrown the bodies of his 99 brothers – this was before his conversion to Buddhism.

The **Mahatma Gandhi Bridge** crosses the Ganga east of the city. On the north bank, near the confluence of the Ganga and Gandak, at **Sonepur**, an animal fair is held in October/November. Further north, **Vaishali**, 40 km (25 miles) away, is the former capital of the Vajian Confederacy (6th century BC), probably the first republic in Asia. The Second Buddhist Council was held here in 383 BC. All that remains is an Ashoka pillar and ruins of Buddhist stupas. The road beyond Vaishali reaches the India-Nepal border at Raxaul. Further east is the village of **Madhubani** (7 hours from Patna), famous for its Mithili style of painting.

About 30 km (20 miles) from the Nepalese border is the town of **Motihari**, where Eric Arthur Blair, the future George Orwell was born in 1903 to an opium inspector. Plans are afoot to make his old two-room house a heritage site and build an "Animal Farm" there.

Mughal monuments

Some of Bihar's finest monuments lie west of Patna. At **Maner**, 30 km (18 miles) away, are two mausoleums. **Choti Dargah**, in a small Muslim cemetery, is the grave of Maneri, a 17th-century ascetic. **Bari Dargah**, on the high bank of an artificial pond, was built in 1620 by Ibrahim Khan, Governor of Bihar under Jahangir, as a mausoleum for Shah Daula, his religious preceptor. At **Sasaram** ㉗, 155 km (96 miles) to the southwest, are monuments from the time of Suri (Afghan) rule, including 16th century Emperor **Sher Shah's Mausoleum**.

Buxar, 110 km (68 miles) west, is the place where Rama is said to have fought the demon Taraka and received, with Laksmana, higher knowledge from the sage Vishvamitra. Rama is said to have left a footprint here at Ram Rekha Ghat. Nearby, in 1764, the British defeated Mir Kasim, the last independent nawab of Murshidabad, adding Bengal and Bihar to theirIndian possessions.

Bihar's biggest spectacle is the month-long Sonepur Elephant Fair, which takes place every October/November at the confluence of the Ganga and Gandak rivers.

BELOW: Patna.

The cradle of Buddhism

Nalanda ㉘, "the place that confers the lotus" (*nalam* means spiritual knowledge), lies 90 km (56 miles) south of Patna. This is the site of **Sri Mahavihara Arya Bhikshu Sanghasya**, a monastic university that flourished from the 5th century until 1199, when it was ransacked by the Afghan invader, Bakhtiar Khilji *(see below)*. Lord Mahavira, the last Jain Tirthankara, and Lord Buddha taught here. Nalanda developed as a centre of Buddhist learning.

Leaving Nalanda for Rajgir, the road passes a small Chinese temple, the **Nava Nalanda Mahavira Research Centre on Buddhism and Pali Literature**, set up by the Bihar Government, and **Wat Thai Nalanda**, a small Thai temple.

Rajgir, or Rajgriha, the "royal palace", 12 km (7 miles) south, was the capital of the Magadha Empire in the 6th century BC. It is a holy place both for Jains and Buddhists. Lord Mahavira taught here for 14 rainy seasons. The Buddha, too, spent five rainy seasons at Rajgir. He had so impressed King Bimbisara on his first visit to Rajgir that, when he returned from Bodhgaya having attained enlightenment, accompanied by 1,000 disciples, the king built a monastery set in a bamboo park for this new order *(sangha)* of monks.

Contemporary Rajgir, a small town, is located north of the ancient site that spreads over seven barren hills surrounding a valley. A 50-km (30-mile) wall with watchtowers built of huge stone blocks used to run round the city. Its remains stand on the hills and at the north and south gates.

Passing by the remains of the **Ajatasatru Fort**, built in the 5th century BC, the road reaches a small square lined with shops. On the right is **Venuvana**, the bamboo park where the Buddha and his disciples lived. A small mound, now covered with Muslim graves, marks the site of the stupa and *vihara* built by Ajatasatru. In the park is **Karanda Tank**, where the Buddha is said to have bathed.

The **Nipponzan Myohoji** is a large Japanese temple and the Centaur Hokke Club caters to the needs of Japanese pilgrims, offering traditional Japanese meals and accommodation. Burmese Buddhists have also built a temple, to the east of the fort, at the foot of Vipula Hill. Further up the hill, past the **Pippla Cave** and the **Jarasandha-ki-Baithak**, a monastery built out of large blocks of stone, is the **Saptaparni cave** where the first Buddhist Council was held. To the south, a cylindrical stone structure, **Manyar Math**, is a former temple to Maninaga, a serpent demi-god, referred to in the Mahabharata. Turning left, the road passes **Jivakamhavana**, the site of the mango grove presented to the Buddha by Jivaka, Bimbisara's physician, and reaches **Maddakuchchi**. From here one has to walk to **Gridhrakuta Hill**, probably the holiest place in Rajgir, where the Buddha delivered most of his sermons. From Maddakuchchi, an

Warning sign at the Mahabodhi Temple, Bodhgaya. The temple stands beside the site of the bodhi tree under which the Buddha is said to have attained enlightenment.

NALANDA

A t its height the university of Sri Mahavihara Arya Bhikshu Sanghasya at Nalanda had a vast library, 2,000 teachers and more than 10,000 students from as far away as Japan, Sumatra, Java and Korea. Legend has it that it contained 9 million volumes and that following the sack of Nalanda in 1199 it burned for six months.

Excavations have yielded nine levels of occupation, six temples *(chaityas)* and 11 monasteries *(viharas)*, all built in red brick. The monasteries are on the eastern side. The main ones are Vihara 1, founded in the 9th century by King Balaputradeva of Sumatra; and Viharas 4 and 5, built by King Kumar Gupta in the 1st century AD. The *viharas* show remains of student cells, lecture halls, bathrooms, kitchens, libraries, storage rooms and wells. To the west are the temples. The most imposing is the Sariputra Stupa, built by Emperor Ashoka in honour of Ananda, the Buddha's first disciple. It is a three-level structure, partly covered with stucco figures of Lord Buddha teaching, and surrounded by stupas erected to the memory of students who died during their studies. Nearby are Chaityas 12, 13 and 14, largely in ruins.

A new site, Sarai Mound, has been excavated to reveal faded frescoes of horses and elephants. East of the ruins is a museum with stone and terracotta sculptures.

aerial ropeway chairlift leads to the top of **Ratna Giri**, a hill at the top of which Japanese Buddhists have built the **Vishva Shanti** (World Peace) **Stupa**, a huge white structure visible from miles around. Four golden statues, one on each side, recall the Buddha's birth, enlightenment, teachings and death.

Map on page 232

Places of pilgrimage

Gaya, 90 km (56 miles) southwest of Rajgir, is an important Hindu site. Lord Vishnu is said to have conferred upon Gaya the power to cleanse one of one's sins. Devotees flock here to perform ceremonies to clear their dead of the burden of sin they might have carried over to the next world. They take a holy dip in the Phalgu River and lay offerings of *pindas* (sweets) and ritual rice cakes on the ghats along the river, before entering the **Vishupada Temple** (closed to non-Hindus) built by the Maharani of Indore in 1787 over the footprint of Lord Vishnu. Within the grounds of the temple stands a banyan tree that is said to be the one under which the Buddha spent six years meditating.

In Rajgir, at the foot of Vaibhara Hill, Jain and Hindu temples have been built around 22 hot springs. Public baths have been set up where one can relax in the hot emerald-green waters.

The Buddha attained enlightenment in **Bodhgaya** 29, 12 km (7 miles) south of Gaya, along the Phalgu River. He first meditated in nearby Dungesvari, eating one grain of rice a day for two years, then nothing for four years. Realising that mortification did not bring enlightenment, he moved to a cave where voices told him this was not the place. He then found a *ficus* – now known as the *bodhi* tree – and sat under it to meditate, vowing not to rise until he attained enlightenment.

King Ashoka erected a shrine near the *bodhi* tree, replaced in the 2nd century by the present **Mahabodhi Temple**. In the 17th century, Hindus took over the temple as the Buddha is considered an avatar of Visnu, and it is now managed by a joint Buddhist-Hindu committee. Inside is a gilded statue of the Buddha, sitting cross-legged, with his right hand touching the ground in acceptance of enlightenment. Around the temple are votive stupas.

BELOW: the Mahabodhi Temple, Bodhgaya.

Along the western wall is the *bodhi* tree, or rather its latest successor. The original is believed to have been destroyed by Emperor Ashoka before his conversion to Buddhism. The replacement was cut down by Ashoka's jealous wife. The next in the line was destroyed by Shasanka, a Hindu king of Bengal. The immediate predecessor of the present tree withered in the 19th century. Under the tree is the **Vajrasana**, the **Diamond Throne**, a stone slab marking where the Buddha was sitting when he attained enlightenment.

Along the north side of the Mahabodhi Temple, the **Chanka Ramana**, a platform built in the 1st century BC, marks the place where the Buddha walked in meditation. Carved stone lotuses indicate the spots where the lotuses sprung from his feet. South of the temple a statue of the Buddha protected by a cobra stands in the middle of a large lotus pond.

Many non-Indian Buddhist communities have built monasteries in Bodhgaya, most of which accept foreign students. More controversial are plans to build a huge bronze Buddha statue which will dominate the site (see www.maitreyaproject.org for more details). The archaeological museum (open Sat–Thur 10am–5pm) displays various sculptures, some of them defaced during the 12th-century Muslim invasion. ❑

Map on page 232

Rajrappa, on the confluence of the Damodar and Bhairavi rivers, is a lively pilgrimage site sacred to the goddess Chinamastika.

BELOW: steelworks ar Jamshedpur.

JHARKHAND

Located on the wild and remote uplands of Chota Nagpur, Jharkhand is home to many Adivasi peoples. It contains much of India's mineral wealth

To the south of Bihar is the new state of Jharkhand. Previously part of Bihar, the new state came into being in November 2000, and largely comprises the mineral-rich Chota Nagpur plateau. A large part of the population is Adivasi, speaking Mon-Khmer languages. The main peoples are the Santhal, Bedia, Birhor, No, Khond, Munda and Oraon. Some are still wanderers, living off hunting. The majority have settled to cultivate maize and millet, and raise cattle and fowl. About 60 percent are Christian. Many Adivasi groups face severe discrimination, and in desperation many have left their traditional villages to find work in the state's new industrial cities.

Ranchi ③⓪, the former summer capital of Bihar, lost its cool climate when its trees were cut to make room for a new industrial town. A few colonial buildings remain: the **Eastern Railway Hotel**, the **Lutheran Church** and **Saint Paul's Anglican Church**, and some eccentric villas on Kanke Road, near Ranchi Hill. Beyond the bazaar area, on top of Ranchi Hill, overlooking Ranchi Lake, stands a **Shiva Temple** of limited interest compared to the 17th-century fortified **Jagannath Temple** at Jagannathpur near the airport. It is open to non-Hindus. The city is also home to the **Tribal Research Institute and Museum** (open Mon–Sat 10.30am–5pm), which has a large ethnographic collection open to the public.

The new state has a great deal of its forest cover (though this is being steadily depleted through logging) and there are many beautiful sites within easy reach of Ranchi. Three spectacular waterfalls lie within 40 km (25 miles) of the capital, the **Hundru**, **Dassam** and **Johna falls**, and a little further are the **Panch Ghagh falls** (55 km/35 miles from Ranchi; so-called because it has five cascades in a row) and the **Hirni falls** (70 km/44 miles from Ranchi).

India's industrial heartland

Jharkhand's mineral wealth is the richest in India and accounts for most of the state's income. As well as substantial deposits of coal and iron ore, there are also reserves of bauxite, copper and mica. The loss of these resources to the already poor neighbouring state of Bihar is potentially devastating.

Jamshedpur ㉛, 170 km (106 miles) south of Ranchi, is the property of the Tata Iron and Steel Company. The city has grown around the first and most productive steel plant in India, built in 1912 by the late Parsi industrialist, Sir Jamshedji Tata, after whom the city is named.

East of Ranchi is "the Indian Ruhr", an industrial zone spreading along the Damodar River into West Bengal. In the northeast of the state is the city of **Dhanbad**; this sits on the largest coal reserves in India and the city is dominated by collieries, technical institutions and research centres. Just to the west is **Bokaro**, the site of India's largest steel complex. To the northwest of Dhanbad, the **Parasnath Hill** is a religious centre noted for its 24 Jain temples of both the Svetambara and Digambara sects, the most interesting ones being the **Samosavan**, **Bhomia Baba** and **Parasvanath**. Of the 24 Jain Tirthankaras, 20 attained *nirvana* here. ❏

Palamau National Park, 140 km (87 miles) west of Ranchi, is both a Project Tiger site and a good place to spot wild elephants, particularly in March and April.

BELOW: a sambar deer.

ORISSA

Map on page 258

Tropical Orissa has much to offer the traveller. Temples abound, notably the Sun Temple at Konark; pilgrims flock to the seaside city of Puri; elephants and tigers inhabit the wildlife parks

Delhi

Most visitors to Orissa seek out Adivasi villages, ancient temples, or wide beaches with migrant turtles, although the state is also known for its dancers and sudden cyclones; in 1999 a huge cyclone hit the state, killing thousands of people and destroying many buildings. Ancient seafarers from Orissa set up colonics in Burma and Java. Buddhism became the religion of the kingdom of Kalinga, as Orissa was called, soon after the faith was established. Buddhist universities flourished at Nrusinghanath and Ratnagiri, near Cuttack.

Orissa is an intensely religious state where devotion is focused on Lord Jagannath, an incarnation of Visnu. Not surprisingly, many elements of Orissan culture stemmed from its temples, where the most remarkable erotic statuary can be found and where Odissi originated, a style of religious dance. Odissi was performed previously in temples by resident dancers *(maharis)* devoting their lives to the temple god. When temple dance was outlawed the style began to disappear; however, Odissi has been revived as a performing art.

LEFT: a Bonda girl.
BELOW: 11th-century Lingaraj Temple at Bhubaneshwar.

Bhubaneshwar: city of temples

Capital of Orissa only since 1956, **Bhubaneshwar ❶** is a city of temples. There were once more than 1,000 of them and many are still active. A large number of temples are located around **Bindu Sarovar**, a tank that is believed to receive water from all the holy rivers of India. The **Lingaraj Temple** to the south, built in 1014 to the glory of Siva, is certainly the most impressive. A massive wall surrounds a 45-metre (150-ft) high *deul* (temple), as well as minor temples to Parvati, Gopalini and Bhubanesvari. All are decorated with a profusion of sculptures of deities, nymphs and amorous couples. Entry is prohibited to non-Hindus.

Vaital Deul is a typical 8th-century temple with an oblong roof *(khakhara deul)*. It is decorated with stone figures of Durga, such as the eight-armed Mahishsuramardini, on the northern wall, piercing the left shoulder of Mahisasura, the buffalo-headed demon, with her trident. Within the sanctum, another *avatar* (incarnation) of Durga, eight-armed Chamunda, often hidden by a drape, sits on a corpse, with an owl and a jackal on each side. She wears a garland of skulls.

Sisiresvara Temple, next to Vaital, has sculptures of lions, elephants, the gods Ganesh and Kartikeya, and the Avilokitesvara Buddha seated cross-legged and accompanied by a deer and a *nag* (cobra), showing how strong Buddhist influence was in Orissa. The **Uttaresvara Temple** on the north bank of the lake has undergone extensive restoration.

Parasuramesvar is one of the oldest of a group of temples east of the lake. Built in the 7th century, it is still well preserved and is decorated with a four-

armed Ganesh, a two-armed Kartikeya mounted on a peacock and killing a snake
amorous couples and rampant lions. **Muktesvara** is the gem of Orissan architecture. Entrance to the temple compound is through a sculptured *torana* (gateway); the *jagamohana* (porch) has diamond-shaped latticed windows and a richly
decorated interior. Temple, gateway and walls are covered with figures of female
warriors, erotic scenes, elephants, women, monkeys in various comic scenes
women worshipping *lingas* and *naginis* (half-snakes, half-women). On each side
of the *deul* is a grimacing lion face, flanked by smiling *ganas* (dwarfs).

Bhubaneshwar has two museums worth visiting. The **Orissa State Museum**
(open Tues–Sun 10am–1pm, 2–5pm; entrance fee) displays Hindu, Buddhist and
Jain sculptures, and early Orissan palm manuscripts. The **Handicrafts Museum** has a collection of traditional art, including Cuttack silver filigree. The
Tribal Research Museum (open Mon–Sat 10am–5pm) is in a cluttered government office, and has a decent bookshop of manuscripts and maps.

Around Bhubaneshwar

West of Bhubaneshwar, on the immediate outskirts, are two hills, **Udayagiri** and
Khandagiri. Both were once inhabited by Jain ascetics who lived in cell
excavated in the rock. Khandagiri has fewer caves than Udayagiri but a smal
Jain temple still stands on top of this hill.

At **Dhauli**, a hill 8 km (5 miles) south of Bhubaneshwar, there is an example
of Emperor Ashoka's edicts. Sculpted elephants mark the site where in 262 BC
the Mauryan emperor Ashoka defeated Kalinga troops, slaying 100,000 people
and taking 150,000 captive. This scene of bloodshed is said to have turned
Ashoka away from violence and led him to adopt Buddhism. To commemorate

*Rajarani Temple in
Bhubaneshwar is
noted for sculptures
of women in
sensuous poses.*

BELOW: the
Jagannath temple,
Puri.

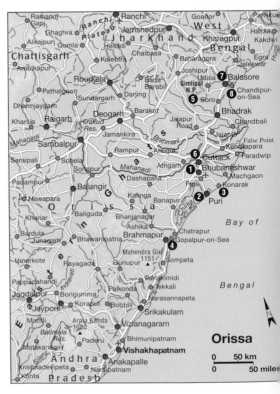

Ashoka's acceptance of Buddhism, substituting the ideal of *dharmavijaya*, spiritual victory, for *digvijaya*, military conquest, Japanese Buddhists have built a white **Peace Pagoda** on top of the hill. Some 10 km (6 miles) south is **Pipli**, a small village specialising in appliqué work in vivid colours unique to this area.

Puri ②, 60 km (37 miles) southeast of Bhubaneshwar, is the holiest place in Orissa for Hindus, and one of the biggest pilgrimage centres in India. The city was once a flourishing port identified with ancient Dantpur.

Puri is known for its cult of Jagannath, originating, some say, in the times when the people of Orissa worshiped trees, hence the practice of carving his image in wood. According to the more popular legend, however, the Lord appeared in King Indrodyumna's dream and commanded him to build a temple for him. The king complied, having the images carved out of a single log of wood found floating in the sea, as the Lord had enjoined in the dream. The climax of Jagannath worship is the *Rath Yatra* festival celebrated every summer at the **Jagannath Temple** *(see page 260)*.

Although the beach at Puri is one of the best in India, the seas can be very rough, with strong and erratic currents. Caution is advised. *Nolia*, lifeguards, easily recognisable by their white cone-shaped straw hats, are not always alert. Be sure to watch the fishermen come ashore through the surf.

The Sun Temple

Going north, 33 km (20 miles) from Puri, is **Konark** (Konarak) **③**, a former centre of Orissan Buddhism, an active port (now silted up) and, in ancient times, a centre for sun worship. A temple to the Sun God was built in the 9th century. The present **Sun Temple** was erected in the 13th century and took 16 years to complete;

Map on page 258

An Orissan temple (deul) consists of a sanctum, one or several front porches (jagamohanas), a dancing hall (nata mandir) and a hall of offerings (bhoga mandapa).

BELOW: a carved wheel at the Sun Temple, Konarak.

1,200 artisans were employed on the task. In its original form the temple consisted of a 70-metre (230-ft) high *deul* with a 40-metre (130-ft) *jagamohana*, representing the Chariot of the Sun; drawn by seven impetuous horses, the chariot rode on a dozen pairs of eight-spoke wheels. The *deul* collapsed in the middle of the 19th century and one horse is missing. The temple no longer stands on the shore since the sea has receded 3 km (2 miles). Despite its dilapidated state the Sun Temple stands out as a fine example of Orissan architecture. Erotic sculptures of couples in sensuous contortions, depictions of nymphs, war, hunting and court scenes, musicians, floral motifs, and elephants are carved on the ruins.

Two lions guard the pyramidal entrance of the Sun Temple at Konarak, and on each side of the temple stands a colossal war elephant, and a warhorse trampling fallen warriors.

South along the coast

South of Bhubaneshwar, along the coast, is **Chilka Lake**, a 1,100-sq km (425-sq mile) shallow inland sea, separated from the Bay of Bengal by a sandy ridge, spreading over 75 km (47 miles) from north to south. From Barkul, the Orissa Tourist Development Corporation operates a two-hour cruise to Kalijai Temple offshore, and to Nalabar Island. The lake has an abundance of fish and shellfish. From mid-December to mid-January migratory birds spend the winter here. Further south, 95 km (59 miles) from Bhubaneshwar, **Gopalpur-on-Sea ❹** was, during the time of the British Raj, one of the finest beach resorts in Eastern India.

Adivasis live in the district of **Koraput**, the Southern Hills area. Most are from the Austro-Asiatic Munda group, and the Bondas are the least acculturated. Women marry boys half their age and the men, armed with arrows, get drunk on sago palm toddy. They dress mostly in beads, though the women wear a stack of nine metal rings around their necks. Market day is the best time to spot them

BELOW: an Adivasi woman, Puri.

an Adivasi woman, Puri.

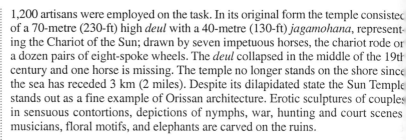

JAGANNATH TEMPLE, PURI

Known as the "White Pagoda", the Jagannath Temple was built in the 12th century. It lies in the midst of a huge complex of buildings where more than 5,000 priests and temple staff live. The main building is 65 metres (213 ft) high, surmounted by the mystic wheel *(chakra)* and the flag of Visnu. It is surrounded by a wall 6 metres (20 ft) high. Non-Hindus are not permitted to enter the temple.

About two weeks before the annual festival of *Rath Yatra*, held in June and July, the images of Jagannath and his brother, Balabhadra, and his sister, Subhadra, are given a ritual bath. On the first day of the festival, the deities are placed on raths, ceremonial chariots 12 metres (40 ft) high, with wheels 2 metres (7 ft) in diameter. Jagannath's chariot is decorated in yellow stripes; Subhadra has a red chariot; Balabhadra's is bright blue. All three are preceded by four wooden horses, but are actually drawn by hundreds of devotees from the temple to Gundicha Mandir (Garden House), 8 km (5 miles) away, where they stay for seven days. The rituals completed, the deities ride back to their temple. The procession is said to commemorate Krisna's journey from Gokhul to Mathura.

Every 12 years the images are replaced by new ones. The old images are then buried in a secret ceremony.

Map
on page
258

In the Northern Hills bordering West Bengal and Bihar, **Simlipal National Park 5** is one of India's most attractive forests, and its 2,750 sq km (1,062 sq miles) are populated with tigers and wild elephants.

Northern Orissa

About 15 km (10 miles) north from Bhubaneshwar is **Nandanakanan**, a park set in the Chandka Forest, where animals are kept in natural surroundings. The main attractions are four white tigers, one-horned rhinos, white-browed gibbons and African lions. There is also a **Botanical Garden**, with a rosarium, Zen temple and a cactus house.

Cuttack **6**, the former capital of Orissa, is situated on a narrow river island 19 km (12 miles) north of Bhubaneshwar. There are a few historical remains, including the blue granite **Barabati** Maratha fort, stormed by the British in 1803; **Qadam-i-Rasal**, a walled compound with corner towers, containing three 18th-century mosques and a domed building housing footprints of Prophet Muhammad engraved on a circular stone. The shrine is visited by both Muslim and Hindu worshippers.

Further north, **Balasore 7** is one of the earliest British settlements in India, granted to the East India Company in 1633. Nearby are three shrines. The Kutopokhari Temple at Remuna is a seat of Vaisnava culture and has an 18-arm granite statue of Durga. Bhudhara Chandi at Sajanagarh, built in the 16th century, contains a three-faced image of Shakti. Panchalingeswar on Devagiri Hill is a temple with five stone *lingams*. To the east is the small resort of **Chandipur-on-Sea 8**, with a beach where the sea recedes by 5 km (3 miles) at low tide. This is a good place from which to visit Simlipal *(see above)*. ❑

The former Buddhist university site of Ratnagiri has the remains of three monasteries, a number of ruined temples, and several stupas.

BELOW: the Rath Yatra, Puri.

Map below

THE ANDAMAN AND NICOBAR ISLANDS

These tropical islands in the middle of the Bay of Bengal are finged with coral reefs and mangrove swamps, and are home to unique groups of indigenous peoples

The Andaman and Nicobar Islands, home to a number of different peoples, lie 1,220 km (760 miles) southeast of Kolkata across the Kala Pani (Black Water). Their existence was reported in the 9th century AD by Arab merchants sailing towards the Straits of Sumatra, but with dense forests, mangrove swamps and shark-infested seas, the 572 islands were considered fit only for political prisoners and Malay pirates. Their development as a tourist destination, attracting scuba divers, birdwatchers and honeymooners, happened only in the past three decades. Nicobar, however, is off limits to visitors to protect the Shompen peoples.

The first Westerners to set foot on the islands were the Danes, who established a settlement in the Nicobars and left in 1768 due to poor health conditions. The British Indian government annexed both groups of islands in 1872 and built a gaol at Port Blair for prisoners serving life terms. The prison was used mainly for political prisioners engaged in the Independence struggle and it was in Port Blair, while under Japanese occupation during World War II, that the Indian flag was first raised.

On 26 December 2004 the islands were hit by the enormous tsunami that

BELOW: the Nicobar Islands, home to the Shompen peoples.

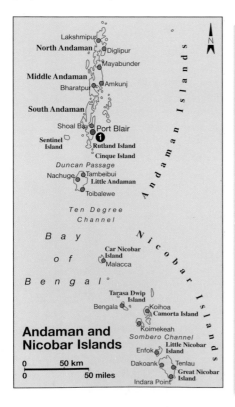

Andaman and Nicobar Islands

also devatated parts of Southeast Asia. The damage was overwhelming and more than 3,000 are offically listed as having been killed, with many more still missing, presumed dead, and thousands more displaced. The damage was so great that six islands have been abandoned altogether, and the task of rebuilding them is proving overwhelming. Although flights have now resumed in and out of Port Blair, much of the infrastructure outside of the capital is in ruins and reconstruction will take some time to complete. Travel beyond Port Blair is still highly problematic and may hamper relief efforts. The tsunami also created several new land masses in the northwest of the islands.

Port Blair ❶, the capital, on South Andaman, was named after Lt. Reginald Blair who conducted a survey of the area in 1789. The **Cellular Jail**, where 400 freedom fighters were held during the struggle for Independence is now a museum. There is also an **Anthropological Museum**, which has mini-reproductions of villages of local peoples, and a Burmese temple at **Phoenix Bay**. Across the harbour is **Aberdeen Market** on **Vyper Island**, where executions used to take place, and **Ross Island**, guarded by World War II Japanese bunkers. It is hard to predict when tourist facilities will be ready to accept visitors; travellers should check with the island authorities before setting off.

Most of the islands are Adivasi reserves and, previously, only a limited number were open to visitors. There was initially great concern about the status of the indigenous peoples following the tsunami. However, subsequent helicopter flights over the islands have shown that they survived remarkably well, as did the native fauna, in part as they tend to inhabit higher, more forested ground, but perhaps also as they would read signs from fleeing animals and birds that told of the impending disaster. ❑

Anthropologists have laid down guidelines for any visitors: these include staying clear of the threatened peoples, and helping to protect the delicate coral gardens from damage by fin strokes and petrol fumes.

BELOW: hunting on the beach.

PEOPLES OF THE ISLANDS

The peoples of the Andaman and Nicobar Islands have maintained their own identities partly because the difficulty of rowing through the ocean currents in shallow canoes limited intermingling. The largest group on Little Andaman are the Onges. They are hunter-gatherers, who collect honey and spear fish, and ritually paint their bodies with clay.

The Sentinelese are an elusive group of 400 people, who fight off intruders with poisoned arrows. They adorn themselves with body painting, beads and bone. The Jarawa, with a population of 300, have a large reserve on South Andaman. In a worrying development a road has been illegally built through the Jawara's territory and the government announced plans to resettle the Jawara forcibly. This increased contact with the outside world threatened game levels in the forests and exposed the Jawara to disease. However, the High Court in Kolkata ordered the government to halt its plans for resettlement and to prevent incursion onto the Jawara's lands. Contact with outsiders practically wiped out the Andamese through disease. Only 30 individuals remain and Strait Island, their new home, is off limits.

On Nicobar, the predominant Nicobaris are of mixed Burmese, Malay, Mon and Shan origin. They cultivate vegetables and tend cows and pigs first introduced by the Danes.

THE WEST

While the bright lights of Mumbai and golden sands of Goa beckon, inland the West is a cultural gem

Washed by the Arabian Sea, the metropolis of Mumbai, formerly Bombay, sets the pace for all western India. Elephanta Island and the exquisite caves of Ajanta and Ellora in Maharashtra may offer up ancient artistry and legend, but the commerce and cinema of Mumbai draws visitors from all walks of life. Pune, in the hills to the east, is not quite in the same league, but provides a less crowded alternative. Western travellers are outnumbered here by spiritual seekers pursuing meditation with Osho, known as Bhagwan Rajneesh before his death.

Goa, a former Portuguese colony, is the watering hole for Mumbai's rich and has become a hedonistic beach centre for clubbers and charter plane groups. Shoestring tourists ride double on hired motorcycles and crowd the slow river ferries. Visitors wash down plates of spicy pork vindaloo with local beer that is chilled enough to cut the glycerine aftertaste. For thundering waves and spectacular skyscapes above the forts and churches, the monsoon season is the time to visit – winter tourists will be long gone.

Diu, a tiny island off the coast of Gujarat, is an alternative beach scene in a more distant setting. Most locals are not yet accustomed to sunbathers, so female tourists are sometimes made to feel like they're in an amateur peepshow.

Gujarat stretches out, sunburnt and dry (alcohol is officially banned in most of the state). The Rann of Kutch shimmers with unearthly mirages above the saltpans, and the patterns are mimicked in the intricate embroidery for which the region is justly famous. Antique scraps of brilliant handiwork can fetch very high prices, keeping alive the needlecraft tradition. In Ahmadabad, the Calico Museum preserves stunning examples of Gujarat's textile heritage. Gypsies wearing layers of petticoats and sequinned headgear resemble walking exhibits as they thread their way through backed-up cars at traffic lights.

In the heart of India, Madhya Pradesh is famed for impressive forts such as Jhansi, Gwalior and Mandu. Nearby are wildlife parks where jungle cats and leopards prowl by night. ❏

PRECEDING PAGES: iron balconies are a feature of Mumbai's architecture.
LEFT: washing at the dhobi ghats, Mumbai.

MUMBAI (BOMBAY)

Renamed Mumbai, India's most populous city is the country's glamorous commercial hub, a magnet to rich and poor, surrounded on three sides by the Arabian Sea

The story of Mumbai is fascinating. From obscure, humble beginnings as a set of seven small islands with tidal creeks and marshes between them, the city has risen to such eminence that today it is India's most important commercial and industrial centre. The seven islands have been merged by land reclamation into one and thus survive only as names of localities like Colaba, Mahim, Mazgaon, Parel, Worli, Girgaum and Dongri. Known until 1995 as Bombay, the Marathi name "Mumbai" derives from the local deity, Mumba Devi. The first Portuguese settlers called the area "Bom Baim" (Good Bay).

Today, Mumbai is booming. Home to the wealthy and the glamorous, it has long been India's Hollywood ("Bollywood"), producing more films each year than any other city in the world. Nowadays, it is also the home of India's own fast-growing satellite and television industries.

Like all big cities, Mumbai has its seamy side, its slums and its overcrowding, the foothills of poverty on which are built towering skyscrapers. And like all success stories, there have been chapters of intrigue, violence, happiness and calm, and the struggles of the pre-independence years, when Mumbai became the political capital of nationalist India. Some of its more disgraceful moments during the 1990s were communal riots between Hindus and Muslims, encouraged by the chauvinist Shiv Sena, and its shady founder, Bal Thackeray.

Mumbai is on India's west coast, running down from Gujarat, through Mumbai to Goa, Karnataka and Kerala. South of Mumbai, narrow beaches and plains sweep up into the forested hills of the Western Ghats. The city has a natural harbour, which was developed by the British and, once the Suez Canal opened in the 19th century, the port never knew a dull moment. Today it handles more than 40 percent of India's maritime trade.

India's largest city now stretches 22 km (14 miles) into the Arabian Sea. The maximum width of the composite island that now constitutes metropolitan Mumbai is no more than 5 km (3 miles). Into this narrow strip are squeezed the majority of Mumbai's 16.3 million people, its major business and commercial establishments, its docks and warehouses, and much of its industry – including almost the whole of its major textile industry, which employs thousands of workers.

Mumbai summers are hot and humid, the winters warm, while the sea breeze brings relief throughout the year. The monsoon hits between June and September, bringing curtains of heavy rain that obscure the view and flood the roads.

A melting pot

Mumbai Municipal Corporation provides primary and secondary education in at least 10 languages, including English. Mumbai has developed its own patter,

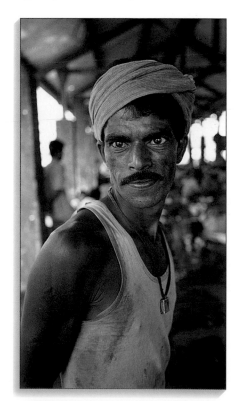

LEFT: cricket team in action on the Maidan.
BELOW: fisherman at Sassoon Dock.

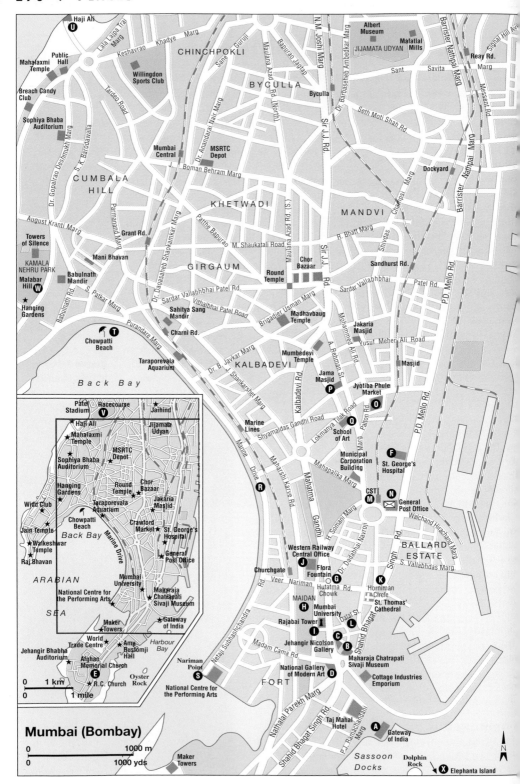

Mumbai (Bombay)

"Bombay speak", which regular Hindi/Urdu speakers find rather comical. It is often caricatured in Indian films and plays. The Hindu population of Mumbai is largely Marathi, though most non-Marathi Mumbaikars are also Hindus, with Jains among the Gujaratis, and neo-Buddhists among the Dalits.

Local Muslim nawabs ruled this region, but handed it over to the Portuguese in 1534 in exchange for support against the Mughals. This was the beginning of Mumbai's large Christian (mainly Roman Catholic) population and its numerous churches, which led to two separate areas in Mumbai coming to be known as "**Portuguese Church**". A few churches retain their Portuguese facades: **St Andrew's** in the suburb of Bandra is a fine example. There are also minor remains of Portuguese fortifications both on the main island and the much larger island of **Salsette** north of the city and now mostly incorporated in Greater Mumbai. (Also being developed is a **New Mumbai** on the mainland, a few miles across Mumbai harbour.) At **Vasai** (Bassein), 50 km (30 miles) from Mumbai, there are ruins of a Portuguese walled settlement.

In 1662 Charles II of England married Catherine of Braganza, a Portuguese princess. As part of the dowry, the British crown received the islands of Mumbai. They were leased to the British East India Company in 1668 at the princely rent of £10 per annum. This company of merchant-adventurers had for some time felt the need for an additional west-coast port, to supplement and ultimately to supplant Surat in Gujarat. Far-sighted governors of this period, such as Gerald Augiers, began the construction of the city and harbour, inviting the settlement of Gujarati merchants and Parsi, Muslim and Hindu manufacturers and traders to help develop the city. This led to the settlement of all these communities in Mumbai.

Cotton boom town

The slow transformation of the swampy islands during the 17th and 18th centuries gave way in the 19th century to rapid change. In 1858, the Honourable East India Company returned the islands to the British crown. In the 1850s came the steam engine and by the end of the century Mumbai was linked with central and northern India by the Great Indian Peninsular Railway and, some time later, with eastern India, too.

During this period, Mumbai became an important cotton town. Raw cotton from Gujarat was shipped to Lancashire, spun and woven into cloth and brought back to Mumbai for sale all over the country. Notwithstanding this, Mumbai's cotton textile industry was established in this period, thanks to the persistence of Mumbai's entrepreneurs. The outbreak of the American Civil War in 1861 and the opening of the Suez Canal gave further impetus to cotton exports. The city's new-found wealth led to the construction of many impressive buildings.

Colaba

The **Gateway of India** Ⓐ on the waterfront at P.J. Ramachandani Marg (previously Apollo Bunder) was conceived as a triumphal arch to commemorate the visit of Britain's George V and Queen Mary for the Delhi Darbar in 1911. The honey-coloured basalt of the arch, designed by George Wittet, faces the sea and

Map on page 270

Auto rickshaws are not allowed into central Mumbai. However, there is a well-run and comprehensive bus service and Mumbai's taxi drivers are generally good at using their meters. Note: the actual fare is calculated using a chart, which you can ask to see.

BELOW: a Jain temple, Mumbai.

catches the light of the rising and setting sun and changes from shades of gold to orange and pink. It was through this arch that the last of the British troops left India by sea. Opposite the Gateway is the **Taj Hotel**. After the industrialist J.N Tata was refused entry to the "European" hotel Watson's, he exacted revenge by constructing a far more opulent hotel nearby. It opened in 1903 and heads of state and celebrities have been passing through its doors ever since.

The foundation stone of the domed **Maharaja Chatrapati Sivaji Museum** **B** (open Tues–Sun 10.15am–6pm, entrance fee), on M.G. Road, was laid by George V in 1905 during his visit to India as Prince of Wales. The museum contains some excellent examples of Indian miniature painting of the Mughal and Rajasthan schools. There are also collections of jade artefacts and chinaware. The **Jehangir Art Gallery** **C**, next to the museum, stages regular exhibitions of contemporary art and crafts. Some exhibits are for sale (open 11am–7pm). Perhaps its greatest asset is the popular Samovar cafe. Opposite the museum, completing the cultural trilogy, is the **National Gallery of Modern Art** **D** (open Tues–Sun 11am–7pm, entrance fee).

The **Afghan Memorial Church** **E** of St John the Evangelist is in south Colaba. The church, on Capt P. Pethe Marg, was established in 1847 and consecrated 11 years later as a memorial to those who fell in the First Afghan War. It is a lovely piece of architecture with Gothic arches and stained-glass windows.

Sassoon Docks is where the city's trawler fleet lands its catch each morning. If you can cope with the overpowering stench, wander around the quays to watch the fish being flung into crates of ice balancing on the heads of waiting porters, who carry them at top speed to the adjacent auction halls for sale. Hundreds of boats tie up here during the day, their flags, masts and rigs forming one

Serving its office workers, Mumbai has a unique city-wide organisation of dabbawallas. They collect dabbas (lunch-boxes containing a cooked meal) from homes during the morning and take them to the office. Each owner and location is identified by markings decipherable by the dabbawallas alone.

BELOW: waterfront, with the Taj Hotel (left) and Gateway of India (right).

of Mumbai's more arresting spectacles. This is also where you will see the city's signature dish, 'Bombay duck', being dried in the salty breezes.

Fort

The **Fort** (downtown) area in South Mumbai derives its name from the fact that the area fell within the former walled city, of which only a small fragment survives as part of the eastern boundary wall of **St George's Hospital** .

Memories of this walled area were preserved in such names as Churchgate, Bazaargate and Rampart Row, all renamed in recent years. Within the Fort was the Castle, the headquarters of the Mumbai Government. Until India became independent, government orders were issued as from "Mumbai Castle", though the castle itself had long ceased to exist.

Flora Fountain ❼ stands in a crowded square at the heart of the Fort area, now called **Hutatma Chowk** (Martyrs' Square). The fountain was erected in honour of the governor, Sir Henry Bartle Edward Frere, who built new Mumbai in the 1860s. The memorial that has given the square its new name – Hutatma – commemorates those who lost their lives in the cause of setting up a separate Maharashtra state in the Indian Union. This has traditionally been the business centre of Mumbai, with major banks and airline offices.

The **Maidan** ❽, just to the west of Hutatma Chowk, is a long stretch of park that runs from Colaba up to the end of M.G. Road. Facing the Maidan are some of Mumbai's finest buildings. The **Old Secretariat** and the **Public Works Department Secretariat** on K. Baburao Patel Marg were designed and built by Colonel Orel Henry St Clair Wilkins during 1867–74, and are high Victorian Gothic in style. Also here are the **University Hall**, funded by Sir Cowasjee Jehangir Readymoney, and the Library and Florentine-style **Rajabai Tower** ❾ (Clock Tower), completed in 1878. On Veer Nariman Road, which bisects the Maidan, is the imposing **Western Railway Central** ❿ office building at Churchgate, built in greyblue basalt with bands of white in 1890, it has towers with oriental domes. West of Hutatma Chowk along Veer Nariman Road is **Horniman Circle** ⓚ. Lined with elegant sandstone buildings, in the centre are very well-maintained gardens. On the southern side is **St Thomas's Cathedral** (1672–1718). Inside there are some wonderful monuments to the British colonial great and good. South of Horniman Circle is the main financial district, centred around **Dalal Street** ⓛ, now shorthand for the SENSEX, or Mumbai Stock Exchange. Also close by is the **Town Hall**, which now contains part of the **State Central Library** (open Mon–Sat 10am–7pm). Along with copies of every book printed in India, the archives include more than 10,000 rare antique manuscripts, among them a copy of Dante's *Divine Comedy* rumoured to be worth US$3 million – Mussolini tried to buy it once but was turned down.

The most impressive High Victorian Gothic structure in Mumbai, designed by Frederick William Stevens, is **Chatrapati Shivaji Terminus** ⓜ (CST, formerly Victoria Terminus, VT) and the adjoining headquarters building of the **Central Railway**, known

Mumbai has a tiny Jewish community. Seven synagogues in the city still serve their dwindling numbers. The house of the Sassoons, Iraqi in origin, left endowments for educational and charitable purposes. Mumbai still has a Sassoon Dock (now used by the fishing fleet) and a Sassoon Library.

BELOW: *dabbawallas* deliver lunch-boxes, Churchgate Station.

One of Mumbai's more unusual spectacles can be seen early in the morning, when groups of people gather simply to laugh. Started in 1995 by Dr Madan Kataria, members of "Laughing Clubs" claim it is beneficial to your health.

BELOW: Mumbai traffic and CST.

originally as the Great Indian Peninsular Railway. Just off Nagar Chowk, i was built between 1878 and 1887 using yellow sandstone and granite with polychromatic stones and blue-grey basalt for decoration.

The **Municipal Corporation Building** opposite CST is another Stevens masterpiece, especially the domed central staircase and the cusped arches in the arcaded storeys. Another building of note near CST is the **General Post Office** 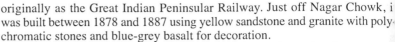, designed by George Wittet. He also left his mark in the **Ballard Estate** area, where his office buildings reflect those of 19th-century London.

Jyotiba Phule Market (previously Crawford Market, built 1865–71) **O** north of CST along Dr Dadabhai Naroji Road, was designed by William Emerson and has bas-reliefs by J.L. Kipling, Rudyard Kipling's father. A fascinating place to explore, you can seemingly buy any kind of foodstuff here.

The Muslims of Mumbai, like the Parsis and Gujaratis, have merged with the rest in the melting pot of urban culture. Yet there are areas in Mumbai where their contributions to city life can still be observed and enjoyed. On **Mohammed Ali Road**, north of Jyotiba Phule Market, one can get *kababs* rolled up in *rotis* (unleavened bread), or hot *jalebi* sweets, at all hours. Close by is the highly ornate **Jama Masjid** **P**, currently under armed guard to protect it from Hindu extremists. Between the Jama Masjid and Lokmanya Tilak Road is **Mangaldas Market**, a covered warren of little stalls selling a huge variety of fabrics.

The **School of Art Q**, on Lokmanya Tilak Road, was built at the same time as Crawford Market. Rudyard Kipling was born and spent his early years here. His father, John Lockwood Kipling, was principal of the school and under his guidance many local artisans prepared panels and motifs to adorn the new buildings of Mumbai. **Elphinstone High School** (1872), with its central tower and canopied balconies, and **St Xavier's College** (1867) are further down. The latter has panels by J.L. Kipling.

Marine Drive

Surrounded on three sides by the sea, life in Mumbai draws much of its character from the beaches, seaside promenades and coastline. Beyond the central city are the beaches of **Juhu**, **Versova**, **Madh Island**, **Marve Manori** and **Gorai**, one-time secluded seaside resorts.

Marine Drive R (otherwise known as Netaji Subhash Road) links Malabar Hill to Fort and Colaba. This long, gracefully curving road along the buttressed sea-coast, viewed from the Hanging Gardens on Malabar Hill, provides at night a view of the glittering "Queen Victoria's Necklace" and, by day and night, a panorama of Mumbai's skyline.

Along Marine Drive runs a wide sidewalk, ideal for the early-morning jogger, evening walker and late night stroller. During the monsoons the turbulent waves splash over the parapets.

In the south Marine Drive ends at **Nariman Point S**. Close by are numerous offices, including those of Air India and Indian Airlines, but at the very tip of the promontory is the **National Centre for the Performing Arts**, set up by the Tata Trust in 1966. One of India's premier cultural centres, it hosts exhibitions and puts on music, dance and drama performances. **Chowpatti T**, at the north end of Marine Drive, is a stretch

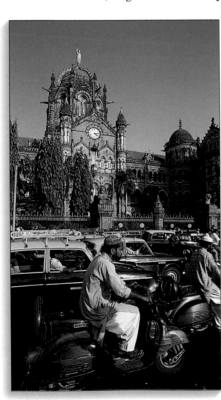

Map on page 270

of sandy beach. In the evenings, it is crowded with people enjoying the cool sea breeze and stalls selling delicious Mumbai *bhelpuri* and other snacks. Chowpatti is famous also for its *kulfi* and ice creams. During the Ganesh Chaturthi festival, processions from the city meet here with images of Ganesh, which are then immersed in the sea. The **Taraporevala Aquarium**, also on Marine Drive, has a good collection of tropical fish (open Tues–Sat 10am–7pm, Sun 10am–8pm).

Sacred places

Gillian Tindall called her historical study of Mumbai *City of Gold* and, certainly, the pursuit of wealth is a major occupation here. But Mumbaikars do not forget the "temples of their gods", though often in pursuit of equally material aims. Appropriately, a major shrine near the racecourse is dedicated to Mahalaksmi, goddess of wealth and prosperity. Many in this cosmopolitan city attend holy shrines, whether of their own religion or of others. Peoples of all faiths queue patiently on fixed days of the week to make their offerings, whether at the tomb of the Muslim saint, **Haji Ali ❶**, on the tidal island off the shore opposite the **Racecourse ❷** at Mahalaksmi; or for the Wednesday "Novenas" at **St Michael's Church** at Mahim; or at the **Siddhivinayak Temple** at Prabhadevi on Tuesdays. Bandra's Fair, in celebration of the feast of St Mary, is centred on an image of St Mary at the **Mount Mary Shrine** and attracts thousands of seekers of succour and favours – with no particular distinction of caste or creed.

Gujaratis from the state north of Mumbai constitute a substantial proportion of the city's Hindu and Parsi populations, and especially of its business community. Fleeing persecution in Persia, the Parsis migrated to Gujarat and moved to Mumbai in large numbers in the 17th century. Being Zoroastrians, they built Fire Temples and a "Tower of Silence" on **Malabar Hill ❸**. The tower is an isolated facility for the disposal of the dead *(dokhura)* by exposure to the elements and vultures *(see page 147)*. Burial and cremation are ruled out for Zoroastrians, since they hold both fire and earth sacred. This very private and sacred site is off limits to visitors.

Cave temples of Elephanta

While Mumbai city has no ancient or even medieval monuments, an hour's ride away by motor launch from the Gateway of India (Tues–Sun), within the waters of the harbour, is the island of **Elephanta (Gharapuri) ❹**, site of a magnificent series of rock-cut cave temples with large sculptured interiors. These were excavated in the 7th and 8th centuries. The centrepiece is a massive 5-metre (18-ft) three-headed bust of Shiva, representing his manifestations as Creator, Preserver and Destroyer. The Portuguese called the island Elephanta after a massive elephant sculpture that once stood in one of the excavated courtyards here, and is now in the Mumbai city zoo.

Some 40 km (25 miles) from the Fort area, near Borivali station on the Western Railway suburban line, is the Sanjay Gandhi national park, within which lies the 2nd-century Buddhist hill caves of **Kanheri**. Sculpture here, too, is on a large scale and matches that of the Ajanta and Ellora caves in eastern Maharashtra. ❑

Close to the Mahalaksmi temples and the tomb of Haji Ali are the extraordinary dhobi ghats. This large and chaotic area is where much of the city's laundry is washed.

BELOW: making *chai* at Sassoon Dock.

Map on page 278

MAHARASHTRA

Away from the steamy metropolis of Mumbai, Maharashtra is rich in historical interest with its breathtaking rock temples, Maratha forts and recuperative hill stations

The metropolis of Mumbai shows the traveller only part of Maharashtra – much of the state is rural, albeit with an important industrial base. The commercial centre of the country, Mumbai contains a cross-section of India's diverse population. However, there is a strong element of Marathi chauvinism in local politics. The Shiv Sena political party, which is in cahoots with the pan-Indian Hindu nationalist BJP, is named after the 17th-century Maratha warrior Shivaji, taking the anti-imperialist message implicit in his battles with the Mughal Empire to justify the communal politics it is pursuing against the city's many Muslims. In Pune you will find the proprietary pride in Shivaji even more pronounced, even though there are those who feel that this constant harking back to a glorious past ensures a less than glorious present. However, this glorious past has left behind treasures for the visitor. The best approach is to use five cities (Pune, Kolhapur, Aurangabad, Nagpur and Nasik) as bases for exploratory trips. If you must choose only one, choose Aurangabad: the caves of Ajanta and Ellora offer riches comparable to those of the Taj Mahal.

Called Poona by the British, **Pune ❶** (170 km/105 miles from Mumbai) has now reclaimed its original Marathi name; it was once the capital of the Maratha Empire. The British captured Pune at the Battle of Koregaon in 1818 and deve

BELOW: Buddhist fresco from the caves at Ajanta.

loped it along the lines of an archetypal army town with the usual uncluttered army cantonment areas in distinct contrast to the busy, crowded old city. Pune became the centre of many Hindu social reform movements; it also became, during the heyday of Bal Gangadhar Tilak, the epicentre of India's independence movement. Industrialisation has changed its character considerably.

Well worth a visit is the **Raja Kelkar Museum** (open 8.30am–6pm, entrance fee), the private collection of Dinkar Kelkar. Its focus is on traditional Indian arts. It has 36 sections, which include carved palace and temple doors, 2,000-year-old excavated pottery, traditional Indian lamps, and 17th-century miniature paintings. Of special interest are a collection of brass nutcrackers (some of them explicitly erotic) and padlocks (including a scorpion-shaped padlock whose "pincers" lock together). Kelkar's collection is so large that the exhibits have to be shown by rotation.

The **Agha Khan Palace** (open Mon–Fri 9am–5.45pm, entrance fee), with Italianate arches and spacious well-mannered lawns, was an unlikely place for a prison, but at one time the British interned Mahatma Gandhi and his wife Kasturba here along with other leaders of the Congress Party. Kasturba died in the palace and a memorial has been erected in the grounds. Mahadji Scindia, one of the Maratha ruling princes, constructed the small black-stone Siva temple **Shinde Chatri** in the 18th century. His descendant, Madhavrao II, built an annexe in Mahadji's memory. His architectural inspiration was not Indian, like Mahadji's, but Southern European. The contrast in the two styles is a monument to the assimilative powers of Indian culture. Mahadji's *samadhi* (mausoleum) stands across a courtyard. There is a likeness of him in silver, topped by a flame-coloured turban. A nearby sign warns you not to open an umbrella as that would be insulting to the prince's memory.

Shanivarvada, in the old city, was the palace of the Peshwa rulers who succeeded to Shivaji's empire. It was built in 1736. All that remains from a massive fire in 1827 are its fortified walls, brass-studded gates, 18th-century lotus pools and the elaborate palace foundations (open 8am–6.30pm, entrance fee). The 8th-century rock-cut **Temple of Patalesvar** stands in the middle of Pune. Carved from a single boulder of awe-inspiring size, it is still used by worshippers. Other fine temples include the **Parvati Temple** on a hilltop on the city outskirts. This was once the private shrine of Peshwa rulers. A Muslim shrine, the **Qamarali Darvesh**, contains a celebrated "levitating" stone, which you might be tempted to investigate.

Maratha forts and temples

Simha Gad, literally "fortress of the lion", stands on a hilltop 25 km (15 miles) from Pune. Some 300 years ago Shivaji's right-hand man, General Tanaji Malsure, with a group of trusted lieutenants, scaled its sheer precipice with the help of ropes and giant lizards especially trained for the purpose. Shivaji won the fortress but his general was killed during the action. Today, most of the battlements are overgrown with weeds.

South of Pune, **Mahabalesvar** ❷ (100 km/60 miles) and **Panchgani** (90 km/55 miles) are cool hill stations that lend themselves to quiet walks with

One of the best routes from Mumbai to Pune is by fast train. The journey through the mountains on the "Deccan Queen" is particularly lovely (Mumbai CST–Pune 5.10–8.30pm; Pune–Mumbai CST 7.15–10.35am.

BELOW: visitors to Ajanta.

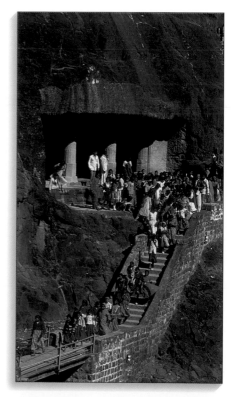

panoramic views. Horse-riding is popular, and horses and ponies can be hired.
Matheran ❸, 94 km (58 miles) east of Mumbai, is inaccessible to cars, which
are prohibited by law. You either walk the last 20 km (12 miles) up a steep hill
or take a train from Neral for the one-and-a-half-hour journey.

The Osho Commune, founded in Pune by the new-age guru Bhagwan Rajneesh in 1974, opens its doors to visitors for guided tours at 10.30am and 2.30pm.

One of the most important pilgrimage centres in Maharashtra is **Kolhapur ❹**,
395 km (245 miles) south of Mumbai. In fact, it's often called **Dakshina Kasi**
(the Varanasi of the South), due to its many temples and the ghats that run down
to the River Panchganga. The temple held in highest esteem is the **Mahalaksmi
Temple** (Ambabai Temple), built in the 9th century. To the east of the city is
Kotiteerth, a temple of Mahadev in the centre of a wide expanse of water.

Kolhapur was the capital of a former princely state and has some splendid
palaces. These include an **Old Palace** of the 18th century and a **New Palace** of
the 19th century. Kolhapur is also known for its wrestlers (its stadium holds
20,000 people). The town is *the* place to go for Kolhapur *chappals* (sandals).

Panhala, 15 km (9 miles) away, is not only a hill station but is also of historical interest, being the scene of a famous Shivaji escape. **Sangli**, 50 km (30

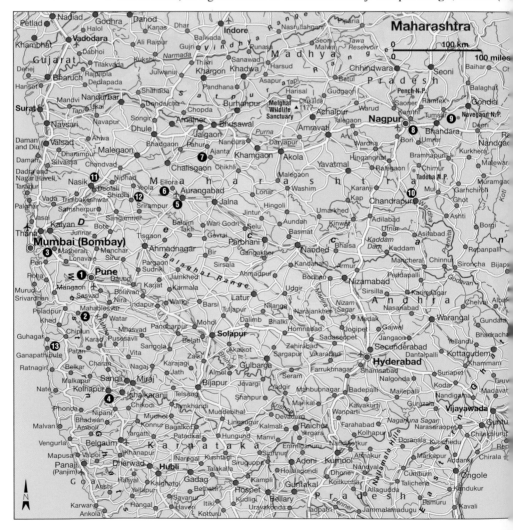

Map on page 278

miles) away, was also the capital of a former principality. It has a fine temple. **Ratnagiri**, 125 km (80 miles) from Kolhapur, is the gateway to the beaches of Southern Konkan. Ratnagiri itself has a fine beach but is better known for its succulent Alphonso mangoes. **Pandharpur**, 200 km (125 miles) northeast, draws pilgrims from all over Maharashtra to its famous **Shrine of Vithal** in July and August. **Sholapur**, 60 km (37 miles) east of Pandharpur, is a busy textile town. It has a formidable fort and a temple surrounded by water.

As its name suggests, **Aurangabad ❺**, 370 km (230 miles) from Mumbai, has a strong Muslim flavour and contains the mausoleum of Emperor Aurangzeb's Begum (**Bibi ka Maqbara**), a poor copy of the Taj Mahal. There is also an interesting medieval watermill, the **Panchakki**, by a Muslim shrine. It recently decided to paint itself pink in an effort to raise the flagging morale of its impoverished population. Three km (1½ miles) from the Bibi ka Maqbara, there are 12 Buddhist caves excavated between the 3rd and 11th century AD. The most interesting are caves 3, 6 and 7; carry a torch.

Daulatabad, 15 km (9 miles) from Aurangabad, has a massive hilltop fort, often described as "totally impregnable" (open 6am–6pm, entrance fee). The site dates from the 12th century, and the seven rings of fortifications are from the 15th–16th centuries. To further deter invaders there is a deep moat, once filled with crocodiles and crossed by a single leather bridge, after which is a dark labyrinth. The views from the top are spectacular. Close by are two sacred sites. At **Khuldabad** is the simple tomb of the Mughal emperor Aurangzeb (1707), surrounded by the graves of Muslim saints. The Hindu **Ghrusnesvar temple** near Ellora was founded in the 8th century and houses one of the 12 *syambu jyotirlingas* ("self-born lingams of light"), and it is an important pilgrimage centre.

Ajanta and Ellora

Among the most important monuments in India are the caves at **Ellora ❻**, 25 km (15 miles) northwest of Aurangabad *(see box overleaf)* and the 30 Buddhist caves of Ajanta, 100 km (60 miles) northeast.

The caves at **Ajanta ❼** (open 9am–5.30pm, entrance fee) not only contain sculptures, but remarkably preserved frescoes as well. They are secluded and were discovered by accident only in the 19th century, which explains why the monuments escaped the depredations of invading armies. To protect the caves from the ravages of pollution, a fleet of environmentally-friendly buses takes visitors up to the site.

The frescoes and sculptures of Ajanta are from the early period after the death of the Buddha when priests felt the need to give a representational form to their teachings, and paintings and sculptures of his life began to proliferate. Thus began the process of Buddhism acquiring some of the sensuousness of Hinduism. People used to the idea of Buddhist thought being essentially a negation of the senses will be startled by the voluptuousness of much of the imagery.

As much as the caves themselves, Ajanta's position in a forested river gorge – with a spectacular waterfall during the monsoon – makes the place very special. Numbered from the entrance, caves 1, 2, 10, 16 and 17 are particularly fine, though all are worth a look.

The ITDC runs good-value tours, with knowledgeable guides, from Aurangabad to Ajanta and Ellora; the latter also taking in Daulatabad and sites in Aurangabad itself. The bus will pick up and drop off at your hotel. ITDC, 210 Labh Chambers, Station Road, Aurangabad, tel: 0240 233 1143.

BELOW: Ajanta, site of numerous early Buddhist caves.

BELOW: Ellora's Kailasa temple is decorated with scenes from the *Mahabharata*.

Other destinations

Nagpur 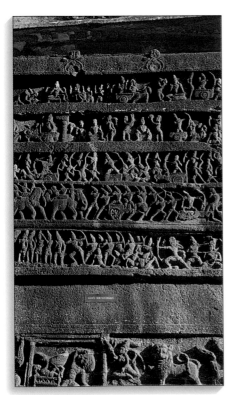, in the northeast of the state, was the capital of the Bhosle branch of the Maratha Empire. Its imperial glory is now revived every winter when today's rulers – cabinet ministers and elected representatives – move from Mumbai to this winter capital of Maharashtra. Nagpur, located at the geographical centre of India, is also famous for being orange-growing country.

Ramtek, 40 km (25 miles) north of Nagpur, is so named because Rama, the popular incarnation of Lord Visnu, stopped here with his wife Sita and brother Laksmana when they were banished from Ayodhya.

Wardha, 75 km (45 miles) from Nagpur, is the alighting point for **Sevagram** and **Paunar**. The village of Sevagram is where Mahatma Gandhi lived in an ashram. This has been well preserved and is a place of modern pilgrimage. Paunar was made famous by one of Gandhi's disciples, Acharya Vinoba Bhave, who lived and died there. He is famous for his *bhudan* (land-gift) movement which encouraged landowners to give away parts of their land to landless labourers. **Nagzira**, 115 km (70 miles) from Nagpur, is a game sanctuary. The Nagzira forests have two all-year-round water tanks that attract wildlife.

Navegaon National Park , 135 km (85 miles) from Nagpur, is a forest rich in wildlife. It has an 18th-century artificial lake. The man who made it has been deified as Kolasur Dev and his shrine lies by the lake. **Chandrapur** , 160 km (100 miles) from Nagpur, has a fort and several temples. From Chandrapur you can head for **Tadoba**, Maharashtra's best-known sanctuary. In the park is a lake held to be sacred by local Adivasis; crocodiles thrive in large numbers. **Chikalda**, 220 km (135 miles) from Nagpur, is the hill station of the region. It is approached through a thick jungle teeming with wildlife.

ROCK TEMPLES OF ELLORA

Ellora (open 5am–6pm), 25 km (15 miles) northwest of Aurangabad, has 34 rock-cut temples representing the Buddhists (caves 1–12), Brahmanic Hindus (caves 14–16) and Jains (caves 30, 32). The term "cave temple" cannot convey the magnitude of the Ellora achievement. These caves were scooped out of the rocks 10 centuries ago. The feat could be compared to carving a whole cathedral out of solid rock. All the caves have been carved out. The work usually started from the top of the temple and moved downwards to eliminate the need for scaffolding.

The centrepiece at Ellora is the Kailasa Temple (entrance fee). Its architects were not modest about their ambitions. Kailasa is, after all, the mythical mountain where the gods dwell. In its galleries are recreated various scenes from Shiva myths. One of them represents the eternal struggle between the forces of evil represented by Ravana, the demon king of Sri Lanka, and the forces of good represented by Shiva and Parvati. Although the carvings at Ellora come from three religions, the structures are often similar, probably due to the demands of the rock formations.

Inside, differences are discernible: the Jain caves are ascetic; the Buddhist caves, inspired by Buddhism's 2nd-century attempt at populism, show an austere richness

Nasik , 150 km (93 miles) northeast of Mumbai, is a holy city. It stands on the banks of the river Godavari, venerated by Hindus. Two thousand temples and many bathing ghats testify to its sanctity. An incident in the Ramayana features Nasik: when Lakshana, Rama's younger brother, tiring of the efforts of the demon Surpanakha to persuade him to marry her, chopped off her nose, it fell where Nasik now stands. The *Kumbha Mela* (known in Nasik as the *Sinhastha Mela*), held once every 12 years, is the high point of a pilgrimage to Nasik, although the focus of the celebrations is at nearby Trimbakesvar. This is safest seen from a distance (at the 2003 *Kumbha Mela* several people were trampled to death).

According to legend, **Trimbakesvar**, 30 km (18 miles) from Nasik, was where a dispute arose between the gods and the demons over the possession of a pot of nectar. In the melée, the nectar spilled. One of the places where some drops fell was Trimbakesvar. The Godavari river rises here from a hill called **Brahmagiri**. The **Trimbakesvar Temple** has an important Shiva *lingam* and is an imposing monument with splendid carvings.

Shirdhi , 75 km (46 miles) from Nasik, is where Sai Baba, the Muslim teacher whose wisdom and miraculous powers made him a saint for people of all religions, including Hindus, lived and died. His followers come in great numbers through the year to pay their respects to his memory. The present (reincarnated) Sai Baba set up his ashram at Puttaparthi in Andhra Pradesh.

The coast

Beaches in Mumbai are far from pristine. It's best to try **Kihim**, 136 km (85 miles) south of Mumbai, or **Murud**, 80 km (50 miles) further, which has a breathtaking approach, an old palace and an island fort less than a mile offshore. ❏

Map on page 278

Ganapathipule , *375 km (230 miles) south of Mumbai, features a white sand beach backed by greenery. It has an old temple of Ganapati on a colossal rock on the shore. The image inside the temple is said to have been made by nature.*

BELOW: fisherwomen at Arnala.

Map
on page
284

GUJARAT

*Walled cities, Jain temples, the rare lions of the Gir Reserve
and the beaches of Diu make a visit to Gujarat,
the birthplace of Mahatma Gandhi, a rewarding experience*

Through the blaring cacophony of bicycles, autorickshaws, cars and bullock carts, a motorcycle with large milk cans tied astride darts through the streets of Ahmadabad with its rider bedecked in a brilliant red turban, flashing golden earrings and a fierce moustache. He is a *Rabari* from the milk-vending community, who has adopted modern transportation while continuing to wear his traditional dress. He is the essence of Gujarat, where tradition and modernity combine in a vibrant, dynamic fashion.

The archaeological finds at Lothal near Dhandhuka in Ahmadabad district and Rozadi in Saurashtra carry the history of Gujarat back to the age of Harappa and Mohenjodaro, 3,500 years ago. In legend, the epics and *Puranas* tell of how Krishna and his brother Balarama left Mathura and settled at Kusathali (Dwarka) on Gujarat's western coast. The name "Gujarat" derives from the Prakrit "Gujja-ratta" or "Gurjara Rastra", which means "land of the Gurjaras". The Gurjaras were an immigrant people who entered India through the northern passes, made their way through the Punjab and settled in lands that came to be known as Gujarat, a name that became popular around the 10th century.

The Gujaratis' flair for maritime and mercantile pursuits developed a strong spirit of enterprise and produced a well-to-do middle class that wielded

BELOW: Indian
Institute of
Management,
Ahmadabad.

considerable influence. Traders and artisans formed powerful guilds and the acquisition of wealth has a strong tradition in Gujarat. The state spreads itself into the regions of Kutch (which was at the epicentre of a devastating earthquake in 2001, *see page 285*), Saurashtra and the verdant territories between the rivers Banas and Damanganga. These are fertile lands of wheat, cotton, peanut and banana plantations. The southern border is hilly, and the former Portuguese colony of **Diu** island offers an escape into holiday ambience.

A more unattractive side of the state is manifest in the popularity of the Hindu chauvinist BJP, who run the state government. This strain of militant Hinduism was seen at its worst during communal riots in 2002. After a terrorist attack on a train carrying *kar sevaks* (Hindu volunteers) to the disputed site in Ayodhya *(see page 101)* gangs of Hindus roamed the streets of Ahmadabad and other major towns and cities, looting, killing and driving out Muslims. Eyewitnesses report the police standing by, or even helping, while the gangs did their worst, prompting speculation that members of the ruling BJP were complicit in the violence.

Ahmadabad's Sunday market on the edge of the Sabarmati River, below Ellis Bridge, comes alive with the Khanmasa Bazaar, a spread of the most fascinating and often preposterous wares.

Mosques, bazaars, museums

The reign of Sultan Allauddin Khalji of Delhi witnessed the creation of the first Muslim empire in India and one of his earliest conquests was the wealthy kingdom of Gujarat in 1300. Ahmad Shah I founded **Ahmadabad ❶** on the site of the ancient city of Karnavati in 1411.

Today, Ahmadabad's belligerent, swerving autorickshaws, modern Ashram Road with its hotels, shops and cinemas, and the heavily populated industrial sections of town, are all manifestations of its character as a great textile and commercial city of western India. Omnipresent is the Sabarmati river over which four bridges connect the old city with the new.

BELOW: village fair in Gujarat.

On one side are the crowded streets leading to **Manek Chowk**, where rows of traders dealing in silver jewellery or printed fabrics lean against spotless white bolster-pillows, waiting for customers. On the upper floors of the buildings on this street are the carved wooden balconies, windows and doorways of old *havelis* (town houses); the most beautiful stand in **Doshivada-ni-Pol**.

The Indo-Saracenic architecture of Ahmadabad blends Hindu and Muslim styles. **Sidi Saiyad's Mosque** near Relief Road is Ahmadabad's most eloquent example of the finest such work in sandstone. Its twin windows of pierced stone, with a lyrical design of a tree with palm leaves and curving tendrils, must be seen. The shaking minarets of **Rajpur Bibi's Mosque** at Gomtipur and **Sidi Bashir's Mosque** at Kalipur are interesting. Pressure exerted on the inner walls of the minarets made them vibrate.

There is, of course, no official "nightlife" in Ahmadabad due to Gujarat's prohibition laws (foreigners who wish to drink can obtain a "liquor licence" at the same time as they apply for their visa), but the substitute it offers is typical of the region. A 15-minute drive out of Ahmadabad on the main highway to Vadodara (Baroda) is the **Utensil Museum** and **Vishala Restaurant** (open Mon–Sat 5–11pm, Sun 10am–1pm, 5–10pm). The museum contains a

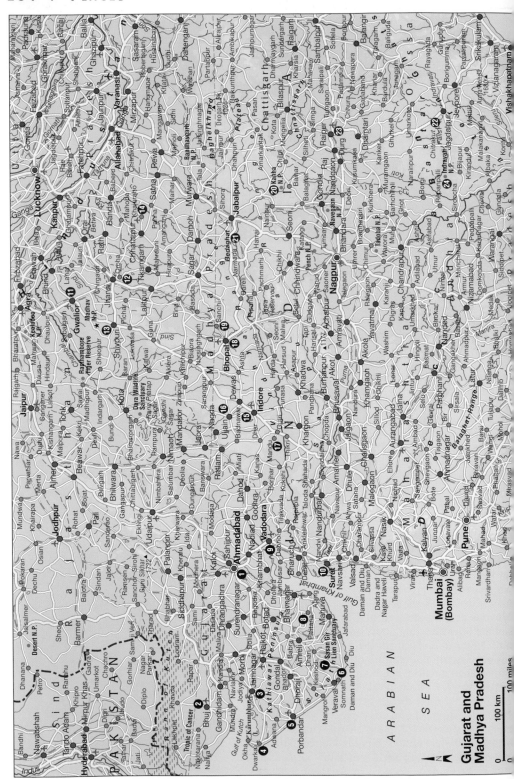

**Gujarat and
Madhya Pradesh**

0   100 miles

0   100 km

Map on page 284

remarkable collection of utensils of every imaginable shape and size. Housed in a building made of mud walls and with a central water tank, the atmosphere is both rustic and evocative of old Gujarat. A traditional Gujarati meal at the **Vishala Restaurant** rounds off the visit. Vegetarian favourites, baked breads, fresh white butter, jaggery and yogurt are served on large brass dishes to the accompaniment of traditional music or puppet shows.

The grace of Ahmadabad's modern architecture must be seen to understand the Gujaratis' appreciation of their own culture and aesthetic sensibilities. The **Indian Institute of Management** in Vastrapur provides a comprehensive education to aspiring managers. The buildings, designed by Louis Kahn, are a fascinating display of the sense of drama that can be created by light and shade, angles and arches.

The **Calico Museum of Textiles** (open Thur–Tues, religious textiles 10.30am–12.30pm, secular textiles 2.45–4.45pm) in Shahibag is located in an old *haveli* which houses the Sarabhai Foundation, a public charitable trust. The exceptionally fine collections include rich brocades and fine embroideries from Kashmir, Gujarat and the southern states, all beautifully displayed.

Hridey Kunj (open 8.30am–6.30pm), Mahatma Gandhi's ashram at Sabarmati, is a set of austere yet beautiful buildings nestling amid mango trees. It was from here that Gandhi experimented in non-violent methods of political struggle. The simple museum, added later, is a fitting tribute. Designed by Charles Correa, a well-known Indian architect, it displays Gandhi's spectacles, sandals, photographs, spinning wheel and cloth spun by him.

Gujarat Vidyapith, a university established by Gandhi, has a vast collection of books, a museum, research centre and the Navjivan Press, which holds the copyright of Gandhi's works. It is located on the busy Ashram Road and visitors can shop for *khadi* (handspun) fabrics and other handmade village industry products at the nearby **Khadi Gramudyog Bhandar**.

Some 17 km (10 miles) north of Ahmadabad is **Adalaj Vava**, a 15th-century step-well, an architectural delight with its geometric and floral patterns on the stone pillars and lintels that line the steps leading to the rectangular well. Tanks and wells have always been artistically treated in Gujarat. This step-well was built during the most glorious period of the Indo-Saracenic style of architecture.

The **Sun Temple** at **Modhera** is a three-hour journey by road north of Ahmadabad. It is one of the finest examples of Indian temple architecture. Built in 1026, during the reign of King Bhima of the Solanki dynasty, the temple is dedicated to the Sun God, Surya, and stands on a plinth beside a stone-stepped tank. It is elaborately carved with figures of gods, flowers and animals.

Rann of Kutch

It is a long drive onwards to Bhuj across the **Little Rann of Kutch**. Kutch (Kachchh) covers 8,750 sq km (3,350 sq miles), bounded by the Gulf of Kutch, the Indian Ocean and the Rann of Kutch, a peculiar landscape described by one Lt. Burnes in his memoirs as "a space without a counterpart in the globe". The

Gujarat has a strong tradition of embroidery. Originally, garments were decorated with fragments of mirror to frighten off wild beasts.

BELOW: chatting on the steps of an Ahmadabad *haveli* (town house).

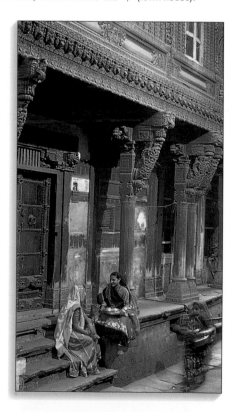

The seaside temple of Somnath was looted and destroyed by Mahmud of Ghazni in 1026. Parts of the building have been reconstructed in the old style.

BELOW: Asiatic lion, an endangered species.

word *rann* derives from the Sanskrit word *irina*, meaning a waste. The expanse is hard, dry, saline and flat and, as the summer heat intensifies, the salt in the baked and blistered earth shines with mirages of dazzling whiteness; herds of galloping wild ass can be seen.

On 26 January 2001 the region was hit by an earthquake which registered 7.9 on the Richter scale. The beautiful walled town of **Bhuj** ❷ was flattened and villages in the surrounding area were devastated. It is estimated that some 25,000 people were killed in the tremors. Governments and individuals donated large amounts of aid to help with reconstruction work, which has started, but the task is huge and it is not known when it will be anywhere near complete. Sub-standard construction due to the avoidance of building regulations was blamed for the collapse of many new concrete buildings; traditional huts survived the quake much better. Hopefully this will lead to the rooting out of corrupt developers and a re-examination of traditional building techniques. Kutch is still getting back on its feet, and facilities for visitors are sparse.

Exploring Saurashtra

The Indian Airlines flight from Bhuj south across the Gulf of Kutch to Jamnagar takes only 13 minutes. **Jamnagar** ❸, the district headquarters, is a walled city with several gateways. The older parts are bursting at the seams but many areas were planned as recently as 1914 and have a systematic layout of facades, squares, circles and broad streets. Textile mill and tie-dyed fabrics both roll out of Jamnagar. The Kotho Bastion of **Lakhota Palace** is located in a tank and approached over a stone bridge. It could accommodate 1,000 soldiers, and now houses a fine museum (open Thur–Tues 10.30am–1pm, 3–5.30pm).

Dwarka ❹, 137 km (85 miles) west of Jamnagar, is a holy spot and was a flourishing port in ancient times. It is said that Krishna established Dwarka 5,000 years ago. The **Temple of Dvarkadish** on the northern bank of Gomti Creek is typical of the architecture of old Hindu temples. It has a shrine, a large hall, a roof supported by 60 columns of granite and sandstone, and a conical spire 50 metres (160 ft) high. The exterior is carved while the inside is simple. The shrine is elaborately ornamented and has a sculpted figure of Ganesh, the elephant deity, over the entrance.

Gandhi's birthplace

For those who have a special interest in the life of Mahatma Gandhi, a visit to **Porbandar** ❺, his birthplace (90 km/56 miles along the coast), is a pilgrimage worth planning. It is a quiet coastal town. Gandhi was born here in 1869, in his ancestral home. With its small rooms, trellised windows and carved balconies, the house has an air of peace and tranquillity.

Driving along quiet coastal roads through Chorwad and Verawal you will reach **Somnath** ❻, 115 km (70 miles) from Porbandar, one of the 12 most sacred Siva shrines in India. It stands majestically, washed by the Arabian Sea. Ransacked repeatedly by northern invaders and rebuilt successively in gold, silver, wood and finally in stone, it is said to have been built by Soma, the moon god, in penance and worship of the

wrathful Lord Shiva who had laid a curse on him. Nearby a temple marks the spot where Lord Krishna is said to have been accidentally killed by a hunter's arrow. Cymbals are played at dusk to mark the time for prayers.

Lions of the Gir Forest

Sasan Gir Lion Sanctuary ❼, 40 km (25 miles) north of Somnath, is one of the last places in the world where Asiatic lions can be seen in their natural habitat. One of the earliest efforts at conservation began in the **Gir Forest**. In 1900 the Nawab of Junagadh, in whose territory most of the forest lay, had invited the viceroy, Lord Curzon, for a lion *shikar* (hunt). When the viceroy accepted, a newspaper published a letter that questioned the propriety of an important person doing further damage to an endangered species. Lord Curzon not only cancelled his *shikar*, but also advised the nawab to protect the remaining lions, which the nawab did. Now the Gir Forest is one of the most important game preserves in India. The Gir lion is a majestic animal with a bigger tail tassle, bushier elbow tufts and a smaller mane than its African cousin. Early in the 20th century there were only 100 lions left in Gir; now they number more than 250.

Mahatma Gandhi was born at Porbandar, Gujarat.

Temple City

Palitana ❽ in Bhavanagar district almost completes the full circle of Saurashtra. Two kilometres (1 mile) from town is the **Shatrunjaya Hill**, the most important centre of Jain pilgrimage, with an incredible 863 Jain temples atop its twin peaks. Palitana is a major marketing centre for chillies, cereals and pulses and has a bustling market for farmers.

BELOW: the Lakshmi Vilas Palace in Vadodara

It is worth heading back in the direction of Ahmadabad via **Surendranagar** and **Wadhwan**. The ancestors of the stone carvers of Wadhwan built Dwarka and Somnath. Skilled stone carvers live and practice their craft near **Hawa Mahal**, a finely conceived but unfinished palace at the edge of the town. Traders in Surendranagar town have a vast collection of old embroideries and artefacts from all over Saurashtra.

The "industrial corridor" of Gujarat is due south of Ahmadabad. In its hinterland lies the exclusively Adivasi belt of Gujarat. The rural societies found here lead very different lives to those of people living in the mercantile centres elsewhere in Gujarat.

The industrial city of **Vadodara ❾** (formerly Baroda) was capital of one of the richest "princely states" in pre-Independence India. The old town has a number of attractions associated with the ruling maharajas. Chief among these is the formerly opulent **Lakshmi Vilas Palace**, built towards the end of the 19th century. Close by is the **Maharaja Fateh Singh Museum** (open July–Mar 10am–5.30pm, Apr–June 4–7pm).

Surat ❿, on the east coast of the Gulf of Cambay, was the first outpost established (in 1608) by the British East India Company and was on one of the old trade routes for silks, embroideries and spices. Despite a dominant Parsi and Muslim influence, its architecture is mostly Portuguese and British. Today it is the centre of the diamond-cutting and *zari* (gold thread) industry. ❑

MADHYA PRADESH

This is the heartland of India, a state packed with surprises, where tigers roam the jungle, and fortified towns, temples, stupas and cave paintings lure the visitor

Map on page 284

Madhya Pradesh, literally translated, means "middle land", and it does spread across Central India. Most of the state is upland plateaus and hills, interspersed with the deep valleys of rivers that flow east into the Bay of Bengal and west into the Arabian Sea. Much of India's forest is located here. It consists of some of the finest deciduous hardwoods in the world – teak, sal, hardwickia, Indian ebony and rosewood. Bamboo is prolific in the hills and there are magnificent fruit and flowering trees. The Mahadeo Hills of the Satpura Range are the home of the tiger, panther, Indian bison and the myriad herbivores that make the jungle their home.

The state is also home to many Adivasi groups. Among the most populous are the Gonds, found across the Madhya Pradesh and into neighbouring Chattisgarh. Western Madhya Pradesh is inhabited by the Bhils, a group of warriors and hunters who once held the powerful Mughal army at bay. Eastern Madhya Pradesh is dominated by the Oraons, now largely Christian.

Madhya Pradesh has many crafts, from the weaving of Chanderi and Maheshwar, to the carpet-making of Vidisha, Mandsaur and Sarguja. Other crafts include carpentry, pottery, textile printing and dyeing, metalworking, woodcarving and leather work.

LEFT: erotic sculptures at Khajuraho.
BELOW: Adivasi girl from Kanha.

Travel and food

Madhya Pradesh is quite easy to reach. One can fly to the state from Delhi, Mumbai and Kolkata. Gwalior, Bhopal, Indore, Jabalpur, Raipur and Khajuraho are on the air map and there are excellent train services throughout the region. Road journeys are interesting because the routes pass through forests and cultivated areas in succession and skirt villages. Most places have adequate, if simple, hotel facilities.

The cuisine varies from the wheat- and meat-based food of northern and western Madhya Pradesh to the rice and fish domination in the south and the east. Gwalior and Indore abound in milk and milk-based preparations. Bhopal produces exquisite meat and fish dishes, of which spicy *rogan josh*, *korma*, *keema*, *biryani* and *kababs* such as *shami* and *seekh* are the most famous. They are eaten with thin slices of unleavened bread called *rumali roti* ("handkerchief bread") and leavened, flat loaves called *shirmal*. Also interesting are the *bafla* (wheat cakes), dunked in rich ghee and eaten with *dal*, a pungent lentil broth, whose tongue-tingling sharpness is moderated by the accompanying *ladus* (sweet dumplings).

The best time to travel is from the mild autumn of October to the spring at the end of March. April to mid-July are very hot. The monsoon months of July, August and September can also be pleasant.

Detail from the painted palace of Man Mandir, one of the many buildings inside Gwalior's mighty fort.

Jewels of the north

The northernmost city, **Gwalior** , was established in the 8th century AD and named after Saint Gwalipa. The city is dominated by its hilltop **fort** (open 6am–7pm, entrance fee), one of the most redoubtable in the world. The Rajput palace of Raja Mansingh, built 1486–1516, is the best preserved section. Located at the northern end of the citadel, it retains much of its original blue tiling. The fort also has one of the finest museums of sculpture in the country (open Sat–Thur 10am–5pm). At the southern end of the fort is the wonderful 8th-century **Teli-ka-Mandir** ("oil man's temple"). Close by is the modern **Sikh gurudwara** commemorating Guru Gobind Singh (1595–1644) who was imprisoned in the fort. The steep road up to the Urwahi Gate passes a series of Jain sculptures dating from the 7th to 15th centuries. The view from the battlements near the ornate pair of 11th-century **Sas Bahu temples** is breathtaking.

The current maharaja, Jyotiraditya Rao Scindia, inhabits part of the **Jai Vilas Palace**, the rest of which is now a museum (open 9.30am–5.50pm, entrance fee). The exhibits range from the usual depressing array of dead tigers, to some very fine stone carving and miniatures. The durbar hall with its huge chandeliers is worth seeing; downstairs you can see the maharaja's silver train set.

Gwalior was also a centre of Indian court music. **Tansen**, the great musician of the court of Akbar, is buried at Gwalior. His 16th-century tomb is set in the pleasant grounds of the impressive domed Mughal **tomb of Muhammad Gaur** Tansen's guru. In his memory a music festival is held here each December.

Gwalior is a good starting point to visit two of the loveliest places in Madhya Pradesh; Orcha and Shivpuri. **Orcha** , 120 km (75 miles) from Gwalior, is a medieval town, which looks today much as it must have in the 16th and 17th centuries, when it was built. It was founded in the 16th century by the Bundela king, Rudra Pratap, on the banks of the sparkling **Betwa River** The countryside undulates gently and the builders of Orcha dotted the landscape with palace and fortress, temple and cenotaph. The architecture is a synthesis of traditional Hindu, hybrid Indo-Saracenic and ornate Mughal One of the finest sights is the view of the architecturally stunning *chatris*, or cenotaphs, from across the blue river with green hills in the background.

About 100 km (60 miles) from Gwalior is **Shivpuri** , the former summer capital of the Scindias of Gwalior. Shivpuri is on the Vindhyan plateau, and the contrast with the Gangetic Plain is immediate. Here are the two lakes of **Sakhia Sagar** and **Madhav Sagar**. Surrounding them is the **Madhav National Park**, home of a variety of deer, *chinkara* or Indian gazelle, sambhar, blue bull, black buck, barking deer and four-horned antelope. Also seen are wild dog and sloth bear. Bird life abounds and

TEMPLES OF KHAJURAHO

One of the greatest sights in Madhya Pradesh is the temple complex at **Khajuraho** in the north of the state. The period 950 to 1050, a mere 100 years, saw a flowering of architecture in this small village that has no parallel. Here the Chandela dynasty built 85 temples. Today 22 survive. These temples are designed to lead one's eyes from ground level ever upwards to the ultimate heaven, *Kailasa*. They are ornately carved, with each frieze and sculpture depicting the genius of the men who carved it and the king who inspired them to their work.

Khajuraho has achieved fame for the sensual appeal of the erotic sculptures, but these form only a small part of the wealth of the site. Taken in totality, the sculptures depict the everyday life of the people and the court in the 10th and 11th centuries. This procession of life itself culminates in the inner *sanctum sanctorum*. The western enclosure houses the main temples (open sunrise to sunset, entrance fee), and the Archaeological Museum (open 10am–5pm; closed Fri) is nearby.

A good time to visit Khajuraho is in March during the annual 10-day dance festival, when India's leading classical dancers perform on the podium of the largest temple, Khandariya Mahadev.

peacocks are to be seen in their hundreds. In the nearby **Karera Bird Sanctuary** is the Great Indian Bustard, an endangered species that has been rescued by sensitive conservation. The lakes are home to the Indian mugger crocodile.

Map on page 284

Indore and Ujjain

In the west is the rapidly growing industrial city of **Indore ⑮** on the Malwa Plateau, known for its cotton fields. On its periphery is **Devas**, made famous by E.M. Forster in *The Hill of Devi*. The land of Malwa is sacred and two of the 12 *jyotirlingam*, or naturally occurring *lingam*, are to be found at the **Mahakalesvar Temple** at **Ujjain ⑯**, 60 km (35 miles) from Indore, and **Mandhata** at **Omkaresvar**. For Hindus, these two places enjoy a sanctity equal to Varanasi. Every 12 years Ujjain has the great fair of *Kumbha Mela*, or *Simhastha* as it is called locally. The *mela* moves every three years between Ujjain, Allahabad and Haridwar on the Ganga, and Nasik on the Godavari River. The sacred river at Ujjain is the **Sipra**. The gods and the *asuras* (demons) fought for 12 days for possession of the *kumbh*, or pot, of *amrit*, nectar of immortality, that came from the churning of the milk-ocean. As they fought, four drops fell on the places where the *Kumbha Melas* are now held. Every 12 years, millions of Hindus congregate to worship at these spots. Ujjain is also a centre for textile dyeing using vegetable dyes and hand-carved teak blocks. The *chipas*, or dyers and printers, are found at **Bherugarh**.

"Dak bungalows" offer simple, clean accommodation. They are maintained by the government and have a khansama (cook-caretaker), who can provide a tasty hot meal at short notice.

Fortress town

Mandu ⑰ is 90 km (55 miles) from Indore. You approach the capital of the Sultanate of Malwa either from the plains of Dhar or from the mountain pass at Manpur. The first sight of Mandu is impressive; there is a chasm, a deep wooded

BELOW: Kandariya Mahadev Temple, Khajuraho.

Rudyard Kipling's
Jungle Book *was
set in the Mahadeo
Hills where the
forests, wildlife and
people are today
almost exactly as
they were in his time.*

ravine that is crossed by a narrow bridge, and on the skyline is the largest-standing fortified city in the world. The walls have a circumference of more than 75 km (45 miles). The **Bhangi Gate**, a fearsome defensive bastion, leads to lakes and groves, gardens and palaces. The **Jahaz Mahal**, or ship palace, floats on its lake, and the **Hindola Mahal**, or swing palace, appears to sway gently in the breeze.

The **Jama Masjid** has acoustics so perfect that a whisper from the pulpit is heard clearly in the furthest corner of the huge courtyard. There is also the **Nikanth Temple**, a standing monument to the tolerance of the Emperor Akbar.

Close by is the **Reva Kund**, said to be filled by the waters of the Narmada River 90 km (55 miles) away and 600 metres (2,000 ft) lower down. Legend has it that Sultan Baz Bahadur met his future queen Rupmati on the banks of the Narmada River when out hunting. He married her on a promise that he would bring the Narmada to Mandu, and Reva Kund is the fulfilment of that promise. On its banks he built a palace for himself and, further up, at the very edge of the escarpment, a pavilion for Rupmati, from the terrace of which she could see the Narmada as a silver thread on the horizon. There is a sheer drop of 600 metres (2,000ft) from the pavilion terrace to the plains of Nimar below.

Bhopal, the state capital

The state capital, **Bhopal** ⓲, was tragically put on the world map in 1984 by the gas leak from a pesticide plant owned by the US multinational Union Carbide, which killed at least 2,000 and affected hundreds of thousands of others. However, Bhopal is far more than this. The city enjoys a moderate climate, and is built on seven hills and round three lakes. The architect Charles Correa designed **Bharat Bhavan**, a fabulous multi-arts centre; it contains a **Museum of Adivasi**

BELOW: the
Buddhist *stupa* at
Sanchi.

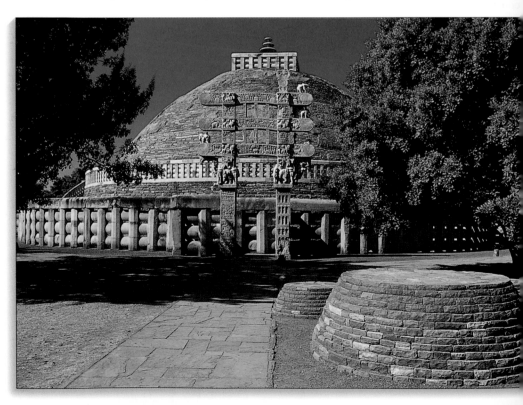

Map on page 284

Art (open Tues–Sun, Feb–Oct 2–8pm; Nov–Jan 1–7pm) that displays striking exhibits. Also noteworthy are the **Archaeological Museum** and **Birla Museum**, with good displays of sculpture. Bhopal is one of the greatest centres of art and culture in the country and a visitor could well spend all their time in the art galleries, museums, theatres and library. Bhopal's industries give the city an air of briskness. State government is its major occupation. The city was founded in the 10th century by Raja Bhoj. The **Bhojpur Temple**, even in its ruined state, speaks of the greatness of this king, as do the remains of the magnificent **Tal** lake, which once covered 600 sq km (230 sq miles) and whose destruction in the 15th century by Sultan Hosang Shah of Malwa altered the climate of the region.

Ancient sites

Thirty km (18 miles) away is **Bhimbethka**, where more than 500 caves with Neolithic rock paintings have been discovered. Five periods have been identified, from the prehistoric upper Palaeolithic to the early historical and medieval. At **Sanchi** ⑲, 46 km (28 miles) from Bhopal, a great stupa covers relics of Gautama Buddha. Noted for exquisite carvings in honey-coloured stone, Sanchi is a place of Buddhist pilgrimage. Northeast of Sanchi are **Vidisha** and **Udaygir** (8 km/5 miles) and **Gyaraspur** (50 km/30 miles), the cradle of Mauryan civilisation and the rocks on which the tide of ancient Grecian conquest broke. The exquisite sculptured *salbhanjika*, or divine attendant of the gods, is preserved here.

South of Bhopal is Kipling country, with the **Narmada River** as the cord which binds the Satpura and Vindhyan Hills together. This is one of the great rivers of India, but it is now part of one of the largest hydroelectric schemes in the world. Its damming and the subsequent displacement of peoples, with little compensation for their loss of land, have provoked fierce protests from local groups and caused international outrage.

The **Kanha National Park** ⑳ and its sister sanctuary, **Bandhavgarh**, are perhaps the state's top attractions. These parks have grassy *maidans* (meadows), which are home for deer. The jungles teem with leopard, bear and wildcat, and there are some tigers. In some cases, the numbers are prodigious, with spotted deer alone numbering more than 17,000. Tiger is king, but not set to rule over gaur, the Indian wild ox; where the gaur browses, the tiger makes a wide detour. Kanha is home to that unique species of 12-horned swamp deer, the barasingha *(Duvaceli branderi)*, the only swamp deer that has adapted to dwelling on hard ground. It faced extinction before the great naturalist and administrator M.K.S. Ranjitsinhji rescued it. The park was the setting for Kipling's *The Jungle Book*.

Two places in Madhya Pradesh deserve special mention: Pachmarhi and Bedaghat. **Pachmarhi** is in the Satpura Hills, 210 km (130 miles) southeast of Bhopal; a special place for trekkers, rock climbers and nature lovers alike. **Bedaghat** ㉑ is 22 km (14 miles) from Jabalpur. Here the Narmada river flows through a 5-km- (2-mile-) long gorge, between towering white marble cliffs, particularly spectacular on full-moon nights. Below the gorge are the **Dhuandhar Falls**, literally "smoky falls". ❏

Large numbers of spotted deer can be seen on the grasslands of Kunha National Park, where the jungle is home to tigers.

BELOW: a common langur.

Map
on page
284

Delhi

CHATTISGARH

*With a name that means either "land of "36 forts",
or "land of the Chedis", Chattisgarh has some of the most extensive
and least-disturbed forest in India*

O ne of India's newest states, Chattisgarh came into being in November 2000 and is perhaps the least-known, and least-urbanised part of the country. Here the hills march in ranks and the forests are primeval. In the **Kanger Valley** is India's largest national biosphere reserve, in which nature has been left totally undisturbed by man. **Tirathgarh Falls** decorate the hills with a 250-metre (820-ft) lace of froth, before disappearing into **Kotamsar**, whose limestone rocks produce caves full of stalactites and stalagmites. Bastar is the home of the bisonhorn Marias, whose dances and drumming can be seen at festivals. It is also the home of the hill mynah bird, which imitates the voice of people. The impressive **Chitrakut Falls** ㉒ on the Indravati river in Bastar is another natural attraction of this remote region.

The state has 44 percent of its area covered by forest, accounting for 12 percent of the remaining forest in India. However, below the forested surface lie some of the richest mineral deposits in the world. In an ominous omen for the region's environment, these vast deposits are starting to be exploited. Mining, huge power plants, steel mills, aluminium factories and copper smelters are already here, with little benefit to local Adivasi populations; even less so since many of the industries have been, or are due to be, privatised.

BELOW: a wild water buffalo.

The state capital

The capital of Chattisgarh is the city of **Raipur** ㉓, which acts as the transport hub for the whole region. Now largely industrial and expanding rapidly, the city is said to have been founded by the Kalchuri king Ram Chandra towards the end of the 14th century, although there seems to have been a settlement on the site since the 9th century. Sights in Raipur include a ruined fortress and a 17th-century temple.

Some 80 km (50 miles) from Raipur is the important site of **Sirpur**. Mentioned as early as the 5th-century AD, excavations in the area have revealed numerous ancient temples, as well as two Buddhist monasteries. Two of the most important buildings still standing are the rare brick-built Laksmana, and the finely decorated Gandesesvara temples.

Indravati National Park

The **Indravati National Park and Tiger Reserve** ㉔ is one of the state's main attractions but, owing to the activities of Naxalite revolutionaries, entry to the park is currently restricted. Established in 1978, and, since 1982, a Project Tiger reserve, the park is part of a vast forest belt that stretches across central India. The Indravati river also flows through the sanctuary. The importance of this park cannot be overestimated. It holds perhaps the only viable population of wild buffalo in central India and is a possible alternative home for the swamp deer of Kanha. Most of the forest is mixed deciduous woodland with teak and large areas of bamboo. There are also large areas of open grassland that are home to herds of chital. Other animals in the park include sambar, nilgai, blackbuck, sloth bear, leopard and jackal. Summers are very hot (up to 49°C/120°F) and the best time to visit, Marxist insurgents permitting, is between January and April.

Rich variety

About one third of the state's population are Adivasi. The most numerous are the Gonds, who once ruled much of central India and after whom **Gondwana** came to be known. They inhabited the Satpura and Kymore ranges and their major branches, the Maria and the Muria Gonds, live in Bastar. Another numerous group are the Oraons, who, having been targeted by missionaries, are now almost wholly Christian converts.

The Adivasis of Chattisgarh have retained their identities and customs, largely because previous state governments have treated them with sensitivity. Their art is not restricted to wood and bamboo: bastar bell-metal casting and clay sculptures are well known. Quality crafts may be found all over Chattisgarh, from household and agricultural items made from bamboo, to exciting jewellery made from a variety of metals, beads, cowries and feathers. Woodcarving is another widely practised skill; fine examples of carved ceilings, doors and lintels can be seen. Similarly, wall and floor paintings display a high degree of skill, particularly traditional *pithora* paintings made to mark life-cycle ceremonies such as marriage and childbirth. These usually include the depiction of a horse, which in the past was considered an auspicious animal to sacrifice. ❑

Rajnandgaon, in the south of the state, is the location of the hilltop Ma Bambesvari Temple. The temple is 480 metres (1600 ft) above the town and is reached by cable car.

BELOW: collecting firewood in Bastar.

GOA

Once the capital of Portugal's empire in the east, the coexistence of Indians and Portuguese, Hinduism and Christianity, gives the tiny west-coast state of Goa its identity

Map on page 298

he state of Goa was taken by the Portuguese on 25 November 1510, after Afonso de Albuquerque defeated Yusuf Adilshah, Sultan of Bijapur, in a fierce battle by the Mandovi River. Thus began four centuries of Portuguese influence on this region. They came looking for spices and stayed to make Goa the centre of their eastern empire.

Tucked away snugly between the hills of the Western Ghats and the Arabian Sea, this territory of only 3,500 sq km (1,350 sq miles), about halfway down the west coast of the Indian peninsula, is covered with bottlegreen hills wooded with jakfruit, mango and cashew groves, cut across by rivers and edged by miles of sun-drenched beaches. A warm languid climate, and friendly, welcoming people complete this compelling kaleidoscope.

Cocooned within its natural boundaries and the colonial cloisters of Portuguese rule, this pocket of South Asia was bypassed as the rest of the country progressed towards Independence and the 20th century, and Goa remained a Portuguese colony, suspended in a web of nostalgia. This all changed when Nehru, in frustration at the lack of movement on the part of the Portuguese Government, sent in the troops to liberate the state in 1961.

Iberian legacy

Since Goa's absorption into the Indian Union, there have been many changes. But one can still drive through peaceful towns with their Iberian-style villas, stop at a small *taverna* (bar) for a potent drink of *feni* (a local brew made from cashew or coconut) listen to the sounds of *mando* (traditional songs) and the strains of a guitar mingling with the lapping of the waves, or bask on the golden sands of idyllic beaches.

There is an almost Mediterranean atmosphere in many of the towns with their red-tiled roofs and narrow streets, and the fishing villages snuggled among coconut groves. Fishermen with faces weathered by sun, salt and wind, catch mackerel, shark, crab, lobster and shrimp. Although the majority of the state's population is Hindu, a fact that is sometimes forgotten by Western visitors, on Sundays and feast days many Christians file into the Baroque-style churches – the women often in European dress and with lace mantillas on their heads, the men in black suits.

Capital town

Panaji (Panjim) ❶, the capital of Goa, situated on the southern bank of the Mandovi River, is centred on a church and the square in front of it. **Largo da Igreja** (Church Square) is an impressive ensemble: a dazzling white-balustraded stairway in front of the **Church of the Immaculate Conception** heightens

LEFT: sea saltpans.
BELOW: a Goan woman.

Motorcycles, mopeds and bicycles are available for hire. Motorcycle taxis are the most popular mode of transport.

the proportions of the Baroque facade, which dominates the square. Built i
1541, its twin towers were the first signs of "home" for the sailors who made th
long voyage from Lisbon.

Panaji has several squares, the houses lining them rising directly above th
wide streets. Most of these villas, painted in pale yellow, green or deep rose, wit
their embellishments picked out in white or some contrasting colour, displa
French windows opening onto wrought-iron balconies.

Particularly quaint is the old residential area of **Fountainahas**, which lie
behind the church, where narrow cobbled alleys weave through a miscellany o
closely knit houses with tiled roofs, overhanging balconies and carved pillars
much as one would expect to find in any provincial town in Portugal or Spain
Winding streets echo to the sputter of motorcycles and the chatter of relaxin
locals. There is never too little time for a drink or a chat. Shops close for sies
ta and the whole town dozes away the golden hours.

Facing the river, along the broad riverside boulevard, are some of Panaji'
public buildings, including the **Secretariat**, built in 1615 by the Portuguese o
the site of the Palacio Idalcao (palace of the Sultan of Bijapur, Yusuf Adil Khan
called the "Idalcan" by the Portuguese), a many-shuttered edifice that was onc
the viceroy's residence. Beyond **Largo da Palacio** (Palace Square) lies th
quay where the catamaran from Mumbai arrives (the service is run by Samudr
Link Ferries: www.sam-link.com).

The **Campal** riverside boulevard is one of the most picturesque spots i
Panaji. In the far distance are the ramparts of the **Aguada Fort** – once one o
the main bastions commanding the entrance into the Mandovi, with powde
rooms, barracks, a church and a lighthouse. It is now used as a prison.

BELOW: Mapusa buffalo market.

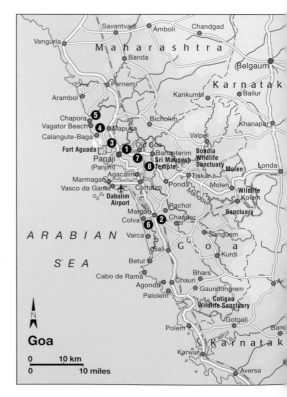

Towns and villages

Margao ②, 27 km (17 miles) south of Panaji, is the second largest town in Goa and the principal commercial centre. In the heart of one of the most fertile districts, Salcete, several prominent landowning families have built themselves town and country houses.

Other towns include **Vasco da Gama**, 20 km (12 miles) northwest of Margao), which is developing into an industrial centre. Goa's port of **Marmagoa**, a further 4 km (2½ miles) west, is one of India's finest natural harbours; **Mapusa**, 13 km (8 miles) north of Panaji, is a traditional market town. But the true voice of Goan culture is much more audible in the villages and outlying regions.

Village houses in Goa are designed around a central courtyard, usually overgrown with banana trees. The style combines Indian elements with the Italianate form prevalent in Europe two centuries ago. An open verandah surrounds the courtyard and leads into airy, spacious rooms, which display carved rosewood furniture, ornate mirrors, chandeliers and a profusion of blue and white porcelain. Some of the larger homes also maintain their own private chapels. The houses are built of red laterite stone and windowpanes are traditionally covered with small rectangles of translucent oyster shell, instead of glass.

Churches and carnivals

As you travel through Goa's villages, the imprint of four and a half centuries of Catholicism is evident. The Portuguese came not only to conquer, but also to preach. Presiding over every village, commanding the heights at hilltops, hugging the shores of rivers, are sparkling white churches, crosses and small shrines, built mostly in the 16th and 17th centuries in the Gothic and Baroque styles.

Map on page 298

The National Institute of Water Sports (Sundial Apartments, A.S. Road, Altinho, Panaji; tel: 0832 243 6550; http://niws.nic.in) can supply information on diving, sailing and windsurfing in Goa.

BELOW: Betim, near to Panaji.

On the feast day of the patron saint – and every village has one – the whole village is in attendance. The image of the saint, brightly decorated, is carried in procession by priests and laity to the chanting of prayers and litanies, recited or sung, accompanied by a violin or even a brass band. A fair normally provides the finale – refreshments, such as black gram, cashew nuts, coconut and jaggery sweets, fancy goods and even utensils are on display for sale.

Often, music and dance accompany such festivities, Christianity having thoroughly mingled with existing religious traditions. Carnival in Goa is comparable to Rio's Mardi Gras, when towns and villages celebrate for three days Masqueraders dance in the streets, and *feni* flows freely everywhere.

Despite the easy availability of ecstacy, cannabis and LSD, narcotics are illegal in India. If arrested for possession, bail is not permitted. One could languish in an Indian jail for years waiting for trial.

Beach culture

Strung along Goa's 100-km (60-mile) coastline, like a lace frill on the edge of a colourful skirt, are some of the most beautiful beaches in the world – dazzling stretches of golden sand and surf edging the vast aquamarine expanse of the Arabian Sea. **Fort Aguada** ❸, 10 km (6 miles) west of Panaji, is near the luxury resorts at **Sinquerim** beach and more downmarket accommodation at **Candolim** beach – now a watersport paradise with jet skis and paragliding. North along the coast 6 km (4 miles) from Fort Aguada is **Calangute** ❹ beach, geared towards Western tourists with a variety of resorts, good restaurants and shopping. This long stretch of beach, lined with restaurant shacks and a favourite with hawkers, ends at the mouth of a small river in **Baga**. Across the river are a few good cafes and rooms for rent. Deck chairs and sukjn umbrellas can be rented on the beach, and you can even have a massage. For good views and fresh seafood try Fiesta.

A walk along a cliff-side path that skirts the ocean leads to **Anjuna Beach**, also

BELOW: Church of St Francis of Assisi, Old Goa.

ST XAVIER, TRAVELLING SAINT

The last time a Christian saint lay in state in the Basilica of Bom Jesus in Old Goa, believers seeking miracles made off with bits of his body. St Francis Xavier, the 16th-century Jesuit missionary who preached in Goa and inspired 30,000 converts, continued to travel widely even after his death. One holy forearm was taken from his ornate Medici vault in Old Goa and sent to Rome, and four years later a bone from the right hand ended up in a Japanese reliquary

This rather grisly precedent was set in 1554 when a Portuguese devotee reputedly bit off a toe while kissing the saintly corpse's feet and then carried it in her mouth back to Lisbon. It proved to be such a powerful cure-all that popular demand for the healing power of St Francis Xavier's skeleton launched a tradition of carrying his remains in a public parade once each decade from the Basilica of Bom Jesus to the Sé Cathedral in Old Goa. Two million onlookers witnessed the spectacle in 1994. The next parade will be in 2014.

The basilica is noted as the best example of baroque architecture in India. St Xavier's tomb was donated by the Grand Duke of Tuscany. Made in Italy from alabaster and Florentine marble, it is inlaid with semi-precious stones and bronze panels depicting scenes from his life.

approachable by road, 4 km (2½ miles) north of Calangute. Once popular with the 1960s flower children, this lovely beachfront is fringed with coconut palms and the gentle sea makes it ideal for bathing, except in the afternoons when local tourist groups descend to view the "naked foreigners", or during the bustling Wednesday flea market. The cafes hidden amid trees are popular for evening parties.

Around the corner from Anjuna are the white sand beaches of **Vagator**, which back onto a residential area with old Portuguese villas. For excellent views of the coastline, climb up to the ruined Portuguese fort at the boat-building village of **Chapora** ❺. Located beside an expansive estuary, this village has some good cafes and rooms for rent. A freshwater lake edged by thick woods is a pleasant surprise at the fishing village of **Arambol**, and makes a good day-trip by road and ferry.

Colva ❻ beach, 25 km (15 miles) south of Panaji, with a 25-km (15-mile) stretch of silver grey sand running to Cabo de Rama, is a remarkable sight. Several luxury hotel resorts have mushroomed here and the formerly pristine beach is no longer tranquil. **Benaulim**, 2 km (1¼ miles) south, has a better beach front. Nearby is the fishing village of **Varca**. A further 40 km (25 miles) south in Canacona district the rocky coast harbours good beaches such as **Palolem**, which is now geared to tourists. **Agonda**, known for big waves, is best for more daring swimmers, and **Polem** beach is a good spot for dolphin-watching.

The beaches of Goa, particularly Anjuna, are well known as a venue for clubbers in search of parties. These have huge sound systems pumping out dance music and a thriving drug culture. While in recent years the full-moon party scene has been pretty active, the Goa police have now started to clamp down on any gatherings, and to impose a 10pm closing time.

On Wednesdays the large and colourful Anjuna Beach Flea Market is a big attraction. Regional handicrafts, New Age trinkets and cooked food predominate.

BELOW: games on Vagator Beach.

Painted face of Goa.

Golden Goa

No visit to Goa is complete without going to the 16th century Golden Goa *(Goa Dourada)*, "Rome of the Orient". The best way to reach **Old Goa ➐** is by boat like the Portuguese, and through the **Viceregal Arch**. Magnificent churches, sumptuous buildings, stately mansions and broad streets characterised Old Goa.

The **Sé** Cathedral (Cathedral of St Catherine) remains one of the greatest monuments of the period. Completed in 1619, it is the largest Christian church in South Asia, and a grand example of Renaissance architecture. The cathedral's 80-metre (260-ft) aisle culminates in a richly carved gilt altarpiece – one of the finest in India. There is a font in the church, possibly a vessel of Hindu origin, said to have been used by Goa's patron saint, St Francis Xavier. Within the compound of the cathedral but facing the opposite direction is the Church of St Francis of Assisi, with a stucco ceiling and a profusion of carvings.

The majestic **Basilica of Bom Jesus** is famous as the site of St Francis Xavier's mausoleum. It's a beautiful building, blending neo-classical restraint with baroque exuberance and a flamboyant late-Renaissance facade. The Jesuits were the first Christians to undertake large-scale missionary activity in Portugal's new Asian possessions, the *Estado da India*, and Francis Xavier, a Basque priest, was their most successful emissary. Housed in a small chapel in the basilica's south transept, his supposedly incorruptible remains are Old Goa's most revered relic *(see page 300)*.

The **Church of St Cajetan**, near the ferry wharf, with two belfries and cupola was modelled on the Basilica of St Peter in Rome by its Italian architect. Also near the river bank stands the **Chapel of St Catherine**, built on the site of the bitterest fighting during Albuquerque's conquest of Goa in 1510.

Map on page 298

A few minutes' walk up the road from the basilica is **Monte Santo** (Holy Hill) where one haunted tower of the **Church of the Augustinian Monastery** is all that remains of a once-splendid vaulted structure. Adjacent to the ruins stands the **Convent of St Monica**, once one of the largest nunneries in the Portuguese empire.

Past the convent's buttresses, on a grassy mound at the edge of a steep cliff, is the shell of the **Church of Our Lady of the Rosary**, one of the earliest to be built in Goa. It contains the alabaster tomb of Dona Caterina, wife of the 10th Viceroy and the first Portuguese woman to hazard the arduous voyage to India.

There is hardly a temple to be seen in the coastal areas. Over the years conversions were forcibly imposed, temples were demolished and churches built in their place. Those who were determined to preserve their ancient faith removed their deities from the shrines and fled to the mountainous interior to the east, where Hindu temples can now be found.

The **Sri Mangesh Temple** ❽ (dedicated to Lord Shiva) and the **Shanta-Durga** (to goddess Parvati) and **Nagesh** temples, 22 km (13 miles) east of Panaji near Ponda, are among the most frequented in Goa. Ornate, Baroque interiors and several-storeyed *dipmals* – elaborate lamp towers – are unique features of these Goan Hindu shrines.

Considerable changes are shaking the somnolence of Goa. Reunion with India has brought water and electricity to the villages, communication with the outside world and Western tourists. The inflow of migrant labour has aggravated the pressures on domestic resources and brought about the growth of a new culture. While Goans fear that the identity of the region will be diluted by the pace of its integration with the rest of the country, much still remains of the fascinating mix of peoples and customs that characterise the state. ❑

So magnificent was the city of Old Goa in the 17th century that it was said, "Quem vin Goa excuse de ver Lisboa" ("Whoever has seen Goa need not see Lisbon").

BELOW: Sri Mangesh Temple near Ponda.

THE SOUTH

Soaring temples, colourful dance-dramas and caparisoned elephants take centre stage in the tropical South

All four states of South India and the westerly Lakshadweep Islands lie within the steamy Tropic of Cancer. Perhaps that explains the slightly more languid pace of life. Coconut palms lash the sky, coconut chutney quenches the fire of the curries, and coconut oil gleams in the hair of passers-by.

South Indian women twine fragrant jasmine blossoms into their hair. Patterns made from flower petals or crushed and coloured rice enhance the entrances of temples and households. Rice is the staple grain here, and people devour gargantuan heaps of the stuff from clean banana leaves. Sweet coffee rather than *chai* is normally offered, and pouring it dramatically at arm's length ensures a delicate foam.

Phrasebook Hindi won't get you very far in this region, where most languages are Dravidian. Linguists would need Telugu in Hyderabad, Kannada in Bangalore, Tamil in Chennai (Madras), and Malayalam in Kochi. However, luckily for travellers, English is widely understood. English is an official government language, so that southern politicians who are loath to speak Hindi, a symbol of northern domination, can communicate with each other.

The vast Deccan plains, the stepped rainforests of the Ghats, and two long coastlines distinguish the south. Temples are truly colourful here: each deity is brushed with a vibrant hue and the steep templetops look as chaotic and crowded as a bazaar. Traces of pigment have been found on venerable carved stone temples, which used to be painted in the same way. Christian churches are especially numerous in the south, and the 16th-century Jesuit missionary Francis Xavier was surprised to find a thriving Christian congregation with links to the apostle St Thomas.

Kerala is noted for its elephants and a unique martial arts tradition. Hyderabad, the gateway to South India, has been famous since Marco Polo's time for the skills of its Islamic craftsmen and the grandeur of Golconda Fort. This glory is almost surpassed by Hampi, a deserted stone city in Karnataka. Bangalore's pubs are a meeting place for men in India's most forward-looking city. And Chennai values its heritage of music, dance and commerce. While it has retained its charm, the South is now throwing off its slightly dreamy traditional image and is the driving force behind India's thriving new technology and software industries.　　　　　　　　　　❑

PRECEDING PAGES: the intricately carved and painted *gopuram* of the Kumbesvara Temple at Kumbakonam, Tamil Nadu.
LEFT: Kerala's beautiful backwaters.

CHENNAI (MADRAS)

*Chennai (formerly Madras), capital of Tamil Nadu,
hugs the sandy southeast shore. The least pressured of India's four
big cities, it is the stronghold of Tamil culture*

Map
on page
310

O
n the southeast coast, Chennai is the fourth-largest Indian metropolis, with 6.4 million inhabitants. The city is aligned north to south along the coast at the northern tip of Tamil Nadu. Chennai is a convenient entry point for southern India and has good links with other parts of India and with Sri Lanka, Burma (Myanmar) and East Asia.

The city has spread north and west to encompass colonial buildings, a coach factory, cycle and car factories and other industries. This rapid expansion has put great pressure on the city's infrastructure, particularly its water supply, and water shortages are common. It has a number of rivers and canals, including the Adyar River and the Cooum. On the Adyar there are some fine buildings: the Madras Club, Madras Boat Club, Chettinad Palace and Theosophical Society.

Dosas and dance drama

Climatically, Chennai goes from hot to hotter and hottest, with relief brought by the northwest monsoon in June and July and the southeast monsoon in December and January. Palm and casuarina trees trim the coastline, sea breezes bring cool freshness to the land and the beaches are beautiful in the early hours and late evenings. The sea here, on the east coast, is not as inviting for the swimmer as the Arabian Sea, but the beaches hum with pic-nickers and political rallies. At night, lights from fish-ing boats can be seen glowing over the dark waters.

Chennai is the gateway to Tamil Nadu, and serves as an introduction to Tamil culture, food, customs and people. Excellent vegetarian food is available in restau-rants serving delicious hot "meals" with boiled rice, lentil curries and tiny portions of vegetables. The crisp fried *dosa* and the steamed *idli* are famous and have come to be identified with Tamil Nadu. The Tamil lan-guage is ancient and poetic, often spoken at breathtak-ing speed. The richness of Tamil literature is matched by Tamil Nadu's music, dance and dramatic traditions.

Kanchipuram silk and cotton saris worn at home and for religious and social occasions are characterised by a combination of brilliant and contrasting colours. The older generation of Tamil Brahman women wear their 9-metre (30-ft) saris in the traditional style, draw-ing one end between the legs and the other over the shoulder. Traditionally the men wear *lungis* or *dhotis*, a length of cloth fastened at the waist and hanging down to the ankles sarong-style. A marriage or a reli-gious procession in Chennai provides a glittering dis-play of heavy 22-carat gold jewellery.

Chennai has a large Christian population. The British occupation from the 17th century left an Anglo-Indian population. Though well integrated into Indian society, their religion, clothes and culture make them distinct.

LEFT: outside a fruit market, Chennai.
BELOW: a pujari at the Kapalesvara temple, Mylapore.

Film-making for the Tamil-speaking market is big business in Chennai.

Chennai today is a curious mixture. While it retains the old legacy of the British East India Company and the subsequent Raj, and is, in some ways, a conservative bastion in social and religious matters, it is also the Bollywood of South India and, simultaneously, a stronghold of traditional Tamil culture. There are churchyards, staid residential areas and prim gardens side by side with giant-size cutouts of cinema heroes and heroines, painted in bright colours and dotted with flashing sequins. As if this contrast were not enough, Chennai has recently started to throw off its traditional image: it now has a thriving software industry, new air-conditioned shopping malls, and one of the best club scenes in the country.

The Tamil film industry has a reputation for producing high-quality films, even if it uses the same ingredients as Bollywood: legends, myths, historical and social themes, all served with a healthy dose of glamour. The songs from its movies, particularly those written by A.R. Rahman, have a country-wide appeal. Tamil film stars have always aspired to even greater glory than celluloid could bring them and have made a big impact on the politics of the state.

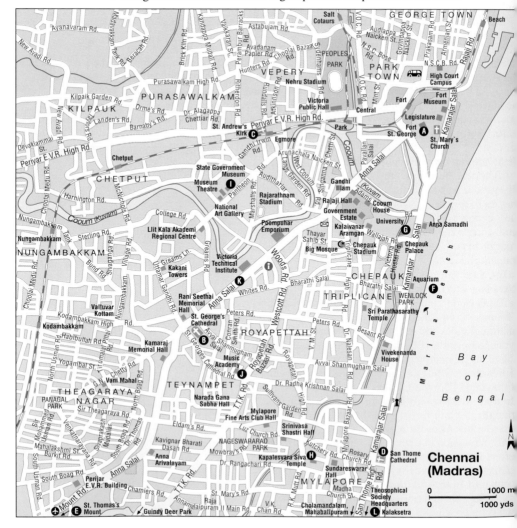

Chennai
(Madras)

The city centre

The British East India Company established one of its earliest seats of power in India in the former Madras. Unlike Mumbai and Kolkata, Chennai does not have a natural harbour. The present breakwaters were built in the 19th century. The construction of **Fort St George** was begun around 1640. The fort was often attacked by Indian and French forces, yet it continued to expand. Today the buildings in Fort St George house the Tamil Nadu Government **Secretariat** and the **Legislative Assembly**. A feature of the East India Company architecture is the use of Madras *chunam*, a glittering whitewash of limestone mixed with crushed seashells. The *chunam*-coated walls of the buildings are dazzling.

Within the fort, a number of other early buildings still stand, of which **St Mary's Church** is the most interesting. It is the earliest English building surviving intact in India and the oldest Anglican church in Asia, consecrated in 1680. The interior of the church is whitewashed, but there are also elaborate carved wooden panels. It was in this church that Robert Clive, victor of the Battle of Plassey in 1759 – which is taken as the beginning of British rule in India – was married in 1753.

The **Fort St George Museum** (open Sat–Thur 10am–5pm, entrance fee) contains displays from the early days of the East India Company and the colonial period. Coins, weapons, pictures and books form part of the collection. Other buildings of importance in the fort are the **Old Government House** and the **Banqueting Hall** (Rajaji Hall), built for the governor's official entertainment during the Clive period. The architectural style of this period drew inspiration from the classical Greeks and Romans with Doric, Corinthian and Tuscan pillars, entablatures and friezes.

Two beautiful churches in Chennai that still have regular services are **St George's Cathedral** and **St Andrew's Kirk**. The latter resembles St Martin-in-the-Fields in London. It was built by James Gibbs. The towering steeples and the strength of the pillars of the facade make it a city landmark. St George's Cathedral, consecrated in 1816, was designed by Captain James Caldwell and Thomas Fiott de Havillard. The interior here has slim Ionic pillars, plasterwork and stained-glass windows.

The **San Thome Cathedral** on the Main Beach Road is associated with the apostle, St Thomas. It is believed that he was martyred on what is called **St Thomas's Mount** and that his remains were enshrined in this church. San Thome was first built in the 16th century and has been rebuilt over the years.

The **Theosophical Society** (open Mon–Fri 8.30–11.30am, 2–5pm) has its headquarters on the banks of the Adyar River south of Mylapore. It houses a vast library of books on religion; in the gardens that lead up to the river and the sea is a sprawling banyan tree, said to be one of the largest in India.

The **Marina**, almost 13 km (8 miles) long, was, before the 2004 tsunami hit the coast, a wide sandy beach. The huge wave dragged much of the sand back into the sea and deposited tons of silt in its place. As a popular place to meet and walk, over 200 people were killed here, and up and down the coast fishing

The "ice factory" on Marina Beach, near the old university, was built in 1842 to store ice shipped from America. Later it was converted into a home for widows.

BELOW: at San Thome Cathedral.

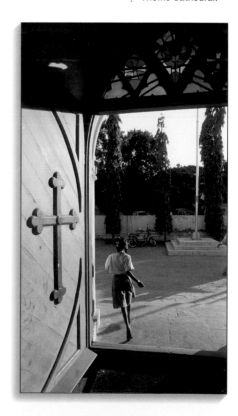

Frisson of symbols: a sign outside the Theosophical Society. Established in 1882, the peaceful library and gardens are a haven from the bustle of the city.

BELOW: traditional Tamil Nadu jewellery.

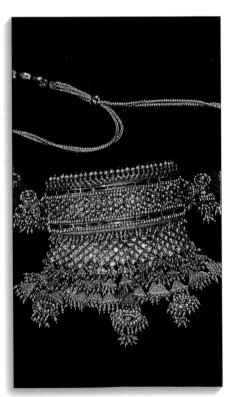

boats and cargo ships were damaged or destroyed. A lot of the clearing up ha now been completed and the municipality has begun planting lawns and tree along the waterfront. Facing the sea are the 19th-century building of the **Pres idency College** and the **Senate House** of the **University** **G**. The universit building and its grounds are noted examples of the Indo-Islamic style used o Indian public buildings in the late 19th century. North of the university ar other interesting structures such as Egmore Railway Station, the Chennai Med ical College, Ripon Building and Victoria Public Hall.

One of the most interesting sections of town is **Mylapore** with a tank, mar ket area and old Brahman houses. At the evening bazaar, crowds of people freshly bathed, make their way to the **Kapalesvara Shiva Temple** **H**. Almos as old is the **Krishna Paratasaraty Temple** on Triplicane High Road.

Mylapore is well-known for its jewellers, who specialise in making gold plated "dance jewellery sets". Silver ornaments are dipped into a gold solutior A bright pink tissue paper is then placed into pre-moulded grooves before bein capped with a pale pink stone. The result mimics the ruby-studded gold tradi tional patterns required for classical dance. The classic headpiece comprises *rakodi*, worn just above the flowers in the hair, flanked by a stylised sun an moon. Ear ornaments come in three parts: a chain, a dangler, and a support fc the lobe. Around the neck is a choker, plus a half-moon-shaped pendar (*padakkam*) suspended from a longer chain. A *vanki* bracelet grips the upper arr and is heavier than the standard gold bangles jingling at the wrist. A broad orna mental belt, called an *odyanan*, completes the costume. Sometimes a *sarpar* hair ornament snakes around the long plait for a final golden touch.

Culture

The **State Government Museum** **I** (open Sat–Thu 9.30am–5pm; www.chennaimuseum.org; entrance fee was established in 1846 and has one of the finest co lections in the country. It houses a rare collection c sculptures from Amaravati in Andhra Pradesh, be longing to the Buddhist period, 2nd century AD. Th white limestone sculptured medallions and panels te the story of the life of the Buddha. The Bronze Galler has a superb collection of Chola bronzes (9th–13t century AD). Some are hardly 4 cm (1½ ins) high an others are over half a metre (1½ ft) tall, all icono graphically sophisticated. The dancing Shivas, Durg; and Ganapatis and the famous Rama, Lakshmana an Sita group are the pride of this museum.

In performing arts, of all the city's **sabhas**, or cor cert halls, the **Music Academy** **J** is the mo renowned. It puts on music and dance programme by eminent artists for discerning audiences, whic inspires the performers, whether of Karnatak mus or *Bharata-natyam*, to memorable heights. Also chec out other venues, such as the **Krishna Gana Sabh;** particularly during the Chennai Festival in Decemb and January, when you can see peformances by Sou India's finest dancers and Karnatak musicians. Th **Sangita Vadyalaya** (759 Anna Salai, behind the Tam Nadu Handicrafts Centre) has an interesting collectic of musical instruments (open Mon–Fri 9.30am–5pm

Anna Salai **Ⓚ** (previously Mount Road) is Chennai's main shopping street. **Higginbotham's**, one of India's best book shops, is here. Chennai is famous for its silk emporia where silk saris, scarves, and material for suiting and dresses are available by the yard. The Government-run **Co-optex** shops have an extensive range of fabrics, and **Poompuhar**, the Government Handicrafts Emporium, has good bronzes. Both these are on Anna Salai, along with a number of other State emporia. At the junction of Anna Salai and Binny Road is Spencer Plaza, an air-conditioned complex with a large number of different shops.

Excursions

South along the coastal road, towards Mahabalipuram, is **Kalaksetra Ⓛ**, an academy of music and dance set up by Rukmini Devi, the doyenne of Indian dance. Her efforts to re-establish temple dance in a staged context have given India a number of leading dancers. Kalaksetra organises dance programmes that are worth attending. On the same coastal road is **Cholamandalam**, the artists' village, where exhibitions, poetry readings and other programmes take place. At Muttukkadu, 28 km (17 miles) from Chennai, is **DakshinaChitra** (open Wed–Mon, 10am–6pm; www.dakshinachitra.org; entrance fee). This exemplary museum has a number of rescued examples of South Indian village architecture and aims to preserve and promote traditional crafts.

Outdoors, the attractions around Chennai are the **Guindy Deer Park** and the **Snake Park**. The former has species of black buck, spotted deer, monkeys and other animals. The Snake Park is the only major reptilium in India. It was started by Romulus Whitaker, who worked towards educating visitors on the types of snakes in India, to prevent the thoughtless killing of reptiles. ❑

Map on page 310

Hallo! Madras contains useful city information and onward travel details. For dance events enquire at the tourist office, 154 Anna Salai (tel: 044-2852 4295).

BELOW: Marina beach, Chennai.

Map on page 316

Delhi

TAMIL NADU

South India's outstanding temple architecture is just one of the highlights of Tamil Nadu, which stretches from the sand dunes of the east coast to the cool Nilgiri Hills in the west

If the truth be told, contemporary Tamil culture is defined by hot food, hot colours, hot music and hot coffee. Film actors and actresses dancing across film hoardings and the aroma of roasting coffee beans are sights and smells that confront the traveller everywhere. Yet tourist itineraries usually substitute a "Brahmanical" perception of local culture in which old stone temples, Karnatak dance and music, and mild vegetarian *thalis* are the main attractions.

Chennai ❶ is the usual starting point for a tour of Tamil Nadu. While there the traveller should try and catch a *Bharata-natyam* performance, a contemporary interpretation of one of South Asia's oldest dance traditions. The dancers once came from a highly trained community of temple dancers, known as *devadasis* or "servants of god", but now mostly hail from urban middle-class backgrounds. *Bharata-natyam* and Karnatak music have become important social accomplishments for young middle-class women. At the Chennai Festival (mid-December to early January), India's leading classical dancers and singers perform for the nation's most discriminating audience. Travellers are also advised to visit a "military restaurant" (as non-vegetarian restaurants are traditionally called) to dismiss the notion that only mild vegetarian *thalis* are available in South India. Fiery Chettinad cuisine uses lamb, quail, crab and

BELOW: religious instruction at Madurai's Minakshi temple.

many spices and lichens for flavouring. The Chettinad area of southeastern Tamil Nadu is also famous for its merchant traders' palatial houses with woodwork in carved Burma teak.

Tamil Nadu has a long coastline, stretching down to Kaniyakumari at the very southern tip of India. The tsunami that hit Southeast Asia at the end of 2004 also badly effected the Tamil coast. Over 8,000 people were killed, some 5,000 of which were from the fishing communities close to Nagapattinam. Carnage from the huge waves was widespread although most of the obvious damage has now been cleared up. Generally the major tourist sights – including the Shore Temple at Mamallapuram and the city of Pondicherry – escaped largely unscathed and they and surrounding hotels and restaurants re-opened quickly.

Tamil, India's oldest living language, has a written history dating back to at least the 3rd century BC. The earliest work we know of is the Tolkappiyam *grammar. The first literary works to be written down appeared in the 1st century BC, of which the most famous is the* Tirukkural *by the poet Tiruvalluvar.*

Politics and the film star

A feature of Tamil temples is the presiding orthodox Brahmans, who still dress in white *dhotis* and display forehead markings, half-shaven scalps and long hair at the back twisted into single plaits. A sacred thread always stands out against their bare chests. Although a minority community, Tamil Brahmans continue to exert much influence in national and international affairs.

In reaction to centuries of Brahman rule, a pan-Dravidian and anti-Brahman movement gathered pace after Independence, claiming that Brahmanical rule and influence were a symbol of northern domination and a continuing Sankritisation of Dravidian culture (leading to Dravidian readings of epics such as the Ramayana in which Rama is seen as the oppressor of the darker-skinned Ravanna). In 1967, a party championing the lower castes, the DMK, won power under C.N. Annadurai, the right-hand man of the great Dravidian campaigner Periyar E.V. Ramaswamy. The DMK was a breakaway party from the DK of P.E.V. Ramaswamy which initially campaigned for an independent Dravida Kalagam; a separate country of "South India". The film star M.G. Ramachandran (known by his initials as MGR) took over as Chief Minister a decade later, controlling the splinter-party AIADMK and attracting a huge level of support. On his death he was succeeded by his former co-star, and "companion", Jayalalitha Jayaram. Voted out in 1996 over allegations of corruption, undaunted, and still attracting fierce loyalty from her supporters, she entered parliament and led her party into coalition with the BJP in 1998. This relationship soon soured, and when she withdrew her support the central government fell. She is presently back in power in Tamil Nadu but her party, the AIADMK, was trounced by its bitter rival, the DMK under M. Karunanidi, in the 2004 general election.

Language was an important element in the pan-Dravidian movement and today still remains a vital part of Tamil politics. The adoption of Hindi as the "national language" (another manifestation of northern arrogance) was greeted with horror in the South, and its official imposition can still spark off riots.

BELOW: Anjuna's penance, carvings at Mamallapuram.

Tamil temples

Temple hopping across Tamil Nadu is a popular post-Chennai option for many visitors. A good place to

Sixty km (37 miles) southwest of Chennai is Sriperumbudur, location of the splendid Adikesava-perumal temple and birthplace of the Hindu philosopher Ramanuja. It is also the place where, in 1991, Rajiv Gandhi was assassinated.

start exploring this ancient heritage is **Mamallapuram ❷** (Mahabalipuram), 50 km (30 miles) south of Chennai. This is the location for some of South India's earliest surviving stone temples; there are 14 cave temples, nine *rathas* and three built temples, as well as a profusion of early carvings. A clean beach put Mamallapuram on the travellers' route in the 1960s and today the World Heritage Site coexists with budget hotels and restaurants. A dance festival takes place here in December/January.

Mamallapuram is still a centre for stone carving and home to the government-run School of Sculpture. The bas-relief of the *Descent of the Ganga* or *Arjuna's Penance* (there is dispute as to what the huge sculpture represents) teems with lively depictions of animals. Further south is the Pallava **Shore Temple**, dating from the 7th century and, unusually, dedicated to both Shiva and Vishnu. This is thought to be the earliest surviving stone-built temple in South India, and one whose design, particularly its towers, influenced temple building across the region. Further along the shore are the five *rathas* (chariots), exquisite 7th-century temple-like structures sculpted from single blocks of stone.

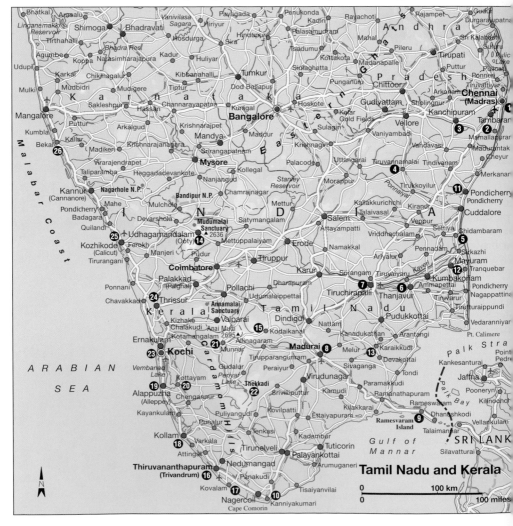

Tamil Nadu and Kerala

Those with an interest in temple architecture should travel on to Kanchipuram, Tiruvannamalai, Chidambaram, Thanjavur and Tiruvarur, Tiruchirapalli and Srirangam, and Madurai, further south. Although each temple town has a distinct character, they share common elements. Processions of the god or goddess are accompanied by the loud temple ensemble of *nagasvaram* (a long oboe with a piercing tone) and *tavil* (barrel drum, played with a stick in the left hand and fingers clad in plaster "thimbles" on the right). The music from the procession is considered very auspicious. The overpowering fragrance of incense and jasmine and marigold garlands, the sight of hundreds of slippers piled up outside temple *gopurams* and the thousands of pilgrims pressing forward for a better view of an idol being paraded on a palanquin are common to all temples during festivals. Visitors should note that many Tamil temples forbid non-Hindus to enter the inner sanctum, although they are usually free to wander around the rest of the complex.

From Mamallapuram it is also possible to begin tracing the development of South Indian temple architecture. Its rock-cut structures emerged during the reign of the Pallavas, the 6th- to 9th-century rulers of a kingdom centred around **Kanchipuram ❸**, a typical temple town 70 km (43 miles) to the northwest. The freestanding *rathas* at Mamallapuram also display the first (now common) temple features such as *garbagrihas*, or womb-like sanctums, capped by modest spires or *vimanas*. **Kailasanatha**, the very fine Pallava temple, in Kanchipuram has an added courtyard, and a high *vimana* crowning the inner sanctum. Prototype carvings of Siva, accompanied by his consort and mythical beasts known as *yalis*, set the standard for carvers. The largest of the town's temples is **Ekambaresvara**, dedicated to Shiva and with a famous "1,000-pillar" *mandapam* (columned hall). The town's silk weavers are renowned for their skill, and use of colour and intricate patterns.

Tiruvannamalai ❹, 100 km (63 miles) to the west of Chennai, is one of the holiest sites in South India, and certainly one of the largest temple complexes, sprawling over 10 hectares (25 acres). The earliest part of the temple, the inner sanctum, dates back to the 11th century, while the huge *gopuram* was built during the Vijayanagar period (14th–16th century).

The temple at **Chidambaram ❺**, the Chola capital from the 10th to the 14th century, is dedicated to Siva in his form as Nataraja (Lord of the Dance). The temple management is the sole preserve of a group of Brahmans known as Diksitars, recognisable by a single tuft of hair over their foreheads.

In **Thanjavur ❻**, (260 km/160 miles southwest of Chennai), the former Chola capital set in the Kaveri delta paddy fields, the **Brihadesvara** temple dominates the landscape. It was constructed in the 10th century by Rajaraja I and features a *vimana* (sanctuary of the god) more than 60 metres (200 ft) high (the tallest in India) and entrance towers *(gopurams)*. Subsequent Chola temples add subsidiary shrines and extended *mandapams* or pavilions to the architectural plan. Close to Thanjavur is the temple town of **Tiruvarur**, birthplace of the South Indian "trinity" of composers, Tyagaraja, Muttusvami Diksitar and

Map on page 316

Between Tiruvannamalai and the coast is the 600-year-old Gingee fort. Set over three hills, this hugely atmospheric site was first developed by the Vijayanagar kings in the 15th century. The fort contains several temples, a mosque and a palace.

BELOW: a local sculptor at work.

The Minakshi Temple in Madurai celebrates the marriage of the local goddess Minakshi (the fish-eyed goddess) to Lord Sundaresvara (Shiva) every April/May with a spectacular procession.

Syama Sastri. A few centuries later saw the developments of the Vijayanagar kings at **Srirangam**, very close to Tiruchirapalli, in the **Sriranganathasvami temple**, dedicated to Vishnu. Temples now had to support an increasing number of social functions. For marriages, for example, the 1,000-pillared *mandapams* (pavilions) were added. The *gopurams* were made taller and water tanks were also introduced.

As well as the nearby temple of Srirangam, **Tiruchirapalli** ❼ is also dominated by a 90 m- (300 ft-) high rock fort containing 7th-century rock-cut temples. At the top of 437 steps is the Tayumanasvami Temple, crowned with a golden *vimana*. From the fort there are remarkable panroamic views (open 6am–8pm).

Madurai ❽, 150 km (93 miles) to the south of Tirucharapalli, is the site of another great Vijayanagar temple, the **Minakshi Sundaresvara temple**. Dedicated to the goddess, and consort of Siva, this is said to be the biggest temple in the country. Its four towering *gopurams* with their brightly painted sculptures are spectacular. The 1,000-pillar *mandapam* here has some beautifully carved columns and displays of art. Other special sights include a monolithic statue of Ganapati, and the temple tank, where the god Indra is believed to have bathed.

The **Ramalingesvara** temple on **Ramesvaram Island** ❾, 150 km (93 miles southeast from Madurai, severed from the mainland by a cyclone in the 15th century, is one of the holiest spots in India. This is believed to be the place where Rama stopped to worship Siva after his conquest of Lanka. Walk away from blaring, devotional songs playing on loudspeakers and catch a bus as far as it will go to the extreme tip of the island for a holy bath at **Danushkodi**. Walk back to the bus stop, 3 km (1¾ miles) across a perfect circle of sand dunes. A pilgrimage

BELOW: bathing at a temple festival, Srirangam.

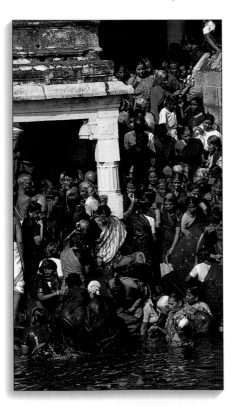

PUDUCHERRY (PONDICHERRY)

Puducherry lies on the coast of Tamil Nadu, 150 km (9 miles) south of Chennai. It came under French rule in the mid-18th century and was finally returned to India in 1954. The town was originally divided by a canal. On one side was the **Ville Blanche** and on the other the **Ville Noir** for the Indian population. **Government Park** formed the heart of the city, around which are now the **Raj Nivas** (residence of the lieutenant governor) and other official buildings. Near the railway station is the Gothic-style **Sacred Heart Church**. The streets of the old French area are cobbled and the waterfront is designed to resemble Nice.

Ten km (6 miles) from the town are the **Sri Aurobindo Ashram** and the new city of **Auroville**. The ashram was set up by Sri Aurobindo, a religious philosopher, who played an active role in the Indian independence movement. His teachings were preserved by his French companion, who became known as "The Mother". These teachings formed the inspiration for Auroville, designed as a model city by the French architect Roger Auger.

Outside Puducherry is **Arikamedu**, an archaeological site that revealed a Graeco-Roman trading centre of the early Christian era, indicating a flourishing trade with the Romans in dyed muslins and spices.

o Varanasi is said to be complete only after bathing at Danushkodi. The town was once a thriving port linking India to Sri Lanka, only 20 km (12 miles) away across the Gulf of Mannar, until it was devastated by a cyclone in 1964.

At the southernmost tip of India is **Kanniyakumari** ⑩, another pilgrimage own, this time to the goddess Kumari. Very popular with Indian tourists, the ndian Ocean, Bay of Bengal and the Arabian Sea all meet here, and in April it s possible to see the full moon and sun on the same horizon.

Map on page 316

Enclaves on the coast

Tamil Nadu's long coastline is washed by diverse influences. **Puducherry** ⑪ *(see box opposite)*, the former French colony, is listed as a Union Territory for administrative purposes (although it is now lobbying for full statehood). In addition to Le Club – arguably the best French restaurant in India – Pondicherry has French-speaking rickshaw drivers, Vietnamese restaurants, the tastiest bottled water in India and Goubert Salai, the cleanest seaside promenade in the country. Mirra Alfissa, the French-born painter and spiritual companion to the Bengali philosopher Sri Aurobindo, founded the new-age community of Auroville in 1968. The city is made up of attractive, experimental housing, and at its centre is the huge, and unfinished, Maitri Mandir meditation centre. Travellers can stay in Auroville to learn more about the place and to participate in voluntary development projects.

Some European settlements on the Tamil Nadu coast are more obscure. The adventurous traveller can experience what is left of the former Danish settlement of **Tranquebar** ⑫ (100 km/62 miles south of Pondicherry) by walking through the old gate, with its coat of arms, down to the sea. A memorial to the first Prot-

Frequent express trains connect the major centres of Tamil Nadu.

BELOW: temple complex at Kanchipuram.

Kochadai, in north Madurai, houses a shrine to the Tamil village deity, Ayyannar. The god's image is paraded through the streets in March.

BELOW: a bullock cart on the road near Nagercoil.

estant missionaries to visit India remembers Bartholomew Ziegenbalg and Heinrich Plutschau. On the right, **Dansborg Fort** overlooks a deserted beach.

Chettinad

On the coastal plain between Tiruchirapalli and Madurai is the **Chettinad** region, homeland of the Chettiar merchant community. Their ancestral villages now partly deserted, have some of the finest family mansions in South India. In the 19th century the Chettiars were known as the bankers of South India and their immense wealth was poured into gold, jewellery and, most impressively their houses. Covering entire blocks, their interiors contain pillars of teak, satin wood and granite, intricately carved teak doors, and Italian marble floors. The walls are gleaming white, covered with a paste made from lime, eggwhite and *myrobalam* fruit. Some of the finest mansions can be found in **Karaikkudi** ⓫ the largest village in the region, and nearby **Kanadukathan**. After Independence the wealth of the community diminished and the money was no longer available to maintain these luxurious dwellings, and now many of them are uninhabited. The Chettiars have, however, left a culinary legacy, of peppery meat-based dishes, flavoured with unusual spices and dried fruits.

Hill stations

In the hills Tamil Nadu preserves a few vestiges of British colonialism. Travellers may arrive at the former summer retreats of **Coonoor**, **Wellington** and **Ooty** (**Udhagamandalam**) ⓮ in the Nilgiri hills (Western Ghats) by an antique steam train. The line, which was opened in 1899, climbs to 2,190 metres (7,230 ft) through steep forests over 31 bridges and through 16 tunnels. The narrow-

gauge train departs from Mettupalayam, but travellers usually start their journey from the industrial city of **Coimbatore**, whose main attraction is its good range of accommodation. Ooty itself is now a very popular resort and much of its colonial charm – perhaps best exemplified by the **Ootacamund Club**, one of the last bastions of suet pudding – has been swamped by overdevelopment. However, the climate and surrounding countryside are some compensation.

In addition to hill stations in the Nilgiris, **Kodaikanal** ⑮, perhaps the most attractive retreat, is in the Palani hills. The Pillar Rocks, three granite spires, provide a stunning view over the plains below. **Yercaud**, the least crowded of the hill stations, in the Shevaroy hills is another former colonial summer escape.

The original inhabitants of the Nilgiris were Adivasi peoples, including the Kotas and Todas. They were initially dispossessed of their land by the British, a process continued by successive Indian governments and, although they have now been given some land back, they continue to face the erosion of their traditional ways of life, many of which have now died out.

Wildlife sanctuaries

As might be expected from a state bounded by the Western and Eastern Ghat mountains and the Coromandel coast, there are still a few pockets of natural jungle, coastal wetland and coral islands where wild animals and birds can thrive. On the coast, **Vedanthangla** and **Point Calimere**, 315 km (196 miles) south of Chennai, play host to a large number of migratory birds during the winter monsoon. **Mudumalai**, in the Nilgiri foothills, 67 km (42 miles) northwest of Ooty, is the home of the gaur (Indian bison), wild elephants and a handful of tigers. The **Annamalai Sanctuary**, 70 km (43 miles) northwest of Kodaikanal, harbours lion-tailed macaques. Access to these sanctuaries is easily granted upon arrival, though it is wise to book accommodation, elephant rides and jeeps in advance.

Lesser-known sanctuaries (which require special government permits) offer the naturalist an extraordinary chance to view rare species. **Mannar Marine Park**, for example, is clustered around 21 low-lying, uninhabited coral islands in the Gulf of Mannar. The sanctuary is the home of the endangered sea cow, the dugong. Myriad other aquatic life forms are also supported by the park's coral reef, as well as more than 100 varieties of seaweed and grass, which change the depths of green in the sea bed. Permission to land on the islands can be granted only by the Chief Conservator of Forests in Chennai, if you convince him that you have a genuine professional reason for visiting. Fears have recently been raised about the long-term survival of the islands, which seem to be slipping into the sea, possibly due to illegal sand extraction.

The **Mukurti Sanctuary**, home of the Nilgiri Tahr (an endangered species of mountain goat) and a few tigers, located high in the Nilgiri, has restricted access. Permission may be obtained from the Nilgiri Wildlife Association in Ooty, but can take a few days. Clefts of tropical rainforest *(shola)* combine with grassland in a beautiful landscape. The altitude (1,800 metres/6,000 ft) gives the park a temperate climate while supporting a variety of tropical wildlife. ❑

Map on page 316

You may be lucky enough to see a performance of the traditional Tamil dance-drama, terukkuttu literally "street drama". Some themes are taken from the Mahabharata, and a popular drama is the story of Draupadi (see page 88).

BELOW: a young Tamil woman.

Map on page 316

Delhi

BELOW: elephant
procession,
Thiruvanantha-
puram.

KERALA

Between the ancient creation myth of Kerala and the modern political fact is a land of lush, physical beauty that contains a rich storehouse of legend, history, culture and tradition

When the victorious warrior-goddess Bhadrakali selected a place on earth where she would reside she chose Kerala in the southwestern corner of India, and today the *thattakkam*, Kerala's local equivalent of a parish, is always under the divine jurisdiction of a goddess. Although legend declares that the land of Kerala was formed when Parsurama, an incarnation of Lord Vishnu, threw his mighty battle-axe into the Arabian Sea, the fertile land that emerged was not established as the state of Kerala until 1956, with the integration of three Malayalam-speaking areas, Malabar and the two former princely states of Cochin and Travancore.

Kerala's attractions are tucked away in the Cardamom Hills and along the Malabar Coast, laced between 41 rivers and plantations of teak, pepper and rubber, all kept green by two monsoons each year. Much of the landscape and wealth of Kerala is dominated by tall, elegant coconut palms. No part of this tree is wasted and the state has a flourishing coir (fibre) industry. Coffee plantations spread across the foothills of the Western Ghats, tea grows at higher altitudes and, in southern Kerala, there are acres of rubber trees. Another important crop, sold to North India, is the areca nut which grows on graceful palms.

The Malabar coast grows the world's best pepper. Half of Europe engaged in

power struggles to command supplies of this small pungent berry. Cardamom and cashew nuts are other important cash crops and no compound is without a few banana trees. The flatter, fertile land supports two or three annual harvests of rice. Tasty Keralan rice – eaten with practically every meal – is parboiled before dehusking, giving a characteristic fat grain flecked with red, a process that preserves the vitamin D.

Modern values

Kerala made its impact on modern India when, in the state's first elections in 1957, it formed the world's first democratically elected communist government – controversially dismissed by the Congress government in Delhi after intense lobbying by Indira Gandhi. The CPI(M), which soon regained power with a huge popular mandate, was led by the great E.M.S. Namboodiripad, who pushed through sweeping land reform, educational and health care programmes. As a result Kerala has the most equitable land distribution in India, near total literacy and low rates of poverty – in the Indian state with the least natural resources.

This high level of literacy (which is also due to the enlightened educational policies of the hereditary rulers of Travancore), coupled with relatively few employment opportunities in Kerala itself, has led to Keralites finding work all over India and in the Gulf states. Gulf workers in particular have proved an important source of income for the state, sending much of their money home to their families. Evidence for this can be seen in the proliferation of "Gulf houses", some of them extraordinary fantasies built of concrete in defiance of the climate and environment; towns such as Chavakad have become "little Dubais".

Women in Kerala have traditionally had a higher profile than elsewhere in India. The Nambudiri Brahmans and Nairs practised matrilineal inheritance and women were in charge of running family property. Although this system has now largely broken down, high literacy levels have empowered Keralan women and they tend to have more freedom than their counterparts in other states.

Any list of Indian writers, poets and musicians features Malayalis prominently: people such as the diplomat turned writer K.P.S. Menon, the novelist Arundhati Roy, the poet Vallathol Narayana Menon (famous for reviving *Kathakali* and founding the Kalamandalam School in Cheruthuruthy), and the great singer of Karnatak music, the late Chembai Vaidyanatha Bhagavatar.

In August, Alappuzha is the venue for the annual Nehru Trophy snakeboat race. The long boats are rowed by more than 100 men, cheered on by enthusiastic crowds.

Religious harmony

Kerala not only has Hindus, Muslims, Christians and Jews but many different castes and communities – all with their own customs and traditions and styles of dress, food, jewellery and marriage. Maybe these contrasting elements explain the genuine religious tolerance found in Kerala, a state remarkably free from the communal violence that haunts other parts of India.

Hinduism in Kerala operates around the twin poles of worship of a complex system of local goddesses, and the Sanskritic traditions of the major temples. The temple of **Chottanikkara**, near Kochi, attracts a growing number of pilgrims who seek release from evil spirits, and the long iron nails driven into the

BELOW: the Sri Ananthapadmanabhasvami temple, Thiruvananthapuram.

The pre-performance application of make-up and wigs by Kathakali *dancers is almost part of the show. Arrive early.*

huge tree near the sanctum of the goddess testify to their successful exorcism. These local practices contrast with the exclusive Brahmanical temple of Sri Padmanabhasvamy in Thiruvananthapuram, the Vadakkunhatha temple to Shiva in Thrissur (Trichur), and the Krishna temple in Guruvayur.

According to popular belief, the oldest of the Christian denominations, the Syrian Christians, was established by the apostle St Thomas in AD 50. The followers of the Prophet Muhammad also came early to Kerala, and although the exterior of the mosque at **Kodungallur** is a brash, modern concrete structure, its interior is still the cool and serene original of India's oldest mosque. The mosque was built on land given by Kodungallur's Hindu ruler – a gesture echoed by the Raja of Cochin in the 16th century when he welcomed Jews fleeing Portuguese persecution in Goa. Although recent emigration to Israel has reduced the community to a handful, their magnificent synagogue at Kochi still stands.

Many of these different factors blend together: for instance, a Marxist politician might prostrate before a Hindu shrine; a Muslim contribute to a temple festival; or a Christian make a Hindu pilgrimage; and buses display the religious icons of three faiths. Saint George is particularly popular across all communities, as he is thought to offer protection against snake bites.

Performance arts and festivals

Kerala has extraordinarily rich theatre. There is the Sanskrit drama of *Kutiyattam* the lyrical dance of *Mohiniattam*, the religious fervour of *Krishnattam* and, above all, the spectacular magnificence of *Kathakali*. These all evolved out of the religious beliefs of their participants and, despite their highly dramatic presentation, are less a theatrical performance than an act of worship. The spectacular *theyyams* of Malabar demonstrate this concept when the fantastically costumed god-actors dance before shrines, possessed with the spirit and power of their Dravidian deities. Costume and make-up play an important part in these ritual dramas. It is worth arriving early at a *Kathakali* dance drama to watch the pre-show transformation of the actors as they apply bright make-up, and don masks and ornate skirted costumes weighing up to 35 kg (77 lbs)

BELOW: a decorated lorry, Thiruvananthapuram.

Only during the monsoon months of June to August is it difficult to find some ritual, ceremony or festival taking place. Although non-Hindus are not usually permitted to enter Keralan temples, temple festivals are accessible and visible to all. In central Kerala the use of elephants brings a regal quality; there can be few sights to beat 30 caparisoned tuskers assembled before the Vadakkunathan Temple in Thrissur on the day of the Thrissur Pooram. Temple festivals are invariably accompanied by traditional music. Look out for the *panchavadyam* (literally "five instruments") drum and trumpet ensembles that accompany processions, the loud but virtuosic *cenda melam* drum-orchestras and the drumming genre *tyampaka*

Southern Kerala

Attractions are plentiful in the capital, **Thiruvananthapuram ⓰** (Trivandrum), former seat of the Maharajahs of Travancore, set on seven hills. The temple of **Sri Padmanabhasvami** that the maharajah built to honour Lord Vishnu physically dominates the bustling old city, but access is forbidden to non-Hindus. Their heirlooms can be seen at their city residence, **Puttan Malika Palace** (open Tues–Sun 8.30am–5.30pm, closed 1–3pm). Their old palace, now just inside Tamil Nadu 63 km (39 miles) south at **Padmanabhapuram** (open Tues–Sun 9am–4.30pm, closed 1–2pm, entrance fee), is worth seeing and is an easy day-trip from Thiruvananthapuram. Window panes of mica cast a magical light into the carved rooms cooled with natural air-conditioning using inner courtyards. An imposing royal bed, a single granite slab, is placed on a gleaming black floor made from egg whites and burnt coconut shell.

The **Botanical Garden and Zoo** (open Thur–Sun 10am–4.30pm and Wed 1–4.30pm), north of the city centre, has the Art Museum, Shri Chitra Art Gallery and Museum of Natural History in its grounds. One ticket gives access to all the museums and gardens. The **Art Museum**, housed in an extraordinary Indo-Saracenic building designed by Robert Fellowes Chisolm for Lord Napier in 1880, has jewellery, ivorywork, Chola bronzes and Keralan woodcarvings. Nearby, the **Shri Chitra Art Gallery** (open 9am–5pm, closed Wed am, Fri, Sat) features oils by Raja Ravi Varma and a good collection of miniatures.

Displays of *Kalaripayattu*, the local martial art, are staged in the gardens by yoga institutes (6.30am–8pm). At **Margi Kathakali School**, West Fort, visitors can to watch *Kathakali* dance-drama classes and enquire about performances.

On the beach

Among Kerala's excellent beaches, the best-known is **Kovalam** ⓱, located 16 km (10 miles) south of Thiruvananthapuram, where facilities at all levels are available. Except for the tourist trade near the beach itself, life in the surrounding

Map on page 316

The city's main markets, well worth exploring, are in the narrow streets of East Fort, opposite the walled old city.

BELOW: sailing through Kerala's backwaters.

countryside and the fishing settlements in the area goes on very much as in the rest of rural Kerala. Ayurvedic massage is relaxing after a swim in rough waters and masseurs are ready on shore to oblige. Massage using herbal oils is said to be most effective at the moment the monsoon breaks in early June.

Varkala, 54 km (32 miles) north of Thiruvananthapuram, is an attractive village with a less commericalised, fine sandy beach at the base of cliffs. Watch out for fishing lines or nets being dragged from the sea around sunset. Though tourists come for the beach, it is also one of Kerala's major Hindu pilgrim centres.

The backwaters

The backwaters are a tangle of brackish channels fed by rivers just inland from the Arabian Sea. They extend from Kochi south to Alappuzha. Sadly, many of the lakes are polluted and have been reduced in area through land reclamation. Another menace is the proliferation of water hyacinth, which now blocks some of the canals.

About 20 km (12 miles) north of Varkala is **Kollam ⓲** (Quilon), a cashew nut port which is the southern gateway to the backwaters. Travellers can journey through a network of narrow canals and wide lakes where people paddle to their daily tasks. Unlike the wave-tossed western seashore, which runs roughly parallel, the backwaters are calm. Boats of all descriptions are punted or sailed along the shallow green waterways with palms arching overhead. Tidy bungalows line up on either side, to give way to great heaps of coconut fibre or clusters of Chinese fishing nets, lit up at night to attract shrimps. Where the waters widen, villagers sometimes can be found up to their necks, picking up fish from the muddy bottom with their toes and flinging them into terracotta pots that float beside them on the surface.

Many tourists take the boats between Kollam (Quilon) and **Alappuzha ⓳** (Alleppey) along the picturesque backwaters. Two companies run the cruises the state Water Transport Department boats are usually slower than Alleppey Tourism. The trip lasts up to eight hours depending on the route. At **Karunagapalli**, shipbuilders fashion *kettuvallam* (literally tied boats) out of jakwood planks sewn together with coir rope. Cruising *kettuvallam*, with rattan-thatched canopies, can be hired for two-day trips. Progress is often slower than by road as the waterways can be unexpectedly shallow and are often choked with waterlilies and duckweed.

BELOW: carrying pots to market.

Inland, past the busy Christian town of **Kottayam ⓴** the roads start to rise into the Western Ghats. Close by, in January, large numbers of devotees of the god Aiyappan start to make their way on foot up to the temple at **Sabrimala**. Aiyappan is very popular across South India, and his followers – predominantly men since only young girls and post-menopausal women are allowed to make the journey – are a common sight dressed in black with *tulsi* beads around their necks.

Also in the Ghats are the tea estates close to the town of **Munnar ㉑**, the highest in Kerala at 1,800 metres (6,000 ft). The scenery around the neat tea gardens is beautiful. **Thekkadi ㉒** is the main town in the popular Periyar Wildlife Sanctuary and Tiger Reserve famous for its herds of wild elephants.

Kochi-Ernakulum

Kochi-Ernakulum ㉓ (Cochin) can be reached from Alappuzha by water, but boat traffic on the way to this major port and naval base is heavy, and many prefer to travel by road or rail. Ferries connect the islands of **Willingdon**, **Bolgatty**, **Gundu** and **Vypeen** to the southern peninsula of Fort Cochin and Mattancherri and to the commercial centre, **Ernakulum**, on the mainland. Semitic traders from Yemen and Babylon used to import dates and olive oil in exchange for peacocks and spices. Kochi is still an important spice port and its *godowns* (warehouses), smelling of pungent spices, are a hive of activity.

Jew Town, a settlement that dates back a millennium, still thrives with antique and spice shops. The small synagogue there is used by the diminishing Jewish community; most families have left for Israel. The synagogue is floored with blue and white tiles from Canton, no two of which are the same.

Matancherry Palace (open 10am–5pm, closed Fri) at Kochi was built by the Portuguese and repaired by the Dutch (renaming it the Dutch Palace), although its architectural style is Keralan. Its frescoes, dating from the 17th century, depict Indian epics in extraordinary vegetable colours. Kochi also has the oldest European church in India, **St Francis's**, built in 1506.

There is little trace of the Arabs, Phoenicians, Chinese, Romans and Greeks who traded at this port. Old colonial churches and warehouses recall the Portuguese, Dutch and British settlers with faded elegance. Dolphins sometimes romp in the current beside the boats near the harbour entrance. By the Chinese fishing nets, facing out to sea in Kochi, is a group of small huts where you can have the freshly caught fish cooked in front of you.

Northern Kerala

Leaving Kochi by crossing to Vypeen island and heading north, you pass a pair of Portuguese forts before rejoining the mainland. Just beyond Azhikod is **Kodungallur**. Steeped in history, this settlement is the ancient port of Musiris, said to have been visited by the Romans, as well as being the site of India's earliest mosque. Travelling further north up the coast from Kochi takes you past the turn-off to the **Palakkad Gap** (Palghat), the lowest point in the Western Ghats, at **Thrissur** ㉔. This is the site of one of Kerala's most important temples, **Vadakkunnatham**, which legend says was founded by Parasurama. Thrissur's small Archaeological Museum on Town Hall Road (open Tues–Sun 9am– 5pm) has interesting examples of temple art. The Krisna temple at **Guruvayur**, 30 km (18 miles) from Thrissur, is the most sacred place in Kerala. The temple painters from this town are particularly skilled. Like most Keralan temples, access is for Hindus only.

Kozhikode ㉕ (Calicut), on the coast, was known to the Phoenicians and Ancient Greeks, who both traded spices here. It is still a thriving port and much of the town is given over to commerce. The **Pazhassi Raja Museum** (open Tues–Sun 10am–1pm and 2–4pm) and **Krishna Menon Art Gallery and Museum** both have interesting displays. Krishna Menon was a prominent Keralan politician after Independence.

Close by, at **Kappad** (16 km/10 miles from Kozhikode), is the place where Vasco da Gama first landed in India in 1498. Further north, past the French enclave of **Mahé** and the attractive coastal town of **Kannur** (Cannanore), is Tipu Sultan's atmospheric fort overlooking the beach at **Bekal** ㉖. ❑

Map on page 316

Elephants, tigers bison, leopards and monkeys may be seen at the Periyar Wildlife Sanctuary, 80 km (50 miles) from Kottayam, surrounding Periyar Lake.

BELOW: a *Teyattam* dancer's intricate make-up, north Kerala.

Map below

Delhi

LAKSHADWEEP

This chain of coral islands is surrounded by crystal-clear seas and fringed by white sand beaches and coconut palms. Only only a handful are inhabited

Scattered 200–400 km (124–248 miles) west of the Kerala coast are the Lakshadweep Islands. Some speculate that the name derives from the estimates of early sailors, who imagined at least 100,000 (a lakh) of these coral islands and atolls. In fact, there are only 22 (depending on how they are counted), of which just 11 are inhabited by some 60,600 people. The group is a continuation of the Maldives and the small islands are similarly characterised by white coral sand beaches fringed with palm trees and translucent lagoons; the islanders of Minicoy have a great deal in common culturally with the Maldives.

Most of the islanders are of Keralan descent: originally Hindu, as the prevalent systems of caste and of matrilineal inheritance bear out. However, Sunni Islam was brought to the islands by Hazrat Ubaidullah in the 7th century and the vast majority of islanders are Muslims. The people speak a dialect of Malayalam; the only exception is on Minicoy island where Mahl (the language of the Maldives) is spoken. Coconut farming and fishing are the main occupations, along with some dairy and poultry farming.

These are some of the few unspoilt coral islands left in the Indian ocean and they have an exceptionally sensitive environment. Tourism by non-Indian nationals is officially restricted to the islands of Bangaram and Kadmat (*see*

BELOW: the beach on Bangaram.

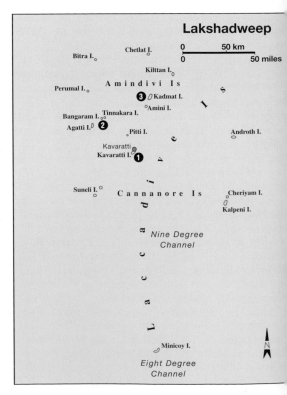

Lakshadweep

Bitra I.
Chetlat I.
Kilttan I.
Perumal I.
Amindivi Is
Kadmat I.
Amini I.
Bangaram I.
Tinnakara I.
Agatti I.
Pitti I.
Androth I.
Kavaratti
Kavaratti I.
Suneli I.
Cannanore Is
Cheriyam I.
Kalpeni I.
Nine Degree Channel
Minicoy I.
Eight Degree Channel

0   50 km
0   50 miles

N

margin). It may, at times, be possible to stay at the tourist resort close to the airport on Agatti. Transfer from Agatti to Bangaram and Kadmat is by boat.

The capital of the island chain is **Kavaratti** ❶, headquarters of the Administration of Lakshadweep. The Ujra mosque here has an ornately carved ceiling, said to be made of driftwood. Kalpeni has a spectacular lagoon containing three uninhabited islands, Tilakkam, Pitti and Cheriyam; Kalpeni has been developed for internal tourism and has watersports facilities and tourist huts. Evidence can still be seen of a huge storm that devastated the island in 1847. The southernmost island is Minicoy. The predominant industry here is tuna fishing and canning. There is also a large 19th-century lighthouse built by the British.

The three islands likely to be of most interest to foreign tourists are **Agatti**, **Bangaram** ❷ and **Kadmat** ❸. The first, on the edge of a stunning lagoon, is the location of the only airport in the island chain. A 20-seater Indian Airlines plane connects with Kochi and Goa. Visitors who are heading on then have a two-hour boat ride to either Bangaram or Kadmat, both uninhabited and on beautiful clear lagoons. This trip takes you outside the reef and is likely to be accompanied by dolphins, porpoises and flying fish, as well as large green and hawksbill turtles. The sea life on the reefs and within the lagoons is equally impressive. As well as a huge variety of corals, there are over 1,000 species of fish, including butterflyfish, clownfish, wrasses, parrotfish, goatfish and lionfish. Among the more spectacular sights are the turtles, harmless sharks and manta rays, and visitors may also encounter dolphins in the lagoons.

Glass-bottomed boats, snorkels or scuba gear are available for close-up encounters, and the resorts offer scuba and snorkel training. If you are planning on diving you will need a certificate of health from your doctor. ❑

Foreign tourists must book through one of two tour operators. For Bangaram Island Resort, contact: CGH Earth (previously the Casino Group), tel: 00 91 484 266 8221, www.cghearth.com; for Kadmat, contact: Lacadives, tel: 00 91 22 666 27381, www.lacadives.com; both operators offer diving packages.

BELOW: the boat from Agatti entering Bangaram lagoon.

KARNATAKA

The southwestern state of Karnataka has much to offer the visitor,
from the sparkling white sands of the coast to the
evocative ruins of Hampi and the opulence of Mysore Palace

Map
on page
332

The State of Karnataka, created in 1956 from the former State of Mysore and renamed in 1973, accounts for a sixteenth of the total landmass of India and has a population of 53 million. It has distinct regional landscapes. A narrow fertile coastal strip to the west, running along the Arabian sea, through which several rivers flow, their banks swelling during the monsoon months from July to September, is backed by the Western Ghats with wet slopes that sustain a narrow strip of dense tropical forest famed for its teak, rosewood and bamboo. These peaks restrict the entry of the rain-bearing monsoon clouds to the Deccan Plateau to the east with its dark volcanic soils and arid regions. In the southwest lie the hills and valleys of the Kodagu district. Amid the profusion of dense tropical rainforests in the southern Ghats roams the Indian elephant, the gaur and the long-tailed langur, the latter frequently breaking into the silence of the sun-freckled forest with gossipy chatter; this is one of the wettest regions of India.

A much visited geographical feature is **Jog Falls ❶** where the upland River Sharavati plunges over four cataracts. The falls are best seen in winter; in the summer the flow reduces to a trickle. The Honnemardu eco-project offers watersports nearby.

LEFT: indigenous forest cleared for cultivation.
BELOW: sculpture at the Channakesvara temple, Belur.

People and culture

Karnataka's people are as varied as its land. The northerners are mostly Lingayats, followers of the 12th-century scholar-saint Basavanna. A Hindu reformer, his message was spread through rhythmic prose called *vachanas*. In the south, in the former princely state of Mysore, the rich farming community of Vokkaligas dominates. Their rivalry continues in Karnataka's politics today.

Coastal Karnataka is inhabited by fisherfolk whose forebears traded with ancient Mesopotamia, Persia and Greece. Portuguese influence can be seen in Mangalore where the Christian community and its churches were established in the 16th century. Chikmanglur, along the border with Kerala, is a major coffee-growing district. Adivasi communities live mostly in the north and the west. The Coorgs of the Kodagu region have a distinctive culture of their own.

The principal language, Kannada, has a rich tradition of poetry and prose. The earliest classic *Kavirajamarga* (9th century) and Kannada inscriptions from the 5th century indicate its antiquity.

Karnataka's traditional theatre, *bayalata*, has many forms, the most famous of which is *yakshagana*. The dance-dramas take their themes from Hindu epics. There is a state-sponsored school in Dharwad for the training of *yakshagana* dance-drama artists. At the

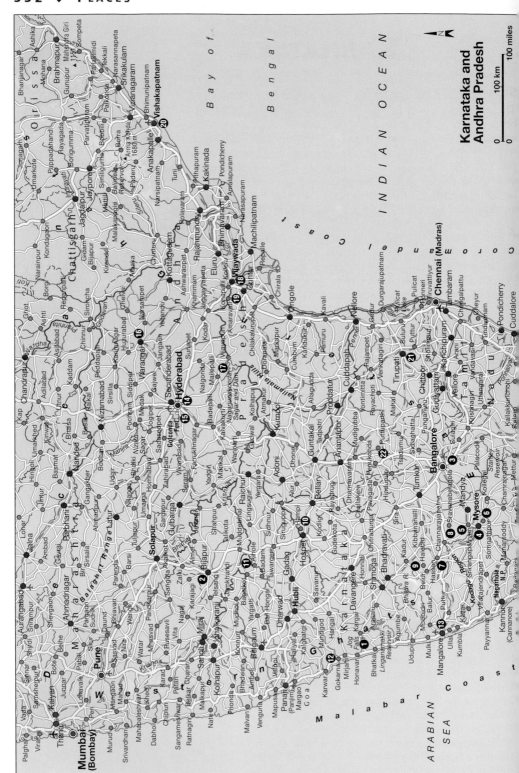

Karnataka and Andhra Pradesh

school, you can see performances by dancers in their elaborate costumes. Traditional crafts of Karnataka include silk weaving, sandalwood- and ivory-carving, Bidri work from Bidar and the popular red clay tiles of Mangalore.

Savoury delights

The cuisine of Karnataka includes the usual South Indian *dosas* (said to have been invented in Udipi), *idlis* and the staple *thali*, but also offers *bisi bele bath*, a delicacy of rice seasoned with lentils, spices and tamarind, *upittu* made of wheat flour, shredded coconut, green chillies and lemon, and *hoalige*, a flat pancake-like wafer filled with molasses, shredded coconut, or copra and sugar, or a variety of lentils and molasses, and fried lightly on a flat skillet. There is a large variety of fruit here, including the cashew tree with its distinctive fruit and nuts from which a potent, vodka-like drink called *feni* is brewed.

A look at the past

Successive Buddhist, Hindu and Muslim rulers dominated the region leaving a trail of architectural wonders. Chandragupta Maurya, India's first emperor, was believed to have converted to Jainism in the 4th century BC at **Sravanabelagola**.

The Hindu Chalukyas (6th–8th century AD) were followed by the Rashtrakutas, other princely houses, and then the Hoysalas of the Vijayanagar Empire who established the capital of their vast empire at **Hampi** in the central eastern region. In the 18th century, Hyder Ali and his son Tipu Sultan were defeated by the British in a battle at **Srirangapatnam** (1799) and the British restored the former Wodiyar Rajas of Mysore as governors. The present state government meets at the Vidhana Soudha in the capital, **Bangalore**.

In the north, the kingdom of **Bijapur** ❷ was founded by Yusuf Adil Shah who was born in Constantinople in 1443. His successors were to enrich the city with such splendid mosques as to rival anything Islam could raise elsewhere. Outstanding is **Gol Gumbaz**, the 17th-century mausoleum of Adil Shah, with one of the largest domes in the world. At **Gulbarga** are the remnants of a fort originally built by a Raja Gulchand and later developed by Allauddin Bahmani, founder of the kingdom of that name. The fort covers several hectares and includes the **Jami Mosque** with 35,000 sq metres (37,600 sq ft) of built-up area in the style of the mosque at Córdoba in Spain. The interior arches are so designed and the pillars so placed that the pulpit can be seen unobstructed from any part of the hall. The acoustics, too, are perfect.

Bangalore (Bengalooru)

The capital of Karnataka, **Bangalore** ❸ (from *Bengala Uru*, "village of beans", the name is now reverting to Bengalooru), was founded in 1531 by a chieftain, Kempegowda, who built a mud fortress here that was later fortified and extended by Hyder Ali and Tipu Sultan. During the British Raj it was a popular garrison town with a pleasant climate, parks and gardens. Bangalore is a research centre for science and technology and the vibrant hub of India's dynamic hi-tech industries. The addition of the computer soft-

Map on page 332

Women at the Sivaratri festival, Bangalore.

BELOW: Maharaja's Palace, Mysore.

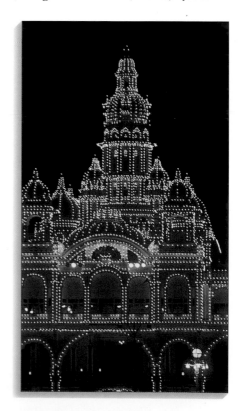

The Maharaja of Mysore opens parts of his palace to the public.

ware industry attracted people from all parts of India and, with a population of around 4 million, it is rapidly becoming overcrowded and congested.

Bangalore is a major transport centre. It compensates for its lack of tourist attractions with a choice of good accommodation and excellent eating places and pub-style bars. These abound in the area around M.G. Road, Brigade Road and St Mark's Road. Try **Commercial Street** for clothes and jewellery shopping, and for contrast visit the colourful city **vegetable and fruit market** on Avenue Road, and the old town with its narrow lanes and bazaars.

The few local sights include public buildings such as the 46-metre (150-ft) high **Vidhana Soudha** (Secretariat and State Legislature) on the northwest of **Cubbon Park**, which is floodlit on weekends and holidays. The peaceful 1,200-hectare (3,000-acre) Cubbon Park was laid out by the British Viceroy in 1864, and the red Gothic **High Court** and **State Central Public Library** buildings stand at its edge.

Another oasis, the **Lalbagh Botanical Gardens** (open sunrise–sunset) in the south of the city, is a 97-hectare (240-acre) park laid out in the 18th century by Tipu Sultan and Hyder Ali. With 1,854 species, it contains India's largest collection of rare tropical and subtropical plants, trees from Iran, Afghanistan and Europe, and a glasshouse similar to the Crystal Palace in London. Lalbagh is the venue for flower shows in January and August.

Tipu Sultan's palace on Avenue Road, southwest of the market, is now a museum, with the ruins of his fort, built on the site of Kempegowda's original fort, nearby. The city offers a surprising variety of entertainment for its size. Bangalore is also famous for its cinema halls, which normally screen films in southern languages. **The Plaza** on M.G. Road and the **Galaxy** on Residency

Road show first-run English films. As a university town, it has several music festivals featuring local rock bands.

The Karnataka State Tourism Development Corporation (KSTDC) at Badami House, N.R. Square, offers city tours and excursions to **Bannarghatta National Park**, 21 km (13 miles) to the south, which runs a wildlife safari and has a crocodile and snake farm (closed Tuesday), and to the **Sai Baba Ashram** 20 km (12 miles) to the east at Whitefield. The helpful KSTDC also publishes a good city map.

Princely Mysore

The town of **Mysore ❹** lies 139 km (86 miles) southwest of Bangalore. Once the capital of a former princely state, today it is a busy city. The best time to visit is in winter, particularly in October when the festival of *divali* is celebrated with royal splendour as the Maharaja leads a richly decorated procession that includes elephants and horses, flowers and incense, through the city streets. Each evening during the 10-day festival, **Mysore Palace** is illuminated.

The former Wodiyar Maharaja's huge, fairytale-castle palace (open 10.30am–5.30pm, entrance fee) was built at great cost by a British architect in 1912 in the Indo-Saracenic style. A part of it is still the residence of the current Maharaja. The interior is an amazing medley of striped pillars, stained glass, carved doors (including one made of solid silver) and mosaic floors. The main parts of the palace are open to the public and include an art gallery, a small museum and some temples set in the grounds.

Sri Jayachamarajendra Art Gallery (open 8am–5pm), housed in the Jaganmohan Palace to the west of Mysore Palace, has paintings dating from the 19th

Map
on page
332

On a hilltop at Sravanabelagola, north of Mysore, stands the 17-metre (56-ft) high granite statue of Gomatesvara, carved in the 10th century.

BELOW: colossus of the Jain saint, Gomatesvara being covered with turmeric at the Mastakabhiseka festival.

TRADITIONAL ENTERTAINMENT

Nothing can be more memorable than a night spent outdoors, sitting on a straw mat watching **bayalata** (field play), the traditional dramas of Karnataka. The drama, which depicts the exploits of heroes and heroines from India's epics, may run from early night until sunrise. The performances are an amalgam of music, dance and drama, and there is the easy camaraderie of people who know what it is all about and are willing to share their knowledge with you.

When the fields are flush with water, there is another sight not to be missed: the **kambala** (buffalo race) that is popular in Karnataka. Run in a paddy field by pairs of special, and cossetted, racing buffaloes, egged on by men riding behind them, in a highly charged atmosphere, the *kambala* is an annual event. The rider crouches behind the buffaloes on a stout wooden shaft yoked to the animals. Not a muscle moves. Only the wind plays on his locks of hair. Suddenly the scene explodes, the man springs up, his hand cocked, his whip held high, and the huge animals lunge forward, bellowing, their hooves churning the muddy waters and sending their wet spray into the hot air, their eyes wide, wild and white. The races are a good excuse for some serious gambling and substantial amounts of money can change hands.

century, including works of Raja Ravi Varma and traditional Mysore gold-leaf paintings. **St Philomenas Church**, built in Gothic style during the 1930s, has beautiful stained-glass windows. It is one of the largest churches in India.

The central area around Sayaji Rao Road has eating places and shops selling the silk and sandalwood for which Mysore is famous. It's a pleasant walk from here to **Devaraja Market**, which sells flowers, fruit, incense and spices.

Overlooking the town is Chamundi Hill, topped by the **Chamundesvari Temple**, patron deity of the city and royal family. There are lovely views on the way up, and a huge statue of Nandi, Siva's bull.

The Chalukya dynasty, responsible for the temples at Aihole, Patadakal and Badami, ruled from AD 547 to 753. The rock-cut temples represent the earliest experiments in what became distinct North and South Indian temple styles.

On from Mysore

At **Srirangapatnam ⑤**, the former capital of Tipu Sultan (14 km/9 miles from Mysore), are the remains of his fort and summer palace, **Daria Daulat**, built in 1784. The palace has a well-preserved interior and is set in gardens. **Somnathpur ⑥**, close to Srirangapatnam, features a splendid, 13th-century starshaped Hoysala temple, its walls covered with frescoes.

Southern Karnataka has two of the finest wildlife reserves in India, with large herds of wild elephants, gaur and a viable population of tigers. **Nagarhole** (93 km/28 miles southwest) and **Bandipur National Park** (80 km/50 miles south) are best approached from Mysore. Bandipur, a continuation of the Mudumalai reserve in Tamil Nadu, was once the maharajas' game reserve and is now a Project Tiger site.

Hassan ⑦ (118 km/73 miles northwest of Mysore) provides a base for exploring other sites, including the Jain pilgrimage centre of **Sravanabelagola ⑧** and the exquisitely carved Hoysala temples of **Belur** and **Halebid ⑨**.

BELOW: carrying coconuts through a sunflower field near Halebid.

Hampi

In northern Karnataka, on the banks of the River Tungabadhra close to **Hospet**, lies the deserted city of **Hampi ❿**, capital of the great Vijayanagar Empire from the 14th century and one of India's archaeological highlights (open: Vittala Temple open 8am–4pm; Royal Enclosure 6am–6pm; entrance fee). Hampi was destroyed in 1565 after the Battle of Talikota, in which the Vijayanagar army was defeated by the Bijapur confederacy. Its many temples and palaces are a World Heritage site. It made its fabulous wealth from the spice and cotton trade, and at one time had a population of half a million people. The spectacular landscape is dotted with ruins and huge boulders and is best explored by bicycle.

Among its many sights, the **Vittala Temple** is noted for its remarkable sculptural details; the **Royal Enclosure** houses the remains of the **Lotus Mahal** and the domed chambers of the **Elephant Stables**.

Aihole ⓫, 100 km (62 miles) north of Hampi, is thought to be the cradle of Hindu temple architecture: it has 125 temples. **Patadakal**, nearby, is another World Heritage site with 10 major temples, and **Badami's fort** and **cave temples** are all worth a visit (25 km/15 miles southwest of Aihole).

The coast

The coast road (NH 17), from **Karwar** in the north to **Ullal** in the south, follows a long stretch of white sand and makes for a spectacular journey along the foothills of the Western Ghats. **Gokarna ⓬** is a popular pilgrimage site famous for its temples and shrines; its secluded beaches have begun to draw some of the travellers from Goa. In the south of the state is the pilgrimage town of **Udipi**, beyond which is the pleasant coastal city of **Mangalore ⓭**. ❑

Map on page 332

Dancing Siva at a Hoysala temple, Halebid.

BELOW: stone chariot among the remains at Hampi.

ANDHRA PRADESH

Many ancient civilisations have left their mark on the east-coast state of Andhra Pradesh. Temples, palaces and ruined forts dot the landscape, offering a wealth of architectural interest

Map on page 332

Geographically one of the oldest land masses in South Asia, Andhra Pradesh has stunning landscapes of hilly, rock-strewn plateaus, fertile river valleys, and a long coastline to its east. Yet it is difficult to explore. The harsh climate – hot and dry for most of the year, interrupted by the flooding of rivers during the monsoon months – causes havoc; monsoons regularly cause fatalities, and during exceptionally hot summers people die in the streets. Cyclones frequently hit the coastal areas during May, October and November, paralysing transportation, and the low-lying coast was also hit by the 2004 tsunami, killing 105 people (most of whom were from Nellore, Prakasam and Krishna districts).

The present state of Andhra Pradesh, the first formed on a linguistic basis, was created in 1956 after considerable agitation, by combining the Telugu-speaking parts of the Presidency of Madras with the former territories of the princely state of Hyderabad. Buddhism, Hinduism and Islam, each with its distinct culture reflected in its architecture, have all flourished here. Ashokan accounts from the 3rd century BC refer to a people called the "Andhras". Later, the Satyavanas ruled from Amaravati and were Buddhist patrons. Recently there have been calls to create a separate state of Telengana out of the poorer northern districts which feel that their interests are often ignored by politicians from the coast and the south.

LEFT: a Lambadi woman, Hyderabad.
BELOW: coconuts, typical produce of southern India.

Andhran culture

Telugu, the principal language of the state, has a rich literature that can be heard in its *padyams* – rolling, sonorous prose narrations of rural life, customs and festivities. *Kuchipudi*, a dance drama originating in the rich delta of the Krishna and Godavari rivers, is thought to have developed out of the traditional *yaksagana* theatre. The skilled workers of Andhra specialise in woodcarving; those from Kondapalli near Vijayawada fashion colourful toys and figures. Bidri workers from Bidar create delicate designs, inlaid in silver or gold on matt black gunmetal hookas, vases, boxes and jewellery. The weavers use distinctive weaves and dye techniques and are famous for their rich brocades, ikats, silks and *himru* fabric – a mixture of silk and cotton. The cuisine of Andhra is well known for its fiery hot curries served with rice or *parathas* in traditional southern "meals". Hyderabad has its own distinct nawabi cuisine, essentially Mughal but adapted to the tastes of the local royalty. Excellent aromatic *biryanis*, delicate kebabs, *halim* (a spiced mixture of wheat and mutton), *bhaghere bain-an* (aubergines) and *mirch ka salan* (green chilli curry) are some specialities.

Hyderabad

Hyderabad ⓮ is the capital of Andhra Pradesh and India's fifth largest city. It has a population of nearly

The eclectic collection of Sir Yusuf Ali Salar Jung, the Nizam's Wazir, is not to be missed. It contains European art, sculpture, manuscripts, textiles, miniatures, toys and Mughal glassware. There are plans to build a permanent gallery in which to display the Nizam's priceless jewels. Afzal Ganj (open Sat–Thur 10am–5pm, entrance fee).

BELOW: sketch showing a bas-relief at Amaravati.

five million. An acute scarcity of water and overcrowding at **Golconda** ⑮, 11 km (7 miles) to the west, led Mohammed Quli of the Qutb Shahi dynasty to build the new capital of Hyderabad on the banks of the Musi River in 1591. In 1687 the Mughal Emperor Aurangzeb overthrew the dynasty and appointed his former general as viceroy. This dynasty of Asaf Jahi, which declared its independence after Aurangzeb's death, ruled as the Nizams of Hyderabad until 1949. The seventh and last ruling nizam, Osman Ali Khan (1911–50), was famous for his eccentricities and enormous wealth, said to have been derived from diamonds and other gems mined by his ancestors around Golconda, in the 17th century the diamond centre of the world. At Independence in 1947 he expressed a wish to join Pakistan, a position he managed to maintain until 1949, when riots in the city gave the Indian army the excuse they needed to invade.

Traditionally a gracious and cosmopolitan centre of learning and the arts, modern Hyderabad and its twin city Secunderabad are separated by **Hussain Sagar Lake**. Besides being a major centre of commerce and industry, transport and communication, Hyderabad is also a processing centre for pearls from the Middle East, Japan and China. It is considered the centre for Islam in South India and yet on the lake is the world's largest statue of Buddha.

The main Mahatma Gandhi Road cuts straight through Hyderabad city, past the central shopping area around Abids Circle, and across the Tank Bund (a popular local promenade overlooking the lake) to continue onwards into Secunderabad. The old walled city area is around Hyderabad's most famous landmark, the **Charminar** (literally "four towers"). Floodlit in the evenings, this magnificent square archway supported by four 56-metre (184-ft) towers was built in 1591 to commemorate the end of a local plague. It is covered with a

WORSHIPPING THE TRISUL EMBLEM
ON A FIERY PILLAR.

From a bas-relief at Amaravati.

GOLCONDA FORT

The huge and once impregnable Golconda Fort, situated on a steep granite hill 11 km (7 miles) west of Hyderabad, was built by the Qutb Shahi dynasty, which ruled during the 16th and 17th centuries. It was their capital until 1590 when the king moved to his new city of Hyderabad. It was used by the last of the Qutb Kings in the 17th century as a bastion against Mughal attack. The fort was encircled by immense walls with 87 semicircular bastions and eight gates with elephant-proof spikes.

Famous for its ingenious acoustics, a remarkable hot and cold water supply system, natural air-conditioning and Turkish baths, the remains of its once splendid palaces and gardens give an idea of its former grandeur. Diamonds and rubies once embellished the walls of the Queen's Palace, and rose water filled a copper fountain. From the three-storey Durbar Hall, the rulers kept watch over their kingdom. Golconda makes an easy full-day excursion and can be reached by local bus or auto-rickshaw. Take a hat or sun-protection. Also worth a visit are the tombs of the kings and their family, a short walk northwest from Golconda's Balahisar Gate (open Sat–Thur 9am–4.30pm, entrance fee).

A sound and light show is held in English at the fort (Wed, Sun; Nov–Feb 6.30pm; Mar–Oct 7pm).

yellow stucco mixed from powdered marble, gram flour and egg yolk. There is a tiny mosque on the second floor where royal children studied the Quran. Nearby stands the sixth largest mosque in India, the black granite Mecca Masjid, said to have bricks made of red clay from Mecca over the central archway. Old bazaars with narrow cobbled lanes lined with rows of tiny shops selling spices, tobacco, grain, perfume oils and Hyderabadi specialities such as seedless Anab-shahi grapes, surround the Charminar. The **pearl market** has varieties of seed pearl, rice pearl and round pearl, sold loose by weight, or strung into jewellery. In other lanes one can find silver filigree jewellery, Adivasi mirrorwork, *lac* bangles, brocades, sandalwood toys, brassware and Bidri work. East of Lad Bazaar is a quadrangular complex of palaces built by the nizams. Other places of interest include the peaceful **Public Gardens**, which house a modest but well-kept **Archaeological Museum** (open Mon–Sat 10.30am–5pm) and a **Gallery of Modern Art**. The **Nehru Zoological Park** (open Tues–Sun 9am–6pm, entrance fee), spread over 120 hectares (300 acres), is supposedly one of the better zoos in India *(see page 173)*. It has landscaped gardens and features a wide variety of animals and birds, an aquarium and a natural history museum. A good spot for sunset views is **Kala Pahad** (Black Mountain) where the **Birla Venkatesvara** temple is perched on the hill top. On the adjacent hill, Naubat Pahad, there is the **Planetarium** with regular shows in English.

Cultural shows are held at Hyderabad's Rabindra Bharati Indoor Theatre, Lalit Kala Thonaram and Max Mueller Bhavan, and in Secunderabad at the Kala Bhavan. Check local papers for listings.

Excursions from Hyderabad

Visits can be made to **Pochampalli**, a village east of Hyderabad noted for its silk saris and ikat weaves, and to **Warangal ⑯**, 150 km (93 miles) to the northeast. This 12th- to 13th-century capital of the Hindu Kakatiyas was renowned for its

BELOW: Golconda Fort and the Qutb Shahi tombs.

Oversized shadow-puppets stitched from goat's leather feature in performances on festival days.

LEFT: a devotee at Tirupati Temple.
RIGHT: celebrating Pongal, a south Indian festival.

now abandoned massive brick and mud fort protected by two rings of walls and a moat. There are a few Chalukyan Siva temples on hills in and around Warangal.

Also interesting is the **Nagarjunakonda Sagar and Dam** ⑰, 166 km (103 miles) south. Built in 1960, this reservoir submerged an entire valley, which had been the site of a series of ancient civilisations. Important Buddhist monuments have been reconstructed at a museum within the ruins of a fort on an island, which was once the top of a 200-metre (650-ft) high hill. Boats depart three-times daily from Vijayapuri for the one-hour trip to the island. **Pochram**, 180 km (110 miles) to the northwest, is a beautiful lake and wildlife sanctuary with a neo-Gothic spired cathedral at nearby **Medak**, built for local Christians between 1914 and 1924.

The Great Stupa

On the banks of the River Krishna, the ancient city of **Vijaywada** ⑱, 240 km (150 miles) east of Hyderabad, was once visited by the Chinese traveller Hieun Tsang. It shows traces of its past in the two ancient Jain temples and the cave temples nearby, and also the hilltop **Kanakadurga temple**, patron deity of the city. Now a busy commercial centre, Vijaywada is useful to the visitor as a base from which to visit **Amaravati** ⑲, 30 km (19 miles) west, the site of early Buddhist settlements. Here the remains of a 2,000-year-old Great Stupa are richly embellished with carvings depicting the life of Buddha. A small museum displays statues of Buddha. The village of **Kondapalli**, 25 km (15 miles) north, at the base of a hill topped by a ruined fort, is famous for its painted toys and figures made of a local species of white cedar. A drive to the coastal town of **Machilipatnam**, 70 km (43 miles) to the east, to see the *kalamkari* process of printing cloth using a *kalam* (pen) and woodblocks, makes an interesting excursion.

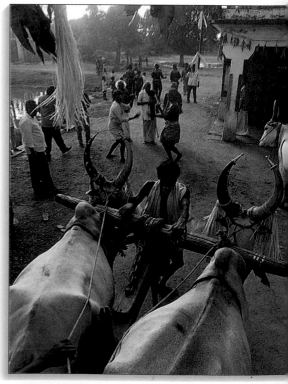

Northeast coast

The naval base and ship-building centre of **Vishakapatnam 20**, on Andhra Pradesh's northeast coast, is the fourth-largest port in India. Its twin city, **Waltair**, built as a resort town by the British and still retaining shady avenues, charming bungalows and marvellous views, can be used as a base to visit coastal Andhra. There are beaches at **Rishikonda** (10 km/6 miles) and at the former Dutch settlement of **Bhimunipatnam** (24 km/15 miles).

In the Kailasa Hills to the west of the city, there is a 13th-century Orissan-style Hindu temple and hot springs at **Simhachalam**. A 70-km (43-mile) drive inland brings you to the ancient **Borra Caves** set in limestone hills with wonderful stalactites and stalagmites. The Adivasi area of the **Araku Valley** on the border with Orissa is nearby.

Southern pilgrim sites

Tirupati 21, with nearby Tirumala Hill on which stands the **Lord Venkatesvara Temple**, is the busiest pilgrimage site in the world, as well as one of the wealthiest. The very efficient temple administration employs around 16,000 people to deal with the 60–70,000 pilgrims a day who come for *darsan* (a view of the god). Many of them shave their heads as a pledge, or to thank the deity. The hair is used to make wigs, which are sold locally and exported. The temple is open to non-Hindus, but they must sign a form declaring their faith in god and respect for the temple's procedures. The steep road up the hill, with 57 hairpin bends, is not for the faint-hearted. **Puttuparthi 22**, bordering Karnataka in Andhra's southwest, is the birthplace of the controversial spiritual leader Sai Baba and the site of his ashram headquarters. ❑

Map on page 332

The temple at Tirumala operates round-the-clock darsan. Pilgrims can either take a paper bracelet that tells them their time of entry or pay for "special darsan", which will get them in quicker.

BELOW: dried red chillies, a common ingredient in Andhran cooking.
FOLLOWING PAGE: painted elephant.

✵ INSIGHT GUIDES
Travel Tips

CONTENTS

Getting Acquainted

The Place

Area 3,287,590 sq. km (1,269,346 sq. miles).
Capital New Delhi.
Largest City Mumbai, with more than 16 million inhabitants.
Highest point Kanchenjunga, in Sikkim (8,586 metres/28,170 ft).
Population estimated at 1,095 billion in 2006, 88 million more than in the 2001 census – about 16 percent of the world's population. Around 40 percent are aged under 15. Total literacy is 65 percent; 76 percent for men and 54 percent for women.
Major Languages Hindi (mother tongue for more than 360 million speakers), Telugu, Bengali, Marathi Tamil and Urdu.
Major Religions Hindu (80 percent); Muslim (11 percent); Christian (2 percent); Sikh (2 percent), Jain, Buddhist.
Time Zones India is 5½ hours ahead of Greenwich Mean Time; 10½ hours ahead Eastern Seaboard Time .
Currency Based on the decimal system with 100 paise to the rupee.
Weights & Measures The metric system is used everywhere. Precious metals, especially gold, are often sold by the traditional *tola*, which is equivalent to 11.5 grams. Gems are weighed in carats (0.2 grams).
Financial outlays and population are usually expressed in *lakhs* (100,000) and *crores* (100 *lakhs* or 10 million).
Electricity The voltage system in India is 220V AC, 50 cycles. DC supplies also exist, so check first. Sockets are of the two round-pin variety normally, but do vary. Take a universal adaptor for British, Irish and Australasian plugs. American and Canadian appliances will need a transformer.
Dialling Codes To call India from abroad, dial the international access code, followed by 91 for India, the local code less the initial zero, then the number. Old Indian numbers need an initial "2" adding to them.

The Land

India lies between latitude 8° north and 36° north, and longitude 68° east and 97° east. It is surrounded by the Arabian Sea on the west, the Bay of Bengal on the east and the Indian Ocean to the south. It shares borders with Pakistan, China, Nepal, Bhutan, Burma (Myanmar) and Bangladesh, and is divided into seven major regions: Himalayas, Indo-Gangetic Plain, Central Highlands, Deccan Plateau, Western Ghats, Eastern Ghats and the bordering seas and islands. *(See also pages 17–19.)*

When to Go

India's climate ranges from the permanent snows of the Himalayas and the tropical conditions along the coasts, to the continental climate of inland areas. There are also many regional and seasonal variations. In general, the best time to visit is after the southwest monsoon.
October to March is the cool season and therefore the best time of year in Peninsular India. On the whole, the weather is beautifully predictable in winter, with blue skies and bright sunshine in most areas. Parts of the south and east see a brief spell of rain from the northeast monsoon, while snow and sleet make the extreme north very cold and often inaccessible.
Summer, from April to June, is very hot and dry for most of the country, and humid along the coasts. Kashmir and the hill stations of Himachal and Uttar Pradesh are particularly lovely at this time of the year.
The southwest monsoon begins to set in along the western coast towards the end of May, bringing welcome respite from the heat and varying amounts of rain as it moves across the rest of the country through June and July and withdraws by late September. Northeastern India has heavy rain during this season, making it one of the wettest regions in the world.

Climate

India's climate ranges from the permanent snows of the Himalayas and the tropical conditions along the coasts, to the continental climate of inland areas. There are also many regional and seasonal variations. In general, the best time to visit is after the southwest monsoon.
October to March is the cool season and the best time of year in Peninsular India. The weather is beautifully predictable in winter, with blue skies and bright sunshine in most areas. Parts of the south and east see a brief spell of rain from the northeast monsoon, while snow and sleet make the extreme north very cold and often inaccessible.
Summer, from April to June, is very hot and dry for most of the country, and humid along the coasts. The hills are particularly lovely at this time of the year.
The southwest monsoon begins to set in along the western coast towards the end of May, bringing respite from the heat and varying amounts of rain as it moves across the rest of the country through June and July and withdraws by late September. Northeastern India has heavy rain during this season, making it one of the wettest regions in the world.

Etiquette

● Removing one's shoes before entering someone's house, or a temple, mosque or *gurdwara* (Sikh temple) is essential. Overshoes are provided in some places of worship at a nominal cost and stockinged feet are usually permissible.
● The *namaskaram* greeting with joined hands, is the Indian form of salutation and its use will be appreciated, though men, especially in the cities, will not hesitate to shake hands with you if you are a man. A handshake would even be appreciated as a gesture of special friendliness.
Most Indian women would be taken aback at the informality of interaction between the sexes common in the West and physical contact between men and women is to be avoided. Men should not shake hands with a woman (unless she first offers to).
● Avoid taking leather goods of any kind into temples as these can often cause offence.
● Always walk around religious shrines clockwise.
● Photography is prohibited inside the inner sanctum of many places of worship. Do obtain permission before using a camera. Visitors are usually welcome to look around at their leisure and can sometimes stay during religious rituals. For visits to places of worship, modest clothing is essential. In Sikh temples, your head should be covered. In mosques, women should cover their head and arms and wear long skirts. A small contribution to the donation box *(hundi)* is customary.
● In private, visitors are received as honoured guests and your unfamiliarity with Indian ways will be accepted and understood. When eating with your fingers, remember to use only the right hand.

Climate

		Jan	Feb	Mar	Apr	May	June	July	Aug	Sep	Oct	Nov	Dec
Agra	Max/Min °C	22/7	26/10	32/16	38/22	42/27	41/29	35/27	33/26	33/25	33/19	29/12	24/8
	Rainfall mm	16	9	11	5	10	60	210	263	151	23	2	4
Ahmadabad	Max/Min °C	29/12	31/15	36/19	40/23	41/26	38/27	33/26	32/25	33/24	36/21	33/16	30/13
	Rainfall mm	4	0	1	2	5	100	316	213	163	13	5	1
Bangalore	Max/Min °C	28/15	31/16	33/19	34/21	33/21	30/20	28/19	29/19	28/19	28/19	27/17	27/15
	Rainfall mm	4	14	6	37	119	65	93	95	129	195	46	16
Bhopal	Max/Min °C	26/10	29/13	34/17	38/21	41/26	37/25	30/23	29/23	30/22	31/18	29/13	26/11
	Rainfall mm	17	5	10	3	11	137	499	308	232	37	15	7
Bhubaneshwar	Max/Min °C	29/16	32/19	35/22	38/26	38/27	35/26	31/25	31/25	31/25	31/23	29/18	28/16
	Rainfall mm	12	25	17	12	61	223	301	336	305	266	51	3
Chandigarh	Max/Min °C	20/7	23/9	29/14	34/19	38/24	39/26	34/24	33/23	33/22	31/17	27/10	22/7
	Rainfall mm	56	25	26	10	13	62	277	263	226	82	5	18
Chennai	Max/Min °C	29/20	31/21	33/23	35/23	38/28	37/28	35/26	35/25	34/25	32/24	29/23	28/21
	Rainfall mm	24	7	15	15	52	53	83	124	118	267	309	139
Darjeelng	Max/Min °C	9/3	11/4	15/8	18/11	19/13	19/15	20/15	20/15	20/15	19/11	15/7	12/4
	Rainfall mm	22	27	52	109	187	522	713	573	419	116	14	5
Delhi	Max/Min °C	21/7	24/10	30/15	36/21	41/27	40/29	35/27	34/26	34/25	35/19	29/12	23/8
	Rainfall mm	25	22	17	7	8	65	211	173	150	31	1	5
Guwahati	Max/Min °C	23/10	27/12	30/16	32/20	31/23	32/25	32/26	32/26	30/25	27/22	25/17	27/12
	Rainfall mm	17	9	73	136	276	351	373	294	190	86	8	7
Hyderabad	Max/Min °C	29/15	31/17	35/20	37/24	39/26	34/24	30/22	29/22	30/22	30/20	29/16	28/13
	Rainfall mm	2	11	13	24	30	107	165	147	163	71	25	5
Jaipur	Max/Min °C	22/8	25/11	31/15	37/21	41/26	39/27	34/26	32/24	33/23	33/18	29/12	24/9
	Rainfall mm	14	8	9	4	10	54	193	239	90	19	3	4
Jaisalmer	Max/Min °C	24/8	28/11	33/17	38/21	42/25	41/27	38/27	36/25	36/25	36/20	31/13	26/9
	Rainfall mm	2	1	3	1	5	7	89	86	14	1	5	2
Kolkata	Max/Min °C	26/12	29/15	34/20	36/24	36/26	34/26	32/26	32/26	32/26	31/24	29/18	27/13
	Rainfall mm	13	22	30	50	135	263	320	318	253	134	29	4
Leh	Max/Min °C	-3/-14	1/-12	6/-6	12/-1	17/3	21/7	25/10	24/10	21/5	14/-1	8/-7	2/-11
	Rainfall mm	12	9	12	7	7	4	16	20	12	7	3	8
Lucknow	Max/Min °C	23/9	26/11	33/16	38/22	41/27	39/28	34/27	33/26	33/23	33/20	29/13	25/9
	Rainfall mm	25	17	9	6	12	94	299	302	182	40	1	6
Mumbai	Max/Min °C	31/16	32/17	33/20	33/24	33/26	32/26	30/25	29/24	30/24	32/23	33/20	32/18
	Rainfall mm	0	1	0	0	20	647	945	660	309	117	7	1
Nagpur	Max/Min °C	29/13	33/15	36/19	40/24	43/28	38/27	31/24	30/24	31/23	32/20	30/14	29/12
	Rainfall mm	15	2	25	20	10	174	351	277	181	62	9	2
Panaji	Max/Min °C	31/19	32/20	32/23	33/25	33/27	31/25	29/24	29/24	29/24	31/23	33/22	33/21
	Rainfall mm	2	0	4	17	18	580	892	341	277	122	20	37
Patna	Max/Min °C	24/11	26/13	33/19	38/23	39/26	37/27	33/27	32/27	32/26	32/23	29/16	25/12
	Rainfall mm	21	20	7	8	28	139	266	307	243	63	6	2
Pune	Max/Min °C	31/12	33/13	36/17	38/21	37/23	32/23	28/22	28/21	29/21	32/19	31/15	30/12
	Rainfall mm	2	0	3	18	35	103	187	106	127	92	37	5
Simla	Max/Min °C	9/2	10/3	14/7	19/11	23/15	24/16	21/16	20/15	20/14	18/10	15/7	11/4
	Rainfall mm	65	48	58	38	54	147	415	385	195	45	7	24
Tiruvanantha-puram	Max/Min °C	31/22	32/23	33/24	32/25	31/25	29/24	29/23	29/22	30/23	30/23	30/23	31/23
	Rainfall mm	20	20	43	122	249	331	215	164	123	271	207	73
Varanasi	Max/Min °C	23/9	37/11	33/17	39/22	41/27	39/28	33/26	32/26	32/25	32/21	29/13	25/9
	Rainfall mm	23	8	14	1	8	102	346	240	261	38	15	2

● Avoid pointing the soles of your feet towards anyone as this is considered a sign of disrespect. Don't point with your index finger: use either your extended hand or your chin.
● Central Government has passed a law banning smoking in all public places, and this has now been enacted by most State governments.

The Government

The Indian Union is a federation comprising 28 states, six union territories and the National Capital Territory of Delhi. Each state, and some union territories, has its own legislative assembly and government, headed by a chief minister. The central (federal) government is headed by a prime minister and council of ministers (cabinet) responsible to the two houses of parliament: the Lok Sabha (Council of the People) and the Rajya Sabha (Council of State). The Lok Sabha is composed of 543 members directly elected by the people on the basis of adult franchise (530 seats for the states and 13 for the union territories), plus two nominated members (a total of 545 members).

The Rajya Sabha (the upper chamber) is an indirectly elected body of 245 members. Each member is elected for 6 years, with a third of the body renewed every two years. The president is elected for a five-year

Place Names

Some places have changed their names, in many cases away from Anglicisations, including the following:
Alleppey Alappuzha
Badagara Vadakara
Baroda Vadodarajh
Bombay Mumbai
Calcutta Kolkata
Calicut Kozhikode
Cannanore Kannur
Changanacherry Changanassery
Cochin Kochi
Capecomorin Kanyakumari
Madras Chennai
Mahabalipuram Mamallapuram
Mercara Madikeri
Ooty Udhagamandalam
Palghat Palakkad
Panjim Panaji
Pondicherry Puducherry
Quilon Kollam
Sulthan Battery Sulthanbathery
Tanjore Thanjavur
Tellicherry Thalassery
Trichur Thrissur
Trichy Thiruchirappalli
Trivandrum Thiruvanathapuram

term by an electoral college consisting of members of parliament and members of the state legislatures. The president, appointed in 2002, is A.P.J. Abdul Kalam, previously head of India's nuclear weapons programme. Each state has its own legislature and is responsible for a number of administrative functions such as health, education, forests and surface transport (except railways).

Elections are normally held every five years but can, in certain situations, be called earlier. India has had 14 general elections since it became an independent country in 1947. There are numerous parties, the six national parties are: Bahujan Samaj Party (BSP); Bharatiya Janata (BJP); The Communist Party of India (CPI); Communist Party of India (Marxist) (CPI[M]); Indian National Congress (INC); and Nationalist Congress Party (NCP).

The 2004 general election saw the greatest upset in Indian politics since Independence. The ruling BJP-led National Democratic Alliance was comprehensively defeated by the Congress and Left parties. Many politcal commentators had assumed that the NDA would win the election, on the back of the newly affluent middle class. However, the electorate threw out the NDA, which had favoured neoliberal economics and had been widely associated with spreading communal discord. The leader of Congress, Sonia Gandhi, turned down the post of prime minister, leaving it for Manmohan Singh, India's first Sikh prime minister and, ironically, architect of the economic liberalisation programmes of the early 1990s. Perhaps the most important legacy of NDA rule is the ongoing negotiations with Pakistan over Kashmir and the reigning in of economic liberalisation.

The next elections are due on 18 July 2007.

The Economy

India has one of the world's fastest growing economies. In the decade since 1996, the economy has grown at an average rate of 7 percent per year, and GDP growth for 2006 was 8.5 percent. India is now among the 15 top industrial nations of the world, and incomes have risen faster in the past decade than at any time in the country's history.

Of the labour force, around 60 percent is employed in agriculture, 12 percent in industry and 28 percent in services, which are a major source of economic growth. Some of this is from business outsourcing: 80–90

percent of the world's business outsourcing goes to India, where pundits believe that it will create 10 million jobs in the next five years. Innovation and high-tech industries are increasingly attracted to India, with a hub at Bangalore.

The rural population represents about 72 percent of the total, with 27 cities having more than one million people. Greater Mumbai is the largest with around 25 million. The rate of population increase has in fact slowed a little in recent years

Despite the agrarian bias of its economy, over the term of the NDA government farmers were largely ignored as the economic orthodoxy began to favour the IT and service industries that generally favour the urban middle class. The relatively low level of exports is partly due to a large volume of domestic consumption. In the matter of production of foodgrains in particular, the advance has been spectacular – once a chronically deficit area, India can now export foodgrains. However, some 25 percent of the population remain below the poverty line, earning less than a dollar a day, compared to 35 percent 10 years ago. Unemployment is just under 8 percent. Only around 64 percent of the villages have access to electricity, but the government has set up a "power for all" goal for 2012. India has half a dozen nuclear power plants, with three more under construction. Renewable power accounts for around 5 percent of output.

Planning the Trip

Arrival

Once through customs the visitor is often besieged by porters, taxi drivers and others. Choose one porter and stick to him. There is a system of paying porters a fixed amount per piece of baggage before leaving the terminal: a tip of Rs5, once the bags are aboard the taxi or bus, is sufficient. If a travel agent or a friend is meeting you, he or she may be waiting outside the building.

Some major hotels operate courtesy buses, and a public service known as EATS (Ex-Serviceman's Transport Service) operates an airport bus service in Delhi, Mumbai and Kolkata with stops at hotels and major points en route to the city centre. There are also offical, pre-paid taxis and coaches.

Customs

Customs procedures have recently been simplified. Visitors fill in declaration forms on the plane, and then proceed to the relevant red or green channels. Keep the slip in your passport for when you disembark.

Prohibited articles

These include certain drugs, live plants, gold and silver bullion, and coins not in current use. All checked luggage arriving at Delhi airport is X-rayed before reaching the baggage collection area in the arrival hall.

Duty-free imports

These include 200 cigarettes (or 50 cigars), 0.95 litres (1 pint) of alcohol, a camera with five rolls of film and a reasonable amount of personal effects, including binoculars, laptop, sound recording instruments, etc.

Professional equipment and high-value articles must be declared or listed on arrival with a written undertaking to re-export them. Both the list and the articles must be produced on departure. As this formality can be a lengthy process, allow extra time, both on arrival and at departure. For unaccompanied baggage or baggage misplaced by the airline, make sure you get a landing certificate from customs on arrival.

Exports

Export of antiques (over 100 years old), all animal products, and jewellery valued at over Rs2,000 (in the case of gold) and Rs10,000 (in the case of articles not made of gold) is banned. When in doubt about the age of semi-antiques, contact the office of the Archaeological Survey of India in Delhi, Mumbai, Kolkata or Chennai (www.asi.nic.in).

Currency declaration

At present, forms for amounts of cash in excess of US$10,000 must be completed at customs on arrival.

Departure

It is absolutely essential to reconfirm your reservations for all outward-bound flights at least 72 hours before departure, especially in the peak season, when most of the flights are overbooked. Security procedures can be intensive and time-consuming, so allow at least two hours for check-in.

For visitors with entry permits, exit endorsements are necessary from the office where they were registered.

Should a stay exceed 180 days, an income tax exemption certificate must be obtained from the Foreign Section of the Income Tax Department in Delhi, Mumbai, Kolkata or Chennai.

Entry Regulations

Tourist visas for all nationalities are issued for six months from the date of issue (not entry). It is preferable to take a multiple-entry visa, in order to have the option of visiting a neighbouring country. Get a visa from the embassy or high commission in your country of residence, rather than risk the complications and delays involved in applying for one in neighbouring countries.

Tourist visas cannot be extended; you must leave the country and re-enter on a new one. It may be difficult to apply for a new visa from neighbouring countries. Five-year visas are also issued to businessmen and students. In addition to visas, special permits are required for certain areas, while other areas are out of bounds to foreigners altogether (see Restricted & Protected Areas overleaf).

If you stay for more than 180 days, before leaving the country you must have a tax clearance certificate. These can be obtained from the foreigner's section of the income tax department in every city. Tax

Departure Tax

Remember before you leave that there is a departure tax of Rs750 – Rs550 for neighbouring South Asian Association for Regional Co-operation (SAARC) countries. This should be included in your ticket, but make sure you check with your airline or ticket agent.

clearance certificates are free, but take bank receipts to demonstrate that you have changed money legally.

Getting There

By Air

The vast majority of visitors arrive in India by air. Mumbai and Delhi airports are the major entry points, with fewer international flights from Europe using Kolkata and Chennai. Kolkata and Chennai especially have flights to and from East Asia. The national carrier is Air India (www.airindia.com), but other carriers which have regular flights between the UK (where many transatlantic passengers can change) and India are British Airways (www.ba.com), Virgin Atlantic (www.virgin-atlantic.com) and Jet Airways (www.jetairways.com).

Other international airports are: Ahmadabad, with flights to and from the UK and the US as well as the Gulf region; Thiruvananthapuram, with flights to and from the Gulf region, the Maldives and Sri Lanka; Hyderabad, with fewer flights to and from the Gulf region; and Dabolin (Goa), with charter flights from Europe.

Agra, Varanasi, Kanpur, Patna, Kozhikode, Kochi and Bangalore are airports with limited international air access and customs and immigration facilities, and are not international airports in the real sense of the term. Agra serves charter flights from the UK. Varanasi, Kanpur and Patna have daily flights from Kathmandu in Nepal and there are connecting flights to Delhi. Kozhikode and Kochi have flights to and from the Gulf region.

Discounts are often available during the off-peak season, so it is worth making enquiries. Many long-haul flights arrive between midnight and 6am.

Once you have bought a ticket, check with the airline to confirm your booking well in advance. **NB**: It is advisable to check in for flights to and from India as early as possible, as planes are often overbooked.

The four major airports – Delhi, Mumbai, Kolkata and Chennai – are constantly improving and all have left-luggage facilities, porters and

Maps

Obtaining good maps of India can be difficult; the government forbids the sale of detailed maps in border areas, which includes the entire coastline, for security reasons; those which can be bought may not be exported.

Some good maps to bring along with you are: Bartholomew's 1:4,000,000 map of South Asia; Lascelles map of the same scale and Nelles Verlag maps.

Tourist offices can supply visitors with larger-scale city maps. The most detailed are held by the Survey of India, Janpath Barracks A, New Delhi 110 001.

Other highly recommended maps are the Eicher series of detailed city maps, including those of Delhi, Chennai and Bangalore, and their India Road Atlas.

Many of these maps are available from www.indiamapstore.com.

licensed taxis, as well as duty-free shops in both the arrival and departure halls.

Airport banks are open 24 hours for currency exchange.

International airport contacts

IGI (New Delhi)
Airport Manager, tel: 011-2569 6179
Terminal 1A, tel: 011-2569 6150
Terminal 1B, tel: 011-2567 5315
International Airport Mumbai
Airport Manager, tel: 022-2838 7046
Terminal 1A, tel: 022-2615 6400
Terminal 1B, tel: 022-2615 6500
International Airport Kolkata
Airport Manager, tel: 033-2232 0501
International Airport Chennai
Airport Manager, tel: 044-2552 9172

Cut Your Carbon

Air travel produces a huge amount of carbon dioxide and is one of the main contributors to global warming. Where possible, take the train while in the country *(see page 334)* as this produces less CO₂. Although nothing can repair the immediate damage of your flight out, it is possible to offset your "carbon load" by, for example, having trees planted as a "carbon sink". A number of organisations can do this for you and many have online "carbon calculators" which tell you how much you need to donate. In the UK, travellers can try www.climatecare.org or www.carbonneutral.com, in the US, log on to www.climatefriendly.com or www.sustainabletravelinternational.com

By Sea

A few cruise ships do call in at Cochin and Mumbai, but India is not a regular cruise destination. Some freighters offer passage to India, with excellent accommodation. Great Eastern Shipping (www.greatship.com), Lloyd Triestino (www.lloydtriestino.it) and the Shipping Corporation of India (www.shipindia.com) have sailings to Mumbai, Kolkata and Chennai.

Overland

It is theoretically possible to take the train from the UK to India. The Eurostar takes you from London to Paris, from there you can get to Istanbul via Vienna and Sofia. A train leaves once a week from Istanbul to Tehran, from where you can make your way to the Pakistani border at Quetta (the line between Kerman and Zahedan on the Iranian side is nearing completion, thus adding the last section of track between Europe and South Asia).

Land services have now resumed between India and Pakistan. The train from Lahore in Pakistan to Delhi in India crosses the Wagah-Attari border. The Samjhota Express to Delhi via Amritsar leaves Lahore at 11am (check in 8am) on Mon and Thurs. There is also a direct bus from Lahore to Delhi leaving at 6am from outside Faletti's Hotel on Egerton Road Tues–Wed, Fri and Sat. The trip takes about seven hours and the fare includes all your food. The new bus between Muzaffarabad and Srinigar is for Kashmiris only. A second rail link with Pakistan reopened in 2006 after a gap of four decades. It now connects the towns of Munabao in Rajasthan to Khokrapar in Pakistan's Sindh province.

The border with Nepal is only open for non-Indian or Nepalese nationals at Birganj/Raxhal, Bairwa and Kakarbitta/Naxalbari.

Indian Embassies

Australia: High Commission of India, 3–5 Moonah Place, Yarralumla, Canberra ACT-2600, tel: 616-273 3774/273 3999; fax: 616-273 3328/273 1308; www.highcommissionofindiaaustralia.org
Canada: High Commission of India, 10 Springfield Road, Ottawa, Ontario KLM 1 C9, tel: 613-744 3751–3; fax: 613-744 0913; www.hciottawa.ca
Great Britain: High Commission of India, India House, Aldwych, London

WC2B 4NA, tel: 0891-880 800 (24-hours recorded visa information); 020-7836 0990 (specific visa enquiries); 020-7836-8484 (general); www.hcilondon.org
US: Embassy of India, 2107 Massachusetts Avenue NW, Washington DC 20008, tel: 202-939 7000; fax: 202-939 7027; www.indianembassy.org

Money

All exchange of foreign currency used to have to be recorded on a currency declaration form, or receipts kept as proof of legal conversion. The laws have eased, but some businesses and hotels may still insist. Visitors staying more than 180 days will have to produce proof of encashment of exchange of currency for income tax exemption and show they have been self-supporting.

Indian currency is based on the decimal system, with 100 paise to the rupee. Coins are in denominations of 1, 2, 5, 10, 20, 25 and 50 paise. Notes are in 10, 20, 50, 100 and 500 rupee denominations. Indian rupees may not be brought in nor taken out of the country. Exchange rates fluctuate against other currencies.

Credit cards are increasingly accepted by hotels, restaurants, large shops, tourist emporia and airlines. It is preferable to have a well-known card such as American Express, Access/MasterCard or Visa. A number of banks will issue rupees against a Visa card, and Amex issues rupees to cardholders against a cheque at their offices. More conveniently, ATMs that issue cash against a variety of cards are found in many places. The ATMs of local banks may only issue cash against their own cards so try and find a machine on an international bank. Traveller's cheques are not worth the hassle.

What to Bring

Clothing

Travelling in southern India, or the North during summer, it is best to wear cotton. Avoid synthetics. In the North during winter, sweaters and jackets are required. Cotton shirts, blouses and skirts are inexpensive and easily available throughout the country. Remember to bring underwear (especially bras) and swimwear.

In winter a sweater – preferably two, one light and one heavy – as well as a jacket or an anorak are necessary, especially in the North where daily temperature differentials can be quite wide. Lighter clothing would be adequate in the South and along the coast. Comfortable footwear, trainers for winter and sandals for summer, is essential. "Trekking" sandals are excellent for wearing in India as they are tough and provide good protection to your feet. Teva and Reef are good brands to look out for.

For their own convenience, women should not wear sleeveless blouses, mini skirts and short, revealing dresses. Cover up – it's a good idea in the Indian sun anyway – locally available *shalwar kamiz* (also known as *churidar*), a long tunic top worn over loose trousers, are ideal.

Film

Colour print film, developing and digital printing facilities are available in all big cities. Colour slide film can only be found in major cities and it may be safer to bring your own.

There are few places offering prompt and reliable camera servicing, so photographic equipment should be checked before the trip. Protect your camera and film from excessive exposure to heat, dust and humidity.

There are strict restrictions on photography of military installations, bridges and dams, airports, border areas and Adivasi/restricted areas.

Other Essentials

If travelling away from the major cities or big hotels, take a sheet sleeping bag, pillowcases and medical kit among other items. Sun cream and sun block (vital in the mountains) are not readily available so they should be brought with you, along with cosmetics and tampons. A hat or scarf to cover your head is a sensible item. A mosquito net and a basin/bath plug are also useful in smaller hotels, which often do not have them.

It is always advisable to obtain good travel insurance to cover the worst possible scenario. Take a copy of your policy and keep it separately as a safeguard.

Restricted & Protected Areas

The country is generally open to tourism, apart from sensitive border regions (essentially those with China and Pakistan) certain areas of the Northeast and some of the islands.
Andaman and Nicobar Islands
Individual tourists may visit the following areas: Port Blair, Havelock Islands, Long Island, Neil Island, Jooly Buoy, South and North Cinque, Red Skin Island, and the entire island of Middle Andaman (excluding the

reserves). All islands in the Mahatma Gandhi Marine National Park except Boat, Holoday, Twin Islands and Pluto Islands need special permission from the Union Territory Administration. The following places may only be visited for the day: Mount Harriet, Mayabunder, Diglipur, Rangat, Ross Island, Brother Island, Sister Island, Barren Island.
Arunachal Pradesh Itanagar, Ziro, Along, Passighat, Deporijo Miao, Namdapha, Tipi Sejusa (Puki), Bhalukpong, Bomdilla-Tawang are open to tourists, as are the following trekking routes:
Passighat–Jengging–Yingkiong; Bhalukpong–Bomdilla–Tawang; Roing–Mayodila–Anini; Tezu–Hayuling. Individual tourists are not allowed. Tourist groups must travel on identified tour circuits only. Maximum period of stay is 10 days.
Lakshadweep Only Agatti, Bangaram and Kadmat are open to foreign tourists. Kavaratti may be used for transiting.
Manipur Foreigners are permitted to visit the following areas for a maximum of 6 days only in a group of four or more: Loktak Lake, Imphal, Moirang INA Memorial, Keibul Lamjao

Deer Sanctuary, Waithak Lake, Khongjom War Memorial.
Mizoram Vairangre, Thingdawl, Aizawl are open to tourists. Individual tourists are not allowed and groups must travel on identified tour circuits. Maximum period of stay is 10 days.
Nagaland Kohima, Mon, Phek, Tuensang, Zunheboto may be visited by individual tourists. A 10-day permit, which may be extended, is needed.
Sikkim Gangtok, Rumtek, Phodong, Pemayangtse Khecepen and Tashiding are open. A permit is needed for Zongri (West Sikkim), Tsangu (East Sikkim), Mangan, Tong, Singhik, Chungthang, Lachung and Yumthang.

Tourist Information

The Ministry of Tourism has a good website (www.tourismofindia.com or www.incredibleindia.org) with a lot of useful information on obtaining visas, places to visit and tour operators.

Indian Government Tourist Offices abroad

Australia: Level 2 Piccadilly, 210 Pitt Street, Sydney, New South Wales 2000, tel: (02) 9264 4855; fax: (02) 9264 4860.

State Tourism Websites

Andaman and Nicobar Islands
http://tourism.andaman.nic.in
Andhra Pradesh
www.aptourism.com
Arunachal Pradesh
www.arunachaltourism.com
Assam
www.assamtourism.org
Bihar
http://bihar.nic.in
Chandigarh
www.citco.nic.in
Chattisgarh
http://cgtourism.nic.in
Daman and Diu
http://daman.nic.in
Delhi
http://delhitourism.nic.in
Goa
www.goa-tourism.org
Gujarat
www.gujarattourism.com
Haryana
http://htc.nic.in
Himachal Pradesh
http://himachaltourism.nic.in
Jammu and Kashmir
www.jktourism.org
Jharkhand
http://jharkhand.nic.in
Karnataka
http://kstdc.nic.in
Kerala
www.keralatourism.org

Lakshadweep
http://lakshadweep.nic.in
Madhya Pradesh
www.mptourism.com
Maharashtra
www.mtdcindia.com
Manipur
http://manipur.nic.in
Meghalaya
www.meghalayatourism.com
Mizoram
http://mizoram.nic.in
Nagaland
www.nagalandtourism.com
Orissa
www.orissa-tourism.com
Pondicherry
www.tourisminpondicherry.com
Punjab
http://punjabgovt.nic.in
Rajasthan
www.rajasthantourism.gov.in
Sikkim
http://sikkim.nic.in
Tamil Nadu
www.tamilnadutourism.org
Tripura
http://tripura.nic.in
Uttar Pradesh
www.up-tourism.com
Uttaranchal
www.uttaranchaltourism.gov.in
West Bengal
www.wbtourism.com

Canada: 60 Bloor Street West, Suite 1003, Toronto, Ontario M4 N3 N6, tel: (416) 962 3787–8; fax: (416) 962 6279.
Great Britain: 7 Cork Street, London W1X 2AB, tel: (020) 8812 0929 (24-hour tourist information); (020) 7437 3677 (general); fax: (020) 7494 1048.
US: 1270 Avenue of America, Suite 1808, New York 10020, tel: (212) 586 4901–3; fax: (212) 582 3274.

Local Tourist Offices

Below is a list of government tourist offices in the major cities:
Agra 191 The Mall
Tel: 222 6368
Ahmadabad H.K. House, Ashram Road
Tel: 2658 9172
Aurangabad Krishna Vilas, Station Road
Tel: 233 1217
Bangalore K.F.C. Building, 48 Church Street
Tel: 2558 5417
Bhubaneshwar B-21 B.J.B. Nagar
Tel: 243 2203
Chennai 154 Anna Salai
Tel: 2846 1459
Fax: 2846 0193
Delhi 88 Janpath
Tel: 2332 0008
Fax: 2332 0109
Domestic Airport
Tel: 2567 5296
International Airport
Tel: 2569 1171
Guwahati G.L.P. Complex, G.S. Road
Tel: 254 7407
Hyderabad/Secunderabad
30-60-140, 2nd Floor Netaji Bhawan, Liberty Road
Tel: 2326 1360
Fax: 2326 1362
Jaipur State Hotel, Khasa Kothi
Tel/fax: 237 2200
Kochi/Ernakulam Willingdon Island, Kochi
Tel: 266 8352
Kolkata 4 Shakespeare Sarani
Tel: 2282 1402
Fax: 2282 3521
Domestic Airport
Tel: 2511 8299
Lucknow P3 Nawal Kishore Road, Chitrahar Building
Tel: 2228 349
Fax: 2221 776
Mumbai 123 Maharishi Karve Marg, opposite Churchgate
Tel: 2203 3144
Fax: 2201 4496
Domestic Airport
Tel: 2615 6920
International Airport
Tel: 2832 5331
Panaji Communidade Building, Church Square

Tel: 222 3412
Patna Sudama Palace, Kankar Bagh Road
Tel/fax: 234 5776
Port Blair VIP Road, Junglighat P.O.
Tel/fax: 233 006
Thiruvananthapuram ParkView
Tel: 232 2517
Airport
Tel: 245 1498
Varanasi 15b The Mall
Tel: 250 1784

Vaccinations

No inoculations are legally required to enter India, but it is strongly advised that you get vaccinations against typhoid (Typhim Vi gives protection for 3 years), hepatitis A (Havrix gives immunity for 1 year, up to 10 years if a 6-month booster is given), polio (a booster is needed every 5 years) and tetanus (booster injection every 10 years). You may need to show proof of a yellow fever inoculation if arriving from an infected area. Other diseases against which vaccinations might be considered, particularly for longer trips, include meningitis, rabies and Japanese B encephalitis. There is no vacccination against Dengue fever, occasionally contracted in India. The only protection is to avoid being bitten *(see also Malaria, under Health)*.

Practical Info

Children

Indians love children and are very tolerant of them, making India a very easy place to travel. Children will find the sights and sounds just as rewarding as adults. The problem is that children can be more easily affected by the heat, unsafe drinking water and unfamiliar food seasoned with chillies and spices. In case of diarrhoea, rehydration salts are vital. Keep the child away from stray animals, especially dogs and monkeys. To avoid the risk of rabies, children should have an anti-rabies vaccine. For infants, it is difficult to find nappies and places to change them. Consider bringing a supply of disposables, or changing to washables. A changing mat is essential, as is a familiar brand of powdered milk. For touring, walking and hiking, a child-carrier backpack is well worth its weight.

Disabled Travellers

Although disability is common in India, there are very few provisions for wheelchairs and special toilets. The roads are full of potholes, and kerbs are often high and without ramps. It may be hard to negotiate street obstacles, beggars, or steep staircases. On the other hand, Indians will always be willing to help you in and out of buses or cars, or up stairs. Taxis and rickshaws are cheap and the driver, with a little tip, will probably help. You could employ a guide to help with obstacles. Another option is to go with a paid companion. In the UK, **Holiday Care**, 7th Floor, Sunley House, 4 Bedford Park, Croydon, Surrey CR0 2AP (tel: 0845-124 9974; www.holidaycare.org.uk), can put you in touch with someone.

Some package holiday operators cater for travellers with disabilities, but ensure that your needs have been understood before making a booking.

Emergencies

Generally speaking, India is a safe place to travel, but a tourist is a natural target for thieves and pick-pockets, so take the usual precautions and keep money, credit cards, valuables and passport in a money belt or pouch well secured with a cord around your neck. A protective hand over this in a crowded place could save you a lot of heartache and hassle.

Do not leave belongings unattended, especially on a beach. Invest in good strong locks (available in India) for your bags. Chaining luggage to the berth on a train, or to your seat on a bus, is a precaution that travelling Indians often take. Watch your luggage, especially during loading and unloading.

Credit card frauds do exist so make sure that shops and restaurants process your card in front of you.

Another sensible precaution is to keep a photocopy of your passport and visa, traveller's cheque numbers and receipts, ticket details, insurance policy number and telephone claims number, and some emergency money in a bag or case separate from your other cash and documents. If you are robbed, report the incident immediately to a police station (be patient, this can take hours).

Gay & Lesbian Travellers

Homosexuality is still a taboo subject for many Indians. Sexual relations between men are punishable with long prison sentences and cruising in public could come under public disorder laws. There is no similar law against lesbians. While general attitudes are discriminatory, things are changing slowly, and at least the issue of gay

and lesbian rights is starting to be discussed, due in no small part to Deepa Mehta's 1998 film *Fire*, which depicted an affair between two married women, and the 2004 film *Girlfriend*. Attacks on cinemas by the religious right brought counter demonstations onto the streets of major cities. However, gay and lesbian travellers should be discreet and avoid any public displays of affection (as should heterosexual couples). On the plus side, hotels will think nothing of two men or women sharing a room.

The male sites http://webbingoyotoms.com/humsafar and www.gaybombay.org have useful information and links. For women, there is **Sangini** (www.sanginii.org), who campaign for lesbian and women's rights.

Health

Medical supplies
Bring along a personal medical kit to take care of minor ailments. This should include anti-diarrhoea medication, a broad spectrum antibiotic, aspirin, clean needles, and something for throat infections and allergies would be a good idea. Take your regular medications, tampons, contraceptives and condoms, as these may be difficult to find in shops.

Also include plasters, antiseptic cream and water purification tablets. All cuts, however minor, should be cleaned and sterilised immediately to prevent infection. Locally available oral rehydration powders (such as Vijay Electrolyte) containing salts and dextrose are an ideal additive to water, especially when travelling in the

summer months or when suffering from diarrhoea. If oral rehydration salts are not available then one teaspoon each of salt and sugar in 500 ml of water is a useful substitute.

Malaria
This moquito-borne disease is very serious and potentially fatal. There are two common strains in India, *P. falciparum* and *P. vivax*, both carried by the Anopheles mosquito. Symptoms are similar to acute flu (including some or all of fever, shivering, diarrhoea and muscle pains) and an outbreak may come on as much as a year after visiting a malarial area. If malaria is suspected then medical attention should be sought as soon as possible.

Prophylaxis is essential for all areas except those above 2,500m (8,200 ft). The usual anti-malarial protection for India consists of a combination of daily proguanil (Paludrine) and weekly chloroquine (Avoclar, Nivaquin). These are now bought across the counter in the UK, and your pharmacist will advise you on the correct dosages (usually 200mg of proguanil daily and 300mg of chloroquin weekly). This is at present the only safe prophylaxis during pregnancy. However, the combination is at best 70% effective and medical advice may change soon. An alternative drug is mefloquine (Lariam), taken weekly. However, this should not be taken by people with a history of epilepsy or mental illness and there has been much anecdotal evidence of long-lasting and serious side effects (although medical evidence suggests that these are no more likely than with the proguanil/chloroquin combination).

High Commissions, Embassies and Consulates

Chennai
British Deputy High Commissioner, 24 Anderson Road
Tel: 2827 3136–7
Fax: 2826 9004
Consulate of Canada, Chamber 2, Business Centre, The Residency Towers, Thyagaraja Road
Tel: 2815 1445
Fax: 2815 7029

Delhi
Australian High Commission, 1-50G Shantipath, Chanakyapuri, New Delhi (P.O. Box 5210)
Tel: 5139 9900
Fax: 5149 4491
www.ausgovindia.com
British High Commission, Shantipath, Chanakyapuri, New Delhi
Tel: 2687 2161 (24 hrs)
Fax: 2687 0065
www.ukinindia.com

Canadian High Commission, 7–8 Shantipath, Chanakyapuri, New Delhi (P.O. Box 5207)
Tel: 2687 6500
www.dfait-maeci.gc.ca
Irish Embassy, 13 Jor Bagh
Tel: 2462 6714
www.irelandinindia.com
New Zealand High Commission, 50N Nyaya Marg, Chanyakapuri, New Delhi
Tel: 2688 3170
www.nzembassy.com
US Embassy, Shantipath, Chanakyapuri, New Delhi
Tel: 2419 8000
Fax: 2419 0017
http://newdelhi.usembassy.gov

Kolkata
Consulate of Canada, c/o R.P.G. Enterprises, Duncan House, 31 Netaji Subhas Road
Tel: 2242 6820/2242 6821

British Deputy High Commissioner, 1 Ho Chi Minh Sarani
Tel: 2288 5172–5
US Consulate General, 5-1 Ho Chi Minh Sarani
Tel: 2242 3611–5/2242 2336–7

Mumbai
Australian Consulate-General, 6th Floor, Maker Towers E, Cuffe Parade, Colaba
Tel: 2218 1071/2218 1072
Consulate of Canada, 41–2 Maker Chamber VI, Jamnalal Bajaj Marg, 220 Nariman Point
Tel: 2287 6027–30/2287 5479
British Deputy High Commissioner, Maker Chambers IV, 2nd floor, 222 Jamnalal Bajaj Marg, Nariman Point
Tel: 2283 0517/2283 2330
US Consulate General, Lincoln House, 78 Bhulabhai Desai Road
Tel: 2363 3611–8
Fax: 2363 0350

In the UK mefloquine is only available as a private prescription.

A newly approved drug is the atavoquone-proguanil combination marketed as Malarone. This is recommended for areas of chloroquine resistance (such as Assam) and is taken once a day. It is expensive and at present only some UK health authorities offer it as an NHS prescription. Other drug regimes are not effective against both strains of the disease.

The best, and only certain, protection against malaria is not to get bitten. Sleep under a mosquito net impreganted with permethrin, cover up in the evenings and use an effective insect repellent such as DEET (diethyltoluamide). Burning mosquito coils, which are easily obtainable in India, is also a good idea.

Fungal infections

Prickly heat is a common complaint caused by excessive perspiration. Try to keep the skin dry by using talcum powder and wearing loose-fitting cotton clothes. Fungal infections are also common, especially during the monsoon, and can be treated by exposure to the sun and/or by the application of Canesten cream.

Diarrhoeas

● **Traveller's diarrhoea** is usually caused by low-level food poisoning and can be avoided with a little care. When you arrive, rest on your first day and only eat simple food; well-cooked vegetarian dishes, a South Indian *thali* and peeled fruits are perhaps best. An upset stomach is often caused by eating too many rich Indian meat dishes (usually cooked with vast amounts of oil and spices) and failing to rest and let your body acclimatise.

Drink plenty of fluids but never drink unboiled or unfiltered water. When in doubt, stick to soda, mineral water, or aerated drinks of standard brands. Avoid ice as this is often made with unboiled water. All food should be cooked and eaten hot. Don't eat salads and always peel fruit.

With all cases of diarrhoea, including dysentery and giardia described below, it is not a good idea to use imobilising drugs such as loperamide (Imodium) and atropine (Lomotil) as they prevent the body ridding itself of infection. These should only be used if you have to travel. The most important thing to do in cases of diarrhoea and/or vomiting is to rehydrate, preferably using oral rehydration salts.

● **Dysentery and giardia** are more serious forms of stomach infection and should be suspected if the diarrhoea lasts for more than 2 days.

Dysentery is characterised by diarrhoea accompanied by the presence of mucus and blood in faeces. Other symptoms include severe stomach cramps and vomiting. Bacillic dysentery comes on quickly and is usually accompanied by fever. It may clear up by itself but its usual treatment is with 500mg of ciprofloxacin or tetracycline twice daily for 5 days. Do not take the powerful antibiotic chloramphenicol as it can have dangerous side effects. Amoebic dysentery has a slower onset and will not clear up on its own. If you suspect you have amoebic dysentery you should seek medical help as it can damage the gut. If this is not available then self-treat with 400mg of metronidazole (Flagyl) three times daily with food for 7 days. You must not drink alchohol when taking metronidazole.

Giardia is a similar infection caused by a parasite. Like amoebic dysentery it comes on slowly and its symptoms include loose and foul-smelling diarrhoea, feeling bloated and nauseous, and stomach cramps. Giardia will not clear up on its own and will recur; its treatment is the same as for amoebic dysentery.

Altitude sickness

This can occur above 2,500 metres. Watch for symptoms of breathlessness, palpitations, headache, insomnia and loss of appetite. With total rest, travellers usually acclimatise within 48 hours. It is important that fluid intake is maintained; at least four to six litres per day is recommended.

Inhaling a few breaths from an oxygen cannister can provide immediate relief in a mild attack. A severe attack, brought on by climbing too high or quickly is marked by dizziness, nausea, vomiting, convulsions, severe thirst, blurred vision, drowsiness, weakness, or hearing difficulties.

The only cure is to descend to a lower altitude at once. Lung damage from lack of oxygen can be permanent if untreated. Allow several days to acclimatise before attempting to reascend in easy stages. In acute cases, as well as immediate descent, it may be useful to give the additional treatment of 250mg of actazolamide twice a day for three days.

A previous trip with no symptoms does not mean that a traveller is immune to altitude sickness. It can strike anyone and being fit does not prevent the problem.

Two other, extremely serious and potentially fatal, conditions can occur at high altitude, primarily to mountaineers: pulmonary oedema and cerebral oedema. The first is the filling of the lungs with fluid (symptoms include coughing up frothy fluid, irrational behaviour and fatigue), the *only* cure and treatment is to descend *immediately*. The second is a swelling of the brain (symptoms here include headache, hallucinations and disorientation, eventually resulting in coma); immediate descent is essential to prevent death. To reduce the swelling it is also possible to give 4mg dexamethasone three times per day, although this is a powerful drug and should only be given with medical supervision or in an emergency.

Sun exposure

The dangers of sunburn are now well-publicised. Cover up and use a high factor sunscreen, even if it is cloudy. The power of the sun is obvious on the plains and in tropical India, but also be careful in the mountains, where thinner air makes the sun very powerful, even if it feels cooler. Overexposure can also lead to the two conditions below:

● **Heat exhaustion** is common, and indicated by shallow breathing, a rapid pulse, or pallor, and is often accompanied by leg cramps, headache or nausea. The body temperature remains normal. Lying down in a cool place and sipping water mixed with rehydration salts or plain table salt will prevent loss of consciousness.

● **Heatstroke** is more serious, and more likely to occur when it is both hot and humid. Babies and elderly people are especially susceptible. The body temperature soars suddenly and the skin feels dry. The victim may feel confused, then pass out.

Take them quickly to a cool room, remove their clothes and cover them with a wet sheet or towels soaked in cold water. Call for medical help and fan them constantly until their body temperature drops to 38°C (100°F).

Hospitals

In an emergency your first call should be to **East West Rescue**, 38 Golf Links, New Delhi; tel: 011-2469 8865; www.eastwestrescue.com. They operate over the whole country and have an extremely good reputation. Other hospitals include:

Delhi

All India Institute of Medical Sciences, Ansari Nagar
Tel: 2686 4851
Kripalani Hospital, Panchkuin Road
Tel: 2336 3788
Safdarjang General Hospital, Sri Aurobindo Marg
Tel: 2616 5060

Hyderabad/Secunderabad
General Hospital, Nampally
Tel: 2234 344
Newciti, Secunderabad
Tel: 2780 5961
Kolkata
Birla Heart Research Centre, 1-1
National Library Avenue
Tel: 2479 2980
Medical College Hospital, 88 College
Street
Tel: 2241 1891
Mumbai
Prince Ali Khan Hospital, Nesbit Road
Tel: 2375 4343

Media

The quality, depth and intelligence of comment and news reporting in the Indian media put the Anglophone West to shame. An essential part of India's vibrant political and intellectual life, the press and broadcast media cover a wide political spectrum and have a long and honourable tradition of holding those in power to account. Star, Asia's biggest media company, provides news and entertainment channels.

Newspapers & Magazines
The large number of English-language dailies and hundreds of newspapers in Indian languages provide a wide and critical coverage of national and international events.

Among the better known national English language dailies are the *Times of India*, *The Indian Express*, *The Hindu* (highly recommended, though this tends to concentrate on the South) and *The Hindustan Times* (all available on-line). All dailies have Sunday editions. The main newspapers in Delhi are the *Asian Age* (good for political gossip) and *The Pioneer*, for which both Churchill and Kipling used to write.

The top news magazines include *India Today*, *Outlook* and the exemplary *Frontline* (also on-line). There are also excellent general-interest magazines such as *Sanctuary* (specialising in South Asian natural history), and travel magazines like *Outlook Traveller* and *India Today Travel Plus* give current information on local cultural events.

International newspapers and magazines are available in Mumbai and Delhi within 24 hours.

There are several glossy magazines in English, including *Society*, many film magazines and city magazines such as *First City*, *Delhi Diary* and *Hallo! Madras*, plus women's magazines such as *Femina*, and Indian editions of *Cosmopolitan* and *Elle*.

Public Holidays

There are many festivals in India, but only a few of these are full public holidays:

● **26 January**: Republic Day.
● **15 August**: Independence Day.
● **2 October**: Mahatma Gandhi's Birthday.
● **25 December**: Christmas Day.

See also *Festivals, page 109*.

Television & Radio Stations
Doordarshan is the government TV company and broadcasts programmes in English, Hindi and regional languages. Local timings vary, but generally the news in English can be heard daily at 7.50am and 9.30pm.

Satellite television is available almost everywhere, including the Star TV's network incorporating the BBC World Service and MTV. NDTV is a local 24-hour news channel that provides good coverage of Indian news and politics. Other stations include Channel V (a local youth-orientated music channel) and Zee TV (Hindi). There are more than 300 channels broadcasting across the nation, some showing sport, American soaps and sitcoms and English-language movies. Up to 90 channels can be picked up in the main cities, half of them free.

All India Radio (AIR) broadcasts on the short-wave, medium-wave and in Delhi, Mumbai and Chennai on FM (VHF). The frequencies vary, so check with your hotel.

Opening Hours

Government offices
Officially 9.30am–6pm Monday to Friday, but most business is done between 10am and 5pm with a long lunch break.

Post Offices
Open from 10am–4.30pm Monday to Friday, and until 12 noon on Saturday. However, in most of the larger cities, the Central Post Office is open until 6.30pm on weekdays, 4.30pm on Saturday. On Sunday some open until noon. Major telegraph offices are open 24 hours.

Shops
Open from 10am–7pm. Some shops close for lunch. Although Sunday is an official holiday, different localities in major cities have staggered days off so that there are always some shopping areas open.

Restaurants
Usually open until 11pm. A few nightclubs and discoteques close very much later. Hotel coffee shops are often open around the clock.

Banks
Opening hours are Mon–Fri 10am–2pm and Sat 10am–noon for most foreign banks and nationalised Indian banks (of which the State Bank is the largest). Some banks operate evening branches, while others remain open on Sunday and close on another day of the week, and some open 9am–1pm. In larger cities many banks now have 24-hour ATMs, often guarded, which are very convenient and safe. All banks are closed on national holidays, on 30 June and 31 December for balancing the books. Most businesses close on public holidays.

Postal Services

The internal mail service is efficient in most areas. It is advisable to affix stamps to letters or postcards yourself and hand them over to the post office counter for immediate franking rather than to post them in a letterbox. Indian stamps do not stick very well so make sure you use the pot of "gum" (glue) that is almost always available.

Sending a registered parcel overseas is a complicated and time-consuming process. Most parcels should be stitched into cheap cotton cloth and then sealed (there are people outside major post offices offering this service). Two customs forms need to be completed. Once the parcel has been weighed and stamps affixed, make sure it is franked and a receipt of registration is issued. Important or valuable material should be registered.

Many shops offer to dispatch goods, but not all of them are reliable. It is usually only safe when handled by a government-run emporium.

Generally poste restante works well, but make sure your name is clearly written. Most towns have only one main post office but there is often confusion between Delhi and New Delhi. New Delhi's main post office is near Connaught Circus while Delhi's main post office is between the Red Fort and Kashmir Gate in Old Delhi.

Courier services
The main international courier firms have agency agreements with Indian companies. DHL, Skypak and IML work under their own brand names while Federal Express operates as Blue Dart. These firms have offices in the major towns and operate international and extensive domestic networks.

Note: The government's Speedpost service delivers quickly at a similar price.

Religious Services

There are few towns in India that are without a church, mosque, or Hindu temple. There are Sikh *gurdwaras* in major towns; a number of synagogues in Mumbai, two in Calcutta and one each in New Delhi and Puné. Your hotel can supply information on the religious institution you are seeking.

Repairs and Tailors

Traditionally, India's use of resources is very efficient, reflected in the way almost everything can be recycled and/or repaired. Since travelling around India can be hard on your shoes, baggage and clothes, this is very useful. Chappal-wallahs, shoe repairers, can be found everywhere, usually sitting by the side of the road with their tools in a wooden box. For an embarassingly small charge, they will be able to glue, nail or stitch almost any pair of shoes or sandals back into shape. (A somewhat less helpful service is offered by the shoeshine boys around Connaught Place in New Delhi. They can throw a dollop of excrement onto your shoe without you noticing, and will then offer to clean it off for an exorbitant fee.)

Indian tailors are very skilful and can run up a set of clothes quickly. Although they can do fair copies of Western fashions, they are, obviously, much better at stitching *sari* blouses or *shalwar kamiz*. The process of buying fabric is one of the great pleasures of visiting India, and if you

Women Travellers

"Eve-teasing" is the Indian euphemism for sexual harassment. Take the normal precautions, especially on crowded local public transport (crowds are a haven for gropers). Do not wear clothes that expose legs, arms and cleavage; *shalwar kamiz* are ideal, and a shawl is handy to use as a cover-all when required.

More serious sexual assaults on tourists are rare and tend to occur in popular tourist areas such as Rajasthan, Goa and Benaras but in case something should happen, call for help from passers-by.

On the up-side, there are "ladies-only" queues at train and bus stations, and "ladies-only" waiting rooms at stations and compartments on trains.

want it made up, most shops will be able to recommend a good tailor.

Tailors will also be able to repair your existing clothes, even badly torn ones, and can stitch up rucksacks which are on the point of collapse.

Telephones

India's telephone system is steadily improving and international calls can now be dialled direct to most parts of the world or booked through the operator. Calling from hotels can be extremely expensive, with surcharges up to 300 percent, so check rates first. Mobile telephones are widely used in India and your own phone may well work while you are there. If not you can buy local SIM cards for use in India.

Privately run telephone services with international direct-dialling facilities are very widespread. Advertising themselves with the acronyms STD/ISD (standard trunk dialling/international subscriber dialling), they are quick and easy to use. Some stay open 24 hours a day. Both national and international calls are dialled direct. To call abroad, dial the international access code (00), the code for the country you want (44 for the UK, 1 for the US or Canada), the area code (without any initial zeros), and the number. Some booths have an electronic screen that keeps time and calculates cost during the call. Prices are similar to those at official telecommunications centres.

NB. Indian telephone numbers are now all 10 digits long (including the area code minus the initial zero). The vast majority of numbers now start with a "2", if you encounter an old-style number (i.e. eight digits long) add a "2" to the beginning and it should work.

Home country direct services are now available from any telephone to the UK, US, Canada, Australia, New Zealand and a number of other countries. These allow you to make a reverse-charges or telephone credit card call to that country via the operator there. If you cannot find a telephone with home country direct buttons, you can use any phone toll-free by dialling 000, your country code and 17 (except Canada, which is 000-167). US international access codes are: MCI 000 127; Sprint 000 137; and AT&T 000 117.

Many privately run telephone services have fax machines and most large hotels have a fax.

E-mail and the internet are very popular and widely available. All large cities, and many smaller places, have internet cafés or similar places where you can surf the net or send e-mails. Charges are usually by the minute or hour, and are usually around 60 Rs

per hour. Two companies, Reliance and Sify, have uniform cyber cafés in most major cities where your membership is accepted.

Tipping

There is no harm expressing your appreciation with a small tip. Depending on services rendered and the type of establishment, this could range from Rs2–Rs10. In restaurants, the tip is customarily 10–15 percent of the bill. Leading hotels add a 10 percent service surcharge and tipping in such places is optional.

Although tipping taxis and three-wheelers is not an established norm, it does not go amiss. Here again, 10 percent of the fare or leaving the change, if not substantial, would be adequate. Porters at railway stations would expect around Rs2 a bag. At airports, a rupee per bag in addition to the fee charged by the airport authority would be welcome.

If you have been a house guest, check with your host whether you may tip his domestic helpers (for instance, the driver or cook) before doing so.

Water

Many water supplies in India are contaminated and are a common source of disease for travellers who have no immunity to water-borne bacteria such as giardia. Bottled water is available. However, there is no guarantee that this is safe and it is extremely bad for the environment (India is accumulating an enormous plastic bottle mountain). It is much better to carry your own water bottle (those made by the Swiss firm Sigg are very tough and hygienic) and fill it from safe water sources (the best is boiled water). This is not always available and portable water filters are an excellent solution. Those made by Katadyn (www.katadyn.com) are considered the best.

Begging

Visitors to India will encounter people asking for alms, especially in the cities, around holy shrines and on railway journeys. Many of them are physically disabled and they have few other options for survival. Small amounts of money (one or two rupees) will be gratefully received and will generally be helping someone out. Try to give discreetly or you might attract unwanted attention.

If you are unsure about whether to give or not, it is fine simply to follow what other people who are around you are doing.

Getting Around

Air Travel

Low-cost domestic airlines are a relatively new idea in India, but they are taking off at a great rate, and domestic air travel is expected to grow at 20 percent a year until 2010.

Indian Airlines (http://indian-airlincs.nic.in), not to be confused with the international carrier Air India, has one of the world's largest domestic networks. Tickets can be booked online. For travel during the peak season (September–March), try and make reservations in advance as flights are usually heavily booked.

With time-consuming check-in and security procedures, you must be at the airport an hour before departure time. Coach services from some city terminals are available. In-flight service is adequate. Alcohol is only available on international flights.

Indian Airlines has a good safety record. Its fares are often lower than those charged for comparable distances elsewhere. The baggage allowance per adult is 20kg and 30kg in business class.

Cancellation charges on tickets purchased locally are extremely high, but none are applicable for domestic sectors issued on international tickets.

The Discover India fare valid for 21 days of travel all over the country and the Tour India Scheme valid for 14 days and limited to six flight coupons are both particulary attractive. These tickets must be purchased abroad, or paid for in India using foreign currency. For details, contact your travel agent or an Air India office abroad, or write to: Traffic Manager, Indian Airlines House, Parliament Street, New Delhi.

Air India (www.airindia.com) carries domestic passengers on its linking flights between Mumbai and Delhi, Kolkata, Chennai and Bangalore. These flights leave from the international terminals in the respective cities.

Budget airlines in the domestic market include Air Deccan (www.airdeccan.net), Jet Airways (www.jetairways.com), which has a particularly good reputation, and Air Sahara (www.airsahara.net), which also flies to Singapore, Kingfisher (www.flykingfisher.com), Spice Jet (www.spicejet.com), Air India Express (www.airindiaexpress.in) and IndiGo (http://book.goindigo.in).

Domestic airline offices

Agra
Indian Airlines
Tel: 236 0948
Fax: 226 3116
Flight information: 230 1180

Ahmadabad
Indian Airlines
Tel: 2550 3061
Jet Airways
Tel: 2754 3304–10
Airport
Tel: 2286 8307/2286 6540

Aurangabad
Indian Airlines
Tel: 2483 392
Fax: 2485 012
Flight information: 2485 421

Bangalore
Indian Airlines, Karnataka State Housing Board Building, Kaveri Bhavan, K.G. Road
Tel: 141
Recorded flight information: 142
Fax: 2227 6334/2527 1234
Jet Airways
Tel: 2227 6620/2555 0856
Airport
Tel: 2526 6898
Air Sahara, Unit G2, Churchgate, 35 Church Street
Tel: 2558 4457/2558 3897
Fax: 2558 4137
Airport
Tel: 2526 2531/2527 0665
Fax: 2526 2531

Bhubaneshwar
Indian Airlines
Tel: 2530 533
Fax: 2530 380
Flight information: 2534 084

Chennai
Indian Airlines, Main Booking Office
Tel: 2855 5200–1
Fax: 2855 5208/2855 3039
Marshalls Road
Tel: 2855 5204
Meenambakkam Airport
Tel: 2234 3131
Jet Airways
City tel: 2855 5353/2620 9622
Airport tel: 2234 0215/2234 6557
Sahara Indian Airlines, 45 Lokesh Towers, 18 Koddambakkam High Road
Tel: 2827 2027/2827 1961
Fax: 2828 3180
Airport:
Tel: 2234 3644/2234 3643
Fax: 2233 0056

Delhi
Indian Airlines, Malhotra Building, F Block, Connaught Place
Tel: 2371 9168/2331 0517
Main Booking Office, Safdarjang Airport (open 24 hours)
Tel: 2462 4332
Reservations tel: 2462 0566/2463 1337
Flight arr/dep tel: 2301 4433
Jet Airways, Jetair House, 13 Community Centre, Yusuf Sarani
Tel: 2652 3345/2685 3700
Fax: 2651 4996
Airport
Tel: 2566 3404
Air Sahara, 14 Kasturba Gandhi Marg
Tel: 2332 6851
Fax: 2566 5362/2566 2312

Guwahati
Indian Airlines
Tel: 2564 420
Fax: 2564 400
Flight information: 2840 401

Hyderabad/Secunderabad
Indian Airlines, Opp. Ravindra Bharti, Saifabad
Tel: 2329 9333
Fax: 2789 6222
Jet Airways
City tel: 2330 1222
Airport tel: 2784 2851

Jaipur
Indian Airlines
Tel: 274 3324
Fax: 274 3407
Flight information: 274 3500
Jet Airways
Tel: 236 0763/237 0594
Airport
Tel: 255 1733
Air Sahara, 203 Shalimar Complex, Opposite Church, M.I. Road
Tel: 237 7637/236 5741
Fax: 236 7808
Airport
Tel: 2553 525

Kochi/Ernakulam
Indian Airlines
Tel: 2352 065
Fax: 2380 131
Flight Information: 2353 826
Jet Airways
Tel: 2369 212/2369 423
Airport
Tel: 2666 509/2668 659

Kolkata
Indian Airlines, Airlines House, 39 Chittranjan Avenue
Tel: 2236 6869
Fax: 2225 6957
Airport (24 hours)
Tel: 2511 9638
Jet Airways
Tel: 2229 0740/2229 2214
Airport
Tel: 2511 6623–4
Air Sahara, 2a Shakespeare Sarani
Tel: 2282 0786/2282 0811
Fax: 2240 7098
Airport
Tel: 2511 9545/2551 8787
Fax: 2511 8442

Lucknow

Indian Airlines, Hotel Clarks
Tel: 222 0927
Fax: 222 6623
Flight information: 243 6132
Jet Airways
Tel: 223 9612–4
Airport
Tel: 243 4009–10
Air Sahara, 7 Kapoorthala Complex,
Sahara Tower, Aliganj
Tel: 232 3126/232 3795
Fax: 237 2742
Airport
Tel: 243 6188
Fax: 243 7771

Mumbai

Indian Airlines, 1st Floor, Air India
Building, Nariman Point
Tel: 2287 6161
Fax: 2283 0832
Airport (24 hours)
Tel: 2611 4433/2611 6633
Jet Airways
Tel: 2285 5788/2283 7570
Airport
Tel: 2615 6666
Reservations
Tel: 2570 3838
Air Sahara, Unit 7, Ground Floor,
Tulsiani Chambers, Nariman Point
Tel: 2283 5671–3/2283 0752–3
Fax: 2287 0076
Airport
Tel: 2611 9375/2611 9402
Fax: 2611 9600

Patna

Indian Airlines
Tel: 222 2554
Fax: 222 7310
Flight info: 222 3199

Port Blair

Indian Airlines
Tel: 230 949
Fax: 231 483

Thiruvananthapuram

Indian Airlines, Mascot Square
Tel: 231 4781
Fax: 231 6271
Jet Airways
Tel: 232 8864/232 1018
Airport
Tel: 250 0710/250 0860

Varanasi

Indian Airlines, Mintt House Motel,
Cantonment
Tel: 234 3746
Fax: 234 8637
Flight information: 234 5959

Boats

Apart from the river ferries there are very few boat services in India. The Andaman Islands are connected to Kolkata, Chennai and Vishakapatnam by boat, as well as to each other. There is a catamaran service between Mumbai and Goa run by Samudra Link Ferries (www.sam-link.com). Kerala has a regular passenger boat system and a number of services operate from Alappuzha and Kollam (formerly Alleppey and Quilon), including the popular backwater trip between the two. There is also a boat service to and from the Lakshadweep islands from Kochi (see http://lakport.nic.in).

Buses

Almost every part of the country is connected by an extensive and well-developed bus system with the railway stations being the natural hubs for both local and regional services. Some of the more rural routes are serviced by noisy dilapidated vehicles, but an increasing number of deluxe and air-conditioned expresses ply the trunk routes.

Many of the trunk routes are now operated by video coaches – if you have never been to an Indian cinema, a night bus journey, for better or (usually) worse, is a highly amplified introduction to the popular variety of Hindi or regional film.

There are many parts of the country where the bus service is the only means of public transport – the Himalayas in particular – and at times may be more convenient (for instance, between Agra and Jaipur).

On many routes, even local ones, reservations can be made. Most baggage is carried on the bus roof, so all bags should be locked and checked on at intermediate stops.

Almost all cities have a bus service; Mumbai's bus service is excellent, the ones in Chennai and Kolkata are not too bad, and the service in Delhi is steadily improving. It is advisable not to use city bus services during rush hour when they become unbearably crowded.

In most cities, however, it is generally preferable to use taxis or three-wheeled "auto-rickshaws".

Regional road transport websites

Most states have a road transport executive responsible for regional bus services. A few have websites *(given below)* with general information and timetables for useful routes.

Andhra Pradesh
www.apsrtc.net
Assam
www.assamtransport.com
Gujarat
www.gujaratsrtc.com
Himachal Pradesh
www.himachal.nic.in/hrtc
Karnataka
www.ksrtc.org
Kerala
www.keralartc.com
Rajasthan
www.rsrtc.org

Tamil Nadu
www.tn.gov.in/transport/stu.htm
Uttar Pradesh
www.upsrtc.com

Cars & Taxis

Chauffeur-driven cars, costing about Rs1,500–2,000 a day, can be arranged through tourist offices, hotels, or travel agents.

Taxis are both air-conditioned and non-air-conditioned (cheaper and sometimes more comfortable). Charges vary, ranging from Rs350 for eight hours and 80 km (50 miles) to Rs500 for an air-conditioned car. For out-of-town travel, there is a per km charge, usually between Rs3–4 per km in the plains (in the hills this rate is often Rs6 per km), with an overnight charge of Rs100. Package tours, sold by travel agencies and hotels, include assistance, guides and hotel accommodation, in addition to taxi charges.

The local yellow-top black taxis are metered, but with constant hikes in fuel prices, charges may often be higher than indicated on the meter. If so, this will be prominently stated in the taxi and the driver will have a card showing the excess over the meter reading that can be legitimately charged.

When taking a taxi or bus into town from the airport, it is advisable to change money in the arrival hall. In Delhi, Mumbai and Bangalore, a system of prepayment for taxis into the city is operated by the traffic police. This saves considerable anguish when the occasional unscrupulous driver takes a long route or tries to overcharge. Elsewhere, enquire at the information desk for the going rate for a journey to your destination before getting into the taxi; and make sure the meter is "down" before you embark. It is alright to share a taxi even if the destination may not be the same (although in the same area). In some cities, for example Mumbai, taxis have fare charts which, when applied to the amount on the meter, give the correct fare. There is often a night surcharge of 10 percent between 11pm and 6am and a rate of Rs1 to Rs2 per piece of baggage.

The fare for three-wheelers is about half that of taxis. Do not forget to ensure that the meter in the three-wheeler is flagged down to the minimum fare.

Driving in India

The best advice to anyone who is thinking about driving in India is, **don't**. Roads can be very congested and dangerous and there are many unwritten rules followed by other drivers. It is far better, and cheaper, to hire a car and driver.

However, if you do have to drive you will need your domestic licence, liability insurance, an international driver's permit and your vehicle's registration papers. Information regarding road conditions can be obtained from national and state automobile associations which periodically issue regional motoring maps, general information regarding roads and detailed route charts.

Contact: the **Automobile Association of Upper India** (AAUI), C-8 Institutional Area, South of IIT, New Delhi - 110016; tel: 11-26965397; www.aaui.org; the **Western India Automobile Association** Lalji Narainji Memorial Building, 76 Vir Nariman Road, Mumbai 400 020, tel: 2204 1085, 2204 7032; www.wiaaindia.com; the **Automobile Association of Eastern India** 13 Promothosh Barna Sarani, Kolkata 700 019, tel: 2475 5131; **Automobile Association of Southern India** 187 Anna Salai, Chennai 600 006, tel: 2852 1162; www.aasindia.in; and the **UP Automobile Association** 32-A Mahatma Gandhi Marg, Allahabad, tel: 260 0332.

Railways

Rail travel is safe, comfortable and by far the best way to get around the country. Trains are slow compared to those in the West, so if you are in a hurry, stick to the expresses. Fares are generally low. Indian Railways has a number of different classes, of varying degrees of comfort. In descending order of price, they are:
● First class AC, very comfortable with lockable cabins of four berths each.
● AC II tier, partitions arranged in groups of 6 berths with curtains that pull across to provide privacy.
● AC III tier, partitions with groups of 9 berths, the middle berths fold down when not used for sleeping.
● AC chair car.
● First class (unfortunately now rare), non-AC but with ceiling fans. Has lockable cabins of four berths each. There is one cabin of two berths halfway down each carriage.
● Sleeper class, partitions of 9 berths with ceiling fans.
● Second class, unreserved with no berths and hard seats.
In the summer months it is best to go AC. When the weather is cooler then first class can be an excellent option as it is possible to see the passing countryside without having to stare through the darkened windows of AC.

All carriages have both Western and Indian-style toilets. If you are up to squatting on a moving train always use the Indian toilets as they are invariably cleaner and better maintained.

Bedding consisting of two sheets, a pillow and a blanket is provided in first class AC, AC II tier and III tier, and is also available from the attendant for Rs20 in first class. In theory, if they want bedding, first-class passengers should contact the Station Manager before travelling, but extra bedding is often available. If travelling sleeper class then it is a good idea to take a sheet sleeping bag (any Indian tailor will run one up for you).

Food can usually be ordered through the coach attendant. On Shatabdi and Rajdhani trains the fare also covers food, drinks and snacks.

Retiring rooms (for short-term occupation only) are available at over 1,100 stations on a first-come first-served basis, but these are usually heavily booked. All first-class waiting rooms have couches for passengers using their own bedding. At both New Delhi and Howrah stations, a Rail Yatri Niwas has been built for transit passengers. Rooms can be booked in advance.

Cloakrooms are available at most stations where travellers can leave their luggage, but bags must be locked; be sure not to lose your reclaim ticket. Check opening times of the cloakroom for collection.

Very useful pre-paid taxi and/or auto-rickshaw services are available at most large stations. Advance reservation is strongly recommended.

Remember to check which station your train departs from and do allow at least half an hour to find your seat/berth. Lists of passengers with the compartment and seat/berth numbers allotted to them are displayed on platforms and on each carriage an hour before departure. The station superintendent and the conductor attached to the train are usually available for assistance.

Reservations and Passes

Reservations are required for all classes other than second class and reserving well in advance is strongly recommended. Many stations now have very efficient computerised booking counters from where you can book any ticket for any route. Reservations may be made up to 60 days in advance.

In the larger cities, the major stations have tourist sections with English-speaking staff to reduce the queues for foreigners and non-resident Indians buying tickets; payment is in pounds sterling or US dollars (traveller's cheques or cash).

If reservations are not available then certain trains have a tourist quota that may be available. Other options are to take a waitlisted ticket or the more assured reservation against cancellation (RAC); the booking clerk should be able to advise you on how likely you are to get a reservation. Tatkal trains (marked with a "T" in timetables) have a certain number of reservations held back, which become available one day in advance for an extra charge, but you forfeit the full amount in case of cancellation. It is also possible to make bookings from abroad through Indian Railways representatives. They will accept bookings up to six months ahead, with a minimum of one month for first class, three months for second.

Cancellations (for which you will need to fill in the same form as for a reservation) can be made with varying degrees of penalty depending on the class and how close the cancellation is made to the time of departure.

The **Indrail Pass** gives unlimited travel on the entire rail network for periods of between 12 hours and 90 days and and can be good value if you plan on travelling nearly every day. They are available to foreign nationals and Indians resident abroad and are paid for in foreign currency. They can cut down on time getting reservations, you pay no reservation

Indrail Pass Fares in US Dollars

	First Class AC		Other AC and FC		Sleeper Class	
	Adult	**Child**	**Adult**	**Child**	**Adult**	**Child**
Half-day	57	29	26	13	11	6
1 Day	95	47	43	22	19	10
2 Days	160	80	70	35	30	15
4 Days	220	110	110	55	50	25
7 Days	270	135	135	68	80	40
15 Days	370	185	185	95	90	45
21 Days	396	198	198	99	100	50
30 Days	495	248	248	126	125	65
60 Days	800	400	400	200	185	95
90 Days	1060	530	530	265	235	120

fees and no sleeper berth surcharge for night journeys for any class of accommodation.

In the UK the pass can be obtained through the very efficient and highly recommended S.D. Enterprises Ltd, 103 Wembley Park Drive, Wembley, Middlesex HA9 8HG; tel: (020) 8903 3411; fax: (020) 8903 0392; www.indiarail.co.uk

They can also book single-journey tickets in advance for you. The Indrail pass can be bought in India at Railway Central Reservations Offices in Chennai, Kolkata, Mumbai Central, Mumbai CST and New Delhi.

Tourist offices at railway reservation centres are helpful in planning itineraries and obtaining reservations (International Tourist Bureau, New Delhi railway station, tel: (011) 2334 6804). There are tourist offices at New Delhi (tel: 2340 5156, 2336 1732), Mumbai Churchgate, Kolkata Fairlie Place, Chennai Central, and some other popular tourist destinations. Railway timetables available at Indian Tourist Offices abroad also contain much useful information.

Indian Railways Websites

For general information:
www.indianrailways.gov.in
For timetables, fares and the current status of trains and your ticket:
www.indianrail.gov.in
To buy tickets online (you will need to register, and delivery or collection of tickets is only available in certain cities):
www.irctc.co.in
For a wide range of links and useful information go to the "rail gateway" website at:
www.raildwar.com
If you really fall in love with the railways, and become a bit obsessive, try the excellent Indian Railways Fan Club site:
www.irfca.org
A great deal of historical information is on the National Rail Museum site:
www.railmuseum.org

Regions

Indian Railways is divided into regional zones. These are given below along with their individual websites, which contain routes and timetable information:
Central Railway
www.centralrailwayonline.com
East Central Railway
www.ecr.indianrail.gov.in
East Coast Railway
www.eastcoastrailway.gov.in
Eastern Railway
www.easternrailway.gov.in
Konkan Railway
www.konkanrailway.com
North Central Railway
http://10.102.2.21
Northeastern Railway
www.ner.railnet.gov.in
Northeast Frontier Railway
www.nfr.railnet.gov.in
Northern Railway
www.uttarrailway.com
Northwestern Railway
www.northwesternrailway.com
South Central Railway
www.scrailway.gov.in
South East Central Railway
www.secr.gov.in
Southeastern Railway
www.serailway.com
Southern Railway
www.srailway.com
Southwestern Railway
www.southwesternrailway.org
West Central Railway
www.westcentralrailway.com
Western Railway
www.westernrailwayindia.com

SPECIAL TRAINS

The Royal Orient This is a luxury, refurbished, air-conditioned, metre-gauge train, using the carriages previously used on the Palace on Wheels. Accommodation is mainly in coupés, with each carriage having a mini-bar, kitchenette and Western toilets. It departs from Delhi Cantonment Station on Wednesdays at 3pm and travels through Chittaurgarh, Udaipur, Mehsana, Ahmadabad, Sasangir (for the wildlife sanctuary), Ahmadpur, Mandvi, Palitana, Sakhraj, Ranakpur and Jaipur over the next six days, arriving back in Delhi at 6am the following Wednesday. The train runs between September and April; a two-berth

Reservation Forms

To buy your ticket you must first fill out a Reservation Requisition Form, which will be available from one of the windows in the booking office. The form is in the local language on one side and English on the reverse. In addition to the obvious information such as where you wish to leave from and go to and when, to fill in the form you also need to know:
● The train number and name. You can get this from a timetable, or, if the train departs from the station you are booking from, it is usually displayed on a board in the booking office.
● The class you wish to travel and whether you require a berth (for overnight journeys, or any journey between 9pm and 6am), or only a seat.
● Whether you require a lower, middle or upper berth. An upper berth is a good idea as it can be used throughout the day, whereas the other two may only be used for sleeping 9pm–6am.

Foreign travellers should also fill in their passport numbers in the column that asks for your Concession Travel Authority Number, which is needed if the ticket is issued under the foreign tourist quota.

cabin costs from $150 to $200 per night. Bookings can be made through travel agents abroad. In India contact: The Senior Manager, Tourism Corporation of Gujarat Limited, 2nd Floor, A-6, State Emporium Building, Baba Kharak Singh Marg, New Delhi 110001, tel: (011) 2336 4724, fax: (011) 2373 4015.
www.indianrail.gov.in/royal_orient.html

The Palace on Wheels Many of the tracks in Rajasthan have now been converted to broad gauge and the original Royal Train, the Palace on Wheels, now has new rolling stock. The 14 carriages leave Delhi at 6.30pm every Wednesday between Spetember and April, and stop at Jaipur, Bharatpur, Chittaurgarh, Udaipur, Sawai Madhopur, Jaisalmer, Jodhpur, Bharatpur and Agra, returning to Delhi on the 8th day. A double cabin costs $350 per night between October and March, and $295 in September and April. See or contact: www.palaceonwheels.net; The Senior Manager, Palace on Wheels, Tourist Reception Centre, Bikaner House, Pandara Road, New Delhi 110 011, tel: 2381 884, fax: 2382 823. The

Timetables

Indian Airlines and Indian Railways have excellent websites that provide all their schedules and fares (see http://indian-airlines.nic.in; www.indianrailways.gov.in; www.indianrail.gov.in; and www.irctc.co.in). These are also available at travel agents and information counters at all major airports and railway stations. In addition, a local travel magazine, Travel Links, publishes air and rail timetables.

Each regional railway prints its full timetable in Hindi, English and the regional language. There is also the monthly Indian Bradshaw, which lists all services across the country, or the concise and comprehensive Trains At A Glance.

trip can also be booked from abroad through travel agents.

Fairy Queen This three-day excursion is pulled by the world's oldest working steam engine. The train leaves Delhi station at 10am and takes you to the Sariska Palace near Alwar. The next day is spent in the Sariska Tiger Reserve, before departing for Delhi the next morning (arriving back at 6.45pm. Contact: The International Tourist Bureau, New Delhi Railway Station, tel: (011) 2340 5156, fax: 2334 3050. www.railmuseum.org

Viceroy of India A 15-day journey on luxury train beginning in Mumbai and calling in Jaipur, Agra, Delhi, Bharatpur, Varanasi and Siliguri before changing to a luxury steam train for the journey to Darjeeling and Kolkata. The meals are provided by the Taj hotel group and feature regional food dependent on your location. Frequent excursions allow you to explore the natural parks and cities along the way. Contact: GW travel, UK tel: 0161-928 9410, US tel: 206-624-7289; www.gwtravel.co.uk.

Hill Trains India also has a number of charming "toy trains" which run from the plains up to certain hill stations. These include the narrow-gauge tracks up to Udhagamandalam (Ooty) in the Nilgiris, the line from New Jalpaiguri to Darjeeling, and the track between Neral and Matheran near Mumbai, as well as the broad-gauge line between Kalka and Simla (this service is known as the Himalayan Queen).

Rickshaws

The most convenient, and classically Indian, way of getting around town is by rickshaw. These come in three types: a cycle rickshaw (a tricycle with a seat for two people on the back), an a motorised three-wheeler known as an "auto" (in Delhi these have all been converted to run on CNG, compressed natural gas) and, only in central Kolkata, rickshaws pulled by men on foot. The latter might seem distasteful to many visitors, but they do perfom a useful function during the monsoon when the streets flood and the other rickshaws will not work.

Autos are, like taxis, supposed to use a meter. You should insist on this and get out if they refuse. Meter rates are subject to periodic changes, and extras for late-night journeys etc., which the driver should show you on a ~ard. In popular tourist spots, during ~sh hour and bad weather, you may ~d it impossible to persuade the ~ers to use the meter. A tactic that

might work is to offer "meter plus five" (the cost plus Rs5). If not, you'll have to negotiate the fare. After a short while in the country you will get a feel for what is acceptable, given that as a relatively well-off foreign tourist you are expected quite reasonably to pay a little more.

In many places it is common for auto drivers to suggest that, for a fixed amount, they take you around the sites for a whole day. This can be convenient and, if you bargain well, good value. Make sure that both of you understand what the price is and where you want to go (i.e. not via endless shops) before you set off.

Cycle rickshaws are more convenient in some places, like the very congested streets of Old Delhi. With these you should negotiate the fare before you set off.

Note: rickshaws are not allowed into central Mumbai; the only transport options are the well-developed bus service or the reasonably priced taxis.

Where to Stay

Accommodation

Accommodation in India is varied to say the least; it runs the full gamut from very cheap and rather unsavoury, to hideously expensive with every conceivable luxury. Between these two extremes are some lovely places to stay. The indigenous five-star hotel chains are extremely well run, but luxury does not come cheap, most charge well over £100 per night.

Perhaps the best, and certainly the most Indian, places to stay are small, cheap hotels which provide basic but usually clean and sometimes attractive accommodation. It is always wise to ask to see the room first before committing yourself (there are some truly dreadful places as well as charming ones). It is also a good idea to ask if there are any discounts, especially out of season.

As well as luxury, business and cheaper hotels, there is also a growing network of "Heritage Hotels" *(see page 281).*

Hotel Listings

ANDAMAN ISLANDS

Port Blair (03192)
Peerless Resort
Corbyn's Cove, P.O. Box 21, Port Blair
Tel: 229 311
Fax: 229 314
A choice of comfortable rooms and cottages set amid beautiful tropical greenery opposite a white-sand beach. Restaurant, bar and diving centre. **£££££**
Hotel Sinclair's Bay View
South Point, Port Blair
Tel: 228 159/227 937
Fax: 227 824
www.sinclairshotels.com
Comfortable hotel on a cliff overlooking the sea. Waves restaurant, bar. Excellent views. **££££**
ANTDC Megapode Nest
Haddo
Tel: 232 076/232 207
Book on tel: 233 659; fax: 232 076
Choice of rooms and AC cottages with great sea views, gardens and good food. **£££**

Hornbill Nest
1 km (½ mile) north of Corbyn's Cove
Tel: 246 042/244 449
Fax: 233 161
Spacious, clean cottages perched on
a coastal hill. Good food if booked in
advance. **££**
Jagannath Guest House
Moulana Azad Road, Phoenix Bay,
Port Blair
Tel: 232 148
Clean rooms in a friendly hotel with a
good, central location. **£**
Youth Hostel
Near Netaji Stadium, Port Blair
Tel: 232 459
Fax: 232 637
Small, basic and very cheap. **£**

ANDHRA PRADESH

Amaravati (08645)
Punnami Amaravati
Tel: 255 332
www.tourisminap.com
Just four non-AC rooms in a tiny
government-run guesthouse. **£**

Hindupur (08556)
Palla Residency
Railway Station Road
Tel: 224 869
Fax: 228 759
A friendly, new hotel with large, clean
and safe AC rooms. Well-run with a
decent veg restaurant. **£**

Hyderabad-Secunderabad (040)
Taj Krishna
Road No.1, Banjara Hills, Hyderabad
Tel: 5566 2323
Fax: 5566 1313
www.tajhotels.com
This gorgeous hotel is designed to
blend in with natural rocks and
waterfalls, though the rooms still have
an indentikit international-business
feel. **£££££**
Taj Residency
Road No.1, Banjara Hills, Hyderabad
Tel: 2339 3939
Fax: 2339 2684
Close by the Krishna is another Taj
luxury outfit with Lakeside views. (Taj
seem to have a monopoly on posh
accommodation in Hyderabad as they
also operate the equally close by Taj
Banjara.) **£££££**
Amrutha Castle
5/9–16, Saifabad, opposite
Secretariat, Hyderabad
Tel: 5563 3888
Fax: 5582 8222
www.amruthacastle.com
Fantasy Bavarian castle, great if
you have a taste for kitsch. Good
rooms and all amenities including
a 5th-floor open-air swimming pool.
£££

The Residency
5/8/231–2 Public Garden Road,
Hyderabad
Tel: 3061 6161
www.theresidency-hyd.com
A comfortable, fairly pricey and plush
hotel near to Hyderabad station. There
is a popular restaurant, Venue, and a
bar and coffee shop. **£££**
Baseraa
9/1–167/8 Sarojini Devi Road,
Secunderabad
Tel: 2770 3200
Fax: 2770 4745
www.baseraa.com
Immaculate AC rooms and good
restaurants make this hotel good
value. **££–£££**
Parklane
115 Park Lane, Secunderabad
Tel: 2784 0466
Fax: 2784 0599
Roomy and clean; non-AC rooms also
available. **££**
Hotel Sai Prakash
Station Road, Nampally, Hyderabad
Tel: 2461 1726
Fax: 2461 3355
An excellent option near Hyderabad
station. Clean, well-maintained rooms
around a large atrium. Two very good
restaurants, the vegetarian
Sukhasaghra, and the Rich'n'Famous,
which serves Mughlai food. **££**

Nagarjunakonda (08680)
Punnami Vijay Vihar
Nagarjuna Sagar
Tel: 277 361
www.tourisminap.com
A pleasant small hotel with AC and
non-AC rooms, and a decent
restaurant. **£–££**

Srisailam (08524)
Punnami Srisailam
Tel: 287 369
www.tourisminap.com
Good value, simple accommodation
close to the pilgrimage site, with a
restaurant attached. **£**

Tirupati (0877)
Bhimas Residency
Renigunta Road
Tel: 223 7376
Fax: 223 7373
Up-market hotel, run by the owners of
the Bhimas Deluxe, and up to their
existing high standards. **££–£££**
Hotel Bhimas Paradise
33–7 Renigunta Road
Tel: 223 7271–6
Fax: 223 7277
www.hotelbhimas.com
Not part of the same group as the
Bhimas Deluxe but well run, with large
rooms, restaurant and pool. **££**
Hotel Bliss
Near Ramanuja Circle,

Renigunta Road
Tel: 223 7770–6
Fax: 223 7774
Modern hotel with clean rooms and
bathooms. Two restaurants,
vegetarian and non-veg. **££**
Bhimas Deluxe
34–38 G. Car Street
Tel: 222 5521
Fax: 222 5471
A lovely, very well-run hotel just
around the corner from the railway
station. Friendly, helpful staff and
management. The excellent Maya
vegetarian restaurant is in the
basement. Recommended. **££**

Vijayawada (0866)
Hotel Raj Towers
Congress Office Road, Governorpet
Tel: 257 1311–8
Fax: 556 1714
Good value and modern AC rooms in a
well-run hotel. The two restaurants
serve vegetarian and non-vegetarian
food. **£–££**
Sree Lakshmi Vilas Modern Cafe
Besant Road, Govenorpet
Tel: 257 2525
Central rooms with or without bath.
The hotel also has a good vegetarian
restaurant. **£**

Vishakhapatnam (0891)
The Park
Beach Road
Tel: 275 4488
Fax: 275 4181
www.theparkhotels.com
Good modern rooms with sea views.
Two restaurants, swimming pool and
direct access to beach. **£££££**
Taj Residency
Beach Road
Tel: 256 7756
Fax: 256 4370
www.tajhotels.com
Vizag's finest and most striking hotel.
All rooms have a sea view. Two good
restaurants and a pool. **£££££**
Hotel Meghalaya
10-4–15 Ram Nagar,
Asilmetta Junction
Tel: 275 5141–5
Fax: 275 5824
www.hotelmeghalaya.com
Friendly hotel with a large range of
rooms (AC and non-AC). It also has a
good vegetarian restaurant. **££**
Railway Retiring Rooms
Good, cheap doubles and a men-only
dormitory. **£**

Warangal (0870)
Punnami Warangal
Opposite R.E.C., Kazipet
Tel: 243 2312
www.tourisminap.com
Simple but clean accommodation
(some AC rooms) and a restaurant. **£**

ASSAM

Guwahati (0361)
Hotel Brahmaputra Ashok
M.G. Road
Tel: 260 2281–4
Fax: 260 2289
Good, government-owned hotel by
the river. Large rooms (some with
river views) and one good restaurant.
££££
Dynasty
S.S. Road, Lakhtokia
Tel: 251 0496–9
Fax: 252 2112
Comfortable hotel in the main Fancy
Bazaar area. Two good restaurants,
one serving Chinese, the other
Mughlai food. **£££**
Bellevue
M.G. Road
Tel: 254 0847
Fax: 254 0848
Charming, quiet and old-fashioned
place by the river, with excellent
views. Large rooms and a good
restaurant. **£££**
Nandan
G.S. Road, Paltan Bazaar
Tel: 252 1476–8/254 0855
Fax: 254 2634
Large hotel opposite the Indian
Airlines office. Comfortable rooms,
two restaurants, including the very
good Utsav, and a bar. **£££**
Ananda Lodge
M. Nehru Road
Tel: 254 4832
Very cheap but small rooms around an
attractive courtyard. **£**
Tourist Lodge
Station Road
Tel: 254 4475
A convenient place to stay with basic
rooms, run by the ATDC. **£**
Railway Retiring Rooms
A few rooms and dormitory
accommodation. **£**

Kaziranga National Park (03776)
Aranya Tourist Lodge
Book through:
Tourist Information Officer, Kaziranga
National Park, Golaghat, Assam
Tel: 266 2423
www.assamtourism.org
A mix of clean and simple rooms,
all with en-suite facilities.
Helpful staff and a pretty good
restaurant. **£–££**
Wild Grass
Kaziranga 785 109
Tel: 266 2085
www.oldassam.com
Simple but attractive huts
and comfortable tents set in
beautiful grounds. Excellent food
and activities centred on local
music and dance. Recommended.
£££

Manas (03666)
Bansbari Lodge
Manas
Tel: 296 824
www.assambengalnavigation.com
Probably the best option close to the
park. This is a pleasant, simple hotel
in lovely surroundings by the river.
Decent food; nature walks can be
arranged with a guide. **£££££**
Mathanguri Forest Lodge
Mathanguri
Book through:
Field Director, Manas National Park,
Assam
Tel: 261 413
Slightly run-down, basic rooms set in
the park itself. Order food and make
preparations in advance. **£–££**

BIHAR

Bodhgaya (0631)
Lotus Nikko Hotel
Tel: 220 0700
Fax: 220 0788
This comfortable hotel is to the east
of the Archaeological Museum. It has
a pleasant ambience and a good
restaurant. **££££**
Root Institute
Near the Thai Temple
www.rootinstitute.com
This is an organisation that runs a
Buddhist meditation retreat. As well
as attending courses, it is possible to
stay in the huts and dormitories as an
independent visitor. Very good
vegetarian meals are provided. **££**
Daijokyo Buddhist House
North of the Giant Buddha statue
Tel: 220 0747
Fax: 220 0407
Although preference is given to
Japanese pilgrims and tour groups,
you might be lucky if you phone ahead
to see if rooms are available.
Excellent Japanese restaurant. **£–££**

Patna (0612)
Maurya Patna
South Gandhi Maidan
Tel: 220 3040
Fax: 220 3060
Patna's top (and most expensive)
hotel with decent rooms, a pool and a
couple of restaurants. **££££**
Pataliputra Ashok
Beer Chand Patel Path
Tel: 222 6270–5
Fax: 222 3467/222 4207
An ITDC run hotel with comfortable
rooms, a swimming pool and a good
restaurant. **££££**
Hotel Republic
Exhibition Road
Tel: 232 0021
A relaxing roof garden and good
vegetarian food. **££–£££**

Hotel Samrat International
Fraser Road
Tel: 222 0560–7
Fax: 222 6386
www.samrat.allhere.com
AC and non-AC rooms with attached
bath and two restaurants. **££**
Amar
Fraser Road
Tel: 222 4157
Basic but pleasant rooms with
attached baths. **£**

CHENNAI (044)

Ambassador Pallava
53 Monteith Road
Tel: 2855 4476/2855 4068
Fax: 2855 4492
www.ambassadorindia.com
Largely a business hotel, it is,
however, in a convenient location
close to Anna Salai and the museum.
Facilities include pool, a beauty
parlour and a couple of decent
restaurants. **£££££**
Taj Coromandel
37 M.G. Road, Nungambakkam
Tel: 2827 2827
Fax: 2825 7104
www.tajhotels.com
Luxurious but hideously expensive
(over £150 per night) with good
service and four excellent restaurants,
including the Southern Spice serving
South Indian dishes. **£££££**
Taj Connemara
2 Binny Road
Tel: 5500 0000
Fax: 5500 0555
www.tajhotels.com
One of the great hotels of India – up
there with the Taj in Mumbai – and
deservedly popular and set in an art
deco building. Excellent value
compared to the Coromandel (around
£100 per night for a standard room).
Good restaurants, including the open-
air Raintree, and Verandah, which has
a great buffet lunch and is a good
place for afternoon tea. **£££££**
The Trident
1–24 G.S.T. Road
Tel: 2234 4747
Fax: 2234 6699
www.tridenthotels.com
Part of the Oberoi chain (and

Hotel Price Categories

The rates below are for a double
room (AC where available) in high
season, including taxes.

£££££	Rs3,700 and above
££££	Rs2,700–3,700
£££	Rs1,700–2,700
££	Rs800–1,700
£	Up to Rs800

therefore a little pricey), this sleek, modern and efficient hotel is out near the airport. It has an excellent coffee shop. **£££££**

Residency
49 G.N. Chetty Road, T. Nagar
Tel: 2825 3434
Fax: 2825 0085
www.theresidency.com
Recommended, with a range of rooms and good restaurant. Good value for what's on offer. Reserve ahead. **£££**

Hotel Kanchi
28 Ethiraj Salai, Egmore
Tel: 2827 1100
Fax: 2827 2928
www.hotelkanchi.com
Large and light rooms that are starting to show their age, but still with a certain charm. Good South Indian food downstairs, great views and OK North Indian dishes in rooftop Geetham restaurant. **££**

Hotel Himalaya
54 Triplicane High Road, Triplicane
Tel: 2854 7522
Fax: 2853 1808
A good, central hotel. Very clean rooms with bath, helpful and friendly staff. Recommended. **££**

Hotel Pandian
9 Kennet Lane, Egmore
Tel: 2819 1010/2819 2020
Fax: 2819 3030
www.hotelpandian.com
Park-side rooms with nice views but no AC. The AC rooms are very cool but dark. It has a reasonable restaurant (the Raj) and useful STD booth in grounds. Friendly staff and convenient for Egmore Station. **££**

Hotel New Woodlands
72–5 Dr Radhakrishnan Road, Mylapore
Tel: 2811 3111
Fax: 2811 0460
www.newwoodlands.com
A large hotel with excellent vegetarian restaurant. The large, clean rooms are popular so book ahead. **££**

YWCA International Guest House
1086 E.V.R. Periyar High Road
Tel: 2532 4234
Fax: 2532 4263
ywcaigh@indiainfo.com
A safe place to stay near the Daily Thandi newspaper office. Rooms with attached baths, some with AC, and also camping facilities. The cost of the room includes breakfast. There is a temporary membership fee of Rs 20. Recommended. **££**

Hotel Mount Heera
287 M.K.N. Road, Alandur
Tel: 2234 9563/2233 0832
Fax: 2233 1236
Noisy hotel near airport, good if you have an early-morning flight. Price includes taxi to the airport. **£–££**

Youth Hostel
2nd Avenue, Indiranagar, Adyar
Tel: 2442 0233
Very cheap but quiet and clean accommodation. **£**

DAMAN & DIU

Daman (0260)
Hotel Gurukripa
Seaface Road
Tel: 225 5046/225 0227
Fax: 225 5631
www.hotelgurukripa.com
The best in town. Good rooms, roof garden, bar and good restaurant serving seafood, *tanduri* and Chinese dishes. **££**

Hotel Sovereign
Seaface Road
Tel: 225 5023/225 0236
Fax: 225 5631
Large, efficient and near the beach. The vegetarian restaurant serves good Gujarati *thalis*. Same owners as the nearby Gurukripa (and same website) but a little cheaper. **££**

Diu (02875)
Kohinoor
Fofrara, Fudam
Tel: 252 209/253 575
Fax: 252 613
A modern hotel with good amenities, including a pool and restaurant. About 2 km (1 mile) outside Diu Town. **£££**

Ankur
Estrada Lacerda
Tel: 252 388
Big, clean rooms, some AC. **£–££**

Hotel Samrat
Collectorate Road
Tel: 252 354
The best hotel in the town itself. AC rooms with bath and balcony, and a good restaurant. **£–££**

Hotel Prince
Rua do Bazar
Tel: 252 265
Clean rooms with balcony; limited restaurant. **£**

Jay Shankar
Jallandar Beach
Tel: 252 424
Simple rooms and a great seafood restaurant. **£**

DELHI (011)

The Ambassador Hotel
Subramaniam Bharti Marg
Tel: 2463 2600
Fax: 2463 2252
www.tajhotels.com
A Taj-run, old-fashioned hotel near Khan Market. Comfortable and not as overpowering as the Taj Mahal or Taj Palace. **£££££**

Ashok Hotel
50b Chanakyapuri, New Delhi
Tel: 2611 0101
Fax: 2687 3216
www.theashokgroup.com
A huge, mock-Mughal luxury hotel. There is a wide range of restaurants, serving Korean, Indian (of various types), Lebanese and French food. As befits a flagship hotel, it has all the luxury trimmings from pool to in-house shopping. **£££££**

The Claridges
12 Aurangzeb Road, New Delhi
Tel: 2301 0211
Fax: 2301 0625
www.claridges.com
Elegant, old-fashioned hotel in the heart of New Delhi. Expensive but excellent service and good North Indian restaurants (*tanduri* at Corbett's and Punjabi food at the Dhaba). **£££££**

The Grand
Nelson Mandela Road, Vasant Kunj
Tel: 2677 1234
www.thegrandnewdelhi.com
The classy, contemporary design helps this property stand out from the bland five-star crowd. Interesting range of restaurants, including Japanese, and a pool and health spa. Convenient for the airport, and the staff are extremely welcoming. **£££££**

Hans Plaza
5 Barakhamba Road (16th–20th floors)
Tel: 2331 6868
www.hanshotels.com
This self-styled boutique hotel has more character than most hotels in the area. The elevated location means it's quiet, and the views from the restaurant are superb. **£££££**

Hotel Diplomat
9 Sardar Patel Marg, Chanakyapuri, New Delhi
Tel: 2301 0204
Fax: 2301 8605
diplomat@nda.vsnl.net
A quiet hotel with a pleasant garden. The elegant, modernist rooms with large windows are popular and advance booking is advisable. **£££££**

Imperial Hotel
1 Janpath, New Delhi
Tel: 2334 1234
Fax: 2334 2255
www.theimperialindia.com
Pretty much as good as it gets in Delhi. Built in 1933, it was the only hotel included in Lutyens' plans for New Delhi. The entrance drive is flanked by huge palm trees, behind which is the pool. The rooms are decorated with lithographs and engravings from the owner's private collection, and it has one of Delhi's best restaurants (the Spice Route). **£££££**

The Manor
77 Friends Colony (West), New Delhi
Tel: 2692 5151
Fax: 2692 2299
www.themanordelhi.com
Delhi's most sleek and attractive luxury hotel. Twelve exquisite rooms, with lots of natural fabrics and wonderful bathrooms. If you have the money and want some class, stay here; if you are after splendor then head for the Imperial. **£££££**

The Oberoi
Dr Zakir Hussain Marg, New Delhi
Tel: 2436 3030
Fax: 2436 0484
www.oberoihotels.com
Elegant, exclusive and very expensive. One of the most comfortable luxury hotels in Delhi. Very good restaurants, including the La Rochelle (French) and Taipan (Chinese). **£££££**

The Maidens Hotel
7 Sham Nath Marg, Delhi
Tel: 2397 5464
Fax: 2398 0771
www.maidenshotel.com
A grand hotel located in Old Delhi – built during the 1900s – and before Lutyens' redevelopment a favourite with visiting bigwigs. The large rooms and attentive service are lovely and not as expensive as you might imagine. The Curzon Room restaurant serves very good food from the British Raj. **£££££**

The Park
15 Sansad Marg
Tel: 2374 3000
www.theparkhotels.com
Some of the funkiest contemporary-style rooms in town, plus an interesting restaurant, poolside bar and great location; the freshest of the five-stars. 224 rooms. **£££££**

Radisson
NH8, close to IGI Airport
Tel: 2677 9191
www.radisson.com
Newly renovated, this is now one smart-looking hotel. The rooms are standard five-star, but the restaurants and coffee shop stand out from the crowd, and the bar has a remarkably long happy hour. **£££££**

Taj Mahal
1 Mansingh Road, New Delhi
Tel: 2302 6162
Fax: 2302 6070
www.tajhotels.com
The luxurious flagship of the Taj Group is primarily a business hotel and the rooms and facilities reflect this. On the plus side, it does have two excellent restaurants (Haveli and House of Ming). **£££££**

Uppal's Orchid
NH8, close to IGI Airport
Tel: 2506 1515
www.uppalsorchidhotel.com
Very classy eco-hotel situated conveniently close to the airport. The facilities are aimed squarely at the business traveller, who should find nothing lacking at this quiet oasis. **£££££**

Vasant Continental
Basant Lok, Vasant Vihar
Tel: 2614 8800
www.jaypeehotels.com
Its contemporary styling and innovative eateries make this luxury hotel stand out. Close to the airport in an up-market residential area, it has a great pool, a lively bar and exceptional food. Great Eggspectations, a breakfast bar with a difference, is highly recommended. **£££££**

Hotel Marina
G-59 Connaught Circus, New Delhi
Tel: 2332 4658
Fax: 2332 8609
A well-established hotel with comfortable rooms, decent coffee shop and good travel service. **££££**

Hotel Nikko
Bangla Sahib Road
Tel: 4250 0200
www. hotelnikkodelhi.com
Part of an up-market Japanese chain, this hotel is an exceptionally well-run place, with distinctly un-Indian levels of efficiency. Well equipped for the business traveller; there's also a good health spa and the best Japanese restaurant in town bar none. **££££**

Nirula's Hotel
L-Block Connaught Circus, New Delhi
Tel: 4151 7070
Fax: 2341 8957
www.nirula.com
Well-established small hotel with clean and comfortable AC single and double rooms. The two restaurants and ice-cream parlour are still very popular but are now starting to show their age. Book in advance. **££££**

Bajaj Indian Home Stay
8A/34 WEA, Karol Bagh
Tel: 2573 6509
www.bajajindianhomestay.com
Promising an experience that's "Indian, altogether", this place prides itself on its homely ambience, treating each guest as one of their own. Certainly stands out from the crowd, and rooms are spotlessly clean. **£££**

Central Court Hotel
N Block, Connaught Circus, New Delhi
Tel: 2331 5013
A somewhat old-fashioned hotel, but the rooms are presentable and the staff very accommodating. No restaurant, but the choice near by is so good that you're unlikely to miss it. Room sizes vary enormously, so see what's available before you decide. **£££**

Good Times Hotel
8/7 WEA Karol Bagh, off Pusa Road
Tel: 4100 5140

www.goodtimeshotel.com
Presentable rooms and a pleasant rooftop restaurant just about make up for the busy, if fairly convenient, location. Staff seem rushed off their feet. This is one of the better-value places around, so book early. **£££**

Jukaso Inn
50 Sunder Nagar
Tel: 2435 0308
www.indiamart.com/jukasoinn
Located in one of Delhi's most desirable residential areas, this is the biggest and best of the several hotels in the area. The 33 rooms are well kept, and the staff go out of their way to please. Book well in advance. **£££**

Jukaso Inn Downtown
L-1 Connaught Circus, New Delhi
Tel: 2341 5450
Fax: 2341 4448
A central hotel just up from Nirula's. The modern and clean AC rooms with attached bath are comfortable and pleasant. **£££–££££**

Hotel Ajanta
36 Arakashan Road, Ram Nagar,
Tel: 2362 0925
www.hotalajanta.com
Away from the Main Bazaar area, this is one of the more up-market options in this part of town. The rooms are perfectly acceptable, and there's a good range of facilities, including a restaurant and travel desk. **£££**

Home Away from Home
D-8 Gulmohar Park (1st floor)
Tel: 2656 0289
permkamte@sify.com
This really is a home, with just two well-equipped rooms in a quiet, leafy area. The owners are extremely helpful and offer discounts to long-term guests. **£££**

Hotel Broadway
4–15a Asaf Ali Road, Delhi
Tel: 2327 3821
Fax: 2326 9966
www.oldworldhospitality.com
A lovely and good-value hotel close to the sights of Old Delhi. Clean rooms, good service and an excellent restaurant (the Chor Bizarre). **£££**

Hotel Fifty Five
H-55 Connaught Place, New Delhi
Tel: 2332 1244/2332 1278
Fax: 2332 0769

Clean AC rooms and attached baths. A little over-priced but in a good, central location. **£££**

Jorbagh "27"
27 Jorbagh
Tel: 2469 8647
guesthouse27@hotmail.com
Set in a residential area, but run more as a hotel then a guesthouse, this 18-room property lacks some of the charm of the more homely establishments, but is efficiently run, clean and well located, with the proximity of Lodi Gardens a real bonus. **£££**

LaSagrita
14 Sunder Nagar
Tel: 2435 9541
Fax: 2435 6956
www.lasagrita.com
Near the zoo in a quiet residential area, this guesthouse offers rooms with comfortable beds and hot water. The staff are great and the food good and relatively inexpensive. The shopping area just around the corner has a great vegetarian restaurant, sweet corner and some good antique shops. Recommended. **£££**

Pal's Inn
East Patel Nagar, Karol Bagh
Tel: 2578 5310
Well-maintained modern rooms in friendly hotel with good coffee shop and attentive staff. **£££**

Yatri House
Corner of Panchkuian and Mandir Margs
Tel: 2362 5563
www.yatrihouse.com
Down a small lane, well set back from the busy main road, this is a clean, well-run guesthouse in a modern family home. Although in somewhat uninspiring surroundings, it's only 1 km (½ mile) from Connaught Place, so one of the quietest options this close to town. **£££**

Choudhary Guest House
H-35/3 Connaught Circus, New Delhi
Tel: 2332 2043
www.indiamart.com/hkchoudharyguesthouse
Small, clean and friendly hotel, in a central location with an exceptionally helpful manager. Can be a struggle to find – it's very tucked away, but well worth tracking down. **££**

Lutyens Guesthouse
39 Prithviraj Road
Tel: 2462 5716
www.lutyensguesthouse.com
Set in a Lutyens-designed bungalow on one of the most exclusive roads in New Delhi, this 15-room guesthouse retains the building's original charm, has a very friendly but unobtrusive feel and, the real deal-sealer, a swimming pool. Be sure to book well in advance. **££**

Master Paying Guest House
R-500 New Rajendar Nagar
Tel: 2874 1089
www.master-guesthouse.com
Four very clean and comfortable rooms with shared bathroom. The guesthouse is run by a very helpful couple and there is a nice common area including a TV and a library created by the guests. Recommended. **££**

Metropolis Tourist Home
1634 Main Bazaar, Paharganj
Tel: 2358 5766
One of the better hotels in Paharganj (generally best avoided). Clean and comfortable rooms, hot water and a good restaurant. **££**

Naari
Tel: 2613 8316
Mobile: 981 067 1603
A women-only guesthouse in South Delhi, with comfortable rooms and a pleasant garden and meals. Very safe and hassle-free for women travelling on their own. Tours can also be arranged from here. Phone ahead for reservations and details on how to reach the hotel. Recommended. **££**

Rail Yatri Niwas
Ajmeri Gate, New Delhi Railway Station
Tel: 2323 3484/2323 3561
Good-value rooms, dormitories and self-service restaurant for travellers holding onward railway tickets (maxmimum 3 days). Book in advance at New Delhi Station. Now privatised, it is drastically cutting down on amenities. There is no running water or even blankets. **££**

Youth Hostel
5 Naya Marg, Chanakyapuri, New Delhi
Tel: 2611 6285
Fax: 2611 3469
www.yhaindia.com
Modern and good value, set in the pleasant diplomatic quarter. You must be a member to stay (there is a wide network of hostels in India so you might want to take out membership before you travel). **££**

YWCA International Guest House
10 Sansad Marg, New Delhi
Tel: 2336 1561
Fax: 2334 1763
www.ywcaindia.org
A recommended, well-run and safe place to stay for both sexes, in a convenient New Delhi location. The spotless AC rooms with attached bath come with a complimentary breakfast at the very good attached restaurant (Ten). There is an STD booth and an efficient travel service on site. **££**

Ajay's
5084A Main Bazaar
Tel: 4154 1226
www.anupamhoteliersltd.com
Part of a group that also includes the

nearby Anoop and Hare Krishna hotels, this place is something of an institution. Offering some of the cheapest accommodation around, it's become a real backpackers' hangout, as much for its excellent bakery as its so-so rooms. **£**

Hotel New City Palace
726 Jama Masjid, Delhi
Tel: 2328 9923
Just behind the mosque in Old Delhi, in the same building as the post office. Basic but clean, air-cooled rooms with attached bath. The rooms at the front have a great view over the mosque. **£**

Hotel Tarra
Mahipalpur Crossing, NH8
Tel: 2678 3677
There are a large number of mostly nondescript budget hotels close to the airport, but the enthusiasm of the manager makes this place stand out. With 10 well-priced rooms, this is a good bet, especially if you're planning to head to Jaipur from Delhi airport. **£**

Major's Den
2314 Lakshmi Narain Street, Paharganj, New Delhi
Tel: 2358 4163
A safe, well-run hotel with clean, air-cooled rooms and attached bath. The best-value accommodation in Paharganj. **£**

Rak International
820 Main Bazaar, Chowk Baoli
Tel: 2358 6508
One of the best-run budget hotels in the area; clean, relatively quiet and with a pleasant rooftop restaurant. **£**

Ringo Guest House
17 Scindia House, Connaught Lane (off Janpath)
Tel: 2331 0605
The pick of the backpacker options in Connaught Place, the Ringo has tiny but clean rooms, a very cheap dorm, a passable restaurant and friendly staff. Overall, it's superior to the nearby Sunny. **£**

Royal Guesthouse
4464 Main Bazaar
Tel: 2358 6176
royalguesthouse@yahoo.com
Another well-maintained budget property, with clean rooms, some with AC, and friendly staff. **£**

Star Palace
4590 Dal Mandi, off Main Bazaar (down lane opposite Khalsa Boots)
Tel: 2356 2400
www.stargroupofhotels.com
There are 31 clean rooms in this relatively quiet hotel, part of a group which includes the slightly cheaper Star View near by. **£**

Wongdhen House
15A New Tibetan Colony, Manju-ka-Tilla
Tel: 2381 6689
wongdhenhouse@hotmail.com

About 2 km (1¼ miles) north of Old Delhi, this predominantly Tibetan colony offers a more peaceful range of backpacker accommodation than Pahar Ganj. This place is by far the most popular establishment, offering a soothing atmosphere and clean, well-priced rooms. **£**

GOA

Anjuna (0832)

Anjuna Beach Resort
De Mello Vaddo
Tel: 227 4499
Mobile: 98221 76753
fabjoe@sancharnet.in
Comfortable rooms with attached baths, some AC, all of which have balconies overlooking the garden. There is also an outdoor, palm thatched, restaurant. Good discounts are available in low season. **££**

Grandpa's Inn
Gaun Waddo, Anjuna
Tel: 227 3270-1
Fax: 226 2031
granpas@hotmail.com
The pleasant rooms of this hotel are set around the flora-filled courtyard of an old Portuguese mansion. The hotel is friendly and well run with a good restaurant. **£££**

Laguna Anjuna
De Mello Waddo
Tel: 227 4305
www.lagunaanjuna.com
Designed by prominent local architect Dean D'Cruz, the resort consists of spacious villas, each one different, set amid palm trees. A very attractive pool is set in lush gardens. The price drops considerably during the monsoon. **£££££**

Lotus Inn
Zor Waddo, Anjuna
Tel: 227 4015
www.lotusinngoa.com
Centrally air-conditioned suites and individually styled double rooms with offbeat decor pitched at well-heeled ex-hippies – in a similar mould to Laguna Anjuna, though not nearly as stylish. Its focal point is a sprawling trefoil-shaped pool overlooked by a swish Italian bar-restaurant. Set back from the shore amid the leafy fringes

of Anjuna and Vagator, the location is tranquil. **££££**

Palacete Rodrigues
Mazal Vaddo, near Oxford Stores
Tel: 227 3358
www.palaceterodrigues.com
A charming traditional Portuguese house crammed full of original furniture. Quiet and peaceful, the veranda overlooking the garden is a lovely place to sit. **££**

Villa Anjuna
Near Anjuna beachfront, Anjuna
Tel: 227 3443
www.anjunavilla.com
Modern, well-run hotels are a rarity in Anjuna; this one is closer to the beach than any of the competition, and has a pool and gym, but it's also only a stone's throw away from Club Paradiso's thumping sound system (the reason most of its clientele stay here). **£££**

White Negro Beach Resort
Near St Antony Chapel
Tel: 227 3326
dsouzawhitenegro@rediffmail.com
Very clean, safe and well run, the rooms here look out on to attractive gardens. The proximity to the beach and good restaurant (lots of fish) make this a decent choice. **££**

Peaceland
Soronto Waddo, Anjuna
Tel: 227 3700
Anjuna's best-value budget place, with clean, well-aired rooms fitted with mosquito nets and backpack racks. The couple who run it are very hospitable. Set back, it's a 15-minute walk to the seafront, in one of the quieter corners of the village. **£**

Arpora (0832)

Nilaya Hermitage
On a hillside 3 km (2 miles) inland
Tel: 227 6793
Fax: 227 6792
www.nilayahermitage.com
Very exclusive with 12 uniquely designed rooms in a startling building. The slightly new-agey interiors have lots of organic curves and there is a wonderful pool out front. Hideously expensive over Christmas but half-price in low season. **£££££**

Baga (0832)

Alida
Saunta Vaddo, Baga Road
Tel: 227 6835
Fax: 227 6285
Pleasant rooms with verandahs in a quiet hotel with peaceful and attractive surroundings. **££**

Jimi's Tepee Village
National Highway 599, Baga Hill
Fax: 227 6124
goa@bay-watch.com
Unusual, but fitting given Goa's hippy

past. Accommodation is in comfortable single and double teepees, as well as a tree house, all set in peaceful surroundings. Open November to March. **£**

Ronil Royale
Baga Road
Tel: 227 6183
www.ronilroyalegoa.com
Clean rooms with balconies in a well-run hotel close to the beach. There is also a decent restaurant. **££**

Villa Fatima
Baga Road, Baga
Tel: 227 7418
www.villafatima.com
Popular backpackers' hotel in the thick of Baga's busy strip, only a short stroll across the dunes from the sea. Fifty clean, en-suite rooms (single, double and family-sized) at low rates for the area. **£**

Benaulim (0834)

Taj Exotica
Cal Waddo
Tel: 270 5666
www.tajhotels.com
Along with the Park Hyatt, this is Goa's flagship luxury hotel: a low-rise palace set amid 22 hectares (56 acres) of lush gardens and flower-filled patios right next to the beach. The facilities of this award-winning complex include a golf course, Ayurvedic spa, four restaurants and kids' clubs. **£££££**

Carina
Vas Vaddo
Tel: 277 0413
Fax: 277 0414
www.carinabeachresort.com
Quiet rooms looking out over the hotel gardens. All have attached baths and hot water heated by solar power. You can also take Goan cooking lessons from the hotel's chef. **££**

Palm Grove Cottages
Tamdi Marti, Vas Vaddo
Tel: 272 2533
Surrounded by a lovely garden this is a clean and pleasant place to stay. The decent restaurant serves Goan dishes and seafood. **££**

Simon Cottages
Sernabatim Ambeaxir
Tel: 277 1839
Most of Benaulim's accommodation consists of no-frills rooms in small guesthouses, or modern tiled annexes tacked onto the side of family homes. This one is a fairly typical specimen, but larger and much better value than most in the village, with big en-suite rooms (some have kitchen space for self-catering) and welcoming owners. It's an ideal first stop if you have just arrived on the plane at Dabolim and need somewhere inexpensive to sleep off your jet lag. **£**

Hotel Price Categories

The rates below are for a double room (AC where available) in high season, including taxes.

£££££	Rs3,700 and above
££££	Rs2,700–3,700
£££	Rs1,700–2,700
££	Rs800–1,700
£	Up to Rs800

Hotel Price Categories

The rates below are for a double room (AC where available) in high season, including taxes.

£££££	Rs3,700 and above
££££	Rs2,700–3,700
£££	Rs1,700–2,700
££	Rs800–1,700
£	Up to Rs800

Succorina Cottages
1711/A Vas Waddo
Tel: 277 0365
A homely little guesthouse on the opposite, south side of the village to Simon Cottages *(see above)*, next to the fishing quarter. It's clean, welcoming and barely five minutes' walk across empty paddy fields to the beach – although it's a bicycle or scooter ride to the village shops and restaurants. **£**

Bicholim (0832)
Goofy's Countryside Hermitage
Assonora, Bicholim
Tel: 238 9231
gats@goatelecom.com
Imaginatively designed "jungle resort" of luxury tree huts and bungalows, hidden deep in the Goan interior. Owner Godfrey Lawrence is an energetic host, leading tours to lesser-visited corners of the state. Transfers from the coast available. **£££**

Bogmalo Beach (0832)
Coconut Creek Resort
Bimmut
Tel: 255 6100
A well-run hotel with stylish rooms set in a peaceful coconut grove. It has a nice pool and decent restaurant. **£££**

Calangute (0832)
Pousada Tauma
Porba Vaddo
Tel: 227 9061
Fax: 227 9064
www.pousada-tauma.com
Very expensive but lovely. 12 suites set around a swimming pool in beautiful grounds. A discreet hideaway, it offers the full works including Ayurvedic treatments and a wonderful restaurant. **£££££**
Concha
Umta Vaddo
Tel: 227 6056
Fax: 227 7555
Comfortable rooms, some with balconies, in an elegant, colonial house with a lovely garden. **££££**
CoCo Banana
1/195 Umta Vaddo
Tel: 227 6478
Fax: 227 9068

Clean and comfortable cottages set around a garden. The Swiss/Goan owners are very helpful. **££**
Kerkar Retreat
Gauro Waddo
Tel: 227 6017
Fax: 227 6509
www.subodhkerkar.com
Six spacious, uncluttered rooms, each with a private balcony as well as en-suite bathroom. There is also a small art gallery (the owner, Subodh Kerkar, is an artist) and restaurant. **££–£££**
Villa Goesa
Cobra Vaddo
Tel: 227 7535
Fax: 227 6182
This quiet hotel, popular with northern European visitors, provides fairly simple rooms with balconies overlooking the lawns and pool. There is also a decent restaurant. **£££**

Canacona (0832)
Dercy's
Agonda beach
Tel: 264 7503
Much the most pleasant and best-value place to stay in Agonda: the accommodation is modern, en-suite and tiled throughout, and equipped with quiet overhead fans; the front rooms open on to a common veranda with lovely sea views. Downstairs, a popular terrace café-restaurant is the ideal place to sample the village's stupendous grilled rockfish. **£**
Dream Catcher
Palolem beach
Tel: 264 4873 or 9822 137446
lalalandjackie7@yahoo.com
Attractive hut camp which has better beds and decor than most of the other places hereabouts, and is situated right next to the river at the north end of Palolem beach. This place is a good fall-back if nearby Cozy Nook *(see page 369)* doesn't have any vacancies – and it's much cheaper. **£**

Candolim (0832)
Casa Seashell
Fort Aguada Road
Tel: 247 9879
A well located place with a pool. The rooms are large and clean with good bathrooms, and the restaurant is recommended for its seafood. **££**
Costa Nicola
Vaddi Vaddo
Tel: 227 6343
Fax: 227 7343
A well-run old Portuguese-style villa in a pretty garden with a pool. Some of the rooms (most pleasant in the old building) have balconies. **£££**
Shanu
Sequeria Waddo
Tel: 227 9606
shanugoa@yahoo.com

Simple, well-kept rooms in a guesthouse whose greatest asset is its location – right on the most peaceful stretch of Candolim beach. Reasonable tariffs, although it's quite a walk to the main strip without some form of transport. **££**
Xavier Beach Resort
Fort Aguada Road
Tel: 247 9489
Fax: 247 9911
www.goacom.com/hotels/xavier
Very good value peaceful and comfortable rooms with sea views. There is also an excellent restaurant and a popular rooftop bar. **££**

Cavelossim (0834)
Dona Sylvia
Tel: 0832-243 4703
Fax: 0832-222 9966
www.donasylvia.com
A resort hotel with nice grounds and a big pool. The rooms – only available as part of a minimum 3-night package – are large and clean, though the restaurant food is bland and not worth the all-inclusive cost. **£££££**
Dona Sa Maria
Tamborim Vaddo
Tel: 274 5290
Fax: 274 5673
www.donasamaria.com
This small, friendly place is good value. Helpful service and simple but clean rooms, and there is the La Afra restaurant serving resaonable Indian food and a swimming pool in the peaceful grounds. **££**

Colva (0834)
Colmar Beach Resort
Tel: 272 1253
By the beach, this popular hotel has good AC and non-AC rooms with attached bath and cottages around a small garden. After the high season, there are good discounts. **££**
Penthouse Beach Resort
Tel: 273 1030
Fax: 273 3737
In the centre of town. Has a group of pleasant cottages surrounding a pool, and a garden with palm trees. **£**
Silver Sands Hotel
Tel: 272 1645
Fax: 273 5816
In the centre of Colva, offers water sports and has a good restaurant. **££**
Vailankanni Cottages
Tel: 273 7747
Centrally located on the main street, has a range of rooms with bath. **£**

Dona Paula (0832)
Prainha Cottages
Tel: 245 3881
Fax: 245 3884
www.prainha.com
Attractive and well-run, with traditional

rooms in cottages close to a secluded beach. **££–£££**

Dona Paula Beach Resort
Tel: 222 7955
Fax: 222 1371
www.opescador.com
Simple but airy rooms overlooking the lawn – some with sea-views – and very close to the beach. **££**

Kankon (0832)
Hotel Molyma
Kindlebaga
Tel: 264 3028
Fax: 264 3081
About 2 km (1 mile) from Chaudi, a modern place with good-value, large rooms. Canacona Palace Udupi Hotel, near the crossroads, serves good vegetarian meals. **££–£££**

Majorda Beach (0832)
Majorda Beach Resort
Tel: 668 1111
Fax: 288 1124
www.majordabeachresort.com
Big, flash and near the beach, this resort has numerous rooms, some luxury villas, three restaurants, pleasant gardens, and good discounts during low season. **£££££**

Mandrem (0832)
Elsewhere/Otter Creek
Mandrem, Pernem
Tel: 253 8451 or 9820 037387
www.aseascape.com
Arguably the most beautifully situated and elegantly restored period property in Goa, Elsewhere's gorgeous pillared veranda looks across empty dunes to a stretch of undeveloped beach. You generally have to rent the house on a weekly basis: three bedrooms accommodate up to six adults, or a family. Hidden from view behind it, along the banks of a tidal inlet, are a row of architectural tents called Otter Creek, offering comparable peace, seclusion and comfort. Friendly staff are on site to serve meals. **£££££**

River Cat Villa
438/1 Junasavaddo
Tel: 224 7928
www.villarivercat.com
A lovely place to stay. Set up by a local artist on the banks of a quiet river, it has good, clean rooms with bath, and an attractive verandah. **££**

Mapusa (0834)
Panchavatti
Kolo Mudi, Corjuem, near Mapusa
Tel: 9822 580632
A palace-cum-guesthouse on a hilltop deep in the idyllic countryside east of Mapusa. From its enormous veranda, scattered with antiques and bowls of floating frangipani flowers, the grounds fall away to a huge pool and view of the distant hills. Its romantically decorated rooms, in-house masseur and fine gastronomic food are other reasons to splash out on a night or two here. **££££**

Satyaheera
Opposite the Municipal Gardens
Tel: 226 2849
Centrally located, with comfortable suites and a good restaurant. **££**

Vilena
Feira Baixa
Tel: 226 3115
The best budget option with clean rooms, some with air-conditioning. **£**

Margao (0834)
Nanutel
Padre Miranda Road
Tel: 270 0901
Fax: 273 3175
nanutelmrg@nanuindia.com
Although rather charmless and modern, this hotel has comfortable and clean AC rooms. Close to the station and good value. **££**

Woodlands
Miguel Loyola Furtado Road
Tel: 272 0374
Fax: 273 8732
Comfortable and clean, this is very popular, so book in advance. **£**

Bhagwan Mahavir (0832)
GTDC Dudhsagar Resort
Tel: 261 2238
Attractive, government-run accommodation, close the Bhagwan Mahavir Wildlife Sanctuary. In a convenient location with good-value rooms and a restaurant. **££**

Palolem (0834)
Bhakti Kutir
Tel: 264 3472
Fax: 264 5211
www.bhaktikutir.com
An eco-friendly resort of 20 cottages made from locally available materials. The open-air bathrooms have stone floors inlaid with shells and decorated with plants. The restaurant dishes up tasty Western food. **££–£££**

Oceanic
Tembi Waddo, Colom, Palolem
Tel: 264 3059
www.hotel-oceanic.com
Thanks to the local municipality's ban on construction near Palolem beach, proper rooms are like gold dust in this area. Efficiently managed by a British couple, these are the most pleasantly furnished of the bunch, and benefit from a small pool and terrace restaurant. **££**

Cozy Nook
Tel: 264 3550
Well-located place to the north of Palolem beach with pleasant sea-facing cottages. Tasty Goan food is available. **£**

Palolem Beach Resort
Tel: 264 3054
A pleasant place with two-bedded tents and a few rooms with shared baths. The restaurant is popular and it can get a bit noisy. **£**

Panaji (0832)
Mandovi
D.B. Marg
Tel: 242 6270
Fax: 222 5451
www.hotelmandovigoa.com
A large business hotel with comfortable rooms which are surpisingly good value; some overlook the River Mandovi. There are two good restaurants and a bookshop. **££££**

Nova Goa
Dr A.B. Road
Tel: 222 6231
Fax: 222 4958
www.hotelnovagoa.com
Centrally located and modern, if a little faceless. Good amenities including a decent restaurant and a swimming pool. **£££**

Panjim (0832)
Casa Britona
Britona, near Panjim
Tel: 241 0962 or 9850 557665,
www.casabritona.com
Set amid the mangroves 4km (2½ miles) up the Mandovi from Panjim, this luxury hotel combines old-world elegance (four-posters, traditional planters' chairs and a wooden deck over the water) with modern amenities such as a swimming pool and smart restaurant. The atmosphere and situation are memorable, but the rates a little ambitious. **£££££**

Panjim Inn and Panjim Pousada
E-212, 31 Janeiro Road, Fontainhas
Tel: 243 5628
Fax: 222 8136
www.panjiminn.com
Two converted old town houses, run by the same owners. The first a Portuguese dating from the 1800s, the second a 1930s Hindu mansion. The rooms have period furniture, the Pousada's interior courtyard ("chowk") is very attractive, and both have displays of contemporary Goan art. **££**

Afonso
St Sebastian Chapel Square, Fontainhas
Tel: 222 2359
Handsomely restored Portuguese-era house in the heart of Panjim's most picturesque quarter, with a range of clean budget rooms and an airy rooftop terrace. **£**

Ponda (0832)
Hotel Atish
Farmagudi, 2 km (1 mile) from Ponda

Tel: 233 5382
Fax: 233 5249
www.hotelatish.com
Clean, AC rooms in a modern, largish hotel a little way out of Ponda. A pool and passable restaurant. **££**
President
Belgaum Road
Tel: 231 2287
Large, clean but basic suites, some AC. Good value. **£**

Salcette (0832)
Longuinho's Beach Resort
Tel: 278 8068–9
Fax: 278 8070
www.longuinhos.homestead.com
A popular and well-run hotel with good rooms overlooking the beach. **££**
Park Hyatt Goa
Arossim beach, Salcette
Tel: 272 1234
Sprawling five-star hotel with more than 250 rooms – some with hidden gardens where you can shower al fresco in complete privacy – built in Indo-Portuguese style. The pool is said to be Indian's biggest, and there's a glamorous spa and Ayurvedic health complex, in addition to all the usual facilities you'd expect from an international hotel. **£££££**

Siolim (0832)
Siolim House
Opposite Wadi Chapel, Siolim, Bardez
Tel: 227 2138
Fax: 227 2941
www.siolimhouse.com
A 300-year-old house, restored using traditional materials, with mother-of-pearl window panes and walls of shell and lime plaster. No AC. **££££**

Sinquerim (0832)
The Aquada Hermitage
Sinquerim, Bardez
Tel: (Beach Resort and Holiday Village) 247 9123; (Hermitage) 227 6201
www.tajhotels.com
This is a luxury complex of three Taj-owned hotels. The most exclusive – and therefore expensive – is the secluded Hermitage, with villas designed for heads of state. The Beach Resort, built on a 16th-century fort, and Holiday Village, "traditional" cottages, are marginally cheaper. All rooms have AC. **£££££**
Whispering Palms Beach Resort
Sinquerim Beach
Tel: 247 9140
www.whisperingpalms.com
A large resort complex with a decent pool and restaurants (the Aahaata serves good Indian food). The rooms – all with balcony and bath – are large and well maintained.
£££–££££

Marbella Guest House
Tel: 227 9551
Fax: 227 6509
In a quiet lane behind the Fort Aguada Resort, an imaginatively restored villa with six spotless rooms with bath. Book ahead. **££**

Tiracol (0832)
Tiracol Fort Heritage
Tel/fax: 226 8258
http://welcome.to/hoteltiracol
This converted fort has superb views over the coast. The quiet, comfortable rooms are set around the courtyard, with suites above. There is also an atmospheric restaurant. **££**

Vagator (0832)
Leoney Resort
Ozram Beach Road
Tel: 227 3634
Fax: 227 4914
www.nivalink.com/leoneys
Well located, with 16 clean, secure rooms and three cottages set around a pool. AC in all rooms. **£££**
Bethany Inn
Tel: 227 3731
www.bethanyinn.com
The best budget option. The spotless rooms have attached baths and fridges. **££**

Vainguinim Beach (0832)
Cidade de Goa
Tel: 245 4545
www.cidadedegoa.com
A well-located resort with two pools and a secluded beach. The food should be good as the resort includes the Academy of Culinary Education. **£££££**

Varca (0832)
Club Mahindra Varca Beach Resort
Varca Beach, Salcette
Tel: 274 4555
www.mhril.com
This well-run complex has spacious and comfortable apartments and a huge range of activites (a good place for children). There is also a good restaurant and wonderful pool. **££££**

Vasco da Gama (0834)
Hotel La Paz Gardens
Swatantra Path
Tel: 251 2121
Fax: 251 3302
www.hotellapazgardens.com
A large, comfortable hotel with good restaurants and a bar. The best in town. **££–£££**
Annapurna
Dattatreya Deshpande Road
Tel: 251 3375
A good budget option with clean rooms. The attached vegetarian restaurant does good North and South Indian meals. **£**

GUJARAT

Ahmadabad (079)
Taj Residency Ummed
International Airport Circle, Hansol
Tel: 2286 4444
www.tajhotels.com
Popular and comfortable, with all the five star trimmings, this is one of Ahmadabad's best hotels. The rooms are pleasant and there is an attractive restaurant. **£££££**
The House of Mangaldas Girdhardas
Opposite the Sidi Sayid Mosque
www.houseofmg.com
This heritage hotel in a 20th-century *haveli* has beautifully converted rooms; very elegant with lovely beds draped with mosquito nets. The attached Agashiye restaurant serves top notch Gujarati food and there is also the pleasant Green House café serving tasty snacks. **££££**
Embassy
Vasant Chowk, behind the Bank of Maharashtra, Lal Darwaza Bus Depot
Tel: 2550 7273
A good mid-budget choice. Rooms are comfortable, some with AC, and there is hot water and room service. **££**
Goodnight
Dr Tankaria Road, Lal Darwaza
Tel: 2550 6997
Very clean AC and non-AC rooms with attached bathrooms. The decent vegetarian restaurant serves Gujarati food. **££**

Bhavnagar (0278)
Nilambag Palace
Tel: 242 4241
Fax: 242 8072
nilambag@ad1.vsnl.net.in
A charming heritage hotel, formerly the royal palace, dating from 1859, with large, comfortable AC rooms, beautiful gardens and a pool. **£££££**
Blue Hill
Opposite Pill Garden
Tel: 242 6951
Fax: 242 7313
bluehill@ad1.vsnl.net.in
AC rooms in a pleasant, efficient hotel with a roof terrace and two good restaurants, the Gokul (Gujarati vegetarian dishes), and Nilgiri (North Indian). **££**
Vrindavan
Darbargadh
Tel: 251 9149
Clean, cheap and central rooms in part of an old palace. Some rooms have air conditioning. **££**

Gir (02877)
Gir Birding Lodge
Bambhafod Naka, Sasan, Gujarat
Tel: 255 514
www.girnationalpark.com
Straightforward and attractive

accommodation set in a mango orchard. Well run by knowledgeable staff. **£££**

Gir Lodge
Sasan, Junagadh 326 132, Gujarat
Tel: 285 521
www.tajhotels.com
A well-run and attractive hotel on the edge of the park, the comfortable rooms have lovely views over the Hiran River. Jeep safaris can also be arranged. **£££££**

Maneland Jungle Lodge
Sasan, Junagadh 362 135, Gujarat
Tel: 285 555
www.maneland.com
This is an excellent and well-priced option with attractive rooms and attentive staff. In a good location for wildlife spotting. **£££**

Gondal (02825)
The Riverside Palace and Orchard
Gondal
Tel: 220 002
Fax: 223 332
ssibal@ad1.vsnl.net.in
A converted royal palace with period English furniture. Accommodation includes the Maharaja's sumptuous railway carriage. Elegant, personal service. This is a good position from which to visit temples and wildlife. The family also run the **Dil Bahar** heritage hotel (a converted hunting mansion) in Bhavnagar. **£££££**

Vadodara (0265)
Express Hotel
R.C. Dutt Road
Tel: 233 0960
Fax: 233 0980
www.expressworld.com
A friendly hotel with modern, comfortable rooms at a reasonable price. There also is a traditionally decorated restaurant serving excellent Gujarati food. **££–£££**

Green
R.C. Dutt Road
Tel: 233 6111
A good, clean budget option in an old house with a great ambience. **£**

HIMACHAL PRADESH

Dalhousie (01899)
Alps Holiday Resort
Khajjiar Road, Bakrota Hills
Tel: 240 775
Fax: 242 840
http://alpsresortdalhousie.com
A modern hotel with a restaurant and a few sports facilities. The rooms are clean and comfortable, and the views from the hotel spectacular. **££**

Aroma-n-Claire
Court Road
Tel: 242 199

A sprawling old-fashioned hotel with character. The rooms are a little basic but some have great views and there is a restaurant and small library. **££**

Grand View Hotel
The Mall
Tel: 242 823
Fax: 240 609
Good suites, now starting to show their age, and a decent bar. **££–£££**

Hotel Mount View
Club Road
Tel: 242 120
Fax: 240 741
www.hotelmountview.com
Another "Victorian-style" building, but one of the better hotels in town. There are good facilities, and the rooms are well maintained and cosy. **£££**

Youth Hostel
Near the bus stand
Tel: 242 189
Fax: 240 929
www.yhaindia.com
Good budget accommodation with meals available. Reservations are recommended. **£**

Dharamsala (01892)
Glenmoor Cottages
Mall Road, McLeod Ganj
Tel: 221 010
Fax: 221 021
www.glenmoorcottages.com
Five self-contained cottages in a forest location. The setting is lovely and quiet, and meals are available on request. **£££**

Chonor House
Near Thekchen Choeling, Mcleod Ganj
Tel: 221 006
Fax: 221 468
www.norbulingka.org
Part of the Norbulingka Institute *(see website for details)*, who also run the **Norling Guest House** in Lower Dharamsala (www.tibet.org/norling), this is a quiet and comfortable hotel, decorated with Tibetan wall paintings. Popular with visiting celebrities, booking is essential. There is also a good Tibetan restaurant. **£££**

HPTDC Bhagsu
South End, Mcleod Ganj
Tel: 221 091
http://hptdc.nic.in
This government-run guesthouse has good value mid-budget rooms; all have attached baths with hot water. **££**

HPTDC Dhauladar
Kotwali Bazaar, Near Bus Stand, Lower Dharamsala
Tel: 224 926
Fax: 224 212
http://hptdc.nic.in
The large, airy rooms all have bath with hot water and a balcony. There are wonderful views from the restaurant terrace. **££**

Surya Resorts
South End, McLeod Ganj
Tel: 221 418
Fax: 221 868
www.suryaresorts.com
Modern and comfortable, the rooms are large and many have excellent views. The service is helpful and friendly, and the attached restaurant has good food. **££**

Hotel Tibet
Bhagsu Road, Mcleod Ganj
Tel: 221 587
Fax: 221 425
Good hotel, popular and well-priced, it has an excellent restaurant and view of the valley. Booking advised. **££**

Om
Near Bus Stand, McLeod Ganj
Tel: 221 313
A few good-value budget rooms, all very clean with attached showers. A small, good restaurant and lovely views complete the picture. **£**

Kangra (01894)
Taragarh Palace Hotel
Taragarh
Tel: 242 034
www.taragarh.com
Built in the 1930s, this was formerly a palace of the Maharaja of Kashmir. It has 16 pleasant rooms with period furniture. There is a good restaurant and a pool in lovely gardens. **££–£££**

Kasauli (01793)
HPTDC Ros Common
Lower Mall
Tel: 272 005
http://hptdc.nic.in
The best hotel and restaurant in town, in lovely surroundings. All rooms have baths with hot water. Book ahead. **££**

Gian
P.O. Road
Tel: 272 244
Decent, budget accommodation with clean, well-maintained rooms. **£**

Kullu (01902)
Span Resorts
P.O. Katrain, National Highway
Tel: 240 138
Fax: 240 140
http://spanresorts.com
A series of quiet and secluded

cottages with comfortable rooms, about 12 km (7½ miles) from Kullu. The resort offers various activities, including yoga. Good food is on offer in the restaurant. **££££–£££££**

Apple Valley Resort
Village Mohal, on National Highway
Tel: 224 115
Fax: 224 116
www.applevalleyresorts.com
Cottages on the bank of the Beas River 6 km (4 miles) from Kullu. Modern and comfortable with a decent restaurant, the resort also offers adventure sports, including rafting on the Beas River. **£££**

Shobla
Dhalpur
Tel: 222 800
Spacious rooms in a friendly hotel overlooking the river. There is also a good restaurant. **££**

HPTDC Hotel Sarvari
Southern end of town
Tel: 222 471
http://hptdc.nic.in
A good base in the town. The rooms are clean and some are quite large. There is a pleasant, cheap, restaurant and good views. (The HPTDC also runs the similar **Silver Moon** 2km/1 mile from Kullu at Shastrinagar.) **££**

Madhu Chandrika
Lower Dhalpur
Tel: 224 395
Fax: 222 720
A good budget option with rooms and dormitories. Near the bus-stand. **£**

Manali (01902)
Ambassador Resort
Sunny Side, Chadiyari
Tel: 252 235
www.ambassadorresorts.com
A well-designed and comfortable hotel with good views, on the eastern side of the Beas River. There is a wide variety of rooms – all of a high standard – and good Chinese and Indian food on offer. **££££**

Banon Resorts
New Hope Orchards
Tel: 253 026
Fax: 252 378
Stylish modern rooms with mountain views, set in a lovely garden. This quiet resort also has a good restaurant. **£££**

HPTDC Log Huts and Hamta Cottages
Old Manali Road
Tel: 252 407
http://hptdc.nic.in
Large, self-catering huts and cottages in a quiet, pleasant location. Comfortable if dated, with a lounge, kitchen and bath. **£££££**

John Banon's Hotel
Manali Orchards
Tel: 252 335
Fax: 252 392

A well-established guesthouse, with good rooms, lovely views and fine food. **££**

HPTDC Hotel Kunzam
Town centre
Tel: 253 197
http://hptdc.nic.in
A government-run hotel in the centre of Manali. Modern, comfortable rooms with attached baths and hot water. **££**

Johnson's Lodge
Circuit House Road
Tel: 253 023
www.johnsonslodge.0catch.com
Well-maintained, self-catering cottages set in an orchard. Food is available from the attached Johnson's Cafe. **££**

HPTDC Hotel Beas
On the river bank, towards Vashisht
Tel: 252 832
http://hptdc.nic.in
An excellent-value hotel in a splendid location. Well-run with decent rooms; meals available on request. **£–££**

HPTDC Hotel Rohtang Manalsu
The Mall
Tel: 252 332
http://hptdc.nic.in
A quiet hotel set in lovely grounds, out towards the Hadimba Temple. The large rooms have good views across the valley. **£–££**

Simla (0177)
Wildflower Hall
Mashroba, Charabra
Tel: 264 8585
Fax: 264 8686
www.oberoiwildflowerhall.com
A fabulous hilltop resort, formerly the residence of Lord Kitchener. Stunning views, luxurious surroundings and a world-class spa make this one of India's finest hotels. **£££££**

Chapslee House
Lakkar Bazaar
Tel: 280 2542
Fax: 265 8663
www.chapslee.com
A Simla institution. A very elegant manor house with wonderful suites, period furnishings and antiques, as well as excellent food. Book in advance. **£££££**

Oberoi Cecil
Chaura Maidan
Tel: 280 4848
Fax: 281 1024
www.oberoicecil.com
A stylish and luxurious Simla landmark, with a fabulous pool, restaurant and well-appointed rooms with excellent views. **£££££**

Hotel Combermere
The Mall, opposite the lift
Tel: 265 1246
Fax: 265 2251
www.hotelcombermere.com
A friendly, modern hotel near the centre of town. Good, comfortable

rooms and helpful staff give the hotel a pleasant air. **£££–££££**

Hotel Shingar
The Mall
Tel: 225 2881
Fax: 225 2998
stylco@sancharnet.in
Good-value, clean rooms and a decent restaurant, situated near the lift. **££**

Hotel Dalziel
The Mall
Tel: 265 2394
Fax: 265 1504
dalziel@sancharnet.in
A reasonable hotel with OK rooms, all with attached bath and hot water. Good Indian meals available. **£–££**

YMCA
The Ridge
Tel: 225 2375
Fax: 221 1016
Very popular. Large, old-fashioned rooms with shared bathrooms. There is also a dining hall. **£**

YWCA
Constantia
Tel: 220 3081
Cheap and clean rooms for both sexes. This good value hostel is in a great position. Book ahead as it is often full. **£**

JHARKHAND

Ranchi (0651)
Railway Hotel
Tel: 220 8048
www.indianrailways.gov.in
An excellent option. A well-kept hotel, run by Indian Railways, in a pleasant old building. Clean rooms (some AC) and a good restaurant. **££**

KARNATAKA

Bandipur National Park (08229)
Bandipur Safari Lodge
Melkamanahalli
Tel: 633 001
www.junglelodges.com
Very well-run basic accommodation in modern cottages (no AC) close to the park entrance. Knowledgeable staff and good Jeep safaris for watching the wildlife. Recommended. **£££**

Country Club Bush Betta
Mangala
Tel: 236 090
www.countryclubindia.net
This resort has over 60 rooms and a
large swimming pool. A little way from
the park entrance but good for
families. **£££–££££**

Forest Department Cottages
For reservations contact:
The Field Director, Project Tiger,
Aranya Bhavan, Ashokapuram,
Mysore 570 008
Tel/fax: 0821-248 0901
www.karnatakatourism.org
Basic accommodation, some of it in
very cheap dormitories, in good
locations. **£–££**

Hotel Mayura Prakruti
Melkamanahalli
Tel: 233 001
www.karnatakatourism.org
Simple budget accommodation but
one of the best options near the park.
Good-value cottages and a decent
outdoor restaurant. **£**

Tusker Trails
Mangala
Tel: 0821-263 6055
Basic (no AC) but clean and
comfortable accommodation in a nice
forested setting. Good opportunities
for wildlife spotting, and safaris are
conducted twice daily. **££££**

Bangalore (080)

The Oberoi
37–9 Mahatma Gandhi Road
Tel: 2558 5858
Fax: 2558 5960
www.oberoibangalore.com
A very expensive but luxurious hotel
with beautiful gardens. The rooms and
suites all have private "sit out" areas
overlooking the gardens. **£££££**

The Park
14/7 Mahatma Gandhi Road
Tel: 2559 4666
Fax: 2559 4029
www.theparkhotels.com
A very swish, modern hotel. The
rooms are elegant and bright, and
there is the excellent Monsoon
restaurant. **£££££**

Shreyas
Santoshima Farm, Near Gollahalli
gate, Nelamangala
Tel: 2773 7102
www.shreyasretreat.com
This is a quiet yoga retreat, often
used for private workshops but can
provide guests with a tailored
wellness holiday. **£££££**

The Taj West End
55 Race Course Road
Tel: 5660 5660
Fax: 5660 5700
www.tajhotels.com
A beautiful old garden hotel,
Bangalore's most attractive five-star.

The lawnside rooms and restaurants
are recommended. The Taj Group also
runs two modern business hotels in the
centre of Bangalore, the **Taj Residency**
on M.G. Road, and the **Gateway Hotel**
on Residency Road *(see the website
above for details)*. **£££££**

Highgates Hotel
33 Church Street
Tel: 2559 7172
Fax: 2559 7799
Very central and well maintained
hotel. Comfortable, good value AC
rooms. Price includes breakfast.
Recommended. **£££**

Hotel Infantry Court
66 Infantry Road
Tel: 2559 1800
hotelic@vsnl.com
Modern, central hotel with
comfortable rooms which are good
value for Bangalore. The price
includes breakfast but watch out for
hidden extras. **£££**

Niligiri's Nest
171 Brigade Road
Tel: 2558 8401
Fax: 2558 2853
nilgrisnest@vsnl.net
A central hotel with large, clean AC
rooms and a restaurant. **£££**

Woodlands Hotel
5 Raja Ram Mohan Roy Road
Tel: 2222 5111
Fax: 2223 6963
wood@bgl.vsnl.net.in
A large but pleasant hotel, well
established, with good-value rooms
and a decent restaurant. **£££**

Hotel Ajantha
22A Mahatma Gandhi Road
Tel/fax: 2558 4321
bagilthay@vsnl.com
Excellent-value large rooms, some
with AC, in good location. There is
also a good vegetarian South Indian
restaurant. **££**

Kamat Yatri Nivas
4 1st Cross, Gandhinagar
Tel: 2226 0088
Fax: 2228 1070
kamat@blr.vsnl.net.in
Located towards the railway station,
this is a modern budget hotel. The 4th
floor South Indian restaurant has
exceptionally good North Karnatakan
vegetarian food. **££**

YHA
65/2 Millers Road, Benson Town
Cantonment
Tel: 2354 0849
bangalore_youthhostel@yahoo.co.in
A modern building with clean AC and
non-AC rooms, and a very cheap
dormitory. Book ahead. **£**

Gokarna (08386)

Hotel Gokarna International
Kumta Taluk, Gokarna
Tel: 657 368/656 848

A comfortable option and good value
for money, though on the main road at
the entrance to the town and thus
prone to traffic noise during the day. **£**

KSTDC Hotel Mayura Samudra
Tel: 256 236
http://kstdc.nic.in
A little out of the way, and with just
three exceptionally good-value, large,
clean rooms. There is a pretty garden
and a basic restaurant. **£**

Nimmu's
Behind the beach
Tel: 656 730
Large budget guesthouse. The rooms
are clean and have bathrooms. Only a
stone's throw away from the temples
and town beach, but a peaceful location
nonetheless. **£**

Hassan (08172)

Hotel Suvarna Regency
97 B.M. Road
Tel: 264 006
Fax: 263 822
An excellent-value modern hotel
with comfortable AC rooms. There is
also a restaurant serving Indian food.
££

Southern Star Hassan
B.M. Road
Tel: 251 816
Fax: 268 916
www.ushashriramhotels.com
A well-run and clean hotel with decent
rooms, most with AC. More expensive
than some but with friendly and
helpful service. **££**

Vaishnavi Lodging
Harsha Mahal Road
Tel: 267 413
Clean and roomy budget
accommodation with a vegetarian
restaurant. **£**

Hampi Bazaar (08394)

Hotel Mayura Bhuvaneshwari
Kamalapur
Tel: 241 574
Fax: 228 537
http://kstdc.nic.in
Good-value AC and non-AC rooms a lit-
tle distance from the site. Good food
is available in the restaurant. **£**

Shanti Lodge
Near Virupaksha Temple
Tel: 241 568
Spotlessly clean rooms with shared
bathrooms, overlooking a shaded
inner courtyard. **£**

Hospet (08394)

Hotel Malligi
6/143 Jambunath Road
Tel: 228 101
Fax: 227 038
Close to M.G. Road. A quite expensive
but popular hotel with bar, restaurant
and a good pool (non-residents may
pay to use the pool). **££**

Hotel Price Categories

The rates below are for a double room (AC where available) in high season, including taxes.

£££££	Rs3,700 and above
££££	Rs2,700–3,700
£££	Rs1,700–2,700
££	Rs800–1,700
£	Up to Rs800

Hotel Priyadarshini
V-45 Station Road
Tel: 228 838
Fax: 24709
priyainn@vsnl.com
AC rooms with balconies, helpful and friendly service and a garden restaurant looking out over the sugarcane and paddy fields. Hot water 6.30–9.30am. **££**

Hotel Shivananda
Beside KSRTC Bus Stand, College Road
Tel: 220 700
Cleanish, good value rooms with attached bath, and a small restaurant. Hot water is available 6–9am. **££**

Mangalore (0824)

Manjarun Hotel
Old Port Road, Bunder
Tel: 566 0420
Fax: 566 0585
www.tajhotels.com
A little way out of town, this modern Taj-run hotel has good-value, comfortable rooms, some with sea view. There is a pool and a restaurant serving Indian and Western food. **£££**

Hotel Poonja International
K.S. Rao Road
Tel: 244 0171
Fax: 244 1081
www.hotelpoonjainternational.com
Very good-value, clean rooms in a large modern hotel. Well run with excellent food in the restaurant. **££**

KSTDC Maurya Netravati
Kadri Hills
Tel: 221 1192
http://kstdc.nic.in
Extremely good-value, large and clean rooms; decent restaurant. **£–££**

Mysore (0821)

ITDC Lalitha Mahal Palace Hotel
Siddhartha Nagar
Tel: 247 0470
Fax: 247 0555
www.theashokgroup.com
Palatial rooms with wonderful period bathrooms, in a neoclassical building sporting a dome modelled on St Paul's cathedral in London. Excellent service and an impressive Wedgewood-blue restaurant, as well as a pleasant pool and gardens. **£££££**

Green Hotel
Chittaranjan Palace, 2270 Vinoba

Road, Jayalakshmipuram
Tel: 525 5000-2
Fax: 251 6139
www.greenhotelindia.com
A charming palace conversion in own gardens a little way out of town. A remarkable project in sustainable tourism through energy-saving and equal-opportunity employment. Good value, attractive rooms and superb food. Highly recommended. **££–£££**

The Viceroy
Sri Harsha Road
Tel: 242 4001
Fax: 243 3391
Clean, modern hotel with well-appointed rooms. The restaurant serves good North Indian food. **££**

KSTDC Mayura Hoysala and Yatrinivas
2 Jhansi Lakshmibai Road
Tel: 242 5349
http://kstdc.nic.in
Extremely good-value large rooms. There is also a decent bar and restaurant and pleasant gardens. The Yatrinivas (tel: 242 3492) adjoining the Hoysala has a very cheap dormitory. **£**

Hotel Ritz
Bangalore–Nilgiri Road
Tel: 242 2668
Fax: 242 9082
Characterful little hotel with only four rooms around balcony with a guest's dining area. The rooms have mosquito nets and attached bathroom with hot water. Good restaurant downstairs. Book ahead. Recommended. **£**

Nagarhole

Forest Department Cottages
Book through:
Conservator of Forests, Kodagu Circle, Aranya Bhavan, Madikeri 571 201, Karnataka
Tel: 08272-225 708
www.karnatakatourism.org
Basic lodges with simple but clean rooms; food is available, as are Jeeps for safaris. **££–£££**

Jungle Inn
Veeranahosalli, Hunsur,
Murkal–Nagarhole Road, Mysore District 570 011, Karnataka
Tel: 0822-246 022
www.jungleinnnagarhole.com
Decent rooms in a well-run resort. The wildlife watching facilities are excellent and safaris within the park are accompanied by a knowledgeable naturalist. **£££££**

Kabini River Lodge
Karapur, Nissana Beltur, Mysore District 571 114, Karnataka
Tel: 08228-264 402
www.junglelodges.com
One of the best wildlife lodges in India. Comfortable accommodation, decent food and excellent advice available from the resident

naturalists. Very good value and highly recommended. **££££–£££££**

Water Woods
19 Karapur, Mysore District 571 114, Karnataka
Tel: 0821-226 4421
www.waterwoods.net
Beautifully kept and comfortable accommodation overlooking the river. Decent buffet food and good access to the park by boat or Jeep. **£££££**

KERALA

Alappuzha (0477)

La Casa del Fauno
Muhamma, Aryakkara
Tel: 286 0862
www.casadelfauno.com
A very classy homestay, about 8 km (5 miles) from Alappuzha. The rooms are spotless and attractive in a kitschy-minimalist sort of way. The facilities include boat hire, Ayurvedic treatments and a pool. **£££££**

Kayaloram Heritage Lake Resort
Punnamada
Tel: 223 2040
Fax: 223 1871
www.kayaloram.com
A peaceful resort 4 km (2½ miles) from Alappuzha (free transfer at 11am, 1pm). Individual Keralan-style wooden cottages, as well as a restaurant and pool. Stays can also be arranged in *kettuvallams* – traditional boats. **£££–££££**

Raheem Residency
Beach Road, Alleppey-688012
Tel: 223 0767
Mobile: 94470 82241
www.raheemresidency.com
A heritage home located on a quiet Kerala beach. Rooms are decorated in Mughal style. Pool, Ayurveda suites and a writers' retreat. **£££**

Emerald Isle Heritage Villa
Kanjooparambil–Manimalathara
Tel: 2703 899
Mobile: 94470 77555
www.emeraldislekerala.com
A highly recommended, peaceful retreat. Four guest rooms with lovely "outdoor" bathrooms, in a traditional house set in idyllic tropical surroundings. Excellent Keralan meals and considerate service. Twelve km (7 miles) from Alappuzha; call in advance so the boat is waiting for you at the jetty to take you to the island. **£££**

Alleppey Prince Hotel
A.S. Road
Tel: 224 3752
Fax: 224 3758
Decent, clean AC rooms, restaurant and pool. Kathakali dance performances are occasionally staged and backwater tours can be organised from here. **££**

KTDC Yatri Nivas
Motel Aram Compound, A.S. Road
Tel: 224 4460
Fax: 224 4463
www.ktdc.com
Good-value rooms AC rooms (very cheap non-AC accommodation) in a government-run guesthouse. **£**

Athirapalli (0480)
Rainforest
Kannamkuzhy
Tel: 276 9062
www.avenuecenter.com
This peaceful resort has superb views over the waterfalls and surrounding forests, which make up for the rather basic rooms and facilities. **£££**

Bekal (0467)
Gitanjali Heritage
Panayal
Tel: 223 4159
www.gitanjaliheritage.com
This is a wonderful place to base yourself. Mr Jagannathan and his family are very welcoming and their 70-year-old home, a traditional *kodoth* house, is beautifully maintained. It is set in a delightful garden and the food is excellent. Mr Jagannathan is also a mine of information on the local *teyyam* dances. This is a highly recommended retreat. **£££**

Guruvayur (0487)
Vrindavan Tourist Home
Next to KSRTC Bus Stand, West Nada
Tel: 255 4033
A rather sweet and well-maintained budget lodge that mainly caters to pilgrims. The staff are welcoming, the rooms clean and very good value. **£**

Kannur (0497)
Royal Omars Hotel
Thavakkara, opposite
Bharat Petroleum
Tel: 276 9091
A flash, modern business hotel near the railway station. Remarkably good-value comfortable rooms and facilities. **££–£££**

Kochi-Ernakulam (0484)
The Brunton Boatyard
Calvetty Road, Fort Cochin
Tel: 221 5461
www.cghearth.com
A luxury hotel in a splendid location, built in the style of early Portugese and Dutch colonial architecture. Elegant and beautifully appointed rooms and bathrooms. A restaurant serves local dishes recreated from historical recipes. **£££££**
Malabar House Residency
1/268–9 Parade Road, Fort Cochin
Tel: 221 6666
Fax: 221 7777

malabarhouse@vsnl.com
Luxury hotel in a refurbished 300-year-old house within the fort area. The rooms are comfortable and furnished with antiques, and the food in the restaurant is excellent. **£££££**
Taj Malabar
Malabar Road, Willingdon Island
Tel: 266 6811
Fax: 266 8297
www.tajhotels.com
One of the best hotels in the state – rooms in the old wing are more atmospheric. There are also good restaurants – especially eating outside overlooking the harbour – and a pool. **£££££**
The Avenue Regent
39/2026 M.G. Road, Ernakulam
Tel: 237 7688
Fax: 237 5329
avenue@md2.vsnl.net.in
A modern business hotel with very comfortable rooms. The restaurant is very good (try the buffet lunch) and the chic Loungevity bar is one of the best in the state. **££££**
Casino Hotel
Willingdon Island
Tel: 266 8221
Fax: 266 8001
www.cghearth.com
Comfortable hotel with a highly recommended seafood restaurant. Very clean and tasteful rooms and a good pool. A little way from the centre of Ernakulam but convenient buses go to M.G. Road. **£££££**
Avenue Center Hotel
Panampilly Avenue,
Panampilly Nagar, Kochi
Tel: 231 5301
Fax: 231 5304
www.avenuehotels.in
A busines hotel and convention center with a good, central location. **£££**
Abad Plaza
M.G. Road, Ernakulam
Tel: 238 1222
Fax: 237 0729
www.abadhotels.com
A good, modern hotel with clean rooms in central Ernakulam. There is a pool and a decent restaurant serving seafood. **£££**
Delight Tourist Resort
Parade Ground, Fort Kochi
Tel: 221 6301
www.delightfulhomestay.com
A quiet little guesthouse with spotless rooms right in the centre of Fort Kochi. Comfy beds, a lovely garden and a helpful travel desk. **££–£££**
Adams Hotel
South Junction, Ernakulam
Tel: 237 7707
A good-value hotel above Pizza Hut, very convenient for the railway station. Rooms are clean and the service efficient. **££**

Woodlands
M.G. Road, Ernakulam
Tel: 238 2051
Fax: 238 2080
woodland1@vsnl.com
A comfortable hotel with clean, excellent-value AC rooms (cheaper non-AC) and a good vegetarian restaurant. **££**
SAAS Tower Hotel
Cannon Shed Road, near Boat Jetty,
Ernakulam
Tel: 236 5319
Fax: 236 7365
This good value hotel has decent if smallish rooms. The attached restaurant has good Indian food. **£–££**
YHA
NGO Qrts Junction, Thrikkakra
Tel: 242 2808
Fax: 242 4399
www.yhaindia.com
A bit out of the way behind Ernakulam Junction, but clean, good value and quiet. Meals are available. **£**

Kollam (0474)
Hotel Sudarshan
Paramesvar Nagar, Hospital Road
Tel: 274 4322
Fax: 274 0480
www.hotelsudarshan.com
Clean, largish AC rooms with attached bath, hot water. There is also a restaurant and snack bar. **££**
KTDC Yatri Nivas
Ashramom, Guest House Compound
Tel: 274 5538
www.ktdc.com
A large, government-run hotel with good-value, basic rooms beside the lake, opposite the jetty. **£**
Government Guest House
Ashramom
Tel: 274 3620
Formerly the British residency, on Ashtamudi Lake. Very atmospheric, it has five spacious rooms and food, if ordered in advance. Backwater trips may be arranged (pick-up from the jetty across from the garden). **£**

Kottayam (0481)
Coconut Lagoon
Vembanad Lake
Tel: (0484) 266 8221
www.cghearth.com
One of the finest resorts in Kerala, about 10 km (6 miles) from Kottayam and only accessible by boat. The facilities are first-class, including the Ayurvedic treatments, and the rooms are tasteful and luxurious. **£££££**
Vembanad Lake Resort
Kodimatha
Tel: 236 1633
Fax: 236 0866
Located 3 km (2 miles) from the town. Comfortable cottages in gardens by lake. A good restaurant on a house

boat serves *tanduri* and seafood dishes. **££**

Hotel Aida
Aida Junction, M.C. Road
Tel: 256 8391
Fax: 256 8399
www.hotelaidakerala.com
Good-value, comfortable rooms, all with en-suite bath and hot water; the restaurant serves Indian dishes. **££**

KTDC Aiswarya
Thirunakkara
Tel: 258 1440
Fax: 256 5618
Pleasant rooms, with optional AC and cable TV; restaurant. **££**

Kovalam (0471)

Coconut Bay
Vizhinjam
Tel: 248 0566
www.coconutbay.com
A well-run and quiet resort, just behind the beach, set out in small bungalows. The staff are discreetly attentive and the Ayurvedic package here is extremely good. **£££££**

The Leela Kovalam
Tel: 248 0101
www.theleela.com
Striking hotel complex (previously the Kovalam Ashok), designed in part by Charles Correa. The hotel now includes the Halcyon Castle, summer palace of the Maharajas of Travancore. Expensive but exceptionally luxurious, with a great pool and in a superb location. **£££££**

Surya Samudra Beach Garden
Tel: 226 7333
Fax: 248 0413
www.suryasamudra.com
An expensive and exclusive resort with accommodation in relocated traditional houses. About 8 km (5 miles) from Kovalam in wonderful, quiet location overlooking the sea. **£££££**

Taj Green Cove Resort
G.V. Raja Vattapara Road
Tel: 248 7733
Fax: 248 7744
www.tajhotels.com
The Taj group doing what it does best: well-run, low-key luxury. Very comfortable rooms and cottages set in lovely grounds; superb pool. **£££££**

Lagoona Davina
Pachalloor
Tel: 238 0049
Fax: 238 2651
www.lagoonadavina.com
Peaceful resort, close to Pozhikkara Beach, run by Englshwoman Davina Taylor. The attractive rooms have four-poster beds; good food, Ayurvedic massage and yoga classes. **££££**

Hotel Sea Face
N.U.P. Beach Road
Tel: 248 1835
Fax: 248 1320

www.hotelseaface.com
A popular hotel close to the beach. Pleasant, clean rooms, friendly staff, good restaurant and pool. **££££**

Hotel Neelakanta
Lighthouse Beach
Tel: 248 0321
Fax: 248 0421
www.hotelneelakantakovalam.com
This hotel is right on the beach front. The rooms have huge windows and balconies, which give you a great view over the sea. **££–£££**

Hotel Rockholm
Lighthouse Road
Tel: 248 0306
Fax: 248 0607
www.rockholm.com
Pleasant hotel at the end of Light House Beach. The spotless rooms have great views and there is a good restaurant. **££–£££**

Maharaju Palace
Tel: (0031) 299 372 597
www.maharajupalace.nl
A Dutch-owned hotel (book through the Netherlands) close to the lighthouse. Very pleasant and quiet and only 30 metres (100 ft) from the beach. **££**

Kozhikode (0495)

Kadavu
N.H. Bypass Road, Azhinjilam
Tel: 283 0570
Fax: 283 0575
www.kadavuresorts.com
Beautifully located hotel, 14 km (8½ miles) from Kozhikode. The comfortable rooms and suites all have spectacular river views, and there is good food in the restaurant. **£££££**

Malabar Palace
Manuelsons Junction, G.H. Road
Tel: 272 1511
www.malabarpalacecalicut.com
Comfortable mid-budget choice with good AC rooms. Friendly service and an excellent restaurant. **££**

Alakapuri Hotel
Moulana Mohamed Ali Road
Tel: 272 3451
Fax: 272 0219
An excellent-value colonial-style guesthouse. The large rooms with bath are full of character. The restaurant serves good Indian food. **£**

Munnar (04865)

The Windermere Estate
PO Box 21, Pothamedu
Tel: 230 512
www.windermeremunnar.com
Attractive, simple rooms in secluded planter's cottages with stunning views over the hills. It is beautifully quiet and very relaxing. **£££££**

The Olive Brook
In the Tata Tea Estate, Pothamedu
Tel: 230 588

Hotel Price Categories

The rates below are for a double room (AC where available) in high season, including taxes.

£££££	Rs3,700 and above
££££	Rs2,700–3,700
£££	Rs1,700–2,700
££	Rs800–1,700
£	Up to Rs800

www.olivebrookmunnar.com
These two bungalows set high above the town are a lovely retreat. The staff are great and there is cooking demonstrations in the evening. Highly recommended. **££££**

Blackberry Hills
Bison Valley Road, Pothamedu
Tel: 232 978
www.blackberryhillsindia.com
A group of cottages 3 km (2 miles) out of town in an idyllic location. Well kept, with stunning views. The staff can arrange treks in the surrounding countryside. **£££–££££**

Edassery East End
Temple Road
Tel: 230 451
Fax: 230 227
www.edasserygroup.com
This large hotel has comfortable double rooms in the main building, and a series of cottages in the well-maintained grounds. Good value for its location and facilities, this is one of the best hotels in the town. **£££**

Isaac's Residency
Top Station Road
Tel: 230 501
A comfortable, modern hotel close to the centre of town. The rooms are spacious and well maintained, and those at the front of the building have excellent views. The in-house restaurant is not bad. **£££**

Periyar Wildlife Park (04869)

Aranya Niwas
Thekkady, Idukki 685 536, Kerala
Tel: 222 023
www.ktdc.com
Set on the banks of the lake, this somewhat dated but still comfortable retreat retains some of its colonial charm. **££££–£££££**

Bamboo Grove
Periyar Tiger Reseve, Thekkady 685 536, Kerala
Tel: 224 571
www.periyartigerreserve.org
Set right inside the park, these simple huts are perfect for serious wildlife observation. Book in advance. **£££**

Jungle Inn
Periyar Tiger Reseve, Thekkady 685 536, Kerala
Tel: 224 571

www.periyartigerreserve.org
A rare opportunity to spend a night in amongst the wildlife of the park. A small, secluded hut that is ideally placed for forest treks. **£–££**

Lake Palace
Thekkady, Idukki 685 536, Kerala
Tel: 222 023
www.ktdc.com
Previously belonging to the Maharaja of Travancore, this small heritage resort is a great base for wildlife-spotting trips. **£££££**

Periyar House
Thekkady, Idukki 685 536, Kerala
Tel: 222 026
www.ktdc.com
Good-value budget accommodation near the park, Clean and comfortable rooms and friendly staff. **££**

Spice Village
Kumily Road, Thekkady 685 536, Kerala
Tel: 224 514
www.cghearth.com
Traditional-style thatched cottages in beautiful grounds. Very comfortable and excellent service. Forest walks and Ayurvedic treatments are on offer. Recommended. **£££££**

Silent Valley

Forest Department Rest House
Mukkali
Book through: Wildlife Warden, Silent Valley National Park, Mannarkkad, Palakkad, Kerala
Tel: 0492-242 2056/245 3225
www.keralaforest.org
Basic accommmodation ranging from simple doubles to a dormitory. You must be accompanied by a forest guard to enter the sanctuary. **£**

Thiruvananthapuram (0471)

The Muthoot Plaza
Punnen Road
Tel: 233 7733
Fax: 233 7734
www.sarovarhotels.com
The city's top business hotel, with very comfortable rooms and good facilities. **££££**

The South Park
M.G. Road
Tel: 233 3333
Fax: 233 1861
www.thesouthpark.com
Swish hotel with a flash lobby, aimed at the business market. The rooms are not quite as impressive and a little overpriced. **££££**

Residency Tower
South Gate of Secretariat, Press Road
Tel: 233 1661
Fax: 233 1311
www.residencytower.com
A modern, comfortable hotel with good facilities. There are good restaurants and a rooftop pool. Good

value for what's on offer. **£££–££££**

Mascot Hotel
P.M.G Junction
Tel: 231 8990
Fax: 231 7745
www.ktdc.com
Pleasant, quiet hotel, originally built to house British officers during World War I. Well-priced rooms and a good restaurant. **££**

Hotel Chaithram
Central Station Road, Thampanoor
Tel: 233 0977
Fax: 233 1446
www.ktdc.com
A clean, good value and comfortable KTDC hotel opposite the railway station. Rooms have AC and attached baths. Good restaurant. **££**

Hotel Highland Park
Manjalikulam Road, Thampanoor
Tel: 223 8800
Fax: 233 2645
A newish hotel with both AC and non-AC rooms at good rates. The rooms are well maintained and there is a decent vegetarian restaurant. **££**

Greenland Lodging
Aristo Road
Tel: 232 3485
Very convenient for the Railway and Bus Stations. A decent, budget hotel with clean rooms. **£–££**

Hotel Prathiba Heritage
Dharmalayam Road
Tel: 233 6442
Very central with clean and safe rooms in a friendly hotel. Filtered water available. **£**

Hazeen Tourist Home
off Aristo Road
Tel: 232 5181
On the second road on the right coming from the railway station. Good, clean rooms in quiet hotel. **£**

Thrissur (0487)

Mannapuram Hotel
Kuruppam Road
Tel: 244 0933
Fax: 242 7692
A modern, attractive hotel with clean, comfortable rooms. Well-run with a good restaurant. Good value. **££**

Ramanilayam Government Guest House
Palace Road
Tel: 233 2016
Strictly speaking for visiting officials only, but you may get in. Huge suites with balconies in a very atmospheric colonial mansion. Food available to order in advance. Excellent value. **£**

KTDC Yatri Nivas
Near Indoor Stadium
Tel: 233 2333
Fax: 233 2122
www.ktdc.com
A good budget option with clean rooms. Snacks available. **£**

Varkala

Taj Garden Retreat
Near Government Guest House, Janardana Puram
Tel: 260 3000
www.tajhotels.com
A luxury resort hotel near to the beach. There are great views from its hilltop position. Good restaurants and pool. **£££££**

Villa Jacaranda
Temple Road West
Tel: 0470-261 0296
www.villa-jacaranda.biz
Spotless, nicely designed rooms in a modern guesthouse. The surrounding gardens are quite beautiful and the views of sunset over the sea breathtaking. **££££**

Waynad

Green Magic Nature Resort
Book through: Tour India, P.O. Box 163, near S.M.V. High School, M.G. Road, Thiruvananthapuram
Tel: 0471-233 0437
Fax: 0471-233 1407
www.tourindiakerala.com
Accommodation is in either a wonderful treehouse or cottages set in the heart of a pristine rainforest. This is an eco-resort in the true sense of the term (they use bio-gas and solar power, serve organic food and only natural cosmetics are allowed). Not cheap, but a unique experience. **£££££**

Jungle Park Resort
52a Vrindhavan Colony, Chevayur, Kozhikode
Tel: 0495-552 1163
www.jungleparkresorts.com
Beautifully located in the Fintser Hills, this eco resort offers the opportunity to stay in traditional-style cottages right in the forest. **££££–£££££**

Forest Rest Houses
In Tholpetty, Muthanga, Kurichat and Thirunelly
Book through:
Wildlife Warden, Waynad Widlife Division, Sulthanbathery
Tel: (04936) 220 454
www.keralaforest.org
A series of simple huts and dormitories in the wildlife reserve. All of them are provided with a cook and a guide. **£**

KOLKATA (033)

Hotel Hindustan International
235/1 J C Bose Road
Tel: 2283 0505
Fax: 2280 0111
www.hhihoteld.com
Ccentrally air-conditioned, 15 km (10 miles) from airport and 5 km (3 miles) from railway station. **£££££**

Hotel Sonar Bangla Sheraton Tower
JBS Haldane Avenue
Tel: 2345 4545
www.welcomgroup.com
Multi-cusine resturants, banquet
rooms, pool, sauna and health club,
cable TV and the usual facilities one
expects in a five-star hotel. **£££££**

Hyatt Regency
JA1 Sector 3, Salt Lake City
Tel: 2335 1234
Fax: 2335 1235
www.hyatt.com
All five-star facilities. **£££££**

MBD Airport Hotel
Netaji Subhas Chandra Bose
International Airport
Tel: 2511 9111
Fax: 2511 9137
www.fhrai.com
Indian and continental cusine.
Conference Hall to seat 300. Bar,
resturant, coffee house, swimming
pool and all regular amenities. **£££££**

The Oberoi Grand
15 Jawaharlal Nehru Road
Tel: 2249 2323
Fax: 2249 1217
www.oberoikolkata.com
A Kolkata landmark. A very elegant
hotel with extremely luxurious rooms
and suites. Excellent restaurants
including La Terrasse (French), and
the Baan Thai. **£££££**

The Park Hotel
17 Park Street
Tel: 2249 9000
Fax: 2249 4000
www.theparkhotels.com
A central five-star hotel, with all the
usual amenities and attractive rooms.
Good restaurants, including one with
Thai and Szechuan food. **£££££**

The Kenilworth
1–2 Little Russell Street
Tel: 2282 3939
Fax: 2282 5136
www.kenilworthhotels.com
Elegant rooms in a quiet hotel. Those
in the new wing are good value. There
is a decent restaurant, bar and
garden. **£££££**

Taj Bengal
34b Belvedere Road, Alipore
Tel: 2223 3939
Fax: 2223 1766
www.tajhotels.com
A very plush five-star Taj Group hotel
with an impressive entrance lobby.
The rooms are very comfortable, if
aimed at the business market, and
there are a number of excellent
restaurants, including the Chinoiserie
(Chinese). Near enough the zoo for
the lion's roar to wake you in the
morning. **£££££**

Tollygunge Club
120 Deshapran Sasmal Road
Tel: 2473 4539
www.thetollygungeclub.com

If you can afford it, and get in, this is
one of the best places to stay in
Kolkata. Beautiful grounds and
excellent sports facilities; in South
Kolkata close to a metro station.
Advance booking is essential. **££££**

Lytton Hotel
14 & 14/1 Sudder Street
Tel: 2249 1872
Fax: 2217 4730
Centrally air-conditioned. Room entry
on electronic key card. **£££– ££££**

The Astor
15 Shakespeare Sarani
Tel: 2282 9957
Fax: 2282 7430
A Victorian house with comfortable
rooms. Centrally located, garden,
good restaurants and bar. **£££**

Fairlawn Hotel
13a Sudder Street
Tel: 2252 1510
Fax: 2252 1835
www.fairlawnhotel.com
A legendary hotel which seeks to
maintain a Raj-era ambience (for
example, the full English breakfast).
Well-run and not without a certain
eccentric charm, it has comfortable
rooms and a pleasant garden. **£££**

Middleton Inn
10 Middleton Street
Tel: 2216 0449
Fax: 2246 8520
mchamber@vsnl.net
Clean, pleasant rooms in a well-run
hotel. All have AC and attached bath
with hot water. Good, central location
though still quiet. **£££**

The Great Eastern
1,2,3, Old Court House Street
Tel: 2248 2311-31
There was a time that The Great
Eastern was mentioned along
with Raffles of Singapore and The
Taj of Bombay. But that was a long
time ago. Built in 1841, it was
amongst the first premises in Calcutta
to get electricity in 1883. But when
the capital was moved from Calcultta
to Delhi, it gradually declined. The
Communist government has sold it to
to a private party and it is waiting to
live again. **££**

Hotel Shalimar
3 S.N. Banerjee Road, next to the
Regal Cinema
Tel: 2228 5016
Fax: 2228 0616
hotelshalimar@vsnl.com
Reasonable AC accommodation in a
central hotel. The attached restaurant
serves Indian and Chinese food. **££**

Hotel Victerrace
1B Gorky Terrace, off Camac Street,
behind Gorky Sadan
Tel: 2283 2753
Fax: 2283 2967
www.victerrace.com
Reasonable AC rooms. **££**

WBTDC Udayachal Tourist Lodge
D.G. Block, Salt Lake
Tel: 2337 8246
www.wbtourism.com
Basic but clean rooms – non-AC much
cheaper – located a little out of town.
Meals and snack are available. **££**

YWCA
1 Middleton Row
Tel: 2229 7033
An excellent option – admits men and
women – quiet and pleasant. Very
clean rooms and a dormitory, the
price includes all meals. **££**

Railway Yatri Niwas
Howrah Station
Tel: 2248 2522/2660 1742
Rooms and dormitories for railway
ticket holders. Overlooks the Hugli,
check-out 10am, maximum stay 3
nights. There is a self-service
restaurant. Book in advance. **£–££**

**Salvation Army Red Shield Guest
House**
2 Sudder Street
Tel: 2245 0599
Clean with very cheap dormitories and
a few more expensive rooms. Well-run
and popular for an inexpensive stay. **£**

Shilton Hotel
5a Sudder Street
Tel: 2252 1512
Fax: 2246 0961
shiltoncal@hotmail.com
One of the best of the cheap hotels
along Sudder Street, with good-value,
large rooms and breakfast. **£**

LADAKH

Alchi
There are a number of places to stay
in the village of Alchi itself. Among
these are the **Alchi Resort and
Restaurant** with 15 double rooms (all
£) and the **Zimskhang Holiday Home**
(8 simple rooms, all **£**, and a small
restaurant). Two others (both **£**) that
might be worth a try are: the **Choskar
Guest House** and the **Monastery
Guest House and Garden Restaurant**
(which also has a camp site). On the
way up to Likir, on the other side of
the Indus, is the very attractively sited
Norboo Guest House (£).

Leh (01982)
Some of the expensive (A class)
hotels have compulsory full-board
during high season (mid-June to
August), which can push the price up
quite a bit. Most hotels and guesthouses in Ladakh close for the winter
(November to March); the prices below
are for high season; outside of this
period, good discounts are available.

Bijou
Shagaran, near the Public Library
Tel: 252 131

Large rooms with bath (hot water morning and evening). Friendly, helpful staff and a pleasant garden make this a good choice. Good discounts are available out of season. **£££**
Hotel Ga-ldan Continental
By the vegetable market
Tel: 252 173
Fax: 252 414
A big, central hotel set around a courtyard. It has good rooms, all with attached bath and hot water. **£££**
Hotel K-sar Palace
Fort Road, next door to the Lha ri mo
Tel: 252 348
Fax: 252 735
kesarbadam@hotmail.com
A largish hotel with good-sized rooms in a quiet spot. Lovely surroundings and views over the valley. **£££**
Hotel Lha-ri-mo
Fort Road
Tel: 252 101
Fax: 253 345
lharimohotel@hotmail.com
A central hotel with good views and pleasant surroundings. The rooms all have attached bath with hot water, and there is a restaurant. **£££**
Hotel Lingzi
Opposite the Dak Bungalow
Tel: 252 020
hotellingzi@vsnl.nct
A comfortable, central hotel; all rooms have en suite bath with hot water. Like most of Leh's A-class hotels, it offers all-inclusive buffet food. **£££**
Hotel Shambhala
Skara
Tel: 252 607
Fax: 251 100
www.hotelshambhala.com
A quiet, all-inclusive hotel outside the city, with a good restaurant and pretty gardens. The rooms are large and transport is provided to the centre of town. **£££**
Hotel Tso-kar
Fort Road
Tel: 253 071
afzalmitoo@hotmail.com
Friendly B-class hotel set around an attractive courtyard. Decent, clean, cheap rooms, as well as an excellent Tibetan restaurant. **££**
Padma
Fort Road
Tel: 252 630
A pleasant guesthouse with very clean rooms which have great views. Rooms in the new wing have en-suite baths. **£–££**
Oriental
Changspa Lane
Tel: 253 153
Located just below the Shanti Stupa at the end of Changspa Lane. This is an excellent option, lovely rooms and great local food. Also open during the winter. Recommended. **£**

Stok

On the way up to Stok is the attractive **Hotel Skittsal** (tel: 01982-242 051; fax: 01982-252 414; hotelskittsal@vsnl.net) set in rather bleak surroundings but with fabulous views. In the village, just below the palace, are the **Hotel Highland** (tel: 01982 242 005; **£££**) and the traditional **Kalden Guest House** (**£**).

LAKSHADWEEP

Bangaram
Bangaram Island Resort
Book through:
Casino Hotel, Willingdon Island, Kochi
Tel: 0484-266 8221
Fax: 0484-266 8001
www.cghearth.com
A peaceful luxury resort. Visitors are transferred by boat from the nearby island of Agatti. The shallow lagoon is fabulously clear and clean, and perfect for swimming. All inclusive board and lodging, but bottled water is extra and charged at a slightly shocking marked-up rate (make sure you have enough cash to cover extras at the end of your stay). Accommodation is in simple huts set back from the beach; although the water in the bathrooms smells strongly of sulphur it is safe. Meals take the form of a buffet, predominantly Indian, with lots of fresh fish. The friendly and helpful staff hold a barbeque on the beach one night a week. There are facilities for snorkelling, scuba diving (some of the best in the Indian Ocean) and sailing (none of which are included in the initial cost). There is a bar on the beach (again, drinks are not included in the price of the package). **£££££**

Kadmat
Kadmat Cottages
Book through:
Lacadives, Lakshmi Niwas, 43/2051 K Colony, Kochi
Tel: 0484-220 6766
www.lacadives.com
A lovely, if simple, resort on a fabulous lagoon. Transfer is by boat from Agatti (where the representative will meet you). The accommodation is in small cottages with AC and attached bathrooms. The price includes all (South Indian) meals but, unlike on Bangaram, alcohol is not allowed. There is a small shop selling basics such as toiletries, snacks and soft drinks. The swimming and diving are excellent. Dive packages are available, including those for beginners, or you can book single dives by the day (for an extra fee). **£££££**

Hotel Price Categories

The rates below are for a double room (AC where available) in high season, including taxes.
£££££	Rs3,700 and above
££££	Rs2,700–3,700
£££	Rs1,700–2,700
££	Rs800–1,700
£	Up to Rs800

MADHYA PRADESH

Bandhavgarh National Park
Bandhavgarh Jungle Lodge
Umaria
Tel: 07627-265 317
www.welcomheritagehotels.com
Modern thatched cottages set in pleasant grounds with a central dining area. Very close to the park entrance. Nature tours and excursions can be arranged through the lodge. **£££££**
Churhat Kothi
Tel: 07627-265 358
www.churhatkothi.com
This highly recommended resort was founded by the naturalist K.K. Singh and is one of the finest jungle lodges in India. It's comfortable and stylish, and the knowlegable staff can arrange excellent trips into the nearby park. Credit cards not accepted. **£££££**
Tiger Trails Resort
Tala
Tel: 07655-265 325
www.indianadventures.com
Simple but comfortable cottages close to the park and overlooking a small lake. Quiet and well run. **£££**
White Tiger Forest Lodge
Tel: 07627-265 308
www.mptourism.com
Slightly run-down but good value accommodation from the Madhya Pradesh state tourism authority. There is also a reasonable restaurant and bar. **££**

Bhopal (0755)
Noor-us-Sabah Palace
V.I.P. Road, Kho-e-Fiza
Tel: 522 3333
Fax: 522 7777
www.noorussabahpalace.com
A heritage hotel set in a 1920s palace. The rooms, some with a lake view, are comfortable and there are a couple of restaurants. **££££**
Jehan Numa Palace Hotel
157 Shamla Hill
Tel: 266 1100
Fax: 266 1720
www.hoteljehanumapalace.com
Hotel set in lovely gardens. Good rooms – the Heritage Suites are the most atmospheric – and a good restaurant. **£££–££££**

Hotel Price Categories

The rates below are for a double room (AC where available) in high season, including taxes.

£££££	Rs3,700 and above
££££	Rs2,700–3,700
£££	Rs1,700–2,700
££	Rs800–1,700
£	Up to Rs800

Hotel Sonali
Radha Talkies Road, off Hamidia Road
Tel: 253 3880
Fax: 251 0337
A friendly hotel with clean rooms, some AC. Pricey for its class and facilities but well run with pleasant staff. **£££**

The Residency Hotel
208 Zone 1, M.P. Nagar
Tel: 255 6001
Fax: 255 7637
A modern hotel with good, clean rooms, all AC. It also has a decent restaurant. **££–£££**

MPTDC Hotel Palash Bhopal
Near 45, Bungalows, Banganga Road, T.T. Nagar
Tel: 255 3006
Fax: 255 3076
www.mptourism.com
Excellent-value, large AC rooms set around a pleasant lawn witha good restaurant. A popular option, so book in advance. **££**

Hotel Ranjit
3 Hamidia Road
Tel: 253 5211
Fax: 253 2242
Simple but clean rooms, some AC, all with attached baths; hot water on request. There is a terrace bar and excellent vegetarian restaurant. **£**

Gwalior (0751)
Usha Kiran Palace
Jayendraganj, Lakshar
Tel.: 244 4000
Fax: 244 4018
www.tajhotels.com
This was formerly the Maharaja's guesthouse, but is now a luxury heritage hotel owned by the Taj Group. It has retained its historic splendour but is equipped with all modern facilities. **£££££**

Hotel Shelter
Padav, opposite Indian Airlines
Tel: 232 6209
Fax: 232 6212
A modern hotel with clean AC rooms and a good restaurant. Good value and close to the railway station. **££**

MPTDC Hotel Tansen
6a M.G. Road
Tel: 234 0370
Fax: 234 0371

www.mptourism.com
A large, old hotel with a good restaurant. Rather dark and a bit run-down, but quiet and with a certain charm. **££**

Hotel Sudarshan
Chappar Wala Pul., 1 Jinsi Road
Tel: 233 5693
Fax: 507 9124
A pleasant modern hotel with clean and comfortable AC rooms. Generally good value with helpful staff and a vegetarian North Indian restaurant (fairly pricey for breakfast). **££**

Indore (0731)
Hotel Balwas International
30/2 South Toukouganj Road, behind High Court
Tel: 252 4934
Fax: 251 7938
balwasindore@mantrafreenet.com
Quiet and clean rooms (non-AC cheaper, **£**) and a good restaurant in a friendly hotel. **££**

Hotel Kanchan
12/2 Dr S.P. Marg, Kanchan Bagh
Tel: 251 8501
Fax: 251 7054
Good-value rooms (a few non-AC), most with bath, and a restaurant. **££**

Hotel President
163 R.N.T. Marg
Tel: 252 8866
Fax: 251 2230
A ritzy, mid-budget hotel with a good vegetarian restaurant. The AC rooms are comfortable and there is a pool and health club. **££**

MPTDC Tourist Bungalow
R.N.T. Marg
Tel: 252 1818
www.mptourism.com
Decent, budget rooms, a couple with AC, in a small, quiet hotel. Breakfast included in the price. **£**

Kanha National Park
Kanha Jungle Lodge
Mukki
Book through:
206 Rakeshdeep, 11 Commercial Complex, Gulmohar Enclave, Green Park, Delhi 110 049
Tel: 011-2685 3760
www.adventure-india.com
Quite pricey but well located, simple and well kept accommodation. Good for bird-watching and with some regard for the environment. **£££££**

Kipling Camp
Morcha Village, Kisli,
Mandla 481 768
Tel: 07649-277 218
www.kiplingcamp.com
Charming accommodation in small cottages. This well-run camp has a very knowledgeable staff of resident naturalists and the wildlife-watching is excellent. **£££££**

Krishna Jungle Resort
Book through:
Hotel Krishna, Bhanvartal Extension, Napier Town, Jabalpur 482 001
Tel: 0761-240 1263
www.krishnahotels.com
Comfortable if dated accommodation in tents and cottages. Well organised; small pool. **££££–£££££**

MPTDC Lodges
Bhagira Log Huts, Mukki; Tourist Hostel, Kisli; Kanha Safari Lodge, Mukki
Tel: 07649-277 227; Kanha Safari Lodge 07637-226 029
www.mptourism.com
A range of simple but clean and decent accommodation, from dormitories to double rooms. All of the lodges have restaurants. **£–££**

Royal Tiger Resort
Mukki 481 111, Balaghat
Tel: 07637-226 038
www.royaltiger.com
Locally inspired cottages in large, wooded grounds. Good amenities including excellent, locally grown organic food. **£££££**

Shergarh
Bahmi, Balaghat 481 111
Tel: 07637-226 086
(in the UK Jun–Oct 07969-804 472)
www.shergarh.com
Extremely well-run and professional camp, with knowledgeable guides and comfortable accommodation. There is a useful section on their website about responsible tourism. No credit cards. Recommended. **£££££**

Khajuraho (07686)
Hotel Chandela
Airport Road
Tel: 272 355
www.tajhotels.com
A luxury hotel run by the Taj Group, now showing its age. Not as good value as the Jass Trident but with nice gardens. **££££**

Jass Trident
By-Pass Road
Tel: 272 376
tjokjr@sancharnet.in
A comfortable, luxury hotel with all the usual amenities including a good restaurant and pool. Good-value rooms overlook the gardens. **£££–££££**

MPTDC Hotel Jhankar Khajuraho
Tel: 274 063
Fax: 272 330
www.mptourism.com
A government-run hotel with AC rooms (non-AC **£**), all with bath and hot water, plus a restaurant. **££**

MPTDC Hotel Payal
Tel: 274 064
www.mptourism.com
A pleasant and quiet hotel with some AC rooms (non-AC **£**), all with bath.

Nice garden, good restaurant. **££**
Marble Palace
Jain Temples Road
Tel: 244 353
Very clean rooms (plenty of marble) with attached baths in a pleasant, airy hotel. Recommended. **£–££**

Mandu (07292)
Hotel Rupmati
Near the SADA barrier
Tel: 263 270
A modern hotel with some AC rooms and a restaurant. Great views from the balconies. **££**
MPTDC Tourist Cottages
2 km (1 mile) south of main square
Tel: 263 235
www.mptourism.com
Pleasant, spacious rooms with bath and a view of the Sagar Talao Tank. There is also a nice open-air restaurant. Book in advance. **££**
MPTDC Traveller's Lodge
Near the SADA barrier
Tel: 263 221
www.mptourism.com
Clean rooms with a good view in a government lodge with a restaurant. Popular so book in advance. **££**

Sanchi (07592)
MPTDC Tourist Cafeteria
near the museum
Tel: 266 743
www.mptourism.com
Only two simple rooms, both very cheap but clean, above a MPTDC restaurant. **£**
MPTDC Traveller's Lodge
Bhopal Road
Tel: 266 723
www.mptourism.com
The best option: clean, simple rooms, a decent restaurant, and lovely gardens. Book in advance. **£**
Railway Retiring Rooms
These two large rooms with bath are good if you can get in. **£**

Shivpuri (07492)
MPTDC Tourist Village
Jhansi Road
Tel: 223 760

www.mptourism.com
Comfortable, modern AC cottages (non-AC **£**) on the lakeside 3 km (2 miles) outside the town. There is also a good restaurant and a bar. Book in advance. **££**

MAHARASHTRA

Aurangabad (0240)
Ambassador Ajanta
Jalna Road, CIDCO
Tel: 248 5211
Fax: 248 4367
www.ambassadorindia.com
Luxury hotel with pseudo-traditional interiors and good value rooms. There is an excellent restaurant and good pool. **££££**
Taj Residency
8-N-12 CIDCO
Tel: 238 1106
Fax: 238 1053
www.tajhotels.com
A plush and surprisingly reasonable luxury hotel with large rooms, 8 km (5 miles) from town. Lovely gardens and pool, and excellent restaurant. Recommended. **£££–££££**
Hotel President Park
R-7/2, Chikalthana, Airport Road
Tel: 248 6201
Fax: 248 4823
www.presidenthotels.com
A comfortable, modern hotel with a great pool, and the excellent Spice Avenue vegetarian restaurant. The good-value rooms look out onto the pool. Check out 9am. **£££**
MTDC Aurangabad
Station Road
Tel: 233 1513
Fax: 233 1198
www.mtdcindia.com
A large, old hotel but with comfortable rooms, a garden and a good restaurant. Check out 9am. **££**
Printravel Hotel
Station Road
Tel: 232 9707
Fax: 233 6036
www.printravel.com
Cheap and basic, but clean rooms

with attached bath (hot water in the morning). There is the handy Patang restaurant downstairs and helpful staff. Recommended. **£–££**
Youth Hostel
Padampura Corner, Station Road
Tel: 233 4892
www.yhaindia.com
Clean dormitories and a few rooms in a well-run hostel; full-board available. A good budget option and popular, so book ahead. **£**

Pune (020)
Taj Blue Diamond
11 Koregaon Road
Tel: 2402 5555
Fax: 2402 7755
www.tajhotels.com
One of the best luxury hotels in Pune; large with comfortable, modern rooms. Has all the usual five-star bits, including a pool and a good Chinese restaurant. **£££££**
Hotel Ashirwad
16 Connaught Road
Tel: 2612 8585
Fax: 2612 6121
hotelash@pn2.vsnl.net.in
A good, modern hotel with comfortable AC rooms. There is good vegetarian food in the restaurant. **£££**
Hotel Sunderban
19 Koregaon Park, next to the Osho Commune
Tel: 2612 4949
www.tghotels.com
An excellent value and well-maintained hotel in a quiet location. There is a wide range of clean rooms, and a Barista Coffee Shop. **££–£££**
Hotel Dreamland
2/14 Connaught Road, opposite the railway station
Tel: 2612 2121
Fax: 2612 2424
Simple, clean rooms, some with AC. The restaurant serves good Indian food. **££**
Hotel Ketan
917/19a Fergusson College Road, Shivajinagar
Tel: 2565 5081
Fax: 2565 5076

Heritage Hotels

Some of India's most atmospheric and romantic hotels are set in converted palaces, forts or *havelis* (merchants' houses). Known generically as "heritage hotels", they are largely found in Rajasthan and Gujarat, though there are some superb old buldings to stay in elsewhere in the country, especially in the mountains.

When the civil list of the Indian aristocracy was abolished by Indira Gandhi in the 1970s, some of the ex-

rulers of the princely states, particularly in Rajasthan, turned to tourism to fund the upkeep of their properties by turning them into luxury hotels. These proved popular, and profitable, and soon many owners of run-down old buildings were busy renovating them and taking in guests.

The facilities can, though not always, be luxurious and expensive, with marble swimming pools, beautifully decorated suites and well-

maintained grounds. Food is usually available to guests, most commonly, in Rajasthan at least, an Indian buffet of about seven different dishes.

Many of the hotels are represented by the Indian Heritage Hotels Association (306, Anukampa Tower, Church Road, Jaipur, Rajasthan; tel: 0141-237 1194; fax: 0141-236 3651). Their website is an excellent source of information: www.indianheritagehotels.com.

www.hotelketan.com
Simple but very clean rooms. All have attached bath and are good value. **££**
Hotel Srimaan
361/5a Bund Garden Road, opposite Bund Garden
Tel: 2613 3535
Fax: 2612 3636
www.littleitalyindia.com
Very clean, pleasant AC rooms in a modern hotel; a buffet breakfast is included in the price. The hotel has a good Italian restaurant. **££**
Railway Retiring Rooms
A very good budget option. **£**

MUMBAI (022)

Bawa International
Vile Parle East
Tel: 2611 3636
www.bawahotels.com
This is a bright, modern transit hotel located next to the domestic airport, Santa Cruz. Courtesy buses to and from the airport are available. **£££££**
The Emerald
Juhu Tara Road, Juhu
Tel: 2661 1150
www.theemerald.com
This Best Western establishment positioned behind Juhu Beach offers a wide range of luxury accommodation, from standard business rooms and suites to apartments with fully equipped kitchenettes. Convenient for the airport, which is just 7 km (4 miles) to the east. **£££££**
Fariyas
25 Arthur Road
Tel: 2204 2911
www.fariyas.com
On the quiet side of Colaba, this small four-star hotel is popular with business clients, though it lacks the cachet of the Taj. The pool is small; harbour views cost extra. **£££££**
Gorden House
5 Battery Street, Apollo Bunder
Tel: 2287 1122
www.ghhotel.com
Hip boutique hotel, with variously themed rooms and suites (eg "Scandinavian", "American Country"). It's bright, stylish, modern and centrally air conditioned, with CD players and cable TV in every room, and a popular "wok" restaurant at street level. **£££££**
Grand
17 Shri SR Marg, Ballard Estate
Tel: 5658 0500
Fax: 5658 0501
www.grandhotelbombay.com
This is a lovely old colonial-style hotel near the docks. It is one of the few places in its class which has an authentic pre-Independence

atmosphere about it – however, it is decidedly overpriced. **£££££**
Intercontinental
135 Marine Drive
Tel: 3987 9999
www.intercontinental.com
Ultra-slick boutique hotel fitted out with designer furniture, in-room broadband, plasma-screen TVs and other up-to-the-minute gadgets. The views over Back Bay from its sea-facing suites are superb; plus there's a fashionable terrace restaurant on the roof, and a very hip vodka bar on the ground floor. **£££££**
Lotus Suites
Andheri Kurla Road, International Airport Zone, Andheri East
Tel: 2827 0707
www.lotussuites.com
This determinedly green hotel bills itself as an "eco-five-star at three-star prices". A convenient, comfortable option close to the international airport. **£££££**
Marine Plaza
29 Marine Drive
Tel: 2285 1212
www.sarovarparkplaza.com
Overlooking the bay, this retro-Art Deco five-star is famous for its glass-bottomed rooftop pool. With luxurious rooms and all the usual facilities, it's a good choice if you want the comfort but find larger five-star hotels too impersonal. **£££££**
The Oberoi
Nariman Point
Tel: 2232 5757
www.oberoihotels.com
Very chic and much beloved of visiting heads of state. From its impressive atrium to the elegant restaurants and rooms, this is a fabulous (and fabulously expensive) hotel. **£££££**
Orchid
70-C Nehru Road, Vile Parle East
Tel: 2616 4040
www.orchidhotel.com
Ground-breaking eco-five-star hotel whose every feature, from the swimming pool right down to the laundry service and coathangers, has been designed to minimise environmental impact. **£££££**
Sea Princess
Juhu Tara Road, Juhu
Tel: 2661 1111
www.seaprincess.com
Most appealing among the rank of swish five-star hotels backing on to Juhu Beach, with pleasantly furnished rooms and a small pool. Only a 30-minute drive from the airport. **£££££**
The Shalimar
August Kranti Marg
Tel: 5664 1000
www.theshalimarhotel.com
Housed in a modern eight-storey tower block amid the bright lights of Kemp's

Corner, just north of Chowpatty Beach, this is a slicker-than-average four-star. The decor is minimalist and contemporary, with warm colours and carpets, and the rooms are spacious for the price. **£££**
The Taj Mahal Hotel
PJ Ramchandani Marg
Tel: 5665 3366
www.tajhotels.com
India's most famous hotel, situated opposite the Gateway of India. Very grand and very expensive with beautiful rooms in both the old and new wings. Excellent restaurants and bar, and a great outdoor pool. **£££££**
Ascot
38 Garden Road
Tel: 2284 0020 or 2287 2105
www.ascothotel.com
Spruce, stylish three-star hotel sporting a trendy new look, though it's been here for years. Excellent value in its bracket, with most of the mod cons you'd expect (including in-room internet access and safe deposits), though no pool. **££££**
Harbour View
Kerawalla Chambers, 25 PJ Ramchandani Marg
Tel: 2284 1197
www.viewhotelsindia.com
At an unbeatable location on Apollo Bunder, the hotel has enormous rooms with some wonderful views, although these come at a premium. This establishment is at its best in the rooftop restaurant, which ranks among the most relaxing places to hang out in the city. **££££**
Hotel Atithi
77 a–b Nehru Road, Vile Parle East
Tel: 2611 6124
Fax: 2611 1998
atithi@bom8.vsnl.net.in
Clean, simple rooms in an efficient hotel close to the airport terminals. Good food in the restaurant. **££££**
Midland
Jawaharlal Nehru Road, Santa Cruz East
Tel: 2611 0413
www.hotelmidland.com
This hotel is among the few reliable two-stars that are within striking distance of the two airports. Room rates include a courtesy bus to and from the airports and breakfast. **££££**
Regent
8 Best Road
Tel: 2287 1854
hotelregent@vsnl.com
Efficient, modern place whose fully en-suite, AC rooms are on the small side, but perfectly comfortable, with sound-proofed windows. **££££**
Sea Palace
Kerawalla Chambers, 26 PJ Ramchandani Marg
Tel: 2284 1828,

www.seapalacehotel.com
Recently refurbished hotel in a rather
grand building facing the seafront
where the P&O steamers used to tie
up. The rooms are equipped with
internet connections, fridges and
cable TVs as standard; there's a
multi-cuisine restaurant. **££££**
West End Hotel
45 New Marine Lines
Tel: 2203 9121
Fax: 2205 7506
www.westendhotelmumbai.com
Very clean rooms in a pleasant hotel
with a good restaurant. Quite pricey,
but in a good location close to Marine
Drive. **££££**
Causeway
43/45 Mathurades Estate, S.B.S
Road, Colaba Causeway,
Tel: 2281 7777
www.hotelcauseway.com
A small, popular hotel on Colaba's
main street. Its 25 rooms all have AC,
contemporary decor and en-suite
bathrooms. Avoid those on the front of
the building, which are noisier (despite
the sound-proofing). Online booking
available. **£££**
Chateau Windsor Hotel
86 Vir Nariman Road, Churchgate
Tel: 2204 4455
www.chateauwindsor.com
A central hotel, close to Churchgate
Station, with simple but clean – and
slightly overpriced – rooms (some non-
AC). No restaurant, but a kitchen is
provided for the use of guests. **£££**
City Palace
121 City Terrace
Tel: 2261 5515
hotelcitypalace@vsnl.net
Right opposite CST (VT) railway station,
and clean enough, though its cheaper
rooms lack windows. AC available.
Convenient if you need to catch an
early morning train. **£££**
Hotel Apollo
Lansdowne Road, behind Regal
Cinema, Colaba
Tel: 2287 3312
Fax: 2287 4996
hotelapollo@vsnl.com
Decent AC rooms in a good location.
Friendly and helpful staff in a hotel
run by the same company as the
Godwin (see below). **£££**
Hotel Diplomat
24–6 B.K. Boman Behram Marg,
Apollo Bunder
Tel: 2202 1661
Fax: 2283 0000
www.hoteldiplomat-bombay.com
Simple but comfortable AC rooms in a
friendly and well-run hotel close to the
Taj. Good value for the location and
service. **£££**
Hotel Godwin
41 Garden Road, Colaba
Tel: 2287 2050

Hotel Price Categories

The rates below are for a double
room (AC where available) in high
season, including taxes.
£££££	Rs3,700 and above
££££	Rs2,700–3,700
£££	Rs1,700–2,700
££	Rs800–1,700
£	Up to Rs800

www.cybersols.com/godwin
Clean rooms, some with a sea view, in
a well-run hotel in a good location.
Helpful staff and good Indian food in
the restaurant. Powerful showers with
lots of hot water. **£££**
Hotel Red Rose
16/76 Gokuldas Pasta Road, behind
Chitra Cinema, Dadar East
Tel: 2413 7845
Fax: 5660 2008
hotelrr@vsnl.net
Good-value, clean rooms with shared
bath. A friendly, well-run hotel in the
north of the city. **£££**
ISKCON
Juhu Church Road
Tel: 2620 6860
www.iskconmumbai.com
One of the city's more eccentric
hotels, run by the International
Society for Krishna Consciousness.
The building and furnishings are an
elaborate fusion of mock-Moghul,
Gujarati and Western styles, and the
rooms are huge for the price you
pay, though certain restrictions apply
(you are not allowed to consume
alcohol, meat or caffeine on the
premises). The hotel's restaurant
offers sumptuous vegetarian buffet
meals. Book between 10am and 5pm
only. **£££**
Residency Hotel
26 Rustom Sidhwa Marg
Tel: 5667 0555
www.residencyhotel.com
Good-value, well appointed rooms in a
modern hotel close to the
International Airport. Good Indian food
available from the restaurant. **£££**
Samrat
3rd Road, Khar West, near Khar
railway station
Tel: 2648 5441
www.hotelsinghs.com
Rudimentary economy hotel in a lower-
middle-class suburb that serves as a
handy budget option if you're passing
through Mumbai. **£££**
Sea Green South
145a Marine Drive
Tel: 5633 6535
Fax: 5633 6530
www.seagreensouth.com
Hotel in glamorous location with great
views, though now showing its age.

Most of the large and airy rooms have
AC and are well appointed. **£££**
Shelley's Hotel
30 P.J. Ramchandani Marg, opposite
the Radio Club, Colaba Sea Face
Tel: 2284 0229
Fax: 2284 0385
www.shelleyshotel.com
A good-value hotel set in a wonderful
1930s building with some period
furniture. Good service and well-
maintained, with attractive rooms
(those with a sea view more
expensive). Breakfast is available.
Recommended. **£££**
Strand Hotel
30 P.J. Ramchandani Marg, Colaba
Sea Face
Tel: 2288 2222
Fax: 2288 0059
www.hotelstrand.com
Slightly overpriced but clean
comfortable rooms (not all with
attached bath), some facing sea. **£££**
YWCA International Guest House
18 Madam Cama Road, Fort
Tel: 2202 5053
Fax: 2202 0445
www.ywcaic.com
A good place to stay for both
women and men. Very clean and safe
rooms and dormitories. Rates include
Rs50 temporary membership,
breakfast and dinner. Make a
reservation with deposit well in
advance. **££–£££**
Aircraft International
179 Dayaldas Road
Tel: 2612 1419
Accommodation around the airport at
the budget end of the scale is
generally ropey, with cramped,
windowless, grubby rooms the
norm. This place, though, is well
maintained and good value, offering
larger than average clean rooms at
affordable rates. It's only 5 minutes'
walk from the suburban railway
station, and a short taxi ride from the
airports. **££**
Bentley's Hotel
17 Oliver Road, Colaba
Tel: 2284 1474
Fax: 2287 1846
www.bentleyshotel.com
An excellent budget option in a city
with few good, cheap hotels. Good-
value, large and very clean rooms in a
convenient location. Price includes
breakfast. **££**
Manama
221–225 P. D'Mello Road
Tel: 2261 3412
No-frills budget place, its main
asset being its location a short
walk from the CST railway station.
Nothing special, but comfy and
clean enough for a night, with
windows, freshly laundered towels
and starched white sheets. Most of

Hotel Price Categories

The rates below are for a double room (AC where available) in high season, including taxes.

£££££	Rs3,700 and above
££££	Rs2,700–3,700
£££	Rs1,700–2,700
££	Rs800–1,700
£	Up to Rs800

the guests are train travellers in transit. **££**

Moti International
10 Best Marg
Tel: 2202 1654 or 2202 5714,
hotelmotiinternational@yahoo.com.in
Small, friendly budget hotel, with a range of inexpensive rooms (from simple bathroom-less doubles to large AC suites) in a colonial-era building. They're cool, quiet and clean (if showing signs of age) and the management is welcoming. **££**

New Bengal
Dr D.N. Marg
Tel: 2340 1951
www.hotel newbengal.com
A good economic option if you want to be in the thick of things, close to Crawford Market and central Mumbai, but only a short taxi ride from Colaba. Aimed at visiting businessmen on low budgets, the accommodation is decidedly no frills, ranging from low-ceilinged, airless dorms to more spacious AC doubles. This is not somewhere for a long stay, but it's clean and safe. **££**

Sea Shore
4th Floor, 1–49 Kamal Mansion, Arthur Bunder Road
Tel: 2287 4237
The most dependable and secure of the low-budget hotels in Colaba. Only half of its rooms have windows and none are en suite, but everything is kept spic-and-span and the management is unfailingly courteous. Handy safe-deposit and left-luggage facilities available. **££**

Salvation Army Red Shield Hostel
Red Shield House, 30 Mereweather Road, Colaba
Tel: 2284 1824
Behind the Taj Mahal Hotel. Double rooms and (much cheaper) dormitories. Lockers and meals are available. A bit institutional and run-down, but good value. **£–££**

Lawrence
3rd Floor, 33 Rope Walk Lane
Tel: 2284 3618
Opposite the Jehangir Art Gallery, this is a small hotel with a few clean and great-value rooms. Very popular and reservations are essential. **£**

ORISSA

Bhubaneshwar (0674)
The Garden Inn
A-112 Janpath
Tel: 251 4120
Fax: 250 4254
gardeninn@hotmail.com
Modern, and expensive hotel in pleasant surroundings. Good restaurant and roof garden. **££££**

Hotel Sishmo
86a/1 Gautam Nagar
Tel: 243 3600
Fax: 243 3351
www.hotelsishmo.com
Very comfortable hotel with good amenities including pool and restaurants. Price includes tea in bed and breakfast. **££££**

Hotel Swosti
103 Janpath
Tel: 253 5771
Fax: 253 4794
www.swosti.com
Pricey but comfortable hotel with two excellent restaurants serving Oriyan specialities. Central and may have discounts in low season. **££££**

New Marrion
6 Janpath, Unit 3
Tel: 250 2328
Fax: 250 3287
www.fhrai.com
Near to both rail and air connections the hotel has a restaurant, bar, health club and swimming pool. **££££**

The Royale Midtown
52–3 Janpath
Tel: 253 6138
Fax: 253 6142
www.royalehotels.com
One of the better-value hotels in Bhubaneswar. Clean and pleasant AC rooms with attached baths and hot water. **££**

OTDC Panthanivas
Jaydev Marg
Tel: 243 2324
www.panthanivas.com
Clean and simple AC and non-AC rooms; attached baths with hot water. Good value with restaurant. **£–££**

Cuttack (0671)
Hotel Akbari Continental
Dolmundai, Haripur Road
Tel: 242 3251
Fax: 242 3254
Pricey but perfectly adequate AC rooms (en-suite bath with hot water) which are starting to show their age. There is also a restaurant and pleasant garden. **£££**

Konark (06758)
OTDC Panthanivas Konark
By the temple
Tel: 236 831
www.panthanivas.com

Basic but reasonable and convenient accommodation with a restaurant. Clean rooms with AC and bath. **£**

Puri (06752)
Hans Coco Palms
Swargdwar, Goubada Sahi
Tel: 230 951
Fax: 230 165
hanscocopalms@hotmail.com
Lovely sea-view rooms with balconies in a renovated modern hotel. There is also a nice restaurant and pretty gardens. **££££**

Toshali Sands
Konark Marine Drive Road, Baliguali
Tel: 250 571
Fax: 250 899
tsands@sancharnet.in
Located 9 km (5½ miles) from the town, the hotel has cottages in lovely gardens, a pool and a good restaurant. **£££–££££**

Railway Hotel
Tel: 222 063
www.indianrailways.gov.in
An excellent option. A well-kept hotel, run by Indian Railways, in a pleasant old building. Clean rooms (some AC) and a good restaurant. **££–£££**

Hotel Samudra
C.T. Road, Balukhand, Sea Beach
Tel: 224 155
Fax: 228 654
A mid-range hotel 1 km (½ mile) from the railway station with sea-facing rooms, some with AC. Friendly and also has a restaurant. **££**

OTDC Panthanivas Puri
Chakratirtha Road
Tel: 222 562
www.panthanivas.com
A large, government-run hotel with a wide range of rooms (some of which are better than others). Located near the beach and with gardens and a restaurant. **£–££**

Z Hotel
C.T. Road
Tel: 222 554
www.zhotelindia.com
The rooms in this old house, now a hotel, are basic but large and some of them have sea views. An atmospheric and popular place, with an attractive garden. **£**

PUDUCHERRY (0413)

Le Dupleix
5 rue de la Caserne
Tel: 222 6999
Fax: 233 5278
www.sarovarparkplaza.com
An elegant and chic heritage hotel set in an 18th-century French villa. The interior has been beautifully restored and the facilities are excellent. **£££££**

Hotel de l'Orient
17 rue Romain Rolland
Tel: 234 3067
Fax: 222 7829
www.neemranahotels.com
An 18th-century neoclassical
mansion, now an elegant heritage
hotel. It has lovely rooms and an
excellent Creole restaurant. **££££**

Anandha Inn
154 S.V. Patel Road
Tel: 233 0711
Fax: 233 1241
www.anandhainn.oom
A comfortable and good-value modern
hotel with two restaurants serving
Indian and continental food.
Recommended. **£££**

Hotel Mass
152–4 Maraimalai Adigal Salai
Tel: 220 4001
Fax: 220 3654
www.hotelmass.com
Clean and good-value AC rooms in a
friendly hotel near to the bus stand. A
nice restaurant with good Chettinad
food. **££**

Seaside Guest House
14 Goubert Salai
Tel: 233 6494
Fax: 233 4447
www.sriaurobindosociety.org.in
An Ashram guesthouse, spotlessly
clean with a magnificent view and
cafeteria with vegetarian food. **£–££**

International Guest House
47 Netaji Subash Chandra Bose Salai
Tel: 233 6699
Fax: 233 4447
www.sriaurobindosociety.org.in
A well-kept, centrally located Ashram
guesthouse with a vegetarian
cafeteria. **£**

PUNJAB & HARYANA

Amritsar (0183)
M.K. Hotel
Shopping Centre District, Ranjit
Avenue
Tel: 250 4610
www.mkhotel.com
A flashy, modern hotel with an
abundance of marble, comfortable
rooms, a pool and a restaurant. **££££**

Hotel Ritz Plaza
45 The Mall
Tel: 256 2836
Fax: 222 6657
ritz@del3.vsnl.net.in
An elegant hotel in a quiet but
convenient location with lawns and a
pool. Clean, functional rooms and a
restaurant. **£££**

Mrs Bhandari's Guest House
10 Cantonment
Tel: 222 8509
Fax: 222 2390
Highly recommended, unusual lodging

in a family-run colonial house, with
three-course meals (only for
residents), garden and pool. **££–£££**

Grand Hotel
Queens Road, opposite railway station
Tel: 256 2424
Fax: 222 9677
grand@jla.vsnl.net.in
A friendly hotel with good-value rooms
and a pleasant garden. Good Indian
food in the restaurant. **££**

Sita Niwas
Near the Golden Temple
Tel: 543 092
Good budget option which is central,
with a range of rooms. **£–££**

Chandigarh (0172)
CITCO Hotel Mountview
Sector 10
Tel: 274 0544
Fax: 274 2220
www.citco.nic.in
A big, luxury hotel set in landscaped
grounds. Large, airy rooms and good
business and leisure facilities
including a pool. **££££**

CITCO Hotel Shivalikview
Sector 17
Tel: 270 0001
Fax: 270 1094
www.citco.nic.in
A large, posh, central hotel with a
good Chinese restaurant. Well-run with
comfortable rooms. **£££–££££**

CITCO Hotel Parkview
Sector 24
Tel: 270 6038
Fax: 271 4061
www.citco.nic.in
Previously the Chandigarh Yatri Niwas;
cheap, clean AC and non-AC (**£**)
rooms, and with a decent restaurant.
Popular and friendly, and the price
includes breakfast. **££**

Ludhiana (0161)
Hotel City Heart
G.T. Road, near Clock Tower
Tel: 274 0235
Fax: 274 0243
Central hotel with comfortable AC
rooms. The attached restaurant has
good Punjabi food. **££–£££**

Patiala (0175)
Green's Hotel
The Mall
Tel: 221 3071
Fax: 221 3070
Good value and well-located rooms in
a pleasant hotel with a decent
restaurant. **£–££**

RAJASTHAN

Ajmer (0145)
Mansingh Palace
Vaishali Nagar

Tel: 242 5702
Fax: 242 5858
www.mansinghhotels.com
This is the top hotel in town. A striking
modern building with large,
comfortable rooms, and a decent, but
expensive, restaurant. **££££**

Hotel Regency
outside Delhi Gate
Tel: 262 0296
Fax: 262 1750
www.bahubaligroup.com
Central and pleasant hotel with simple
rooms (some AC). Good vegetarian
restaurant. **££**

Alwar (0144)
Hotel Alwar
26 Manu Marg
Tel: 270 0012
Fax: 234 8757
ukrustagi@rediffmail.com
Good rooms (AC and non-AC) with
attached bath. Restaurant and a
pleasant garden. **££**

Hill Fort Kesroli
Kesroli, 12 km (7½ miles) from Alwar
Tel: 01468-289352
www.neemranahotels.com
Ranged around a lush inner courtyard
full of bougainvillea and palm trees,
this 14th-century fort has been
sensitively converted into an
atmospheric hotel, deep in the Aravalli
countryside. The views from its
ramparts over the surrounding fields
and hills are the main attraction,
though the rooms have retained plenty
of traditional flair. **££££**

Bharatpur (05644)
RTDC Hotel Saras
Saras Chauraha, Agra Road
Tel: 223 700
www.rajasthantourism.gov.in
Simple but adequate accommodation
(some AC) in a government-run hotel
with restaurant, close to the park. **££**

Bikaner (0151)
Lallgarh Palace Hotel
Tel: 254 0201
Fax: 252 3963
www.maharajagangasinghjitrust.org
An impressive red sandstone
palace, now run as a hotel by a
trust that supports local projects.
Some rooms have the original
furnishings. Part of the palace is also
a museum. **£££–££££**

Hotel Basant Vihar Palace
N.H. 15, Sri Ganganagar Road
Tel: 225 0675
Fax: 225 0676
www.basantviharpalace.com
A quiet palace hotel on the outskirts
of town. Slightly shabby but large
rooms; not luxurious – and a bit
overpriced – but with a certain run-
down charm. **££££**

Karni Bhawan Palace
Gandhi Colony
Tel: 252 4701
Fax: 252 2408
www.hrhindia.com
Previously the residence of the
Maharaja of Bikaner. Wonderful period
rooms in a late art deco (1940s)
house. The restaurant serves good
local dishes. **£££**

Maan Bilas
Lallgarh Palace Complex
Tel: 252 4711
Fax: 252 2408
www.hrhindia.com
Comfortable rooms in converted
buildings in the grounds of the
Lallgarh Palace. Good value and
atmospheric. **£££**

Hotel Shri Ram
A-228 Sadul Ganj
Tel: 252 2651
Fax: 220 8071
www.hotelshriram.com
Well-run budget accommodation with
very clean rooms (some AC) and
cheaper dormitories. The rooms have
attached baths and all meals are
available. **££**

RTDC Hotel Dhola Maru
Major Puran Singh Circle
Tel: 252 9621
www.rajasthantourism.gov.in
A central hotel with a range of rooms,
from dormitory to mid-budget. Good,
inexpensive food. **£**

Bundi (0747)
Hotel Braj Bhushanjee
Below the palace
Tel: 244 2322
www.kiplingsbundi.com
Cavernous 250-year-old *haveli*
belonging to the family of a former
prime minister, sandwiched between
the old walled town and the palace.
The views from its various roof terraces
and pavilions are superb, as are the
antique furniture and original murals.
Room rates vary widely according to
size and levels of comfort. **£££**

Lake View
Bohra Meghwahan, Ji-ki-Haveli
Tel: 244 2342
This friendly, rather ramshackle
guesthouse on the lakeside, occupying
a small 200-year-old *haveli*, offers a
great chance for budget travellers to
stay in a period house that still holds
heaps of traditional charm – though it is
far from a luxury palace, and prone to
pilfering raids by monkeys if windows
are left open. A couple of the pricier
rear-side rooms have lovely views over
the Nawal Sagar tank. **£££**

Dungarpur (02964)
Udai Bilas Palace
Tel: 230 808
Fax: 231 008

www.udaibilaspalace.com
A fascinating mid-19th century palace,
now a hotel, in a wonderful lakeside
location. Art deco rooms and
bathrooms, and eccentric decor.
Recommended. **££££**

Jaipur (0141)
Jai Mahal Palace Hotel
Jacob Road, Civil Lines
Tel: 222 3636
Fax: 222 0707
www.tajhotels.com
A top-class Taj-group hotel. Classy and
well-designed rooms, lovely gardens
with a good pool, and an excellent
restaurant. **£££££**

The Oberoi Rajvilas
Goner Road
Tel: 268 0101
Fax: 268 0202
www.oberoihotels.com
This is as good as it gets: an ultra-
luxurious and ultra-expensive 13-
hectare (32-acre) complex, 12 km (7½
miles) outside the city. Elegant rooms
and suites in beautiful gardens with
every conceivable amenity. Excellent
food and a beautiful pool. **£££££**

Rambagh Palace Hotel
Bhawani Singh Road
Tel: 221 1919
Fax: 238 5098
www.tajhotels.com
The ultimate art deco palace for film-
star fantasies. Plush interiors,
beautifully decorated rooms and
suites, and an indoor pool. Good food
and lovely gardens. **£££££**

Samode Haveli
Ganga Pol
Tel: 263 2370
Fax: 263 1397
www.samode.com
An excellent place to stay. This 150-
year-old converted *haveli* has 20
spacious rooms and two wonderfully
decorated suites (no. 115, covered in
wall-paintings, and no. 116 decorated
with mirror-work and overlooking the
garden and pool). **££££–£££££**

Raj Mahal Palace Hotel
Sardar Patel Marg, C Scheme
Tel: 510 5665
www.royalfamilyjaipur.com
The old British Residency converted
into a tasteful lodging. A decidedly
colonial ambience. **£££–££££**

Alsisar Haveli
Sansar Chandra Road
Tel: 236 8290
Fax: 236 4652
www.alsisar.com
A beautiful, quiet converted mansion
with clean, elegant and atmospheric
rooms. There is a wonderful roof-top
swimming pool. **£££**

Jas Vilas
C-9, Sawai Jai Singh Highway
Tel: 220 4638

www.jasvilas.com
Good-value, clean and simple rooms
in a well-run family house hotel. Good
local food and a nice pool. **£££**

Madhuban
237d Behari Marg, Banipark
Tel: 220 0033
Fax: 220 2344
www.madhuban.net
20 rooms, some AC (standard rooms
better, deluxe rooms a little dark), in a
very friendly, family-run hotel. Quiet
and secluded, and a nice garden with
a pool. **£££**

Narain Niwas Palace
Kanota Bagh, Narain Singh Road
Tel: 256 1291
Fax: 256 1045
Roomy and regal, with 19th-century
royal relics of the Kanota chieftan's
family and a vegetarian restaurant.
The rooms overlooking the garden and
pool are lovely. **£££**

Bissau Palace
Chand Pol, near the Saroj Cinema
Tel: 230 4397
Fax: 230 4628
www.bissaupalace.com
Grand building with Rajput warrior
decor. Lovely gardens and a pool.
Some of the excellent-value rooms
lack AC, but with lofty ceilings stay
cool. **££–£££**

Diggi Palace
Diggi House, S.M.S. Hospital Road
Tel: 237 3091
Fax: 237 0359
www.hoteldiggipalace.com
A good deal for budget travellers. A
beautiful old palace with lawns and a
good terrace restaurant. **££**

Hotel Arya Niwas
Sansar Chandra Road, behind Amber
Towers
Tel: 237 2456
Fax: 236 1871
www.aryaniwas.com
Probably the best budget hotel in
Jaipur. Very clean and comfortable, AC
and non-AC rooms. Also has a cheap
and spotless, self-service restaurant,
which will appeal to those who like
being institutionalised. Pleasant
terrace overlooking the front lawn.
Recommended. **££**

Athiti Guest House
1 Park House Scheme Rd, opposite
All India Radio
Tel: 0141-237 8679
This family-run hotel-cum-guesthouse
is one of the cleanest, brightest, most
welcoming places in the state. The
rooms, which open on to a courtyard,
are modern and simple, but spacious,
and there's a great rooftop terrace for
lounging on, plus a popular residents-
only restaurant on the ground floor. **££**

Jai Niwas Guest House
3 Jalupura Scheme, Gopinath Marg,
off M.I. Road

Tel: 236 3964
Fax: 236 1871
www.aryaniwas.com
Clean, simple and convenient accommodation run by the same people as the Arya Niwas. No restaurant. **£–££**
Jaipur Inn
B-17 Shiv Marg, Bani Park
Tel: 220 1121
Fax: 220 0141
www.indiamart.com/jaipurinn
Clean rooms (some AC) and a dormitory. Food is served in a pleasant rooftop bar, and there are camping facilities. Very popular so book ahead. **£–££**
YHA
Janpath, near S.M.S. Stadium
Tel: 244 0515
www.yhaindia.com
Cheap but clean and safe rooms and dormitories a little way out of town. Food is available. **£**

Jaisalmer (02992)
Fort Rajwada
Hotel complex, Jodhpur–Barmer Link Road
Tel: 253 533
Fax: 253 733
www.fortrajwada.com
An impressive complex built of local sandstone, with attractive, cool rooms. Fabulous pool and elegant surroundings. **££££**
Jawahar Niwas Palace
1 Bada Bagh Road
Tel: 252 208
Fax: 252 288
A beautiful, old *haveli* converted into a hotel. The spacious rooms are quiet with wonderful views. There is a restaurant in the garden. **££££**
Killa Bhawan
A445 Kotri Badda
Tel: 251 204
www.killabhawan.com
Nowhere else in Jaisalmer fort cuts quite as much dash as this boutique hotel, which occupies a couple of bastions quite near the palace. Draped with embroidery, mirrorwork quilts and silk cushions that contrast beautifully with the ochre walls and antique wood carvings, it is featured in lifestyle articles across the world. The smaller rooms are not all en suite. **££££**
Narayan Niwas Palace
Tel: 252 408
Fax: 252 101
www.narayanniwas.com
A delicate 19th-century building with simple AC rooms of mixed quality. Good Indian food and pleasant surroundings. **££££**
Gorbandh Palace
1 Tourist Complex, Sam Road
Tel: 253 801
Fax: 253 811

www.hrhindia.com
A luxury hotel on the outskirts of town. Traditionally decorated AC rooms, tasty Rajasthani food and a good pool. **£££–££££**
Hotel Dhola Maru
Jethwai Road
Tel: 252 863
Fax: 252 761
Although this is some way out of town, this is a attractive place to stay – if over-priced – with a knowledgeable owner. **£££–££££**
Simla
Fort
Tel: 253 061
Six romantically furnished rooms with divan beds in a quiet north corner of the fort. Recently restored and a model conservation project of its kind, with environmentally friendly plumbing and waste disposal. **£££**
RTDC Moomal Tourist Bungalow
Amar Sagar Road
Tel: 252 392
www.rajasthantourism.gov.in
A range of clean rooms, some of them with AC and some of which are in round huts, with bath. There is a restaurant and and the staff are helpful. **££**
Suraj
By the Jain Temples
Tel: 251 623
A few large rooms with bath in a beautiful old converted *haveli*. Wonderful views and a vegetarian restaurant. **££**

Jodhpur (0291)
Umaid Bhawan Palace
Tel: 251 0101
Fax: 251 0100
www.amanresorts.com
A magnificent, expensive hotel set in India's most spectacular art deco palace, the 347-room home of the Jodhpur royal family. Spacious rooms with original furniture, large gardens, restaurants and a superb underground pool. **£££££**
Ajit Bhawan Hotel
opposite the Circuit House
Tel: 251 0674
Fax: 251 0674
www.ajitbhawan.com
A well-maintained palace converted into an hotel with attractive garden rooms. Good traditional meals. Recommended. **£££–££££**
Rohet Garh
Reservations via P.W.D. Road, Jodhpur 342 001
Tel: 243 1161
Fax: 264 9368
www.rohetgarh.com
Located 40 km (25 miles) outside Jodhpur on the road to Pali, this family-run hotel has not changed hands since 1622. Each room is

Hotel Price Categories

The rates below are for a double room (AC where available) in high season, including taxes.

£££££	Rs3,700 and above
££££	Rs2,700–3,700
£££	Rs1,700–2,700
££	Rs800–1,700
£	Up to Rs800

individually decorated and the food is as genuine as the hotel. **££££**
Hotel Karni Bhawan
Defence Lab. Road, Ratanada
Tel: 251 2101
Fax: 251 2105
www.karnihotels.com
A charming 1940s sandstone bungalow with attractive rooms. There is a lovely pool and *dhani* huts for dining in the gardens. Excellent food and good value. Recommended. **£££**
Indrashan
593 High Court Colony, 3 km (2 miles) south of town
Tel: 0151-244 0665
Model homestay place in a smart suburb of the old city, with hospitable owners (who host internationally acclaimed cookery courses as a sideline). Just five rooms (all en suite). A bit of a trek from the centre but correspondingly peaceful. **££**
RTDC Hotel Ghoomer
High Court Road
Tel: 254 4010
www.rajasthantourism.gov.in
A wide range of acceptable rooms, some AC, in a central hotel with restaurant. **££**
Shahi
Gandhi St, opposite Nursingh temple, Old City
Tel: 262 3802
Small, intimate guesthouse in a 350-year-old *haveli* overshadowed by the Meherangarh cliffs, deep in the blue city. Its rooms are simply furnished, but the terrace is a superb place to hang out, and the host family especially warm. Rickshaw-wallahs will tell you it is closed, or some such nonsense, as they don't get commission. **££**
Cosy Guest House
Novechokiya Road, Brahm Puri
Tel: 261 2066
Clean, simple rooms in a traditional "blue house" a little way out of the centre. Good meals available on the roof terrace. **£**
YHA
Circuit House Road, Ratanada
Tel: 251 0160
Fax: 261 9911
www.yhaindia.com
Cheap hostel accommodation;

Hotel Price Categories

The rates below are for a double room (AC where available) in high season, including taxes.

£££££	Rs3,700 and above
££££	Rs2,700–3,700
£££	Rs1,700–2,700
££	Rs800–1,700
£	Up to Rs800

convenient and clean. All meals are available as well as cooking facilities for guests. **£**

Keoladeo Ghana (05644)
The Bagh
Agra–Achnera Road, Bharatpur 321 001
Tel: 228 333
www.thebagh.com
Elegant accommodation with excellent bathrooms. The rooms open out onto beautiful gardens. Good food and convenient for the park. **£££££**
Chandra Mahal Haveli
Peharsar, Nadbai
Tel: 05643-223 238
The turn-off for this lovely 1850s *haveli*, set in the middle of a small village, is 22 km (14 miles) out of town down the Jaipur–Agra road. There are suites with a terrace overlooking the charming garden, and a good restaurant. **££££**
Falcon Guest House
Saras
Tel: 223 815
A peaceful and homely budget guesthouse run by the amiable Mrs Rajni Singh. The rooms are clean and the larger ones have private balconies and softer mattresses. The owner's husband is a keen ornithologist willing to share his knowledge. Home-cooked meals are served in the garden restaurant. **£–££**
Hotel Eagle's Nest
NH 11
Tel: 225 144
A comfortable place, close to the park, with large, clean rooms. The restaurant is very good and serves a large variety of non-vegetarian North Indian and Chinese dishes as well as beer. The owner is a reputed ornithologist. **££**
ITDC Hotel Bharatpur Ashok
Keoladeo Ghana National Park
Tel: 222 722
www.theashokgroup.com
Situated inside the park, this friendly hotel has good rooms with balconies, and a restaurant. Very convenient for early-morning bird-watching. Book in advance. **££££**
Jungle Lodge
Gori Shankar
Tel: 225 622

Clean rooms, hot running water, shady marble-floored verandas, a beautiful green garden and a library make this one of the best choices within the park precincts. The service is great and there is a small but nice restaurant. Cycles, binoculars and two motorcycles can be hired. **£**
Kadamkunj
NH 11
Delhi tel: 09891-458 220
A jungle lodge situated in an idyllic setting with picturesque views of the nearby bird sanctuary. The rooms are quiet, comfortable and located around a grassy quadrangle. Good meals available at the restaurant. **£££**
Kiran Guest House
364 Rajendra Nagar
Tel: 223 845
Has five spacious and immaculate rooms with a lovely terrace-top restaurant serving good food and chilled beer. Great personal service, homely and good value for money. The hotel arranges rides to and from town, and bikes and binoculars are available. **£**
Laxmi Vilas Palace
Kakaji ki Kothi
Tel: 231 199
www.laxmivilas.com
This former palace on the outskirts of the city dates from 1899. It has attractive suites and rooms; the food and the service are excellent. **£££££**
Spoonbill
Agra Road, close to the Saras
Tel: 223 571
Decent rooms with shared bathrooms and dormitory beds. Very good food and friendly service. **£–££**

Kota (0744)
Brijraj Bhawan Palace Hotel
Civil Lines
Tel: 245 0529
Fax: 245 0057
A former palace by the river, still run by the royal family. Pleasant rooms with a colonial feel, and good food in the restaurant. Recommended. **£££**
Umed Bhavan Palace
Station Road
Tel: 232 5262
Fax: 245 1110
www.welcomheritage.com
A palace built in 1905 and designed by the British architect Swinton Jacob. A splendid Indo-Sarcenic building a little way out of town with lovely Raj-era interiors. **£££**
RTDC Hotel Chambal
near Chatravilas Park, Nayapura
Tel: 232 6527
www.rajasthantourism.gov.in
A government-run hotel with reasonable rooms and a dormitory, and a reasonable restaurant. **££**
Hotel Navrang

Civil Lines, Nayapura
Tel: 232 3294
Fax: 245 0044
A comfortable and well-run hotel with some AC rooms. The restaurant serves good vegetarian food. **££**

Mahansar (01595)
Narayan Niwas Castle
Mahansar village
Tel: 264 322
One of Rajasthan's quirkier, more down-to-earth heritage hotels, in a labyrinthine mansion still occupied by the "royal family". It has a dozen rooms of various sizes, from simple backpackers' cells to Arabian Nights suites with old carved wood doors and windows – all at affordable prices. Excellent food too. **££**

Mount Abu (02974)
Cama Rajputana Club Resort
Adhar Devi Road
Tel: 238 205
Fax: 238 412
www.camahotels.com
125-year-old converted club building. Comfortable rooms which retain the feel of the club lodgings. There are good sports facilities in the lovely gardens. **££££**
Jaipur House
Tel: 235 001
Fax: 235 176
www.royalfamilyjaipur.com
In a fabulous position overlooking Nakki Lake, this was a guesthouse of the ruling family of Jaipur. Beautifully converted, it has elegant, comfortable rooms and restaurant with a lovely view. **££££**
Palace Hotel (Bikaner House)
Delwara Road
Tel: 235 121
Fax: 238 674
A quiet, well-run former hunting lodge. Large rooms and extensive gardens with a private lake. Advance booking advised. **£££–££££**
Connaught House
Rajendra Marg
Tel: 238 560
www.welcomheritage.com
A British bungalow, previously the summer residence of the Chief Minister of Marwar, with 14 period rooms and peaceful gardens. Good value so book ahead. **£££**
Sun Set Inn
Sun Set Road
Tel: 235 194
Fax: 235 515
A quiet hotel with large rooms (AC and non-AC). The restaurant serves good vegetarian food and there are pleasant grounds. **£££**
RTDC Hotel Shikar
near the petrol pump

Tel: 238 944
www.rajasthantourism.gov.in
A wide selection of rooms in a good
position above the town. Good value
and excellent views. All meals
available. **££**

Shri Ganesh Hotel
Near Sophia High School
Tel: 237 292
Clean, efficient, friendly budget
travellers' guesthouse on the
outskirts of Mount Abu, with en-suite
rooms, rooftop terrace and a good
kitchen serving tasty Rajasthani
curries. Owner Lalit leads popular
guided walks into the rocky terrain
around the resort. **£**

Nimaj (02939)
Chhatra Sagar
Nimaj, District Pali
Tel: 230 118
www.chhatrasagar.com
These 11 tents are set on the edge of
a calm lake. **£££££**

Pushkar (0145)
Hotel Pushkar Palace
Choti Basti, Pushkar Lake
Tel: 277 3002
www.pushkarpalace.com
Probably the best place in town. A
wide range of rooms in a 400-year-old
Maharaja's palace, some with a lake
view. Good vegetarian restaurant.
Book ahead. **£££–££££**

Pushkar Resorts
Motisar Road, Village Ganhera
Tel: 277 2017
Fax: 277 2946
www.pushkarresorts.com
Out of town accommodation in attractive
and comfortable cottages. Good pool
and restaurant in extensive grounds.
The helpful staff will arrange tours. **£££**

New Park
Panch Kund Rd
Tel: 277 2464
www.newparkpushkar.com
A secluded, modern, mid-scale place,
set 4 km (2½ miles) out of town amid
its own rose gardens, close to the
hills. The marble-lined and tiled rooms
on two storeys are all kept fastidiously
clean and tidy, there is a small
pool (residents only) and a couple of
restaurants decorated with gorgeous
local textiles. **££**

VK Tourist Palace
close to the Pushkar Palace
Tel: 272 174
A popular and cheap hotel with clean
rooms. Attached baths with hot water
and an excellent restaurant in the
garden. **£**

White House
near Pushkar Sarovar
Tel: 277 2147
www. pushkarwhitehouse.com
Well-maintained backpackers'

guesthouse, managed with great
efficiency by a hospitable mother-and-
son team. It's impeccably spruce and
has a delightful rooftop terrace
overlooking the narrow lanes of the
brahmin quarter, where you are
served complimentary welcome cups
of mango tea on arrival. **£**

Ranthambore National Park (07462)
RTDC Jhoomar Baori
7 km (4 miles) from railway station
Tel: 220 495
Set atop a hill, this former hunting
lodge provides stunning views of the
lush green forests surrounding it. The
rooms are good, though a little run-
down, and continental food is
available. Discounts on rooms
Apr–June. **££**

Sawai Madhopur Lodge
3 km (2 miles) from station
Tel: 220 541
www.tajhotels.com
In the past this was the Maharaja of
Jaipur's hunting lodge. It has now
been converted into a Taj group hotel
offering all the five-star amenities in
swanky rooms and luxury tents. **££££**

Sher Bagh
Park edge
Tel: 252 119,
Delhi tel: 011-2331 6534
Originally designed for the Maharaja of
Jaipur and his guests' hunting
expeditions, this forest-friendly camp
has 12 luxury tents with attached
bathrooms. The meals are
scrumptious and the special evening
talks with conservationists who have
dedicated their lives to Ranthambore
and its animals are a real treat. Highly
recommended. **££££**

Vanyavilas
Ranthambore Road, 10 minutes from
railway station
Tel: 223 999
www.oberoivanyavilas.com
The latest Oberoi resort is lavish and
luxurious: extremely expensive tent
accommodation with colonial-style
baths and spacious private
compounds, all set in perfectly
landscaped gardens. **£££££**

Tiger Safari
Ranthambore Rd
Tel: 221 137
www.tigersafariresort.com
Sawai Madhopur's budget
accommodation leaves a lot to be
desired, and it is worth splashing out
a little more than you might normally
for a room in this friendly, comfortable
mid-range hotel, 4 km (2½ miles) from
the train station on the way to the
park. Its centrepiece is a well-tended
garden, and there's a breezy rooftop
terrace restaurant offering fine forest
views. **££**

Samode (01423)
Samode Palace and Bagh
Tel: 240 014/240 235
www.samode.com
A sister concern of the Samode
Haveli, this country palace of Jai
Singh II's finance minister was built
on a much grander scale than his
town house, and is the main attraction
of this small village. Towering above a
warren of cobbled streets, it is a fairy-
tale Rajput pile, with interconnected
courtyards on several levels, a lavishly
decorated Durbar Hall and Sheeh
Mahal mirror pavilion. The rooms are
luxurious and beautifully furnished,
and it has a great pool. Excellent
service and a fine attention to detail.
3 km (2 miles) from Samode village is
the – cheaper – Bagh ("garden"). Run
by the owners of the palace,
accommodation is in luxury "tents",
with attached bath, set in beautiful
gardens. Lovely swimming pool.
Recommended. **£££££**

Shekhavati
Hotel Castle Mandawa
Mandawa
Tel: 01592-223 124
Fax: 01592-223 171
www.castlemandawa.com
Castle Mandawa has tasteful rooms,
all individual (non-AC much cheaper)
with attached bath and period
furniture, in an evocative 18th-century
fort. **£££££**

Roop Niwas Palace
Nawalgarh
Tel: 01594-222 008
Fax: 01594-223 3388
A large, comfortable palace with
simple but attractive rooms. The
gardens are lovely, and there is a
good restaurant and pool. Friendly
service. **£££–££££**

Dundlod Fort
Dundlod
Tel: 01594-252 519
Fax: 01594-252 199
www.dundlod.com
An atmospheric 17th-century fort
converted into a hotel with a range of
rooms, some renovated and with a
great view. Friendly service and
interesting local tours. **£££**

Piramal Haveli
Bagar
Tel: 01592-221 220
www.neemranahotels.com
A sympathetic conversion of a 20th
century haveli with a small number of
quiet and attractive rooms. Friendly
staff, and good Rajasthani food is
available. **£££**

Apani Dhani
Nawalgarh (Samode village, 50 km/
30 miles north of Jaipur)
Tel: 01594-222 239
Fax: 01594-224 061

www.apanidhani.com
Low-impact eco-resort of traditional mud and thatch huts, fitted out with Western amenities (including miraculously odourless compost loos) around a bougainvillea-filled central yard. Most of the produce used in the kitchen comes from their own organic garden. A congenial, well-run base from which to explore the painted *havelis* of the little-visited Shekhawati region. Excellent value. Recommended. **££**

Shekhawati Restaurant
Nawalgarh, near the Roop Niwas Palace
Tel: 01594-224 658
Fax: 01594-224 658
www.shekhawatirestaurant.com
Cheap and clean rooms with hot water. This admirable little hotel tries to limit its environmental impact and the restaurant serves excellent local vegetarian food. **£**

Udaipur (0294)
Devi Garh
Delvara, Nathdvara
Tel: 02953-289 211
Fax: 02953-289 357
www.deviresorts.com
Very swish, very elegant and beautifully designed (but shockingly expensive), this impressive fort is now one of India's finest hotels. Very luxurious with a wonderful pool and excellent food. Located 26 km (16 miles) from Udaipur. **£££££**

Shiv Niwas and Fateh Prakash Palace
City Palace
Tel: 252 8016
Fax: 252 8006
www.hrhindia.com
The magnificent guest apartments of the City Palace have been converted into an exclusive hotel. Some rooms have an excellent view of the lake, and there is a lovely pool. Part of the City Palace complex is now the Fateh Prakash, with lovely, exclusive rooms and suites. The restaurant, with wonderful views of the lake, serves excellent afternoon teas. **£££££**

Taj Lake Palace Hotel
Pichola Lake
Tel: 252 8800
Fax: 252 8700
www.tajhotels.com
An exquisite, luxurious hotel, said to be the most romantic in the world. The suites are all beautifully furnished, and the view over the lake from the restaurant is one of the great sights of India. **£££££**

Udaivilas
Haridasji ki Magri
Tel: 243 3300
Fax: 289 357
www.oberoihotels.com
Unbelievably luxurious, and as

expensive as it looks, this, one of the Oberoi's latest hotels, oozes wealth and comfort. Amenities run from private swimming pools to your own butler. **£££££**

Hotel Hilltop Palace
5 Ambavgarh, Fatehsagar
Tel: 243 2245
Fax: 243 2136
hilltop@bppl.net.in
An efficient, modern hotel with comfortable rooms and friendly staff. Great views and decent food from the rooftop restaurant. **£££–££££**

Shikarbadi Hotel
Goverdhan Vilas
Tel: 258 3200
Fax: 258 4841
www.hrhindia.com
Formerly the Maharaja's hunting lodge, 4 km (2½ miles) from the railway station, this attractive hotel has good AC rooms, all large and comfortable. There is also a restaurant, swimming pool, gardens and a deer park. **£££–££££**

Amet Haveli
Hanuman Ghat
Tel: 243 1085
Exquisite 350-year-old *haveli* with romantic rooms, whose carpeted window seats look through delicate arches across Pichola Lake to the City Palace and Lal Ghat – Udaipur's trademark view. A prime spot, with architecture and service that do it justice. The hotel also hosts a top-notch restaurant, Ambrai. **£££**

Jagat Niwas Palace Hotel
23–5 Lalghat
Tel: 242 0133
Fax: 241 8512
A popular converted *haveli* with elegant rooms. Beautifully restored, the hotel is very pleasant with friendly staff. The restaurant is excellent. **£££**

RTDC Hotel Kajri
Shastri Circle
Tel: 241 0501
www.rajasthantourism.gov.in
A government-run hotel with safe, clean rooms in a modern bloc. Central and good-value, if not as atmospheric as elsewhere. There is a garden and restuarant. **££**

Kankarwa Haveli
26 Lal Ghat
Tel: 241 1457
Fax: 252 1403
www.indianheritagehotels.com
A lovely converted *haveli* overlooking the lake with cosy rooms. Friendly service and good value. Snacks and meals (ask in advance) available on the roof terrace. Recommended. **££**

Ratan Palace Guest House
21 Lalghat
Tel: 256 1153
Friendly and clean budget

accommodation with attached bath. A frendly and safe hotel with a rooftop restaurant. **£–££**

Lalghat Guest House
33 Lalghat
Tel: 252 5301
Fax: 241 8508
A well-known travellers' haunt with a wide range of rooms and dormitory beds. Some rooms have attached baths; snacks are available on the terrace, from which there are good views. **£**

SIKKIM

Gangtok (03592)
Nor-Khill
Paljor Stadium Road
Tel: 205 637
Fax: 205 639
www.elginhotels.com
Formerly the Chogyal's guesthouse, built in 1932. Luxury rooms with character; well-run hotel with decent amenities, including a good restaurant. **£££££**

Netuk House
Tibet Road
Tel: 222 374
Fax: 224 802
netuk@sikkim.org
Family-run hotel with traditional rooms and a restaurant serving excellent Sikkimese food. **££££**

Hotel Tashi Delek
Mahatma Gandhi Marg
Tel: 222 991
Fax: 222 362
www.hoteltashidelek.com
A central and famous luxury hotel complex. Friendly with good rooms. Very good restaurant and rooftop cafe with stunning views. **££££**

Hotel Tibet
Paljor Stadium Road
Tel: 222 523
Fax: 226 233
www.sikkiminfo.net/hoteltibet
A comfortable and friendly hotel with decent rooms. Excellent local and Tibetan food in the restaurant. **£££**

Hotel Sonam Delek
Tibet Road
Tel: 222 566
Fax: 223 197

Hotel Price Categories

The rates below are for a double room (AC where available) in high season, including taxes.

£££££	Rs3,700 and above
££££	Rs2,700–3,700
£££	Rs1,700–2,700
££	Rs800–1,700
£	Up to Rs800

www.sikkiminfo.net/sonamdelek
Well located, excellent value rooms.
There is a pleasant garden and decent
restaurant serving good local food. **££**
Denzong Inn
Denzong Cinema Chowk, Lall Bazaar
Road
Tel: 222 692
Fax: 202 362
www.hoteltashidelek.com
Run by the same owners as the Tashi
Delek, this is a very good-value place
to stay. A wide range of rooms, all
with attached bath and hot water, a
restuarant and a nice terrace. **£–££**
Siniolchu Lodge
Enchay, near the Enchay Gompa
Tel: 222 074
A very good budget option run by the
Sikkim government. A little out of town
but with superb views. There is a
restaurant and tours can be booked
from the desk. **£–££**

TAMIL NADU

Chidambaram (04144)
Hotel Saradharam
19 V.G.P. Street
Tel: 21336
Fax: 22656
Simple rooms in a hotel that is
starting to show its age, with AC and
non-AC rooms. However, it does have
a good restaurant. **££**
Hotel Akshaya
17 East Car Street
Tel: 220 192
Decent rooms in a central hotel (close
to the temple) with non-AC, and a few
AC, rooms. **£–££**
Hotel Ritz
2 V.G.P. Street
Tel: 223 312–4
Good, clean rooms, some AC, in a
small, friendly hotel. **£–££**

Coimbatore (0422)
Heritage Inn
38 Sivasamy Road, Ramnagar
Tel: 233 1451
Fax: 233 3233
www.hotelheritageinn.com
Modern, comfortable and well-
maintained rooms. A clean hotel with
good restaurants. **£££**
Nilgiri's Nest
739a Avinashi Road
Tel: 221 7132
Fax: 221 7131
nilgiris@md3.vsnl.net.in
Good and comfortable AC rooms.
There is a great restaurant and useful
shop. Convenient for the railway
station. **££–£££**
Sree Annapoorna Lodging
47 East Arokiasamy Road, R.S. Puram
Tel: 254 7722
Fax: 254 7322

www.sreeannapoorna.com
Good-value rooms, some AC, in a well-
established hotel. Tasty vegetarian
food in the restaurant. **££**
TTDC Hotel Tamilnadu
Dr Nanjappa Road
Tel: 230 2176
Fax: 230 3511
www.tamilnadutourism.org
A quiet hotel near the bus-stand.
Good-value clean rooms, some AC
(non-AC **£**) with attached bath. **£–££**

Coonoor (0423)
Taj Garden Retreat
Church Road, Upper Coonoor
Tel: 223 0021
Fax: 223 2775
www.tajhotels.com
Luxury cottages set in beautiful
gardens. Excellent food in the
restaurant (particularly the buffet).
Surprisingly reasonable and good
discounts during off season. **££££**

Kanchipuram (04112)
Baboo Soorya Hotel
85 East Raja Veethi Street
Tel: 222 555
Fax: 222 556
Very clean rooms, both AC and non-
AC, in a friendly hotel. There is also a
very good vegetarian restaurant. **£–££**

Kanniyakumari (04652)
Hotel Singaar International
5/22 Main Road
Tel: 347 992
Fax: 347 991
singaar@sancharnet.in
A clean and modern hotel with some
pricey AC rooms (non-AC a much
better deal). There is a good pool and
a restaurant. **£££**
TTDC Hotel Tamilnadu
Beach Road
Tel: 246 257
Fax: 246 030
www.tamilnadutourism.org
A wide range of cottages, rooms,
dormitories, some AC. Decent food
available and in a good location. **£–££**

Kodaikanal (04542)
The Carlton
Lake Road
Tel: 240 056
Fax: 241 170
www.krahejahospitality.com
A lakeside colonial house converted
into a luxury hotel with comfortable
rooms. Good sports facilities and an
excellent restaurant. **£££££**
Hilltop Towers
Club Road
Tel: 240 413
Fax: 240 415
www.indiamart.com/hilltoptowers
A good-value hotel near the lake, with
comfortable, well-furnished rooms.

There is also a decent restaurant and
bakery. **££**
Hotel Jewel
7 Road Junction
Tel: 241 029
Fax: 240 518
glentravels@vsnl.com
Good-value, non-AC, comfortable
rooms with attached bath and hot
water, and a restaurant. **££**
Greenland's Youth Hostel
St Mary's Road, near Coaker's Walk
Tel: 241 336
Fax: 241 340
Probably the best budget option,
though it can get crowded. Clean, but
very basic, rooms and dormitories.
Lovely views and nice gardens. **£**

Madurai (0452)
Taj Garden Retreat
40 T.P.K. Road, Pasumalai
Tel: 237 1601
Fax: 237 1636
www.tajhotels.com
Madurai's top hotel; based around an
old company guesthouse dating from
the days of the Raj. The rooms have
lovely views, and there are pretty
gardens and a pool. **£££££**
Hotel Chentoor
106 West Perumal Maistry Street
Tel: 235 0490
Fax: 235 0499
Modern and comfortable rooms, some
AC, in a friendly hotel with a good
vegetarian restaurant. **££**
Hotel Supreme
110 West Perumal Maistry Street
Tel: 234 3151
Fax: 234 2637
www.supremehotels.com
A modern hotel with a good rooftop
restaurant with temple views. The
rooms are clean and modern. **££**
Hotel Sree Devi
20 W. Avani Moola Street
Tel: 274 7431
Good-value, clean rooms (some AC,
non-AC **£**) with attached bath. Great
views of the temple *gopurams* from
the roof. Filtered water available on
ground floor. **£–££**
Hotel International
46 West Perumal Maistry Street
Tel: 234 1552
Fax: 274 0372
Good-value, non-AC rooms (some with
views) in a clean and friendly hotel. **£**
TTDC Hotel Tamilnadu
Alagarkoil Road
Tel: 253 7461
Fax: 253 3203
www.tamilnadutourism.org
Quiet rooms (some AC) in a
government-run hotel. There is also a
good restaurant. **£**
Railway Retiring Rooms
Good-value budget rooms on the first
floor of the railway station. **£**

Hotel Price Categories

The rates below are for a double room (AC where available) in high season, including taxes.

£££££	Rs3,700 and above
££££	Rs2,700–3,700
£££	Rs1,700–2,700
££	Rs800–1,700
£	Up to Rs800

Mamallapuram (04114)
Fisherman's Cove
Covelong Beach, Kanchipuram District
Tel: 272 304
Fax: 272 303
www.tajhotels.com
Lovely, renovated beachside hotel, 8 km (5 miles) from Mamallapuram. Rooms with a sea view and beachside cottages. There is a great swimming pool and very good seafood restaurant. **£££££**
Mamalla Bhavan Annexe
104 East Raja Street
Tel: 242 060
Fax: 242 160
Good-value budget rooms, some with AC, in a modern, clean hotel. There is also an excellent vegetarian restaurant. Recommended. **££**
TTDC Hotel Tamilnadu Beach Resort
Tel: 242 361
Fax: 242 268
www.tamilnadutourism.org
AC and non-AC cottages, a bit run-down, in a lovely, quiet setting. There is a good pool and a restaurant. **££**

Mudumalai National Park (0423)
Bamboo Banks
Masinagudi
Tel: 252 6211
www.bamboobanks.in
A highly recommended place to stay. Well appointed cottages in wooded grounds. Good Parsi food using locally grown vegetables. Excellent value for the position and facilities. **£££**
Forest Rest Houses
Abhayaranyam, Kargudi, Masinagudi and Teppakadu
Book through:
Wildlife Warden, Mahalingam Buildings, Coonoor Road, Udhagamandalam 643 001, Tamil Nadu
Tel: 244 4098
Simple accommodation in a number of locations. Catering is provided on request. **£**
Jungle Retreat
Bokkapuram, Masinagudi 643 223
Tel: 252 6469
www.jungleretreat.com
An excellent, and very reasonable, place to stay. Straightforward and pleasant accommodation. Wonderful

views from the grounds (which also have a pool). Friendly service and excellent opportunities for wildlife-watching. **££££**
Jungle Trails
Masinagudi
Tel: 252 6256
Simple but clean and decent accommodation for the true wildlife enthusiast. The resort is run by the naturalist Mark Davidar, who is a mine of information on the natural history of the surrounding area. **££**
Monarch Safari Park
Bokkapuram, Masinagudi 643 223
Tel: 252 6250
www.hojoindia.com
Well-sited with some great views. Simple, raised huts with attached bathrooms. Decent food in the restaurant and good bird-watching from the grounds. **££–£££**

Udagamandalam (0423)
Savoy Hotel
77 Sylks Road
Tel: 244 4142
Fax: 244 3318
www.tajhotels.com
Forty rooms, some in cottages evocative of the Raj. Fires are lit in the guest rooms when the evenings get cooler. Lovely gardens, restaurant and coffee shop. **££££–£££££**
Hotel Nahar Nilgiris
52a Charing Cross
Tel: 244 2173
Fax: 244 5173
Good-value and comfortable rooms in a friendly, central hotel. Convenient and with a decent restaurant. **££**
YWCA Anandagiri
Ettines Road
Tel: 244 2218
Popular for its good-value rooms, dormitories and restaurant. Often full so book ahead. **££**
TTDC Hotel Tamilnadu
Charing Cross
Tel: 244 4370
Fax: 244 4369
www.tamilnadutourism.org
Good-value rooms and dormitories in a friendly and cheap hotel. Good views and a decent restaurant. **£–££**

Ramesvaram (04573)
TTDC Hotel Tamilnadu
14 Sannathi Street
Tel: 221 277
Fax: 221 070
www.tamilnadutourism.org
Clean, sea-facing rooms, some AC (non-AC **£**), and a dormitory. Also has a good restaurant. **£–££**
Railway Retiring Rooms
Tel: 221 226
Good value and clean budget accommodation. **£**

Thanjavur (04362)
Hotel Parisutham
55 Grand Anicut Canal Road
Tel: 231 601
Fax: 230 318
www.hotelparisutham.com
A comfortable, modern hotel, with good rooms overlooking the canal. There is a decent restaurant and a great swimming pool. **£££££**
Hotel Sangam
Trichy Road
Tel: 239 451
Fax: 236 695
www.hotelsangam.com
Pricey, modern hotel with comfortable rooms. Good restaurants and pool in a nice garden. **£££££**
Hotel Gnanam
Anna Salai
Tel: 278 501
Fax: 235 536
www.hotelgnanam.com
Good-value, clean rooms in a central, pleasant hotel. There is also a good vegetarian restaurant. **££**
TTDC Hotel Tamilnadu
Gandhiji Road
Tel: 231 421
Fax: 231 970
www.tamilnadutourism.org
Large and comfortable rooms in a good-value hotel, with a restaurant and garden. **£–££**
Hotel Ganesh
2905/3–4 Srinivasan Pillai Road
Tel: 231 113
Fax: 272 517
hotelganesh-97@hotmail.com
Simple but clean, good-value rooms close to the railway station. The hotel has a good vegetarian restaurant. **£**
Railway Retiring Rooms
Six double rooms on the first floor of the railway station. Try and book.

Tiruchirapalli (0431)
Hotel Sangam
Collector's Office Road
Tel: 241 4700
www.hotelsangam.com
A comfortable, fairly expensive hotel with good AC rooms. There is a pool, and a restaurant with tasty Indian food. **£££££**
Jenney's Residency
3/14 Macdonalds Road
Tel: 241 4414
Fax: 246 1451
jennys@satyam.net.in
A pleasant up-market hotel, with good-value, large AC rooms. There is a pool and two good Indian restaurants. **£££**
Femina Hotel
109 Williams Road, Cantonment
Tel: 241 4501
Fax: 241 0615
try_femina@sancharnet.com
Comfortable AC rooms, some with

balconies, in a good-value hotel. Good vegetarian restaurants and a swimming pool. **££–£££**

Ashby Hotel
17a Rockins Road
Tel: 246 0652
chinoor@yahoo.com
Large, atmospheric rooms (non-AC much cheaper) with verandas around a courtyard. There is a good restaurant. **£–££**

TTDC Hotel Tamilnadu
Macdonalds Road, Cantonment
Tel: 241 4246
Fax: 241 5725
www.tamilnadutourism.org
A wide range of cheap, if a little shabby, rooms (AC and non-AC). There is also an attached restaurant. **£–££**

Railway Retiring Rooms
A good budget option. **£**

Vellore (0416)

Hotel Prince Manor
83 Katpadi Road
Tel: 222 7106
Fax: 225 3016
hotelprincemanor@vsnl.net
Good-value and comfortable AC and non-AC rooms in a well-run and friendly hotel. It has an excellent restaurant. **££**

Hotel River View
New Katpadi Road
Tel: 222 5251
Fax: 222 5672
A modern hotel with some AC rooms. Very good restaurants and pleasant gardens. **££**

UTTRANACHAL

Corbett National Park

Camp Corbett
Corbett Nagar
Tel: 05942-242 126
www.campcorbett.net
An excellent and friendly place to stay. Pleasant cottages, a good library and nearby bird-watching all add to its attractions. The food is particularly good. **££££**

Corbett Ramganga Resort
Jhamaria
Book through: WelcomHeritage, 31 First Floor, Siri Fort Road, New Delhi 110 049
Tel: 011-2626 6650
www.welcomheritagehotels.com
An up-market resort beautifully situated by the river. Well maintained grounds and attractive cottages. Not as eco-friendly as some, but with lots of activities for children. **£££££**

Forest Rest Houses
Dhikala
Must be booked through:
Main Reception Centre, Ramnagar,

Nainital, U.P.
Tel: 05947-251 489
Basic accommodation, from dormitories to private bungalows, in various locations within the park itself. Recommended for early morning or evening animal-spotting. Book well in advance. **£–££**

Infinity Resorts
Dhikuli
Tel: 05947-251 279
www.tigercorbettindia.com
Formerly Tiger Tops Corbett, this is a classic jungle lodge. Comfortable and with a certain charm, there are at least some efforts to be eco-friendly. The staff can arrange extended safaris in the sanctuary. **£££££**

Jungle Brook
Ramnagar
Tel: 0091-98998 09710
www.junglebrook.com
Lovely thatched cottages and "tents" in delightful surroundings. Quiet and secluded with great walks in the immediate area. **££££–£££££**

Tiger Camp
Book through:
Tiger Camp, B-9, Sector 27, Noida 201 301
Tel: 0120-255 1963
www.tiger-camp.com
Attractive, local-style cottages and rooms with en-suite bathrooms. There is a good restaurant and well-run Jeep tours. **£££**

Dehra Dun (0135)

Hotel Great Value
74c Rajpur Road
Tel: 274 4086
Fax: 274 6058
www.greatvaluehotel.com
A modern, clean and comfortable hotel with a good Indian restaurant. Recommended. **£££**

Hotel President
6 Astley Hall, Rajpur Road
Tel: 265 7082
Fax: 265 8883
prestrav@sancharnet.in
AC rooms in a well-run hotel. Friendly with a good restaurant and efficient travel desk. **££–£££**

GMVN Drona
45 Gandhi Road
Tel: 265 4371
Fax: 265 4408
A basic and central hotel with Large rooms, some AC, and a men-only dormitory. Good Indian restaurant. **££**

Motel Kwality
19 Rajpur Road
Tel: 265 7001
Fax: 265 3994
Comfortable and clean rooms, some AC, in a 1960s hotel now showing its age. There is also a decent restaurant. **££**

Haridwar (0133)

Haveli Hari Ganga
Pilibhit House, 21 Ramghat
Tel: 222 6443
Fax: 226 5207
hariganga@sancharnet.in
A restored *haveli* with 20 nice rooms overlooking the Ganga and a good vegetarian restaurant. **£££–££££**

Hotel Midtown
Railway Road
Tel: 222 7507
Fax: 222 6049
Simple, quiet accommodation (some AC, non-AC cheaper) in a modern hotel. **££**

Sagar Ganga Resorts
Niranjani Akhada Road, Mayapur
Tel: 242 2115
Fax: 242 8478
A riverside hotel with bags of charm and large, pleasant rooms. food is available. **££**

Uttaranchal Tourism Rahi
Station Road
Tel: 242 6430
A range of rooms and dormitories set amid pleasant gardens. Centrally located and close to the bus-stand. Good budget option, book ahead. **££**

Mussoorie (0135)

Jaypee Residency Manor
Barlowganj
Tel: 263 1800
www.jaypeehotels.com
A luxury hotel 5 km (3 miles) out of town. Swish and comfortable, and in a lovely, quiet location. **£££££**

The Claridges Nabha
Air Field, Barlowganj Road
Tel: 263 1426
Fax: 263 1425
An old bungalow, now a fully refurbished and comfortable hotel. Well-managed and surrounded by a lovely garden, it is quiet and peaceful with lovely views. **££££–£££££**

Kasmanda Palace
The Mall
Tel: 263 2424
Fax: 263 0007
www.welcomheritage.com
Originally built in 1836, this historical building is now a comfortable and atmospheric hotel. Lovely, quiet grounds. **£££**

Carlton's Plaisance
Off Charleville Road
Tel: 263 2800
Quiet and relaxing hotel with period furnishings. A pleasant garden and good restaurant. **££–£££**

Filigree
Camel's Back Road, Kulri
Tel: 263 2380
Fax: 263 2360
A pleasant, friendly hotel with comfortable rooms, some of which have a great view. There is a

good restaurant and a pleasant terrace. **££–£££**

Hotel Peak View
Camel's Back Road
Tel: 263 2052
peakview@mailcity.com
A good budget hotel with a wide range of rooms (some "flats" with a kitchen). **££**

Valley-View Hotel
The Mall, Kulri
Tel: 263 2324
Clean and comfortable rooms in a mid-range hotel. There is a good restaurant and bakery. **££**

Nanda Devi

GMVN Tourist Bungalow
Joshimath
Tel: 01389-222 118
www.gmvnl.com
Small, basic but clean rooms run by the tourism development corporation. Very cheap dormitory beds are also available. **£**
The **Johar Valley Trek**, which takes in part of the Valley of the Flowers, can be booked through:
Shakti
3rd Floor, E-82 Greater Kailash 1, New Delhi
Tel: 011-5173 4788
www.shaktihimalaya.com

Nainital (05942)

The Manu Maharani
Grassmere Estate
Tel: 237 341
Fax: 237 350
manumaharani@vsnl.com
Very comfortable modern rooms with great views. There is a nice bar and a good Chinese restaurant on the premises. **£££££**

Vikram Vintage Inn
Near ATI, Mallital
Tel: 236 177
Fax: 236 179
Elegant rooms in a quiet wooded location. No pool but other sports facilities. **££££**

Alka Hotel
The Mall
Tel: 235 220
Fax: 236 629
www.alkahotel.com
A recommended hotel with pleasant rooms with a lake view. Well-managed with a good restaurant. Good reductions in rates during low season. **£££**

Belvedere Palace
Awagarh Estate, Mallital
Tel: 237 434
Fax: 235 082
www.welcomheritage.com
A converted palace with large rooms and views over the lake. Lovely gardens and a pleasant restaurant. Good value. **££–£££**

YHA
Ardwell, Mallital
Tel: 236 353
www.yhaindia.com
Great value dormitories and rooms, with meals available. Very popular and in a peaceful location. Book ahead. **£**

Rishikesh (0135)

Ananda in the HImalayas
Palace Estate, Narendra Nagar
Tel: 01378-227 500
Fax: 01378-227 550
www.anandaspa.com
A very expensive but fabulous spa 18 km (11 miles) from Rishikesh. Set in an old palace, it has elegant rooms with lovely views. The spa has a wonderful pool. **£££££**

Hotel Ganga Kinare
16 Veerbhadra Road
Tel: 243 1658
Fax: 243 5243
hotelgangakinare@hotmail.com
A comfortable hotel a little way out of town. A lovely position on the riverbank and a good restaurant.

Inderlok Hotel
Railway Road
Tel: 243 0555
Fax:243 2855
A well-established central hotel, with pleasant rooms and a vegetarian restaurant. There is a nice terrace garden affording lovely views. **££**

GMVN Rishilok
Badrinath Road, Muni ki Reti
Tel: 243 0373
Fax: 243 0372
Good-value mid-budget cottages and rooms, which are set in pleasant grounds. Quiet with a decent restaurant. **£–££**

UTTAR PRADESH

Agra (0562)

Amarvilas
Taj East Gate Road
Tel: 223 1515
Fax: 223 1516
www.oberoihotels.com
By far the most luxurious of the five stars, up to the usual Oberoi standards (and prices). An imposing building with great views of the Taj, lovely spa and pool and sumptuous rooms. **£££££**

Clarks Shiraz
54 Taj Road, Cantonment
Tel: 222 6121
Fax: 222 6128
www.hotelclarksshiraz.com
Comfortable hotel on a large estate with good facilities, now starting to show its age. Good restaurants (especially the rooftop one), and a nice pool and gardens. **£££££**

Hotel Price Categories

The rates below are for a double room (AC where available) in high season, including taxes.

£££££	Rs3,700 and above
££££	Rs2,700–3,700
£££	Rs1,700–2,700
££	Rs800–1,700
£	Up to Rs800

Mughgal Sheraton
Taj Ganj
Tel: 233 1701
Fax: 233 1731
www.welcomgroup.com
A well-designed hotel built and furnished in "Mughal" style. A very pleasant enviroment with good, but expensive, restaurants. Nice gardens with a good pool, some (more expensive) rooms have a view of the Taj. **£££££**

Taj View Hotel
Fatehbad Road, Taj Ganj
Tel: 223 2400
Fax: 223 2420
www.tajhotels.com
A bland, modern hotel with distant views of the Taj Mahal. Comfortable rooms within a functional exterior, and nice twin swimming pools in the grounds. **££££–£££££**

Hotel Amar
Tourist Complex, Fatehbad Road
Tel: 233 1884
Fax: 233 0299
amaragra@sancharnet.in
An impersonal, modern hotel with comfortable AC rooms. Has a restaurant and pool. **£££**

Grand Hotel
137 Station Road, Cantonment
Tel: 222 7511
Fax: 222 7510
grand@nde.vsnl.net.in
Faded hotel in large grounds with facilities for camping. Has a nice garden, restaurant and bar. **£££**

Joshi Tourist Complex
21 km Stone, N.H. 11, Agra–Jaipur Highway
Tel: (05613) 244 556
Fax: (05613) 213 109
www.joshiresort.com
A lovely village complex with traditional huts (some with AC), close to Fatehpur Sikri. There is a pool and a restaurant serving excellent local vegetarian food. **££**

Lauries Hotel
M.G. Road
Tel: 222 7511
Fax: 222 7510
laurieshotel@hotmail.com
A well-known but now rather decrepit hotel with facilities for camping. Has a nice grounds, and a restaurant and bar. **££**

Mayur Tourist Complex
Tourist Complex, Fatehbad Road
Tel: 233 2302
Fax: 233 2907
bibhab@nde.vsnl.net.in
Slightly run-down AC cottages around peaceful and well-maintained gardens with a pool and fountains. **££**

UP Tourism Rahi Tourist Bungalow
Delhi Gate, near Raja ki Mandi Railway Station
Tel; 235 0120
Fax: 215 3472
www.up-tourism.com
A good range of accommodation in a clean, government-run hotel. Out of the way but quiet and good value. **££**

UP Tourism Hotel Tajkhema
Taj Ganj
Tel: 233 0140
Fax: 223 0001
www.up-tourism.com
Safe, clean rooms in a government hotel close to the Taj. Good views, a good selection of rooms and a restaurant. **££**

Tourist Rest House
Kachahari Road, Baluganj
Tel: 236 3961
Fax: 236 6910
trh@vsnl.com
The best low-cost place to stay in Agra. Clean rooms with attached bath around a courtyard. Friendly owners and good vegetarian food. Recommended. **£**

Allahabad (0532)
Hotel Allahabad Regency
16 Tashkent Marg, Civil Lines
Tel: 260 1519
Fax: 261 1107
Elegantly furnished and good value. A clean, comfortable hotel, with a restaurant and pool. **££–£££**

Hotel Yatrik
33 Sardar Patel Marg, Civil Lines
Tel: 260 1799
Fax: 260 1434
yatrik@vsnl.com
A popular, well-managed hotel with AC rooms and a lovely tropical garden and restaurant. **££**

Presidency
19d Sarojini Naidu Marg, Civil Lines
Tel: 262 3308
Fax: 262 3897
starhotels@vsnl.net
A pleasant, comfortable and moderately priced guesthouse, with a pool and foreign exchange. Book in advance. **££**

UP Tourism Rahi Illawart Tourist Bungalow
35 M.G. Marg, Civil Lines
Tel: 260 1440
Fax: 261 1374
www.up-tourism.com
Large rooms, some with AC with attached bath and hot water. Nice

garden and a restuarant. Close to the bus station. **££**

Railway Retiring Rooms
Good budget room and a very cheap dormitory. **£**

Dudhwa National Park
Forest Rest Houses
Book through:
Chief Wildlife Warden, 17 Rana Pratap Marg, Lucknow 226 001
Tel: 0522-220 6584
www.up touricm.com
Basic huts in different locations across the park. Those at Dudhwa and Sathiana (which have canteens) have bedding, while for Bankatti, Sonaripur and Kila you will have to bring your own and also arrange food before arrriving. There is an extra charge for the generator at Sathiana and Sonaripur; there Is no electricity at Kila. Best to book in advance. **£–££**

Tharu Huts
Dudhwa
Book through:
Field Director, Project Tiger, Palia, Dudhwa Tiger Reserve, Lakimpur Kheri 262 701, U.P.
Tel: 05872-252 106
Basic hut accommodation. Project Tiger also has a dormitory which might be available. **£–££**

Faizabad (05278)
Hotel Shan-e-Avadh
by the Civil Lines Bus-Stand
Tel: 223 586
Fax: 226 545
Comfortable, clean rooms with hot water and a restaurant. **£–££**

Hotel Tirupati
by the Civil Lines Bus-Stand
Tel: 223 231
A modern hotel with some AC rooms, and a good restaurant. **£–££**

Jhansi (0517)
Hotel Sita
84 Shivpuri Road
Tel: 244 2956
Fax: 244 4691
One of the best places in town. A modern hotel with pleasant rooms, some AC, and a good restaurant. Recommended. **££–£££**

Jhansi Hotel
Shastri Marg, opposite Head Post Office
Tel: 247 0360
Fax: 247 0470
A colonial-era bungalow that is now decaying but still retains some of its charm. Some rather overpriced AC rooms, pleasant grounds and a restaurant. **££**

UP Tourism Rahi Veerangana Tourist Bungalow
near the Circuit House
Tel: 244 2402

www.up-tourism.com
A wide range of accommodation (some AC rooms) in a government-run hotel with a decent restaurant and nice gardens. **£–££**

Raj Palace
Shastri Marg
Tel: 247 0554
Near the bus-stand. Decent, clean mid-budget rooms (some AC) with attached bath. **£–££**

Samrat
Chitra Chauraha
Tel: 244 4943
Good budget rooms in a friendly hotel with a restaurant. Near the railway station. **£**

Kanpur (0512)
The Landmark
10 Somdatt Plaza, The Mall
Tel: 230 5305
Fax: 230 6291
lmknp@sancharnet.in
The best, if most expensive, hotel in Kanpur. Comfortable, modern rooms, as well as good restaurants and a coffee shop. **£££££**

Hotel Gaurav
18/54 The Mall
Tel: 231 8531
Fax: 231 4776
hotel_gaurav@rediffmail.com
Good value, comfortable AC rooms. Also has a restaurant and a nice garden. **££**

Hotel Swagat
109/423 80 Feet Road, Brahmnagar
Tel: 254 1923
Fax: 254 2100
Reasonable accommodation with good-value AC rooms (non-AC cheaper). Also has a restaurant. **££**

Hotel Meera Inn
37/19 The Mall, opposite the Reserve Bank of India
Tel: 231 9972
Good-value, clean air-cooled rooms (a few AC, **££**). The hotel also has a basic restaurant. **£–££**

Lucknow (0522)
Taj Residency Hotel
Vipin Khand, Gomti Nagar
Tel: 239 3939
Fax: 239 2282
www.tajhotels.com
Lucknow's top hotel, very luxurious and peaceful with lovely gardens. Excellent restaurant serving Avadhi food. **£££££**

Hotel Clarks Avadh
8 Mahatma Gandhi Marg
Tel: 262 0131
Fax: 261 6507
www.hotelclarks.com
A comfortable, if a little dated, luxury hotel located in the centre of town. Helpful, friendly staff and good restaurants, especially the rooftop

Hotel Price Categories

The rates below are for a double room (AC where available) in high season, including taxes.

£££££	Rs3,700 and above
££££	Rs2,700–3,700
£££	Rs1,700–2,700
££	Rs800–1,700
£	Up to Rs800

Falaknuma serving very rich Avadhi dishes. **£££££**

Carlton Hotel
Ranapratap Marg, Hazratganj
Tel: 222 2413
Fax: 223 1886
A long-established, legendary hotel, somewhat faded, with old-fashioned rooms and baths (non-AC much cheaper). An impressive colonial building with a lovely garden, restaurant and bar. **££**

UP Tourism Hotel Gomti
6 Sapru Marg
Tel: 221 4708
Fax: 221 2659
www.up-tourism.com
A very good option; a clean hotel well-run by UP Tourism. Some good-value AC rooms as well as a restaurant and bar. **££**

Capoor's Hotel
52 Hazratganj
A run-down but well-known hotel, with AC rooms and a good restaurant. Not without charm. **££**

Mrs Sharma's Guest House
Mall Avenue, Sudharshan Seth
Tel: 223 9314
A highly recommended small guesthouse run by the widow of a retired brigadier. Very clean and friendly, with good home-cooked meals available on request. **£**

Chowdhuri Lodge
3 Vidhan Sabha Marg, near the General Post Office
Tel: 222 1911
Cheap, safe and friendly accommodation, though the lodge has become rather run-down and could be cleaner. **£**

Mathura (0565)
Radha Ashok
Masani By-Pass Road, Chatikara
Tel: 253 0395
Fax: 253 0396
www.mathura-vrindavan.com
A very well-kept and attractive, modern hotel featuring comfortable rooms, pleasant gardens with a swimming pool and a very good vegetarian restaurant. **£££–££££**

Hotel Madhuvan
Krishna Nagar
Tel: 242 0064

Fax: 242 0684
bhtul@nde.vsnl.net.in
Clean air-conditioned rooms with attached bath; the hotel also has a swiming pool and pleasant restaurant. **££**

Hotel Mansarovar Palace
Mansarovar Crossing, Chowki Bagh Bahadur
Tel: 240 8686
Fax: 240 1611
mansarovar@vsnl.com
A pleasant hotel with good-value AC and non-AC rooms and a decent restaurant. **££**

Sarnath (0542)
Jain Paying Guest House
Tel: 259 5621
www.visitsarnath.com
A small but very friendly guesthouse. Clean rooms, doubles with attached shower and toilet (singles have attached shower and shared toilet). Good, home-cooked vegetarian food. **£**

Namo Buddha
S10/81 C-2 Mohalla Baraipur, 3rd house behind Mishra General Store
chrisnehrulal@yahoo.com
A small guesthouse with simple but comfortable rooms. The atmosphere is friendly and the accommodation good value. **£**

Varanasi (0542)
Taj Ganges
Nadesar Palace Grounds, Nadesar
Tel: 234 5100
Fax: 250 2724
www.tajhotels.com
One of the top hotels in town. Comfortable rooms, two good restaurants, and a nice swimming pool. **£££££**

Hotel Clarks Varanasi
The Mall
Tel: 234 8501
Fax: 250 2736
www.indiamart.com/hotelclarksvaranasi
Well-established and atmospheric, with good amenities including a swimming pool. It also has an excellent restaurant. **£££££**

Hotel Ganga View
Assi Ghat
Tel: 236 8640
Fax: 236 8703
Highly recommended. An old mansion converted into an atmospheric and well-run hotel. Comfortable, very clean AC rooms with good attached baths. Great views from an upstairs terrace. Drinks and snacks available, vegetarian dinner (ask in advance) served at 8pm. **£££**

Hotel India
59 Patel Nagar, Cantonment
Tel: 250 7593
Fax: 250 7598
www.hotelindiavns.com

Large hotel with big, comfortable and very clean AC rooms with good bathrooms. Nice garden and a good selection of restaurants. **£££**

Hotel Pradeep
C-27/153 Jagatganj
Tel: 220 4594
Fax: 220 4898
www.hotelpradeep.com
A friendly hotel with well-maintained and clean AC rooms. Very good value for money and also has the excellent Poonam restaurant. Recommended. **££**

Diamond Hotel
Bhelpur
Tel: 227 6696
Fax: 227 6703
diamotel@satyam.net.in
Good value AC and non-AC rooms in comfortable hotel with a restaurant and garden. **££**

Hotel Malti
C-31/3 Kashi Vidyapith Road
Tel: 222 3878
Fax: 222 4857
A well-run and friendly hotel with clean AC and non-AC (**£**) rooms with balconies. **££**

UP Tourism Rahi Tourist Bungalow
Parade Kothi, Cantonment
Tel: 234 3413
Fax: 251 1638
www.up-tourism.com
Good-value rooms (non-AC **£**) in a quiet and clean hotel. Friendly and efficient, there are also nice gardens and a passable restaurant. Recommended. **££**

Hotel Surya
S20/51 5a Nepali Kothi, Varuna Bridge, Cantonment
Tel: 234 3014
Fax: 234 8330
Hassle-free and clean hotel with decent, safe rooms (some AC). Good restaurant and nice garden. Recommended. **£–££**

WEST BENGAL

Darjeeling (0354)
Windamere Hotel
Observatory Hill
Tel: 225 4041
Fax: 225 4043
www.windamerehotel.com
A legendary hotel with famous clientele and an old-fashioned grandeur. Plenty of nostalgia; not as comfortable as it might be, but worth it for the experience. **£££££**

Elgin Hotel
Robertson Road
Tel: 54114
Fax: 54267
www.elginhotels.com
An elegant but expensive, colonial hotel. Comfortable rooms and a

good restaurant. Like the Windamere, the Elgin wallows in Raj-era nostalgia. **£££££**
Dekeling Resort at Hawk's Nest
2 A.J.C. Bose Road
Tel: 225 3092
Fax: 225 3298
www.dekeling.com
A late-19th century building in a fabulous position. Lovely wood panelled rooms with excellent views. Friendly staff and good food. Recommended. **£££**
Bellevue Hotel
The Mall
Tel: 225 4075
Fax: 225 4330
www.darjeeling-bellevuehotel.com
A friendly, Tibetan-owned hotel. The large, characterful rooms all have attached baths and hot water. This claims to be the "original" Bellevue. **££**
Dekeling Hotel
51 Gandhi Road
Tel: 225 4159
Fax: 225 3298
www.dekeling.com
A friendly and attractive hotel with pleasant rooms (the ones in the attic are best), some with a good view; attached bath and hot water. There is also the good Deveka's restaurant in the hotel. **££**
WBTDC Maple Tourist Lodge
Old Kutchery Road
Tel: 254 413
www.westbengaltourism.com
A little way out of town but quiet with good-value rooms and hot running water. **££**
WBTDC Tourist Lodge
Bhanu Sarani
Tel: 254 411
www.westbengaltourism.com
Not as good value as the Maple Tourist Lodge but in a more convenient location. Fairly standard rooms, with hot water available. **££**
Main Old Bellevue Hotel
Chowrasta, The Mall, 1–5 Nehru Road, above the Bellevue
Tel: 54178/53977
Fax: 54330
www.darjeelinghotels.com
An old Raj-era wooden house with decent, large rooms. The staff are friendly and the garden is lovely. All in all, very good value. Recommended. **£–££**
Andy's Guest House
102 Dr Zakir Hussain Road
Tel: 253 125
Very good-value, clean rooms with hot water in a small friendly guesthouse. Good views from the roof. **£**
Youth Hostel
Dr Zakir Hussain Road
Tel: 252 290

www.westbengaltourism.com
This is a very popular place to stay with budget travellers. Very cheap, it has renovated dormitories and a few rooms. Good views. **£**

Kalimpong (03552)
Silver Oaks
Upper Cast Road
Tel: 255 296
Fax: 255 368
www.elginhotels.com
The 1930s home of a British jute planter now a delightful hotel. Surrounded by lovely gardens and with characterful rooms, it also has a good restaurant. **£££££**
Himalayan Hotel
Upper Cart Road
Tel: 255 248
Fax: 255 122
www.himalayanhotel.biz
A lovely conversion of an old house, previously the residence of the Macdonald family. It has a variety of comfortable rooms and suites, as well as a good restaurant and beautiful garden. **£££**
Kalimpong Park Hotel
Rinkingpong Road
Tel: 255 304
Fax: 255 982
parkotel@satyam.net.in
A peaceful hotel with large rooms. Friendly with a good restaurant and nice garden. **££–£££**
WBTDC Hill Top Tourist Lodge
Tel: 255 654
www.westbengaltourism.com
Clean and simple rooms in a well-run government lodge. Meals available. **£–££**

Murshidabad (03482)
Hotel Manjusha
Lalbagh
Tel: 270 321
A clean and cheap hotel with restaurant, in a pleasant location. **£**
Youth Hostel
Lalbagh
Book through Kolkata
Tel: (033) 2210 9206
Very cheap but clean and safe. **£**

Santiniketan (03463)
Chhuti Holiday Resort
241 Charupally, Jamboni
Tel: 252 692
Mobile: 0943 401 2872
www.chhutiresort.com
Accommodation in thatched cottages, some with AC, set in pleasant grounds. There is also a decent restaurant. **££**
WBTDC Santiniketan Tourist Lodge
Tel: 252 699
Fax: 252 398
www.westbengaltourism.com

A good variety of accommodation, from a dormitory to AC rooms (non-AC **£**) in a government-run hotel. There are nice gardens and an average restaurant. **££**

Sundarbans National Park
WBTDC Tourist Lodge
Sajnekhali, Gosaba, South 24 Parganas 743 331, West Bengal
Tel: 03219-252 560
www.wbtourism.com
Basic rooms and a dormitory in a secluded building. Food is available, but you need to book in advance. **£**
Tours can also be arranged through the Kolkata office of **Pugmarks**:
10 Meher Ali Road, Kolkata
Tel: 033-2280 8917
www.pugmarksholidays.com

Vishnupur (03244)
WBTDC Tourist Lodge
Near the tank
Tel: 252 013
www.westbengaltourism.com
The best option in Vishnupur; this government-run hotel has small and clean rooms (some of them good-value with AC), and a decent restaurant. **£**

Where to Eat

Eating

Some of the best food is found in hotel restaurants, particularly in the luxury hotels where it can be excellent. Where a hotel has a particularly good restaurant it has been mentioned in its description (*see pages 362–88* for recommendations). Don't get confused if you see a restaurant described as a "hotel", as this is a common name for restaurants in India. Most places are open for lunch and dinner, usually from around noon–3pm, and then 6pm–10.30pm, though cheaper places might be open all day. Booking is not usually necessary; though it might be wise to phone restuarants in the luxury hotels beforehand.

One of the biggest problems, especially in North India, can be tracking down good, authentic local food. Many restaurants rely on a menu of old, pan-North Indian favourites such as *sag panir*, *tandoori* breads and chicken dishes, and various *kormas*; all of which can become very repetitive and heavy after a while. To find more unusual dishes, look for places full of locals, with a quick turnover to ensure freshly cooked ingredients.

In the South, local "meals" places are generally excellent, cheap and very clean. Look for places with a high lunchtime turnover (the traditional time for the day's big meal) to find the best food. "Meals' usually come in the form of a *thali*, literally a "tray" with a pile of rice in the middle and small pots containing different vegetable and *dal* dishes, as well as some curd, around the edge.

Street food from stalls, provided it is fresh and cooked in front of you, can be very good and tasty. Snacks range from *chana dal* and *puris*, to omelettes laden with green chillies, to freshly cooked *paratha*. As with most things, use your common sense and only buy from stalls that appear hygienic.

Western-style fast food, breads and cakes are now becoming widely available. For more information on eating *see pages 137–9*.

ANDAMAN ISLANDS

Port Blair
Annapurna Café, Aberdeen Village. Good South Indian food (some non-vegetarian) and tasty breakfasts.
China Room, Aberdeen Village. Excellent seafood and vegetable dishes for surprisingly moderate cost.

ANDHRA PRADESH

Hyderabad-Secunderabad
Kamat's There are several outlets of this clean and inexpensive Udupi-style vegetarian chain in the city; in the Ramalaya and Alladin complexes on Sarojini Devi Road in Secunderabad, and on Secretariat Road and Station Road in Nampally.
Laxmi, Nampally, close to the railway station. Good value and tasty vegetarian and non-vegetarian North and South Indian dishes.
Paradise Cafe and Stores – Annexe Persis, M.G. Road, Secunderabad. A complex of stalls offering good Indian and Chinese food to eat in or take away. Very good *biriyani*.
Utsav, 221 Tivoli Road, Secunderabad. Excellent North Indian vegetarian food served in pleasant surroundings.

Nagarjunakonda
Punnami Ethiopothala, Punnami Vihar A small eating place about 11 km (7 miles) from Nagarjuna Sagar, though many tour buses stop here. It is in a wonderful position beside a gorge with an impressive waterfall.

Tirupati
Punnami Srinivasam, Tirupati, A good vegetarian restaurant attached to a government-run hotel.

Vijayawada
Hotel Santhi, near the Apsara Theatre, Governorpet, A clean restaurant with good vegetarian food.
Punnami, Berm Park, A riverside restaurant attached to a large government-run hotel. The food is decent and the position is lovely.

Vishakhapatnam
Dakshin, Hotel Daspalla, Suryabagh. Very tasty – and spicy – Andhran non-vegetarian food.
Punnami Yatri Niwas, opposite the Appu Ghar Site, Beach Road, M.V.P. Colony, a decent restaurant attached to a government-run hotel. The menu is wide-ranging and the food is well prepared.

ASSAM

Guwahati
Paradise, G.N.B. Road, Chandmari. Good Assamese food with great *thalis* and daily lunchtime specials.
Utsav, Hotel Nandan Building, H.P. Brahmachari Road. Decent but generic Indian and Chinese food.
Woodlands, G.S. Road, Ulubari (also A.T. Road). Clean vegetarian restaurants serving South Indian food; good *thalis*.

BIHAR

Patna
Abhiruchi, Marwari Awas Griha Compound, Fraser Road. Tasty Marwari and generic North Indian vegetarian food.
Amrali, Hotel Kautilya Vihara building, B.C. Patel Path. A good restaurant with excellent vegetarian food served in pleasant surroundings.

CHENNAI

Annalakshmi, 804 Anna Salai. Excellent Southeast Asian vegetarian food prepared by volunteers (all profits go to charity).
Buhari's, 83 Anna Salai. Well-prepared and tasty tandoori food.
Chungking, 67 Anna Salai. Reasonable Chinese food served in rather dark surroundings.
Cozee, by the beach, Besant Nagar. Excellent kebabs and other non-vegetarian offerings from a well-known open-air stall and restaurant.
Dakshin, ITC Park Sheraton, 132 T.T.K. Road. This South Indian restaurant is one of the best in the country, with unusual dishes from all four states and the Chettinad region. Recommended.
Dasaprakash, 806 Anna Salai, next to Higginbotham's. Udipi fast-foods in an up-market environment but at reasonable prices.
Kaaraikudi, 10 Sivasvamy Street, Mylapore. Excellent Tamil food, including non-vegetarian Chettinad dishes.
Kabul's, 35 T.T.K. Road, Alwarpet. Expensive but very good NWFP and Mughlai food.
Mavalli Tiffin Room, G.N. Chetty Road, T. Nagar. The first branch of this long-established restaurant outside Bangalore serves up wonderful vegetarian dishes – you can also buy spices and pickles to take away.
Midnight Express, T.T.K. Road. The only late-night eatery outside of the posh hotels. Good for a fix of *dosa* or *idli* when everything else is shut.

Sangeetha Vegetarian Restaurant, Ethiraj Salai, Egmore. One of a chain of decent vegetarian eating halls in the city. Clean with a wide range of tasty South Indian food.
Saravana Bhavan, many branches including Shanti Theatre Complex, 44 Anna Salai; Central Railway Station; 77–9 Usman Road, T. Nagar; 209 N.S.C. Bose Road, George Town. An excellent chain of clean, cheap and tasty South Indian vegetarian meals halls. Open all day.
The Cascade, 15 Khader Nawaz Khan Road, Nungambakkam. Expensive but very tasty Chinese and Thai food.
Velu's Military Hotel, Valluvar Kottam High Road, Nungambakkam. You can't get much better than this long-standing institution for a superb binge on traditional Chettinad non-vegetarian food. It is possible to get a sample plate so you can try lots of different dishes.
Woodlands Drive-in, Agri Horticultural Gardens, 30 Cathedral Road. Set in a horticultural garden. Better on *channa-bhatura* (North Indian food) than on its own Udupi cooking. Open all day.

DAMAN & DIU

Daman
Samrat, Seaface Road. Vegetarian, with very good Gujarati *thalis*.

DELHI

Appetite, 1575 Main Bazaar. Tempting Nepali, Indian and Italian fare. The *lassis* are really special, and the pastries not bad either.
Basil & Thyme, Santushi Shopping Complex, Chanakyapuri. A pleasant and quiet lunch spot, with good and reasonably priced Western food, including excellent cheesecake.
Big Chill, 35 and 68A Khan Market, tel: 4175 7533. Superlative range of Italian dishes plus desserts and home-made ice cream to die for, this place is deservedly popular, particularly at weekends, when you may have to queue for a table.
Boyarin, Ashok Hotel, 50B Chanakyapuri. One of the more remarkable recent additions to the Delhi dining scene must be this opulent Russian restaurant. The velvet-draped interior lends a dramatic air, while the menu and drinks are nothing if not authentic.
Bukhara, Maurya Sheraton Hotel, Sardar Patel Marg, Diplomatic Enclave. Beautifully prepared food from NWFP in a pricey but well-designed restaurant.
Café 100, 20-B Connaught Place, New Delhi. A very popular fast-food place (eat-in or take-away). Good noodles, juices and ice-creams.
Café Turtle, Full Circle Bookshop, 5B Khan Market. There's a laid-back, if slightly cramped, feel to this innovative café; the pastas and salads are good, but the cakes are even better.
Chor Bizarre, 4/15A Asaf Ali Road, tel: 2327 3821. Reliably delicious Mughlai and Kashmiri fare in interestingly quirky surroundings. The salad buffet is housed in a classic car, while the tables are made from all manner of oddments, including a four-poster bed. Reservations highly recommended.
Dilli Haat, off Aurobindo Marg, between Kidwai Nagar West and Lakshmibai Nagar. The "Foods of India" complex has very cheap and clean stalls, run by different state tourist development corporations. A good place to try unusual dishes, such as Minicoy fish curry. Entry Rs10, open 10.30am–10pm.
Dum Phukt, Maurya Sheraton, Sardar Patel Marg, Diplomatic Enclave. Expensive but delicious Avadhi dishes prepared by lengthy steaming in a sealed pot.
Everest Bakery Café, Dal Mandi, near Star Palace Hotel. This has a very relaxed, grotto-like feel. The *momos* (dumplings) are the main attraction here, but the pies are not far behind.
Flavors, C52 Moolchand Flyover Complex, Defence Colony, tel: 2464 5644. Italian-owned and run, Flavors dishes up some of the most authentic Italian cuisine in town. The portions are huge, but hard to resist. The recent addition of a licence to serve alcohol has added to the appeal. The garden terrace is still the place to sit, making this a better place for lunch than dinner.
Havemore, 11–12 Pandara Road Market, tel: 2338 7070. The handful of up-market *dhabas* here are all equally good, but this has the most tempting name. The location of these late-closing Punjabi restaurants so close to India Gate makes them a good place to have lunch while taking in the sights.
Imperial Garden, E3 Masjid Moth, Greater Kailash II, tel: 2922 7798. One of the city's best Chinese restaurants – the food and the atmosphere are equally authentic.
Kake's, Plaza Building, H Block, Connaught Place. A simple but well-established and perennially popular Punjabi *dhaba*. The food here is dependably tasty and extremely good value, which, combined with the lightning-quick service, makes this place a winner.

Karim's, Gali Kababiyan, Matia Mahal, near Jama Masjid, Delhi. The best Muslim food in the city. Mouthwatering non-vegetarian *tandoori* dishes and excellent breads. There is a more expensive, and less good, branch in Nizamuddin, South Delhi.
La Piazza, Hyatt Regency, Bhikaji Cama Place, Ring Road, New Delhi. Italian restaurant in a very flash hotel. Slightly dated, though has good pizza and interesting desserts (avoid the sorbet). Good service but imported wine is very expensive.
Lodi The Garden Restaurant, Lodi Gardens, Lodi Road, tel: 2465 5054. This restaurant has a beautiful location in Lodi Gardens. The expansive terrace is the biggest draw, although the Mediterranean food comes a close second. Sunday brunch makes for a particularly pleasant experience.
Mag Pappa's Odysseia, M45 Connaught Place, tel: 2341 6842. The most authentic Greek food in town, married with Spanish guitar music, makes for a lively evening. New in town but already deservedly popular.
Malhotra Restaurant, top end of Main Bazaar. Astounding range of cuisines, but all done to a reasonably high standard, with the refurbished interior adding to the experience.
Moti Mahal, 3704 Netaji Subhash Marg, Daryaganj, tel: 2327 3661. If you would rather enjoy your Mughlai cuisine in more refined surroundings, this is the place to go. For many years the standard bearer in the world of Delhi's North Indian restaurants, it still serves food of a consistently high quality, in its soothingly calm, if somewhat dimly lit, interior.
Nirula's Pot Pourri, L-Block, Connaught Place, New Delhi. This popular restaurant with Continental and Indian food is now starting to show its age, though it is still a good place to go for breakfast.
Oh! Calcutta, E Block, International Trade Towers, Nehru Place, tel: 2646 4180. Delhi's first real attempt at bringing the cuisine of West Bengal to the capital's diners, and initial responses have been overwhelmingly positive. This is first and foremost a seafood restaurant, and particularly highly recommended are the *kangra chingri bhapa*, Thai-style steamed cakes wrapped in banana leaves, filled with crab and prawns and flavoured with lime and mustard.
Olive's Bar & Kitchen, Haveli No. 6–8, One Style Mile, Mehrauli, tel: 2664 3914. Easily the city's best Mediterranean eatery; the menu is varied and consistently of a high standard, the service is discreet but polished and the decor superb. Set in

a whitewashed old *haveli*, with a choice of dining inside or out, this could almost be a villa on the Med. Has been a hit with Delhi's smart set since day one – don't even think of going without a reservation.

Orient Express, Taj Palace Hotel, 2 Sardar Patel Marg, tel: 2611 0202. The best of traditional fine dining that the city has to offer, and certainly the only place where your seven-course meal will be served in a stationary railway carriage. The food is classic Continental. Smart dress.

Parikrama, Antriksh Bhavan, 22 K.G. Marg, New Delhi. Revolving restaurant with excellent views and surprisingly good North Indian, Chinese and Continental food.

Park Balluchi Restaurant, inside the Deer Park, Hauz Khas Village, New Delhi. An award-winning restaurant serving rich Mughlai and Afghan dishes. In a lovely setting on the edge of the park.

Ploof, 13 Main Market, Lodi Colony, tel: 2464 9026. One of the city's only seafood specialists, and easily the best. Fish is flown in daily, so you need not fret about freshness, and some of the preparations are sublime, particularly those from South India.

Punjabi by Nature, 11 Basant Lok, Vasant Vihar, tel: 4151 6666. The ultimate in Punjabi cuisine, the food at this place gets consistently rave reviews, and is hugely popular with local diners – worth booking ahead.

Q'BA, E42/43, Inner Circle, Connaught Place, tel: 4151 2888. One of the trendier joints in town, this is a cavernous but comfortable space serving a variety of tasty fare in super-stylish surroundings, arranged over three floors.

Rodeo, 12-A Connaught Place, New Delhi. Good Tex-Mex food and cocktails served by waiters in cowboy outfits. A pleasant place for a drink, must be with food after 7pm.

Sagar, Shahid Bhagat Singh Marg, New Delhi; 18 Defence Colony Market. Very popular, and extremely clean, South Indian restaurants, part of a chain. Good *thalis*, *dosas* and coffee.

Sakura, Metropolitan Hotel Nikko, Bangla Sahib Marg, New Delhi. Excellent and beautifully presented Japanese food (there is an extensive menu in Japanese). Good wines by the glass. The set meals are good-value.

Sam's Café, Vivek Hotel, 1534–50 Main Bazaar. The strident interior marks this place out as modern, but for a quick bite it's as good as anywhere, with the tasty salads a welcome change.

Saravana Bhavan, 46 Janpath, New Delhi. Excellent vegetarian South Indian, with good *dosas* and *thalis*.

Very clean, good value and efficient. Open all day.

Spice Route, Hotel Imperial, 1 Janpath, New Delhi. Superb restaurant, beautifully decorated with wooden pillars and carvings. The wall paintings were done by painters from the Keralan temple town of Guruvayur. Fabulous, if pricey, Keralan and Southeast Asian food.

Spirit, E34 Connaught Place (1st floor), tel: 4101 7006. Classy bar/restaurant offering some of the best Mediterranean food around – Lebanese is a speciality. They also have a better wine list than most, and tend to play music at a volume low enough that conversation remains a possibility – another rarity.

Swagath, 14 Defence Colony Market, tel: 2433 7538. Under the same management as Sagar, this South Indian seafood restaurant maintains the same high standards as its close neighbour. The slightly functional interior and bright lights are soon forgotten once the food arrives, although don't make the mistake of ordering anything but fish.

Ten, 10 Sansad Marg, in the YWCA International Guest House. Pleasant restaurant with a good selection of Continental food, such as pasta, and Indian dishes.

Terrace in the Sky, The Village Bistro Complex, 12 Haus Khaz Village, tel: 2685 3857. There are a number of restaurants in this complex, but the pick of them is on the roof terrace, overlooking the floodlit remains of Siri. The food is up-market Mughlai, and very tasty it is too, but the views are what you'll savour longest.

Thai Wok, Top Floor, Ambawatta Shopping Complex, Mehrauli, tel: 2664 4289. The beautifully decorated roof terrace overlooking the Qutb Minar, the soft lighting and ambient music all help you to unwind before you even look at the menu. The Thai cuisine doesn't disappoint either, being authentically fiery, and the portions are huge. Definitely worth the journey to get there.

360, Oberoi Hotel, Dr Zakir Hussain Marg, tel: 2436 3030. The city's hippest restaurant, and in many ways its most refined. The interior is cutting-edge contemporary, as are the glass-fronted kitchens, where an amazing variety of Japanese, Continental and Indian delicacies are rustled up before your eyes.

United Coffee House, E15 Connaught Place. The food is only part of the attraction here – it's the original cake-icing decor and the ambience that set this place apart. Equally popular with locals and travellers, there's always a mixed crowd in here, and the beer's

cold and well priced, another major draw.

Veda, H27 Outer Circle, Connaught Place, tel: 4151 3535. Decorated with help from one of Delhi's leading fashion designers, the candlelit, baroque-style interior sets this place apart from the moment you enter. The Indian food is also a break from the norm, coming from all over India rather than just the North. The wine list is impressive, and the cocktails well put together. Overall, it's expensive but does much to justify the cost; the maître d' is outstanding.

The Village Bistro Restaurant Complex, 12 Hauz Khas Village, New Delhi. A group of decent restaurants serving Indian (the **Village Mohalla**, **Khas Bagh** and **Top of the Village**, the latter a rooftop *tandoori* with lovely views over the ruined *madrasa* and tomb of Firoz Shah Tuglaq), Chinese (**The Village Kowloon**) and Continental food (**Le Cafe**).

Wenger's, A-16 Connaught Place, New Delhi. Tasty and cheap take-away pastries, bread and cakes.

Zen, B-25 Connaught Place, New Delhi. A Chinese restaurant, very popular with Delhi's middle class, which also serves good Japanese dishes. Good for people-watching.

GOA

Anjuna

Blue Tao, Beach Road. A fantastic breakfast spot serving delicious sour-dough rye and brown breads, healthy tahini-based and nut-butter spreads, as well as herb teas and freshly squeezed juices (including wheatgrass shots).

Arambol

Double Dutch, Main Street. Netherlands expats Axel and Lucie threw away their passports and went into business a decade ago selling their sublime Dutch apple pie around the resorts. Their operation has since expanded into a full-blown café-restaurant up in Arambol where you can lounge under the palm canopy enjoying delights such as the famous "mixed stuff" (stuffed mushrooms and capsicums with sesame potato), delicious cakes, pasties and biscuits, and fragrant South Indian coffee.

Fellini's, Beachfront. Most of the tourist population of Arambol converges on this Italian-run restaurant each evening for its wonderful pasta dishes, pizzas and gnocchi, served with a choice of over 20 different sauces at backpacker-friendly prices.

Baga

Britto's, by the beach. Good Indian food and reasonable prices make this a popular eating place.

Citrus, Tito's Lane. Classy, pure vegetarian cuisine, devised by a former animal-rescue volunteer from Birmingham in England. Drawing on worldwide influences, her recipes are all original creations, such Turkish meat-less balls with smoked couscous or blue cheese and caramelised onion galettes. The wine selection is one of the best in Goa, too, and they serve proper Italian coffee.

Fiesta, Tito's Road, above the beach. A lovely restaurant in a great position serving good Mediterranean and Italian food.

Infantaria Pastelaria, next to St John's Chapel. A sub-venture of the famous Souza Lobo restaurant on the seafront, Calangute's busiest bakery pulls in streams of locals and tourists for its croissants, apple pies and traditional Goan sweets and cakes (including *dodol* and *bebinca*). You can eat under paddle fans on the open-sided ground-floor terrace, or on the first floor, where they serve main meals in the evenings.

J&A Little Italy, Little Baga, opposite the river. An atmospheric but pricey restaurant serving good Italian food.

Lila Café, Baga Creek. Five minutes' walk up Baga Creek from the box bridge, this German-run bakery-café is a relaxing place for breakfast or to escape the midday heat. Lounging on low-slung bamboo chairs, you can peruse the papers over fresh coffee and healthy snacks such as aubergine pâté or buffalo "ham" with Nilgiri cheese and home-baked bread.

Benaulim

Durigo's, Sernabatim, north of Maria Hall crossroads. Rough-and-ready locals' fish restaurant where you can sample real Goan seafood for a fraction of the price at Martin's Corner (*see below*). Order at least one plate of mussels *(shenanio)*, lemonfish *(modso)* and barramundi *(chonok)*, either smothered in fiery red *rechead* paste or pan-fried in crunchy *rawa* millet.

Betalbatim

Martin's Corner, close to Betalbatim beach. Known for its excellent Goan food. A family-run business, with impeccable service. Can become crowded at weekends.

Calangute

After Eight, Gauro Waddo, Calangute, near the Lifeline Pharmacy. Swish gourmet restaurant in a candlelit garden close to St Anthony's Chapel on the main Candolim–Calangute drag. Most people come for the juicy steaks, but they also serve delicious seafood prepared in innovative Indo-Italian fusion style, plus there's plenty of choice for vegetarians. And be sure to leave room for the sublime chocolate mousse.

Florentine's, Saligao, 4 km (2½ miles) inland from Calangute, next door to the Ayurvedic Natural Health Centre (ANHC). The reputation of this no-frills Goan eatery at Saligao, a short drive inland from Calangute, rests on just one dish: Mrs D'Costa's famous chicken cafreal. Chefs from the Taj have even been known to sneak in to sample the flavour-packed curry, and the prices are as down to earth as the ambience. An absolute must.

Oceanic, Calangute Market Place. A wide range of good food and pleasant surroundings. A long-standing restaurant with many repeat visitors.

Plantain Leaf, Calangute Market Place. Cheap and clean South Indian food with excellent *dosas* and *thalis*.

Souza Lobo, Calangute Beach. A long-standing restaurant with good seafood and friendly service.

Canacona

Cozy Nook, Palolem Beach. Salads are generally to be avoided in India, but you can enjoy them in perfect safety at this hip little beachside restaurant, situated on the north side of Palolem next to the tidal creek. Every lunchtime, they lay on an "eat-as-much-as-you-like" buffet, prepared fresh with leaves and vegetables that have been washed thoroughly in chlorinated water.

Dercy's, Agonda beach. It's worth travelling down to Agonda just to eat at Dercy's, a small family-run place set back from the beach, where there's generally only one thing on the menu: local rockfish. Steeped in heavenly garlic butter, portions are huge and the chips cooked to perfection.

Droopadi, Palolem beach. Sophisticated North Indian dishes prepared right on the beach by a top-class Mughlai chef. The tandoori fish, chicken tikka masala and lamb kebabs are mouth-watering, and the creamy curries, laced with saffron and dry-roasted almonds, are sublime when scooped up with a naan bread crisp from the oven.

Candolim

Amigo's, 3 km (2 miles) east of Candolim at Nerul bridge, tel: 240 1123 or 9822 104920. From its ramshackle appearance, cowering on the muddy river banks beneath Nerul bridge (which played a bit part in the 2004 Matt Damon movie, *The Bourne Supremacy*), you'd never guess this place ranked among the best seafood spots in Goa. But the fish, rustic atmosphere and prices are in a class of their own. Everything – from their house speciality, grilled snapper, to the giant crabs hauled out of the creek each night – comes straight from the family boats.

Cuckoo Zen Garden, 1.5 km (1 mile) north of Candolim, off Chogm Road. Hidden down a winding sandy lane (signposted off the main Candolim–Calangute drag), this oriental restaurant is run by a team of enthusiastic young Taiwanese and Japanese. The cooking is painstakingly authentic, using imported and cleverly adapted local ingredients to rustle up sushi and other eastern delicacies. Ask for a seat on the lantern-lit rooftop.

Palms 'n' Sands, on the beach. Serves good seafood and has great views of the sea.

Pete's Shack, Escrivao Waddo, Candolim. Beach cafés tend to have their ups and downs, but this one, near Shanu's guesthouse at the north end of Candolim beach, has been steadily improving for years. Choose from their ever-expanding repertoire of hygienic salads, dressed with real olive oil and balsamic vinegar, or main dishes of seafood sizzlers and tandoori specialities. For dessert, they also serve a knockout chocolate mousse.

Sea Shell, Fort Aguada Road, Candolim. Popular multi-cuisine restaurant, spread across the terrace of a stately 19th-century Goan *palacio* on Candolim's main strip. It caters mainly for British charter tourists, with copious sizzlers, steaks and fresh seafood, as well as a full range of Chinese and Indian dishes. Genuinely hospitable and very good value for money.

Sheetal, Murrod Waddo. The best place in north Goa for quality Mughlai cuisine. Served in shiny copper *karais* on charcoal braziers, the chicken, mutton and vegetable dishes bubble in creamy concoctions that will put your local Bangladeshi take-away in the shade. If hot spices aren't really your thing, try the milder *murg malai* – chicken in delicious cashew-nut sauce.

Stone House, Fort Aguada/Chogm Road, Candolim. Groaning portions of beef steak and kingfish fillets, accompanied by baked potatoes, are the trademarks of this lively restaurant in south Candolim. Laid out on a terrace in front of the eponymous stone house, it has a great location and loads of atmosphere, staying open late most nights, when owner Chris D'Souza cranks up his beloved blues music at the bar.

Chapora

Bean Me Up, Near the Petrol Pump. Refined wholefood cuisine that's as healthy as it is tasty. Home-made tempeh in cashew sauce and spicy tofu stew are the house specialities, served with steamed organic spinach and home-baked breads with dips. Plus they do a range of tempting desserts (including a delicious banana pudding with soya cream).

Colva

Kentuckee, Colva Beach. Very fresh and well-cooked seafood. In a nice sea-front location.

Mapusa

F.R. Xavier's, Municipal Market complex, Mapusa. The perfect pit stop if you've worked up an appetite shopping in Mapusa's Friday market. F.R. Xavier's has done a roaring trade with the local middle classes for decades, and its style and menu have changed little since the 1930s. The veg and beef flaky pastry "patties", prawn curry and Goan-style samosas are all delicious, but the old-world atmosphere is the main appeal here.

Margao

Banjara. A comfortable restaurant serving decent North Indian food.
Longuinho's, near the Municipal Buildings. Excellent Goan food, including a good pork vindaloo.

Panjim

Delhi Darbar, M.G. Road, opposite the Magnum Centre. A very popular restaurant with nice surroundings and good tandoori and North Indian food.
Kamat Hotel, 5 Church Square. A popular restaurant serving excellent Udipi-style South Indian food.
Sher-e-Punjab, 18th June Road. Another popular North Indian restaurant, with good tandoori and Punjabi dishes.
Shiv Sagar, Mahatma Gandhi Road, Panjim. The capital's slickest South Indian fast-food joint, or udipi (the waiters wear black ties and waistcoats), though you still have to squeeze into formica booths to eat here. The crunchy masala dosas (which you can order with spinach mixed into the batter), idly-wada-sambar and samosas are excellent, as is their popular Bombay-style bhaji-pao; and they make wonderful freshly squeezed fruit juices and lassis.
Viva Panjim!, 178 Rua 31 de Janeiro, behind Mary Immaculate High School, Fontainhas, Panjim. Crammed into a

narrow alleyway amid the colour-washed backstreets of the capital's 19th-century enclave, Fontainhas, this is the perfect spot to sample traditional Indo-Portuguese and Goan food: prawn xacutis, ambot tik, grilled kingfish rechead and chicken cafreal. Everything's fresh and carefully vetted by the lady patronne before it's whisked sizzling to the tables outside.

GUJARAT

Ahmadabad

Gopi Dining Hall, opposite Town Hall, Ellis Bridge, Ashram Road. A popular Gujarati and Kathiawadi vegetarian restaurant with tasty food.
Mirch Masala, 7–10 Chadan Complex, Swastik Char Rasta Navrang Pura. Very good Punjabi dhaba food and Gujarati chats.
Sheeba, C.G. Road, Navragpura. A large restaurant with good-value Punjabi dishes.
South Land, C.G. Bungalow, Lal Darwaja. Good-value, clean and decent South Indian food.

Vadodara

Khichdi (Havmor), Yash Kamal Building, Sayajigunj. Good-value and tasty Indian food.

HIMALCHAL PRADESH

Dalhousie

Kwality's, Gandhi Chowk. A wide range of Indian and Chinese food in a decent restaurant.
Milan, Gandhi Chowk. A friendly and pleasant place, serving good Indian and Chinese dishes.

Dharamsala

Chocolate Log, Jogibara Road, McLeod Ganj. Cakes, pies, quiches and other goodies. There is also a roof terrace café.
McLlo, Central Square, McLeod Ganj. A good selection of Western food.
Nick's Italian Kitchen, Bhagsu Road, McLeod Ganj. Italian dishes and great desserts.
Shambala, Jogibara Road, McLeod Ganj. Good-value Indian vegetarian food as well as good breakfasts and delicious cakes.

Manali

Chopsticks, The Mall. Excellent Chinese and Tibetan food, including great momos, as well as being good for breakfast.
German Bakery, The Mall and Old Manali. Very tasty Western-style pastries, pies, bread and health food.
Johnson's Café, The Mall. A garden

restaurant on the way to Old Manali (before Johnson's Lodge). Excellent Continental food.
Mount View, The Mall. A popular restaurant with good Chinese, Japanese and Tibetan food.
Shiva Garden Café, Old Manali. A popular budget restaurant, with plenty of atmosphere and good food.

Simla

Devico's, 5 The Mall. Popular Indian, Chinese and Western fast food, milk shakes and bar. Open all day.
Baljees, 26 The Mall. A very popular snack bar with a very good restaurant upstairs with a wide range of dishes. Open all day.
Choice, Middle Bazaar. A wide range of good, budget Chinese food.

KARNATAKA

Bangalore

Barista Coffee House, M.G. Road. One of a number in the city, very popular with young Bangaloreans. Good for real espressos and cappuccinos, as well as cakes and snacks.
Casa Piccola, Devatha Plaza, 131 Residency Road. Fast food and good coffee. Imaginative, informal decor and sensible prices. Recommended.
Chalukya, 44 Race Course Road. Good-quality Udupi dishes.
Chinese Hut, 1st Floor, High Point 4, 45 Palace Road. Very good food, mainly Cantonese and Szechuan.
Coconut Grove, Spencer's Building, 86 Church Street. Pleasant restaurant with outdoor seating. Excellent Andhran, Malabar, Konkan, Kodagu and Chettinad dishes.
Crescent Avenue, 2a–b Crescent Road, High Ground. Good-value and tasty Thai food in nice surroundings.
Gangotree, 45 Palace Road. Excellent spicy vegetarian snacks, and even better sweets.
Kamat Yatrinivas, 4 1st Cross, Gandhi Nagar. Excellent South Indian vegetarian meals and snacks.
Koshy's, 39 St Mark's Road. A Bangalore institution and favourite meeting place. Relaxed surroundings and extensive menu of well-cooked food. Open all day.
Mavalli Tiffin Rooms, Lalbagh Road. Very good Udupi-style food. Opens very early, good for breakfast.
Megh Malar, 80 Hospital Road. Good South Indian food; excellent dosas.
Nagarjuna Residency, 44/1 Residency Road. Hot and spicy non-vegetarian Andhran food; excellent biriyanis.
Orange Country, The Central Park, 47 Dickenson Road. Live jazz and decent Cajun and Creole dishes. Good

service and fun cocktails. A good place for women to have a drink.
Prince's, 9 First Floor, Curzon Complex, Brigade Road. Good-value with nice surroundings and good service.
The Only Place, Mota Royal Arcade, 158 Brigade Road. Legendary restaurant serving very good and reasonably priced Western food (including excellent steaks).

Hospet
The Waves, Hotel Malligi, 10-90 Jambunath Road. Pleasant rooftop restaurant serving average Indian and Chinese dishes.
Manasa, Hotel Priyadarshini, V-45 Station Road. Garden restaurant looking out on sugarcane and banana plantations. Good vegetarian and non-vegetarian food; also serves beer.

Hassan
Hotel Suvarana Regency, B.M. Road. Excellent South Indian vegetarian meals and snacks.

Mangalore
Lalith, Balmatta Road. A decent restaurant with a good range of North Indian and Chinese dishes.
Surabhi, Near the KSRTC stand. Excellent North Indian meaty and vegetarian *tandoori* dishes.

Mysore
Hotel Dasaprakash, Gandhi Square. Good vegetarian restaurant serving meals and Udupi cuisine, *dosas* a speciality.
Ilapur, 2721/1 Sri Harsha Road. Andhran restaurant serving excellent vegetarian meals, with some non-vegetarian and Chinese dishes.
Lalitha Mahal Palace Hotel, Siddhartha Nagar. Superb food, try the *birlyanis*, served in opulent surroundings accompanied by live Hindustani music. Recommended.
Shilpastri, Gandhi Square. Popular and central rooftop restaurant serving mostly North Indian food.

KERALA

Alappuzha
Arun Komala Hotel. Good vegetarian meals in a small restaurant attached to a hotel.
Indian Coffee House, Mullakai Main Road. Coffee and basic meals from the state-wide chain; a good place for breakfast.

Guruvayur
Indian Coffee House, Kizhakkenada, a dependable venue in this town, which is mostly given over to feeding pilgrims.

Kochi-Ernakulam
Bimby's/Southern Star, Shanmukam Road, Ernakulam. Bimby's is a great place for cheap Indian fast food. The Southern Star upstairs does very good and reasonably priced sit-down meals.
Canopy Coffee Shop, Abad Plaza Complex, M.G. Road, Ernakulam. Tasty continental and fast food, good place for breakfast. Open all day.
Caza Maria, 6/125 Jew Town Road, Mattancherri, Kochi. This restaurant on the first floor of a historic building has been beautifully decorated. The food is an imaginative mixture of Indian and European dishes on a menu that changes daily.
The Cocoa Tree, The Avenue Regent, M.G. Road, Ernakulam. A great modern coffee shop attached to the hotel. Good coffee, light meals and excellent pastries. Open until 1am.
Gokul Restaurant, M.G. Road, Ernakulam. An excellent place for South Indian meals and snacks, the *dosas* and *uttapams* are particularly good.
Indian Coffee House, Cannon Shed Road, Ernakulam. Good snacks and coffee in a somewhat run-down building.
Pandhal, M.G. Road, Ernakulam. Very clean restaurant serving good North Indian and Keralan dishes.

Kollam
Indian Coffee House, Main Road, Chinnakkada. Decent snacks and coffee from this popular chain.
Sri Suprabathan, Clock Tower. A cheap and cheerful vegetarian place, with tasty food.

Kottayam
Indian Coffee House, T.B. Road, also at M.L. Road and the Medical College. The usual non-vegetarian snacks and good coffee. Convenient for the bus station.
Thali Restaurant, Homestead Hotel. Decent vegetarian meals served on the eponymous metal tray.

Kovalam
The best option outside of the bigger hotels, and certainly the most atmospheric, is to eat at one of the many beach-front cafés/restaurants serving freshly caught fish, grilled or fried and served with chips and salad. Make sure you choose your fish carefully. Finish off with fruit from the women selling mango, pineapple and papaya along the beach.

German Bakery, South End of Lighthouse Beach. Something of a Kovalam institution, the bakery-cum-restaurant sells strudel and bread, as well as dishing up a good selection of

Thai and European dishes (mainly pasta).
The Lobster Pot, above Ashok Beach. An excellent viewpoint on top of the cliff and under the coconut palms. Decent enough Indian food, but the location is better.

Kozhikode
Kalpaka Tourist Home, Town Hall Road. Reasonable Indian food, conveniently near the railway station.
Sagar, I.G. Road. A restaurant very popular with locals, so sometimes you have to queue to get a table. However, the wait is worth it as the Indian food is excellent.
Woodlands, G.H. Road. A good, and cheap, vegetarian meals hall in the centre of town.

Thiruvananthapuram
In addition to restaurants in hotels, try the traditional "meals" places across the road from the Secretariat on M.G. Road. Very clean and cheap.
Annapoorna, Pazhavangadi, opposite the Ganesh Temple. A good meals place with an air-conditioned first-floor "family room". The *dosas* and *uttapams* are particularly good, and the fresh fruit juices (make sure you order without ice) are also worth a try.
Arul Jyothi, M.G. Road, opposite the Secretariat. A very clean meals hall with excellent food. This is some of the best vegetarian food in the city. Good for juices.
Casa Bianca, 96 M.P. Appan Road, Vazhuthacaud. This lovely café and restaurant run by Ingrid, a Swede settled in Thiruvananthapuram, is a little out of the ordinary for the city. A well-designed interior is the setting for very tasty Italian and Indian food (the pizza is excellent). Open daily 11am–10pm.
Coffee Beanz, Magnet, Thycaud. A modern café, opposite the women's college, serving excellent coffee and snacks such as chips and sandwiches. A popular hang-out for students and young people. Open Mon–Sat 11am–10pm, Sun 9am–10pm.
Indian Coffee House, Central Station Road. City landmark, beside the bus stand. Great coffee and snacks served in spiral building designed by Laurie Baker. Good for breakfast. Another branch near Spencer Junction, M.G. Road.
Park Field Gardens, Cotton Hill, Vazhuthacaud. A pleasant restaurant serving good Indian and international dishes. The combination meals, with a wide variety of Indian dishes, are particularly good.
Hotel Sri Bhadra and Hotel Sree Padmanabha, opposite the temple tank, Fort. A pair of decent vegetarian

restaurants serving meals – *dosas* and the like – with not much to choose between them. They both have good views of the temple from the first floor and can be very pleasant in early evening.

Thrissur
Hotel Anupam, The Round. Decent vegetarian meals, with plenty of tasty extras, not far from the north gate of the temple. "Meals" are served on the first floor.
Indian Coffee House, Round South, also at C.B.D., Kuruppam Road and K.A.U. Mannuthi. Another set of places from the Keralan cooperative. They all serve good coffee and a reasonable selection of light meals and snacks.

Varkala
Like Kovalam, Varkala has a whole string of restaurants lined up along the sea front. Most of them have great views out to sea and the food is all of a similar standard (the usual combination of North Indian dishes, noodles and some seafood). Near the road try the **Somatheeram Beach Restaurant** or the **Sea Face** (both on Main Beach, Papanasam), or the slightly more up-market **Marine Palace** just above.

KOLKATA

Aheli's, Peerless Inn, 12 Jawaharlal Nehru Road. Excellent, if pricey, Bengali food; very authentic. Recommended.
Amber Bar & Restaurant, 11 Waterloo Street. Very good North Indian, especially the *tandoori* dishes, and some Continental food.
Beijing, 77/1 Christopher Road. A bar/restaurant serving a wide variety of Tangra-style Chinese food.
Blue Fox, 55 Park Street. Good Continental, Thai and Indian dishes, especially the seafood. Friendly and popular with a good bar.
Flury's, 18 Park Street. Popular coffee shop serving pastries and ice-creams. Open all day.
The Indian Coffee House, 15 Bankim Chatterjee Street. Famous coffee shop near the university; a meeting place for Bengali intellectuals. Snacks available, open all day.
Kewpie's, 2 Elgin Lane. Exceptionally good Bengali food, with tasty fish. In a very pleasant family house with lovely service. Recommended.
Kwality, 17 Park Street. Decent, if not outstanding, North Indian and Continental food. Very popular.
Mainland China, Uniworth House, 3a Gurusaday Road. The best lobster in

black bean sauce you'll probably ever eat. Also features a 15-course buffet.
Mocambo, 25b Park Street. All-round good restaurant with a wide selection of dishes; the Bengali ones are particularly well-cooked.
Oberoi Grand, 15 JL Nehru Road. Best Thai food in town.
Oh Calcutta, 1b 172 Sector 3 Salt Lake City. Offers a variety of quick bites – the pizzas, burgers and sandwiches are especially good, not to mention the *dosas*. Modern wrought-iron furniture contrasts with sketches of old Calcutta. Good place to rendezvous.
Peter Cat, 18a Park Street. Tasty Mughlai food, some Rajasthani and Gujarati dishes, and a good bar. Rather slow service.
Red Hot Chilli Peppers, Bengal Intelligent Park, Sector 5, Salt Lake City. A yuppie hangout that serves Chinese and Continental food in a fusion of Oriental and Western decor.
Sare Chuattor, 213 Sarat Road. Designed in the style of a rural Bengali home, it attracts Bengalis looking for genuine Bengali food.
Suruchi, 89 Elliot Road, near A.G. School. Restaurant serving excellent Bengali food, run by a local women's group. Open all day, closed half day Sunday.
Tamarind, 64 Sarat Bose Road. The city's only South Indian restaurant serving vegetarian and non-vegetarian food. **Zaranj**, 26 Jawaharlal Road. Very good North Indian food with excellent kebabs. Recommended.
Zurich, 3 Sudder Street. A very popular travellers' hang-out, serving the usual banana pancakes, etc.

LADAKH

Hemis
An outdoor café (and earth toilet) just below the monastery. Attractive wooded surroundings. Basic but good bowls of noodles and glasses of tea.

Leh
Café World Peace and Pumpernickel German Bakery, Main Street, almost on the square, on the side of an alley. A large range of breads, pasta, muesli, cakes and teas, all tasty and freshly cooked; wonderful apple pie. Good for breakfast. A travellers' favourite. Recommended.
Dreamland, Fort Road. Popular restaurant with Continental and Chinese dishes. Very meat-heavy. Nice environment but average service.
Tibetan Kitchen, Hotel Tso-Kar, Fort

Road. Pleasant and friendly restaurant with seating in a lovely courtyard. Simple but tasty Tibetan dishes; try a bottle of the delicious Gul Badan apple juice.
Norlakh Tibetan Restaurant, Main Street. On a first floor, close to Explore Himalayas. A very friendly place that is highly recommended. Freshly cooked cheap and tasty Tibetan food; for pudding they offer big bowls of banana and custard.

MADHYA PRADESH

Bhopal
Bagicha Restaurant, 3 Hamidia Road. A garden restaurant with good North Indian food. Open all day.
India Coffee House, Hamidia Road; New Market. Two decent South Indian restaurants with vegetarian dishes.
Kwality, Hamidia Road; New Market. Reasonable and rich North Indian vegetarian and non-vegetarian food.
Jyoti, 53 Hamidia Road. Cheap but very tasty vegetarian *thalis*.

Gwalior
Indian Coffee House, Station Road. Good South Indian meals and snacks, and decent breakfasts (opens early).
Kwality, Din Dayal Market, M.L.B. Road. Rich North Indian vegetarian and non-vegetarian food. Average service, but it has air conditioning and is well-lit.

Indore
Gypsy, 17 M.G. Road. A fast-food place serving good snacks, ice creams and sweets.
Woodlands, Hotel President, 163 R.N.T. Marg. Excellent South Indian vegetarian food in clean, pleasant surroundings.
Status, 565 M.G. Road. A good budget option. Excellent vegetarian food and *thalis* at lunch. Located below the Hotel Purva.

Khajuraho
La Terazza, off the Main Square. Continental and Indian food served in clean, pleasant surroundings.
Mediterraneo Ristorante Italiano, Jain Temple Road. Pleasant rooftop café owned by an Italian–Indian couple. Good pasta and other dishes.
Raja Cafe, Main Square. Popular but strangely unfriendly place serving Western and Indian dishes; also has a book and curio shop.
Safari, Jain Temple Road. Excellent western-style food and snacks. Good for breakfast.

MAHARASHTRA

Ajanta
MTDC Ajanta Restaurant. Slightly run-down but has a reasonable selection of Indian and Chinese dishes.

Aurangabad
Angeethi, 6 Meher Chambers, Jalna Road, Vidya Nagar. Very dark but once you have penetrated the gloom the North Indian food is very good. Has AC and is popular with couples.
Bhoj, Central Bus Stand Road. Cheap but clean with very tasty vegetarian Indian dishes.
Dwarka Executive, near Railway Station. Very clean and brightly lit with good service and decent vegetarian and non-vegetarian Indian food.

Ellora
MTDC Ellora Restaurant. Cheap and very clean restaurant serving tasty vegetarian and non-vegetarian North Indian food.

Pune
Coffee House, 2a Moledina Road. Excellent coffee and South Indian vegetarian dishes.
Darshan Snacks, 759–60 Prabhat Road. Very clean with tasty Continental vegetarian food and excellent juices.
Kwality, 6 East Street. The usual, but generally tasty, rich North Indian non-vegetarian food.
Mayur, Mumbai–Pune Highway, Chinchwad. A pure-vegetarian restaurant with excellent Gujarati thalis. Closed Thursday.
Poona Coffee House, 1256 Deccan Gymkhana. A wide variety of very popular non-vegetarian food.
Sher-e-Punjab, Alankar Theatre Building 16, Connaught Road. Very good, and very non-vegetarian, Punjabi food; try the butter chicken.
Shravan, 1145 F.C. Road, Shivaji Nagar. Very good vegetarian food, especially the North Indian dishes.
Vaishali, Fergusson College Road, 1218 Shivajinagar. Very clean and very popular. One of Pune's best-known institutions with excellent vegetarian snacks.

MUMBAI

All Stir Fry, Gorden House Hotel, 5 Battery Street, Apollo Bunder, tel: 2287 1122. Designer Oriental restaurant with sparse white decor and Chinese-style wooden benches. You pick your own ingredients and sauces, then watch them being wok-fried in showy style by the chefs.
American Express Bakery, Clare Road, Byculla. Decent fast food and tasty pastries.
Apoorva, Vasta House (Noble Chambers), SA Brelvi Road, tel: 2287 0335. Sublime Konkan seafood – including what might well be the world's tastiest prawn gassi – served in a typically cramped "Mangalorean" with low ceilings and tacky decor, just off Horniman Circle (look for the fairy lights wrapped around the tree). They also do a definitive Bombay duck, best enjoyed with steaming hot appams and cold beer. Just as good as Trishna's (see below), but at half the price.
Bade Miya, Tullock Road, behind the Taj Mahal Hotel, Colaba. A Mumbai institution. An open-air pavement grill, famous for its tasty kebabs. Operates evenings only.
Badshah Juice and Snack Bar, opposite Crawford Market, Lokmanya Tilak Road. Tall glasses of brightly coloured rose syrup and milk swimming with maize-flour vermicelli, falooda is the quintessential Mumbai soft drink, brought here by Irani Zoroastrians from Persia in the 1920s. This cramped little café opposite Crawford Market is its undisputed spiritual home. Royal falooda is the most popular choice, but they also do a delicious kesar-flavoured falooda, made with real saffron, as well as a range of fresh mango preparations, from pure juice to milkshake, melba and kulfi (India's own sweet version of ice cream).
Bagdadi, Tullock Road, on the southern corner, Colaba. Cheap and very clean North Indian Muslim food. Mutton and chicken masala, good egg and vegetable biriyanis. Very popular.
Barista. A city-wide chain of modern coffee shops serving snacks and very good coffee.
Brittania Café, opposite the GPO, Sprott Road Ballard Estate. Delicious Irani and Parsi food.
Busaba, 4 Mandlik Marg, tel: 2204 3779. One of the city's hippest restaurants, serving sumptuous dishes from across Asia: Tibetan momos, Vietnamese fish sizzlers, or Korean glass noodle salad. DJs play on Friday and Saturday.
Café Basilico, Arthur Bunder Road, Colaba. This clean and modern bistro and deli serves very tasty Mediterranean snacks and pastries, as well as good coffee.
Café Samovar, Jehangir Art Gallery, 161 B M.G. Road, Kalaghoda Fort. The popular gallery café, with a good range of snacks and drinks. Daily specials for lunch (1–3pm). In a lovely cool position overlooking the gardens.
Cha Bar, Oxford Bookstore, 3 Dinsha Vaccha Road, Churchgate. Trendy bookshop café, frequented mainly by rich students from the university on the opposite side of the maidan, which offers teas from all over India (from disgusting Ladakhi yak-butter chai to more fragrant, fine-tipped Nilgiri). They also do a range of grilled sandwiches and other light meals and snacks. Open 10am–10pm.
China Garden, Kemp's Corner, 250–550 August Kranti Marg, near Chowpatty Beach, tel: 2495 5589. Owner-chef Nelson Wang only had Rs27 in his pocket when he arrived in Mumbai in the early 1980s. He's since become a multi-millionaire thanks to the reputation of his restaurant, the most authentic Chinese in the city and a much-loved haunt of the glam set. It's said there hasn't been an empty table here for over 11 years. Try the Mongolian Steamboat soup and famous Peking chicken. Reservations essential.
Copper Chimney, Dr A.B. Road, Worli; Kalpak Corner, Guru Nanak Road, Bandra Junction. Excellent but pricey tandoori and North Indian dishes.
Crystal, Chowpatty Seaface, near Wilson College. Authentic Punjabi home cooking, dished up to homesick North Indians in what must be the grimiest-looking restaurant on Back Bay. Crystal is proof that appearances really can be deceptive: the vegetarian food – palak paneer (spinach and soft cheese), dal makhini (black lentils in a creamy sauce) and bhindi bhaji (okra curry) – is unfailingly delicious and well worth the trip to Chowpatty.
Haji Ali Juice Centre, Lala Lajpat Rai Road, Haji Ali Circle. Situated just outside the entrance to Haji Ali's tomb, this place is famous across the city for its fresh pomegranate, chickoo (sapodilla), mango, orange and lychee juices, though they also offer faloodas, lassis and various milkshakes loaded with ice cream.
Ideal Corner, 12 F/G Hornby View, Gunbow Street, tel: 2262 1930. Renowned Parsi restaurant in the heart of Fort where the dishes remain as traditional as ever, despite a recent facelift. If they're offered, try khichidi prawn, lamb dhansak or the chicken farsha. And be sure to leave room for the quirky British-inflected house dessert, "custard lagan". Closed evenings and Sunday.
Indigo, 4 Mandlik Marg, tel: 2236 8999. South Mumbai's most fashionable place to eat, with A-list celebs swanning in and out (the Clintons ate here once, and you can spot Bollywood stars most weekend evenings). For all that, a laid-back atmosphere prevails, and both the refined Indian fusion food and sophisticated decor warrant the hype.

Jimmy Boy, 11 Bank Street, Vikas Building, off Horniman Circle, tel: 2270 0880. There aren't many places left in Mumbai where non-Parsis can sample traditional Zoroastrian wedding food, but Jimmy Boy prides itself on keeping the traditions alive with its pomfret in green chilli sauce and mutton *pulao* with *dhansak* – though the atmosphere is decidedly Western.

Joshi Club, 31-A Narottamwadi, Kalbadevi Road, tel: 2205 8089. Gujaratis love wholesome, subtly flavoured vegetarian dishes made from elaborate blends of mild spices, and you're unlikely ever to come across a finer example than the *thali* served here – not that you'd guess it from the downbeat, grubby-walled dining hall. One of the city's gastronomic highlights, but hard to find – head north for 10 minutes up Kalbadevi Road from the Metro cinema on Dhobi Talao, and ask a local for "Joshi bhonalaya".

Kailash Parbat, 1 Pasta Lane, near the Strand cinema. "KPs" is Colaba's best-loved snack and sweet joint, famous for its *sindhi pakora* (vegetable chunks deep-fried in maize flour), *rasgulla* (sponge balls soaked in rose syrup) and yummy cashew-nut *barfi* (milk sweet). They also offer a full multi-cuisine menu, including all the usual delicious South Indian standards, across the street.

Kamat, Sahid Bhagat Singh Marg (Colaba Causeway). Very cheap and tasty South Indian meals and excellent *dosas*.

Khyber, 154 M.G. Road, Kala Ghoda Fort. Pricey but excellent menu of North Indian dishes, including some unusual breads and vegetable dishes. Aloof service, but a nice cool interior.

Konkan Café, Taj President Hotel, Cuffe Parade, tel: 5665 0808. Haute cuisine from coastal Maharashtra, Goa, Karnataka and Kerala at surprisingly restrained prices. Signature dishes include tiger prawn in sour *kokum* sauce, snappers steamed in banana leaves and divine pepper-garlic crab. The flavours are all painstakingly authentic and the service five-star.

Kyani's "House of Cakes" Bakery, opposite Metro cinema, Dhobi Talao. The definitive old-school Irani café, verging on decrepit but still going strong on a diet of *bun maska* (essentially buttered white rolls) and biscuits dunked in fierce orange *chai*. Worth at least a pit stop en route to or from the nearby movie houses.

Leopold Café, Sahid Bhagat Singh Marg (Colaba Causeway). A legendary travellers' haunt, immortalised in the book *Shantaram*. Good, if slightly pricey, Western food and a bar.

Ling's Pavilion, 19–21 Mahakavi Bhushan Marg, Colaba, just down from the Regal Cinema. Chinese restaurant with an excellent menu from soups to seafood. Good, varied and interesting vegetable dishes. Gracious service.

Mahesh, 8D Kawaji Patel Street, Fort. Extremely good, and very fresh, South Indian and Goan seafood. Well-priced and very popular.

Mezzo Mezzo, JW Marriott Hotel, Juhu Tara Road, by Juhu Beach, tel: 5693 3000. Home of Danio Galli, Mumbai's most celebrated Italian chef, who specialises in Tuscan and Sardinian cuisine. His menu changes every three months or so, but there are always succulent wood-fired pizzas on offer. Everything's imported fresh from Italy – hence the sky-high rates. A favourite of the glitterati, who then move on to the Enigma nightclub in the same hotel.

Mocha Bar, V.N. Road, tel: 5633 6070. If you've ever wanted to try a hookah pipe, this fashionable terrace bar on V.N. Road, decked out like a Turkish queen's boudoir with carpets and bolster cushions, will satisfy your curiosity. That said, fresh coffee, made on a proper coffee machine, is why most of its punters come here. Inside, the air-conditioned dining room offers more substantial Mediterranean *mezes* accompanied by pricey New World wines.

Olive Bar and Kitchen, 14 Union Park. Tucked away down a sidestreet and serving sophisticated Mediterranean food. Very trendy.

Olympia Coffee House and Stores, Rahim Mansion 1, Sahid Bhagat Singh Marg, Colaba. Delicious non-vegetarian Muslim food; excellent mutton dishes and *biriyani*. Lovely, mirrored 1920s interior.

The Pearl of the Orient, Ambassador Hotel, V.N. Road, tel: 2204 1131. The regional Chinese food served in this four-star hotel's rooftop restaurant may not be as authentic, nor as inventive, as some of Colaba's pan-Asian places, but it really doesn't matter because the views over the city and Back Bay are astounding. Moreover, as the whole structure revolves 360° in an hour and a half, they change constantly. Arrive at least 30 minutes before sunset. Reservation recommended.

The Sea Lounge, Taj Mahal Hotel, Apollo Bunder. Afternoon tea and cakes at a window seat in the Sea Lounge, overlooking the Gateway of India, is *de rigueur* for Raj-ophiles, and a good way for anyone not lucky enough to be staying at the Taj to sample its genteel charms.

Shamiana, Taj Mahal Hotel, Colaba. The lunchtime buffet here (12.30–3pm) is extremely good. Very good value as well considering you can eat as much you can stuff in of the very tasty food. Excellent desserts.

Sidewok, NCPA, Nariman Point. In the National Centre for Performing Arts complex, an attractive if expensive restaurant with good East/Southeast Asian food. Very good juices and lots of vegetarian options. Spotless toilets.

Soul Fry, Silver Croft, Palli Malla Road, Bandra, tel: 2604 6892. Traditional Konkani seafood, served in incongruously trendy surroundings, but at low rates (the taxi ride up here is likely to cost more than your bill). Come at lunchtime for the wonderful Goan-style fish *thali*, comprising a couple of crisp-fried Bombay Ducks, slices of pomfret or *surmai*, spoonfuls of clams in coconut *masala*, *rotis*, *papads* and pickle, all for under Rs100. In the evenings, the pricier à la carte takes over. A lively bar serves beers and spirits.

The Tea Centre, Resham Bhavan, 78 V.N. Road. A cup of top-quality tea can be surprisingly hard to come by in Mumbai, but even aficionados should be impressed by some of the single-estate Assams, Darjeelings and Nilgiris on offer at this charming Raj-era establishment. A perfect place to catch your breath, only five minutes' walk from the seafront and tourist office.

Trishna's, 7 Rope Walk Lane, Kalaghoda Fort. Excellent, if a little pricey, Indian seafood dishes in a very popular restaurant.

Vithal Bhelwala, 5 A.K. Naik Marg (Baston Road), close to CST (VT) Station. Vithal Bhelwala is credited with inventing Mumbai's best-loved snack, *bhel puri*, and this is a safe, hygienic place to try it. There are 25 or more varieties on offer, along with other tasty nibbles such as *samosas* and *aloo tikki* (fried potato patties).

Yezdani's Bakery, 11-A Cowasji Patel Road, Fort. This is one of the few traditional Irani bakeries left in the Fort district. People from all over south Mumbai still order their Portuguese-style bread-roll buns and flaky-pastry puffs from here, along with wholegrain brown loaves and other new-fangled breads from the West. Step in to the worn wooden interior and ask the proprietor, the irascible Mr Zend M. Zend, for a piece of the famous Yezdani apple pie.

ORISSA

Bhubaneshwar

Much of the best food is in the hotel restaurants. Try also:
Banjara, Station Road. Very good and tasty Mughlai and *tandoori* food.

PUDUCHERRY

La Terrasse, 5 Subbaiyah Salai. Excellent and good-value Continental dishes. Closed Wednesday.
Le Club, 33 rue Dumas. An expensive but excellent French restaurant, probably the best in India. Authentic food, wine and great service; also good for breakfast. Closed Monday.
Rendezvous, 30 rue Suffren. A popular Continental restaurant with a pleasant rooftop area. Good for breakfast.
Satsanga, 13 Lal Bahadur Shastri Street. A very good restaurant serving European dishes. Lovely surroundings and good value. Closed Thursday.

PUNJAB & HARYANA

Amritsar

Bhiranwan-da-dhaba, near the Town Hall. Excellent vegetarian food. Small menu but very good *thalis*.
Kesar-ka-Dhaba, Passian Chowk. Exceptional vegetarian Punjabi food; all very rich.
Kwality, Novelty Building, Lawrence Road. Decent Indian food; snack bar and ice-cream parlour with an adjoining AC restaurant.
Odeon, The Mall. Very good North Indian dishes.

Chandigarh

Bhoj, 1090–1, Sector 22B. Recommended for Indian vegetarian food, good *thalis*.
Hot Millions, S.C.O. 73–9, Sector 17D. One of a chain serving Western and Indian fast food; there is a good salad bar.
Mehfil Hotel & Restaurant, S.C.O. 183–5, Sector 17C. Good North Indian and other dishes. Very popular.

RAJASTHAN

Ajmer

Honeydew, Station Road, next to King Edward Memorial. Dependable multi-cuisine option with a relaxing garden terrace where you can order the standard range of North Indian vegetarian and non-vegetarian dishes, as well as passable pizzas. The only smartish restaurant in the centre of Ajmer, and very popular, especially at weekends.

Sheesh Mahal, Mansingh Palace Hotel, Ana Sagar Circular Rd. Attached to Ajmer's sole luxury hotel, on the outskirts of town on the shores of Ana Sagar lake, this self-consciously up-market restaurant serves a predictably overpriced menu in its Western-style dining hall. Not somewhere worth making the special trip to eat at, but convenient if you are staying here.

Bundi

Garden, Bohra Meghwahan, next to Lake View Guesthouse. "Rajasthani pizza" – processed cheese, tomato and Indian *tulsi* basil on a *chapatti* base, with onions and garlic – is one of those hybrid creations that crop up at tourist centres across the state – with varying results. Served on a threadbare lawn by the water, the version prepared here is tastier than average, and the setting is perfect.

Jaipur

Anokha Gaon, 14 Vishwakarma Road, near Jodla Power House. Definitive Rajasthani cuisine prepared using rustic wood fires and clay ovens and served village-feast style on long, low tables. Live folk cabaret and camel rides round the evenings off. Avoid it at weekends, when it can get horrendously busy.
Chanakya Restaurant, M.I. Road. Very well-presented food in posh surroundings. Has a reputation for the best traditional Rajasthani food in Jaipur. However, this may be a shock to the unwary – lots of *ghee* is used in the cooking, which may not sit well on a weak stomach.
Chokhi Dhani, 15 km (9 miles) south of Jaipur on the Tonk Road. Middle-class Jaipuris pour south down the main highway on Friday, Saturday and Sunday evenings to eat at this open-air "special village" restaurant, where you can enjoy sumptuous traditional *thalis* and live music, dance and puppet shows. Camel and elephant rides will amuse the kids. Worth the trip, although the food isn't quite up to the standards of Anokha Gaon.
Copper Chimney, Maya Mansions, M.I. Road. Very good Continental and Indian food served in comfortable surroundings.
Lassiwala, M.I. Road. A series of streetside stalls serving snacks and renowned clay cups of *lassi* to long queues of customers. Early morning to late evening.
LMB, Johari Bazaar. Zealously pure-veg place in the old city. Despite a garish recent facelift, it has served pretty much the same menu of traditional, high-caste *satvik* cooking since the 1950s. The Rajasthani

deluxe *thalis* are especially popular on Sundays. For a quick bite, try the scrumptious cashew nut and potato *tikkis*, served with a blob of sweet mango pickle from a stall on the street outside.
Niros, M.I. Road. A cool, AC restaurant, very clean and central. Tasty food and prompt service from an extensive menu of Indian, Chinese and Continental dishes. A little more expensive than other places in town.
Om, Best Western Om Tower, Church Road, off M.I. Road, tel. 236 6683. Revolving restaurant atop Jaipur's newest and glitziest skyscraper, from which you can survey the entire city over delicious Rajasthani and other North Indian specialities. Each revolution takes 45 minutes. A popular night out for more well-heeled locals and business types. Advance reservation recommended.

Jaisalmer

Natraj, opposite Salim Singh ki Haveli. A pleasant rooftop restaurant with decent Indian and Chinese food.
Trio, Gandhi Chowk. A very popular and friendly restaurant, partly under tents. Good food and drinks, and live traditional music.
Vyas Meals Service, near Jain temples, Fort. Home-cooked *paratha* curd and *masala chai* breakfasts, lunchtime *thalis* and filling traditional *dal batti* suppers served by an endearing, elderly couple. Don't come if you are in a hurry for your food.

Jodhpur

Kalinga, near the Railway Station. Good, and inexpensive, Indian food (vegetarian and non-vegetarian) in a friendly restaurant.
Mehran Terrace, Meherangarh Fort, tel: 0291-254 9790. Candle-lit Rajasthani meals served on the outermost rampart of the fort, its arched windows, filigreed stonework and illuminated domes soaring behind you, with the old city spread 125 metres (400 ft) below. The location is unbeatable, though the food itself (unexciting vegetable *thalis*) is overpriced and gets mixed reviews. Evenings only; reservation essential.
Mishri Lal, Gateway south of the Clock Tower. This place is a Jodhpuri institution, serving mega-rich *makhania* lassis to a steady flow of silently appreciative, sweet-toothed local aficionados. Flavoured with saffron, cardamom and buffalo cream, the *lassis* are a bit on the sugary side for most foreign palates, but you should definitely still come here once for the old-world atmosphere.
On The Rocks, next door to Hotel Ajit Bhawan, Airport Rd, tel: 0291-230

2701. On the southern edge of town, a popular, lively garden restaurant frequented by a mix of well-heeled locals and foreign tourists staying at the adjacent Ajit Bhawan. The menu is similarly eclectic, but strongest on kebabs, grilled chicken and non-veg curries.

The Pillars, Hotel Umaid Bhawan. Umaid Bhawan has four restaurants, but its tea garden terrace is the most affordable and atmospheric, with peacocks strutting picturesquely over the grass and grand views of the distant city and desert. Come here for a gourmet sandwich at lunchtime, afternoon tea or mocktail sundowner.

Mount Abu

Jodhpur Bhonalaya, near the Taxi Stand. Traditional Rajasthani *thali* joint, renowned above all for its *churma*: crumbly, slightly sweet dumplings spiced with cardamom. Delicious cooking, and inexpensive, though the dining hall can be busy.
Kanak, near the Bus Stand. Gujarati *thalis* differ from their Rajasthani counterparts (they are lighter on oil and chillies, and often a touch sweeter, with unique combinations of flavours) and this place serves the best one in town. Servings are unlimited – you may have to stop the waiters spooning second helpings on to your plate.
Veena, Nakki Road. Great pan-Indian fast food, from Southern-style *dosas* to Bombay *pao bhaji* (spicy lentil-and-tomato stew served with griddle-fried butter rolls). You can eat outside on a convivial roadside terrace around an open fire in the evenings.

Pushkar

Pushkar's religious significance means that no meat, fish, eggs or alcohol are legally served in its restaurants.
Om Shiva, off the lane between Mian Bazaar and the Pushkar Palace. All-you-can-eat Rs50 buffets are the main attraction of this perennially popular café-restaurant, another hippy hangout close to the eastern shores of the lake, which offers better cooking than average and a relaxed garden setting.
Raju Garden, near Ram Ghat, Main Bazaar. Simple, traveller-oriented place on a rooftop terrace festooned with fairy lights and plants in pots. The food consistently outstrips the competition in this popular end of town (try their tasty veg shepherd's pie or wood-baked pizza), as do the wonderful lake views.

Udaipur

Ambrai, Hanuman Ghat. Occupying a spit of land that juts into Lake Pichola from Hanuman Ghat, this ranks among Udaipur's best-situated restaurants, with superb views across the water. And for once, the cuisine – mostly rich Mughali and Rajput specialities prepared by the Maharaja's former head chef – rates as highly as the views.
Berry's Restaurant, Chetak Circle. Good Indian dishes and reasonable Western snacks. Very clean and open all day.
Lake Palace, Lake Pichola, tel: 0294-252 8800. India's classic luxury dining experience, on Udaipur's glamorous "floating palace". At Rs1,500 per head for a mediocre buffet (including a launch ride from the palace jetty), it is way overpriced, though some think the experience deserving of the hype. Dress smartly and bring a warm wrap in mid-winter, when the breezes off the water can be chilly. Reservations essential.
Natraj, New Bapu Bazaar, behind Ashok Cinema. Filling, unlimited North Indian *thalis* served in a grubby dining hall in the north of the city. Hard to find and invariably jam-packed, but worth hunting out for the delicious food, cooked fresh each day and a bargain at Rs50 per head. Udaipur's best budget eating option.
Natural, 55 Rang Sagar. An excellent, laid-back restaurant serving Continental and Tibetan food; a good place for breakfast.
Purohit Cafe, Anand Plaza, near Ayad Bridge. Very good, and inexpensive, South Indian food; excellent *dosas*.
Savage Garden, east side of Chand Pol. Trendy fusion cuisine (mainly pasta with delicately spiced Indian sauces) served in a stylishly converted 250-year-old *haveli*. Prices reflect its strong reputation, based on the designer lounge-groove decor rather than the food.

SIKKIM

Gangtok

Porky's Restaurant, Deorali Bazaar. Definitely non-vegetarian. A good range of snacks, fast food and ice-creams. Open all day.
Shaepi Restaurant, Hotel Mayur, Paljor Stadium Road. Good *tandoori*, Chinese and Sikkimese food.
Wild Orchid Restaurant, Central Hotel, 31a N.H. Good, cheap Chinese and Tibetan food. Open all day.

TAMIL NADU

Chidambaram

Hotel Saradharam, 19 V.G.P. Street. A run-down hotel with a popular restaurant serving a wide range of tasty dishes.

Kanchipuram

Saravana Bhavan, 504 Gandhi Road; 66 Anna Indira Gandhi Road, near the Bus Station. Two branches of the excellent, cheap and very clean chain of South Indian vegetarian restaurants.

Kanniyakumari

Hotel Saravana, Sannathi Street. A good, clean meals place serving excellent *dosas*.

Madurai

Meenakshi Bhawan, West Perumal Maistry Street, near the Anna Bus Stand. Excellent and popular South Indian food, including Chettinad dishes.
New Arya Bhavan, 268 West Masi Street. Good-value and tasty North and South Indian vegetarian food. Open all day.

Thanjavur

Ananda Bhavan, Gandhiji Road, close to the Hotel Tamilnadu. Clean with extremely cheap and very tasty vegetarian meals.
Coffee Palace, Eliamman Kovil Street. The best place in Thanjavur for real South Indian coffee and snacks.
Golden Restaurant, Hospital Road. Another vegetarian meals place, but with a good local reputation.

Udagamandalam

Nilgiri Woodlands, Ettines Road. This hotel serves up good-value, and very tasty, vegetarian meals and snacks.

UTTARAKHAND

Dehra Dun

Atithi, 101 Rajpur Road. Good Indian food, especially the vegetarian dishes.
Daddy's, 3 Astley Plaza, Rajpur Road. Popular Indian, Western and Chinese meals and snacks.
Kumar, 15a Rajpur Road. Very good North Indian vegetarian food in a cheap, popular restaurant.

Haridwar

Chotiwala, Lalta Rao Bridge, Upper Road. Popular since 1937. Famous for pure vegetarian food and *thalis*.
Aahar, Railway Road. Good *thalis*, Punjabi dishes and Chinese food.

Mussoorie

The Tavern, The Mall, Kulri. A popular restaurant and bar, though noisy during the high tourist season.
Windsor's Whispering Windows, Library Bazaar, Gandhi Chowk. Good Indian and Chinese food, and a decent bar. Open all day.

Nainital
Kumaon Restaurant, Grassmere Estate, Mallital. An excellent restaurant serving very tasty Pahari food. Recommended.
Sakley's, The Mall. A popular Western restaurant and bakery with good sweets.

UTTAR PRADESH

Agra
Capri, Hari Parbat. Very good North Indian food, especially the *tandoori* dishes, in a friendly and pleasant restaurant.
Dasaprakash, Meher Theatre Complex, 1 Gwalior Road, Cantoment. Very good South Indian food, especially the *dosas*, and sinful desserts. Very clean and well run.
Kwality, Sadar Bazaar. Like all Kwality restaurants, this is pleasant and serves good North Indian vegetarian and non-vegetarian food.
Zorba the Buddha, E13 Shopping Arcade, Gopi Chand Shivhare Road, Sadar Bazaar. A very clean and popular vegetarian restaurant serving tasty and imaginative dishes. Run by followers of Osho. Closed during the summer. Recommended.

Allahabad
Coffee House, M.G. Marg, Civil Lines. Popular with good South Indian vegetarian snacks and great coffee.
El Chico, 24 M.G. Marg, Civil Lines. A good, comfortable restaurant with a choice of Indian, Western and Chinese dishes and an adjacent snack shop and bakery (the **Espresso Snack Bar**). Open all day.
Hot Stuff, 21c Lal Bahadur Shastri Marg, Civil Lines. A very popular place for a variety of Western fast food. Open all day.
Jade Garden, Hotel Tepso, M.G. Marg, Civil Lines. Good Chinese food.
Kwality, M.G. Marg, Civil Lines. The usual Kwality service with decent North Indian food.

Jhansi
Holiday, Shastri Marg. A clean AC restaurant with good Indian food and some Western dishes.

Kanpur
Chung Fa, 94b Canal Road, The Mall. A long-standing restaurant serving decent Chinese food.
Kwality Restaurant, 16/97 The Mall. Reliable North Indian vegetarian and non-vegetarian dishes. Open all day.
Pandit, opposite Green Park, Civil Lines; Katahari Bagh, Cantonment. Tasty pure vegetarian food, especially the *pakoras*.

Sarovar Restaurant, 3a Sarodaya Nagar. Good North, and a few South, Indian dishes. Open all day.

Lucknow
The basic "meals" places by the M.G. Marg/University Road roundabout, close to the Clark's Avadh, serve safe and decent North Indian food, including *tandoori* dishes.
Dasaprakash, Jopling Road. South Indian vegetarian.
Indian Coffee House, Ashok Marg, near the Post Office. Decent South Indian snacks and coffee.
Mu Man's Royal Cafe, 51 Hazratganj. Very good Chinese food in a pleasant, friendly restaurant.
Nirula's, Shahnajaf Road. India's answer to McDonald's.
Shanghai Surprise, Sapru Marg. Tastefully furnished, decent portions and good service.
Tunde Kabab, in the Chowk. A Lucknow institution. Famous kebabs, Lucknaivi-style, served with very tasty breads.
Vyranjan, Ashok Marg. Good-value vegetarian food.

Varanasi
Bread of Life, B3-322 Shivala, off Sonarpur Road. A bakery selling great bread and cakes. The attached restaurant serves safe and tasty Western food. A good place for breakfast. Open all day.
Kerala Cafe, Bhelupura Crossing. One of the best places to get vegetarian South Indian food in Varanasi; very good *dosas* and *idli*.
Keshari, off Dasasvamedha Ghat Road. Excellent Indian vegetarian food; try the *thalis*.
Sindhi, Bhelupura, by the Lalita Theatre. Varanasi's traditional pure vegetarian food; tasty and good value.

WEST BENGAL

Darjeeling
Deveka's, 52 Gandhi Road. Popular restaurant serving good Western and Indian food.
Glenary's, Nehru Road. A well-established restaurant, bar and café with a good bakery and sweet shop. A good place for breakfast and Raj-style "high tea".
New Dish, J.P. Sharma Road. This restaurant is famous locally for its excellent Chinese food and friendly service.

Outside of the sometimes dubious pleasures of Goa, India is not famed for its nightlife. However, things are slowly changing in the large cities as the young middle class adopt more "western" lifestyles. Many places are in the large, luxury hotels, all of which have strict admission policies. Visitors from abroad may well find Bangalore's famous "pub culture" over-hyped. Bars are still largely a male preserve and lone women may find them intimidating. For up-to-date listings check on the www.explocity.com site.

Bangalore
180 Proof, St Marks Road. A very popular bar with music and dancing; also has decent Southeast Asian food.
Pub World, 65 Residency Road. Basically lots of beer and cocktails; more comfortable than some.
NASA, 1–4 Church Street. Space Shuttle-themed pub – lots of metal – with very loud music.
Peco's, Rest House Road, off Brigade Road. Slightly "alternative" bar (well, pictures of Frank Zappa anyway) on two levels, less in-your-face than some.
Underground, 65 M.G. Road. A very popular bar disguised as a London tube station.

Chennai
EC41, on the beach. Open until dawn with a sprinkler system to cool things down. Opens 10.30pm.
Hell Freezes Over, Quality Inn Aruna, 144 Sterling Road. Reopened in 2003, this popular venue is still one of Chennai's top clubs.

Delhi
Elevate, on the top floor of Centre Stage Mall. **Fabric**, on the Mehrauli Gurgaon Road.

Mumbai
Fire and Ice, Phoenix Mills Complex, 462 Senapati Bapat Marg. One of the biggest clubs in the country, and very popular.
Not Just Jazz by the Bay, 143 Marine Drive. A restaurant and bar with live bands, DJs and karaoke nights.
Café Mondegar, S.B. Road. A fairly lively place with a decent bar and food.
Enigma at J.P. Road and **Insomnia** at the Taj Mahal Hotel are also worth checking out.

Shopping

What to Buy

The assortment of goods on offer is staggering, so look around first and check out the differing quality and prices before you buy anything.

Places selling handicrafts (of all kinds) are a good first stop. Carpets are available in different sizes and knot-counts. Unless you know a lot about carpets, shop at a Government Emporium. Less expensive are rugs and *dhurries* from all over the country. There is a huge assortment of precious and semi-precious gemstones, jewellery set in both gold and silver, traditional as well as modern, often much cheaper than in Europe.

India is famous for its textiles which come in a bewildering array of natural and man-made fibres, textures, weaves, prints, designs and colours.

Carved sandalwood figures and elaborately worked wooden panels are found in the South. There are also many objects in brass, copper and gun metal, inlaid, enamelled, worked or beaten.

Marble inlay work and papier mâché items with intricate designs, reproductions of miniature paintings on paper or cloth, and leather wallets, shoes and bags are all good buys. Hand-painted pottery, and cane goods ranging from table mats to furniture, are popular, and so are ready-made clothes.

Antiques and semi-antiques are governed by strict laws limiting their export; also beware of fakes. Export of skins, furs and ivory is strictly forbidden.

Major credit cards such as Visa and MasterCard are widely accepted in shops. Do be careful not to let your card out of your sight as fraud has been reported in India (sometimes multiple copies of card receipts have been made and charged later on). Most cities will now have a number of ATMS where cash can be withdrawn. Local bank ATMS may not accept international cards, so try and find one of the multinationals, or one of the larger national banks.

Where to Shop

Agra

Agra is famous for its carpets and inlaid marble. As elsewhere, be careful about what you buy and look around before making any purchase. Many items passed off as marble are soapstone or chalk. Check if the stone is translucent (will light up from the other side) and whether it leaves a mark when rubbed on a rough surface; marble will light up and will not leave a mark. Silk carpets change colour and sheen when viewed from different directions.

The **Harish Carpet Company** is on Vibhav Nagar Road. You can see a demonstration of the weaving, washing and trimming of the carpets, and also inspect the raw yarns they are made from: either wool, wool/silk mix or pure silk yarns, all with natural dyes (the yarns are sourced from Kashmir). Most designs are traditional Indo-Persian patterns. You should expect to pay from around Rs600 per square foot (30 square cm) for wool, Rs800 for wool/silk mix, and Rs1,200 for pure silk.

For marble inlay work, the best place in town is the government **U.P. Handicrafts Development Centre** (Handicraft Nagar, Fatehbad Road). They have their own factory employing some 500 people. Some of the work is exquisite and a large piece can take up to 18 months to complete. A small box costs from around Rs600. They also sell fabrics, *saris*, shawls and ready-mades, all at fixed prices.

Bangalore

M.G. Road and Brigade Road are Bangalore's main shopping streets, with the usual array of shops selling Lacoste and Adidas. For general shopping, the government emporium, **Kaveri**, is on Brigade Road.

Brigade Road has a post office and a Citibank **ATM** (there is another on Infantry Road). Just off Brigade Road is the **Premier** bookshop with a wide selection of titles. Other bookshops include the **Select** on St Mark's Road, and the **Strand** in the Manipal Centre.

Thomas Cook are on M.G. Road and there is a branch of **Foodworld** at No. 86, with a good fruit stall outside (there is another fruit stall at the bottom of Brigade Road).

Bhopal

New Market has a wide variety of handicrafts, handlooms and garments (closed Sun–Mon). **Chowk** is good for silver jewellery, crafts and silk (closed Mon–Fri). The **MP State Emporium**, T.T. Nagar, sells traditional textiles.

Chandigarh

Try **Sector 17 Shopping Complex**, Haryana State Emporium Phulkari, for embroidered silk, woodwork and Punjabi shoes.

For handlooms and block-printed garments try **Khadi Gramodyog**, **Uttar Pradesh State Emporium**, and **Hotel Shivalik View**.

Chennai

Chennai is one of the best places in India to buy books. The following shops are all very helpful, have a good stock and will post books back for you: **Landmark Books** in Spencer Plaza is said to be Asia's largest bookstore, with a huge number of books and CDs; **Bookpoint**, 160 Anna Salai is also recommended; **Higginbothams**, 814 Anna Salai, is one of the largest bookshops in India; and **Giggles** in the Taj Connemara Hotel has also been recommended for its knowledgeable owner and eclectic stock.

Close by the Connemara is Spencer Plaza, a large, air-conditioned shopping centre. This has an American Express exchange on the ground floor (and a local rival with better rates opposite), some internet places and a **Foodworld** supermarket, where you can buy familiar food and toiletries, including Tampax.

Chennai is also a good place for clothes and fabrics, particularly Kanchi silks. Try the government shops (and others) at the top end of Anna Salai, in particular the **Central Cottage Industries Emporium** at No. 476 and **Poompuhar** at No. 818. For ready-mades, Naidu Hall in Pondi Bazaar, T. Nagar is recommended.

Delhi

Central Delhi

Connaught Place was built as the commercial centre of Lutyens' new city. Nowadays it is full of restaurants, Western sports shops and places trying to lure in tourists. It is probably best to avoid shopping here as the prices are inflated, although the bookshops are worth having a browse through. Of the bookshops, **The Bookworm** at 29-B has a particularly good stock of fiction, non-fiction and academic and reference works. Also avoid the tourist traps in the underground Palika Bazaar. Connaught Place does, however, have a number of useful 24-hour ATMS.

The **Tibetan market** at the top of Janpath has stalls selling Tibetan curios. Opposite, at Jawahar Vyapur Bhavan, Janpath, is the government-run **Central Cottage Industries Emporium** (Mon–Sat 10am–7pm). The fixed prices and wide variety of goods, spread over 6 floors, make it a good place to start looking. It is a particularly good place to buy fabrics. Also on Janpath is the **Survey of India Map Sales Office** (2a Janpath Barracks), where you can pick up large-scale maps (**NB**: any maps over 1:250,000 may not be exported but they may be used while you are in the country). Another good place for maps is **International Publications** (40 Hanuman Lane, Connaught Place).

Baba Kharak Singh Marg, near Connaught Place, is where all State Emporia and the **Khadi Emporium** can be found (as well as the very popular government **Coffee Home**). The pavements have recently been tidied up and widened. Among the best of the emporiums are: **Cauvery** (Karnataka) with good silks; **Poompuhar** (Tamil Nadu) with some exquisite, but expensive, bronzes; the **Handicrafts Development Corporation**, with lots of silks; **Lepakshi** (Andhra Pradesh) with good gold and pearl jewellery; **Rajasthali** (Rajasthan), with a very large and well presented selection of everything from fabrics to jewellery; and **Gurjari** (Gujarat) with an excellent selection of cotton textiles.

Old Delhi

Between **Chandni Chowk** and **Chawri Bazaar** are the bazaars of Old Delhi. **Ghantewale** on Chandni Chowk is one of the oldest and best sweet shops in Delhi. Running south off Chandni Chowk, just past the Jain Mandir, is Dariba Kalan, the jeweller's street, once famous for its gold but now mostly selling silver. **Katra Neel**, west of the town hall on Chandni Chowk, is a warren of small shops selling fabrics, particularly silk, by the metre. **Nai Sarak**, which runs between Chandni Chowk and Chawri Bazaar has bookshops, mostly of educational publications. By the Jama Masjid is the extraordinary spare car-parts bazaar.

South Delhi

In **South Delhi** is the swish, air-conditioned **Ansal Plaza**, on Khel Gaon Marg. A good place to visit to see how the other 5 percent live, it has the Shoppers Stop department store, and a branch of Music World with a good range of Indian CDs.

For books try the **Om Book Shop** at E77 South Extension Part 1 (also at 45 Basant Lok, Vasant Vihar).

The **Hauz Khas Village Complex** has numerous designer shops selling *shalwar* and *lehengas*. Try **Nasreen Qureshi** (26 Hauz Khas Village), a Pakistani designer from Lahore, now living in Delhi. **Expressionist Designs** (1a Hauz Khas Village, tel: 651 8913) stock the clothes of Delhi designer Jaspreet. For a large stock and the

work of several Delhi designers go to **Marwari's** (15 Hauz Khas Village).

Next to Marwari's at No. 14 is the excellent **Village Gallery**, whose knowledgeable staff showcases Indian artists working in a variety of media. The exhibitions change every month and back-stock may be viewed on the first floor.

Near the zoo, **Sunder Nagar Market** has several art and antique stores. The **Crafts Museum** at Pragati Maidan has a very good shop.

Diplomatic Area

Near this area there is a chic shopping complex called **Santushti**, run by the Airforce Wives Association. There are branches of the Jaipur-based designers' shop **Anokhi**, and of **Padakkam**, which sells fabrics and accessories from South India, mostly Keralan. South of this and next to Chanakya Cinema, **Yashwant Singh Place** has several shops selling leather items. **Sarojini Nagar Market**, nearby, is another "colony" market selling many goods including vegetables, household items, export surplus clothes and shoes.

Khan Market has good bookshops – try the **Times Book Gallery** – and is a good place to pick up groceries. It also has a branch of **Anokhi**, an outlet for the Biotique range of Ayurvedic skin-care products, and **Padakkam**, with a pleasant balcony where you can drink coffee.

Other "colony" markets worth visiting are **South Extension**, **Defence Colony**, **Greater Kailash** (N and M Block Market), and **Lajput Nagar Central Market**.

Gangtok

Try **New Market**, M.G. Road for Tibetan curio shops. **Lall Market** is the local market on Paljor Stadium Road where you can buy Tibetan and Sikkimese curios. The **Directorate of Handicrafts and Handloom**, on the National Highway, has a showroom selling carpets and paintings of *thankas* among other things.

Goa

The shops in Goa are mostly near the beaches and offer a range of handicrafts, curios and jewellery from other parts of India.

Basic swimwear and scarves for beach wraps are available. Fancy leatherware shops offer a choice of bags and other items.

Beach hawkers selling Rajasthani clothes, scarves and jewellery are a nuisance, but you can haggle with them and obtain a bargain.

The flea market held every Wednesday at **Anjuna Beach** is the best place to head if in a shopping

mood. You may find interesting handmade jewellery, antique silver buckled belts, clothes and swimwear from Bali, home-made cakes, biscuits and other goodies. Keep a hand on your purse or wallet and don't be tempted to buy the drugs that will be on offer.

Hyderabad/Secunderabad

Hyderabad is the pearl capital of India, and pearl jewellery and silver filigree work are the best buys in the city. Hyderabad is also famed for its glass and lacquer bangles and Lambadi silver jewellery. Venkatagiri and Pochampalli handloom saris, Dharmavaram silk fabrics, Kalamkari "painted" cloths, and carpets from Warangal and Eluru are also good buys. Kondapalli wooden toys and inlaid bidriware are other well-known Andhran handicrafts. All these products are available at **Lepakshi** in the Mayur Complex.

The **pearl market** is on Petherghati Road near the Charminar in Hyderabad. Nearby are the famed bangle shops. In this area too are numerous silversmiths and bidriware craftsmen.

Other good shopping areas are **Abid's** (particularly good for fabrics) and **Basheer Bagh** in Hyderabad and **M G Road** in Secunderabad.

Jaipur

Traditional tie-dyed textiles made by knotting the material and dipping it in dye to form delicate *bandhani* patterns are worth looking out for. The block prints of Sanganer, many with *khari* (over-printing with gold); *ajrah* prints from Barmer; *jajam* prints from Chittor; and the floral prints from Bagru can be found in the bazaars in the old city. The **Rajasthali Government Emporium** (just off M.I. Road) is the only government-run shop. It sells fabric by the yard, or made up into garments and wall hangings, gemstones and other jewellery. Another good place for fabrics and clothing is the **Gramya** khadi handicraft emporium (Panch Batti, M.I. Road). Jaipur is also the home of **Anokhi** (2 Tilak Marg, C Scheme). They sell elegant *shalwar* (in colours that will appeal to Western tastes), T-shirts, skirts, bed linen, throws etc., all in good-quality fabrics that are reasonably priced and ethically sourced.

Jaipur is famous as a centre for semi-precious gemstones. If you do want to buy these, check what you are buying very carefully. Rajasthali, above, is recommended, as is **The Gem Palace** on M.I. Road. This long-established jewellers has beautiful, and expensive, work. If you are buying gems from elsewhere, ask to take them to the government's **Gem Testing Laboratory** (Chamber 1, 3rd Floor, M.I. Road). The tests take about two hours and the charge is around Rs200 per stone.

Jaipur and Sanganer are famous for their "blue pottery". These hand-painted vessels are decorated with floral motifs and geometric patterns in combinations of blue, white and occasionally other colours.

Leather workers using camel and other hides produce a variety of traditional footwear, including *jhutis* with their turned-up toes. In Jaipur the cobblers also make *mojadis*, which are soft slippers embroidered with bright colours.

Carpets and *dhurries* are made both for local and export markets. Jewellery can be found in the **Johari Bazaar**. Although it is well-known for its silver, the gold-work is finer. Make sure you bargain hard. Jaipur has the best selection of *pichwais* or cloth paintings. Try the **Friends of the Museum Master Craftsmen and Artists** display room inside the main courtyard of the City Palace, where you can watch the artists at work. Engraved brassware, and exquisite enamel work and inlay is also available; the best enamel work is done by **Kudrat Singh** (1565 Rasta Jarion, Chaura Rasta).

Kerala

The state government emporium is known as **Kairali**, with branches in Ernakulam (on M.G. Road), Kozhikode (on M.M. Ali Road) and Thiruvananthapuram, where it is called the SMSM **Handicrafts Emporium** (just behind the Secretariat building).

Among Kerala's exports are items made from coir (coconut fibre), spun and made into all kinds of mats, carpets and bags. Alappuzha is the centre of the coir industry and is probably the best place to look.

All towns have their fabric shops. In Thiruvananthapuram try **Partha's** on Powerhouse Road (they also have a branch in Ernakulam on M.G. Road), which has a huge selection of dress fabrics and ready-made clothes, or **Alapatt Silks** in East Fort. In Kochi a lovely modern shop selling designer clothes and items for the home is **Cinnamon** (Ridsdale Road, by the Parade Ground; tel: 0484-221 7124).

Traditional gold jewellery can be exquisite, with delicate interwoven strands and characteristic small bobbles. It is generally sold

by weight, and the day's gold price should be displayed in the shop. Don't expect jewellery to be cheap, especially if gems are included in the piece. Do make sure, as well, that you buy from a reputable jeweller. One of the largest chains in the state is **Alukkas**. They have branches in Thiruvananthapuram (East Fort), Ernakulam (M.G. Road), Alapuzzha (Boat Jetty Road) and Thrissur (Round East, by the temple). Another very reputable chain is **Josco**. They can be found in Thiruvananthapuram (East Fort), Kottayam (K.K. Road), Ernakulam (M.G. Road), Thrissur (M.O. Road) and Palakkad (G.B. Road).

Although the rules for exporting antiques from India are very strict, you can find some very fine items (all passed for export) at **Natesans** on M.G. Road in Thiruvananthapuram.

Other useful shops in Thiruvananthapuram are the **Modern Book Centre** close to M.G. Road, and further up, opposite the South Park Hotel, is **Spencer's Supermarket**, handy for toiletries and bits and pieces to eat and drink.

Kochi-Ernakulam

For a huge selection of fabrics and ready-mades, try **Partha's** on M.G. Road. The government emporiums are also along M.G. Road.

Kolkata

The **Government Emporium** (7 Jawaharlal Nehru Road) offers local handicrafts. Close by antique shops sell Rajasthani jewellery, old prints and postcards.

Handicrafts can be found at **Good Companions** (13c Russell Street) and chic Indian clothes at **Sacha Ritu's** (46a Rafi Ahmad Kidwai Road).

New Market off Lindsay Street is huge and has a vast amount of items for sale. The bazaar area in North Kolkata spreads over a third of the city with individual streets devoted to one item. There are shops and *gaddies* with elevated floors where hawkers sit selling bags, secondhand books and records, pets and animals (**Natibagan**), secondhand furniture (**Mullick Bazaar**), electrical goods (**Paddar Court**), shoes (**Bentinck Street**), jewellery (**P.B. Sarkar, P.C. Chandra**, Dharamtola Street, **Bow Bazaar**).

Silks can be purchased at **Indian Silk House**, Gangadeen Gupta, 1 Shakespeare Sarani, in the air-conditioned market.

For contemporary Indian art try: **Gallerie 88** (28b Shakespeare

Sarani); and the **Centre Art Gallery** (87c Park Street).

Every year, at the end of January, the **Kolkata Book Fair** on Cathedral Road on the Maidan attracts more than a million visitors.

Other books can be found at **Oxford Book and Stationery**, 17 Park Street, and at the **Modern Book Depot**, 15a Jawaharlal Nehru Road.

Lucknow

Chikan Corner, near the Chota Imambara, is the place to buy clothes and scarves. Before looking elsewhere, check out **Gangotri**, the **Uttar Pradesh Government Emporium**, Hazratganj, for quality handicrafts/handloom fabrics, including Lucknow's fine *chikan*-work embroidery. The fixed prices will help you when you shop around.

Ram Advani on Hazratganj is an excellent bookshop, with a very good stock of modern fiction and academic titles. **Asghar Ali Mohammed Ali**, Aminabad, is the place to buy – or try – Lucknow's famous perfume oils (*ittar/attar*) like amber, *khus* and *gulab* (rose).

Mumbai

Most shops are open Mon–Sat 10am–7pm, and are closed Sun. Some of the bazaars remain open until 9pm. **Jyotiba Phule Market** has a wide range of food and household items. Nearby is the huge **Mangaldas Market**, full of textiles. Try **Shaheed Bhagat Singh Marg** for leather items and clothes. **"Fashion Street"**, otherwise known as M.G. Road, is lined with stalls selling export surplus Western clothes.

For handicrafts, try the **State Emporia** in the World Trade Centre, Cuffe Parade, and Sir P.M. Road, Fort. The **Central Cottage Industries Emporium**, 34 Shivaji Marg (near the Gateway of India) has the widest range. **Natesan's** in the Jehangir Gallery Basement has some wonderful, if pricey, antiques and works of art.

Crossword, 22b Bhulubhai Desai Road, has a good range of books, as does **Strand**, off P.M. Road, Fort. **Planet M**, Times of India Building, D.N. Road, has a huge range of CDs. Bookstalls line M.G. Road, from the museum to Hutatma Chowk, mostly selling novels and university and school textbooks.

Mysore

Mysore is famous for silk and sandalwood. An excellent place to buy fabrics is the **Mysore Silk Emporium** (3 Nethra Nivas, Hotel Sandesh Complex, Nazarbad Main Road).

Check the purity of the silk by burning a strand or two. If the fibres burn away to ash that just crumbles in your fingers then it is pure silk, if there is a residue then the fabric is wholly or partly synthetic.

Sandalwood is found all over Mysore, but check that sandalwood oil comes in a metal bottle from the licensed factory just outside of town. The **Handicrafts Sales Emporium** (Ramson's House, opposite the zoo) has a good selection of sandalwood carvings, jewellery, bronzes and fabrics, all at fixed prices.

Thiruvananthapuram
Natesans on M.G. Road has fine examples of Indian art, all very expensive. **The Modern Book Centre** close by has a very good range of titles. Further up M.G. Road, opposite the South Park Hotel, is **Spencer's Supermarket**, handy for toiletries.

Wildlife

There are about 70 national parks and more than 330 sanctuaries in India, home to hundreds of species of mammals, birds and reptiles *(see also pages 143–7)*. Of these, Gujarat's **Geer Forest** is famous for its population of Asiatic lions, **Periyar** (in Kerala) for elephants, **Manas** and **Kaziranga** for one-horned rhinoceroses, Manipur's **Keibul Lamjao Park** for Thamin deer, and **Corbett** and **Kanha** for tigers. A selection of some notable wildlife sanctuaries follows.

Wildlife Parks

Bhandhavgarh (Madhya Pradesh)
Sal and mixed forest with bamboo breaks. Excellent game viewing and birdlife. Tiger, leopard, gaur, chital, sambar, dhole, nilgai, wild boar, sloth bear, chinkara. Elephant riding.
Best time: November–June
Contact: Director, Bandhavgarh National Park, Umaria P.O., Shadol District, Madhya Pradesh

Corbett (Uttaranchal)
Tiger, mugger, gharial, deer, most other large species. Mahseer and other fish in Ramganga river.
Best time: February–May
Contact: Field director, Project Tiger, Corbett National Park, Ramnagar P.O., Nainital District, Uttar Pradesh

Dhangadhra Sanctuary (Gujarat)
This special sanctuary in the Little Rann of Kutch was set up for the Indian wild ass. The Rann is a flat saline wilderness with little vegetation. Other animals include blackbuck, a few chinkara, wolf and desert cat.
Best time: January–June
Contact: Field Director, Dhangadhra Sanctuary, Little Rann of Kutch, Gujarat

Dudhwa (Uttar Pradesh)
Tiger, leopard, sloth bear, rhinoceros, swamp deer, hog deer, chital and an excellent range of birdlife.
Best time: December–June
Contact: Director, Dudhwa National Park, Lakhimpur Kheri, Uttar Pradesh
Indravati National Park & Tiger

Reserve (Chattisgarh)
This park has perhaps the only viable population of wild buffalo in central India and is a possible alternative home for the swamp deer of Kanha. Other animals seen include sambar, nilgai, chausingha, chinkara, blackbuck, gaur, sloth bear, wild boar, leopard, wolf, hyena and jackal.
Best time: late January to April.
Contact: Field Director, Indravati National Park, Chattisgarh

Jawahar National Park (Bandipur Tiger Reserve, Karnataka)
This park has one of the best-planned road systems among Indian parks, which provides excellent opportunities for game viewing, especially for elephant, leopard and gaur.
Best time: November–February
Contact: Field Director, Project Tiger, Bandipur Tiger Reserve, Mysore

Kangchendzonga National Park (Sikkim)
Wet temperate forest rising to the rock and snow of the very high Himalayan peaks on the Nepalese border. The park has an impressive range of animals and birds: leopard, clouded leopard, tahr, musk deer, bharal, serow, snow leopard, red panda and binturong.
Best time: April–May, August–October
Contact: Field Director, Kangchendzonga National Park, Sikkim

Kanha (Madhya Pradesh)
Considered by some to be India's greatest national park, the area is certainly an excellent place to see many species in their natural habitat. Barasingha (swamp deer), tiger and other species.
Best time: February–June (closed July–November)
Contact: Field Director, Project Tiger, Mandla P.O., Madhya Pradesh

Kaziranga (Assam)
Famous for rhinoceros, wild buffalo, swamp deer and hog deer. Tiger, wild boar, Hoolock gibbon, capped langur and ratel can also be seen. Well-trained elephants can be hired.
Best time: November–March
Contact: Director, Kaziranga National Park, Bokakhat P.O., Jorhat District, Assam

Kumbalgarh (Rajasthan)
This large sanctuary in the Aravalli hills is perhaps the only area in India where the highly endangered wolf is breeding successfully. Other animals include leopard, sloth bear, chinkara, chousingha, ratel and flying squirrel.
Best time: September–November

Birdlife

Chilika (Orissa)
Lake, shore and hinterland on the Bay of Bengal coast support white chital and blackbuck. Extensive birdlife includes wading birds and flamingo. Dolphins can sometimes be seen.
Best time: December–March
Contact: DFO, Ghunar South, Khurda P.O., Puri District, Orissa

Keoladeo Ghana (Rajasthan)
One of the world's greatest heronries is situated here. Famous for waterbirds including crane and migratory fowl. Mammals include sambar, blackbuck, chital, nilgai, fishing cat, jungle cat, otter and mongoose.
Best time: breeding, August–October; migrants, October–February
Contact: Chief Wildlife Warden, Keoladeo National Park, Bharatpur, Rajasthan

Contact: Wildlife Warden, Kumbalgarh Sanctuary, Udaipur District, Rajasthan

Mudumalai Sanctuary (Tamil Nadu)
This sanctuary with mixed deciduous forests is bounded to the north by Bandipur National Park in Karnataka and to the west by the Wynad Sanctuary in Kerala. It has good animal viewing and facilities.
Best time: March–June, September–October
Contact: Field Director, Mudumalai Sanctuary, Tamil Nadu

Nagarahole National Park (Karnataka)
An extremely attractive park, separated from Bandipur by a large reservoir. Large groups of gaur, elephant, the occasional tiger and leopard, chital and sambar are seen. Over 250 species of birds have been recorded here.
Best time: October–April
Contact: Field Director, Nagarahole National Park, Karnataka

Namdapha (Arunachal Pradesh)
Fascinating mix of Indo-Burmese, Indo-Chinese and Himalayan wildlife. Tiger, leopard (clouded leopard, snow leopard), gaur, goral, takin, musk deer, Hoolock gibbon, slow loris, binturong and red panda. Hornbill and pheasant are among the great range of birds.
Best time: October–March
Contact: Field Director, Project Tiger, Miao P.O., Tirap District, Arunachal Pradesh

Nanda Devi (Uttar Pradesh)
A World Biosphere Reserve with limited access, and the site of India's second-highest mountain, Nanda Devi Peak (7,816 metres/25,643 ft). Animals here include mountain goat, snow leopard and musk deer.
Best time: April–October
Contact: DCF, Nanda Devi National Park, Joshimath, Chamoli District, Uttar Pradesh

Periyar (Kerala)
India's southernmost tiger reserve. Elephant viewing excellent, some tiger, monkey. There are woodland birds in abundance. Boats and dugouts available.
Best time: September–May
Contact: The Field Director, Project Tiger, Kanjikuzhi, Kottayam, Kerala

Ranthambore (Rajasthan)
An impressive range of animal species including sambar, chital, nilgai, chinkara, monkey, wild boar, sloth bear, hyena, jackal, leopard and tiger. Excellent birdlife including crested serpent eagle.
Best time: October–April
Contact: The Field Director, Ranthambore National Park, Sawai Madhopur, Rajasthan

Sunderbans (West Bengal)
Most of the area is a vast estuarine mangrove forest and swamp inhabited by crocodiles and turtles. The Gangetic dolphin can also be seen. The park holds more tigers than any other reserve.
Best time: December–February
Contact: Field Director, Sunderbans Tiger Reserve, Canning P.O., 24 Parganas District, West Bengal

Silent Valley National Park (Kerala)
This was set up to protect the peninsula's last substantial area of primary tropical rainforest. Elephant, lion-tailed macaque and tiger are among the animals seen. Restricted access.
Best time: September–March
Contact: Field Director, Silent Valley National Park, Kerala

Sasan Gir (Gujarat)
Last home of the Asiatic lion and one of the last of the Indian wild ass *(see also Dhangadhra)*. The park has more than forty species of animals and more than 450 species of birds, some migrant from Africa.
Best time: December–April
Contact: Conservator of Forests, Sardar Baug, Junagadh, Gujarat

Language

With 18 official languages, hundreds of others and countless dialects, India can present a linguistic minefield. Luckily for the traveller, English is often understood and it is usually possible to get by. However, attempts to speak the local language are always appreciated. The language most widely spoken in the North is Hindi, while in the South, Tamil has the highest profile.

Indian languages are phonetically regular, based on syllables rather than an alphabet. Important differences are made between long and short vowels, and reteroflex, palatal and labial consonants – listen hard to get a feel for the vocabulary below. There are various systems of transliteration and you may see many of the words below spelt different ways in English. Where a consonant is followed by "h" this is an aspirated sound, "c" is usually pronounced "ch" (followed by "h", "chh"), and "zh" in Tamil stands for a sound somewhere between a reteroflex "l" and "r".

Traveller's Hindi

Basics
Hello/goodbye *Namaste*
Yes *Ji ha*
No *Ji nehi*
Perhaps *Shayad*
Thank you *Dhanyavad/shukriya*
How are you? *Ap kaise hai?/Ap thik hai?*
I am well *Me thik hu/thik hai*
What is your name? *Apka nam kya hai?*
My name is (John/Jane) *Mera nam (John/Jane) hai*
Where do you come from? *Ap kahan se aye?*
From (England) *(England) se*
How much (money)? *Kitna paise hai?*
That is expensive *Bahut mahenga hai*
Cheap *Sasta*
I like (tea) *Mujhe (chai) pasand hai*
Is it possible? *Kya ye sambhav hai?*
I don't understand *Mujhe samajh nehi*
I don't know *Mujhe malum nehi*
Money *Paisa*
Newspaper *Akhbar*
Sheet *Chadar*
Blanket *Kambal*
Bed *Palang*

Room *Kamra*
Please clean my room *Mera kamra saf kijie*
Clothes *Kapre*
Cloth *Kapra*
Market *Bajar*

Pronouns

I am *Mai hun*
You are *Ap hain*
He/she/it is *Voh hai*
They are *Ve hain*

Verbs

To drink *Pina*
To eat *Khanna*
To do/make *Karna*
To buy *Kharidna*
To sleep *Sona*
To see *Dekhna*
To hear/listen to *Sunna*
To wash (clothes) *Dhona*
To wash (yourself) *Nahana*
To get *Milna or pana*

Prepositions, adverbs and adjectives

Now *Ab*
Right now *Abhi*
Quickly *Jaldi*
Slowly *Dirhe se*
A bit *Bahut*
A little *Tora*
Here *Yaha/idhar*
There *Vaha/udhar*
Open *Khola*
Closed *Bund*
Finished *Khatam hai*
Big/older *Bara*
Small/younger *Chota*
Beautiful *Sundar*
Old *Purana*
New *Naya*

Questions

What is? *Kya hai?*
Where is? *Kahan hai?*
Why? *Kyun?*
Who is? *Kaun hai?*
When is? *Kab hai?*
How? *Kaisa?*
Most straightforward sentences can easily be turned into a question by putting *"kya"* on the front and raising the pitch of the voice at the end of the sentence, e.g. *"Dhobi hai"*, "There is a washerman", *"Kya dhobi hai?"*, "Is there a washerman?"

Days of the week

Monday *Somvar*
Tuesday *Mangalvar*
Wednesday *Budhvar*
Thursday *Guruvar*
Friday *Shukravar*
Saturday *Shanivar*
Sunday *Itvar*
Today *Aj*
Yesterday/tomorrow *kal*
Week *Hafta*

Months

January *Janvari*
February *Farvari*
March *March*
April *Aprail*
May *Mai*
June *Jun*
July *Julai*
August *Agast*
September *Sitambar*
October *Aktubar*
November *Navambar*
December *Disambar*
Month *Mahina*
Year *Sal*

Relatives

Mother *Mata-ji*
Father *Pita-ji*
Sister *Behen*
Brother *Bhai*
Husband *Pati*
Wife *Patni*
Maternal grandmother *Nani*
Maternal grandfather *Nana*
Paternal grandmother *Dadi*
Paternal grandfather *Dada*
Elder sister (term of respect) *Didi*
Daughter *Beti*
Son *Beta*
Girl *Larki*
Boy *Larka*
Are you married? *Kya ap shadishuda hai?*
Are you alone (male/female)? *Kya ap akela/akeli?*
How many children have you got? *Apke kitne bache hai?*
How many brothers and sisters have you got? *Apke kitne bhai behen hai?*

Health

Doctor *Daktar*
Hospital *Aspatal*
Dentist *Dentist*
Pain *Dard*
I am ill *Main bimar hun*
I have been vomiting *Mujhe ulti ho rahi thi*
I have a temperature *Mujhe bukhar hai*
I have a headache *Mere sir men dard hai*
I have a stomach ache *Mere pat men dard hai*

I have diarrhoea *Mujhe dast ar raha hai*
The English word "motions" is a common expression for diarrhoea.

Travel

Where is (Delhi)? *(Dilli) kahan hai?*
Bus station *Bus adda*
Railway station *Tren stashan/railgari*
Airport *Hawai adda*
Car *Gari*
How far is it? *Kitni dur hai?*
In front of/opposite (the Taj Mahal) *(Taj Mahal) ke samne*
Near *Ke nazdik/ke pas*
Far *Dur*
Ticket *Tikat*
Stop *Rukh jaiye*
Let's go *Chele jao*
I have to go *Mujhe jana hai*
Come *Ayie*
Go *Jayie*

Food

I want (a thali) *Mujhe (thali) chahiye*
Without chilli *Mirch ke bina*
Little chilli *Kam mirch*
Hot *Garam*
Cold *Thanda*
Ripe/cooked *Pukka*
Unripe/raw *Kachcha*
Basics
Mirch Chilli
Namak Salt
Ghee Clarified butter
Dahi Yoghurt
Raita Yoghurt with cucumber
Chaval Rice
Panir Cheese
Pani Water
Dudh Milk
Lassi Yoghurt drink
Nimbu pani Lime water
Tandur Oven
Pilao Rice cooked with *ghi* and spices
Biriyani Rice cooked with vegetables or meat
Mithai Sweets
Breads (Roti)
Puri Deep-fried and puffed-up wheat bread
Chapatti Flat, unleavened bread
Nan Leavened flat bread
Tandoori roti Similar to *nan*

Hindi Numbers

1	ek		30	tis
2	do		40	chalis
3	tin		50	pachas
4	char		60	sath
5	panch		70	setur
6	che		80	assi
7	sat		90	nabbe
8	arth		100	sau
9	nau		1,000	hazar
10	das		100,000	lakh
20	bis		10,000,000	kror

Paratha Chapatti cooked with ghee
Vegetables (Sabzi)
Palak Spinach
Aloo Potato
Gobi Cauliflower
Bindi Okra
Pyaz Onion
Sarsun Mustard greens
Matter Peas
Tamata Tomato
Baingain/brinjal Aubergine
Dal Dried pulses
Meat
Gosht Lamb
Murg Chicken
Machli Fish
Fruit
Kela Banana
Santra Orange
Aum Mango

Traveller's Tamil

Basics

Hello Vanakkam
Goodbye Poyvituvarukiren
(Reply Poyvituvarungal)
Yes Amam
No Illai
Perhaps Oruvelai
Thank you Nandri
How are you? Celakkiyama?
What is your name? Ungal peyar
yenna?
My name is (John/Jane) Yen peyar
(John/Jane)
Where is the (hotel)? (Hotel)
yenge?
What is this/that? Idu/Adu
yenna?
What is the price? Yenna vilai?
That is very expensive Anda vilai
mikavum adikum
I want (coffee) (Kapi) Vendum
I like (dosa) (Dosai) Pudikkum
Is it possible? Mudiyuma?
I don't understand Puriyadu
Enough Podum
Toilet Tailet
Bed Kattil
Room Arai
Train Rayil
Sari Pudavai
Dhoti Vesti
Towel Tundu
Sandals Ceruppu
Money Punam
Temple Kovil

Verbs

Come (imperative) Varungal
Go (imperative) Pongal
Stop (imperative) Nillungal
Sleep Tungu
Eat Sappidu
Drink Kudi
Buy Vangu
Pay (money) Punam kodu (literally
"give money")
See Par

Wash (clothes) Tuvai
Wash (yourself) Kazhavu

Prepositions, adverbs and adjectives

Quickly Sikkirum
Slowly Meduvaka
A lot Mikavum
A little Koncam
Here Inge
There Ange
This Idu
That Adu
Now Ippodu
Same Ade
Good Nalla
Bad Ketta
Hot Karam
Cold Kulirana
Dirty Acattam
Clean Cattam
Beautiful Azhakana
Sweet Inippu
Big Periya
Small Cinna
Old Pazhaiya
New Pudiya

Days of the week

Monday Tingal
Tuesday Cevvay
Wednesday Putam
Thursday Viyazhan
Friday Velli
Saturday Ceni
Sunday Nayiri
Today Inraikku
Week Varam
Month Matam
Year Varutam

Questions & "and"

How? Yeppadi?
What? Yenna?
Who? Yar?
Why? Yen?
Where? Yenge?
When? Yeppodu?
How much? Yettanai/Yevvalavu?
Questions in Tamil are usually formed
by adding a long "a" to the last word
of a sentence (usually the verb), e.g.
"Ningal venduma?" "What do you
want?". "And" is formed by adding
"um" to the end of the nouns (with an
extra "y" if the noun ends in a vowel),
e.g. "Kapiyum, dosaiyum", "Coffee
and dosa".

Pronouns and relatives

I Nan
You Ningal
He/She/It Avan/Aval/Avar
**We (including addressee)/
(excluding addressee)** Nam/Nangal
They Avakal
Man Manidan
Woman/Girl/Daughter Pen
Boy/Son Paiyan
Children Pillaikal

Baby Pappu
Mother Amma
Father Appa
Husband Kanavan
Wife Manaivi

Health

I am sick (vomiting) Utampu
cariyillai irukkiradu
I have a pain Vali irukkiradu
I have diarrhoea "Motions"
irrukkiradu
Doctor Taktar
Help! Utavi cey!

Food (Sappadu)

Tunnir Water
Sadum Rice
Puzham Fruit
Kaykuri Vegetables
Pal Milk
Mor Buttermilk
Minakay (iilamal) (without) chilli
Tengay Coconut
Mampazham Mango
Valaippazham Banana
Kapi Coffee
Ti Tea
Iddli Steamed rice cakes
Dosai Pancake made from fermented
dough
Vadai Deep fried snack made of dal
Rasam Thin, spicy soup, usually with
a tamarind base
Sampar Thick soup made from dal
Poriyal Dry vegetable curry
Kolikarri Chicken curry
Attukkari Lamb curry
Mils "Meals", similar to a North
Indian thali, traditionally served on a
banana leaf
Payasam Sweet milk-based dish
served at festivals

Tamil Numbers

1	onru
2	irandu
3	munru
4	nanku
5	aindu
6	aru
7	yezhu
8	yettu
9	onpadu
10	pattu
11	patinonru
12	pannirandu
20	irupadu
30	muppadu
40	rarpadu
50	aimpadu
60	arupadu
70	alupadu
80	yenpadu
90	tonnuru
100	nuru
100,000	latcam
10,000,000	kodi

Further Reading

History

Amritsar: Mrs Gandhi's Last Battle, by Mark Tully and Satish Jacob (Jonathan Cape, 1985). Account of Operation Blue Star, the storming of the Sikhs' Golden Temple, and the aftermath which scarred a nation following Indira Gandhi's assassination.
An Autobiography, or My Experiments with Truth, by M.K. Gandhi (Penguin, 1982). A translation from the original Gujarati which shows the complex and at times flawed nature of one of India's greatest popular leaders.
The Discovery of India, by Jawaharlal Nehru (Asia Publishing House, 1966). Revealing history by India's first Prime Minister, which tells as much about the author as its subject.
Freedom at Midnight, by Larry Collins and Dominique Lapierre (Tarang, 1975). Gripping popular history of the birth of the Indian nation.
The Great Moghuls, by Bamber Gascoigne (Cape, 1971). Well-researched book which describes the dynasty that for two centuries ruled India, in turn both enlightened and decadent, austere and brutal. Sumptuous photographs complement highly readable text.
A History of India, Volume I, by Romila Thapar (Pelican, 2003). New edition of this highly acclaimed history. Volume 1 traces the history of South Asia from ancient times through to the Delhi sultanate. Volume II, by Perceval Spear, continues from the Mughals to the assassination of M.K. Gandhi.
An Introduction to India, by Stanley Wolpert (Viking 1992). Informative account of India's complexities by an American academic.
India: a History, by John Keay (HarperCollins, 2000). A one-volume history by a well-respected writer. Also by Keay, **India Discovered** (Collins, 1998) documents the unearthing of India's past by British scholars and adventurers.
Liberty or Death: India's Journey to Independence and Division, by Patrick French (HarperCollins, 1997). Readable and well-researched account of the freedom struggle and Partition.
The Nehrus and the Gandhis: an Indian Dynasty, by Tariq Ali (Pan, 1985). A gripping account of India's famous political family. Now out-of-print but secondhand copies can still be found.
No Full Stops in India, by Mark Tully (Viking, 1991). Essays on modern political India by the BBC's ex-South Asia correspondent.
Tea: Addiction, Exploitation and Empire, by Roy Moxham (Constable, 2003). A fascinating history of the skullduggery and economics behind one of India's most valuable crops.
Travels of Ibn Batuta, by Ibn Batuta and Tim Mackintosh-Smith (Picador, 2002). The story of a 14th-century adventurer.
They Fight Like Devils, by D.A. Kinsley (Greenhill Books, 2001). Stories from Lucknow during the Great Uprising in 1857.
This Fissured Land, by Madhav Gadgil and Ramachandra Guha (Oxford University Press, 1993). Searching and thought-provoking ecological history of South Asia.
Traders and Nabobs: the British in Cawnpore 1765–1957, by Zoe Yalland (Michael Russell, 1988).
Wicked Women of the Raj, by Coralie Younger (SOS Freestock, 2005). Stories about the women who married Indian Rajas.
The Wonder that Was India, by A.I. Basham (Rupa, 1967). Learned historical classic in idiosyncratic, rapturous prose.

Society, Culture & Religion

A Book of India, by B.N. Pandey (Rupa, Delhi, 1982). A real *masala* mix of philosophies, traveller's notes, poetry and literary trivia, revealing a quixotic India. Recommended.
The Argumentative Indian, by Amartya Sen (Penguin, 2006). Reflections on culture, history and identity by India's Nobel Prize winner.
Changing Village, Changing Life, by Prafulla Mohanti (Viking, 1990). Wry account of village life in Orissa.
Conversations in Bloomsbury, by Mulk Raj Anand (Oxford University Press, 1986). In turns, amusing, scathing and enlightening account of an Indian author's meetings with 20th-century luminaries of the British literary scene.
Everybody Loves A Good Drought, by P. Sainath (Penguin, 1996). Stories from India's poorest district, by an award-winning investigative reporter who looks at the human face of poverty.
Gods, Demons and Others, by R.K. Narayan (Heineman, 1986). Retellings of some of India's most popular religious myths by one of the country's greatest writers. Also worth looking out for are his retellings of

The Ramayana (Penguin, 1977), based on the Tamil Kamban version, and **The Mahabharata** (Heineman, 1986).
The Idea of India, by Sunil Khilnani (Hamish Hamilton, 1997). Intellectual *tour de force* examines concepts about an ancient civilisation and its status as a relatively new nation.
India: A Literary Companion, by Bruce Palling (John Murray, 1992). Another compilation of impressions taken from literature, letters and unpublished diaries, skillfully presented.
Indira: the Life of Indira Nehru Gandhi, by Katherine Frank (HarperCollins, 2002). An in-depth biography of one of post-Independence India's most charismatic leaders.
Intimate Relations: Exploring Indian Sexuality, Sudhir Kakar (University of Chicago Press, 1990). This study throws light on many aspects of Indian marital and family relations.
I Phoolan Devi, by Phoolan Devi with Marie Therese Cuny and Paul Rambi (Little Brown, 1996). The autobiography of an illiterate low-caste woman who fought convention, led a gang of bandits, and surrendered to the Indian government after years on the run. When freed from prison, she went on to win a parliamentary seat. A controversial insight into caste politics.
An Introduction to Hinduism, by Gavin Flood (Cambridge University Press, 1996). Perhaps the best general introduction to the complexities of this diverse religion. Recommended.
Lucknow: Last Phase of an Oriental Culture, by Sharar Abdulhalim (Oxford University Press, 1989). The classic account of this highly cultured city derived from articles written in Urdu from around 1913. Recommended.
Maximum City, by Shukut Meta (Headline Review, 2005). Bombay lost and found.
May You Be the Mother of a Hundred Sons, by Elisabeth Bumiller (Penguin, 1990). Women's issues tackled head-on, everything from dowries to infanticide, with dozens of poignant interviews.
A Million Mutinies Now, by V.S. Naipul (Heineman, 1990). The misanthropic scholar returns to seek his roots and finds a cast of characters not easily pigeon-holed. A more positive follow-up to his earlier, jaundiced, **India: A Wounded Civilisation** (Penguin, 1979).
The Mind of India, by William Gerber (Arcturus, 1967). Snippets from The Vedas, Buddhism, ancient and medieval commentaries and modern mysticism all help to understand a Hindu perspective.

The Other Side of Silence: Voices from the Partition of India, by Urvashi Butalia (Penguin, 1998). Tales of families torn apart for 50 years, compellingly told by India's leading literary feminist.

Outcaste: A Memoir, by Narendra Yadav (Viking Books, 2003). A story of a dalit's life, or how the other 95 percent live.

Plain Tales from the Raj, ed. Charles Allen (Rupa, 1992). First-hand accounts from ex-colonialists.

The Remembered Village, by M. Narasimhachar Srinivas (Oxford University Press India, 1999). A reprint of the classic anthropological study of a South Indian village.

Savaging the Civilised: Verrier Elwin, his Tribals and India, by Ramachandra Guha (University of Chicago Press, 1999). Biography of the great champion of India's beleaguered Adivasis.

South Asia: the Indian Subcontinent (The Garland Encyclopedia of World Music), ed. Alison Arnold (Garland Science, 1998). The ultimate reference work on the performance traditions of South Asia, written by leading academics.

Subaltern Studies: Writings on South Asian History and Society, I–X, various eds (Oxford University Press India). An ongoing series of volumes dealing with Indian history, gender, class and violence. In turns fascinating, challenging and inspiring.

Temptations of the West, or How to be Modern in India, Pakistan and Beyond, by Pankaj Mishra (Picador, 2006). Insightful travelogue by the author of *Butter Chicken in Ludhiana*.

Fiction

Calcutta Chromosome, by Amitav Ghosh (Harper Perennial, 2001). A scientific thriller set in India, New York and Egypt.

Clear Light of Day, by Anita Desai (Penguin, 1982). The difficulties of post-Partition India seen through the eyes of a Hindu family living in Old Delhi.

Delhi, A Novel, by Kushwant Singh (Viking, 1989). A bawdy saga that takes us through 600 years of temptresses and traitors to unravel the Indian capital's mystique. Narrated in turns by a eunuch, an irreverent wag, potentates and poets. Superb. (It took this popular author 20 years to write.)

The English Teacher, by R.K. Narayan (various editions). Narayan depicts infuriating and endearing characters which inhabit Malgudi, a composite South Indian village. Also in various editions, are **Malgudi Days**, a series of short stories.

A Fine Balance, by Rohinton Mistry (Faber & Faber, 1996). Beautifully written but sad story of two tailors who move from their village to the city.

The Gift of a Cow, by Premchand (Allen & Unwin, 1968). The great Hindi novelist's tragic classic about the hardships endured by a North Indian peasant.

The God of Small Things, by Arundhati Roy (Random House, 1997). The Kerala backwaters are evoked in a hauntingly personal novel set in a small village pickle factory in the 1960s. Recommended.

Hungry Tide, by Amitav Ghosh (Harper Collins, 2005). An atmospheric novel set in Sundarbans.

In Custody, by Anita Desai (Heineman, 1984). The last days of an Urdu poet, made into a beautiful Merchant-Ivory film.

Kanthapura, by Raja Rao (Oxford University Press, 1947). A lyrical novel about a village in Karnataka which implements Gandhi's methods of non-violent resistance to British rule.

Kim, by Rudyard Kipling (Penguin Books, 2000, ed. by Edward Said). The wonderful adventures of a boy who wanders across North India in search of the Great Game.

Midnight's Children, by Salman Rushdie (Jonathan Cape, 1981). Rushdie burst onto the literary scene with this dazzling novel of post-Independence India. Sardonic. **The Moor's Last Sigh**, on Mumbai, also dazzles (Jonathan Cape, 1995).

A New World, by Amit Chaudhuri (Picador, 2000). Naturalistic contemporary tale of divorced Indian man, resident in America, who takes his young son back to his parents in Kolkata for the holidays.

Out of India, by Ruth Prawer Jhabvala (Morrow, 1986). A collection of strong short stories that amuse and startle.

A Passage to India, by E.M. Forster (Penguin, 2000). The classic novel of the misunderstandings that arose out of the East-West encounter. After a mysterious incident in a cave Dr Aziz is accused of assaulting a naive young Englishwoman, Adela Quested. The trial exposes the racism inherent in British colonialism.

Pather Panchali, by Bibhutibhushan Banerji (Rupa, 1990). Outstanding Indian novel which outdoes the film by Satyajit Ray, depicting richness of spirit amid poverty in Bengal.

The Raj Quartet, by Paul Scott (University of Chicago Press, 1998). Four novels – **The Jewel in the Crown, The Day of the Scorpion, The Towers of Silence** and **A Division of Spoils** – set during the last days of the British Raj and charting its decline and fall.

Red Earth and Pouring Rain, by Vikram Chandra (Viking, 1996). Acclaimed debut novel, quick-paced and audacious.

A River Sutra, by Gita Mehta (Viking, 1993). Gently wrought stories which linger in the imagination.

The Romantics, by Pankaj Mishra (Random House, 2000). East meets West in Banaras.

Samskara, by U.R. Anantha Murthy (Oxford University Press, 1976). A tale of a South Indian Brahman village in Karnataka, where one Brahman is forced to question his values. Beautifully translated by A.K. Ramanujan.

The Scent of Pepper, by Kavery Nambisan (Penguin, 1996). This beautifully written family saga is set in South India.

A Suitable Boy, by Vikram Seth (Phoenix Press, 1994). A huge and multi-faceted novel set during the run up to Independent India's first elections, which centres around a mother's search for a suitable husband for her daughter. Highly recommended.

Train to Pakistan, by Kushwant Singh (various editions, 1954). Gripping story of the excesses of partition, penned when scars of the divided sub-continent were still fresh.

Untouchable, by Mulk Raj Anand (Penguin, 1986). Grinding tale of poverty and discrimination.

Women Writing in India: 600BC to the Present, ed. Susie Tharu and K. Lalitha (Feminist Press, 1991). Wonderful and eclectic anthology bringing to light the neglected history of Indian women. Volume 1 includes writings from 600BC to the early 20th century; volume 2 concentrates on the 20th century alone.

Yaarana: Gay Writing from India, ed. Hoshang Merchant, and, **Facing the Mirror: Lesbian Writing from India**, ed. Ashwini Sukthankar (both Penguin, 1999). Anthologies of short stories, extracts from novels and poetry from gay and lesbian Indian writers.

Travel

Butter Chicken in Ludhiana: Travels in Small Town India, by Pankaj Mishra (Penguin, 1995). An urban Indian novelist casts a jaundiced eye over modern Indian life.

City of Djinns, by William Dalrymple (HarperCollins, 1993). The respected travel writer's account of a year spent in Delhi, full of historical references.

Desert Places, by Robyn Davidson (Viking, 1996). A woman's story of living and travelling with the desert nomads of Rajasthan.

Exploring Indian Railways, by Bill Aitken (Oxford University Press, 1996). Highly informed and occasionally idiosyncratic tour of the Indian railway system written by a clear enthusiast.

A Goddess in the Stones, by Norman Lewis (Cape, 1991). The founder of Survival International travels among the Adivasis of Bihar and Orissa. Entertaining.

The Great Hedge of India, by Roy Moxham (Constable, 2000). One man's bizarre quest to find the hedge that marked the old British customs line. Very entertaining and packed full of historical detail. Recommended.

Leaves from the Jungle: Life in a Gond Village, by Verrier Elwin (Oxford University Press, 1992). Very entertaining account of this early anthropologist's stay with a central-Indian Adivasi group.

Old Delhi: Ten Easy Walks, by Gayner Barton and Lorraine Malone (South Asia Books, 1997). Very useful guide to the confusing maze of streets in Old Delhi.

Open the Eyes: Travels in Karnataka, by Dom Moraes with sketches by Mario Miranda (Roli Books, 2005). One of the last books by the Mumbai-born writer.

Sorcerer's Apprentice, by Tahir Shah (Penguin, 1998). Travelogue of the author's attempts to learn the secrets of illusion and fraud of India's street magicians.

Food, Language & Images

Dakshin: Vegetarian Cuisine from South India, by Chandra Padmanabhan (Angus and Robertson, 1999). An excellent guide to wonderful foods of South India.

Hanklyn-Janklin, or a Stranger's Rumble Tumble Guide to some Words, Customs and Quiddities Indian and Indo-British, by Nigel B. Hankin (Banyan Books, New Delhi, 1992). Lives up to its title and is a delightful reference work.

Hobson-Jobson (Routledge and Kegan Paul, 1968). The 1886 glossary on which Hankin modelled his modern etymology. The pair complement each other.

India: Decoration, Interiors, Style, by Henry Wilson (Watson-Gupthill, 2001). Exquisite photography of a number of North Indian palaces and houses (in Delhi and Rajasthan), demonstrating the inventiveness and sense of design to be found in this part of India. Recommended.

Lucknow City of Illusion, by Rosie Llewellyn-Jones (Prestel Verlag, 2006). An historical survey of the city with fabulous photos from the Alkazi collections.

Mansions at Dusk: the Havelis of Old Delhi, by Pavan K. Varma (Spantech, 1992). Atmospheric photographs by Sondeep Shankar illustrate this homage to the now decaying mansions of Muslim Delhi.

Wildlife

The Cult of the Tiger, by Valmak Thapar (New Delhi, OUP, 2002). A short book by a renowned tiger expert, which explores the myths and legends surrounding this animal and their implications for its survival.

The Last Tiger, by Valmik Thapar (New Delhi, OUP, 2006). A history of conservation of the tiger and Thapar's current views on how to save it from extinction.

A Book of Indian Birds, by Salim Ali (Bombay Natural History Society. 2002). Thirteenth revised edition of the classic guide to Indian birds, suitable for novice and experienced bird-watchers.

Pocket Guide to the Birds of the Indian Subcontinent, by Richard Grimmett, Carol Inskipp and Tim Inskipp (New Delhi, 1999). Illustrated guide for keen ornithologists, in a handy size.

Feedback

We do our best to ensure the information in our books is as accurate and up-to-date as possible. The books are updated on a regular basis, using local contacts, who painstakingly add, amend and correct as required. However, some mistakes and omissions are inevitable and we are ultimately reliant on our readers to put us in the picture.

We would welcome your feedback on any details related to your experiences using the book "on the road". Maybe we recommended a hotel that you liked (or another that you didn't), as well as interesting new attractions, or facts and figures you have found out about the country itself. The more details you can give us (particularly with regard to addresses, e-mails and telephone numbers), the better.

We will acknowledge all contributions, and we'll offer an Insight Guide to the best letters received.

Please write to us at:
Insight Guides
PO Box 7910
London SE1 1WE
United Kingdom
Or send e-mail to:
insight@apaguide.co.uk

ART & PHOTO CREDITS

Cartographic Editor **Zoë Goodwin**
Production **Linton Donaldson**
Design Consultants
Carlotta Junger, Graham Mitchener
Picture Research **Hilary Genin**

Index

*Numbers in italics refer to
photographs*